KING OF THE
DINOSAUR
HUNTERS

KING OF THE
DINOSAUR
HUNTERS

The Life of John Bell Hatcher and the
Discoveries that Shaped Paleontology

LOWELL DINGUS

PEGASUS BOOKS
NEW YORK LONDON

KING OF THE DINOSAUR HUNTERS

Pegasus Books Ltd.
148 W 37th Street, 13th Floor
New York, NY 10018

First Pegasus Books edition December 2018

Interior design by Maria Fernandez

Library of Congress Cataloging-in-Publication Data is available.

ISBN: 978-1-68177-865-5

10 9 8 7 6 5 4 3 2 1

Printed in the United States of America
Distributed by W. W. Norton & Company

Dedicated to the Descendants of John Bell and Anna Matilda Hatcher

Contents

Glossary of Genera

Note: Unless otherwise referenced in the text, generic synonymies are standardized based on the data contained in http://fossilworks.org/

Abderites: Small, rodent-like, frugivorous marsupial

Acaremys: Small, ground-dwelling, herbivorous rodent related to guinea pigs

Acdestis: Small, rodent-like, omnivorous marsupial

Aceratherium: Seven- to eight-foot-long, herbivorous, browsing rhinoceros, weighing about one ton

Achaenodon: Six-foot-long, herbivorous, pig-like entelodont or terror pig, weighing about 500 pounds

Acipenser: Carnivorous sturgeon

Aciprion: Ominovorous lizard related to other iguanas

Acrocyon: Swift, wolf-like, carnivorous marsupial

Adelphomys: Small, ground-dwelling, herbivorous rodent related to guinea pigs

Adinotherium: Five-foot-long, quadrupedal, herbivorous, hippo-like, notoungulate mammal, weighing about 250 pounds

Adjidaumo: Small, ground-dwelling, herbivorous relative of pocket gophers and kangaroo rats

Aelurodon: Large, hyaena-like, bone-crushing dog

Aepycamelus: Ten-foot-tall, ten-foot-long, browsing camel, weighing about a ton

Aetobatis: Marine, eagle ray

Agriochoerus: Clawed, even-toed, herbivorous ungulate

"Alethesaurus": Extinct lizard now called *Chamops*

Aleurocyon: Weasel- or badger-like, carnivorous predator related to weasels and otters

Albanerpeton: Salamander-like amphibian

Allacodon: Small, herbivorous, multituberculate mammal

Allognathosuchus: Extinct, five-foot-long, carnivorous alligator

"Allops": Large, herbivorous, odd-toed ungulate now called *Megacerops*

Allosaurus: Large, bipedal, carnivorous saurischian dinosaur about 25–30 feet long and weighing around 2.5 tons

Alphadon: Quick, ground-dwelling, omnivorous marsupial mammal

Alphalagus: Herbivorous rabbit

Amia: Piscivorous bowfin fish

Amphicaeonpus: Browsing rhinoceros

Amynodon: Large, semi-aquatic, hippo-like, browsing, odd-toed ungulate related to rhinoceroses

Analcimorphus: Herbivorous ground sloth

Ancodon: Large, hippo-like, herbivorous, browsing, amphibious, even-toed, ungulate mammal

Ankylodon: Ground-dwelling, insectivorous elephant shrew

Apatosaurus: Long-necked, long-tailed, herbivorous sauropod dinosaur about 70 feet long and weighing 25 tons; now once again called *Brontosaurus* by some

Aphelops: Moderate-sized, herbivorous, odd-toed rhino, weighing up to three tons

Aramus: Ground-dwelling, two-foot-tall, carnivorous bird or limpkin

Archaeotherium: Large, pig-like, omnivorous, even-toed, hoofed "terror pig," three feet tall, six feet long, weighing over 500 pounds

Ardynomys: Ground-dwelling, herbivorous rodent

Aspidertes: Aquatic, carnivorous, soft-shell turtle

Asterostemma: Armored, tank-like, omnivorous mammal called a glyptodont related to armadillos

Astrapothericulus: Hefty, herbivorous ungulate mammal

Astrapotherium: Eight-foot-long, hefty, herbivorous ungulate mammal, weighing around a ton

Astrodon: Long-necked, four-footed, herbivorous, sauropod dinosaur, around 30 feet tall and 50-60 feet long

Aublysodon: Large, carnivorous, bipedal dinosaur, closely related to other tyrannosaurs including *Tyrannosaurus*

"Aulocetus": Carnivorous, suspension-feeding, baleen whale now called *Cetotheriopsis*

Axestemys: Aquatic, carnivorous or piscivorous, softshell turtle

Baena: Aquatic, carnivorous turtle

Barbourofelis: Lion- to lepoard-sized, saber-toothed, carnivorous predator only distantly related to true cats

Barosaurus: Extremely long-necked, 85-foot-long, herbivorous sauropod dinosaur, weighing about 20 tons

Basilemys: Enormous terrestrial turtle

Bathygenys: Small, even-toed, hoofed, herbivorous, pig-like oreodont, weighing about 15 pounds

Batodon: Small, insectivorous, placental mammal

Belonostomus: Carnivorous, ray-finned fish

Blastomeryx: Herbivorous, even-toed, hoofed, 2.5-foot-long musk deer with enlarged canines, weighing about 35 pounds

Borhyaena: Four- to five-foot-long, swift, wolf-like, carnivorous marsupial, weighing around 50 pounds

Bothriodon: Pig-sized, even-toed, hoofed, hippo-like ungulate

Brachychampsa: Nine-foot-long, amphibious, carnivorous crocodile

Brachyrhyncocyon: Relatively small, ground-dwelling, carnivorous "bear dog" or amphicyonid

"Brontops": Small elephant-sized, rhino-like, horned, odd-toed, hoofed, browsing mammal, 8 feet tall at shoulder, 15 feet long, weighing about 3 tons and now called *Megacerops*

"Brontotherium": Small elephant-sized, rhino-like, horned, odd-toed, hoofed, browsing mammal, 8 feet tall at shoulder, 15 feet long, weighing about 3 tons and now called *Megacerops*

Bufo: Large, stocky, carnivorous toad

"Caenopus": Cow- or tapir-sized herbivorous rhino around 8 feet long, weighing about 800 pounds and now called *Subhyracodon*

Calamagras: Carnivorous snake related to modern boas

Calyptocephalella: Amphibious, helmeted water toad

Camarasaurus: Stocky, herbivorous sauropod dinosaur about 50 feet long and weighing around 20 tons

"Camelomeryx": Deer-like, browsing even-toed ungulate now called *Leptoredon*

Campestrallomys: Burrowing, herbivorous mountain beaver

Camptomus: Small, multituberculate mammal

Captorhinus: Two- to three-foot-long, lizard-like, carnivorous reptile

Carcharhinus: Requiem shark

Carcharodon: White shark, close relative of modern great white shark, sometimes now called *Carcharocles*

Caudiverbera: Stout, amphibious frog

Centetodon: Small, shrew-like mammal

Ceratodus: Lungfish

Ceratops: Herbivorous, horned dinosaur

Ceratosaurus: Large, bipedal, carnivorous saurischian dinosaur, about 17 feet long and weighing one to 1.5 tons

Chamops: Polyglyphanodontian lizard

Champosaurus: Five- to 10-foot-long, aquatic, carnivorous reptile resembling a crocodile, although not closely related

Chrysemys: Aquatic, omnivorous painted turtle

Cimolestes: Quick, ground-dwelling, insectivorous placental mammal

Cimolomys: Small, herbivorous, multituberculate mammal

Cimolodon: Small, herbivorous, multituberculate mammal

Cimolomys: Small, herbivorous, multituberculate mammal

Cimolopteryx: Carnivorous shore bird

Cladosictis: Swift, somewhat hyaena-like, carnivorous marsupial

Clidastes: Seven- to 20-foot- long, marine monitor lizard called a mosasaur that probably ate fish and squid

Cochlops: Tank-like, armored, omnivorous glyptodont related to armadillos

Coelurus: Eight-foot-long, carnivorous, bipedal, theropod dinosaur, weighing about 40 pounds

Colodon: Ground-dwelling, odd-toed, browsing tapir

Colpodontosaurus: Extinct lizard

Coniophis: Small, burrowing, carnivorous snake

Contogenys: Extinct lizard

Coriops: Bone fish

Corythosaurus: Thirty-foot-long, crested, herbivorous, duckbill dinosaur, weighing about three tons

"Creosaurus": Large, bipedal, carnivorous dinosaur now called *Allosaurus*

Crocodylus: Crocodile

Cuttysarkus: Amphibious salamander now called *Prodesmodon* by some paleontologists

Cylindrodon: Ground-dwelling, herbivorous rodent

Cyclopedius: A 4-foot-long, sheep-like, ground-dwelling, herbivorous oreodont

Cynodesmus: Coyote-sized, omnivorous true dog

Cynodictis: Small, martin-like, carnivorous "bear dog" or amphicyonid, about three feet long

Daemonelix: Large, corkscrew-shaped, fossilized burrow up to 6–8 feet long made by *Palaeocastor*

Daphoenus: Coyote-sized, carnivorous bear dog, distantly related to modern dogs

Deinodon: Large, carnivorous, bipedeal dinosaur closely related to *Tyrannosaurus*

Deinosuchus: Enormous alligator up to 35 to 40 feet long and weighing as much as 8 to 9 tons

Delotrochanter: Ground-dwelling, carnivorous "bear dog"

Desmatolagus: Ground-dwelling, grazing or browsing rabbit

Diadectes: Eight-foot-long, stocky, herbivorous, terrestrial, four-footed animal

Diadiaphorus: Swift, four-foot-long, somewhat horse-like, herbivorous, proterotheriid placental, mammal, weighing around 150 pounds

Diceratherium: Ground-dwelling, browsing rhinoceros, weighing about one ton

Didelphodon: Opossum-like and sized marsupial mammal

"Didelphops": Small, marsupial mammal now called *Didelphodon*

Dimetrodon: Ten-foot-long, fin-backed, carnivorous early relative of mammals

Dinictis: Leopard-sized, cat-like, saber-toothed carnivore only distantly related to true cats

Dinohyus: Enormous, omnivorous, pig-like, "terror pig" with skull as long as 3 feet and standing almost 6 feet tall at the shoulder

Diplacodon: Large, browsing, odd-toed ungulate called a brontothere

Diplocaulus: Three-foot-long, boomerang-headed, primarily aquatic, carnivorous amphibian

Diploclonus: Large, quadrupedal, herbivorous, odd-toed ungulate called a brontothere

Diplodocus: Long-necked, long-tailed, small skulled, herbivorous sauropod dinosaur up to more than 80 feet long and weighing about 15 tons

"Dipriodon": Small, multituberculate mammal now called *Meniscoessus*

Domnina: Small insectivorous shrew

Dryolestes: Small, insectivorous mammal

Dryptosaurus: Carnivorous, 25-foot-long, bipedal dinosaur, closely related to *Tyrannosaurus* and weighing about 3000 pounds

Echmatemys: Aquatic, herbivorous turtle

"Ectoconodon": Opossum-like, marsupial mammal now called *Didelphodon*

Edaphosaurus: Ten-foot-long, fin-backed, herbivorous early relative of mammals

Edmontonia: Twenty-foot-long, herbivorous, tank-like, armored, nodosaurid dinosaur, related to ankylosaurs

Edmontosaurus: Bipedal, herbivorous, duckbill dinosaur up to 40 feet long, weighing 10 tons

"Elosaurus": Enormous, long-necked, herbivorous sauropod dinosaur, now called *Apatosaurus* or *Brontosaurus*

Elotherium: Large, omnivorous, pig-like entelodont or "terror pig," also called *Ammodon*

Entelodon: Large, 4.5-foot-tall, pig-like ungulate or entelodont, informally called a "terror pig"

Eocardia: Small, ground-dwelling, herbivorous rodent related to guinea pigs

Eomoropus: Large, browsing, odd-toed ungulate called a chalicothere

"Epigaulus": Horned, ground-dwelling, gopher-like rodent, now called *Ceratogaulus*

Epihippus: Two-foot-tall, browsing horse

Epoicotherium: Insectivorous relative of the pangolins or "scaly anteathers"

Eporeodon: Moderate-sized, even-toed, herbivorous, ruminating oreodont, weighing around 250 pounds

Equus: Modern genus of horse

Eryops: Eight-foot-long, semi-aquatic, carnivorous amphibian

Essonodon: Arboreal, herbivorous, multituberculate mammal

"Euangelistes": Ground-dwelling, omnivorous or frugivorous placental mammal now called *Gypsonictops*

Eucholoeops: Omnivorous ground sloth

Eucinepeltus: Armored, tank-like, omnivorous mammal called a glyptodont related to armadillos

Euhapsis: Amphibious, browsing beaver

Eumys: Six-inch long, herbivorous, mouse-like, ground-dwelling rodent

Eusmilus: Eight-foot-long, cat-like, saber-toothed carnivore only distantly related to true cats

Exostinus: Carnivorous anguimorph lizard

Galeocerdo: Tiger shark

Gavia: Ground-dwelling, carnivorous loon

Geochelone: Large, ground-dwelling, herbivorous tortoise

Glasbius: Small, herbivorous or frugivorous marsupial mammal

Glyptodon: Five-foot high, 11-foot-long, tank-like, omnivorous, armored mammal related to armadillos, weighing around two tons

Glyptops: Extinct, side-necked or cryptodire turtle

Glyptosaurus: Ground-dwelling, insectivorous or carnivorous, anguid lizard

Gomphotherium: Ten-foot-tall, four- to five-ton relative of elephants

Goniopholis: Six- to 12-foot-long, semi-aquatic, carnivorous, crocodile-like reptile

Gopherus: Burrowing, herbivorous tortoise

Gregorymys: Browsing pocket gopher

"Griphippus": Small, herbivorous, three-toed, grazing horse now called *Pseudhipparion*

Gypsonictops: Ground-dwelling, omnivorous or frugivorous placental mammal

Habrosaurus: Five-foot-long, carnivorous salamander

Hadrosaurus: Large, herbivorous, duckbill dinosaur

"Hadroleptauchenia": Herbivorous oreodont now called *Leptauchenia*

"Halodon": Small multituberculate mammal now called *Meniscoessus*

Hapalops: Three-foot-long, primarily herbivorous ground sloth with some arboreal ability

Haplocanthosaurus: Large, long-necked, herbivorous sauropod dinosaur with spines on back, about 50 to 60 feet long and weighing around 13 tons

"Harpagosaurus": Carnivorous lizard now called *Exostinus*

Hatcheritherium: Small, omnivorous, marsupial mammal

Hayoceros: Browsing, antelope-like pronghorn

Hegetotherium: Herbivorous notoungulate mammal

Heliscomys: Ground-dwelling, herbivorous rodent related to pocket gophers

Helodermoides: Carnivorous and insectivorous anguid lizard

Hemiauchenia: Six-foot-tall, seven-foot-long, herbivorous, llama-like camel, weighing about 600 pounds

Hemipristis: Ground shark

Hendryomeryx: Ground-dwelling, fruit-eating, even-toed, hoofed ruminant

Heptacodon: Large, hippo-like, browsing ungulate called an anthracothere

Hesperocyon: Primitive, 3-foot-long, slender, fox-like dog, weighing around five pounds

Hesperomys: Ground-dwelling, herbivorous mouse

Hipparion: Six-foot-long, six-foot tall, herbivorous horse weighing about 1000 pounds

Homalodotherium: Six-foot-long, herbivorous notoungulate mammal, weighing around 650 pounds

Homogalax: Browsing, tapir-like, odd-toed ungulate

Hoplophoneus: Leopard-sized, cat-like, saber-toothed carnivore only distantly related to true cats

Hyaenodon: Relatively large, massive skulled, small-brained, hyaena-like mammal, among the largest carnivores of it time

"Hyopotamus": Browsing, hippo-like anthracothere now called *Bothriodon*

Hyopsodus: Swift, omnivorous, ungulate mammal called a condylarth

Hypertragulus: Small, even-toed, deer-like ruminant, weighing about 15 pounds and related to chevrotains

Hypisodus: Small deer-like, even-toed, hoofed ungulate related to chevrotains

Hyracodon: Swift, 5-foot-long, slender-legged rhino, probably forest and open grassland browser

Ictops: Ground-dwelling, insectivorous or carnivorous mammal related to *Leptictis*

Iguanavus: Lizard

Interatherium: Two-foot-long, quadrupedal, herbivorous notoungulate mammal

Ischyrocyon: Carnivorous "bear dog" or amphicyonid, weighing about 350 pounds

Ischyromys: Early, 2-foot-long, squirrel-like, arboreal rodent

"Ischyrotomus": Ground-dwelling, herbivorous rodent now called *Pseudotomus*

Isectolophus: Browsing, tapir-like, odd-toed ungulate

Isurus: Mako shark

"Kindleia": Carnivorous or piscivorous bowfin fish now called *Cyclurus*

Labidosaurus: Three-foot-long, heavily built, lizard-like, insectivorous reptile

"Lanceosaurus": Extinct lizard now called *Chamops*

Leidyosuchus: Large, carnivorous crocodile

Leptictis: Primitive, 2- to 3-foot long, weasel-like mammal, possibly insectivorous

Leptauchenia: Ground-dwelling, even-toed, hoofed, herbivorous oreodont, weighing about 80 pounds

Lepisosteus: Large, carnivorous gar

Leptoceratops: Primitive, herbivorous, seven-foot-long member of horned dinosaurs weighing about 150–400 pounds

Leptochamops: One-foot-long, insectivorous lizard

Leptochoerus: Chevrotain-like, rabbit-sized, swift, hoofed ungulate, browsing herbivore

Leptomeryx: Three-foot-long deer-like, even-toed, hoofed, herbivorous ruminant

Leptoreodon: Browsing, deer-like, even-toed ungulate

Leptotomus: Ground-dwelling, herbivorous rodent

Leptotragulus: Browsing, deer-like, even-toed ungulate

Licaphrium: Swift, somewhat horse-like, herbivorous, proterotheriid, placental mammal

Limenetes: A 4-foot-long, sheep-like, ground-dwelling, herbivorous oreodont

Lisserpeton: Extinct salamander

Litakis: Polyglyphanodontian lizard

Lysorophus: Salamander-like, aquatic amphibian with reduced limbs

Mammut: Large, elephant-like mastodon

Mammuthus: Huge, elephant-like mammoth

"Mastodon": Large, elephant-like mastodon, now called *Mammut*

Megacerops: Small elephant-sized, brontothere; rhino-like, horned, odd-toed, hoofed, browsing mammal, 8 feet tall at shoulder, 15 feet long, weighing about 3 tons

Megalagus: Large, ground-dwelling, herbivorous rabbit

Megalonychotherium: Large, herbivorous ground sloth

Megatylopus: Browsing, 14-foot-tall camel, weighing about two tons

Melvia: Carnivorous bowfin fish

Meniscoessus: Small, herbivorous, multituberculate mammal

Meniscognathus: Extinct lizard

Menoceras: Small, browsing, rhino about 5 feet long

"Menodus": Large, herbivorous, rhino-like, odd-toed ungulate now called *Megacerops*

Merychippus: Three-toed, hoofed, grazing, 3-foot-high horse, with different species weighing up to 200 pounds

Merychyus: Pig- or sheep-like, even-toed, hoofed herbivorous ruminant, weighing about 200 pounds

Merycochoerus: Enormous, pig-like, even-toed, hoofed ruminating oreodont, weighing up to 900 pounds

"Merycodesmus": Browsing, deer-like, even-toed ungulate now called *Leptoreodon*

Merycodus: Ground-dwelling, herbivorous, browsing and grazing, antelope-like ruminant

Merycoides: Moderate-sized, even-toed, herbivorous, ruminating oreodont, weighing around 150–250 pounds

Merycoidodon: Pig-like, even-toed, hoofed, herbivorous ruminating oreodont, four- to five-foot-long and weighing 200–300 pounds

Mesatirhinus: Large, herbivorous, odd-toed ungulate called a brontothere

Mesocyon: Small, carnivorous dog, weighing between 8 and 15 pounds

Mesodma: Small, herbivorous, multituberculate mammal

Mesohippus: Two-foot-tall, four-toed, browsing horse that stood and ran primarily on its middle toe

Mesonyx: Four-foot-long, carnivorous, wolf-like mammal called a condylarth

Mesoreodon: Large, pig-like, even-toed, hoofed, herbivorous grazing ruminating oreodont, weighing up to 500 pounds

Metamynodon: Large, amphibious, browsing, rhino-like, odd-toed ungulate

Metarhinus: Large, browsing, odd-toed ungulate called a brontothere

Metopotoxus: Armored, tank-like, omnivorous mammal called a glyptodont related to armadillos

Miacis: Weasel-like and sized, carnivorous, placental mammal

Microbiotherium: Small, opossum-like, insectivorous marsupial

Micropternodus: Shrew-like, insectivorous placental mammal

Microtus: Ground-dwelling, herbivorous vole

Miohippus: Four-foot-long, three-toed, browsing horse, weighing about 60 pounds

Moropus: Large, odd-toed, clawed, herbivorous chalicothere, weighing up to 650 pounds

Mosasaurus: Up to 55-foot-long marine monitor lizard called a mosasaur that fed on fish, turtles, ammonites smaller mosasaurs, birds, pterosaurs, and plesiosaurs

Mylagaulus: Beaver-like, herbivorous rodent

Myledaphus: Carnivorous mackerel shark

Mylodon: Ten-foot long, herbivorous ground sloth, weighing around one ton

Mytonomys: Ground-dwelling, herbivorous rodent

Nanomyops: Small, herbivorous, multituberculate mammal

Necrolestes: Six-inch-long, somewhat shrew-like, insectivorous, non-therian mammal

Nematherium: Large, herbivorous ground sloth

Neohipparion: Four-foot tall, three-toed, grazing horse, weighing about 300 pounds

Neoreomys: Small, ground-dwelling, herbivorous rodent related to guinea pigs

Nesodon: Nine-foot-long, herbivorous, quadrupedal, hippo-like, notoungulate mammal, weighing about 1200 pounds

Nimravides: Swift, carnivorous, five- to six-foot long, tiger-like cat, weighing about 225 pounds

Nothocyon: Meat-eating and omnivorous, true carnivore most closely related to bears

Notorhynchus: Sevengill shark

"Nyssodon": Small, carnivorous or insectivorous, opossum-like, placental mammal now called *Cimolestes*

Odaxosaurus: Anguid lizard

Odontaspis: Carnivorous, sand tiger shark

Oligospermophilus: Small, fruit or seed-eating squirrel

Opisthodactylus: Large, ground-dwelling, herbivorous bird called a rhea

Opisthotriton: Extinct salamander

Opthalmosaurus: Twenty-foot long, carnivorous, dolphin-like marine reptile called an ichthyosaur

"Oracodon": Small, herbivorous, multituberculate mammal now called *Meniscoessus*

"Oreodon": Herbivorous, sheep-like oreodont now called *Merycoidodon*

Oreonetes: Small, browsing, even-toed, hoofed, pig-like ruminant called an oreodont

Ornithomimus: Twelve- to fifteen-foot-long long, bipedal, toothless saurischian dinosaur weighing about 350 pounds

Orthacanthus: Ten-foot-long, carnivorous, fresh-water shark

Ourayia: Arboreal, insectivorous primate

Oxydactylus: Herbivorous, long-legged camel, weighing between 250 and 300 pounds

Pachycephalosaurus: Fifteen-foot-long, bony helmeted, herbivorous dinosaur, weighing about 1000 pounds

Pachyrukhos: One-foot-long, rabbit-like, herbivorous, notoungulate mammal

Palaearctomys: Seed- or fruit-eating squirrel

Palaeocastor: Two-foot long, burrowing beaver responsible for *Daemonelix* burrows

"Palaeoelaphe": Carnivorous, rat snake now called *Elaphe*

Palaeolagus: Early, ten-inch long, ground-dwelling, herbivorous rabbit

Palaeosaniwa: Carnivorous monitor lizard

Palaeoscincus: Large, herbivorous, tank-like, armored, nodosaurid dinosaur related to ankylosaurs

Palaeospheniscus: Ground-dwelling, carnivorous penguin

Palaeospiza: Small, omnivorous mousebird

Palaeosyops: Large, browsing, odd-toed ungulate called a brontothere

Palaeothentes: Small, rodent-like, omnivorous marsupial

Panoplosaurus: Six-foot-high, 15- to 25-foot-long, tank-like, herbivorous, armored, nodosaurid dinosaur

Paraderma: Extinct, carnivorous monitor lizard

Paradjidaumo: A small, ground-dwelling, herbivorous relative of pocket gophers and kangaroo rats

Parahippus: Three-toed, three-foot-tall, grazing horse

Paralbula: Carnivorous ray-finned fish

Paramys: Ground-dwelling, herbivorous rodent

Parasaniwa: Carnivorous relative of monitor lizards

Parictis: Small, primitive bear

Paronychodon: Small, bird-like, carnivorous dinosaur closely related to *Troodon*

Pediomys: Ground-dwelling, insectivorous marsupial mammal

Peltosaurus: Lizard, possibly insectivorous, related to modern anguids such as glass lizards

Pelecyodon: Large, omnivorous ground sloth

Pelecyornis: Swift, ground-dwelling, carnivorous "terror bird" now called *Psilopterus* by some paleontologists

Peltephilus: Ground-dwelling, omnivorous armadillo

Peradectes: Opossum-like marsupial

Peratherium: Opossum-like marsupial

Perchoerus: Herbivorous or omnivorous peccary

Perimys: Ground-dwelling, herbivorous rodent

Phenacocoelus: Pig- or sheep-like, even toed, hoofed, herbivorous ruminating oreodont, weighing about 160 pounds

Phororhacos : Swift, eight-foot-tall, ground-dwelling, carnivorous "terror bird," weighing almost 300 pounds (also sometimes spelled *Phorusrhacos*)

Piceoerpeton: Extinct aquatic salamander

Planops: Large, omnivorous ground sloth

Platacodon: Omnivorous bowfin fish

Platycarpus: Fourteen-foot-long, marine monitor lizard called a mosasaur that probably ate fish and squid

Plesiarctomys: Ground-dwelling, herbivorous rodent

Pliohippus: Six-foot-tall, eight-foot-long, grazing horse, weighing about 1,000 pounds

Pliolagostomus: Ground-dwelling, herbivorous rodent

Poebrotherium: Primitive, 3-foot-tall, 3-foot-long, slender, long-legged camel, possibly a mixed browser and grazer

Prepotherium: Large, herbivorous ground sloth

Priconodon: Large, tank-like, four-footed, herbivorous, armored, nodosaurid dinosaur, distantly related to ankylosaurs

"Prionosaurus": Carnivorous lizard now called *Exostinus*

Priscodelphinus: Carnivorous, toothed whale

"Proamphicyon": Coyote-sized, carnivorous "bear dog," distantly related to modern dogs now called *Daphoenus*

Probaena: Herbivorous tortoise

Procamelus: Llama-like, 4-foot-tall, even-toed, hoofed, browsing camel, weighing about 120 pounds

Procaimanoidea: Extinct, carnivorous alligator

"Prodaphaenus": Arboreal, carnivorous member of Carnivora now called *Miacis*

Prodesmodon: Amphibious salamander

Proeutatus: Ground-dwelling, insectivorous armadillo

Proictinia: Carnivorous hawk

"Proinia": Carnivorous, dolphin-like, toothed whale now called *Prosqualodon*

Promeycochoerus: Three-foot long, hippo-like, even-toed, hoofed oreodont, probably amphibious

Propalaeohoplophorus: Relatively small, heavily armored, tank-like, omnivorous, glyptodont mammal related to armadillos

Prosciurus: Burrowing, herbivorous mountain beaver

Prosqualodon: Carnivorous, dolphin-like, toothed whale

Prosthennops: Omnivorous peccary

Protemnocyon: Ground-dwelling, carnivorous or omnivorous dog

Proterotherium: Swift, somewhat horse-like, herbivorous, proterotheriid, placental mammal

Prothylacynus: Swift, wolf-like, carnivorous marsupial

Protitanotherium: Large, browsing, odd-toed ungulate called a brontothere

Protoceras: Three-foot-long, browsing, deer-like, even-toed ungulate with horn-like ossicones on skull, weighing from 120 to 200 pounds

Protohippus: Three-toed, grazing horse

Protolambda: Small, omnivorous, marsupial mammal

Protomeryx: Ground-dwelling, browsing camel

Protoptychus: Ground-dwelling, herbivorous rodent

Protoreodon: Clawed, even-toed, herbivorous ungulate called an oreodont

Protamandua: Ground-dwelling, insectivorous anteater

Protylopus: Two and a half-foot-long, browsing, camel-like, even-toed ungulate, weighing about 55 pounds

Protypotherium: One-foot-long, quadrupedal, rodent-like, herbivorous notoungulate mammal

Prozaedius: Ground-dwelling, insectivorous armadillo

Pseudocylindrodon: Ground-dwelling, herbivorous rodent

Pseudhipparion: Large, grazing horse

Pseudotomus: Ground-dwelling, herbivorous rodent

Psilopterus: Swift, two and a half-foot-tall, ground-dwelling, carnivorous "terror bird," weighing around 10 to 15 pounds

Pteranodon: Large, crested, fish-eating, flying reptile with webbed wings up to 20 feet across

Reithroparamys: Ground-dwelling, herbivorous rodent

Rhineura: Legless, amphisbaenian or worm lizard

Rhinoptera: Cownose ray

Rutiodon: Ten- to 25-foot-long, crocodile-like, carnivorous reptile called a phytosaur

Saniwa: Five- to six-foot-long, carnivorous relative of monitor lizards

Saurornithoides: Seven-foot-long, bird-like, bipedal, carnivorous dinosaur closely related to *Troodon*

"Serridentinus": Mastodon-like proboscidean now called *Gomphotherium*

Scapherpeton: Extinct salamander

Scaptohyus: Pig-like, omnivorous entelodont, informally called a "terror pig"

Schismotherium: Large, omnivorous ground sloth

Schistomys: Small, ground-dwelling, herbivorous rodent related to guinea pigs

Sciamys: Small, ground-dwelling, herbivorous rodent related to guinea pigs

"Scottimus": Six-inch long, herbivorous, mouse-like, ground-dwelling rodent now called *Eumys*

"Selenacodon": Small, multituberculate mammal now called *Meniscoessus*

"Serridentinus": Large, herbivorous, browsing, elephant-like gomphothere now called Gomphotherium

Sespia: Small, even-toed, hoofed, herbivorous, pig-like ruminant called an oreodont, weighing about 10 pounds

Simidectes: Swift, carnivorous mammal called a mesonychian

Sipalocyon: Swift, somewhat hyaena-like, carnivorous marsupial

Spaniomys: Small, ground-dwelling, herbivorous rodent related to guinea pigs

"Stagodon": Opossum-like, marsupial mammal now called *Didelphodon*

Stegosaurus: Plated, spiked, herbivorous armored dinosaur 15 feet long and weighing 2.5 tons

Stegotherium: Ground-dwelling, insectivorous armadillo

Steiromys: Small, ground-dwelling, herbivorous rodent related to guinea pigs

Stenotephanos: Hippo-like, herbivorous notoungulate mammal

Stenomylus: Two-foot tall, gazelle-like, even-toed, herbivorous camel

Stenotatus: Ground-dwelling, insectivorous armadillo

Stichomys: Small, herbivorous, ground-dwelling rodent related to guinea pigs

Stygimoloch: Large, bone-helmeted, bipedal, herbivorous dinosaur, sometimes now called *Pachycephalosaurus*

Stylemys: Ground-dwelling tortoise

Stilotherium: Small, shrew-like, insectivorous marsupial

Subhyracodon: Eight-foot-long, browsing rhinoceros, weighing about 800 pounds

Sunkahetanka: Relatively small, bone-crushing dog, weighing around 30 pounds

Syllaemus: Mullet fish

Symborodon: Large, herbivorous, browsing brontothere

Synechodus: Aquatic, carnivorous shark

Tanymykter: Ground-dwelling, browsing camel, weighing about 300 pounds

"Tayra": Swift, weasel-like carnivore, now called *Eira*

Telacodon: Small, insectivorous, placental mammal

Teleoceras: Large, short-legged, odd-toed, hoofed, hippo-like rhino, weighing up to 1.8 tons

Telmatherium: Large, browsing, odd-toed ungulate called a brontothere

Temnocyon: Small, carnivorous "bear dog" weighing about 50 pounds

Terrapene: Omnnivorous box-turtle

Testudo: Tortoise

Theosodon: Six-foot-long, llama-like, herbivorous, macrauchenid mammal, weighing about 350 pounds

Thescelosaurus: Bipedal, herbivorous ornithischian dinosaur, 10 to 15 feet long, weighing around 500–600 pounds

Thescelus: Baenid turtle

Thinohyus: Ground-dwelling, omnivorous peccary

Thoatherium: Swift, two-foot-long, somewhat horse-like, herbivorous, proterotheriid placental mammal

Ticholeptus: Pig-like, even-toed, hoofed ruminant, weighing up to 300 pounds

"Titanops": Large, herbivorous, browsing brontothere now usually called *Megacerops*

"Titanotherium": Large brontothere now called *Megacerops*

Trachodon: Large, herbivorous, duckbill dinosaur

Torosaurus: Twenty-five to thirty-foot-long, three-horned, herbivorous dinosaur, weighing around six tons

Triceratops: Quadrupedal, three-horned, herbivorous ornithischian dinosaur, up to 30 feet long and weighing 6 to 13 tons

Trigonias: Seven-foot-long, hornless rhino, weighing about 800 pounds

Trimerorhachis: Three-foot-long, primarily aquatic, carnivorous amphibian

Trionyx: Carnivorous, soft-shelled turtle

Triplopus: Gracile, long-limbed, browsing rhinoceros

"Tripriodon": Small, herbivorous, multituberculate mammal now called *Meniscoessus*

Troodon: Seven-foot-long, swift, agile, bird-like, carnivorous dinosaur, fairly closely related to *Velociraptor*

Tylosaurus: Forty- to 45-foot-long, marine monitor lizard called a mosasaur that probably ate fish, sharks, marine birds and other mosasaurs

Tyrannosaurus: Bipedal, carnivorous, saurischian dinosaur up to 40 feet long and weighing 15 tons

Uintatherium: Thirteen-foot-long, five- to six-foot-tall, herbivorous, knobby-skulled mammal called a uintathere, weighing around two tons

Vulpes: Carnivorous to omnivorous fox

Xiphactinus: Enormous, predatory, bony fish up to 20 feet long that resembled a tarpon, but was not closely related to it

Ysengrinia: Ground-dwelling, carnivorous bear-dog, weighing about 160 pounds

Yumaceras: Horned, antilope-like, browsing ruminant

Prologue

At the turn of the 20th century, while prospecting for fossils across the harsh plains of Patagonia, John Bell Hatcher, a slight, wiry, steely-blue-eyed fossil collector from Princeton University, scanned his surroundings from beneath his dusty Stetson and found himself crimped for cash to get home. His precarious and audacious plan? Teach Patagonians how to play poker:

> *The professor passed through every hamlet from Bahia Blanca to the Straights; the lessons were always the same . . . as a rule the loose change of the community passed on to the bone hunter to be spent on science. When the famous night finally arrived on which Hatcher was to leave[,] San Julian dropped in to exact revenge. The game started early and was one of those friendly Western games with everyone's sixshooter on the table. The stacks of pesos in front of Hatcher climbed up and up until he was almost hidden behind them; the whistle of the steamer sounded down the harbor. Hatcher announced that he must go. Someone suggested that they would not*

let him. He picked up his gun and his pesos and backed through the door with a "Good night, gentlemen!" No one made a move.[1]

Part of being a successful paleontologist involves taking risks, since challenging situations arise on almost any extensive expedition to remote field localities. As his Patagonian escapade illustrates, Hatcher certainly possessed a knack for remaining calm and coldly rational under perilous pressure.

Although millions of museum visitors every year marvel at the skeletons of dinosaurs and other creatures he collected, few recognize this intrepid collector's name. Yet, among his contemporaries and modern-day successors, he is widely acclaimed as a "King of Collectors." But how did he attain such lofty laurels?

SECTION I
1861–1884

1

Becoming Marsh's Minion

erely six months after the Civil War began to rip the country asunder in 1861, John Bell Hatcher first opened his eyes in Cooperstown, Illinois, on October 11. He was the second son of John B. Hatcher, born in Stark County, Ohio, in 1835, and Margaret Columbia O'Neal, born in Brown County, Illinois, in 1842. The genealogical roots of John B. are entwined with the "Quaker and Dorset Hatchers from England," according to the Hatcher Families Genealogical Association, who document that this lineage comprised two relatively unconnected families known to be related through DNA testing. The largest was Quaker and began with William, born about 1705 in Buck Co, Virginia. Many of William's descendants migrated to Virginia's Loudoun and Fauquier Counties before heading due west, where many settled in Ohio. The second, smaller family, with primarily Catholic roots, arrived around 1850 from Dorset, England, and settled in Minnesota. In all, John B. and Margaret would foster a plentiful set of siblings for John Bell that included four brothers and six sisters, the last being born in 1887. But like his forebearers, John B. was restless and, soon after John Bell was born, migrated from Cooperstown, Illinois, southeast to the fertile farmlands near the town of Cooper in Greene County, Iowa. There, John B. mixed labor in the fields with teaching at the nearby schools during the winter months. Scant material survives with which to paint a detailed portrait of John Bell's early life. However, according to an account from Hatcher's father, John Bell's quest for intellectual satisfaction started early on and was manifested in:

> . . . the lad's determination when he was but a mere boy to amass useful knowledge, patiently sitting for hours pouring over his books when his comrades of like age about him were bent upon sports and pastimes. He was an indefatigable student of books and a very keen observer. . . .

Often sickly as a child, John Bell studied under his father's tutelage, in addition to attending local schools when he was able.[1]

Throughout his life, Hatcher chronically suffered from an ailment that he characteristically called "rheumatism." Although the severity of these episodes seemed to vary, during instances when the affliction was especially acute, Hatcher could be disabled from performing mundane daily activities for weeks or even a month or two at a time. Today, there is a strong suspicion among some members of the families descended from John Bell that the source of his chronic ailments was a disease called Type 1 osteogenesis imperfecta (OI), a name that basically means "imperfect bone formation." The descendants' suspicion derives from the fact that this disease, which can be genetically transmitted, has been diagnosed in some of their family members. Sometimes referred to as "brittle bone disease" in common parlance, OI results from "a faulty gene that reduces either the amount or the quality of type 1 collagen throughout the body," and symptoms range from bone pain, common fractures due to low bone density, fatigue, short stature, spinal curvature, "triangular" skull shape, brittle teeth, and loose joints. Given Hatcher's physical characteristics, complaints, and strenuous fieldwork, it's clear that if he suffered from OI, it was a relatively mild type of the disorder.[2]

Fortunately, the onset of adolescence saw the boy gain strength to the point where he began to work in the nearby coal mines, which allowed him to stash away some savings. While laboring in the mines, he occasionally came across fossils of plants and other ancient organisms preserved in the 300-million-year-old layers of rock. Naturally fascinated, he amassed a modest collection and developed an interest in geology and paleontology to a degree that he used his hard-earned savings to enter Grinnell College in 1880 or 1881. However, he soon aspired to obtain the best education possible on his favored subjects and invested the remainder of his savings to enter and study at Yale's Sheffield Scientific School in 1882. Playing into Hatcher's decision was an unfortunate natural disaster that befell Grinnell and its college community; a tornado devastated the town on June 17, 1882, decimating the campus and killing thirty-nine people, including two students.[3]

One obvious advantage of gaining an education at a prestigious university such as Yale is the knowledge one obtains, especially in the discipline that one desires to pursue. However, a less commonly acknowledged, yet equally essential, benefit is the contacts one fosters with prominent professionals already established in the field. As a student at Sheffield, Hatcher would cross paths with some of the most preeminent and powerful scientific professionals in the world, let alone the nation. As a young man, Hatcher had become especially attracted to Yale through its highly acclaimed professor of geology, James Dwight Dana, whose books he had zealously studied. But how had the "Sheff," as it is endearingly nicknamed, gained such scientific prominence?[4]

Although Yale College was founded in 1701 as an institution to train young men as ministers in the Congregational Church, Sheffield Scientific School did not arise until 1847. During much of that interim, especially from the late 1700s on, the administration of Yale was deeply engaged in, and often divided by, the contemporary controversies that pitted advocates for the establishment of a full-fledged university against those who continued to resist the expansion in the curriculum that would be required to elevate the institution beyond a seminary.

In the 1730s, students for old Yale College were drilled during their program in Latin, Greek, and occasionally Hebrew. Supplementary subjects included logic, metaphysics, mathematics, physics, and especially rhetoric and oratory, as would be required for members of the clergy. By the 1740s, freshmen still focused predominantly on Latin, through Virgil and Cicero, some New Testament Greek, and arithmetic. But sophomores broadened out into Horace, logic, geography, algebra, geometry, and the intricacies of grammar. Juniors also tackled trigonometry and natural philosophy, while seniors emphasized metaphysics and ethics, to explore "the tough problem of how to reconcile man's newly emancipated reason and natural law with the old theology and Christian Law."[5]

Strong currents of the sea change heralding the expansion of scientific education did not break on Yale's shores until the hiring of Benjamin Silliman as a professor of chemistry and natural history in 1802, and no one was more shocked than Silliman himself, who had studied law but never studied chemistry. But there were few if any professionals proficient in both chemistry and natural history in the United States at that time. So Silliman delayed the start of his actual teaching for two years and crammed for his new gig by studying chemistry at the medical school of the University of Pennsylvania, before embarking for London and Edinburgh to continue his preparation where he became interested in geology. Silliman was an excellent teacher, as well as an influential public lecturer on the benefits of science—so much so that he is often anointed as the "patriarch" of science in the United States, despite the fact that he wasn't an equally influential scientific researcher. Another accomplishment was his acquisition of numerous collections of minerals and other objects related to natural history, which served as the foundation of the collections for the Peabody Museum of Natural History at Yale.[6]

Even more formidable waves washed ashore in New Haven during 1847, when the Department of Philosophy and the Arts was established to provide instruction in the natural sciences, among others. It was out of this department that the graduate school and Sheffield Scientific School would eventually evolve.[7]

From 1836 to 1837, Silliman employed a precocious young scientist named James Dwight Dana as his assistant after he graduated under Silliman's tutelage in 1833. Having worked for the US Navy as a mathematics teacher in the interim, Dana then joined the prestigious United States Exploring Expedition led by Charles Wilkes, where he served as a mineralogist and geologist when the first American global geographic and scientific foray sailed throughout the Pacific between 1838 and 1842. His voluminous monographs that resulted from his research on the journey ranged from volcanoes to corals and crustaceans. These, along with his seminal works on mineralogy, including his *System of Mineralogy* of 1837 and *Manual of Mineralogy* in 1848, catapulted Dana into the upper echelon of the nation's scientific community. Dana succeeded Silliman to become the Silliman Professor of Natural History and Geology, in 1850, and persistently promoted the expansion of Yale College into a full-fledged university that had begun with the establishment of the Department of Philosophy and the Arts in 1847, the same year that Harvard, Yale's then and current archcompetitor in the academic arena, initiated the Lawrence Scientific School. At the commencement ceremony of 1856, just a year after his hiring, Dana declared:

> . . . *Yale is determined to be up to the times. The desire is manifest that the College, as it now stands, shall not longer mark the limit of American training in literature or science. . . . Why not have here, The American University—where nature's laws shall be taught in all their fullness, and intellectual culture reach its highest limit.*[8]

In the same address Dana prophetically advocated for the establishment of a museum of natural history to support learning and research in the natural sciences:

> *The museum . . . should be a spacious one, containing collections connected with all the subjects taught in the school. . . .* [with specimens in natural history, presumably including fossils; seeds; soils; and collections illustrating mines and metallurgy] *In fact, the museum should lecture to the eye. . . . It should be a place*

where the public passing in and out, should gather something of the spirit, and much of the knowledge, of the institution.[9]

In 1858, New Haven financier Joseph Earl Sheffield donated over $100,000 to purchase the old Medical Department building, complete with two newly renovated wings for the scientific school. In recognition of Sheffield's patronage, Yale's Corporation christened this institution the Sheffield Scientific School during the commencement of 1861. By 1883, an armada of prominent scientific instructors had landed at Yale to teach a burgeoning Sheffield student body of 207 graduates and undergraduates from no fewer than twenty-five states and the District of Columbia. Among the sixteen professors, notables included the chairman and executive officer, George J. Brush, who handled mineralogy; Daniel C. Eaton, in charge of botany; and Addison E. Verrill, who headed up zoology and geology. Tuition for an undergraduate cost $150 per year—roughly $3,400 in modern dollars.[10]

As stated in the Sheffield's Annual Reports published in 1883 and 1884 when Hatcher was a student, the school's mission was formulated to fulfill the scientific and technological needs of Connecticut:

> *It is in its purposes, and in the kinds of work it undertakes, pecu-*
> *liarly adapted to the wants of our State. We are preeminently an*
> *industrial community, but industrial in those departments which*
> *are based upon the most extended studies of natural science, and*
> *upon the application of the most recent results of these studies.*
> *Consequently it is here that a school devoted to the pursuit and*
> *encouragement of such studies finds its natural field.*[11]

Requirements for admission to the freshman class were daunting. Candidates, in addition to being at least fifteen years old and providing references from former instructors or other "responsible persons" documenting sufficient moral character, were required to pass a broad battery of exams administered over five days—three in late June and two in mid-September. The subjects for examination ranged from the more classical, such as English, history of the United States, geography and Latin, to the more scientifically pertinent disciplines of arithmetic, algebra, geometry, and trigonometry.[12]

A three-year course of instruction followed, including two terms of courses taken by all students during the first year and a regimen of more specialized courses conducted over the final two years, once the student had chosen what we would call his major area of interest. During the more generalized freshman year, first-term classes encompassed German, English, composition, spherical trigonometry, plane analytical geometry, physics, chemistry, and elementary drawing. In the second term, students continued to tackle the subjects of language, physics, chemistry, and plane analytical geometry, while also delving into physical geography, botany, and various aspects of drawing, including isometric drawing, shading, tinting, and the principles of orthographic projection.[13]

Having successfully run the gauntlet of these intimidating courses, juniors and seniors could finally set sail toward their preferred professional goal, with their options including chemistry, civil engineering, dynamic engineering, agriculture, natural history, premedical studies or premining and metallurgy studies. Hatcher, of course, chose natural history, which the faculty at the time saw fit to divide into four subdisciplines: geology, mineralogy, zoology, and botany. So his junior year entangled him in classes involving theoretical chemistry, qualitative analysis, mineralogy, botany, German, French, zoology, physiology, and physical geology. During his senior year of 1884, he would have continued to investigate geology, including field trips and lab work; zoological lab practices, lectures, and excursions; botanical studies in the herbarium and the field; vertebrate anatomy; meteorology; and French. Presciently, his final year culminated with the submission of his first research paper, a graduation thesis entitled "On the Genus of Mosses termed *Conomitrium*." Although no transcripts recording Hatcher's performance in these courses still exist, his scholarly determination as a student culminated in the spring of 1884, when he secured his bachelor of philosophy degree.[14]

During the course of his rigorous routine of studies, Hatcher showed his collections of Carboniferous fossils from the coal mines to George J. Brush, professor of metallurgy and director of the Sheffield Scientific School. Brush, who, along with professor of paleontology Othniel

Charles Marsh, was one of the three original curators and a trustee of the Peabody Museum, recognized Hatcher's self-motivated initiative and, in turn, introduced Hatcher to Marsh. Like Hatcher, Marsh had studied under Brush while a student at Yale. As soon as he had his diploma in hand, Hatcher, the consummate poker player, laid his cards on Marsh's table. In the early summer of 1884, Hatcher marched with calm confidence into Marsh's office. At stake were his years of self-financed education, as well as his future. When Marsh inquired as to the newly minted scientist's purpose, Hatcher was direct: "I want a job collecting fossils, anywhere, anytime, at any salary." It might have been the most subservient statement that Hatcher would ever make for the rest of his career.[15]

In showing his hand to the ever imperious and often pompous Marsh, Hatcher was, in effect, bidding to join in a burgeoning revolution surrounding scientific and especially paleontological knowledge in the United States. For the most part, American geology and paleontology, as well as other scientific disciplines, languished in the shadows of European universities and museums throughout the early 1800s, with American students traveling to Europe for scientific training, as we saw with Silliman. But in the wake of Thomas Jefferson's Louisiana Purchase in 1803 and his subsequent commission for the Lewis and Clark expedition from 1804 to 1806, during which their Corps of Discovery explored the northern extent of the nation's new territory, the US government eventually passed the Pacific Railroad Survey bill in 1853 to find the best routes for railroads from the Mississippi to the Pacific coast. This initiative further triggered a number of federally funded surveys after the Civil War that brought together explorers, engineers, scientists, and topographers in a common effort to chart the western landscape under the leadership of dauntless expeditionary luminaries such as John Wesley Powell, Clarence King, Ferdinand Hayden, and George Wheeler. These forays found a significant number of vertebrate fossils that were first evaluated primarily by Joseph Leidy, a professor of anatomy at the University of Pennsylvania and a member of the prestigious Academy of Natural Sciences in Philadelphia, and Europe began to take note of North America's evolutionary riches soon after Darwin published his seminal study *On the Origin of Species*. But by the 1870s, Leidy found his role as the nation's most prominent paleontologist under threat by two young, ambitious, and wealthy competitors, who began to explore the American West for fossils themselves. One was Edward Drinker Cope, whom Leidy fostered in Philadelphia at the Academy of Natural Sciences, and the other was the person to whom Hatcher made his appeal, O. C. Marsh. Just five years before Hatcher enrolled at Sheffield, both field crews of Cope and Marsh had made momentous discoveries of new dinosaur species in the frontiers of Colorado and Wyoming. So with his bold bid to Marsh, Hatcher stood on the precipice of joining this remarkable and raucous paleontological revolution. But would his gambit work?

2

Marsh: The Master

The second child of farmer Caleb Marsh and his wife Mary Peabody of Lockport, New York, O. C. Marsh tasted tragedy at the tender age of three when his mother died of cholera. Overall, he spent a listless childhood that was not sparked until he met Col. Ezekiel Jewett, also an accomplished field paleontologist, who opened the boy's eyes to the wondrous world of fossils in the tailings of the recently dug Erie Canal, just a mile from the Marsh farm. At last intellectually motivated, O. C. received financial support about 1851 from a settlement of property held for him by his father and, like Hatcher, determined to invest it in attaining an education at the prestigious Phillips Academy in Andover, Massachusetts.[1]

But after graduating from Phillips, Marsh would need substantially more financial resources to follow his path toward paleontology. Fortunately, he held that financial ace in his genealogical hand in the form of a most unusual uncle, George Peabody. Born as he was into a poor family in South Danvers, Massachusetts, young Peabody's schooling ended at the age of eleven, when he began to hone his extraordinary skills for business as an apprentice in a general store. By fifteen, he set out for the nation's capital, becoming a partner in a dry goods business in Baltimore, where he amassed a small fortune of $40,000 by age twenty. Gradually, he expanded into international trade and finance, eventually settling in London, where he established the banking house of George Peabody and Company, specializing in foreign exchange and American securities.[2]

As he neared retirement, Peabody gave away most of his massive fortune, totaling more than $9 million, to fund housing for the poor and educational causes, one of which involved supporting his nephew, O. C. Marsh, who received his bachelor of arts degree with honors from Yale College in 1860. Marsh then received a Berkeley Scholarship from Yale to pursue graduate studies in mineralogy, geology, and chemistry at Sheffield and was awarded an MA from Yale in 1863. After consulting with his advisors at Yale, including James Dwight Dana, he was advised to pursue graduate work in Europe, where he focused his studies on mineralogy and chemistry at several univerisities in Germany in hopes of becoming a hard rock geologist and eventually joining the Yale faculty. However, while there, he began purchasing some vertebrate fossils. His aspiration for a faculty position at Yale came to pass in 1866, when Marsh, under the guidance of Brush, Dana, and Benjamin Silliman Jr., professor of practical chemistry and the son of Yale's first scientific faculty member, negotiated with his famous uncle to provide a $150,000 grant in order to found Yale's Peabody Museum of Natural History. Since Dana held the professorship for hard rock geology, Marsh was appointed as the nation's first professor of paleontology, an essentially unpaid position without much teaching responsibility that he held until his death, in addition to being a trustee and founding curator at the Peabody Museum. The museum opened to the public in 1876. Unfortunately, Peabody did not live to see it, as he died in London in 1869, where his body received the rare privilege of a temporary burial in Westminster Abbey before being brought to America for final burial in Peabody, Massachusetts—his birthplace renamed in his honor.[3]

Marsh received an inheritance of $100,000 after Peabody's death, with the stipulation that most of it was to remain invested so that he could live off the income. He used his inheritance to fund his decades-long quest for vertebrate fossils, fossil footprints, invertebrate fossils, osteological specimens, as well as archaeological and ethnological artifacts. During his career he published around four hundred scientific studies of the fossils he and his large staff of assistants and collectors brought back to Yale. In 1898, a year before his death, Marsh presented his extraordinary collections to Yale, along with his mansion, which is now on campus.[4]

By the time Hatcher and Marsh crossed paths, Marsh was already famous for his discoveries of dinosaurs in the American West. Their names now roll off the tongue of any five-year-old aficionado: *Brontosaurus*, *Stegosaurus*, and *Allosaurus*, among others. Yet Marsh's achievements are virtually impossible to view in isolation, for his career, almost from the start, became entangled in his long-running, vitriolic feud with Edward Drinker Cope of the Philadelphia Academy of Sciences, often referred to as the "Bone Wars." Numerous treatments of their rancorous rivalry have already been written, including *The Gilded Dinosaur* by Mark Jaffe and *The Fossil Feud* by Elizabeth Noble Shor, and their dynamic provides a suitable context into which we can place the world Hatcher was being primed to enter upon his graduation from Yale.[5]

Born in 1840, as the eldest son of a family of well-to-do Quakers on the fringe of Philadelphia, Cope, like Marsh, lost his mother at the age of three. Although his father long wished him to take root in the family's farming, Edward was uninterested in such labors and used his time investigating the flora and fauna that inhabited the surrounding countryside. By 1860, Cope had published a study on the scientific classification of salamanders, the first of around 1,300 scientific papers that would consummate his career, and was taking anatomy classes at the University of Pennsylvania under Joseph Leidy, one of America's most prominent professors of anatomy and natural history at the time. By 1863, with the Civil War raging, Cope's father sent Edward off to Europe, where he toured the great museums and universities and met many of the Continent's prominent paleontological and zoological scientists. It was during this sojourn that Marsh and Cope first met and spent several amicable days together in 1864, when Marsh was, likewise, studying in Berlin, after he had left the United States soon after the war broke out. Signifying their mutual respect, Cope even named an early fossil relative of tetrapods (including amphibians, reptiles and mammals)—*Colosteus marshii*—for his new colleague in 1867. Marsh returned the favor by naming a giant fossil sea lizard, called a mosasaur, *Mosasaurus copeanus* in 1869.[6]

Having returned to the United States after the conclusion of the Civil War, Marsh settled in New Haven, where he helped oversee the development of the Peabody Museum, and Cope moved to Haddonfield, New Jersey, in 1868, where the nearby marl pits had produced the first fairly complete dinosaur ever found in the Americas in 1858. Leidy named that duckbilled dinosaur *Hadrosaurus foulkii* and had it mounted in the Philadelphia Academy of Sciences around the same time Cope had started working in the collections there. Alerted to the possible presence of more fossil bones found by workers in the quarry in 1866, Cope rushed to the Haddonfield marl quarries and recovered the fossil remains of an enormous carnivorous dinosaur, which he christened *Laelaps aquilungis* the same year. Cope's discovery caught the eye of Marsh, who visited Cope at Haddonfield in the spring of 1868. They spent a week touring the marl pits in search of fossils before Marsh apparently departed. However, unbeknownst to Cope, Marsh slyly reconnoitered with the owners of several marl pits and contracted with them to send any fossils they found to him rather than Cope. This usurpation of Cope's prior claim to the fossil fields at Haddonfield most probably lit the fuse in Cope's mind for the feud to come.[7]

In the early 1870s, both competitors turned their attention to the promising potential of numerous fossil localities along the eastern flank of the Rocky Mountains and the adjacent Great Plains. Both Marsh and Cope had been receiving intriguing remains from geologists and amateur collectors roaming these regions; as the transcontinental railroad was constructed through the region, settlers continued to migrate into the vast open spaces, and their governments and universities continued assessing the potential for natural resources. After an initial reconnaissance trip along the unfinished railroad line in 1868, during which he acquired a set of vertebrate fossils at the stop in Antelope, Nebraska, that convinced him of the region's paleontological potential, Marsh was the first to field forays into these fossil fields by organizing four expeditions from 1870 through 1873. Marsh manned these expeditions with adventuresome students from Yale who paid their way. Through his connections with the US government, Marsh secured letters of support and introduction from military luminaries such as General William Tecumseh Sherman, now the top commander of the Army, General Philip Sheridan, commander of forts throughout the western frontier, and regional commander General E. O. C. Ord. These endorsements guaranteed logistical support and armed security as the expeditions traversed territory still claimed by hostile Native American tribes.[8]

Between bison hunts and campfire tales from guides and scouts, including William Cody (better known as "Buffalo Bill"), Marsh and his crew of 1870 collected an amazing array of fossils, including early horses and rhinos from the Miocene beds of western Nebraska along the Loup Fork and North Platte Rivers; Oligocene brontotheres, oreodonts, turtles, rhinos, and birds from sites in northeast Colorado; fossil fish from the Eocene lake beds of the Green River Formation in Wyoming; allosaur teeth from Jurassic sediments in Utah near what is now Dinosaur National Monument; as well as Cretaceous mosasaurs, two knuckle bones of the pterosaur called *Pteranodon*, and part of a shin bone of the four-foot-tall, toothed bird called *Hesperornis*, the first toothed bird ever found in the Americas, all from the chalk beds of the Niobrara Formation in western Kansas.[9]

The 1871 field season saw Cope join the fray on the western frontier. By early July, Marsh's crew was, once again, successfully crawling over the Niobrara chalk in search of more pterosaur specimens, which confirmed Marsh's original estimate, published in 1871, that the wingspan of his flying reptile, still called *Pteranodon*, was not less than twenty feet. They then moved west for a six-week assault on the Eocene beds of the Bridger Basin, near Fort Bridger in southwest Wyoming, where the crew discovered specimens of the new, primitive horse *Orohippus*, along with rhinos and tapirs.[10]

Following in Marsh's wake, Cope invaded the Cretaceous chalk buttes of western Kansas during August and September and discovered his own mosasaur skeleton, as well as turtles, pterosaurs, and fish. When Marsh found out that Cope had collected in the Kansas chalks, he was incensed by what he considered an act of paleontological trespassing, ironically similar to his own actions at Haddonfield. No doubt further enflaming Marsh's mania was Cope's published announcement in March 1872 that his pterosaur had an even longer wingspan than Marsh's, making it the largest yet found on the continent.[11]

But it was not their conflict over the Kansas chalk beds that caused their festering feud to reach critical mass. Instead, that bomb detonated over the dry, desolate badlands of the Bridger Basin in 1872. Cope had hitched his paleontological wagon to the federally sponsored United States Geological and Geographical Survey of the Territories led by Ferdinand V. Hayden, who engaged Cope as the survey's lead paleontologist. By June, Cope descended on Fort Bridger ready to begin prospecting, but struggled to find horses and wagons because Hayden had appropriated them all for his own fieldwork. Hoping to be reimbursed, Cope bought a wagon and four mules for $500 and hired another team and driver, along with a cook, guide and packer, before setting out for the badlands. Within a few days, he reported back to the fort that he'd hit pay dirt, finding "25 or 30 species of which 10 are new." Marsh was not in the field yet, but he had hired a couple of men to collect for him in the Bridger Basin, including B. D. Smith and an opportunistic character named "Sam" Smith. Leidy, a much more mild-tempered third ring in this paleontological circus, soon arrived in the Bridger area and quickly discovered remains of an enormous, intimidating, multi-horned mammal with fearsome, saberlike canine teeth, which he named *Uintatherium*. Meanwhile, Cope had been called by a colleague on the Hayden survey to Black Buttes, about forty-five miles northeast of Fort Bridger, where he'd come across bones that Cope excavated and named *Agathaumas sylvestris*, which represented only the third-known dinosaur skeleton from North America. Later, on Bitter Creek, Cope discovered a similar horned mammal to that of Leidy's, which he named *Loxolophodon*, although due to a mistaken transcription in Cope's hastily written telegram back to Philadelphia, it was announced as *Lefalaphon*. In all, Cope felt he had discovered around fifty new species of fossil organisms, and much to

Marsh's dismay, a steady stream of preliminary announcements, important in establishing Cope's priority for naming and describing these discoveries, began flowing out of Philadelphia.[12]

Marsh hastened his small 1872 crew of four Yale students into the field. Their first stop was in the chalk beds of Kansas, where their brief efforts were rewarded by the discovery of the first skull of *Hesperornis regalis.* As Marsh quickly moved on the Bridger Basin, Cope left to begin collecting in the nearby Wasatch Basin, where he discovered skulls and skeletons of another horned mammal, for which he coined the name *Eobasileus.* By the fall, all three paleontologists had returned to their home bases in the East, but with all the preliminary reports regarding discoveries, some of which seemed to represent very similar fossil vertebrates, it became unclear who had actually discovered what first, since the rules and procedures for naming new animals were not rigorously standardized and adjudicated. The basic rule holds that the name first published for a given organism is the legitimate one that has priority. In terms of the enormous, multi-horned, Eocene mammal that Cope, Leidy, and Marsh had all found fragmentary specimens of, Leidy published the name *Uintatherium* for it on August 1, followed shortly thereafter by Cope's name *Loxolophodon* on August 17 and Marsh's two names, *Tinoceras* and *Dinoceras* on August 19. Marsh had named a specimen of this animal "Titanotherium anceps" in July 1871, but since that name had already been used for another animal, he renamed it *Tinoceras anceps.* Another Cope name, *Eobasileus,* appeared in a publication describing a more complete specimen of the same animal on August 20. Suffice it to say that at that time, confusion reigned.[13]

By January of 1873, Marsh in effect declared war on Cope. Having received a note from Cope congratulating him on his announcement of *Hesperornis,* along with a box of specimens, Marsh fired off a vicious salvo:

> *I am glad you appreciated my bird with teeth . . .*
> *Your paper on the "Proboscideans"* [meaning *Uintatherium,* which Cope incorrectly thought was a relative of elephants] *came the 20th inst., with postmark 18th of January, although bearing the date 16th. Why don't you send your papers more*

promptly, as I invariably do. I am willing to accept as publication
even an uncorrected proof (as we agreed). . . .

The Kansas fossil you sent came all right, where are the rest? and
how about those from Wyoming?

The information I received on this subject made me very angry,
and had it come at the time I was so mad with you for getting away
with Smith (to whom I had given valuable notes about localities
etc.) I should have "gone for you" not with pistols or fists, but in
print. I came very near publishing this with some of your other
transgressions . . . but my better judgement prevailed. I was never
so angry in my life.

The rogue Smith was "Sam" Smith, one of the collectors whom Marsh had hired to collect for him in the Bridger Basin. For a while the previous summer, "Sam" Smith had switched his allegiance and worked for Cope.[14]

Cope immediately fired off a four-page retort, in which he decried that it was "more irritable" for him to be accused of "dishonorable acts" than to lose possession of fossils or priority to name new species. He further admonished Marsh by asserting, "All the specimens you obtained during August 1872, you owe to me. Had I chosen they all would have been mine." Cope claimed that Smith had left before he discovered a new locality, and when Smith returned, Cope allowed him to collect for Marsh, which resulted in Cope losing "several fine things." In view of all this, Cope demanded that Marsh retract his accusations of unethical actions. But Marsh promptly refused, responding, "I feel I have been deeply wronged by you in numerous instances. These wrongs I have usually borne in silence. . . . After the Smith affair last summer, I made up my mind that forbearance was no longer a virtue."[15]

Throughout the spring of 1873, a torrent of vituperative diatribes rumbled through the scientific press. Marsh charged that Cope had nefariously predated several of his scientific papers in an attempt to dishonestly establish priority for the names of new species and genera he had published. Marsh also cited what he considered to be numerous errors in Cope's anatomical descriptions. Cope responded that Marsh's anatomical criticisms were simply misinterpretations of what Cope had written and that Marsh's charges of predating the papers were "either criminally ambiguous or untrue."[16]

Relations between the two rising paleontological titans would continue to deteriorate throughout the mid-1870s. Although both antagonists continued to butt heads in the Cretaceous chalks of western Kansas and the Eocene badlands of southwestern Wyoming, each extended their collecting efforts to important new regions. Most notably, in late 1874, Marsh was invited by General Ord of the Army to collect in the stunningly scenic, light gray badlands near the Lakota Sioux Red Cloud Agency in what is now south-central South Dakota. Known today as Badlands National Park, the Oligocene and Miocene sediments have produced a wealth of fossil mammals, including bizarre, knob-headed beasts called titanotheres, about which Marsh became particularly enthralled. With Red Cloud's permission, Marsh made a significant collection and, in the process, became a champion for Red Cloud and his tribe by returning to Washington and fiercely lobbying the federal government for better treatment and supplies for the tribe. Not to be outdone, Cope expanded his efforts southwest into New Mexico in 1874, where he also attached himself to Lieutenant Wheeler's geographic and geologic survey of the region. In the process, Cope discovered the fossil-rich Eocene sediments of the San Juan Basin, and more importantly, the even older Paleocene fossil beds along the Rio Puerco near Nacimiento (now Cuba, New Mexico).[17]

As each amassed his impressive collection of fossils, the value of the specimens clearly transcended mere treasured objects and obscure names. Not surprisingly, Cope and Marsh envisioned different views regarding the evolutionary stories the specimens told, especially in relation to Darwin's theory of evolution by natural selection, which had been published in 1859 as both Cope and Marsh were beginning their careers. Cope, at least in part due to his religious beliefs as a Quaker, could not accept Darwin's view of evolution as a random result of natural variations in organisms selected on the basis of their fitness to the environment they inhabited. To him, there had to be an overarching mechanism of design guiding the process. For Cope, variations were created by the "acceleration or retardation" of characteristics as organisms grew and acquired new traits during their life as they interacted with their environment, and ancestors could pass these acquired characteristics on to their descendants. In essence, Cope's belief was a rejuvenated version of Lamarck's earlier evolutionary ideas, famously illustrated by the supposed story that giraffes attained their long necks by stretching them to reach tender leaves high in the treetops. Marsh, on the other hand, had quickly accepted the legitimacy of Darwinian evolution by natural selection, and carefully observed the fossils coming into his collection for the evidence they provided for that process. In fact, by 1876, he would have the opportunity to demonstrate the power of his collection for documenting Darwinian evolution to the world.[18]

Darwin's chief supporter was a tenacious anatomist and naturalist named Thomas Henry Huxley, and in August of 1876, he arrived for the first time in the United States to deliver some landmark lectures on evolution in Baltimore and New York. But first, having heard of Marsh's burgeoning collection of vertebrate fossils, he paid a visit to the then newly built Peabody Museum. Darwin and Huxley knew that one key to scientifically demonstrating Darwin's theory of evolution would be to document the transitional forms of organisms between an ancestral form and its modern living descendant. However, the fossil record, even today, let alone back in 1876, is universally recognized to be woefully incomplete, due both to the rare environmental and depositional conditions required to preserve fossils and the constant destruction of fossils due to erosion once they are exposed near the surface of the ground. Nonetheless, Huxley had already tried to document the evolution of the horse based on fossils from Europe, where he thought the horse had originated. He examined how the teeth and legs grew longer and the number of toes decreased through geologic time, but there were many transitional forms missing. Based on his collections, Marsh was convinced of two things. The horse had first evolved in North America, not Europe, and he had the specimens to document the transitional forms from the early ancestors with short legs, short teeth, and many toes to the modern horse with long legs, long teeth, and just one toe. Huxley spent two full days skeptically questioning Marsh and probing his collections of horse fossils from the American West. Each time Huxley confronted his host with a challenge to produce a specimen illustrating a particular transitional characteristic, Marsh would instantly send an assistant into the collection to retrieve a demonstrative specimen. Amazed and somewhat stunned, Huxley exclaimed, "I believe you are a magician. Whatever I want, you just conjure up." Thoroughly convinced by Marsh's overwhelming fossil evidence, Huxley went on to highlight Marsh's demonstration of horse evolution in his lectures, thereby enhancing Marsh's standing in the eyes of both the scientific community and the public.[19]

As the later 1870s rolled into view, both Cope and Marsh began to rely increasingly on freelance fossil collectors to handle their collecting operations in the field. Marsh eventually abandoned going to the field by the late 1870s. So the conundrum of collectors, like "Sam" Smith, switching their allegiance between Cope and Marsh would continue to bedevil both. A prime example is represented by Arthur Lakes, an Oxford-educated schoolteacher and minister imbued with a profound interest in geology and natural history, who settled in Colorado. He discovered what are now known to be 150-million-year-old, late Jurassic dinosaur bones in 1877, near the city of Morrison. Lakes immediately wrote Marsh and provided a sketch of the specimen, and Marsh volunteered to try and identify the bone if Lakes sent it. By the time Lakes received Marsh's response, he had found the end of a limb bone fourteen inches in width. Although Marsh astonishingly failed to respond immediately, Lakes nonetheless sent Marsh ten crates of bones weighing in at 1,500 pounds. By the time Lakes finally did receive Marsh's response, requesting that Lakes keep the discovery quiet, along with a check for $100, Lakes had already sent another sample of bones to Cope. Marsh immediately sent Benjamin Mudge, one of his collectors, to evaluate Lakes's fossil locality, and Mudge managed to secure rights to collect there for $100 to $125 per month after confirming the significance of the site. Within weeks, Marsh had published an announcement about the discovery of "a new and gigantic dinosaur," estimated to be between fifty and sixty feet long, thus "surpassing any land animal hitherto discovered." He initially coined the name "Titanosaurus" for it, but after his archenemy Cope complained that that name had been previously used for a dinosaur found in India, Marsh changed it to *Atlantosaurus*. Within a couple of months, Mudge and Lakes had gleaned ten crates of bones weighing 2,500 pounds from Lakes's outcrop and sent them to Marsh.[20]

While all this was happening, Cope had been examining the teeth and bone fragments sent by Lakes and was ready to purchase them, but before he could prepare a paper for print, he received a letter from Lakes requesting that he forward the fossils to Marsh because Marsh had already bought them. Although no doubt disappointed, Cope's displeasure was diminished because he had already received another shipment of late Jurassic bones from around a town about 120 miles from Morrison called Cañon City. The sender was O. W. Lucas, a local superintendent of schools interested in botany. Among Lucas's assortment was a large vertebra that, in a hastily penned paper, Cope characterized as belonging to an enormous animal "which exceeds in proportions any other land animal hitherto described, including the one found. . . by Professor Lakes." Cope named his behemoth *Camarasaurus*, and needless to say, the "bone rush" for dinosaurs was on.[21]

Upon hearing of Cope's coup in Colorado, it was Marsh's turn to be disappointed—not only because Cope had found a way to enter the fray but also because the bones he was getting were better in terms of preservation. Beyond that, according to Mudge, whom Marsh sent to Cañon City to check, Cope's bones from there were 10 to 30 percent larger than Marsh's bones from near Morrison. Marsh telegraphed Mudge to "Secure all possible [bones]. Jones has violated all agreements." (Jones was the code name for Cope in correspondence between Marsh and his collectors.) But Mudge informed Marsh that Lucas would send all the bones of the skeleton he was working on to Cope. However, Marsh might have a chance to obtain subsequent finds if the price was right. In fact, if Marsh had not been so distracted or delinquent, he could have had the bones coming out of Cañon City, too, because another of his collectors, David Baldwin, had alerted Marsh to their presence at least a month before Lucas wrote to Cope about them.[22]

But not to worry, for in mid-July Marsh received a letter written on the nineteenth from two railroad workers from around Laramie in the Wyoming Territory, informing him of their discovery of fossil bones, including a shoulder bone 4' 8" in length and a vertebra 2.5' in diameter.

The men, who went by the aliases of Harlow and Edwards, sent a few fragments and indicated, "We would be pleased to hear from you, as you are well known as an enthusiastic geologist, and a man of means, both of which we are desirous of finding—especially the latter." Marsh sent a check for $75 payable to Harlow and Edwards and requested that they ship the specimens to him. After a delay of several weeks, they shipped the bones but informed Marsh that they couldn't cash the check and were not sure they could keep their discoveries secret. Convinced of the bones' significant value, Marsh immediately dispatched his most trusted and highly trained collector, Samuel Wendell Williston, to Laramie to investigate. Williston soon discovered that the men had used phony names in their letter to Marsh in order to avoid drawing attention to their discovery. Their real names were William Edward Carlin (aka Edwards), the station agent at Como, Wyoming, and William Harlow Reed (aka Harlow), the section foreman. The financial arrangements were quickly sorted out, and Williston was told,

> [The fossil bones] *extend for seven miles and are by the ton. . . . The bones are right by the station but there are only four or five persons that know about them. . . . The bones are very thick, well preserved, and easy to get out. . . . I will send a ton a week. . . .*

The railroad men then led the stunned Williston on a tour of the fossil beds exposed along a ridge called Como Bluff. Upon regaining his composure, Williston duly informed Marsh, "Cañon City and Morrison are simply nowhere in comparison with this locality both as regards perfection, accessibility and quantity."[23]

Indeed, from November of 1877 to March of 1883, Marsh's field crews, led primarily by the former section foreman Reed, shipped a total of 152 crates and 84 cans of bones and teeth to Marsh. In turn, Marsh paid his crewmen over $8,000 for their labor, about $175,000 in today's currency. But for Marsh, it was certainly worth it, for the bones from Como Bluff allowed Marsh to describe a tremendous team of 150-million-year-old, dinosaurian all-stars, known today as *Allosaurus* Marsh, 1877; *Apatosaurus* Marsh, 1877; *Brontosaurus* Marsh, 1879;

Diplodocus Marsh, 1878; *Stegosaurus* Marsh, 1877; and *Coelurus* Marsh, 1879. Beyond that, one of Reed's Como Quarries (No. 9) produced a dazzling array of minute, 150-million-year-old mammal teeth and jaws that Marsh eagerly named and described. At the time, they were among the oldest mammal teeth ever found and still play an important role in modern studies of mammalian evolution. Although Carlin eventually abandoned Marsh for Cope and found fossils for him in the area, there's no doubt that Marsh bested his rival at the battle of Como.[24]

As the "bone rush" for dinosaurs was playing out in Colorado and Wyoming during the late 1870s, Cope and Marsh were engaged in another battle back east. This one was political, and it would greatly affect the funding for paleontological projects provided by the federal government. Cope had been elected as a member of the prestigious National Academy of Sciences (NAS) in 1872, and he used this position to help gain access to US government funding through his participation as a paleontologist on several government-funded surveys in the West, including Ferdinand V. Hayden's United States Geological and Geographical Survey of the Territories, through which Cope received partial funding for his collecting in the Eocene sediments near Fort Bridger, and Lieutenant G. M. Wheeler's United States Geographical Surveys West of the One Hundredth Meridian, from which he received some funding to collect in the Eocene and Paleocene deposits of New Mexico. These and other surveys in the West had been administered under the supervision of the US military. Marsh, on the other hand, had not received direct funding from these surveys, although he had sought and received logistical and protective security from the US Army during his expeditions in the early 1870s. Nonetheless, in 1874 Marsh was also elected to the NAS, receiving thirty-seven out of thirty-eight votes. As Marsh's biographers pointed out in a somewhat less than cryptic conclusion: ". . . remembering the rising heat of the Marsh-Cope quarrel at this time, it is not difficult to figure out who was the lone dissenter."[25]

Marsh became acting president of the NAS in 1878 and eventually served two six-year terms in that office beginning in 1883. Most importantly, it was while Marsh was serving as acting president that Congress requested that the NAS develop a plan to consolidate all the various, relatively independent government surveys into a more efficient governmental system under civilian control in order to save money and eliminate the ongoing duplication of efforts that characterized the various surveys at the time. Marsh, as the head of the NAS, was charged with heading up this effort. Marsh set up a committee of thirty-two NAS members to develop the plan, and upon completion, thirty-one members voted to approve the plan and send it on to Congress. Again, it's not hard to guess who dissented. The subsequent approval by Congress resulted in the formation of the United States Geological Survey within the Department of Interior in March of 1879.[26]

Eventually, Major John Wesley Powell, a Civil War hero who lost his arm at the Battle of Shiloh but nonetheless famously went on to lead a daring expedition of exploration down the Colorado River through the Grand Canyon, was appointed the second director of the USGS in 1881. With Marsh having led the charge to establish the USGS, Powell, in turn, appointed Marsh as the official vertebrate paleontologist of that agency in August of 1882. For a decade after 1882, Congress would pass legislation allocating some amount of funding for that year's projects conducted by the USGS, and through the budgeting process, Powell would authorize a portion of that funding to Marsh for work related to vertebrate paleontology. Thus, in essence, Cope found his federal funding frozen out under the direction of Marsh, and this, along with some bad mining investments that caused his fortune to simultaneously dwindle, placed Cope and his collecting program in decidedly dire straits, which naturally augmented Cope's abhorrence of Marsh.[27]

But what was bad news for Cope was good news for a 22-year-old, newly minted graduate of the Sheffield Scientific School. For it was with his USGS funds in mind that, in 1884, Marsh gazed at John Bell Hatcher standing steadfastly in front of his desk at the Peabody Museum. Although he had little actual field experience, except for the geologic excursions around New Haven during his time at Yale and his work in the Iowa coal mines where he collected some plant fossils,

This June morning, something in Hatcher's quiet manner, his wiry physique, or the look in his steady gray-blue eyes must have further

impressed him. . . . Marsh had Federal money at his disposal, and shortly after Commencement he sent Hatcher out to Long Island, Kansas. . . .[28]

Hatcher's gamble had paid off, albeit at the modest sum of $50 per month, a bit less than $1,200 per month in today's dollars. The agreement between Hatcher and Marsh, dated June 24,1884, covered one year from July 1, 1884 to June 30, 1885, and stipulated that three months of that year would be spent in New Haven. Marsh provided a $100 advance, representing salary for the first two months. The contract also included an option for Hatcher to work another year at the same rate, but with traveling expenses "to be extra." Marsh might have reasoned that if Hatcher didn't work out as a collector, the money expended on his salary was minuscule, and he would know about Hatcher's collecting abilities within a few months. But as with Hatcher's gambit, Marsh would also reap tremendous rewards.[29]

SECTION II
1884–1893

3

Wrestling with Rhinos, as well as Authority

As Hatcher set out for Kansas on his first assignment for Marsh, Marsh himself had already engaged a prolific, freelance fossil collector, Charles H. Sternberg, to excavate at the Long Island site. Originally a New Yorker, Sternberg was born into a family of theologians in 1850 and grew up along the Susquehanna River just south of Cooperstown, but at the age of seventeen, he joined his brothers when they moved to a ranch near Ellsworth on the Smoky Hill River in northern Kansas, where Charles spent his leisure time collecting leaf fossils in the Cretaceous Dakota Formation. Eventually he determined to devote his life "to collect facts from the crust of the earth; that thus men might learn more of 'the introduction and succession of life on our earth.'" In the aftermath of the Battle of Little Bighorn in 1876, Cope hired Sternberg to collect with him in the Judith River badlands along the Missouri River east of Fort Benton, Montana, where he helped Cope collect 1,700 pounds of fragmentary fossils, including specimens of the first horned dinosaurs ever found. That winter, Cope invited Sternberg to visit his home in Haddonfield, and in subsequent years, Sternberg collected for Cope in far-flung localities across the West, from the Miocene John Day beds in Oregon to the Permian red beds in Texas.[1]

But in 1884, Sternberg, attracted by the funding Marsh was capable of offering, switched patrons and signed on with Marsh to collect at the Long Island Quarry that Sternberg himself had discovered and proclaimed to be the most fabulous fossil locality he had found in a decade. Ironically, it had all been an accident. Usually, new fossil sites are discovered either by collectors who are familiar with what fossil-bearing rock layers look like in the region where they are seaching or by locals who stumble upon bone fragments weathering out of the ground and bring them to the attention of a paleontologist at a nearby university or museum. If one is searching for a particular kind of fossil, one must prospect in areas where rocks representing the right age and environment are exposed on the surface of the landscape. Today, geologic maps and satellite photos can help narrow these areas to be examined. But in this case, while resting near the Long Island site in 1882, Sternberg had let his team of horses ramble, later retrieving them along a stream in a ravine, whose walls were replete with an exceedingly rich trove of fossil rhinoceroses that, as it turned out, seemed to represent a different species than had ever been found before. Endlessly on the lookout for new fossil species, Marsh hired Sternberg to excavate the quarry. Serendipitously, Marsh probably wanted Hatcher to hone his fossil collecting skills under Sternberg's experienced hand, while gathering a large enough sample of specimens to describe the species.[2]

Within three days after arriving, Hatcher wrote Marsh on July 10 in disgust over having to labor under Sternberg's supervision. This seems to represent the first instance of what would become Hatcher's chronic complex of direct, if well-intentioned, insubordination. Marsh had charged Hatcher with writing a weekly report detailing what he had collected, but Sternberg dictated that the whole crew work together. "I would be glad to keep such a report," Hatcher pleaded, "if I could work somewhat independently." Most damningly, Hatcher disparaged Sternberg's carelessness in excavating the fossils, emphasizing that "taking more pains in raising the bones after they have been uncovered" would yield more useful and complete specimens. Also, in contrast to what Sternberg believed, Hatcher told Marsh, "This locality is by no means exhausted in fact only a good commencement has been made . . . many good specimens can yet be obtained with little difficulty." Impressively, Hatcher's geologic training even led him to offer an initial assessment of how the fossils came to be preserved in the way they were: "The bones here all lie in beds of sand or gravel, they have been washed in [by river currents] apparently after they were disjointed and lie scattered about promiscuously, two bones belonging together seldom if ever being found together."[3]

In any event, fossils were flying out of the ground, with Hatcher reporting on July 13 the recovery of three rhino skulls, several lower jaws and tusks, two mastodon teeth and two tusks, along with a set of rhino teeth and a foot preserving all the bones in place. He skeptically intimated to Marsh that he hoped Sternberg packed the teeth well and decried the fact that Sternberg had broken the foot bones a bit in the process of excavating them. In his off hours, the aspiring apprentice crammed from William H. Flower's *Introduction to the Osteology of the Mammalia* in order to help him recognize and properly excavate the bones he was encountering in the quarry. Again, he stated, "I hope it will be so after a while that I can take out what I find myself and send you a weekly report. . . ." In all, he optimistically declared, "I think this work agrees with me for I feel better than I did when I left New Haven."[4]

The next week brought more success, including what Hatcher felt might be some fossil seeds that none of the other workers had noticed, and which he hoped Marsh could identify. Although the bones were thinning out, he uncovered two more rhino skulls and some hollow bones Sternberg thought might have belonged to a bird. Increasingly miffed about not working independently, Hatcher lamented, "You said . . . that you wanted me to take out, pack & label my own specimens & to keep and send you a daily report of my collecting at least once a week. I should like very much to do so but the way Mr. Sternberg works it, it is impossible to do so."[5]

By July 31, with his patience for Sternberg's supervision exhausted, Hatcher exclaimed to Marsh in exasperation:

> *If you keep me with Mr. Sternberg this season I should either like the privilege of taking out and packing what specimens I find myself, or if you can't grant me this privilege please do not estimate my work by his. He is a hard working, industrious man but quite careless, and in a hurry about taking out and packing specimens* [before more respectfully qualifying his diatribe by concluding] *at least in my opinion. I think you had better write him about properly packing those he has collected before shipping them.*[6]

Hatcher's next missive on August 11 revealed that the owner of the land on which the quarry was located, James M. Overton, wanted Sternberg to cease work, although Hatcher didn't know why. Sensing a brewing brouhaha, Marsh defused the situation by dispatching his tried-and-true troubleshooter, Samuel Williston, to the site, who informed Hatcher that Marsh wanted him to continue working there. Hatcher indicated Overton had no objection to this as long as Hatcher paid him the same amount that Sternberg had offered—$50 per month. In addition, Williston arranged for Hatcher to open a quarry on the opposite side of the ravine from where Sternberg was working. Hatcher drew up an agreement between Overton and Marsh that stated the terms, which both eventually signed. Hatcher further negotiated a deal with Overton's son to help open his quarry by scraping off overburden using a scraper and Overton's team of horses for a couple of days at $3 per day. Finally, by boarding with Overton for $2.50 per week, Hatcher could essentially achieve full independence from Sternberg, and assured Marsh that he'd put in ten-hour days and keep an accurate account of his expenses as well as submit a daily report of his activities every week. Seeking Marsh's approval, Hatcher made his pitch for Marsh to send him funds at once: "If you can send me . . . $50.00 to use in buying packing material, hiring team etc. I can get along quite well. . . . Sternberg has borrowed every cent of money I had & I don't know when I shall be able to get it." In a final dig at his soon-to-be former supervisor, Hatcher asked Marsh how the teeth he collected that Sternberg sent did in the mail, adding that he hoped "they were not too badly broken, for they were splendid specimens & well preserved."[7]

After attacking the overburden on the opposite side of the ravine from Sternberg's quarry with a horse-drawn scraper and then picks and shovels, as was the norm at the time, Hatcher immediately proved the value of his independence by inventing a novel fossil collecting technique that is still used today. As he had previously reported to Marsh, most of the skeletons were all jumbled up rather than having all the bones of one individual preserved side by side as they had fit together in life. It was as if a flood or some other event had scattered the different parts of individual carcasses after the animals died. In order to clearly record where he found each separate part of a rhino skeleton or other bone, Hatcher divided the floor of his fossil quarry into a grid of seventy-eight five-foot squares, then numbered each square and recorded the position of each bone he excavated on a hand-drawn map of the quarry, which still exists. With each bone individually labeled to correspond with its image on the map, the positions of all the bones could be precisely reconstructed after they were carefully packed and shipped back to Yale. This kind of map is commonly used in excavating fossils today as the basis for a branch of paleontology called taphonomy—the study of the events and processes, such as burial in sediment, transportation, and decomposition, that affect the remains of an organism after it dies. In addition to spatially recording each specimen, Hatcher exercised much greater care in excavating the bones and teeth than Sternberg had. Fossils are usually cracked and fractured by natural geologic forces after being buried, so excavating them requires meticulous care in order to keep the fractured pieces together. Sternberg tended to hack the fossils out of the ground with hammers and chisels as fast as was praticable before quickly wrapping them and haphazardly loading them into crates for shipment. Follwing a formal set of collecting procedures that Marsh gave all his collectors beginning in 1875, Hatcher excavated his specimens with greater care before more carefully wrapping them in cotton or encasing them in a hard covering of cloth soaked in flour paste and more securely loading them into crates padded with straw to protect them during shipment. This more painstaking approach greatly increased the chances that the fossils would be in better shape and preserve more delicate details of their anatomy when the shipment arrived at the Peabody for study by Marsh. Beyond that, the training Hatcher received at the Shef on short geologic forays into the field gave him another advantage over most other fossil collectors, as the paleontological historian Url Lanham notes:

> *Fellow bone hunters thought* [Hatcher] *had a sixth sense that led him to exposures of rock that contained fossil bone. His uncanny skill was based in part on a close study of rock that enabled him to imagine from the appearance of the rock the current flow in long-vanished streams, or reconstruct an eddy where a floating carcass might have come to rest and been buried.*

In Long Island, Hatcher received $70 from Marsh to fund his work, and as the latter half of August rolled by, Hatcher reported finding isolated rhino bones and teeth, a turtle shell, the lower jaw of a camel, "deer" limb bones, a horse pelvis, and some isolated bones of a mammalian carnivore.[8]

At the end of August, Williston had departed, and Hatcher was "hard up" for funding. The monthly payment to Overton was due, as well as the fee to Overton's son, who had helped with the scraping and team of horses. Williston had told Hatcher to write Marsh for Overton's first month's pay, but Hatcher matter-of-factly confided to Marsh:

> *I would rather have nothing to do with Mr. Sternberg's business but if you care to place the paying of his* [Sternberg's] *assistant in my hands I will see that he is paid, get a receipt from him for the money and send it to you. If I pay young Mr. Overton I shall want $150.00. Fifty dollars each for the Overtons and fifty more for expenses which I think with what I have on hand will pay all expenses as long as I am here. Please send $150.00 at once.*

In the meantime, Hatcher kept an eye out, as Marsh had requested, for bones of small animals, and reported retrieving numerous specimens of two small rodents including one nearly complete skeleton, along with a good rhino skull, snake vertebrae, a bird's bill, and a carnivore thigh bone. The dutiful submission of his expense account recorded purchases for a memo book, tools, lumber and nails for boxes, fees for the scraping team, twine, and paper. Through the first half of September, fossils continued to flow out of Hatcher's quarry, including two good rhino skulls, small bird bones, and specimens from small animals. Marsh, anxious to see the quarry and Hatcher's new mapping process, visited the site from September 13 to 15, 1884 and was duly impressed.[9]

In the wake of Marsh's visit, Hatcher began packing specimens that Sternberg had previously collected and stored in his tent and at Long Island, Kansas. On September 17, Hatcher reported he'd completed packing specimens from the tent except for three rhino skulls that Sternberg planned to take home and had started on the specimens in town. Marsh had apparently directed Hatcher to search for a specimen of a rhino foot that Sternberg had mentioned, but an exasperated Hatcher replied, "I almost know beforehand that the search will be fruitless." Hatcher reported that Sternberg intended to keep some fine specimens, despite the fact that Marsh wanted all the best fossils, but Hatcher was loathe to confront Sternberg because the packing was going well, according to his standards. Even though Sternberg protested it was proceeding too slowly, Hatcher insisted on doing it properly. Marsh had further charged Hatcher with negotiating with Overton for continued access to the site, and Hatcher indicated he was confident of concluding that arrangement in the next week or two. After another week of packing in Long Island, Hatcher complained that Sternberg's specimens were in bad condition, "almost powder." Although he packed them in boxes with plenty of straw around them, he feared no amount of packing would get them through in good shape, but the much-desired foot specimen could not be found.[10]

At the end of September, Hatcher prospected at a site near Logan, Kansas, where Sternberg claimed there were abundant horse fossils. Although he and Sternberg found several isolated bones, Hatcher was skeptical that the site was worth sending a crew to work it, especially compared with the Long Island quarries that yielded rhinos, including some bones of juveniles, several bones and lower jaws of small rodents and other animals, a neck vertebra of a mastodon, horse hooves, snake vertebrae, and some nearly complete frog skeletons. Sternberg thought that he'd about exhausted his side of the draw and that he could exhaust Hatcher's side in about a month if he had the privilege of crossing. But Hatcher resisted, reporting that he would have plenty of work for the fall and maybe another month next year if he returned.[11]

On October 5, Hatcher reported expanding his quarry and finding another rhino skull, but he lamented, "Mr. S. has found 4 since you left but broke three of them up pretty badly taking them up & the fourth one is not entire." Then, even though bones were still plentiful and increasingly well-preserved as he scraped back farther into the bank, Hatcher began to close up the quarry for the season, alerting Marsh that he'd need $75 for boxes and payments to the Overtons. One "very" fine skull of an adult rhino and another of a juvenile appeared, as well as isolated bones of "deer," horse and camel. By October 19, Hatcher was frustrated at Marsh's failure to send the requested funds for Overton, peevishly complaining, "I wrote for it some three weeks ago & he is needing it & should have had it before this.... [Send it] as soon as possible as I will want to leave here about Nov. first according to your orders when you were here."[12]

Finally, Hatcher received the requested funds by October 26 and reported that Sternberg had gone home. But by the time he reached the railroad station in Orleans, Nebraska, with the crates of fossils for shipping, he "rec'd word last evening that my mother was not expected to live. Must leave here at once. All the boxes are in the car & car nailed up." His note concluded with the news that the long-lost rhino foot had finally been found and sent to Marsh by express. Marsh could only have been pleased in November when a massive shipment of 143 crates of fossils representing the combined efforts of Hatcher and Sternberg arrived in New Haven, each weighing between 250 and 1000 pounds.[13]

In the end, although Hatcher had proved difficult to work with and there had certainly been tension and tests of wills between Hatcher and Sternberg, Charles was more magnanimous when he recalled his encounter with the young collector in his autobiography:

That year, 1884, . . . was a memorable one, not only because we secured a large carload of rhinoceros bones, but also because we had with us Mr. J. B. Hatcher, who afterwards helped to build up three great museums of vertebrate paleontology . . . Yale and Princeton and the Carnegie Museum. . . . A bright, earnest student, he gave promise of a future even then by his perfect understanding of the work in hand and the thoughtful care he devoted to it. I have always been glad that I had the honor of being his first teacher in the practical work of collecting, although he soon graduated from my department and requested me to let him to take one side of the ravine while I worked the other. He employed Mr. Overton's son with a plow and scraper and got out a magnificent collection with no further instructions from me. [14]

Today, the valid scientific name of the fossil rhino from Sternberg's Long Island Quarry is *Teleoceras fossiger*. Interestingly, its name represents remnants of research by both Hatcher and Cope, for Hatcher coined the name of the genus soon after he left Marsh's employ in 1894, but the species name was conceived by Cope in 1878 based on specimens he had acquired. Although Marsh, possibly to irritate Cope, named a skull from the Long Island Rhino Quarry *Aceratherium acutum* in 1887, that name was shown to be invalid in terms of priority by 1904. With a general body form like a hippo's, this barrel-chested grass-grazer, whose legs, although stout, were barely long enough to reach the ground below its stocky body, lived around five or six million years ago in the late Hemphillian Land Mammal Age of the late Miocene on the North American Great Plains. Although there is good evidence to show that *Teleoceras* ate grasses, since some specimens have been found with fossilized grass particles associated with their teeth, there is still scientific debate about whether this ancient rhino was primarily terrestrial, like modern rhinos, or aquatic, like modern hippos.[15]

However, Hatcher's collection from the 1884 season at Long Island, Kansas, totaling 708 specimens that are all housed at the Smithsonian's National Museum of Natural History (USNM), represents much more than just *Teleoceras*. As noted in appendix 2, this diverse fauna included another rhino (*Aceratherium*), the elephant-like *Mastodon*, the carnivorous amphicyonid "bear dog" *Aelurodon*, the saber-toothed carnivore *Barbourofelis*, a weasel (*Tayra*), six genera of horses ("Griphippus," *Hipparion*, *Merychippus, Neohipparion, Pliohippus, and Protohippus*), the pocket mouse *Perognathus* and two other mice (*Hesperomys* and *Microtus*), a peccary (*Prosthennops*), three species of frogs (*Bufo*), a tortoise (*Terrapene*), a snake ("Palaeoelaphe"), a mousebird (*Palaeospiza*), and a falcon (*Proictinia*).

All in all, the season for Hatcher was a triumph. He had transcended his frustrating apprenticeship and was ready to roam on his own. But to do so successfully would challenge his physical and mental abilities to the max. He clearly loved being enveloped in natural settings, but would his health hold up to the extent required to conduct long, physically demanding field seasons? His innate intellect and rigorous education at Yale had trained him well in the basics of geologic and paleontologic exploration. He possessed acute powers of observation and the patience to spend long hours analyzing the rock units exposed around him while focusing intently on the outcrops in search of small bone fragments and teeth weathering out of the ground. Also, since he came from a relatively humble, rural background, perhaps he had a chip on his shoulder regarding his more aristocratic and highly educated superiors, such as Marsh, which drove his determination to demonstrate that he could stand toe-to-toe with them when it came to collecting or researching the scientific significance of his fossil discoveries. Now, after years of preparation, he finally had the opportunity to prove himself—both in his own eyes and theirs.

4

Messin' with Texas and Returning for Rhinos

B y early December, Hatcher was preparing for a winter season of collecting near Wichita Falls, Texas. His purchases funded by Marsh's account included a tent, blankets, pen, ink, and a rubber suit, perhaps for warmth. On December 11, he purchased a ticket for just under $35 (about $960 in today's dollars) and boarded a train in New Haven for a five-day rumble to Fort Worth via Cincinnati and St. Louis. Thus, less than two months after finishing his first field season in Kansas, Hatcher's first solo foray found him wandering around Wichita Falls on Christmas Day 1884. His charge was to collect fossil vertebrates from Permian rock layers in the area that were between 280 and 270 million years old.[1]

In essence, Marsh was sending Hatcher on a mission to compete with Cope. When ensconced in the Wheeler Survey for the US government, Cope had traveled to Texas in 1877, the same year the "Bone Wars" for dinosaurs descended on Colorado and Wyoming further to the north. While working in Texas, Cope met a local fossil collector named Jacob Boll, who was born in Switzerland in 1828 and belonged to a family that had established the utopian society called La Reunion in Dallas during the mid-19th century. Apparently fond of fieldwork, Boll discovered the first vertebrate fossils from the Permian red beds near the Wichita and Red Rivers, and Cope hired him to collect. It was primarily through Boll's collection that Cope began describing in 1878 the ancient amphibians and reptiles that had inhabited the region around Wichita Falls around 275 million years ago. Lending credence to the hazards of such fieldwork back in those days, Boll actually died in 1880, when he was bitten by a venomous snake while on a collecting trip in the area. From then on, Cope hired William F. Cummins, a Missouri-born Methodist minster and former Confederate soldier turned geologist, to lead his collecting efforts in the region.[2]

But also in 1878, Marsh had purchased some Permian fossils from nearby New Mexico, discovered by David Baldwin, an enigmatic freelancer who especially loved to collect fossils all alone—except for his burro, some cornmeal, and his pickax—during the dead of winter to avoid the summer heat and take advantage of snowy meltwater. Marsh rather deviously described Baldwin's fossils before Cope described his from Texas, further inflaming their feud, as illustrated by the following incident:

> In the winter of 1877–1878, Jacob Boll of Dallas collected for Cope remains of animals . . . from the Texas redbeds, and the discovery was announced by Cope at a meeting in Philadelphia. It is said that Marsh, present at the meeting, left early to catch a train for New Haven, having remembered that he had purchased (but up to then neglected) a collection of bones, apparently also Permian in age, from New Mexico. He appears to have opened one or two packages and to have hastily written a short paper, which was

published within a few weeks. Marsh, despite his knowledge of Cope's work, calmly stated that "hitherto no Permian vertebrates have been identified in this country." His work of identification was so superficial that of two species described as belonging to a single genus, one is an amphibian, the other a mammal-like reptile! Cope, quite naturally, was aggrieved at this treatment; and when his own paper was published, appears to have compounded the tangle by claiming it to have been distributed about three weeks earlier than was the case. And so the battle continued.[3]

All this work helped open a new chapter in paleontological history, as the world was introduced to several new fossilized superstars, such as the giant, salamander-like amphibian *Eryops* and the fabulous, fin-backed early relative of mammals *Dimetrodon*—both top predators of their day.

When Hatcher arrived on the scene, he resourcefully hired a driver with a horse-drawn wagon for $2.66 per day, or about $73 per day in modern currency, who knew where Cope's Cummins-led crew had collected. Having purchased tent poles, groceries, a notebook, and towels on December 23, he informed Marsh that they would depart the next day for a two-week reconnaissance trip. But it would not be conducted under cushy conditions—the temperature was twelve degrees below zero and the small towns that dotted the harsh landscape were fifty to sixty miles apart. In addition, those towns seemed to be rather poorly tended by local law enforcement: "There was rather an amusing though serious instance [that] occurred here the other day. Two men quarreled, one shot and killed the other. The authorities arrested and imprisoned the dead man & let the living one go." Before parting, Hatcher reported that he hadn't heard from Cope's former collector David Baldwin yet. In what would become a recurring refrain, he requested that Marsh immediately send $100 to sustain the operation so it would be there when he returned to town.[4]

Eleven eventful days later, Hatcher chronicled the trials and tribulations on January 3, 1885. While they were in the field, two men in the region froze to death, and David Ballow, the old settler guiding Hatcher, suffered a frozen foot. Hatcher, however, remained healthy. Their travels were aided by the rivers being frozen, which facilitated crossing and allowed them to cover fifty miles during the nine-day trip. Hatcher located three fossil beds, but due to the sub-zero temperatures, the ground was too hard to quarry because it was frozen solid. Yet Hatcher was able to gather fragments of bone on the surface and sent Marsh a few samples for evaluation. Overall, the prospects seemed good for success once the weather warmed, leading Hatcher to confidently proclaim, "I know that the locality is inexhaustible and I think that if I could have 2 or 3 men to help me for as many months and good weather I could easily get a carload [ie. rail boxcar] of bones." He had a couple of men in mind, including Ballow and a younger local named James Lyons, a cowboy who could double as cook, but they would charge $40 per month, a salary much higher than journeymen in Kansas. After asking for Marsh's guidance, he closed with his soon-to-be common chorus, "Have not heard from you since I came. Have not rec'd the money I wrote for yet. I am out of money and can not go out again untill [sic] I get money."[5]

Marsh finally rode to the rescue with a $100 check that Hatcher received on January 7, and with the weather having significantly improved, Hatcher set out for the hinterlands on the eighth. He informed Marsh that he expected to be gone about two weeks.[6]

Upon his return about January 20, Hatcher was, once again, more than miffed to find no letter from Marsh. As he waited for another week, his simmering frustration built up to a roiling boil by the twenty-seventh:

I have received no answer to my letter of Jan. 3. When I left for Texas you authorized me to expend $50.00 for help if it was needed, before hearing further from you. I have already expended a little over that amount & have not heard anything as yet from you about the matter. I have been waiting for over a week to hear from you. I like to do as nearly as possible and directed. We are having good weather now and I feel as though I should be at work, but will wait until I hear from you. I collected & packed three large boxes of bones while out on my last trip and collected & left out there about 250 lbs. which I had not lumber for boxes to pack in. I am fully convinced of the richness of the locality and if I could

have anything or anybody to do with & knew what to do I could
& would do a great deal here by the first of April or time to go to
KS. But I do not feel very much encouraged so far.

As far as hearing from you often is concerned that does not matter
but I don't like to lay around waiting & doing nothing when a
word or two would let me know what to do.

If you want me to do anything here please write and let me
know as the $50.00 have already been expended and send check
for $100.00."

In terms of fossils, his letter only states that he had collected several jaws with teeth, many toe and leg bones and one skull over a foot long, but he made no attempt to identify them.[7]

In addition to the letter, he must have sent Marsh a telegram complaining about Marsh's lack of correspondence with additional funding. For the next day on the twenty-eighth, Marsh telegraphically replied, "Letter Jan 3 answered promptly. Keep on with work." On the twenty-ninth, Hatcher wrote Marsh that he'd received the telegram and was again heading out with Lyons, even though he hadn't received Marsh's letter. As to why the letter hadn't arrived, news in town seemed to suggest an answer: "There seems to be considerable trouble in getting mail through this postoffice [sic]. I understand that the present postmaster has been arrested for destroying mail & that another will take his place. Hope it will be for the better." Hatcher ended with another plea to send a total of $150 to fund continued work.[8]

A weary Hatcher trundled back into Wichita Falls on February 8, only to find that there was still no letter from Marsh. Having only received $100 during the last six weeks, Hatcher's woeful missive to Marsh the next day detailed the dire state of his financial affairs: "I can not pay my board, hire a man & team, buy provisions, packing material, lumber etc. for six weeks on a hundred dollars. I have not money enough to buy a postal card nor have not had for some time." Regardless, Hatcher reported that he'd collected a box of good specimens on the trip and would send some teeth and toe bones by mail before lamenting that he wouldn't have come in so soon, ". . . but some one came when we were off at work and stole three pair of blankets and a lot of provisions so that we had to come in for more. . . . But I have nothing to get either with."[9]

At long last, fortunately, Marsh's check was in fact in the mail and arrived the next day, on the tenth. Flush with $150, Hatcher paid his bills for lumber, hardware, groceries, packing material, and overdue salaries for himself, Ballow, and Lyons. Then he wrote Marsh that he planned to be out for five or six weeks, near Seymour in Baylor County, until it would be time to head back to the Long Island Rhino Quarry in Kansas. Marsh must have badgered him about the burgeoning expenses for the trip, because Hatcher assured him that he would do his best to keep them down, but he needed Lyons to help him handle the thousand pounds of broken specimens he'd already accumulated. As evidence for his economic restraint, Hatcher said he wouldn't need to buy blankets, since he'd been able to borrow some to replace the stolen ones. However, he ominously intimated to Marsh, "When I go out I am going to visit all the cow camps in the vicinity & if the boys have the blankets I will have them or something else." Looking forward, Hatcher implored Marsh to send $200 so it would arrive in three weeks, if he wanted him to leave for Kansas in April, which at that point, Hatcher was more than willing to do. The funds would be needed to wrap up, pay bills, and ship the specimens from Fort Sill, now Lawton, Oklahoma.[10]

Needless to say, when Hatcher arrived back in Wichita Falls on March 8, there was no letter or check from Marsh to greet him, making it impossible for the road warrior to wrap up his work and head off to Kansas. Infuriated, Hatcher let loose with a lecture:

> . . . In order to be there promptly as I have always tried to be prompt with you I walked about sixteen miles & waded the Big Wichita River when there was ice in it only to find when I got there that there was nothing for me & I have received nothing yet.
>
> I do not know why it is that you have been holding back on me since I came here unless you are in some way dissatisfied with me. If you are, I don't feel that I can better matters for I have done my best since I commenced in July. I like the work and should like to continue in it if I thought I could please you. But I do not like the

way matters have been since I came to Texas. When I promise men money at such a time I expect to get it there for them and I don't like to tell them when the time comes that I haven't it.

Unless there can be a change I had rather stop work.

Adding to Hatcher's frustration was the fact that he'd had a verbal battle with Ballow and had to dismiss him because the old codger had complained that Hatcher rode his mule too hard. Yet despite all the trouble, Hatcher had secured seven boxes with between 1,500 and 2,000 pounds of specimens that were ready to ship as soon as Marsh's check for $200 was received.[11]

Hatcher had to cool his heels for another ten days before funds arrived, along with Marsh's explanation that he had taken ill. In his response on the seventeenth, Hatcher expressed hope that Marsh had entirely recovered before informing him that he'd leave for Kansas the next day and had written Overton to expect him there by April 1. But it turned out that Hatcher had not wasted his time while waiting; instead, he'd gathered some juicy intelligence for Marsh:

I have become acquainted with Prof. W. F. Cummins who has been collecting here the past four years for E. D. Cope. He would like to collect for you during this coming summer. I told him that I would stop off in Dallas as I went through & see him. I think he would be a good man at any rate the best one in this part of the country.

He also spoke to me of some fossil birds he wanted to dispose of to you. He says Cope has written him to send them to him, but that he is waiting to hear from you.[12]

It seems Hatcher might have had a hidden agenda for hoping that Marsh would engage Cummins to carry on with the collecting in Texas, for Hatcher's closing commentary regarding the region is less than complimentary:

I think Texas is the worst place outside of "Hades." I have done the best I could under circumstances since I came here & have found a great many specimens though most of them are badly broken up. I am not satisfied with my work here for I have had to lay still & do nothing half of the time simply because I had nothing to do [it] *with.* . . .

If you ever want me to come to Texas again, this Fall for instance, I am willing to come but I want to pick some northern man out to come with me.[13]

And with that, as far as the records show, Hatcher would never return to Texas to collect. It seems that as far as he was concerned, he had gathered his evidence, formed his opinion, and delivered his verdict. In all, collecting the seven crates now constituting thirty-one catalogued Permian fossils in the Peabody collection had cost $532.93, which Hatcher, in his eagerness to calm Marsh's nerves about his field expenses, meticulously calculated to average out at only $177.64 per month—a mere $4,200 in today's money.[14]

Nonetheless, Hatcher gleaned a respectable, if not spectacular, set of specimens from the rugged landscape. In general, most of the material Hatcher collected during his tenure with Marsh was shipped from the field to the Peabody Museum at Yale, even though technically Hatcher was employed through the USGS. For the most part, it wasn't until after Marsh died in March of 1899 that a comprehensive program was conducted to split Hatcher's massive collection between the Peabody and the Smithsonian's National Museum of Natural History, in Washington, D.C. A search through the online collections of both institutions reveals that Hatcher's 1885 specimens from around Wichita Falls were split rather unevenly between the Peabody, which retains thirty-one specimens, and the USNM, which possesses only one.

Still housed in the Peabody's collection are a skull, vertebrae, and other skeletal fragments of a bizarre, boomerang-headed amphibian called *Diplocaulus*, which, with its sharp teeth and three-foot-long body, plied the Permian streams in search of prey around 275 million years ago. Other specimens include a skull, lower jaw and limb bones of *Eryops*, a 275-million-year-old, six- to nine-foot-long amphibian that probably used its sturdy four limbs to punt through the swampy rivers or occasionally haul out on land in search of prey, which it would grasp with its teeth before tossing its head up and backwards like a crocodile in order to swallow the meal. A fairly closely related amphibious form, called *Trimerorhachis*, is also represented. Two types of fin-backed, terrestrial, early relatives of mammals also adorn the Peabody's collection—the dazzling, carnivorous *Dimetrodon* and the equally elaborate, herbivorous *Edaphosaurus*. Another Peabody denizen from Hatcher's Texas sojourn is *Diadectes*, a seemingly bloated, six- to nine-foot-long beast that was among the first fully terrestrial, herbivorous animals ever to evolve to such a large size. Finally, there are two specimens of a salamander-like amphibian, named *Lysorophus*, which was probably a fully aquatic form, based on the size of its tiny reduced limbs, and three specimens of the nimble reptilian insectivore called *Labidosaurus*. Also represented is a freshwater shark named *Orthacanthus*. The only fossil at the USNM from Hatcher's Texas haul that is fully identified is a specimen of *Captorhinus aguti*.[15]

After fleeing Texas, Hatcher arrived back in the friendly confines of his Long Island Rhino Quarry on March 22 to find the Overtons glad to see him, especially since he hoped to hire Overton and two of his sons to help with the work and sought Marsh's approval. By April 3, Marsh, apparently concerned about costs, sanctioned the hiring of one man, and Hatcher concurred, "I am glad you only want one man to work here with me for I think I can do better work. . . . With one man here the expenses will not be above $120 per month." Although work was going well, with the discovery of two good rhino skulls, Hatcher needed another $100 for salaries and scraping overburden to expand the quarry. By the twelfth, Hatcher's submission of his weekly activity report listed 727 bones collected and packed into thirteen crates, including four rhino skulls of which three were "perfect," one mastodon lower jaw, and some rhino hyoid bones that Marsh had indicated he was especially keen to see. On the twentieth, with a $100 check in hand and a good deal of glee, Hatcher noted that the crew was having even better luck than the previous year.[16]

Although hampered by rainy weather and a "strained" and painful left hand the following week, Hatcher nonetheless reported finding a skull with lower jaws and a mastodon tusk, along with a tally of twenty-one full boxes, on the twenty-sixth. In early May, after paying the Overtons and purchasing tent poles, twine, glue, straw, and nails, Hatcher still needed more funds for lumber to build crates. He was working in the same quarry as the previous year but believed he'd need to move soon because there was so much dirt and stone in the twelve feet of overburden to move that continuing there would be very expensive. Despite that, by May 10, the quarry had produced ". . . two of the finest skulls . . . we have ever found." He now had a total of thirty-one packed boxes containing 2,100 bones, mostly rhino except for a few small animals. Regarding his accommodations, he reassured Marsh, "I live alone in my tent & have it right at the quarry where I can watch everything. It is awful lonely." He again bemoaned his lack of lumber and other supplies, before hopefully concluding, "but I suppose you have already sent the money I wrote for." However, a week later he complained, "I now have over 300 bones out unpacked & no lumber for boxes to pack them in, nor money to get any with & it rained all day yesterday on them and is raining today." Perhaps to spur Marsh's payment, he warned that Henry Fairfield Osborn of Princeton had written young Overton about working there and having Overton work for him. Then he softened the blow with the fact that if Osborn hired Overton, Overton would have to work somewhere else on the property if Marsh said so, adding, "I have no doubt though that I can arrange all that peaceably."[17]

The leverage worked, for Hatcher received a $100 check by May 24 and reported that they had now packed 41 boxes. Confidently projecting forward at that rate, he anticipated having at least 140 boxes by November 1, or 23 more than the previous year. But weather continued to weigh down the pace with hard rain and hail so everything was "drowned out." Nonetheless, Hatcher reported the finding of two fine rhino skulls, a horse bone, and a mastodon tooth by the thirty-first.[18]

Marsh must have inquired again about Osborn, because on June 7, Hatcher told him:

> *I have heard nothing more of Mr. Osborn and young Overton. But had a talk at the time with Mr. Overton himself on the matter, and he told me that as long as you wanted me to dig bones here you need not be uneasy about his letting anyone else in. The old gentleman*

knew nothing about Osborn's & young Overton's correspondence
until I told him, the boy having kept it from everyone but the man
he got to read Osborn's letters for him as he could not read them
himself & this man was the first to tell me. I am quite convinced
that Sternberg is at the bottom of all of it. But Mr. Overton &
myself are on the best of terms & there will be no trouble. [19]

Given the greater responsibilities that he was assuming for managing
the project, over and above just collecting fossils, Hatcher apparently felt
that he deserved a few more dollars, and in his characteristically steadfast
and straightforward way, he addressed Marsh:

When I hired to you last June I agreed to stay two years at $50.00
per month if you wanted me & you said at that time that if I did
well you might be able to do better by me. Now that my first year is
nearly up I would like to know if you want me another year & if so
how much better you can do? During the past year I have worked
pretty hard & and just about come out even. I should like to feel
like I was making a little clear after the 1st of July. I think while
I am out here in the field at work $75.00 per month would not be
far from right & $50.00 during the winter while in the museum.
Please let me hear from you about this. [20]

To bolster his proposed bargain he expanded on his very successful
week, as shown on his daily report: one good rhino skull and two pair
of good lower jaws, as well as an ulna and tibia of some kind of new
animal entirely different from those found before. He further noted that
he now had fixty-six packed boxes all from the same quarry he worked
the preceding year, adding that the bones were getting better, but they
now had to move twelve to fifteen feet of overburden to get to the bone
layer. [21] By June 21, Marsh, in addition to sending a $100 check, had
decided to see the operation for himself. Hatcher was glad to hear he was
coming out during the summer and reported that the railroad would be
completed by the time he arrived all the way to Long Island. But Hatcher
implored that if Marsh also went to Europe, he please send money to keep

them going while he was gone. They now had sixty-six packed boxes and 5,102 numbered bones, all drawn in position on the gridded quarry map, including some good bird bones. Of course, he reassured his mentor, all the horse and camel bones were carefully collected, but they were rare where they were presently excavating.[22]

In early July, Hatcher visited home for ten days. The timing of this trip seemed to reflect a natural break, for on the sixteenth, he told Marsh that he had finished his quarry with 117 boxes and would now move back across the ravine next to where Sternberg worked in 1884. Hatcher had neither heard nor seen anything of Sternberg. Apparently to counter Osborn's feelers for collecting in the area, Hatcher also enclosed two copies of a possible contract signed by D. J. Miller, whom Hatcher believed almost surely had bones on his land. The agreement was drafted so that Marsh could control any bones there for the next three years without it costing a cent, although Miller would receive $50 per month for working under the direction of Marsh's field supervisor. Hatcher didn't expect to work there himself but rather to keep others out. Noting that Marsh had spoken the previous year of securing the rights to work on other places, Hatcher felt that there were two other men with whom they should do the same thing if Marsh wanted to control all the Miocene fossil beds in this area. Then Hatcher moved on to another chronic plea for funds:

> About five weeks ago I wrote to you to send me $125.00. You have neither sent it nor told me why you did not. By the enclosed balance sheet you will see that I have up to yesterday paid out nearly $75.00 more than received. There will also be $70.00 due Mr. Overton the 29th of this month, 20 of which has been due for some time. I must have money and I want enough to do me a while without being broke all the time. I want $350.00 (three hundred & fifty) dollars. Send this amount in two checks, one for $125.00, the other for $225.00. Please send it at once for I am needing part of it.[23]

By the twenty-seventh, Marsh had sent a $125 check and signed the contract. Meanwhile Hatcher was keeping a good lookout for all kinds of bones in his new quarry and finding "a great many that I do not know." Accordingly, he kept everything, anticipating, "I have no doubt that when the collection from this place is worked over many new things will be found." Beyond that, despite discouragingly wet weather, he found another rhino skull and two lower jaws, along with two hundred other bones, and reported he'd still not seen or heard of Sternberg. On the thirty-first, Hatcher chronicled the unusual discovery of an articulated partial skeleton of a horse and bones of a small carnivoran, along with an aggravating expense report that showed he'd still laid out $63.63 more than he'd received from Marsh, adding:

> *Mr. Overton's July salary is now due. I must have more money. . . . I must have some more lumber soon. There will soon be due young Overton's $20.00, Mr. Overton's July and August salary $100, lumber $12.00, and $63.63 now due me, in all over $200.00. I wish you would send me at once $250.00 as both myself and Mr. Overton are needing it very badly. Please send it at once.*[24]

Despite Hatcher's impassioned pleas, Marsh judiciously doled out a check for only $125 in his response on August 1. Miffed, Hatcher responded on August 7, "You want to know how work is progressing. Very well I think considering . . . the intense heat & amount of dirt & rock we have to move to get to bones." So far, the season's haul totaled eighty-seven boxes of bones, already as much as had been sent in the previous year. Hatcher's luck with the horses continued, "At present we are getting some very fine horse bones which is something of a change from all the rhinoceros." But he'd need more money by September 1 for scraping fees, lumber, packing materials, and salary for young Overton and Mr. Overton. By the twenty-first, as he continued to expand Sternberg's old quarry, Hatcher's next dispatch noted the discovery of many bones of animals not found before, including a lower jaw with teeth and several other bones of a very large carnivore, bones of small carnivores, a lower jaw with teeth and bones of a small ungulate, a nearly complete skeleton of frog, and many good horse bones. Yet his financial woes wore on. "Have expended nearly $150.00 more than I have received and

I must have more money or stop work." He now could boast of securing ninety-five boxes of bones.[25]

Although two fine rhino skulls and other new kinds of bones continued to appear, by September 1, Hatcher lamented that the expense of getting to them was great due to the amount of overburden removal required, and he asked Marsh if he should continue here or open another quarry. More scraping was needed, but he had no money for it. They had packed 103 boxes with over nine thousand bones so far. His balance sheet for August revealed a continuing deficit of $130.58, including charges for newspapers and cotton for packing, a pick, scraping fees, twine, lumber, and salaries. Yet, always with his pupils peeled for potential poachers, Hatcher asked Marsh if it wouldn't be a good plan to secure the rights to collect at "Bone Mound," where Cope's crew had worked for about three months one year.[26]

As September blazed on, Hatcher coaxed more material out of the quarry, including rhinos, horses, "deer" and other small ungulates, carnivorans, and two fine skulls and two lower jaws of camels or other large ungulate. But by the thirteenth, Hatcher erupted once again at Marsh for funds.

By the end of October, when the field season concluded, Hatcher had shipped 115 crates of fossils to the Peabody—a prodigious haul, indeed. His 1885 collection from Long Island is now split between Yale's Peabody Museum of Natural History and the Smithsonian's National Museum of Natural History, with 1,299 specimens being housed at the former and 25 at the latter.

In all, the great majority of the 1885 Long Island, Kansas, specimens represent the rhinoceros *Teleoceras fossiger*, about which we've already spoken, totaling 1,163 in the Peabody. Other intriguing members of the 1885 fauna housed at the Peabody and USNM include another rhino, *Aphelops*; a primitive mastodon, *Gomphotherium*; a small, distant relative of antelope, *Merycodus;* and an advanced, three-toed horse, *Pliohippus*.

Despite being smaller, the 1885 collection by Hatcher that still resides in the USNM is somewhat more diverse than that of the Peabody, based on the current collection records. For example, four members of the camel family are present: *Procamelus, Aepycamelus, Megatylopus*, and the early relative of llamas, *Hemiauchenia*. The antelocaprid, *Merycodus*, is again represented, along with the somewhat elk-like, but not closely related, *Pediomeryx* or "Yumaceras." Carnivorous mammals are represented by the bone-crushing, amphicyonid "bear dog" named *Aelurodon* and a catlike, saber-toothed carnivore called *Barbourofelis*. Among rodents, one finds a relative of modern mice, *Hesperomys*. Especially noteworthy in the USNM collection, the unusual horned mylagaulid rodent is specifically named "Epigaulus" *hatcheri*, in honor of its discoverer. Frogs are represented by the genus *Bufo*. Reptiles include a giant tortoise, *Geochelone*, as well as a bird that was a relative of the limpkin, *Aramus*.

In addition, the USNM specimen catalogue also contains two entries for the crocodile-like phytosaur named *Rutiodon*, which lived in the Triassic about 225 million years ago. Interestingly, there seems to be no mention in Hatcher's correspondence that he took a separate collecting trip to North Carolina where these specimens were collected.

On the strength of all his success in Kansas and Texas, and clearly indicative of Marsh's growing confidence in Hatcher's abilities, Hatcher's request for a raise was granted. As the new agreement, dated March 6, 1886, stated,

> *I hereby agree to remain with Prof. Marsh on U. S. Geolog. Survey till July 1st 1887, or one year from the expiration of present agreement for ninety dollars* [90] *per month* [almost $2200/mo. in today's dollars], *provided the Govt gives the same or a greater amount for paleontology than this year.*
>
> *I further agree to remain four years more, or till July 1st 1891, on above conditions, for $100 per month.* Signed J. B. Hatcher[27]
> (See appendix 1)

5

Thunder Beasts

uoyed by the substantial salary increase, Hatcher enthusiastically focused his pervasive gaze on another kind of big
game—enormous evolutionary relatives of rhinos and horses
called brontotheres that originated as pig-sized mammals inhabiting
the dense forests of North America about 55 million years ago, but
eventually evolved into huge beasts that shook the earth as they trod.
The first scientific descriptions of brontotheres hatched from the hand of
Joseph Leidy, who described the genus *Megacerops* based on fragmentary
specimens from Colorado in 1870. But as with many other groups of
fossil vertebrates, Leidy's lead was quickly subsumed by the vicious feud
between Cope and Marsh. Marsh and his students had discovered specimens of "Palaeotherium" or "Titanotherium" in the Oligocene White
River badlands of northeast Colorado during the Yale College Scientific
Expedition of 1870. Marsh's early efforts continued through 1874, when

he made the famous foray into the Big Badlands of what is now South Dakota in the cold of November and met with the Oglala Lakota chief Red Cloud to get his blessing to collect in the wake of Custer's expedition to the Black Hills earlier in the year, which had discovered gold. The Native Americans were extremely skeptical that Marsh truly intended to travel through the area at the beginning of winter simply for a bunch of seemingly worthless bones, but Marsh eventually convinced them that he had no interest in gold and would carry their complaints about the inferior quality of the meat and supplies the government was providing them back to Washington. With that they briefly relented and agreed to provide a guard of several warriors; however, Red Cloud balked when Marsh's entourage, complete with a contingent of soldiers marching in formation, arrived at the chief's agency, where Red Cloud announced that his people could not be convinced that the expedition was not intended to find gold. So Marsh surreptitiously snuck out in the middle of the night for the Badlands. Throughout the short excursion, Marsh's party was trailed by Native American sentinels, but nearly two tons of valuable fossil bones were collected at the site before a party of friendly braves, reputedly sent by Red Cloud, warned Marsh that hostile northern warriors were on the way to attack. The next day was spent furiously packing the bones, and Marsh's contingent beat a hasty retreat to Fort Robinson less than a day before the war party arrived. True to his word, Marsh brought Red Cloud's complaints about the inferior government-provided provisions and supplies all the way back to President Grant's office, and a commission was convened that uncovered and punished the corrupt officials responsible. From then on, Red Cloud considered Marsh not only a friend but "the best white man I ever saw," and their bond of mutual respect culminated in a visit that Red Cloud paid Marsh at New Haven in 1883, memorialized by the famous photo of the two passing a pipe of peace and a belt of wampum. But in the hunt for brontotheres, by 1873 Cope was hot on Marsh's heels by way of discovering what he thought were new kinds of brontotheres in Colorado, including a brontothere he named *Symborodon*, which is now sometimes known as *Megacerops*. A feisty competition ensued, with Marsh formally naming the group Brontotheridae, which he later changed to Brontotheriidae, and also being the first to recognize that brontotheres were related to other perissodactyls, including horses, rhinos, and tapirs. Not to be outdone, Cope published his thoughts about how the brontotheres then known were related to one another. A summary of the history of paleontological studies regarding this group, along with a comprehensive analysis of the group's evolutionary relationships, can be found in Mihlbachler (2008). Thus, Hatcher's primary agenda for the 1886 season flowed from the ongoing feud between Marsh and Cope, when Marsh charged Hatcher with collecting more complete material for a species he had named "Brontops robustus"—now known as *Megacerops robustus*, the last and largest member of the group, which lived around 34 million years ago.[1]

But for the opening act of his 1886 odyssey, Hatcher boarded a train in New Haven with a $47.80 ticket to Republican City, Nebraska, a fare equivalent to about $1,150 in modern money. From there Hatcher once again landed briefly in Long Island on March 24 to secure the rights for excavating at the Overtons', as well as at the nearby Miller place, where he had conducted negotiations during the previous season. Once those arrangements were "fixed up" and the contracts recorded, he moved on to Bone Mound, but the owner was not around. Nonetheless, Hatcher sleuthed out that the proprietor was a land speculator who lived in Nebraska. Given that, Hatcher advised Marsh, "I think the better plan is to say nothing to him about the right to dig bones on his land and run the risk of other parties not knowing anything about it."[2]

By April 17, Hatcher reached Chadron, Nebraska, and met with Hank C. Clifford, who had helped guide Marsh's 1873 student expedition during its loop through northwestern Nebraska, as well as on the famous 1874 trip to the Big Badlands region near the Red Cloud Agency. It was during the latter trip that Clifford had discovered the first-known specimen of the brontothere that Marsh eventually named "Brontops robustus," and Marsh commanded that Hatcher co-opt Clifford to guide him back to the fossil locality where it had been found to see if more bones of it could be recovered. Clifford, described as a "handsome squaw man" by Marsh's biographers, expressed his desire to work with Hatcher that summer. Hatcher, believing they could get along well and desiring his knowledge of the region, struck a deal with

Clifford, subject to Marsh's approval, for $175 per month, or around $4,250 in today's currency, to furnish team, driver, wagon, and cook and to keep things in repair. But until Clifford became available on May 20, Hatcher forged an initial foray by hiring another man and team for a month at $135, explaining to Marsh that the rate was the best he could get because men could work for the railroad for $4.00 to $4.50 per day—around $100 now.[3]

In setting out for the area around the Big Badlands, he was focusing his efforts on what, at that time, were known as the Titanotherium beds and Oreodon beds. Our geologic terminology, as well as the age, for these beds has been greatly revised and refined since Hatcher's day. Below is a table that, in general, translates the geologic terms Hatcher utilized for these rock units into the geologic names and the associated ages that geologists and paleontologists use today. The sediments forming these beds and formations originated in the rising Rocky Mountains to the west and were carried eastward by rivers flowing out of the highlands down across the floodplain that we recognize today as the Great Plains.[4]

Modern Geologic Units for Fossils Collected by Hatcher's Crews in South Dakota and Nebraska (MA=millions of years ago)

Hatcher's term	Geologic Formation	N. Amer. Land Mammal	Age/MA
Upper Loup Fork	Upper Harrison Fm.	Hemingfordian	16–19 MA
Daemonelix beds	Lower Harrison Fm. Monroe Creek Fm.	Arikareean	19–30 MA
	Brule Fm. (Poleslide Member)	Whitneyan	32–30 MA
Oreodon beds	Brule Fm.	Orellan	32–34 MA
Titanotherium beds	Chadron Fm.	Chadronian	34–37 MA

When Hatcher reemerged from the countryside on May 4 to pick up mail, he, as usual, had to wire Marsh with the familiar refrain, "Am here waiting for check why don't you send it." Fortunately, it arrived the next day, and Hatcher more amicably assured Marsh:

> *Had had good success on my last trip. Brought in four boxes of good specimens and took out about 1,200 lbs more which I had not packing material enough to pack and bring in. Among them are four Brontotherium skulls. I got quite a number of limb bones of Bron. which are much better than any I have seen in the museum.*

He now thought he could do as well without Clifford, having found a good young man with a good team and wagon named L. Drury, who would work for $85 per month, or about $2,000 today, with board. But he left the decision up to Marsh, adding, "Men don't like to hire out here . . . unless they are boarded. And I will not go out and live on cornbread and bacon the way they would want to live if they boarded themselves." After relaying that he'd go out again until the twentieth, he concluded by imploring Marsh to send $100 by then to save the expense of a hotel stay.[5]

The crew was probably pleasantly shocked when they returned on the appointed day to find Marsh's check waiting for them. Hatcher was further delighted to declare,

> *I have up to date packed eighteen boxes of bones or about 4,000 lbs. They will average as good as the bones I collected in Kansas. Would have made it twenty boxes but my driver was taken very sick and I had to come in with him day before yesterday . . . will start out with Clifford today for one month. Will get the rest of the big Brontotherium the first thing.*
>
> *Among the bones I have already got some of the best are four Bront. skulls, two forelegs & feet perfect and bones in [life] position, one foreleg and foot of Oreodon bones in position.*

These were massive objects, with skulls and limb bones two to three feet long. To excavate them without breakage, Hatcher and his crew had to dig trenches completely around them before covering them with burlap soaked in flour paste, which they had to let dry. Then the blocks had to be undercut and rolled over to cover the bottom in pasted cloth. Often such large blocks required wooden struts to strengthen the blocks before they could be somehow lifted onto the wagon and transported by horse team to the nearest railroad for shipment to Yale. Hatcher queried Marsh about whether he wanted them to work in the "Bront. Oreodon & Mylodon beds or in the horse beds in the Running Water country." In any event, he said he hoped to get a carload of good bones by the time he shipped in the fall and would work hard to do it. By the twenty-fifth, Marsh had engaged Clifford, who apparently was concerned about working on the reservation, but Hatcher was confident there would be no trouble because Clifford's only enemy there had been removed and replaced by a Major Bell. Nonetheless, Hatcher promised to take every precaution to avoid trouble but keep working.[6]

By June 7, when Hatcher returned to Chadron for lumber and provisions, he reported having "27 boxes of good bones packed & know where there are lots more." He planned to be in the field until the twentieth, when Clifford's money was due. Then he'd need to hire another team to haul a load in, but having already paid out $120 more than received, he badgered Marsh to please send $250 by then and tell him definitively whether he wanted to retain Clifford and whether he wanted Hatcher to work in the "Horse or Brontotherium beds." His monthly balance sheet documented the shortfall in funds and purchases for groceries, hotel stays, packing materials, lumber, fees for the team, glue and brush, nails, water keg, plaster of Paris, oats, a horse with a saddle and bridle along with saddle straps and the crew's salaries.[7]

On the twenty-fifth, Hatcher tersely telegraphed Marsh to inquire, "Have you sent check for June 20 as requested—answer." It arrived the next day. Hatcher wrote again on July 10, especially to justify the job he'd done:

> . . . I have been pushing ahead to see all the localities Clifford knew of, and get lots of bones, too. Had to buy a horse, pay Mr. Drury & paid Clifford nearly $120.00 besides paying all other expenses.

As long as the bones I collect go to the government . . . I expect to charge for everything I spend on the work and nothing more. Whenever my bones are going to Yale I am ready to do as much for Yale as anyone. I have now 45 boxes packed [with] bones . . . and can make my car load by cold weather, and when I get through I think the collection will excel any ever made from here.

The last trip I went on to the Running Water, wanted to see the localities, got three good horse skulls & lower jaws perfect, but somewhat rotten . . . quite a number of perfect horse feet and limbs, and a perfect rhinoceros skull. 10 boxes of good bones.

He'd visited many of the localities throughout that country, then written them up and mapped them. Regarding his crew, "Drury will do more in a week than Clifford will in a month. Hank no doubt is a good . . . guide, . . . but here where there is a farmer every half mile . . . I had rather have a man who will take hold of a pick and shovel and go to work." With Drury, expenses would total only $200 per month, or about $4,800 now, and although Clifford had offered to work for $150 per month, Hatcher preferred Drury at any price. "Hank and I are good friends, and I think the best way [is] just to let the matter drop where it is. I have paid him off and will hire Drury unless you want Hank at $150 per month." Hatcher planned to return the twenty-second and requested a check for $100. He also noted he'd gotten a letter from his man watching things for him in Kansas, who said everything was fine and no one was collecting there. Osborn's Princeton crew was in Colorado. But conditions were brutal, and Hatcher bemoaned that it had hit 105 in the shade the previous week in Running Water.[8]

Hatcher received a check on the twenty-first, although it was only for $100. He then left for the field with Drury, vowing to keep his outfit, comprising the wagon, team, and camp gear, out there until it got too cold to work. At the end of the month, he reported that July expenses totaled $255.60, over $6,200 in today's dollars. So to ease Marsh's concerns about getting his money's worth, he noted they now had fifty boxes of bones packed and expected to glean another box a day where they were collecting near Hermosa, South Dakota, just south of Rapid

City and east of the Black Hills. Their site was on the reservation about twenty-five miles from Battle River, the nearest town on the railroad about eighty miles from Chadron. To continue, Hatcher requested that Marsh send a check for $100 at Battle River, Custer County, Dakota Territory.[9]

By August 16, Hatcher railed that he hadn't received the $150 requested two weeks earlier, adding, "I am out of money and everything else. Pawned my watch and chain today for money to buy lumber, packing material and provisions with. Send me $150.00 more so it will be here by Sept 1st." To sweeten his solicitation, Hatcher told Marsh they'd taken out three good "Brontotherium" skulls—one of a very young animal and perfect. In all, he now had sixty-three boxes packed, boasting that he was finding just as many good specimens as in Kansas, although it was awful hot and hard work. "If the expenses are too high here just let me know what you can afford to lay out per month and I will limit expenses to that and do what I can." But he needed two men to work successfully. Then Hatcher noted that an alternative means to obtain specimens had arisen. "There is man here named Clarke who has two pretty fair Brontotherium skulls & quite a collection of other fossils for sale. He wants $500.00 for all [about $12,000 today]. . . . I think I can get them for much less than he asks. . ." This seems to be the first time Hatcher offered to be a purchasing agent for Marsh in the field, a role he would assume with greater frequency in the future.[10]

The crew's collection swelled to seventy-three boxes by the end of August, including "12 Bront. skulls, 2 Hyracodon [rhino], & many thousands of other bones." Hatcher received a check for $150 but needed another hundred to continue because the $150 had only paid for supplies for the next foray, redeemed his watch, and provided "money enough to give the men to keep down mutiny." Adding to his woes, Clifford had apparently complained to Marsh about being dismissed, for Hatcher, reflecting the biased attitude at the time of many western settlers in the wake of the Battle of the Little Bighorn, bluntly bellowed, "Can not help it if Clifford did get mad. He is not worth anything for work. Has too much of the Indian in him." Hatcher then confidently predicted that he'd have a carload by mid-October or November 1.[11]

Hatcher had wrangled with Clarke to purchase his collection for the amount Marsh wanted to pay by September 15, and matter-of-factly mentioned that they now possessed eighty-nine packed boxes, containing, in part, fourteen "Brontotherium" skulls. But by October 1, Hatcher had again reached his boiling point about bucks, reporting, "I have spent to date $360.00 more than . . . received," an astonishing sum for an apprentice paleontologist that amounts to $8,700 in today's money. He then matter-of-factly admonished Marsh:

> I wrote you more than two weeks ago to send $150.00 but have received nothing from you. On the 22 of this month there will be two months wages due the men working for me, $250.00. I expect it would be as well to close work [then] as it will take me about two weeks . . . to get my boxes freighted to the railroad. I will be back here again the 15 . . . and must have money. Send me $650.00 . . . $360.00 now due me, $250 to pay [the crew], and $40.00 for freighting.

In an attempt to stave off his superior's financial fury, Hatcher confirmed collecting four more good "Brontotherium" skulls to add to the 103 boxes now packed.[12]

Mollified, Marsh capitulated and sent the amount demanded by mid-October, and Hatcher reassured him by confirming that Clarke's collection was now ready to ship, along with 118 other crates. Hatcher hailed the season's success by exclaiming, "I am sure it is by far the largest shipment of fossils ever made to the government, [and] am well satisfied with Summer's work."[13]

Except for three uncatalogued crocodile teeth that Hatcher found, along with twenty-two specimens of the rhino *Menops* that were collected by and purchased from Clarke, all of the 227 specimens that Hatcher collected during the 1886 season in the Great Plains are now housed at the Smithsonian's National Museum of Natural History, as listed in appendix 2 for the specimens that are catalogued and identified to the generic level. The great majority appears to be from the Orellan-aged deposits of the Brule Formation, which are between 34 and 32 million years old, including several genera of brontotheres now called *Megacerops*, several genera of rhinos ("Caenopus," *Hyracodon*, "Menodus," *Subhyracodon*, *Trigonias*), a horse (*Miohippus*), the hippo-like anthracothere called *Ancodon*, the pig-like entelodont *Archaeotherium*, a sheep-like oreodont (*Merycoidodon*), an oreodont-like ungulate (*Agriochoerus*), three small deer-like forms (*Hypertragulus, Hypisodus, Leptomeryx*), a carnivorous "bear dog" (*Cynodictis*), a large predatory creodont (*Hyaenodon*), the saber-toothed carnivore *Hoplophoneus*, the rodent *Eumys*, the rabbit *Palaeolagus*, and the tortoise *Stylemys*. The small fauna from the 37- to 34-million-year-old Chadron Formation comprised one creodont (*Hyaenodon*), one horse (*Mesohippus*), and one rhino (*Trigonias*). Hatcher also appears to have collected two saber-toothed carnivores from the 9- to 5-million-year-old Long Island Rhino Quarry (*Barbourofelis* and *Nimravides*), as well as a suite of horses (*Equus, Pliohippus, Psuedhipparion*), a rhino (*Aphelops*), a camel (*Procamelus*), and a "bear dog" (*Ischyrocyon*) from other Miocene deposits in Nebraska.[14]

With that, he departed Chadron on October 21 for a week's visit home before returning to New Haven. In all, the season's haul, which will be detailed later, totaled 21,136 pounds of precious fossils. But Hatcher's triumphant field season had taken a terrible toll on his chronically frail frame, and he would not be able to return to the field for five months. For long spells during that winter of discontent, Hatcher was confined to a hospital bed in New Haven, struggling to recover from the bout of "inflammatory rheumatism" that racked his own fragile bones. Nonetheless, he did work around Washington, D.C., Virginia, and North Carolina for a bit at the start of 1887.[15]

But by mid-March of 1887, Hatcher was once again on the hunt for "thunder beasts." While he was on his way west, with his arm in a sling due to a bout with "rheumatism," Marsh directed him to evaluate a related collection owned by a Mr. Phillips of Minneapolis. On the fourteenth, Hatcher reported that although Phillips did indeed have specimens of "Brontotherium," the rhino *Hyracodon* and the pig- or sheep-like "Oredon," only one of the "Brontotherium" skulls seemed scientifically significant, since its horncores exhibited unusual protuberances near the top. Given that, Hatcher told Marsh to negotiate a price for the collection if he was interested, since he didn't feel the specimens justified an offer. Nonetheless, Hatcher did provide a recommendation for Phillips, who wanted to collect for Marsh that summer in Cretaceous deposits in northern Minnesota.[16]

From there, Hatcher rumbled on to Rapid City, South Dakota, where Marsh wanted him to arrange to borrow a brontothere skull from a Professor Frank D. Carpenter of the Dakota School of Mines so Marsh could illustrate and describe it. On the twenty-fifth, Hatcher sent Marsh a copy of the loan agreement, adding that Carpenter had undertaken extraordinary efforts to speed the loan through the school's bureaucracy and praising him as ". . . a thorough gentleman and a scientist with a true scientific spirit. No speculator or bone shark." These side trips effectively allowed Hatcher to continue his recuperation, which he acknowledged in closing by intimating to Marsh, "I am improving every day, am writing with this lame hand." With that, Hatcher headed for the field in earnest on April 1 by catching a train to Chadron, Nebraska, after purchasing pliers, glue, labels, blankets, and packing material.[17]

April 5 found Hatcher back in the field with two new assistants, Joseph Brown, who drew a monthly salary of $85 with his wagon and team of horses, and A. G. Tinker, who charged $40 per month as a collector. All were after brontotheres, and Hatcher reported "some success" in the search for the missing elements of the holotype, or first-known specimen, of "Brontops" *robustus*, now called *Megacerops robustus* (YPM VP 12048). He also seemed to be searching for other odds and ends, including more of a horse skeleton identified as "Anchitherium" that he had collected in 1886, alerting Marsh that he had found one of the forefeet.[18]

Returning to town on the twentieth to find no check waiting for him from Marsh he reminded him that Brown and Tinker would expect their salaries on May 1, along with an assurance that they were having fair success despite wet weather, including the discovery of a good "Brontotherium" skull. Finally the check arrived on the twenty-eighth, at the same time when Hatcher came in for lumber to crate up three more brontothere skulls, but now Hatcher needed the $285 monthly advance for salaries, which he requested Marsh to send by the first. By May 8, the crew was, at least for the moment, fully funded, and Hatcher relayed that they had six good brontothere skulls, but the weather hadn't cooperated. "Had one of the worst storms I ever saw May 1st. Hundreds of cattle perished." Yet the weather wasn't the only irritant Hatcher was enduring. Apparently, the commanding officer at Fort Robinson wasn't showing Hatcher or Marsh what the former considered due respect:

> *I do not know what is the matter with Maj. Burt. But he must not think for a moment his title or rank an excuse to ride over me. I don't go a cent on rank. He attacked me (so to speak) or contradicted a statement which I know to be correct. Said that you had "done him dirt" two or three times etc. And I naturally a little quick tempered replied to him a little more sharply than I ought. However, I have no apologies to make. But he must not speak to me as he evidently would a "Buck Soldier."*[19]

By the twenty-fifth, despite heavy storms that left mud knee-deep, the count for "Bront. skulls" had risen to eight, but Hatcher had even better news for his mentor from Hat Creek, where Marsh had collected in 1874: ". . . one skeleton almost perfect excepting ribs and vertebrae. All four of the legs & feet, both scapulae [shoulder blades], in fine condition & pelvis. . . ." The skull was crushed. But the teeth were all fine, and the lower jaws were almost in their natural position—a rarity, since the lower jaws often separate from the skull when the carcass decays or is scavenged and undergoes burial in sand or mud before becoming fossilized. Beyond that, Hatcher, presumably at Marsh's behest, was also angling to purchase the brontothere skull he'd borrowed from Carpenter. He was confident of obtaining it for "a very reasonable consideration." Accordingly, he hoofed it to Rapid City to negotiate, and on the thirty-first, notified Marsh that Carpenter would raise the matter with the board of the School of Mines and was sure the transaction would be approved. Additional limb elements of the specimen had reportedly been found, and Hatcher hoped to be able to visit the locality to recover more. Marsh had also apparently raised the idea of Hatcher collecting along the southerly Atlantic coast during the winter, to which Hatcher expressed enthusiasm and sought more information so he could prepare during the summer season.[20]

As May turned to June, the crew got another good skull, making nine for the season, and planned to move twenty miles west in a day or two. Hatcher hesitated going north, because although he knew he might get more skulls there, he thought he might find more skeletons where they were. But the crew wasn't the only group finding what they wanted: ". . . mosquitoes very bad even in the heat of the day." But on the sixth, Hatcher decided to move north, shipping twenty-two boxes, including the eleven skulls found so far. He also prodded Marsh for the May payment, pleading, ". . . the men want their money before they go [north]. I have advanced them all the money I have to spare."[21]

Five days later, Marsh still hadn't complied, and Hatcher lashed out: "I have been here nearly a week now waiting. I would not care myself but the men must have their money before they go as they have bills to pay before leaving." He enclosed Prof. Carpenter's letter describing the actions of the Dakota School of Mines regarding the skull and thought the price quoted seemed rather high, but apparently it was just what it cost them. He needed to know if Marsh wanted it and whether he should go see where it was found to get what other bones might still be there. They would next be based in Hermosa, Dakota, along the Cheyenne River. Marsh's check for $223.50 for the School of Mines brontothere showed up by the fifteenth, along with another check for $285, allowing them to move camp.[22]

Within a few days, Hatcher was off to Rapid City, where he paid for the bronthothere skull and made arrangements to visit the site to secure more of the skeleton. But unfortunately, in the process, he said, "My horse tried to play circus the other day and fell over backwards on to me injuring one of my legs a little but not seriously. It might very easily have been much worse." Adding to Hatcher's difficulties, by the twenty-eighth there was an issue with his crewman Tinker: "He concluded that digging bones was not much of a picnic & quit & I paid him off." Beyond that, Hatcher reported:

> *I have only found one skull since I came up here* [to Hermosa] *& I have rode and climbed all over. I can work as hard as any one but I must find something. Yesterday I left camp at 5 o'clock A.M.*

and rode until nearly sundown without a mouthful of anything to eat. I felt well satisfied though for I found one fine skull with lower jaws in position. I will get it and look the ground over well in that region for more & if I find none will go about 70 miles N.E. of here & see what I can do there.

He planned to return in ten days or two weeks and wanted the checks for June there by then. Frustrated, he asked Marsh for advice, ". . . for I can not stay here & find nothing." He got a Mr. Caple to try and show him where he'd found the Rapid City skull, but they ". . . rode all day and he could not find the place" and told Hatcher that the bones Prof. Carpenter showed him did not belong with it. While in Rapid City, Hatcher purchased George A. Clarke's Indian collection, adding that he thought Marsh would like some of the things and would be glad if he would take it all.[23]*

Returning to Hermosa as planned on July 12 to receive the monthly $285 check, Hatcher exalted a long-awaited change of luck:

Now I am going to surprise you & I hope at the same time please you. On this last trip we took out and packed 13 skulls. How is that? The 4th of July was the banner day, on that day we got three skulls. You will have no chance to complain this Winter about my skulls all being small for some of them are the largest I ever saw. I have two with horn cores like the one from Rapid City.

He joked that given the "beastly hot weather," Marsh could congratulate himself that he wasn't out there among the white bluffs. With the monthly money in hand, Hatcher could pay for food, lumber, hardware, a telegram, feed, hotel stays, nails, horse medicine, rail fare, salaries, and blacksmithing.[24]

At the end of July, Hatcher returned to Hermosa to briefly chronicle the discovery of seven more brontothere skulls, along with a greater variety of forms than he'd ever seen before. On August 12, he mailed his final correspondence to Marsh for the season, having taken out ten skulls and six pairs of lower jaws on his last trip, including one skull that had the lower jaws in place.[25]

Hatcher's haul from the 37- to 34-million-year-old Chadron Formation contained no less than eight genera of brontotheres ("Allops," "Brontops," "Brontotherium," *Diploclonus, Megacerops, Symborodon,* "Titanops," "Titanotherium"). Several of these are now known as *Megacerops.* His slightly younger sample from the 34- to 30-million-year-old Brule Formation includes the enormous, pig-like entelodont *Archaeotherium* and the sheep-like oreodont *Merycoidodon.*

After about six weeks, presumably back in New Haven, Hatcher was on the road again to collect around Washington, D.C., as well as in coal mines around Richmond, Virginia, and Egypt, North Carolina. With his salary now set at $100 per month, his first assignment involved an "examination of Potomac Formation for vertebrate fossils . . . to secure specimens sufficient to determine age of formation . . . and report to Director [Powell] or Mr. McGee in his absence." Then "make careful search for mammals at Deep River Coal localities in North Carolina or other stratigraphic equivalents." By October 5, Hatcher had hooked up with McGee and prospected the most promising locality, where he spent a few minutes looking around and found a few good teeth, "probably Cretaceous." He then left for some downtime in the West, especially Long Pine, Nebraska, confident that he could find some good things in the East, but cautioning Marsh, ". . . you must not expect too much of me." After returning to Washington, he confirmed on the twenty-third that fossils were abundant but small. The process was simple but required intent focus while he sorted through small piles of sand and silt with a small brush or sharp tool and separated the shiny teeth and bones from the other sediment. By examining only a bushel of matrix, Hatcher gleaned about two hundred teeth, one piece of skull showing occipital condyles, foramen magnum, and a portion of the base of the skull, and two vertebrae. They appeared to represent remains of fish, reptiles, and mammals, as well as bivalve and univalve mollusks, all of which Hatcher felt were probably new. The locality appeared inexhaustible but would require moving considerable dirt, necessitating some extra expense. Hatcher informed Marsh that the owner, a Col. Soot, provided authorization, in Soot's words, "to go ahead and employ one or two darkies to work with you," with Hatcher clarifying to Marsh, "this is confidential."

But Hatcher was concerned about where the extra money would come from and preferred to have "whitemen work with me when I have any." While waiting for Marsh's advice, Hatcher worked through the latter part of October, finding several new teeth, bones, and what appeared to be the mandible of a turtle. Despite getting very sick and enduring a good deal of rainy weather, he was amassing an impressive bounty of one hundred fossils a day.[26]

As had been the case with Sternberg and would often be the case in the coming years, Hatcher quickly began to doubt the geologic observations of his predecessors and superiors in the region, as he reported to Marsh on November 6:

> *I don't believe these people here know which is Potomac & which is not. . . . McGee drove me around & showed me what he said was Potomac & what Quaternary & showed me the only place where fossils had been found in the Potomac. Now I have made a large collection from that very spot & the fossils show conclusively that it is Eocene. I think that either the Potomac is Eocene or that they do not know here just which is & which is not Potomac. . . . You will undoubtedly be able to determine when you get collection. . . . I had Mr. McGee walking the floor yesterday afternoon at a rapid pace. I suspect that he feels that he has made a blunder in calling certain formations Potomac which are not. But don't say anything to him, for he is a nice man and a good friend. If this proves to be Eocene we've done something [constructive] anyway. Have we not?*
>
> *Now you never answer any questions I ask you. But if this is Eocene I want you to write & tell me what to do & if possible let me try the real Potomac at once.[27]*

Marsh had evaluated a set of fossils Hatcher sent by the twelfth and confirmed that they were Eocene but not from the Potomac. Hatcher expressed regret at the mix-up but maintained that McGee had showed him the locality and never expressed any doubt about it being Potomac, even providing Hatcher with a very elaborate description of how to distinguish Potomac from Quaternary from a stratigraphic point of view.

Hatcher concluded, "Perhaps he will not go so much on stratigraphy or structure for determining the age to which a geologic formation belongs hereafter."[28]

Determined to transcend the snafu, Hatcher spent the next week searching for fossils in typical Potomac Formation exposures around Washington and Baltimore, very unsuccessfully. Despite Maj. Powell having urged Marsh to focus on Potomac localities that had "already yielded vertebrate remains in small numbers," Hatcher could find no one who knew of any such localities. By the twenty-second, he had found and sent to Marsh a box of fossils partly from typical Potomac and partly from the remainder of the Tertiary collected at Good Hope Hill, requesting that Marsh let him know if they were of any value. Marsh responded on the twenty-fifth, and Hatcher led McGee out to where he'd found several bone fragments in one of the iron ore beds. A chastened McGee was uncertain if it was Potomac or not, leading Hatcher to confide to Marsh,

. . . *what I find seems to prove that much of that usually considered . . . Potomac is not Potomac at all.*

I do not think there is any one here able to say just which is & which is not Potomac. In fact I know there is not, for I have proven that which they have referred me to as Potomac to be something more recent. The bones I sent you came from the red & bluish clays which no one would ever have thought of calling anything else but Potomac if it were not for finding those bones in them.

You seem to think I am wasting my time here. I don't know what to do. I know I am trying hard enough. I have depended upon Mr. McGee for localities. I do not believe there is any two miles between here & Balt. in which I can not find such bones as the last I sent you & in the red and bluish clays too. Please answer with regard to bones sent you at once.[29]

Marsh wrote Hatcher confirming he'd finally found fossils typical of the Potomac by the twenty-eighth, and Hatcher was confident he could now find more, especially if he could hire two men to "pick and shovel" and get the water pumped out of the iron ore pit at Muirkirk, Maryland, where he was working, a task that McGee and Powell offered to help fund. Hatcher would also need a camp outfit, as out west, for "People mostly know nothing of hospitality here & it is a great expense of time and money to return to Washington every night," as evidenced by most of his bills for November consisting of hotel and transportation charges. At least his spirits were high: "I never felt better in my life . . . & if I can stay South all Winter I believe I'll be a new man in the Spring. Have been improving all along since leaving that mudhole on Good Hope Hill." Accordingly he hoped to soon "send . . . a large box of good bones from the typical Potomac."[30]

Hatcher next informed Marsh he'd found the first bones from undisturbed clay at Muirkirk on December 8, "at bottom as I expected not top as McGee believed I would." They comprised several vertebrae, bone end fragments, a terminal phalanx, and several pieces of reptilian skulls. It required an immense amount of work to get them because of the thirty feet of overburden and the bones' rarity, and Hatcher feared finding enough to determine the age of the formation would be difficult. Then he launched into a rant about his lazy colleagues in the region:

> *I think men who delight to call themselves Geologists & who have made a study of this particular formation as they say (boastingly) for years . . . & who . . . live within 30 minutes ride of where an abundance of fossils have been taken* [out] *for the past 30 years . . . ought to have accomplished a little more & should be somewhat ashamed. But there is considerable fireside Geology in the country.*

A few days later, Hatcher came across some cones of a conifer that Professor Ward identified as from *Sequoia*, and by the thirteenth, Hatcher also expressed several complete phalanges, two limb bones, vertebrae, and several fragments of a skull that he hoped would help accurately determine the Potomac's age. Despite all the difficulties, Hatcher pledged he'd camp "all winter if it is necessary . . . [but] am also very willing to get through & get out of here as soon as possible."[31]

On the sixteenth, Hatcher wrote Marsh with a proposition made by Mr. C. E. Coffin, owner of the Muirkirk ore pit, which Coffin had quit mining two years earlier because it wasn't profitable. Coffin offered to lay track and put his engine, cars, and seven men to work for two months mining for ore and bones if Marsh would pay half the expense, which wouldn't exceed $5 a day. But Marsh must commit for two months. Hatcher argued this would increase the chances of securing a good collection, unless Marsh only required a few more bones to determine the Potomac's age. Marsh concurred by the nineteenth and apparently planned to visit, because Hatcher provided directions—about 2.5 miles southeast of Muirkirk Station of the Washington branch of the Baltimore and Ohio Railroad. In any event, excavations began immediately. As Hatcher had hoped, larger bones began to appear in the pit, but it was still "impossible to get these large bones out except in pieces," which Hatcher hoped Marsh's fossil preparators back at the Peabody could glue back together.[32]

Christmas brought some good news for Hatcher, as he noted when Marsh sent the proofs of a scientific article. "Many thanks for appreciation you have taken occasion to show of my work. I hope I shall prove myself worthy of the praise you have given me." However, on the twenty-seventh, Hatcher was frustrated with the mining crew's holiday hangover. "I went out to resume work today but not a single man showed up despite saying they would be on hand today." He closed his note somewhat bitterly with "I suppose you all had the proverbial Merry Christmas & I can wish you a Happy New Year." Marsh visited during the second week of 1888, and by January 28, Hatcher, having sent four more metapodials, one phalanx, a piece of skull with four teeth, a piece of pelvis, and one tooth resembling that of an allosaur but much larger and stronger, left Coffin and his men to continue working the iron ore pit. Hatcher's plan was to finally move on to the coal mines around Richmond.[33]

On the way, Hatcher watched for exposures of the Potomac and saw numerous outcrops of Potomac sandstone similar to those around Hanover, with sandstone overlying iron ore beds and no examples of the iron ore clays overlying the sandstone, which would be expected if the clays were younger than the sandstone. Hatcher wanted to resolve that issue and thought he could, even offering to spend a month's vacation on it sometime. Then switching gears, he prospected in the Richmond coal mines for mammalian fossils on the thirtieth but found "no vertebrate remains whatever, not even a tooth or piece of bone" and decided to travel on to Greensboro, North Carolina, on February 1.[34]

Hatcher wrote Marsh from Gulf in Chatham County on the second, reporting that he visited one mine and, dressed in his "Go to Meetin" clothes, found one tooth of Emmou's "Palaeosaurus carolinensis" but no mammals. Nonetheless, having retrieved his trunk and tools, he was hopeful of finding more and would not give up until "satisfied that it is useless to try further." In subsequent days, he sent Marsh four reptilian teeth and other fossils from the Taylor mine but still no mammals. One day was devoted to the old Egypt shaft that Marsh wanted targeted, but Hatcher found nothing at all, finding instead that it hadn't been worked for years and all slates were so decomposed that the prospect of finding fossils in them was not promising. Regardless, he vowed to examine all the mines thoroughly before giving up, adding, "I am sure you are not more anxious than I to get mammals from here." But by the twelfth, Hatcher threw in the towel, lamenting to Marsh that it was only a waste of time to remain here longer, since none of the mines were being worked, all were full of water, and the slates were so decomposed they yielded nothing. With that, he retreated to Washington before returning to New Haven to prepare for his season out west.[35]

Today, all of the specimens collected by Hatcher on this trip in late 1887 and early 1888 appear to be housed in the Smithsonian's National Museum of Natural History, and most are now catalogued to have come from the Patuxent Formation, although the iron-bearing beds from Muirkirk are now referred to the 112-million-year-old Arundel Formation. As currently identified in the USNM collection, the specimens include the carnivorous dinosaur "Allosaurus medius," which Marsh described in 1888 but Gilmore reassigned to *Dryptosaurus* in 1920, as discussed by Weishampel et al. (1990). Also the immense herbivorous sauropod, "Astrodon," which Marsh described and named in 1888, is now called *Pleurocoelus nanus*. The carnivorous dinosaur *Coelurus gracilis*, which Weishampel et al. consider to be specifically and generically indeterminate, is also listed, along with two other dinosaurs that Marsh named in 1888—*Ornithomimus affinus* and *Priconodon crassus*—which are considered to be dubious names by Weishampel and colleagues. Finally, the tortoise, *Glyptops caelatus*; and the crocodile, *Goniopholis affinus*, are also represented.[36]

In addition, younger marine fossils from the 15- to 18-million-year-old beds of the Calvert Formation include several kinds of sharks and a ray. Among them are the purportedly more than 50-foot-long relative of the great white shark, *Carcharodon megalodon* (now often referred to as *Carcharocles*), as well as a requiem shark *Carcharhinus*, a tiger shark *Galeocerdo*, a weasel shark *Hemipristis serra*, a mackerel shark *Isurus hastalis*, a broadnose sevengill shark *Notorynchus primigenius*, and a cownose ray *Rhinoptera*.

By April 1, after a "long & tedious journey" due to delays from high water, Hatcher found himself back in the more familiar fossil fields around Chadron, Nebraska, reporting on the eighth that he was shipping several whole bones of the brontothere #2048 that they were able to find, along with one partial skeleton of the rhino "Hyracodon" with complete fore and hind feet. He then set out for Hat Creek. By the eighteenth, he finished collecting missing fragments of another previously discovered skull, along with several good foot bones, caudal vertebrae, and two sternals. Also included were small bones and teeth that Hatcher suspected represented many new species from a locality where they were very abundant, adding that he should spend one season there collecting other things besides brontotheres because he could make a magnificent collection. He then set out about thirty miles west for a strip of badlands in Wyoming for the remainder of the month, requesting that the monthly check be sent to Crawford, Nebraska. But on the thirtieth, as usual, he wrote Marsh in complaint: ". . . no checks are here. What is the reason? The vouchers were sent in good time."[37]

Although brontotheres were a primary focus of the 1888 season, they were not the only one, for Marsh also charged Hatcher with prospecting in the Missouri Breaks in Montana where Cope and Sternberg had found the first specimens of horned dinosaurs in 1876. On May 1, Hatcher told Marsh he would be ready to go to Ft. Robinson and Crawford the next day, and if Marsh's money had arrived, he would then be ready to start for the Judith River region unless Marsh should write otherwise. In retrospect, this venture for ceratopsians would come to dominate the rest of Hatcher's tenure with Marsh and catapult Hatcher into the pantheon of the greatest paleontological collectors of dinosaurs who ever lived.[38]

Beyond that, on the tenth, as Hatcher and his crew passed through Hermosa along the muddy roads on their way to Miles City, Montana, the vouchers for salaries he submitted to Marsh reveal that he was joined on the journey by W. H. Burwell and Olaf August Peterson. This is the first time Peterson is mentioned in Hatcher's correspondence, but it would be far from the last. For, in addition to becoming one of Hatcher's most accomplished assistants, he was also Hatcher's brother-in-law; Hatcher had married Olaf's sister, Anna Matilda Peterson, in 1887. But for the moment, Burwell, by virtue of the use of his team of horses for the expedition in addition to his role as a collector, drew a salary of $85 per month, or a bit over $2,000 now, while Peterson, hired only as a collector, drew a salary of $40 per month.[39]

Upon reaching Miles City on the twenty-second, Hatcher was pleased to find Marsh's monthly check for $310 waiting, but there was a problem:

> *We will have to stay here three or four days as I can not get your check cashed here until they send it to New Haven & the bank there wires back that it is all right. I don't want to go off up in there without plenty of money. I wish you would send drafts on New York hereafter. I always have trouble with personal checks where I am not acquainted.*

After shipping Marsh some Indian relics, antelope skulls, and hides and buffalo horns he had found along the way and purchasing a map, nails, pliers, wrench, staples, paper, lumber, and feed, Hatcher's crew left on the twenty-ninth for Judith, hoping to arrive there in a week if the weather held.[40]

Hatcher wrote next from Flat Willow Creek in Montana on June 4, saying they had three more days to the Judith River before adding in a cranky tone: "Had much rather be digging than 'looking at the country.' We had a bad time crossing the Musselshell River. . . . Swam our horses & I thought once we were not going to make it." Correspondence would be difficult from the Breaks, with the crew only getting mail once a week overland from Billings, two hundred miles away. Accordingly, Hatcher urged Marsh on the ninth to send checks immediately so they would get them by the first week in July. He reminded Marsh to divide the monthly payment into two or three checks or drafts, which were much better out there, where he was a stranger, and went on to note that their prospecting had yielded some good bones but no rich localities. By the twenty-fifth their luck hadn't changed, with Hatcher suspiciously suggesting, "I am commencing to think Sternberg lied about rich fossil beds . . . here." There were many water-worn fragments, few good bones, and lots of duckbill tooth fragments, but not a single good tooth yet. Their meager haul so far amounted to less than two boxes of fossils, leading Hatcher to query, "In case I find nothing here what shall I do? I can not stand it here more than three or four weeks more if I find nothing." And the locals where they were camped, about forty miles down the river from Judith, weren't all welcoming. "I killed a bear here the other day." Their take had doubled to four boxes by July 2, but the quality of the fossils was still not sufficient. So they planned to cross the river and prospect on the other side, where they met with more success, as Hatcher reported on the seventeenth: ". . . packed six boxes on this trip. Bones are mostly broken up pretty badly. I find plenty of teeth but no skulls. Find a good many good bones." However, Hatcher was pretty fed up with the Breaks by the end of the month, reporting poor success and threatening that unless he could do better he'd leave for the Dakota Territory in a week or ten days. He'd followed the formation as far as it extended both up and down the Missouri River on the north side and as far down as it extended on the south side, but he hadn't prospected its upper limit on the south side.

> Judith is on Missouri River about ½ mile below the mouth of the Judith River. I have found little. . . . Passed through Cretaceous No. 4 [apparently Pierre Shale] all the way up. Plenty of baculites, ammonites, etc. but few vertebrates.
>
> I have so far packed (12) twelve boxes of bones . . . and have . . . enough for another box. There are quite a number of good bones . . . ,

*many good vertebrae & teeth but no skulls. I have not failed
entirely . . . but I can not call it a success unless I strike something
yet, which I shall try hard to do, but I have little hope. I was very
anxious to come up here & dreamed only of success, which I have
tried hard to have. I am sorry that I have not found more bones
but I have worked as hard as I could & to the best advantage I
knew how. I will not leave until I am fully satisfied that it is useless
to work longer. Then I suppose the blame will all be mine & I will
take the consequences.*[41]

True to his word, Hatcher shipped fifteen crates of fossils through
the quartermaster at Fort Assinibonine around August 4 and headed
for the Dakotas. But on his way in mid-August, he received notice at
Fort Maginuis in Montana that Marsh wanted him to proceed to Ferris,
Wyoming, and meet a man named Lamothe, who claimed to have found
some fossils.[42]

Despite Hatcher's downbeat assessment of his Judith collection, an
intriguing assortment of 75- to 80-million-year-old specimens still
resides in the collection of the USNM. Among them are the horned
dinosaur "Ceratops montanus," which Marsh named in 1888, but is
now thought to belong either to *Avaceratops* or some close relative of
Centrosaurus; the armored dinosaurs *Edmontonia, Panoplosaurus,* and
the dubiously named ankylosaur, "Palaeoscincus costatus"; the duckbill "Hadrosaurus paucidens," which Marsh named in 1889 and is now
thought to possibly belong to *Lambeosaurus*; another duckbill called
Corythosaurus; and three carnivorous forms, *Ornithomimus tenuis,*
which Marsh named in 1890, *Troodon formosus,* and the *Tyrannosaurus*
relative *Aublysodon.* In addition, there are two turtles, *Aspideretes
granifer* and *Baena*; the crocodile-like reptile *Champosaurus*; and a
shark, *Synechodus.* Intriguingly, the Peabody collections contain only
one specimen listed in their catalogue that may have come from this
trip. It's a tooth identified as belonging to the family Tyrannosauridae
(YPM VP 054465), but it came in a box (#12) that suggests it was
collected in the Judith River region, in which case it might instead
be the tooth of *Deinodon horridus.*

It wasn't until the thirty-first that Hatcher wrote Marsh from North Battle River, Wyoming, to confirm that he'd met a local man named Louis Lamothe, who owned some bones:

> . . . *went out to see Mr. Lamothe's "beast" this morning. I dont* [sic] *think it is all there & it is in rather poor condition. Mr. Lamothe is in very hard circumstances but I did not feel justified in giving him anything more than he had agreed to give the man who found the beast for it. He wanted $500.00 for it but I told him that I would pay the $100 promised to the man who found the skeleton & give him $75.00 to work with me one month & show me other skeletons which he says he has found & to show me other fossil bearing regions that he had explored. And as an incentive I told him that if he was successful & found lots of good things while he was at work I might want him longer.*
>
> *The one skeleton might be worth the whole $175 but I dont* [sic] *believe it is worth much. I will make the most out of the skeleton & Mr. Lamothe too & if he really does know what he claims to or a small portion of it I will try to find out $175 worth before I get through with him, & if there is good work here we can hire him right along for what is right I believe, for apparently he is an honest and true old man & deserves a chance.*

Although he spent a week prospecting with Lamothe, it seems that Hatcher's skepticism about the potential of this region around Rawlins and the value of Lamothe's specimen delayed the discovery of *Triceratops* for about nine months. For, as he wrote Marsh on September 24, ". . . I concluded that [Lamothe] had lied about all of [his finds] & so I left him." However, Hatcher would come to recognize, once he became more familiar with the badlands of southeast Wyoming and with this beast in particular, that Lamothe's weathered skeleton represented the first remains of *Triceratops* ever encountered by a paleontologist. Hatcher was on the right track but as yet lacked the proper search image. Nonetheless, there is also a specimen in the USNM collection identified as *Triceratops* sp (V 5804), which, if truly collected during this trip, would be the earliest scientific specimen of the genus found, even though it was not described. In addition, Hatcher collected one specimen of the crocodile-like reptile called *Champsosaurus*.[43]

After stopping in Wyoming, the crew headed back to their more familiar haunts around Hermosa in the Dakotas, where on September 24, Hatcher related that there had been, ". . . lots of indian [sic] scare out here the past month. But I think it will all amount to nothing." Much more importantly, Hatcher intimated, "Had a letter from home a few days ago stating that we had a fine boy there."[44]

Although Marsh's monthly check had not arrived by October 8, prompting another impassioned plea, Hatcher was having splendid success with brontotheres, taking out eight skulls, eight lower jaws, one pelvis, one scapula, and a very peculiar pair of horncores and nasals. One lower jaw seemed to represent a juvenile even younger than that smallest one he had gotten two years earlier, since there were only two teeth in it, and he had another lower jaw with the permanent teeth just beginning to erupt. But the success of his expeditions had fueled a burgeoning bone rush, with Hatcher lamenting, "Since I came back here this fall the country has been swarming with 'bone hunters.' Joe Brown that worked for me [the last two years] was over with another man & they were just going to take all the bones & skulls in the country & a half dozen other parties all stayed about a week, found nothing & left disgusted." Apparently still feeling guilty about his lack of success in the Judith, Hatcher was determined to work around Hermosa through November to make this year "show up yet."[45]

On the twenty-second, Hatcher's crew brought in 3,150 pounds of fossils, including eight skulls and several pairs of lower jaws. Overall, they'd tallied sixteen skulls, despite considerable competition: "Bone hunters in the Bad Lands are as thick as sparrows in New Haven." One party had found a good skull, ". . . but they did not know what it was & dug right down through the top of it to the teeth to find out." Acting as Marsh's agent, Hatcher bought their best skull for $25, presuming his mentor would want it, and asked if Marsh would want him to purchase others if possible. Essentially, Hatcher was setting up a satellite operation, since "there are four of them & they have been at work over three weeks

& are still sticking at it. I can't keep away from them & they follow me wherever I go. I can buy their skulls if you want them very cheap." But, of course, he would need more money.[46]

Speaking of money, the start of November saw Hatcher fire off a familiar salvo:

> *The last three months you have sent . . . $300 per month instead of $310 & you have not sent the $50 I paid to L. Lamothe, making $80 in all that I have not received that vouchers have been sent for. You say to buy all the skulls I can get cheap. The man I got the other skull* [from] *says he has ten more & that I can have all I want . . . if I will pay* [for] *shipping & packing & take them up myself & give him ½ of what I sell them for. But I must advance him $10 on each skull before I leave here. If you want them . . . send $100.00 as I asked you before . . .* [and] *the $80 not yet received so that I will get it when I come in again.*

For their part, Hatcher's crew proper had taken up twenty-two skulls and twenty pairs of lower jaws, along with two fine pelvis specimens and a lower jaw of something entirely new as part of the 3,160 pounds of bones they brought in on the second. Their treasure in the depot now tipped the scales at over nine thousand pounds.[47]

Marsh mailed the check for $180 by the fifteenth, and Hatcher contracted with his competitor Gus Craven for eight of his skulls, making the season's total twenty-nine skulls, twenty-four pairs of lower jaws, three pelvic arches, and one nearly complete skeleton with, he thought, every vertebra represented. But there was more: "I have five more skulls to take up . . . and several other things which will keep me busy until in December." In all, he had sixty-two boxes packed and proclaimed he'd never had such good luck. On the twenty-seventh, he was still on a roll, but Burwell and Peterson were tiring of the "severe" weather. So he promised to pay them their full salary for December if they'd work until December 12, for, he said, "I hate to leave here without taking up all the skulls I have found." In the end, Hatcher reported shipping seventy-one boxes weighing 15,140 pounds on December 3, having collected and packed everything they'd found. On the way out, he planned on the crew driving to Porcupine Creek to see the fossil beds Hank Clifford had talked so much about before proceeding to Valentine, Nebraska, by the tenth. From there, he'd take the train from Valentine but stop at his home with Anna in Long Pine, Nebraska. In his assessment of the season's work, he boasted to Marsh, "My collection here is magnificent."[48]

That 1888 collection, along with those from the region collected in 1886 and 1887, is now housed for the most part in the USNM and contains specimens from three different geologic rock units: the White River Group, the Eocene Chadron, which ranges from about 37–34 million-years old and the Oligocene Brule Formation, about 34–30 million years old. As currently identified, the diverse assemblage from the Chadron consists of fourteen mammalian genera. There are eight brontotheres, including "Allops," "Brontops," "Brontotherium," *Diploclonus, Megacerops, Symborodon,* "Titanops," and "Titanotherium," most of which are now included in the genus *Megacerops.* There are four rhinos, including "Caenopus," which is now called *Subhyracodon,* "Menodus," and *Trigonias.* The one horse is *Mesohippus.* The imposing, pig-like entelodont *Archaeotherium* also appears, along with the fearsome mammalian carnivore *Hyaenodon.* The fauna from the White River collection is less diverse, containing only six genera of vertebrates: the iguana *Aciprion,* the relative of the Gila monster *Helodermoides,* a worm lizard *Rhineura,* a monitor lizard *Saniwa,* the insectivore-like *Leptictis,* and the rhino *Subhyracodon.* Finally, Hatcher's collection from the Brule contains seventeen genera: a sheep- or pig-like oreodont, *Merycoidodon;* the ungulate, *Agriochoerus;* the entelodont, *Archaeotherium;* an even-toed ungulate called an anthracothere *Ancodon;* the small, antelope-like *Leptomeryx* and *Hypertragulus;* the rhinos *Hyracodon* and *Subhyracodon,* the horse *Miohippus,* the rodents *Eumys* and the relative of pocket gophers and kangaroo rats *Heliscomys;* the primitive rabbit *Palaeolagus,* and the carnivorous amphicyonid "bear dog" *Cynodictis.* Also in 1888, Hatcher acquired, possibly by purchase, one noteworthy specimen now at the Peabody Museum from the Chadron Formation of Pennington County, South Dakota—Marsh's holotype for the giant tortoise "Testudo" *brontops* (YPM VP 608), which is the largest tortoise specimen known from the White River Badlands.[49]

After dismissing his crew and reaching Long Pine on the eleventh, Hatcher beamed, "Found Mrs. H and boy well." He sought Marsh's permission to take a two-to three-week vacation to "fix up a little on my ranch here before I go East." While he was in the field, he had had a "fine barn" built on his place and now had it full of "nice horses and mares." Marsh, in appreciation of his efforts, sent copies of his article on "Horned Dinosauria." The day before Christmas, Hatcher said he'd leave for New Haven in a few days and would be ready to return to North Carolina anytime after he arrived.[50]

Curiously, the catalogue of the USNM also records a collection of specimens from the sauropod dinosaur "Astrodon," now called *Pleurocoelus,* as well as a specimen of the crocodile relative *Goniopholis* among Hatcher's acquisitions during the 1888 season.

6

Tracking *Triceratops* and Mining Mini-Mammals

atcher couldn't have been in New Haven for more than two weeks, because he was in Washington on January 18, 1889, where he returned to the Muirkirk iron ore beds but found nothing of consequence. Two days later, he wrote from Gulf, North Carolina, and related he'd found several fine fish teeth in coal slates. A large company had just starting pumping out the old Egypt shaft where North Carolina State geologist Ebenezer Emmons had found his "mammal" remains, but it would be a long time before they mined any coal. One other nearby mine had not had any work done on it since the previous year. He vowed to give the place a fair trial, but he knew his chances would be better if coal was coming out. By the twenty-fifth, Hatcher sent Marsh several teeth and dermal plates or skull fragments of reptiles, some fish teeth, a few bones from Muirkirk, and a nearly complete skull of an ichthyo-saur or plesiosaur missing only the front of the snout. He proclaimed it "undoubtedly the best thing that has ever been found here in the line of reptiles," although the specimen does not seem to be listed in the records of either the Peabody or USNM. Yet he'd failed to find any mammals despite braving frigid days of rain with a heavy cold and a very sore throat. Another week's work produced more reptile bones and teeth, but the search for mammals remained unsuccessful.[1]

Fortunately, prospects seemed to be brightening for the coming season out west, for on February 1, Hatcher responded to Marsh about a pos-sible dinosaur skull his mentor had gotten wind of: "I am glad you're going to get other horn core & fragments from Guernsey & hope we may get skull soon." This seems to be the first reference to what would become the first scientifically documented specimen of *Triceratops*, and according to a cowboy on Guernsey's ranch who had seen the skull, it sported "horns as long as a hoe handle and eye holes as big as your hat." In another comment, Hatcher revealed that he had set up an investment for Marsh's older sister, Mary, in his hometown, reassuring Marsh that he hoped "the bank at Long Pine will transact that business satisfactorily to the young lady and yourself & that she will be well pleased with her investment. I know everything will be done right."[2]

Despite the dearth of mammals at Gulf, Hatcher argued to Marsh on the seventh that he already had "much better material from here than [Emmons] had." In addition, Hatcher had a letter from the bank in Long Pine "saying they . . . would send the young lady her papers just as soon as they get them closed and recorded." He also reported that he'd received "a letter from Mr. Guernsey [that] says he will start for Wyoming today & he will be pleased to show me the skull from which he got horncores & assist me in getting it when I come west in the Spring."[3]

The note from Guernsey led to unraveling a remarkable case of mis-taken identity. In 1887, Marsh had received an enormous pair of fossilized bony horns from Whitman Cross, a geologist for the Federal Survey in Denver, which had been discovered by George Cannon Jr. along Green Mountain Creek. Marsh immediately identified them as belonging to "one of the largest American bovines" and christened them with the name "Bison alticornis" and assigned a Pliocene age to the specimen. But that age didn't conform with the fact that Cross had been finding remains of dinosaurs in the same beds from which the fossilized horns were collected, leading him to suspect that the Denver beds were either Cretaceous or very early Cenozoic in age. Were these bony horncores really from an ancient bison? It fell upon Hatcher to solve the mystery.[4]

Upon reaching Long Pine by February 26, Hatcher said Peterson was lined up for the season and was pleased with the gift of a watch from Marsh. He hoped Burwell would be on board soon. On a more personal level, Hatcher intimated, "Mrs. H wishes to thank you for the presents sent her and the baby." Regarding the investment for Marsh's sister, Hatcher indicated that Mary's money was loaned on the lot and building to be built adjoining the bank. The building was insured with good security, and interest would be paid promptly, so "she need not be at all uneasy for her investment is a good one." With that, Hatcher planned to leave and meet Guernsey in a day or two at Lusk, Wyoming.[5]

Once in Lusk, Hatcher had to wait for Guernsey to return from Chicago, so he wrote Marsh to send the money to Chadron for March, a full $200, because he had bought $50 of fruit trees for his farm, and the sooner he planted, the sooner he'd have fruit. If Marsh couldn't send $200, then "send $150 & credit me for $50 on my note as per agreement." The $200 seems to represent Hatcher's monthly salary plus a $100 fee for use of Hatcher's team and wagon. This is the first mention of Hatcher borrowing money from Marsh. Hatcher then explained that the papers for Mary's investment had been delayed due to sorting out a previous mortgage on the property, but that it was still a "good, safe investment" that would draw 10 percent from February 1, with interest paid semi-annually.[6]

It wasn't until March 19 that Hatcher reported he "didn't get that big skull as Mr. Guernsey could not find it." But his ranch foreman, Edmund Wilson, who originally found it, would be back in the spring and guide Hatcher to it. Having seen the country, Hatcher was confident he could take a fully supplied crew there that summer and have good results, but he couldn't do anything without a crew, since there was no means of subsisting. In the meantime he'd go to Rapid City to see Craven and Burwell, then stop at Long Pine to check on his farm and the investment.[7]

From Long Pine on the twenty-fifth, Hatcher wrote that Gus Craven had three brontothere skulls and one nice pelvis, as well as the fact that Carpenter had an excellent skeleton that Marsh could probably purchase. So during the summer, Hatcher hoped to hopscotch from Carpenter's site near Rapid City, to Burwell's brontothere sites around Chadron, and back to Guernsey's potential dinosaur locality around Lusk. Again, he asked Marsh to send $150 and credit him $50 on his note. He further informed Marsh that Mary's investment papers had been sent and intimated, "Our boy is very sick."[8]

Meanwhile, Marsh laid out his priorities for Hatcher's season on March 28 in a confidential memorandum, stating his desire for him to work a good deal in the Laramie Formation, with the possibility of calling on George L. Cannon Jr. of Denver and getting him to show Hatcher the typical localities in the region where previous fossils had been found, including the eastern slope of Green Mountain, where two thirds of a large dinosaur skeleton was possibly preserved based on specimens already sent to Yale. Hatcher was to secure all the remaining bones and the rights to the locality. Marsh also directed Hatcher to visit a locality where Eldridge had found lots of bones, because Marsh had seen portions of six "Ceratops" or allied skulls from the Denver region, so there must be good skulls there. He might also want Hatcher to visit Colorado Springs and Cañon City to see typical Jurassic localities, but Hatcher should say nothing to Cannon or others about his plans. Regarding the geologic relationships, Marsh would send Cross's paper, adding that although his stratigraphy and lithology were admirable, he was wrong about the age, which Cross concluded was Tertiary rather than Cretaceous.[9]

Back in Long Pine on the twenty-eighth, Hatcher wrote saying there was a basin of Laramie badlands on Buck Creek in Wyoming thirty to forty miles northeast of Lusk where Guernsey's big skull was. They were several miles in extent and would take several months of work to prospect thoroughly but would require a complete field outfit because the nearest ranch was twenty miles away. He'd require two men, three horses, and a camp outfit costing about $300 per month. Regarding the other prospects, he thought the Rapid City specimen well worth pursuing, and they ought to keep an eye on the brontothere beds, too. In terms of Mary's investment, it would go towards building a two-story, double brick building 60 x 120 feet, with the upper story to be used as a Masonic temple and the lower to rent for two storerooms. Hatcher informed Marsh the same group had secured the two adjoining lots and planned to build on them. They intended to borrow $4,000 at 8 percent, which Hatcher thought would be a good investment for five years for Marsh, since the building and lots would be worth two or three times the amount loaned and would have the Masonry behind it. Finally, a concerned Hatcher lamented, "Our boy has been very sick the past week and I have had no sleep since I got home . . . and am not feeling very first rate."[10]

Marsh must have been anxious to get Guernsey's skull, for on April 4 Hatcher responded, "I know of no other way of getting the big skull than to wait for Mr. Wilson to come back and show it to me. Guernsey has promised to do all he can toward getting it for me & I can only rely on his promise." More bad family tidings followed: "My wife's mother is expected to die any moment so that I do not want to leave here until there is a change one way or the other. But that will come soon." On the eighth, Hatcher expected to go out with Wilson for the skull within ten days, even though Anna's mother was still "very low." Hatcher said he'd leave on the thirteenth for Lusk to meet Wilson.[11]

However, on the nineteenth, Hatcher revealed he and Anna had been dealt an even more devastating blow:

It seems my bad luck never will stop this Spring. My little boy died yesterday & my wife is very sick now. The baby was very sick about two weeks ago & then he got better & the doctor said was out of danger when my wife's mother was taken down. She got better & I was ready to start work Saturday the 13th when the baby suddenly got worse again. So as to lose no time I started Peterson with team outfit & saddle horse for the field in Wyoming intending to overtake him by R.R. at Chadron or Lusk. I thought sure the baby would get better & the Dr. said all along that he was in no danger but I watched him closely & felt differently about it. We did all we could for him & as he never was sick scarcely a moment of his life before I did certainly think his strength would pull him through.

I suspect you think I am doing nothing this Summer, but you do not know all I have had to contend with this Spring. I came home from the West as we agreed that I should to spend two weeks getting things started on my place so that I could be gone for the summer. Have been here three weeks & sickness has kept me busy night and day & I have seen nothing but misfortune.

I do not know what to do & can not tell you anything until my wife gets better, which I hope she will soon. But it will be very lonely for her here all alone now, he was so much company to her. Perhaps I may have to stay here with her awhile anyway. You see just how I am situated so take what action you see fit. If left to myself I shall certainly try to do the best I can for you & as soon as I can. If you are tired waiting on me longer, you can send out someone to take my place & I will give them all the help in my power. What shall I do with my men and teams? They are up there somewhere now. If you want to trust the securing of the big skull to them I can write them and have them do the best they can. Do as you see fit. I no longer have any suggestions to offer. . . .

Unfortunately, the name of Anna and John Bell's first son is not now known; he is listed simply as "Child Hatcher" in the Hatcher Family Association records.[12]

A series of telegrams and letters on the twentieth and twenty-first established that Wilson had returned and awaited Hatcher, who requested $250 from Marsh. Marsh, although anxious about the skull, nevertheless simply counseled "use your best judgment about work." Hatcher sent Peterson and Burwell on to Lusk to go out with Wilson, "look after" the skull, and prospect for others. He'd catch up as soon as possible. Then Hatcher pleaded over his plight to Marsh:

I asked you if you could send me $250.00. When I was ready to go before the baby died I just had money enough to run me a month in the field. Now I have to borrow money to pay Dr. bill, funeral expenses & for lot in graveyard. If you will let me have it, I will pay you whatever rate of interest you think right &

will pay the note at the rate of $50 per month (after I have paid the other note) until paid. You have accommodated me so often that it seems like an imposition to ask you to accommodate me now when I still owe you $100.00. But unless I get the money of you I shall either have to sell some of my stock here for just what people are amind to pay me or borrow the money & pay 3% a month on it.

Please let me know if you can let me have the money, & if you can, make out the note as you would like to have it & send it to me & I will sign it. Answer by telegram yes or no. . . .

My wife is a little better and I hope to be able to leave soon.[13]

Struggling to return to a more business-focused mind-set six days later, Hatcher reported that Peterson and Burwell had found Guernsey's skull, and with Anna feeling better now, he hoped to go and pack it up in a few days, if he could get the money to "straighten up his affairs." Marsh came through with the money by loaning Hatcher $250, which Hatcher received on May 2. Profoundly grateful, Hatcher responded, "You do me a great favor by letting me have the money. . . ." Since Marsh declined to set the interest rate, Hatcher designated it at 10 percent. Hatcher also advised Marsh about the buildings in Long Pine in which Marsh was considering investing, cautioning that the building must be smaller than originally conceived and only veneered in brick rather than solid. Although they would still pay 8 percent on the $6,500 borrowed, the security would be based on the honor of the Masonic lodge there, "not the mortgaged property that it should be."[14]

Shortly after, Hatcher set off for the skull and sent a dispatch from Lusk on May 7:

The big skull is ours. . . . It is badly broken up, but was in good condition when found three years ago. They broke the horncores off it and rolled it down the bluff & broke lots of it into small pieces some of which we found over 100 yds. below. I doubt if we can ever find all the pieces. Lower jaws were there. When packed it will weigh 1000 lbs. or over. It will probably be a week before I can

get it packed & in here, let me know whether to express or freight.
Express will cost about $100.00.

And it got better: "Yesterday . . . , I found very fair Hadrosaurus skull about 300 yards below big skull in nearly same horizon . . . also a fragment of another big skull." Wilson, who found the first skull, wanted to work for Marsh, and Hatcher recommended him as young, ambitious, honest, and intelligent. Hatcher pledged to keep expenses down to $300 per month but couldn't run the operation for less. Then he ended with a request to send $100 "to pay the boys . . . and Wilson."[15]

By the twentieth, Hatcher was planning his trip to Denver on June 1. He'd need $100 per month plus expenses, but that wouldn't leave much to pay for help if fossils were found. He wasn't sure how Peterson and Burwell would do, since they hadn't found anything significant during his previous absence, but he hoped "to find some good localities for mammals & other small things and set them to work on them" while he was gone. He was sending five crates containing the big skull and a lower jaw of a hadrosaur, along with a package containing four or five species of Laramie mammals. The lot also included some fossil fish fragments, reptiles and birds found in the same bed with mammal teeth, along with the humerus of a mole-like mammal. He'd yet to receive the $100 requested to pay Wilson and men for the previous month and needed $300 for everything this month. He reminded Marsh to credit him for $50 on his loan and added a note about the mammals:

> *I hope you will be pleased. . . . They are by no means abundant.*
> *The few I send you requiring several days careful search after the*
> *localities were found. I hope you will not despise them because they*
> *are few in numbers & will make the best of them.*
>
> *If you describe the big skull, give Edwin B. Wilson & Chas. A.*
> *Guernsey credit for finding it. I have dug the ground over and over*
> *again for pieces of it, but I feel sure that many of them will never*
> *be found. I saw no teeth.*

He closed by noting he'd been suffering terribly from "rheumatism" in his hand and left hip the last two weeks.[16]

Over the next two weeks, another skull and skeleton of *Triceratops* were found and partially collected, so on the thirty-first Hatcher shipped another five crates to Marsh, including the lower jaws, a maxillary, three vertebrae, and various other bones. It would take another week or ten days to finish collecting the skull because Hatcher was afraid to remove it simply by pasting, for it was so large and clumsy it might break of its own weight. So he pleaded for patience, since it was much more complete than Guernsey's specimen. He noted the teeth were like that of a hadrosaur and thought a little jaw he had sent last summer from Montana belonged to one of these horned dinosaurs rather than a hadrosaur. Stratigraphically, he believed that if the horn-cores from Denver were from typical Denver beds, there can be little doubt of their being Cretaceous. He also gleaned a few more mammal teeth, but Marsh apparently thought they weren't packed well enough, so Hatcher defended his technique: "I do not think the fossils I sent . . . were so poorly packed as to receive any damage. The mammals were in a little box with plenty of cotton." He thought Marsh might want to decide for himself the age of the formation independent of his opinion, and went on to defend himself further:

> *You seem to find considerable fault with me this Spring about not writing often & various other things. No doubt you had cause to be exasperated with my slowness this Spring but then I could not possibly be away from home then, and no one regretted it worse than I did. You complain all the time about my not writing oftener. I write you every time I come to town as fully as I can. You must remember that there are no street corners with letterboxes on them out where I am at work. And since it takes me 3 days to go to town and back if I do anything I can not be in town very often. I have to do everything up here myself so far this summer as neither of my men are worth h-l room. If I send them to hunt for specimens they never find any & if I set them to work on anything they break it all in pieces before they get it up. I am doing the very best I know how*

to do, and I would like you to realize it. Of course I make mistakes but I try to do what is best for all.[17]

Things seemed to be patched up between Marsh and Hatcher by the eighth, but Marsh wanted the crew to stop work on dinosaur skeletons and intensify the search for mammals. Hatcher confirmed that almost all mammals sent recently were from a locality where the big skull was, but he had found mammal fossils in four different localities, although he had spent no time looking for them. So he'd focus on that next week and send them all when he came in to pick up Marsh's student Charles Emerson Beecher. Hatcher's receipts reveal that Peterson's salary had increased to $60 per month, while Burwell's was $50. On June sixteenth, apparently in response to Marsh's query, Hatcher wrote that he'd found no dermal or sternal plates with the ceratopsian skeleton and couldn't say whether the new skull was larger than Guernsey's since the latter was so broken up. He repeated that the mammals and dinosaurs were from forty miles north of Lusk, and since he'd now found mammals in ten or twelve isolated localities, he couldn't say if they were all from the same horizon because of the distance between them and the disturbed condition of the strata. He hoped Beecher could manage his crew when he left for Denver and wanted Marsh to visit during his upcoming trip west. With that, he shipped four crates of ceratopsian bones and three cans of small specimens including mammal teeth. But the work in the rain was taking a toll: "I am troubled terribly with rheumatism at present. It comes on by spells." He also needed a better reference to help him identify the bones he was excavating: "Can you get me a copy of Leidy's Cretaceous reptiles? That [Cope's] miserable Judith Basin paper isn't fit for a fire lighter."[18]

The crew wrestled the big skull out of the outcrop and packed it securely by the twenty-seventh, with Hatcher admonishing Marsh to make a plaster bed for it at the Peabody before taking it out of the crate and beginning to prepare it. Then another plaster bed should be prepared before turning it over to prepare the bottom. He'd spent weeks excavating and packing it, so he didn't want "a little carelessness there [to] destroy" the details of the internal or external anatomy, which could be clearly revealed down to a row of small tubercles surrounding a large bony plate (frill). He added that "Beecher's suggestions have been of great value . . . & it now remains to be seen what you will do with it there." Beecher had even made sketches to guide the preparation. Hatcher inquired about Wilson working with them, but he didn't want any novices. Then, apparently in response to Marsh's demands for more mammals and concerns that the crew was slacking off in collecting them, he blasted Marsh broadside:

> *You seem to think that Laramie mammals are everywhere abundant out here & that all that is necessary is to go out and scoop them, notwithstanding what I have said to the contrary. They are very rare & about two teeth represents an average patient day's work. They are getting more rare every day & unless we find a new locality you need not expect any more. The first locality I found has afforded 10 times the material of all the rest. However I will do the best I can & hope to be able to report rich localities when I come in again. Peterson has become very proficient in finding these small things & is doing well. You need not be afraid that I or any man under me will soldier on you. The reason we dont [sic] send you more and better mammals is because we cant [sic] find them & not because we do not try.*

After expressing his displeasure, he confirmed sending a box that day with several mammals and small things, before making a confession of sorts based on his newfound knowledge of horned dinosaurs:

> *I now have to write something which you will say exposes my carelessness. But nevertheless I will write it. I now believe that the skeleton that Lamothe had last fall was one of these Ceratops. And that a certain flat bone which I only partially uncovered & which was very cracked up was a part of the large bones on the back of the skull over five feet across. If this be true the skull would be fine. It is a reproach to me but after seeing the skull I feell [sic] almost certain that it is another one. However I may be mistaken. I wish I was there now for two hours with any pick or oyster opener.*

Then he was back on attack about money, noting that he had incurred "considerable extra expense the last two months . . . coming to town so often . . . for extra materials . . . [for] packing and I think you ought to bear part of it." Hatcher was having a house built and needed the money, and he wanted to see Marsh that summer "to have a talk" with him.[19]

For his part, Marsh had already pumped out a paper about the new Cretaceous mammals (Marsh 1889) for which Hatcher received the proofs, along with a $200 check, by July 6. Hatcher was pleased, "especially for the credit you give me in your paper," and was able to reciprocate by mailing three packages containing over five hundred mammal teeth besides many bones. "You will have . . . at least 800 teeth of Laramie mammals, abundant material for two more papers. I broke the record yesterday by finding 87 mammal teeth in one day." After complimenting Peterson and Beecher for their help, he revealed the secret of their success: "We sifted all the anthills in the two best localities & were rewarded a hundred fold." He elaborated on this curious collecting method in a later paper published in 1896:

> *The small mammals are . . . never abundant and on account of their small size are seen with difficulty. They will be most frequently found in what are locally known as "blow outs"* [areas where the wind has eroded into the ancient channel sands of the Laramie or Lance Creek Formation] *and are almost always associated with garpike scales and teeth, and teeth and bones of other fish, crocodiles, lizards and small dinosaurs. . . . In such places the ant hills, which in this region are quite numerous* [usually conical and 12–18 inches high], *should be carefully inspected as they will almost always yield a goodly number of mammal teeth. It is well to be provided with a small flour sifter with which to sift the sand contained in these ant hills, thus freeing it from the finer materials and subjecting the coarser material remaining in the sieve to a thorough inspection for mammals. By this method the writer has frequently secured from 200 to 300 teeth and jaws from one ant hill.*[20]

Nonetheless, Hatcher was miffed about his still missing money, complaining, "I will be out of money when I pay for supplies today & unless check gets here will have to borrow when I come in again. Please send as soon as possible." Again changing tone and recalling his college days, he exclaimed, "very glad Yale won boat race" and noted that he'd "have to congratulate Beecher on his new [PhD] degree." The next day Hatcher wrote again to announce that he'd begun excavating a new skeleton found two weeks previously that preserved at least several ribs, some foot bones, vertebrae, and several other unidentified bones. If complete, it would be "a monster," since the vertebral centra were over seven inches in diameter. He hoped the skull was attached. Then, again based on what he'd seen, he critiqued Marsh's identification of *Bison alticornis*:

> *You say . . . "Skull no.1* [YPM VP 1820] *has a horn on nasals about a foot or more back of beak" also that you have three feet of beak together & nowhere near back to horncores yet, also that both horncores are in place now so that you know just where you are. This is very strange. I am sure you are mistaking the back of the skull for the front; this would be a very natural thing for you to do, especially if you should follow your "Bison alticornis" for a guide, for I am sure you have them turned wrong. I think that the horn which you think you have found on the beak will turn out to be one of several situated on a large frill on back of skull. If this be the case, it will be a consolation to me to know that I was not the only person puzzled by this exceedingly strange form of skull. I presume you have already received Beecher's drawings, & they'll doubtless help you a great deal. Those Ceratopsidae were queer birds.*[21]

More mammals, more mammals—Hatcher mailed another 150 mammal teeth to Marsh on July 13, along with a list of the mammal localities from which the teeth in Marsh's publication were collected. But he cautioned that the flow of teeth would subside unless the crew found new localities. He also confirmed that he'd check with Craven about purchasing his season's collection of brontothere skulls that had been featured in a newspaper article earlier in July. Finally, he inquired if Marsh knew where William Berryman Scott's party from Princeton was headed, as he had not seen them and didn't expect to, since the mammals Hatcher's crew was finding were not complete skeletons. The receipts submitted show that both Peterson and Burwell were now receiving salaries of $40 per month. On the sixteenth, as the "fearfully hot" summer simmered on, Hatcher and Beecher brought five more crates in for shipment. After reminding Marsh to send the check for July, he admitted that he should have waited until the following year to build his house because it had made him "very hard up." So he requested that Marsh allow him to skip payments on his loan for a couple of months. In a letter on the twenty-first, Hatcher confirmed he'd written Craven about his skulls. Marsh must have expressed interest in their finding more hadrosaur material, because Hatcher indicated they'd not found any skulls so far but "hoped to run on to one any day." Elaborating on the new ceratopsian skulls, he reported,

> One . . . has four cervicals right in position . . . the atlas, axis and next two. The frill is very beautifully scalloped on border, something we have not noticed in any previous skull. The beak should be entire as it sticks straight down in the rock. The other one Mr. Beecher found within eight rod of this one & it is also very good. These skulls when taken out will weigh about three thousand pounds each. Hence . . . we have some work ahead of us. But I have an abundance of "self conceit" & it does not frighten me at all & you may be sure we will get them out & packed all O.K. I think if it were possible [they should] remain at Yale.

Marsh had apparently approved of hiring Wilson, who was to start on the twenty-eighth, and despite his bravado, Hatcher was glad to have another man to help handle the massive skulls.[22]

Money matters were foremost in Hatcher's mind when he wrote to Marsh on August 3, as he acknowledged receiving a $250 check that seemed to indicate Marsh had credited $50 to his loan despite Hatcher's request to the contrary. He groused,

> I will try to get along. But I can not run this party any longer for $300 per month. I had left last month less than $80. This will not

pay for my time & horses, wagon & harness. When it comes to paying $15.00 for materials for 2 boxes & other things in proportion I can not stand it. It will cost me nearly $100 to get those two boxes with the big skulls in them to Lusk. Now you know that this is too much to ask of me for the wages I get. I am not asking for any increase in salary but I can not stand this extra expense any longer. I have obligations to meet that I must make.

He had hoped Marsh would come out to "see how work goes here," and they could discuss it, but Marsh had no plans to come. He then indicated that Lucien Warren Stilwell was trying to purchase Craven's collection, but Craven agreed to wait two weeks for Hatcher, so he and Beecher were heading to the "Bad Lands" to deal. They struck a bargain with both Craven and Joseph Brown for $300 by the fifteenth, and Hatcher shipped four brontothere skulls, including "a new prong horned fellow." Despite a lack of communication between Marsh and Hatcher regarding the price Marsh was willing to pay, Hatcher considered his acquisition "cheap" and defended his decision to pay that amount. They also saw Stilwell's collection in Deadwood, which featured an entelodont skull called *Elotherium* for $150 and two rhino skulls of *Metamynodon* for $150 and $100.[23]

Returning to Wyoming, the two new ceratopsian skulls were crated and ready to ship by the seventeenth, with Hatcher proclaiming, "If No. 2 made you happy Nos. 3 & 4 ought to make you one hundred fold more so" (No. 2 is YPM VP 1821; No. 3 is YPM VP 1822; No. 4 is YPM VP 1823). The icing on the cake in the shipment would be another can of mammals. But still stewing over finances, he fumed,

After paying for freighting [the skulls], *I will be about $8.00 worse off than if I had not dug bones at all this month. In other words, I pay $8.00 for the privilege of working a month & furnishing an outfit that has cost me over $500.00. I want to work and do the best I can for you but I ought to do something for myself too I think. I have been disappointing people all Summer. If I can not do any better I will have to close up & come in pretty soon. All I* *want is my salary & pay for the use of my horses & outfit above the other expenses.*

As Beecher headed back east around the twenty-third, Hatcher planned to check on his spread in Long Pine and paint his house for ten days, but before leaving he again pleaded with Marsh to come out and "look over ground with me this Fall if only for a day or two." Anticipating Marsh's concerns, he warned that since Wilson had been working that month, he'd need more funding than he'd been needing because he'd covered a great deal of extra expense. He figured about $400 for August would about get him even. He promised to make an itemized expense report for the period since he left New Haven so Marsh could see the problem for himself and again pleaded, "I am actually losing money this month by working at $300 per month & furnishing everything. I have taken . . . great . . . pains this season to get things up in good shape & have gone to lots of expense to do it . . . but can go no farther."[24]

Marsh came through with the $400, along with reprints of his Ceratopsidae and Laramie mammals papers by September 3, as Hatcher set out on his return to the field. Marsh apparently was also contemplating a visit to the Wyoming badlands, because Hatcher advised him to give advance notice so they could meet him because it would be hard to find them otherwise, and Hatcher urged him on by warning, "If you don't come out this fall . . . I shall think you do not care much for our Laramie mammals, Ceratopsidae, etc." The "etc." may have been for hadrosaurs, for he expressed hope of still finding one of their skulls. Then he closed by recounting that his farm looked well, the house nearly finished and the crops good. Hatcher's next correspondence on October 5 alerted Marsh to watch for another shipment of big boxes and contained a hope that he got home safely, implying he'd visited in the interim. They must have worked out their financial foibles, because another $400 check arrived by October 5 to cover that month's expenses. Another shipment of crates and mammals followed on the eleventh, and Hatcher cheerily headed for Long Pine, proclaiming, "Thought I would come home & celebrate my birthday which is today." He was glad Marsh enjoyed his trip to Denver and succeeded in getting some nice Navajo blankets. He promised to mail a pair of moccasins that Marsh had gotten at Hat Creek and left at camp. Wilson was pleased with the "charm" Marsh had gifted him, and Hatcher added that all enjoyed his visit with them and wished to be remembered to Marsh. Hatcher expected to be back at camp by the twenty-third and would be ready for Denver by November 1.[25]

Snow covered the ground as Hatcher departed for Denver on the first, after deciding to leave one of Burwell's ceratopsian specimens in the ground until next season and directing the crew to concentrate on excavating Skull No. 5 and prospecting for more mammal localities. He added, "Glad the big boxes are there safe. You can't imagine what a relief it is to me to get those boxes off my hands in good shape. They were bad things to handle out here without any tools & in such a miserable place to get out." Before boarding the train he'd send about two hundred mammals by registered mail.[26]

From Denver on the seventh, Hatcher reminded Marsh to send the check for October so he could pay the men and cover his expenses in Colorado. He'd been unable to begin his survey of fossil sites due to heavy snow and expressed his general state of displeasure. "I wish I was out of this thing. This man Cannon I do not like very well." Hatcher claimed George L. Cannon, a local high school teacher, had already presented a paper before the October meeting of the Denver Scientific Society based on information delivered from Marsh's articles in the *American Journal of Science*, as well as unpublished information that Marsh personally provided him with when he was there, "in which he at least anticipates if he doesn't state precisely those facts which my finds here (if I make any) are sure to establish." Beyond that, the man in charge of the Survey in Denver informed Hatcher that there was no saddle horse available, so Hatcher would have to hike to the localities. By the eleventh, Hatcher had only spent one day in the field and found nothing, again grousing, "Unless snow goes off pretty soon & we get good weather, I shall want to leave."[27]

A check arrived for $200, but Hatcher telegraphed for another $100 on the twenty-first, arguing that the money would run out before the end of the month, and "if the weather is good I do not wish to lay up here for want of money." Evidently, Hatcher had had enough:

I want to quit here the end of the month no matter what happens. I have been in the field now almost regularly since I got out of the hospital in New Haven, almost three years ago. And I want to come in for a while this winter. The past month is enough to take the enthusiasm out of any one. I have had nothing but wet feet, sore throat & colds for the last month. The snow is still on the ground, though not so deep as it was. I stayed in this morning to write letters. Practically, I had just as well stay in all the time. I tell you I am sick of this work here & want to come in for a while & then I can go to work with new enthusiasm in the Spring. I can do nothing here & I am tired of trying.

Ever a man of his word, Hatcher returned to Lusk by December 3, paid off his men with half a month's extra bonus to boot, and closed the camp. From Lusk he would head to Long Pine and stay there until he received his salary settlement from Marsh, then head east to New Haven.[28]

Clearly the dinosaurs Hatcher collected are the most spectacular discoveries he made in the eyes of the public, but the mammals are at least as important scientifically because they begin to shed light from more than 66 million years ago on the evolutionary origins not only of our own human lineage but also the mammalian lineages with which we still share the earth today. Beyond their being minute and difficult to find, it's fairly safe to say Hatcher almost certainly paid a price in pain when he collected them, because the ants that inhabit the anthills from which many of the teeth were gathered take onerous offense to their domicile being demolished and are capable of delivering searing, stinging bites to defend their home. Among the minuscule mammalian jewels that Hatcher snatched from the 66-million-year-old sediments of the Lance Formation were, as now identified in the USNM and Peabody collections, numerous genera of the herbivorous, rodent-like multituberculates (*Allacodon, Cimolodon, Cimolomys, Meniscoessus, Mesodma, Camptomus*; as well as "Dipriodon," "Halodon," "Oracodon," "Selenacodon," and "Tripriodon" [all now called *Meniscoessus*]; "Nanomyops" and "Nanomys" [now called *Cimolodon*]). There were also five genera of early marsupials (*Alphadon, Didelphodon, Pediomys,*

Protolambda, Hatcheritherium, which was named for Hatcher; as well as "Ectoconodon" and "Stagodon," which are now called *Didelphodon*) and more of our own placental relatives (*Cimolestes, Gypsonictops, Batodon,* and *Telacodon,* as well as "Nyssodon," now called *Cimolestes*). The catalogues also record the small, swift, insectivorous mammal *Dryolestes.* In addition, seven genera of lizards are recorded (*Chamops, Colpodontosaurus, Leptochamops, Iguanavus, Odaxosaurus, Peltosaurus, Paraderma,* and "Harpagosaurus" [now called *Exostinus*]). Amphibians are represented by *Albanerpeton,* as well as the salamanders *Lisserpeton, Piceoerpeton,* and *Scapherton,* while turtles in the fauna included *Trionyx* and *Baena.* Another reptile was the alligator *Allognathosuchus.* Six ray-finned fish called *Belonostomus, Coriops, Melvius, Paralbula, Platacodon,* and "Kindleia," which is now called *Cyclurus,* are represented. Finally, the dinosaurian stars of the show included the horned dinosaur *Triceratops,* for which Hatcher had given both Marsh and the world their first look at the true size and spectacular anatomy of this genus that has since become one of the most famous and popular dinosaurs of all time. Other dinosaur discoveries included the horned cousin of *Triceratops, Leptoceratops,* the duckbill *Trachodon,* the bone-helmeted herbivore called *Pachycephalosaurus,* the carnivores *Paronychodon* and *Troodon.* For good measure, the 1889 season also yielded a sharp, serrated tooth of arguably the most famous dinosaur ever found, *Tyrannosaurus.* However, there was not yet enough of this animal's skeleton known to recognize it as a new genus, so it would be another sixteen years before *Tyrannosaurus* took its place on the Cretaceous stage with *Triceratops.* Nonetheless, Hatcher found specimens of the tyrannosaur cousin *Aublysodon,* along with the shorebird *Cimolopteryx.*

In addition, Hatcher's 1889 collection contains a couple of specimens of sharks from the 18- to 15-million-year-old Calvert Formation—the great white "Carcharodon," which is now sometimes called *Carcharocles,* and the sand shark, *Odontaspis.* Furthermore, the Peabody houses one specimen of the sauropod called *Barosaurus,* which was collected by Marsh with the assistance of Hatcher from the Morrison Formation in the Black Hills of South Dakota, and Marsh used the specimen to redescribe the genus in 1890. In addition, six fossils of its evolutionary cousin "Astrodon," which is now called *Pleuroceolus,* now reside at the USNM.[29]

7

Pondering Other Options

After Hatcher took a six-week respite from the field, he wrote from Gulf, North Carolina, in mid-January 1890 that he was again attempting to find Jurassic mammals but hadn't succeeded, even though they were now mining coal from an old shaft. He considered it useless to search for mammals there. A specimen might be found, but it would only be a chance find, and "to say that the circumstances are discouraging expresses it but mildly." Still laboring futilely at the Egypt mine on the twenty-seventh, Hatcher planned to follow Marsh's directive and travel to Archer, Florida, where he planned to collect next. But before leaving, he revealed to Marsh that he'd had an offer from Georg Baur to join him in a commercial fossil-collecting venture he was starting. Born in Germany, Baur came to the United States and became one of Marsh's assistants at Yale in 1884 after finishing his doctorate at the University of Munich in 1882. A specialist in the embryology and morphology of living and extinct vertebrates, Baur remained with Marsh until 1890, when, dissatisfied, he left to lecture at Clark University in Massachusetts before eventually joining the University of Chicago as the chairman of the osteology and vertebrate paleontology department in 1892. But regardless of Hatcher's association with Baur as a colleague under Marsh, Hatcher was wary about joining Baur in his business:

> *Of course it is impossible for me at present to go into such a business with anyone without doing you an injustice & even if I were inclined to I could not now under my present financial conditions. I think I offended him in my reply as I have not heard from him since. However, I will state definitely so that there may be no misunderstanding between you and I that until my time with you is up I shall enter into no such business with anyone unless it be by your consult & approval. And further, I never expect to make a business of collecting to sell. Great as my success as a collector has been I think I am as well prepared to judge of the cost of getting fossils ready for market as any one & I know what the profits would be.*[1]

Baur's flight from Marsh's lab had been triggered when the Cope-Marsh feud exploded onto the front pages of the popular press. On January 12, 1890, the *New York Herald* led its Sunday edition with a headline in bold, black type: SCIENTISTS WAGE BITTER WARFARE, while subsidiary headlines explained that Cope was bringing "Serious Charges" against Marsh and the director of the USGS, the famous, one-armed Civil War hero and Grand Canyon explorer John Wesley Powell. Cope had conspired to bring his long-simmering stew of scandalous accusations against Marsh through enlisting the help of an acquaintance and freelance journalist with questionable credentials and integrity named William H. Ballou, to whom Cope turned over all the supposedly incriminating documents and evidence he'd collected and sequestered in the lower drawer of his desk for the previous twenty years. Among the more serious charges was an allegation that Marsh had plagiarized his papers on the evolution of horses from the work of Russian paleontologist Vladimir Kowalevsky, along with the charge that many of Marsh's research papers had actually been written by his laboratory assistants, including Williston for Marsh's research on toothed birds (Odontornithes) and other dinosaurs, as well as Cretaceous mammals, and Baur for the horned mammals called Dinocerata. Baur, somewhat differently, claimed that Oscar Harger wrote the Odontornithes monograph and the descriptive part of the Dinocerata volume. Much to the horror of numerous leading paleontologists of the day, Cope provided Ballou with correspondence from numerous colleagues, including Henry Fairfield Osborn and William Berryman Scott of Princeton, as well as Samuel W. Williston and George Baur of Marsh's own laboratory to back up his claims. Regarding the USGS, Cope alleged that Powell and Marsh had conspired to fill the ranks of the National Academy of Sciences with people directly associated with and dependent on the Survey, thereby facilitating the distribution of federal funds to Marsh and his cronies to the detriment of adversaries such as Cope. Powell and Marsh passionately and comprehensively sought to refute each charge and raise countercharges, many of which have already been mentioned, against Cope in subsequent voluminous follow-up articles that ran in the *Herald* on January 13, 14, 19, 20, and 26. Part of Marsh's counterattack involved soliciting statements of denial from the colleagues and assistants that Cope had cited as providing evidence against Marsh. Hatcher was only marginally enmeshed in this melee, having only been listed as a person "in a position to offer evidence" regarding Marsh's alleged "incompetence, ignorance and plagiarism" in Ballou's lead article on the twelfth. Hatcher's denial, dated January 10, 1890, stated, "I have never authorized Professor E. D. Cope or anyone else to use my name in any way in any attack against you or the United States Geological Survey." A similar statement by Baur was quoted in which he stated, "I hereby voluntarily state that I have never in any way authorized the use of my name in any attack on you or your work." But Baur became a casualty in the battle between Cope and Marsh in the *Herald*. Marsh had badgered Baur to state in writing that he had not "dictated" any of the generalizations in Marsh's volume on the Dinocerata to Marsh. Baur eventually complied, but his statement also noted that Baur had advised Marsh on "all the points," especially how the animals were scientifically classified. However, Marsh only provided the *Herald* with Baur's first sentence in which Baur confirmed that he had not dictated any of the generalizations. Incensed upon seeing only part of his statement in print, Baur immediately resigned his position in Marsh's lab, which apparently led him to offer Hatcher a partnership in the commercial collecting enterprise that he considered establishing in the wake of his resignation.[2]

Having abandoned his collecting effort in North Carolina, Hatcher shortly headed south via rail to Charleston and on to Florida, where he wrote on February 13 that he had begun work near Williston, Florida, at a locality about 1.5 miles from the post office on the farm of J. J. Mixon (also sometimes spelled Mixson), eleven miles southwest of Archer. Situated in an orange grove, it was by far the most promising locality he'd seen, so he secured the right to collect and hired Mixon's son to help at $50 per month. The bones were badly broken up but included many specimens of mastodon and rhinos, including a rhino skull with a beautifully complete set of teeth. Hatcher's crew was working in yellow clay on level ground, and Hatcher anticipated having a nice collection to supplement the Kansas collection. Looking ahead, he suggested Beecher might come down to oversee the operation when Hatcher left for Wyoming, and he sought Marsh's advice about rehiring his former crew out there as well as the route Marsh wanted him to take when he left about March 10. Marsh telegraphed Hatcher on the seventeenth to return to New Haven to discuss plans for the summer season and advised Hatcher to close operations there at the end of February. But on the eighteenth, Hatcher replied that it was very inconvenient for him to leave immediately "for I have not money enough to square up here and take me to New Haven." He asked Marsh to send two drafts on his New York bank—one for $25 and the other for $50—as soon as possible, for the nearest bank was thirty miles away. Then he would come at once, despite the fact that they were still having good success, because he realized the Wyoming work was more important. Although the trip was truncated, a search of the USNM Paleobiology collections reveals that seventeen specimens were collected from Mixon's Bone Bed during 1890, presumably by Hatcher and his assistants. These include one of the rhino, *Aphelops*; fourteen of the rhino, *Teleoceras*; one of the early relative of elephants, "Serridentinus," now called *Gomphotherium*; and one of the camel *Procamelus*. The yellow clay in which the fossils were found suggests that all of these mammals lived around a quiet body of water, such as a lake, that also hosted crocodiles and alligators during the late Miocene, about eight to nine million years ago, and this site represented the first rich fossil locality ever found in Florida, as well as the first major Miocene or Pliocene fossil locality ever found in the eastern United States.[3]

As with the previous year, Marsh prioritized Hatcher's tasks for the 1890 season around Lusk in a document dated March 7: (1) secure horn-core fragments of Skull No. 1; (2) secure other fragments of the small three-toed foot now here and investigate if the vertebrae sent with it were found close by and from one animal; (3) get all fragments of Skull No. 6 (labeled No. 5 when sent) and all fragments of other specimen found twenty yards from it; (4) take up Skeleton A (called Skull 3 in last year's list); (5) the skull labeled No. 5 last year should retain that number, and try to find more fragments of it since it seems to be distinct from others; (6) the large concretion showing fragments of ribs and other bones projecting may be named the "brown concretion," and left for present after stabilizing it; (7) Burwell's specimen in bluff on south bank of "Big Skull Cañon" should eventually be taken up if it's worth it and pre-dental bone is found; (8) but first, go for the big skulls, "Ceratops" and "Hadrosaurus," and don't let any other party interfere; (9) next push on with the mammal hunt, especially where there is chance of getting new things or more complete specimens. The directive ended by emphasizing, "With these few suggestions, I leave everything to your own good judgment, in full confidence that you, on the ground, will know best the relative importance of the various kinds of work before you. With your party as a whole, and with every member of it, your word is law."[4]

In pursuance, Hatcher arrived in Long Pine on the eleventh to find "Mrs. H well and everything in good shape." She was again grateful for the presents Marsh sent. But Hatcher was suffering from a cold and sore throat and thought he'd soon be better if it didn't turn into pneumonia. Still sick on the eighteenth, Hatcher strained his back wrestling a haystack off his wagon, adding to his misery. Guernsey had been on Hatcher's train from Chicago and said he'd received Marsh's letters asking to send the horncore from Skull No. 1, but since Marsh "did not seem to be willing to give him either credit or money he had decided not to send it." Guernsey also said that the horncore already sent to Marsh was to be held at the Peabody subject to his orders, and he wanted it sent it to him at Westford, New York. Hatcher told him he thought the horncore was more valuable to Marsh, since Marsh had the skull, and asked Guernsey to set a price. But Guernsey set an enormous one, $250, almost $6,400 in today's currency, for sending the missing one and letting Marsh keep the one in New Haven. So Hatcher asked if they could be cast and Guernsey said he might allow that. Hatcher intimated that Guernsey "was evidently very . . . displeased at something you had said or written or not written," but he was very friendly with Hatcher and invited him to take a trip with him that spring. Then Hatcher opined, "Of course, the horncore is not worth $250.00 & you are foolish if you give him that." Hatcher hoped to start for Lusk the next day and round up his crew, before cryptically adding:

> . . . *will tell you frankly now that I don't like this man* [T. C. Beecher, Charles Beecher's brother] *& that if I had hired him independently myself I never would take him to camp with me.*
>
> *I invited him as a gentleman to come and stop with me until we went on west. He drinks all the time. On the way out from Chicago he associated himself with a drinking crowd & was drunk and noisy all the way out. Drinking from a bottle openly in the car every few minutes. I think he might at least have had respect enough for my wife and myself to remain sober when he knew he was going home with me where I had not been for three months. He has got drunk every time he's been in town since I got here. I do not believe his brother* [Charles] *knows what he is or if he does he never ought to have recommended him to come out here. I am not an angel by any means, but I don't approve of his conduct.*[5]

With a little snow still lingering on the outcrops, the crew pitched camp by the twenty-fourth, and Hatcher left for a short excursion with Guernsey that introduced him to a great deal of new and intriguing geology in the region. Hatcher responded to a telegram from Marsh by assuring him that he wouldn't dismiss his irritating and inebriated sidekick, because he apparently knew a lot about the area. Nonetheless, Hatcher still loathed him: "I do not want men to tell me what to do, but do what I tell them. Perhaps you should start another party & put him in charge of it." Hatcher then offered to resign. Regarding his spread in Long Pine, Hatcher confided, apparently in response to a query, that he hadn't bought more stock but had purchased more fruit trees, flowering trees and "forest trees" that he would have to go home and plant in April. Marsh responded on the twenty-ninth, saying that he and Charles Beecher agreed that he should let T.C. go without delay.[6]

Despite continued snow, Hatcher had uncovered many more elements of the three-toed foot Marsh had mentioned in his orders by the 30th, along with two massive Skulls (Nos. 7 and 8), one of which he thought would be better than any collected the previous year, especially because it seemed to be connected to at least part of a skeleton, including several limb bones. In addition, Peterson, who was now making $66.66 per month, was exposing another skeleton, and "keeps finding more bones all the time as he goes in." These finds were the result of a systematic search Hatcher initiated: "I start in at the mouth of a canyon & ride up and down every branch of it. I have done this with every cañon on the right hand side of Lance Cr . . . & if I remain here I propose to do it with every cañon in the whole country." Then Hatcher disgustedly revealed that Beecher's brother was "not over his protracted spree yet," but despite Peterson being the only man to help collect, they were having good success so far. To enhance efficiency, Hatcher proposed to do the freighting to the railhead himself if Marsh would pay him as much as he would need to pay someone else, which would put money in Hatcher's pocket and save the time Hatcher would expend in finding someone else. In closing, Hatcher dropped what must have seemed like a massive bomb to Marsh:

> *Now Prof. I'm going to ask you for something you have promised me several years ago. You told me when I hired to you that if I did well & ever wanted to get a permanent position anywhere you*

would give me a recommendation & your personal influence. I have decided to try to get a permanent position somewhere this summer, and have a place in view where they have already spoken to me. Now what I want is a general letter of recommendation as a collector from you stating how long I have been in your employ & in what capacity & whether or not I have given satisfaction. It is with a great deal of reluctance that I have thought of closing my connections with you, for I have much to be thankful to you for. But during the past year matters have so shaped themselves that I no longer feel contented. Perhaps I am too sensitive but I feel sore over some things, & if I am, it is my fault, & I will have to suffer for it. You no longer have a place for me in the museum winters, & at times I think you are only waiting for an opportune moment to get rid of me in the field. During the time I have worked for you I believe I can truthfully say that I have never let an opportunity pass of doing you a favor, & have always worked for your interest, so that I think I can reasonably ask you for a recommend in full faith that you will give it me, & I can assure you that wherever I go I will work as energetically for them as I ever have for you. The position I have in mind is in a Western institution & not with any of your enemies. I am perfectly willing & will be glad to continue the work here for you until I get another position, but about that you must be the judge. If you want me, allright [sic] & if you dont [sic] want me allright [sic] to [sic]. As long as I do work for you I will work for your interest alone, as I always have worked, & you need have no uneasiness on that score I assure you. If I do not succeed in getting the position I have in view I shall try elsewhere. What I want is a place where I can work & become identified permanently with what I do. Hoping to hear from you favorably . . .[7]

Hatcher responded to Marsh's suggestion that he fire Beecher's brother on April 1 by saying he'd rather not at the moment because he feared the blame would be placed on him, which is why Hatcher hesitated in taking him on the trip. But Hatcher insisted the brother had no one to blame but himself regarding his inappropriate conduct and again reported that the brother had done no work to speak of because he'd been "sick" almost all the time. Yet Hatcher held no ill will toward Charles Beecher.[8]

An eight-page opus that Hatcher penned to Marsh from Long Pine followed on the sixteenth. Unfortunately the skull he thought was complete did not turn out to be, but there was a good deal of a well-preserved skeleton associated with it, including the complete pelvis. He still hoped to find the rest of the skull nearby. Wilson had rejoined the crew, and since Marsh apparently inquired, Hatcher reiterated the situation with Guernsey before berating Marsh about it: "It has now been more than a month since I wrote you & it seems you have never written him. This is no way to do." On another front, Charles Beecher had written his brother, who admitted to Hatcher that he had behaved badly and apologized. But Hatcher refused to fire him, telling Marsh, "You hired him & in his case you are the one to do the discharging." Another seething soliloquy followed:

> Since you did not send me a recommend I suppose you had rather not give me one or think me unworthy of one. As for giving Yale the first chance & the National Museum the second I will say that I had rather be connected with either of those institutions than any other in the world for it is there that the results of six of the best years [sic] work of my life are stored. But when I work as I have I like to go up one round at least in the ladder instead of being pulled down two or three as you have done with me the past year. You tell me "that you and Beecher agreed after discussing the matter fully" that it was the proper thing in your last article to state that I "aided" you in securing certain things which I secured for you. I have several times had a friend who I wanted with me & one who I could personally vouch for as a good man (I mean W. W. Russ) & an agreeable one but you always found some excuse for not taking him, but the minute Beecher asks a place for a man who is a perfect "tenderfoot" you take him at once although he is an utter stranger to both of us, & keep him when you know he did everything he could to make himself obnoxious. I do not think that Mr. Beecher has any more right to interfere with my work than I have with his &

I would not think of making a single suggestion with regard to his, but on the other hand you have to consult with him as to whether I ought to have any credit or not for what I do. As I understood it Mr. Beecher came out here last Summer in the first place to photograph and make drawings of Skull No. 2. Of the value of those drawings you yourself are the best judge, as for any other aid that he rendered in the field I have never seen that his services were of any more value than those of any other new man. I tried to treat him right and I believe I did in every respect. But when you and he mutually agree that it is right to speak of me in your article I will tell you plainly that I consider you both very ungrateful to me. I also think that when you furnished the material for the series of articles in the American Field last winter you might at least have given me some credit instead of taking all to yourself. Especially since I have collected 75 percent of all your fossils from that region & I first made known how rich the locality was in fossils.

I have always worked for your interest first of all & Yale College & the National Museum second & have never failed in securing every good thing for you that I ran across. In return I think as a Yale graduate I am deserving of a little better treatment than I have had the past year, especially from a Yale graduate and professor. Of course you will show this to Beecher as it is no longer possible for one of you to know any thing that the other does not know. You used to think ourselves competent to run one party in the field & we have always had good success & everything ran smoothly. All I have to say is if we can not run our own business as we used to without a third party why then let's quit at once. If we can & you are willing to give me full credit for what I do why then I am willing to go on and work with all my energy for you or Yale College or the National Museum as long as you want me & for a reasonable salary & in any field you want me. I think what I ask of you is only reasonable & what I offer perfectly fair.[9]

Returning to more routine business on the eighteenth, Hatcher submitted vouchers for April and part of March totaling $498.33, with a request to credit him with $75 on his note before sending the remaining $423.33 to him at Lusk so it would be there by April 30. In other news, he recommended that Gus Craven and a collector named George A. Clarke would both do good work in the "Bad Lands" if Marsh didn't have enough fossils from there. Craven had seven more brontothere skulls and wanted Hatcher to look at them, so Hatcher inquired whether Marsh wanted him to go. He didn't know what W. H. Burwell was doing, but he'd been talking of working in mines. Hatcher planned to return to Lusk that day and have four or five thousand pounds of fossils to ship by May 1. He'd learned that Prof. Scott of Princeton was coming out this summer, so Hatcher anticipated lots of bone hunters in the country. But he intended "to have the bulge on all of them and . . . keep it too."[10]

At that point, a six-week hiatus ensued until May 1, when Hatcher composed another lengthy epistle to plead that he'd expended $78.09 more than he'd received, mostly as a result of purchasing a buckboard as Marsh had directed, and he needed that money, especially since he was trying to repay his debt to Marsh. He also reported that a crew from Minnesota was due out around May 20, and that Baur had gotten a position at Clark University and intended to collect in Kansas that summer. Regarding Hatcher's own crew, Beecher's brother had left that day after an annoying incident. He'd failed to properly tie Hatcher's horse when he dismounted, so when it spooked, it skedaddled four or five miles back to camp, destroying the saddle and slicing his hide as it fled. Infuriated that the brother had risked Hatcher's horse, especially because that had happened before and he knew better, Hatcher discharged the brother even though Marsh and Charles Beecher would think he'd done wrong. Still disgusted, Hatcher vowed, "I never again want a man whom I do not know myself" on his crew. Adding to Hatcher's troubles, Wilson, who was drawing $50 per month, quit because ". . . he prefers life on [the] ranch over our quiet life & for the present . . . can command better wages." He seems to have been replaced by a Peter Olsen, who was paid $53.33 per month. Regardless, the crew's luck was good, with eleven crates packed and material for forty to fifty more in sight, including four more skulls, one of which was rather small. He'd blasted open the "brown concretion" and found a continuous series of vertebrae. Burwell's specimen was ready to haul down the bank, and skeleton B seemed more slender than the typical "Ceratops." To top it off, the crew had gleaned another large collection of mammal teeth, all of which led Hatcher to sarcastically quip, "So you see if you have been busy & are nearly sick from overwork & worry I have not been altogether idle." That dig preceded a pronouncement from Hatcher on May 1 regarding his quest for a permanent position on May 1: "I now have three chances of getting such a position," and he wanted a letter of recommendation from Marsh. He bemoaned the fact that ". . . now after the fossils go into the box in the field & are put on the depot platform ready to ship I have nothing more to do with them," and he longed for the opportunity to prepare and mount them for exhibition. He pledged to continue working with all the energy he had, but he couldn't accept that there would be "no chance for me ever to do anything of any account but work in the field as long as I am with you." He fumed at Marsh's claim, "You say you rather give me too much credit instead of too little. I should like to know in what instance you have given me too much credit." In all, Hatcher argued, ". . . I am getting to that age when I ought to make up my mind & settle down to something. I now have a chance of getting a position & I may never have another such a chance if I let this one go."[11]

This fully unveiled warning triggered, given the mail at the time, a rapid and rare handwritten response on USGS letterhead from Marsh on May 9, in which he sought to salvage the continued employment of his ace collector:

> *Dear Mr. Hatcher.*
>
> *I suppose you rec'd my telegram of the 7th inst., so I will now write fully as I promised.*
>
> *Let me say first of all that I have fully appreciated your remarkable ability, the past success you have achieved, and especially what you have done for Science in so many ways. I decided some time ago to show all this, when your time with me was up, not merely by giving you the strongest recommendations, and securing for you the best place I could get, but by much more substantial testimonial.*

I was pleased, moreover, when our agreement was completed, to do all I could to benefit you either to continue with me, directly or indirectly, either on the Survey, in my division or in some other, if you wanted field work, or partly with field, and partly here or at the National Museum, if you preferred less field work.

I made arrangements, when last in Washington, to have you spend next winter there (if you wished to) preparing your own specimens for exhibition and putting them in place yourself. If you preferred New Haven, I could give you the same chance here.

Now as to salary. If all goes as usual with the Geol. Survey so far as appropriations go, I can promise you from the 1st next July (1890) an increase of $50 per month, making $150 monthly.

I hope you will consider this a "fair salary," the term you use in your proposition of April 16th. The other conditions you mention, I accept fully, and will do better. How you ask. When I see you, we will talk about the more distant future. Your ability and knowledge will command a good position at any time, but I cannot see why you should leave Yale or the National Museum when your services are so much needed, and will be fully appreciated more and more as the results of your work are made known.

If, after a while, you prefer the West to the East, I trust we can still retain your services to increase our Collections here and at Washington, in a way that will be of benefit to us both.

At all events, let me assure you that, now or at any time, I am ready to do you any service in my power.

Will you not kindly let me know by telegraph that you have rec'd this letter, and I hope you will answer it with same spirit I have written it.

Yours ever,
O. C. Marsh (signed)[12]

Apparently, Marsh also sent a telegram, for on the twelfth, Hatcher, in addition to alerting his boss that he'd brought in a load of boxes and informing him that he was excavating a skeleton "quite different than anything yet" in its short massive bones and humungous horncores, further stated:

> *Have not yet received the letter you speak of in regard to a permanent position. I would be glad to have position either at Yale or the National Museum & will gladly accept one if permanent. I have an offer of a place to collect 3 or 4 months in the year & take entire charge of the collection in the museum. I will accept this offer unless I can get an equally good one at Yale or the National Museum. As soon as I get your letter stating what the position is you have in view for I will let you know.*

He ended by saying he'd not sent the Minnesota party any information about localities and didn't intend to before asking how many payments Marsh had credited him on his note.[13]

By the eighteenth, he sent in the monthly $375 worth of vouchers for May with a request to credit him $75 on his loan and send the rest to Lusk by the end of the month. There was a "fine sacrum" with skeleton C, along with ten vertebrae, and he'd discovered another ceratopsian skull. A week later, in addition to shipping nineteen crates, he'd received a camera and a slew of letters from Marsh, including Marsh's new employment proposal, which offered a $50 per month raise. In response, he wrote on the twenty-fourth that although Marsh's offer was "very liberal," he would only accept it if it came with a permanent position.[14]

The shipment primarily consisted of *Triceratops* material (Skeletons B and C, Skulls Nos. 7, 8, 9, and associated elements), along with one turtle. That was followed on the thirty-first by a newsy account that acknowledged receiving Marsh's monthly check for $375 and contained the balance sheet for May, which documented that expenses exceeded the money received by $113.94 due to blacksmithing and purchases of a new tent, buckboard and harness, lumber, plaster of Paris, and other "unusual" items. Beyond that, Hatcher realized he'd made a mistake in the balance sheet for March and April, either neglecting to include some items or adding it up incorrectly, so he corrected it in the May statement. He'd now finished skeleton C, proclaiming it "the finest thing we have found yet." He'd also heard from Baur, who was collecting in Kansas, and thanked Marsh for his account of the Yale boat race. Hatcher's receipts revealed that he'd also hired a new assistant at $40 per month—one William H. Utterback, who would, like Peterson, stick with Hatcher, at least off and on, for most of the rest of his career.[15]

Hatcher finished skeletons C and D by June 8 and found at least thirteen little "horncores" united at their base, evidently forming part of the dermal skeleton of D (possibly tubercles rimming the frill). He wondered, "Can it be possible that portions of the exterior of these animals were covered by these little horns like the body or arms of the star-fish are covered with peduncles and pedicles? We evidently don't know all about *Triceratops* yet." The bones of the skeleton were much more slender than others found heretofore. He also sent a few Laramie mammals in the same package, including an upper jaw of "Platacodon" that he thought would throw some light on the true position and character of teeth that Marsh already had. Hatcher was working on a complete skull, but it was in such hard rock and the bones were so soft that he feared he couldn't do much with it, since it was "cracked in ten thousand different ways." In closing, he wondered when Marsh thought he'd be out there. Clearly trying to make amends with his skittish collector, Marsh's check for the $114 in extra expenses arrived by the tenth, just as Hatcher shipped the rest of Skeletons C and D, with which the "little horncores" were found. Baur wasn't having much success in Kansas, and although Craven's skulls had not impressed Marsh, he'd written to say he'd found nine more, one of which Craven claimed was the best he'd ever seen. Hatcher lamented that Beecher must be "on the outs" with him, since Hatcher hadn't received a letter from him since discharging his brother, but he repeated his vow: "I shall never have anything more to do with any relatives of my friends. Nine times out of ten they think they can treat you as they please & that you must stand it and say nothing." He passed along the news from Anna that Long Pine had suffered from severe wind, rain, and hail that blew down several houses and windmills; killed lots of colts and calves; completely destroyed crops; blew Hatcher's buggy shed and chicken house over; and killed all the chickens except twelve out of one hundred.[16]

As the summer sizzled, Hatcher set off for Hermosa, South Dakota, to negotiate with Craven for his cache of brontothere skulls, which Marsh via telegram on July 1 authorized him to purchase if offered at a "fair price." In Hatcher's mind, haste for securing any scientifically significant specimens was imperative, since Scott of Princeton was on his way there. But brontotheres weren't the only commodity in view, as Hatcher informed Marsh that he had eleven more crates of fossils from the Laramie ready to ship. To the south, Baur was now having some success in Kansas and was contemplating a visit to Hatcher's camp near Lusk. Hatcher was unfazed, reassuring Marsh, "I think I have it all corralled & they can do no damage." Besides, he had "quite a lot of mammals ready to send." The negotiations with Craven resulted in Hatcher buying nine skulls of his relatively high-quality collection on July 4, for $690, around $17,500 in modern dollars. One had a lower jaw in place with canines and incisors, which Hatcher considered as good a skull as YPM VP 2048. Thus, he concluded the price was reasonable, and he thought it better to wrap everything up before Scott arrived. As the mercury soared to 107 in the shade, Hatcher informed Marsh that he expected Baur to arrive on the nineteenth and vowed to treat him as a guest and take possession of anything he found. Crates 28 through 38, all containing *Triceratops* material including portions of Skeleton A, shipped on the eighth. But Marsh was uneasy about Baur's visit, telegraphing on the thirteenth not to allow it: "He is now [an] open enemy of [the] Survey and me, and doing all he can against both. His visit will lead to serious trouble." Undaunted, Hatcher telegraphed back the next day: "No injury shall occur to you through B's visit." Intent on minimizing Marsh's malaise, Hatcher reported Baur arrived on the fifteenth and only planned to stay a day or two, but Hatcher communicated by letter, which would not arrive until after Baur had left. He then left for Long Pine to ship Craven's 4,450-pound collection, which also included a set of *Elotherium* jaws and a large ammonite.[17]

Upon receiving Hatcher's missive, Marsh must have remained on edge; on the nineteenth, Hatcher apologized for Baur causing so much uneasiness. Hatcher reassured Marsh that Baur had only been in camp one day and that he'd informed Baur that he was receiving him as a friend and a gentleman. Thus, Baur would be expected "to make no use of anything he saw while with me in any way." Then Hatcher gently turned the table on Marsh: "If you think Baur can use me to your injury in any way you do me an injustice. I have always protected myself & you out here & I am not at all alarmed yet, nor would I be if Baur, Scott, Cope and all should invade my territory." Then Hatcher cheerily went on to announce more "splendid success."

> *Found four Tri. skulls one of which I know is new & another I think* [is]. *The horncores have a deep groove on inner side running whole length.*
> *I also found a skeleton which bids fair to surpass anything yet. I never saw such fine toe bones; they equal those of the rhinoceros in Kansas.*

All the bones in a foot are not commonly found together because they are relatively small and easily dispersed by currents in rivers after the connective tissues deteriorate before being buried in sediment. Hatcher reminded Marsh that he'd promised to raise Hatcher's salary by $50 if Marsh got the ususal appropriation from the government. Marsh telegraphed on the twentieth to say he would send all the money "on answer to my letter."[18]

That letter seemed to involve financial complexities related to paying for Craven's collection. On the twenty-second, Hatcher wrote from Long Pine to say he was disappointed that Marsh hadn't already sent the required funds. Hatcher needed to make the payment to free up funds for his return to Lusk, since he had paid an advance installment to Craven and had apparently expended funds on his farm. At issue was a loan of $75 that Marsh had made to Craven the previous winter. Hatcher angrily wrote, "I know nothing about that. . . . However my deal has nothing to do with your old one. I bought the collection for $690 . . . and sold it to you at same price . . . and I thought I was doing you a favor when I did it." He went on to say that Scott wouldn't be out before August 1, so his stay would be short.[19]

No check from Marsh had arrived by August 1, so Hatcher proceeded to continue prodding, ". . . not yet received check for balance of Craven's collection nor for July & I am very much in need of money." He knew that appropriations for government departments had been extended for thirty days in the beginning of July, so the delay in passing the civil servants bill should have nothing to do with the last month. Then he lashed out in a temperamental tirade: "I want to pay off my indebtedness to you & close up and quit this business. I am thoroughly disgusted with the way everything has gone the past year. You never pay any attention to my requests nor anything I write you." But by the seventh, two checks for $350 and $190 arrived that had ostensibly been delayed in the mail. In the interim, Scott had arrived and entered the field, but he wouldn't collect in the Laramie. Then Hatcher calmly laid down his royal flush in front of Marsh:

> *I think I will be able to secure a position commencing October 1st Prof. & I think I shall accept it, for then I can be at home all of the year but about 3 or 4 months when I would be collecting. I like collecting, but I am tired of having 12 months in a year of it as I have had the past three years, and I must give it up.*[20]

The four big skulls, although unfortunately not as complete as had been hoped, were ready to ship by August 9, so Hatcher headed into Lusk. Yet, one seemed entirely new in terms of the horncores and the condyle that attached it to the neck. It possessed one jaw in which all the teeth were preserved, and Hatcher also had found and packed a number of good foot bones. In all, there were twelve crates. Shortly thereafter, the crew's camp was decimated by a "regular Wyoming 'Jimicane'" that blew the tent down and generally tore things up, but they had another twelve boxes ready to ship.[21]

Uncharacteristically, Hatcher promptly received the $350 check for the September salaries on the twentieth when he came in to ship another sixteen crates. Success continued to follow the crew, although the recent haul contained only "good things" and nothing spectacular. Hatcher was disappointed that Marsh would vacation back east, for he desperately wanted to see Marsh in person, especially after receiving Marsh's proposal in his letter of May 9:

I should like very much the work of preparing the specimens for exhibition in Washington you speak of. But I have fully decided to accept a permanent position this fall. I have endeavored during the last seven years . . . to show you that I was worthy of a permanent position. . . . Since my marriage three years ago, instead of considering my changed position & trying to make matters more agreeable to me, you have kept me in the field constantly. . . . I now have an offer of just such a position [with] 4 months in the year collecting & the remainder . . . working on collection with an assistant & at the same salary that you are now giving me. It looks hard to leave the immense collection I have made . . . but if I have to break off, the sooner the better.

I wish you would come out here and bring my notes with you. For I want to settle up everything with you & leave in a perfectly friendly, fair & honorable way.

Hatcher also revealed that because one of Marsh's "bosom friends" had told him in New Haven the previous winter that Marsh considered Hatcher "an element of discord in the museum," he had "at once commenced looking for another position." He closed by noting he'd received a blank "Oaths of Office" apparently related to his USGS position with the government but would not return it, since he didn't suppose there would be any need for it.[22]

On the thirty-first, Hatcher revealed another reason for wishing to remain closer to his family. "A letter from Long Pine tells me that we have another young bone-hunter at our house. I hope he will live longer than the other one did." The boy was christened Earl Madison Hatcher. John Bell also alerted Marsh to expect a very good coracoid bone in a previous lot of eleven boxes, and they had another very peculiar bone ready to pack, probably a scapula, about four feet, four inches long averaging about one foot in width. It was complete and different from anything he'd seen. The crew was preparing fifteen to twenty more crates for shipment. He still hoped Marsh would come out but acerbically added, ". . . of course, it is much pleasanter and more interesting for you at Newport or Bar Harbor." In an echo of the truly Wild West, Hatcher chronicled that the country was infested by a band of horse thieves that had stolen about two hundred horses during the summer. They'd run off with one of his two weeks before, and he'd never found any trace of it. But three thieves had been caught the previous week. To handle all the loading and hauling, Hatcher had added a crewman named W. L. Magoon for $40 per month, and the monthly expenses now totaled $425, although that was reduced by Hatcher's request to credit his loan with a $75 payment. The extra help allowed Hatcher to comment on September 19, "We are getting the field pretty well cleaned up so far as we have looked over it." Marsh finally broke his several-week silence after returning from vacation by telegraphing Hatcher on the twentieth: "Best congratulations on arrival of new bone-hunter. Will write fully. Shall come out soon as some Washington matters permit. Will telegraph before I start. Could you meet me at Chadron if necessary." No doubt pleased with this development, Hatcher telegraphed back that he would.[23]

The resulting tête-à-tête at Chadron precipitated a monthlong lacuna in their letters that was broken on October 16, when Hatcher wrote in hopes that Marsh had safely reached New Haven. They'd finished packing the ceratopsian skull Peterson had been excavating when Marsh was there, and Hatcher had finally repossessed his pilfered horse. He included a list of contents for crates 55–67, which all contained *Triceratops* material, including Skulls No. 14 and 15, as well as Skeleton H and Burwell's specimen. Monthly costs totaled $295 without Hatcher's usual $75 credit on his loan. On the twenty-eighth, Hatcher wrote saying he hoped to wrap up the season by November 11 and asked if Marsh wanted him to see Craven and buy his collection. Marsh responded on November 7 that he did and wanted Hatcher to see other collectors in the region and secure all the important specimens without paying too much. The same day, Hatcher shipped the last seven crates of the season as snow began to fall, including what he thought might be the most important specimens yet from the Laramie: "two lower jaws [of] either a carnivore or ungulate." He tracked down Craven and purchased another thirty-one boxes of fossils for $675 on the thirteenth, then headed home to Long Pine.[24]

Accounts of Craven's collection reveal that it featured eighteen brontothere skulls and eight lower jaws, along with two turtles. Hatcher considered the price fair and intimated that Craven wanted more and didn't seem satisfied, but Hatcher couldn't justify a higher evaluation. He had also purchased seven boxes of fossils from Joseph Brown and Burwell. Regarding his own situation, Hatcher responded on November 16 to a letter that Marsh had sent:

> *Received your letter in regard to house on reaching home today. If I should remain with you I shall certainly buy a small house & lot in New Haven. But owing to the uncertainty do not lose an opportunity of renting it on my account.*[25]

The tally for Hatcher's 1890 trips included two rhinos (*Aphelops* and *Teleoceras*), one camel (*Procamelus*), and one elephant relative ("Serridentinus") from the 9- to 8-million-year-old Alaucha Clay in Florida, as well as one brontothere (*Megacerops*) from the 37- to 34-million-year-old Chadron Formation and a specimen of the creodont carnivore *Hyaenodon* from the 34- to 30-million-year-old Brule Formation in the Great Plains. A much larger sample came from the 68- to 66-million-year-old sediments of the Lance Formation in Wyoming, including multituberculates (*Cimolodon, Cimolomys, Essonodon, Meniscoessus,* and *Mesodma*); marsupials (*Alphadon, Didelphodon, Pediomys,* "Didelphops" and "Stagodon," now called *Didelphodon*); and a placental (*Gypsonictops*). The ranks of ray-finned fish contained *Belonostomus* and "Kindleia." Six salamanders were found: *Scapherpeton, Habrosaurus, Lisserpeton, Piceoerpeton, Prodesmodon,* and *Opisthotriton*. A trio of turtles is also recorded (*Baena, Basilemys,* and *Thescelus*), along with the lizard *Litakis* and the alligator *Procaimanoidea*. Hatcher's hunt for dinosaurs greatly expanded the known record for late Cretaceous forms in North America with the discoveries of the duckbill *Edmontosaurus,* the bird-mimic *Ornithomimus,* the bone-helmeted *Stygimoloch,* the herbivore *Thescelosaurus,* the carnivore *Paronychodon,* the king of them all *Tyrannosaurus,* its close cousin *Aublysodon,* the close relative of birds *Troodon,* and the shorebird *Cimolopteryx*—not to mention a full treasure chest of *Triceratops* skulls and bones that provided for the first time a nearly complete portrait of this superstar's skeletal anatomy, along with another specimen of its smaller cousin *Leptoceratops*.

Given the work needed around his farm, he didn't anticipate reaching New Haven before December 5. Numerous financial transactions ensued to wrap up business regarding the crew and the purchases of fossils over the rest of November. And Hatcher wrote that he might have to return to Wyoming to retrieve his horses and outfit due to some "Indian excitement." But he didn't think it would be necessary because "they now have enough troops at Pine Ridge to wipe out the whole Sioux tribe & I hope they will disarm the Indians or force them to fight." Finally, on December 4, with Anna and, presumably, the new baby in tow, Hatcher informed Marsh that they were in Washington, D.C. and planned to travel to New Haven shortly.[26]

Ostensibly throughout the middle of December, Hatcher and Marsh conducted face-to-face negotiations regarding Hatcher's future at Yale. Those efforts culminated on the twentieth with the signing of a new contract, handwritten by Marsh, which made Hatcher an assistant in geology at Yale's Peabody Museum for the next five years (1891–1896) and, crucially, gave him the responsibility to work on his own collections whenever he was back home in the East.[27] (See appendix 1)

Hatcher's new contract represented a ramification of the poker game he'd once again been playing with his professional career. This time it involved not only Marsh but also Osborn at the AMNH. Correspondence from August 1890 reveals that Hatcher had first requested a position from W. B. Scott of Princeton, but apparently Scott did not have the funding for it. Nonetheless, when Hatcher met Scott in the field in late July or early August, Scott told him that Osborn was then "in a position" to offer Hatcher a job at AMNH, and Hatcher immediately wrote Osborn on August 7 to pass along his pleasure at hearing the news, adding, "I will be greatly pleased to accept a position there," while at the same time requesting more information regarding what Osborn had in mind. Osborn was in the process of founding a department of vertebrate paleontology at the AMNH and sought to staff it with the very best young paleontologic researchers and collectors he could find. Clearly, that would cost a considerable amount of money, but Osborn, like Marsh at Yale, was well connected to the aristocracy on the East Coast. His father, William Henry Osborn, was a wealthy merchant and president of the

Illinois Central Railroad, and his uncle was none other than the legendary financier J. Pierpont Morgan. After receiving Hatcher's letter, Osborn replied on August 15 that he envisioned Hatcher conducting fieldwork during the climatically "favorable months," then working at the AMNH to supervise the unpacking and preparation of fossils for exhibition and research with the help of Hatcher's own assistant, and finally spend the rest of his time on his ranch in Long Pine—all at the same salary that Marsh had been providing. He could immediately guarantee that position for one year but would need to confirm the arrangement with the museum's trustees before committing to future years. Also, Osborn insisted that Hatcher tell Marsh that this offer had resulted from the request for a new position by Hatcher and not from an initiative by Osborn. On the nineteenth, an uncharacteristically giddy Hatcher exclaimed to Osborn that the position was "exactly what I've been wishing for," before confirming his annual salary of $1,800 and explaining that he currently received one month of vacation per year, which would be plenty for him to devote to his ranch. Hatcher also intimated that he was proud of the collections he'd garnered, "but of something over 700 large boxes of fossils which I have collected I have never had the pleasure of seeing a single one of them put on exhibition and I have given up all hopes of ever doing anything but collect. . . ." So Hatcher would accept Osborn's gurarantee of one year with the understanding that if he performed satisfactorily, the position would be made permanent, and Hatcher would inform Marsh that he had sought the position, which he did in his previously discussed letter to Marsh on August 20. Through the end of August into early September, Hatcher and Osborn discussed further details regarding the position, but Osborn envisioned Hatcher finishing the year for Marsh before joining the AMNH around June 1, 1891, whereas Hatcher, writing Osborn on September 8, seemed anxious to fly Marsh's coop as soon as possible and begin collecting for Osborn in the Laramie on October 1, 1890. Here, Hatcher seems to have misplayed his hand, for on September 20, Osborn resisted Hatcher's request, writing, "It seems to me best to start in Spring [1891]. . . . You can give your present employer due notice [and] I will have ample time to complete all the arrangements in the Museum. . . . I fear if you start this Fall, it will be said that you ought to have given at least a month's notice. . . ." On September 25, Hatcher dejectedly relented and told Osborn he'd wait until the next spring, but he wouldn't be working for Marsh because he'd already given Marsh notice. A somewhat stunned Osborn quickly telegraphed Hatcher on the thirtieth to begin collecting for AMNH in the Laramie, focusing on mammals and reptiles. But this episode of cross-country whiplashes continued, with Hatcher informing Osborn on October 11 that an "anxious" Marsh had met him in Long Pine as previously mentioned and implored Hatcher to continue working for him through the winter, which Hatcher agreed to do. Osborn applauded Hatcher's decision on the seventeenth but wanted to make sure Marsh didn't lay claim to new collecting areas over the winter, so Hatcher reassured Osborn that Marsh would probably not.[28]

After Hatcher and Marsh had hashed out Hatcher's new contract, a seemingly stressed and depressed Hatcher wrote Osborn on December 22 from New Haven to say:

> For various reasons I have concluded to remain where I am for a while and then quit the collecting business altogether and settle down on my ranch out west.
>
> I fully appreciate the spirit both you and Prof. Scott have shown toward me. . . . You have been fair with me all the way through and I fully intended and hoped to commence work with you in the spring; but rather than to inflict the discomfiture which this would cause to others I prefer to quit the business and seek a livelihood in some other line.

An understandably astounded yet seemingly annoyed Osborn replied on Christmas Eve:

> I can hardly tell you how surprised I was by . . . your letter. From what Scott and Baur have both told me of your character, I believe your word is as good as your bond. . . . I can well understand the influence and pressure you have been under to write me as you have. I . . . will stop in New Haven to see you. . . . This seems to me the best way.

It's unclear if that meeting took place, but regardless, it seems that Hatcher's impatient gamble to flee the clutches of Marsh had, at least for the moment, foiled his best chance and led to an extremely rare, self-inflicted, existential crisis of confidence in Hatcher's own view of his heretofore promising paleontological career.[29]

8

Hail the Hadrosaurs and Trumpet *Torosaurus*

atcher apparently continued to deliberate over his new contract during the holidays, and after the turn of the New Year, Marsh and Hatcher added an amendment in which all of the clauses conferred more benefits on Hatcher, including choosing and supervising his own crews in the West, publishing on the geology of the Brontotherium and Ceratops beds, and overseeing the preparation and arrangements of specimens he collected. Marsh also granted Hatcher a raise to $2,000 per year and agreed to help him find a new position if funding issues forced the termination of his contract (appendix 1).[1]

Seemingly satisfied, Hatcher headed off for Lusk near the end of January 1891; however, his post card en route from Chicago revealed that a personal concern loomed over the trip: "As I received no message here I take it that my child is no worse; hope he is better." He reached Lusk by the thirty-first, but not until 3:00 A.M. due to heavy snow, and immediately traveled to Utterback's. He couldn't return to Lusk until February 2, and even then, he wrote, "[I] froze one of my ears." Since the previous field season ended, Henry Fairfield Osborn of AMNH had tried to raid Hatcher's crew and poach one of his best fossil prospectors, Utterback. But Hatcher countered by matching Osborn's offer of $75 per month and agreeing to employ Utterback, whom Hatcher characterized as a "smart, shrewd western man of some ability," throughout the year to protect Marsh's sites from being plundered by competing paleontologists. Seemingly now back firmly within Marsh's sphere of influence, Hatcher intimated to Marsh that he now viewed Osborn's attempt to hire him as a ruse to "throw me off" so he could poach Utterback, which seems far-fetched, since Hatcher initiated the negotiations for the position Osborn offered him. Nonetheless, Hatcher closed with: "If Osborn wants to try the trick business with me in this country or any of his gang, I am ready for them & if they come into this region this season they will find it out. They are on their own "dung-hill" east, but this is mine out here."[2]

Adding to Utterback's usefulness, Hatcher intended to employ Utterback's ranch as a staging area for baled hay, grain, provisions, and lumber until the weather improved. Photography seemed to be a priority this season, since Hatcher wanted Beecher to send a bottle of single fluid developer for a camera and a ruby lantern, which he couldn't get out west. Then he expressed concerns about the loyalty of his brother-in-law, who had apparently also spent part of the winter in New Haven and apparently was plotting to collect for Osborn:

> Now a few words confidentially about Peterson. He has been trying last fall & this winter to cut into me out here. He is very foolish to do so, for as you know I have shown him all he knows about this work & have helped him along in many ways. I knew from the way he acted back there that something was up, but he was dumb to me. However I know it all now. He can not work with me in the spring. It is important perhaps that Osborn will not employ him & I do not believe he will try to for I never told him anything

about him. When he (Peterson) finds that his schemes out here fail
he will probably apply to Osborn. I suggest this remedy. You let
him take my place there in the museum cleaning up boxes for the
national museum. You could put him on the National Museum
pay roll as you did me at say $75 per month to July 1st, this would
be about equivalent to $50 out here & I think would induce him
to stay there. Thus you would save his salary from your own fund.
You have promised to make this exhibit in Washington & I think
you can & ought to do it. At any rate I dont [sic] want him here
with me next Spring, especially should Osborn come out to go to
work. Later should it appear advisable for him to come out at his old
salary or any that you & he agree on, why well & good, but I will
not agree to keep him if he trys [sic] anything like he has been up to.

   I am very much obliged to you for the messages regarding my
child, for it was a great relief for one to know that he was getting
along alright. When Mrs. Hatcher leaves please do not let her take
the Derby road. I had to change five times between New Haven
& Albany.

With Burwell expected imminently, Hatcher would have a party of three, which he felt through experience would be "the most effective in this work for the money expended."[3]

Marsh approved of Hatcher's strategic proposals regarding Utterback and Peterson, so Hatcher spent all of February stowing supplies at Utterback's in between blizzards with blinding winds, temperatures twenty degrees below zero and drifts ten to twelve feet deep that left "several people frozen to death and great losses with stock." Hatcher was relieved to hear that his child had recovered from illness by the fourteenth. He also submitted the monthly vouchers early in hopes of getting the funds by the twenty-fourth, since his mortgage would be due March 1 and he would need to apply some of his salary to that as well as borrow money. Then on the twentieth, Anna also requested $100 from Marsh to be loaned on March 1, perhaps for her trip back west, because Hatcher requested that Marsh help make sure her ticket was purchased through to Long Pine with all of her checked baggage. In short, despite Marsh's image as a miserly curmudgeon, he continued to be the Hatchers' source of first resort for extra funds. Hatcher received Marsh's check for $250 by the twenty-fifth and expressed appreciation for saving him the trouble of borrowing elsewhere. But he was still making little progress on starting to collect, due to bad weather making the rutted dirt roads impassible; on the twenty-seventh, he reported, "It snowed & blowed all day." Beyond that, expenses were high, which, given the lack of results, made Hatcher worry so much he didn't charge Marsh for the use of his own horse teams. The balance sheet for mid-January through February showed charges for photo developing and printing, block and tackle, express mailing, repair of clinometer, rail tickets, hotel stays, plaster, paint, hardware, photo apparatus, groceries, blacksmithing, rope, salaries, livery, and lumber. In addition, salaries were a bit higher than previously mentioned, with Burwell drawing $65 per month, Utterback $90 per month, and Hatcher $250 per month, including his team and wagon.[4]

Conditions had still not improved enough to start collecting by March 12, although they were improving, but Hatcher had to request a $100 check, since he was out of funds as a result of his mortgage payment. When he submitted the vouchers for March, which included his quarterly bonus of $50, they totaled a staggering $500, more than $12,500 in today's currency. Nonetheless, he was relieved that Anna and his son had made it to Long Pine safely and passed his gratitude along to Marsh, declaring, "Many thanks for your kindness to them." Still another blizzard blasted the land around Lusk on the twenty-third, leaving Hatcher to once again lament that it seemed the weather would never let up and promise to try to make it up when better weather arrived. Osborn had sent Hatcher a copy of his scientific article reviewing Marsh's paper on the Cretaceous mammals, along with copies of the correspondence between the two regarding the possible position at American Museum of Natural History in New York City. Hatcher didn't think Osborn planned to collect much in the region that spring. Finally, by the twenty-sixth, Hatcher made it to the camp, despite six inches of snow still on the ground. He was anxious to begin work on Skull No. 18, in spite of suffering a bout of "rheumatism" in his right hip. He indicated that he'd probably need to hire a man to temporarily fill in for Utterback, who needed to travel in April.[5]

Hatcher complained that he was "crippled with this miserable rheumatism" on April 1 and hadn't been able to do anything the past two days, as he'd been working alone because Utterback hadn't been able to return from town due to bad roads. But he had made a good start on Skulls 18 (YPM VP 1829) and 19 (YPM VP 1830), which were turning out very well. Number 18 was from a young animal and largely disarticulated but with the nasal horncore, whereas 19 was from a much larger animal with a nearly complete but short nasal horncore. In all, Hatcher viewed 19 as being very different from Nos. 1 (YPM VP 1820), 16 (USNM 1201), and most other skulls from the Lance Creek area. The beak had broken off, but he had most of the pieces. The squamosal bones of the skull were the most slender he'd seen, and the maxillary bones that formed the upper jaw were probably present. This would turn out to be the first-known specimen of *Torosaurus*, a horned dinosaur closely related to *Triceratops* that differs most obviously in having holes in its shield or frill that forms the back of the skull. He'd also found another skull in large concretion. Anticipating a large operation, he foresaw one man continually hauling, while the other helped him with the big skulls. He hoped to have both skulls ready to box in about three days if his "rheumatism" abated; otherwise he'd need "to stop and go doctor up for it" since he couldn't even get on and off his horse alone. Fortunately both the weather and his malady improved, so he had the skulls ready to crate by the fourth. Three days later, No. 18 was ready to ship, but his "rheumatism" had returned with a vengeance, confining him to camp for a day, but on the seventh he still hoped to have No. 19 on the road in about three days.[6]

Although he had the two skulls ready to ship by around the sixteenth, road conditions would make it impossible to haul them to the railhead until June or July. With his "rheumatism" still raging, Hatcher headed home on the fourteenth to doctor it up, and if that didn't help, he planned "to go to Hot Springs Dakota for a week or two." He also revealed that he had indeed hired a new field assistant, A. L. Sullins, who was drawing $55 per month as a collector even though Utterback worked throughout April. Hatcher thought Sullins was a good worker and queried Marsh about keeping him. Home cooking was improving his condition, but he admitted to Marsh, ". . . it is pretty rough to be ripped up in camp." In contrast, "Mrs. H and the young bone-hunter are well & send their best regards."[7]

Soon after his return to Lusk, Hatcher reported on May 1 that he anticipated having "five good skulls" ready to ship in ten days, along with various other bones and quite a collection of mammal teeth—"some nice things [that] I am sure you will be glad to see." He further foresaw that his healthy young boy would "soon be ready to take to the field to hunt bones." Hatcher sent even better news to Marsh on the thirteenth, when he reported expressing a small box "containing a portion of the skull of some new animal (Hadrosaurus & one other very curious bone)." He also had three *Triceratops* skulls boxed with three more in sight, so this dinosaur, which had essentially been unknown just two years before, was now represented by a substantial sample. Peterson was apparently becoming antsy cooped up in the Peabody, for Hatcher told Marsh, "You and Peterson can settle it between yourselves whether he comes or stays." But new discoveries were burgeoning with the finding of another skull within ten feet of No. 20. Although the top and most of the frill were missing, the maxillaries and lower portions were good, so Hatcher queried, "Shall I take it or leave it? Answer at once." In about a month's work, he now had nine boxes ready to ship. But Hatcher had received a letter from Osborn that troubled him terribly:

> *Enclosed you will find a letter from Prof. Osborn, which please return to me. You will see that it announced my appointment to a position in the American Museum. Can it be possible that you have made the representations to Mr. Jessup as to my character referred to in the first paragraph of this letter. It could have come from but two persons.*

Osborn's letter, written on April 27, started by stating Osborn had, with some difficulty, hired Hatcher as an assistant in paleontology in his fledgling Department of Vertebrate Paleontology at AMNH. The difficulty involved Osborn convincing the head of AMNH, Morris K. Jessup, to overlook imperfections in Hatcher's character about which some unspecified person had informed Jessup. Having convinced Jessup of Hatcher's worthiness, Osborn now expected Hatcher, as an "honorable man," to accept the position Osborn now offered and start work on May 1 as Hatcher had already allegedly and previously agreed to do, according to Osborn. Hatcher was directed to begin collecting in the Laramie beds, and Osborn would soon visit him there. In response, Hatcher wrote Osborn a short note on May 13, stating, "I regret that I am not at liberty to accept the position at the American Museum."[8]

Marsh, upon receiving the letter from Hatcher with Osborn's letter enclosed, quickly telegraphed Hatcher on May 16 to claim, "Statement implied in enclosed letter absolutely false." Then Marsh followed that up with a longer explanation to Hatcher on the eighteenth, in which he expressed surprise at Osborn's statement and denied saying anything disparaging about Hatcher's character to Jessup. He continued, "What I said to him was in your favor, if rightly understood. I met him twice accidentally and [emphasized] the importance of your services to Yale and the Geologic Survey, and the unfairness of Osborn's attempt to make you break your written contract already signed and witnessed." Marsh offered to explain more fully when they next met and implored Hatcher to let him know if Osborn attempted any further shenanigans. Nonetheless, Osborn's pursuit of Hatcher continued throughout the summer, as documented by correspondence between Osborn and his colleague and close friend at Princeton, William Berryman Scott. On July 24, Osborn intimated to Scott, as mentioned earlier, that if Hatcher would be willing to work at the AMNH, Osborn would hire Hatcher for a year with the intention of extending the position if both Hatcher and Osborn were satisfied with the arrangement. Hatcher would receive the same salary he was presently receiving from Marsh, since Osborn "would not like to have it said that I had tempted him by higher wages." Osborn followed up by stating to Scott on August 14 that he'd written Hatcher to inform him of Osborn's proposal. Quite possibly in reference to Osborn and Scott's support for Cope in his quarrel with Marsh, Osborn confided that hiring Hatcher would provide "grist for our mill" while "paralyzing 'the Greatest American Paleontologist.'" By September 2, Osborn told Scott he and Hatcher had corresponded, and that Osborn believed he would receive a positive response from Hatcher, even though Hatcher was also being courted for another position by Charles Otis Whitman at Clark University in Worcester, Massachusetts. According to historian Ronald Rainger, a key reason for Hatcher rejecting Osborn's offer was that, as Rainger states, "Osborn was offering [Hatcher] a position at an institution where Osborn himself did not yet have a formal appointment," so Hatcher terminated the discussions. In the end, however, as Marsh states above, Marsh was also unwilling to let Hatcher break his contract with him and the USGS. Returning to the fieldwork, Marsh implored Hatcher, "We need a Hadrosaurus skull badly, especially the front parts." If the skull near Skull 20 could be collected without too much work, Marsh would like it, but if Hatcher had something better, he should secure that first, especially since, as Marsh wrote, ". . . as you say you have one or more set of poachers in the country this summer."[9]

The same day, Hatcher wrote Marsh to document he truly had a lunker on the line: Skull No. 18 weighed in at 3,100 pounds and took two days to load, haul, and unload. He was shipping it specially through the quartermaster at Fort Robinson, then he'd send the other nine crates, as advertised earlier, simply as fast freight, although Hatcher loathed having to judge which specimens might be most scientifically significant when they were still in the martix that surrounded the bone. He had not started on Burwell's specimen because he preferred to focus on skulls while the roads were good. Although not snake-bitten, his luck in terms of his health seemed to be since he'd mashed his left thumb that day between two crowbars. Not having heard back in detail from Marsh on the subject, he admitted, "I do not know what to think about Osborn's letter." Then Hatcher closed with a financial update after submitting the vouchers for May, "I suspect you think I am never going to pay what I owe you but I am some time if I live." He'd run up some expenses with Anna's trip to New Haven, along with buying mares and constructing a windmill at their farm in Long Pine, but he intended to resume paying off his debt to Marsh in July.[10]

For his part, Marsh telegraphed on the nineteenth that he was sending more troops in the form of his assistant, Thomas A. Bostwick, in early June, and Peterson the first of July. Hatcher responded on the twenty-fifth that he was pleased to hear it, especially since the last shipment had weighed a total of 5,400 pounds. The list of contents showed that *Triceratops* Skulls 18 and 20 were included, as well as two skulls both numbered 19. These were designated 19 (YPM VP 1830) and 19A (YPM VP 1831) when they arrived at the Peabody on June 20, 1891. Marsh's fossil preparatory, Hugh Gibb, began unpacking the skulls on August 6, and Marsh quickly began studying them. Within nine days, Hatcher received a note from Marsh stating that No. 19 was undoubtedly a new and important type of horned dinosaur. This specimen became the basis for Marsh's 1891 description of a new genus of horned dinosaurs that he christened *Torosaurus*, now the Peabody Museum's official mascot.[11]

Hatcher closed out May by shipping three more crates (15–17) weighing 2,700 pounds and containing Skull No. 22 (YPM VP 1834), which he also considered of equal or greater importance than No. 3 (YPM VP 1822), given its hardness and completeness. It was associated with a sequence of vertebrae ten to fifteen feet long that would clarify the true number of cervicals (neck) and dorsals (rib-bearing). He hoped the whole vertebral column would be in the ledge that these came from, along with the limbs. This spectacular specimen now resides in the State Collections of Bavaria, having been acquired from Yale in 1964.[12]

Hatcher continued to be bullish on Skull No. 22 and its skeleton when he came in to pick up Thomas Bostwick on June 6 and to ship three more crates (18, 19, 23), which contained the remainder of the skull, some ribs, and the pelvis. He believed the specimen was getting better as they went further into the ledge. His balance sheet for May showed purchases for groceries, nose bags for horses, hotel stays, pick handles, salaries, use of outfit, hardware, help with boxes, blacksmithing, saw sharpening, livery, and lumber. A week later Hatcher reported that Skull No. 20 (YPM VP 1833) would be coming in the next day, along with two other crates containing fragments of Skulls Nos. 21 (YPM VP 1832, which is now at the Naturalis Biodoversity Center in Leiden, Netherlands) and 22. But the heavy loads were taking a toll, as Hatcher reported on the seventeenth: ". . . we have had the misfortune to break the king-bolt of one of our wagons loaded with Skull No. 20 & it has been raining so we have been unable to get another." But with the rain, skulls were popping out of the ground like spring flowers on the prairie. Hatcher hoped to transport Skull No. 23 (YPM VP 1836) soon; it had been found about fifteen feet from Skull No. 20. Regarding Marsh's "poachers," Hatcher reported that the University of Nebraska's Erwin H. Barbour was nearby. "Have just heard indirectly through a party of amateur collectors of the prayer-meeting class that Barbour & a classmate of mine would be out here in a few days. I have never heard a word from either of them . . . & know nothing of their plans and intentions. I feel sure that Barbour will accomplish nothing for I can . . . control my classmate." Hatcher apparently felt sure of himself even though he was "all knocked out with this infernal rheumatism again . . . can get around but in misery." Vouchers submitted for June totaled $510 with Hatcher's quarterly bonus.[13]

Still having good luck despite bad weather, Hatcher indicated the crew would haul Skull No. 20 to the railroad on June 20, before he maligned Marsh about his paranoia regarding perceived "poachers" and competitors who might move into the area where Hatcher was working for Marsh and take fossils from territory where Marsh thought only his crews had the right to collect:

> *I think you are a long way ahead of Cope so far as material is concerned & do not see why you should let him get ahead of you on the literary part of the work, with all your assistants back there to help you. I will certainly try to keep the end out here a good, long pull ahead of any party that attempts to come in. I think the idea of keeping a corner on fossils of any kind should be given up & the work of cleaning up & describing pushed more vigorously. You certainly have an abundance of material & much more already than Cope can ever have. Of course it is the proper thing to go on collecting for only by such work are the new things brought out. But if Osborn or Cope or any one else see fit to send collectors into this rich field (which they have a right to do) there are bones here for the millions & it would be the utmost folly for one to attempt to keep them from getting some of them. I should not have written as*

I have only for the repeated mentions you have made in your letters
about poachers etc. insinuating that everything rested with me.[14]

Less than a week later on the thirtieth, when Hatcher sent a number of steel tools back to New Haven to be tempered and re-sharpened so that they would stand up to the hard sandstone containing some of the specimens, he informed Marsh that Skull No. 24 (YPM VP 1828), the largest yet found, and most of its skeleton were ready to box. This behemoth tested Hatcher's crew to the extreme, for it weighed in at 6,850 pounds. As if that weren't enough, recovering it required prying the jacketed block out of the outcrop with wooden boards or crowbars and hauling it out of a ravine fifty feet deep with horses before transporting it safely over trackless ground and through streams for forty miles to the nearest railhead. After achieving this feat, Hatcher yodeled, "I would not be afraid to tackle one now that weighed ten thousand pounds." Hatcher's crew member Charles Beecher beamed in amazement and testified that achieving this task "is really a monument to the collecting skill of Mr. Hatcher. I do not believe any other collector would attempt to take up such a large and fragile specimen whole." But Hatcher had just begun and further reported, "I found yesterday a skeleton of some small animal, probably Hadrosaurus. There are 15 or 20 feet of the vertebrae in position, some of the limb bones & other bones in sight. All are in good condition. I believe the skull is in position on the vertebral column but can not say definitely."[15]

Marsh again strained to satisfy his disgruntled field general by appointing him to an additional position at the Peabody, but Hatcher was having none of it:

I am sorry you should have put yourself to any trouble about it as
it is only an honorary position carrying with it no responsibilities,
quite different from the one I might have had at the American
Museum & should have been only too glad to have accepted if you
would only have let me gone. I foresee in the coming five years only
a repetition of the past seven with no change whatever. I presume
now that this is the first vacancy to which you referred last winter
& said I should be appointed.

Then he continued by saying he'd telegraphed about Peterson and had nothing more to say, since Peterson had refused to say earlier in New Haven if he wanted to work with Hatcher that summer. Hatcher was miffed that Peterson tried "to influence men here not to work for me." Hatcher then stated defiantly that he had no trouble getting good men and was, therefore, not dependent on having any one man on his crew. He enclosed a list of contents for crates 1–40 and shipped seven that day, including the remainder of No. 22 and some bones of No. 24. He then proposed a plan for work that winter: to work in Wyoming as late as possible, then sift a lot of mammal sand and ship it to Long Pine, then pick through it that winter to obtain a large collection of mammals. He said he had a little house on his place that was light and warm in which to work, before peevishly adding, ". . . it would keep me away from New Haven where I am not wanted and at home this winter where I should be at least a portion of my time." He could meet Marsh in person in Washington during a meeting of the International Geological Congress to plan the following season's work. Regarding other competitors, he wrote, "I know nothing about what Wortman may do. But I do not think he will come here. Have heard nothing further from Barbour." At that time, Jacob Wortman was working for Osborn at AMNH.[16]

A pair of rapidly fired telegrams flew through the wires between New Haven and Lusk on the thirtieth, with Marsh saying he couldn't decide about sending Peterson until he heard further from Hatcher, and Hatcher again simply responding that Marsh should suit himself and Peterson, then wire if he came. On July 1, Hatcher, clearly not wishing to bow, wrote again to stubbornly state, "It does not make a penny's difference to me whether he comes out or not. You & he must arrange it between yourselves. Yours in haste, J.B. Hatcher."[17]

Returning to more mundane matters on July 3, Hatcher submitted his balance sheet for June, documenting that he'd expended $108.80 more than he'd received, largely due to purchasing the great deal of lumber that was required to build crates for the large blocks with skulls and skeletons (although the total for lumber was curiously only $14.75). Marsh telegraphed on the sixth to approve Hatcher's plan for the winter's work and say he'd come out west September 1, then wrote on the tenth to send the $108.80 check for overages. Attempting to mollify his minion, Marsh agreed it was ". . . only natural that you prefer to be in your own house . . . with your family" over the winter. If Hatcher wanted to attend the Geological Congress, that was fine, but Marsh wouldn't be there. Instead, he'd participate in an excursion out west with some of the participants to the conference, and he wondered if Hatcher wouldn't prefer to meet him at Yellowstone or Denver on that excursion. Marsh emphasized that it was becoming more important to know about the horizons in the Laramie, and since Hatcher was in charge of that, he hoped Hatcher would focus on that if he went to Yellowstone or on a trip "north" with Thomas Bostwick. Marsh added, "The region where you have worked so much appears to be essentially one horizon, but further north you are sure to find several others, and some of the lower ones will be very important." So Marsh asked Hatcher to respond and say what he preferred to do.[18]

Meanwhile, Hatcher was wrestling with a mix-up involving the shipping form for the crates that he thought were sent on the thirtieth, leading him to report that he'd ship those along with fifteen more shortly, making twenty-two in all. Included would be a nearly complete skeleton of a small animal similar to *Iguanodon*, a large herbivorous dinosaur distantly related to duckbills, with all four feet present, along with the pelvis and most of the spinal column. There were small fin-like spines on the caudal (tail) vertebrae, but unfortunately the skull was gone, having stuck out of the bank and washed away. Most impressively, all the bones were in their natural position. The mammals were in box 49 with some interesting foot bones. Responding to Marsh's query about his other hadrosaur skeleton, he assured him, "Yes I know the skull of Hadrosaurus having seen Cope's specimen. I am not sure that the skeleton I have found has the skull but . . . there is a good chance. . . . Have not commenced work on it yet, but hope to soon." He didn't think he'd take a trip north this summer because he disliked leaving here with so much work in sight. Bostwick would be disappointed, but he'd either have to forego the trip or stop everything to go. Marsh telegraphed on the sixteenth in praise of the crew's good luck, adding that Peterson was still in New Haven.[19]

After receiving several missives from Marsh, Hatcher responded from Chadron with disappointment on the nineteenth that Marsh didn't want him to go to the Congress in Washington, but he would look forward to the Yellowstone trip if it could be arranged. He had no interest in Denver. He went on to criticize Marsh for getting his hopes up about the Congress. "I see that I ought not to have referred . . . to my going to Washington. But as your invitation last winter seemed so hearty I thought it would cause a pleasant break in my long season's work; as I will have been in the field seven months & shall probably have three months more before it closes & as I had never been East during that season." At Marsh's direction, he had started on the trip north with Bostwick despite having rather stayed in camp and "pushed work along." They planned to go to the Pine Ridge Agency, then across the reservation to the "Bad Lands," and directly north to Slim Butte to spend a few days prospecting. Then they'd return through Minnesella, Deadwood, and the Black Hills. After submitting his July vouchers for $460 and asking Marsh to credit him for $50 on his note, Hatcher reminded Marsh that, by contract, his time for fieldwork would be up on July 31, when he'd have been in the field for just six months. Then he added, "If you wish me to work out here I am of course willing to do so. But I want a written statement that it is your wish."[20]

On their northern trip, Bostwick especially enjoyed the reservation, where he saw a "Shinny game and an Omaha dance." Craven was still "boss farmer," and Joe Brown had "one Bront. Skull, one Elotherium, one rhino and some small things," which Hatcher bought for $75. Hatcher told Brown he'd pay him to go back where he'd gotten the bizarre, antelope-like *Protoceras* skull that Hatcher had bought from him last winter and get another good one. Marsh, still trying his best to please his discontented chief collector, telegraphed on July 28 that if Hatcher wanted to go to the Congress, he'd be glad to have him go, and if not, he could join the party at Yellowstone.[21]

Still on the road, Hatcher wrote from Deadwood on August 4 that he'd received the monthly check of $410 minus a $50 credit to his loan and agreed to meet Marsh's party at Yellowstone. They were back at camp on Doegie Creek by the seventh, where Hatcher immediately met with astounding success by finding an anthill with 230 mammal teeth on it. The skeleton he thought was a hadrosaur was, instead, a sixteen-foot-long vertebral column of *Triceratops* that was associated with the pelvis, sacrum, and several limb bones. Hatcher was pleased to hear Scott would not be coming to their field area. A week later, Hatcher headed home to his family in Long Pine for the first time since April after receiving good news from Marsh: "Glad that 19 [*Torosaurus*] is so important. I thought it would be new as I wrote you." The crew already had No. 24 boxed, and two more awaited excavation. They shipped eight crates through the quartermaster, including the six with the *Triceratops* vertebrae and hindquarters. Hatcher was now thinking he'd rather come to the Congress than see Yellowstone. On the fifteenth, he mailed two hundred mammals teeth to Marsh.[22]

But Marsh, unaware of Hatcher's change of heart, also telegraphed on the fifteenth to say he hoped to see him soon at Yellowstone and was sure Hatcher would enjoy it, along with encouraging him to continue on with them to Denver. Marsh offered to cover all expenses. Yet apparently later that same day, after receiving a telegram from Hatcher, Marsh replied, saying he'd be happy to see Hatcher back east, where they planned to meet on the twenty-sixth.[23]

Although no record exists of their meeting, Hatcher returned to Long Pine by September 7, where he found that "Mrs. H and the boy are well" before he set off for Lusk. The crew finished excavating No. 25 by the fifteenth, but Hatcher was especially pleased with his new collector, A. L. Sullins:

> *Sullins distinguished himself while I was gone. . . . I told him to go north . . . where there was some very promising looking country & look for bones. He . . . found a pair of Hadrosaurus lower jaws & another Hadrosaurus skeleton. Most of skull is there. The complete series of vertebrae & ribs to the end of the tail in position. The pelvis & both hind legs & feet all in position. [Also] scapulae, but alas front legs and feet they were exposed & badly broken up as was . . . the front of the skull and lower jaws. All the rest is in fine state of preservation. We will take it up as soon as possible & ship at once.*

This specimen is now housed at the Smithsonian's National Museum of Natural History and catalogued as USNM V 2414. But other crew members weren't faring as well as Sullins. Burwell gave up and went home sick. Utterback wanted to quit in November, but he offered to work later on "that old woman's skeleton in the Jurassic east of the hills" if Marsh wanted. Meanwhile, Hatcher was "all crippled up" with "rheumatism" and had to hire a cook to replace Burwell. Nonetheless, whatever had passed between Marsh and Hatcher in Washington rendered Hatcher unusually reflective and grateful:

> *I do not know how I will ever repay you for what you have been doing for me of late. But depend upon it that nothing but my health will keep me from giving you the best service there is in me the next five years. I am going to do the right thing by myself & you too & my family as well in the future.*

His list of contents for crates 40–62 revealed that most crates contained *Triceratops* material, including Skull No. 25, except for Sullins's two lower jaws of a hadrosaur. The month's vouchers totaled $455 plus his quarterly bonus of $50.[24]

The crew was still wrangling with the hadrosaur skeleton on the twenty-first when Hatcher next wrote with an update to say they'd taken up the skull, neck vertebrae, hind legs, and feet. The rest had been exposed to reveal that a portion of the tail was missing. Skull No. 25, which had just shipped, was very good and included a complete beak and nasal horncore. His list of contents for crates 60–71 documented, again, Skull No. 25, as well as several now packed with parts of the new hadrosaur skeleton (No. 1). But as always, Marsh continued to clamor for more mammals, so on the thirtieth, Hatcher promised to reexamine Peterson's old Quarry and Quarry 1 to see what they might find, even though they were twelve miles removed from their present camp. They now had all of hadrosaur Skeleton No. 1 packed in crates and ready to ship. With that done, Hatcher was ready to face Skull No. 24: "Will have to get another team & a still heavier wagon and another team. I believe it will weigh between 5000

& 6000 lbs. By far the heaviest yet." They were making good progress on Skull No. 26 and had brought a load in weighing 4,600 pounds that day. But discoveries continued, with Hatcher announcing that they were just starting to uncover another "fine little skeleton." Hatcher then requested the $200 Marsh had promised him in Washington, while also promising in return to repay Marsh $100 per month until they were square.[25]

Continuing their furious pace, the crew had three more Skulls (26–28: USNM V 2100, 5740, 6679) lined up—one ready to box, one nearly ready, and a third awaiting excavation—along with lots of other good things in sight. But Hatcher was concerned Utterback wasn't turning in everything he found, especially mammal teeth. Utterback, who wanted to quit November 1, wanted Marsh to return his contract. So Hatcher said he could quit if he thought the weather was too bad, and Marsh wouldn't trouble him about the contract if he didn't come back here and begin digging bones for himself or others. But Hatcher recommended that Marsh retain Utterback's contract. Utterback had just left for Hot Springs to see about building a house, and if he found work there, Hatcher suspected his bone hunting days were over. In any event Hatcher didn't think he'd want Utterback anymore. Hatcher next planned to visit the old mammal quarries and check for fragments of Skull 19A. There had been three snowstorms already, and his "rheumatism" had returned with the weather, wet feet, clothes and bed, and so much heavy lifting. On the tenth, Hatcher provided detailed instructions for preparing Skull No. 24: ". . . leave it on edge just as it comes & take the box from around it down to within about two feet of the bottom . . . then work off all the rock without shifting position of skull."[26]

Skulls 27 and 28 were ready to box by the nineteenth, and Skull 26 was almost ready. Hatcher had also taken up the little *Triceratops* skeleton, which only had the pelvis, sacrum, and twelve tail vertebrae. He had found mammal teeth at Quarry 1 and Peterson's Quarry. Utterback, still at Hot Springs, said that he was ready to quit for the year, so Hatcher submitted vouchers for $450 and asked Marsh to credit him with $100 on his loan of $370 and promised to send the remainder by the end of the month. As October closed, Marsh sent Hatcher a map of Wyoming on which to mark his localities, and Hatcher shipped the loose fragments of 19A he'd found, along with ten other crates containing Skulls 26, 27, and the small hindquarters. Regarding Utterback, Hatcher disappointedly reported:

> While I was gone home & in Wash. he spent most of his time looking for bones but claimed to have found none. Instead of going to the Springs to build, I found on getting back here today that he has moved his family here & bought a team, wagon & harness & I've heard indirectly that he intends to go bone hunting. Of course, if he is, he had found some good things of which he has said nothing, for no man would go to the expense of buying a team, etc. at this season of the year unless he knew exactly what he could do in the bone business. Of course he did not expect to find me here yet & was very anxious to know when I was going to close up. If he comes over in that country collecting I shall not recognize him as the owner of any specimens he may find on government land. He understood distinctly when I paid him for this month that it was on the condition that he should engage in some other occupation until Feb. 14 when his year would be up. . . . I [will] hire another man for Nov. & keep him & Sullins taking up bones and hauling them in & I will spend my time looking. I have spent only three days . . . all summer so far looking for bones.[27]

Hatcher's list of contents for crates 77–87 on the twenty-ninth documented Skulls 26 and 27, along with a hadrosaur thighbone. By November 9, he sent the marked-up map, noting that Bull Creek and Crazywoman Creek were known by locals as Doegie Creek and Buck Creek. A couple more mediocre skulls had been found, but he still thought them worth taking if they could deal with an overhanging rock about fifteen feet above ground that might cause some "bad luck getting them down." His list of contents on the twenty-first for crates 88–99 showed Skull 28 and other *Triceratops* specimens except for one hadrosaur lower jaw and two hadrosaur limb bones. Utterback had indeed returned to collect, but Hatcher didn't expect him to stay out long, since it had been and still was stormy. Hatcher had heard that Osborn had hired Utterback for the following season and encouraged Marsh to intervene legally, since Hatcher thought specimens from US government land should go to the government. With his "rheumatism" now raging, Hatcher headed home after submitting $415 worth of vouchers and a request to credit him with a $100 payment on his loans and then send the rest to Long Pine. They'd cached a considerable amount of "mammal sand" in camp to pick through during bad weather when they weren't taking out the three skulls "in sight." So Hatcher was able to send "quite a number" of good mammal teeth and bones to Marsh.[28]

Marsh was characteristically concerned about Utterback's activities and told Hatcher that he had shut him out of working for the AMNH. Nonetheless, Hatcher reassured Marsh that he'd leave Long Pine for Lusk on December 3 to gather whatever information he could. But to add to the troubles with their former and now wayward collectors, Hatcher informed Marsh that Anna had received a letter from Peterson saying he was visiting New York before going out west with AMNH's collector Jacob Wortman. Hatcher foresaw other parties collecting at their localities north of Lusk in the following year, and he considered Marsh lucky that they'd not come before. Although he still believed they could legally prevent anyone from working in the same region on government lands, he doubted if it would be "policy" to ban an AMNH party, although since the Peabody had discovered the locality, it would only be just for others to work elsewhere until Marsh and Hatcher were through. He even thought Wortman would agree if it was presented to him in that light. In any event, Hatcher thought it would be wise to keep two men in Lusk that winter. By the fourth, Utterback had returned empty-handed to Lusk, feeling "beaten at his own game," according to Hatcher. Nonetheless Hatcher still suggested that Burrell and Sullins stay in Lusk over the winter at a combined salary of $120 per month, and he offered to furnish them a team for nothing. They could sift "mammal sand" from Quarry 1, Peterson's Quarry and other good quarries, working some over in camp and shipping the rest to New Haven and Long Pine for Hatcher and Marsh to sift through. But Hatcher emphasized that in justice to himself, he should work indoors this winter, since he almost constantly suffered from "rheumatism" now.[29]

As of December 7, Utterback had still not found any mammals, unless he had kept some he'd collected during the previous summer with Hatcher. But according to Hatcher, Utterback had "looked & acted awful sneaking" one day, prompting Hatcher to enquire whether Marsh had shut him out from the AMNH for good or only for the winter. Due to the bad weather that kept Utterback in, Hatcher's crew had sorted out quite a lot of mammal teeth, and despite it, they'd managed to get a skull and skeleton of *Triceratops* ready to ship. Work on Skull 29 (USNM V-4928) had revealed by the fourteenth that its complete nasal horn was spoon-shaped on back, and the frill, instead of being solid, seemed to be composed of four bones distinct from each other—that is, two squamosals and two parietals. Both orbital horns were complete, along with the beak and the upper and lower jaws. There were many other good bones with it, too, but it required a lot of plastering, so Hatcher asked Marsh to get some rubber dishwashing gloves so he could "paste" in the cold weather. They'd amassed thirty wagonloads of mammal sand from Quarry 1 and Peterson's Quarry for working over the winter, so ". . . if P & W [Peterson and Wortman] come out expecting to reap a rich harvest from there or any other of the old localities they will be very badly fooled."[30]

By the nineteenth, as he'd expected with temperatures plummeting to eighteen below, Hatcher's hands were very sore from being exposed while applying burlap soaked in flour paste to Skull 29. He also reported having sifted eleven wagonloads of sand for mammals. He assured Marsh,

> *You need not fear Wortman's taking any specimens I find. I am fully prepared & competent to prevent any such proceedings. I am glad Utterback is out at the American Museum. I consider him nothing but a common thief. In 10 days . . . we will have the mammal localities all taken care of, & I think P & W or W & P will have to rustle for themselves when they come & besides they*

will be at the disadvantage of not knowing the territory that has been worked over this year.[31]

Hatcher hoped to finish by December 29 and head home, so he was still at the camp outside Lusk on Christmas when Marsh told him that despite his protests to Osborn, Peterson was apparently coming out with Wortman. Hatcher dismissively responded, "I am glad he is gone though for I do not care to have him work for me any more. I think it is much better for him and Wortman to come in here without U. [Utterback] than with, for he knows the country we have worked over this year and they do not." Hatcher would try to get Peterson to furnish a team for them, because if he did, that would ensure that Peterson and Wortman would exclude Utterback. Blizzards and Hatcher's "rheumatism" were preventing the crew from hauling Skull 29 in, but they had sifted most of the mammal sand in preparation for picking through it over the winter. He now hoped to finish around January 10–15, and closed by pointedly telling Marsh, "Hoping you've had a better Christmas than I," before wishing him a Merry New Year.[32]

By the end of 1891, Hatcher had lassoed another magnificent menagerie from the Lance Formation's 68- to 66-million-year-old strata, including the multituberculates (*Allacodon, Cimolomys, Meniscoessus, Mesodma, Tripriodon,* and "Oracodon," which is now called *Meniscoessus);* the marsupials (*Alphadon, Didelphodon, Glasbius, Pediomys, Protolambda,* and "Didelphops," "Ectoconodon," and "Stagodon," which are now called *Didelphodon);* and the placentals (*Batadon, Cimolestes,* and *Gypsonictops).* The ray-finned fish *Belonostomus* also appears. Salamanders included *Habrosaurus, Lisserpeton, Opisthotriton,* and *Scapherpeton.* The list of lizards contains *Alethesaurus, Exostinus, Iguanavus, Chamops,* and "Lanceosaurus," which is now called *Chamops,* in addition to the crocodile *Brachychampsa* and the turtles *Baena* and *Basilemys.* The dinosaurs corralled encompassed the duckbill *Trachodon,* the herbivore *Thescelosaurus,* the bird-mimic *Ornithomimus,* the bird relative *Troodon,* the ever-imposing *Tyrannosaurus,* along with its cousin *Aublysodon* and another slew of *Triceratops,* as well as its close cousin *Torosaurus.*

A spirited scientific debate has sprung up in recent years over whether *Triceratops* and *Torosaurus* are truly separate genera and species, as was proposed by Marsh and has long been accepted by today's paleontological community. More specifically, Montana paleontologists Jack Horner and John Scannella argued in 2010 that specimens of *Triceratops* with solid frills simply represented young or juvenile individuals of a horned dinosaur genus whose adult form was represented by *Torosaurus* with its perforated frill. In 2012, Yale paleontologists Nick Longrich and Daniel Field countered that conclusion by examining three predictions of the Horner-Scannella argument.

The first prediction specified that if *Triceratops* and *Torosaurus* represented different growth stages of the same species, their fossils should be found in the same geographic areas and in rocks of the same age. Longrich and Field found this to be true: "Both *Torosaurus* and *Triceratops* are known exclusively from the late Maastrictian [about 66-million-year-old rock units] of western North America."

Second, if *Triceratops* and *Torosaurus* represented different growth stages of the same species, their specimens should show consistent differences in anatomical maturity. But Longrich and Field found that several specimens of *Torosaurus* "appear to be near or at maturity, but others lack the full suite of features expected for a mature animal. . . . Furthermore, many *Triceratops* skulls exhibit extensive cranial fusion and heavily rugose bone surface texture, suggesting that they are adults."

Third, if *Triceratops* and *Torosaurus* are simply different growth stages of the same genus, there should be intermediate forms linking the two stages. Scannella and Horner suggested that "Nedoceratops hatcheri" (USNM 2412) might be one in which the solid frill of the younger growth stage found in *Triceratops* is beginning to develop the holes in the frill seen in the adult stage represented by *Torosaurus*. But Longrich and Field deem the hole in the frill of "Nedoceratops" a pathology clearly resulting from disease, since the position of the opening in relation to the bones of the skull is different from the position found in *Torosaurus*. In addition, Longrich and Field found that the number of epiparietal bones—the small, triangular-shaped knobs that adorn the margin of the bony frill or shield at the back of the skull—is consistently different in *Torosaurus* and *Triceratops*, with *Torosaurus* having ten or more, and *Triceratops* five to seven, suggesting that *Torosaurus* and *Triceratops* represent different genera. But at this time, several other paleontologists have entered the fray, and the debate continues.[33]

In short, this debate represents a perfect example of how specimens that Hatcher collected over 125 years ago, including his skulls of *Triceratops* and *Torosaurus*, still influence and inform present paleontological research. It is exactly for this that Hatcher remains such a reverential figure in our field.

9

An Unexpected Ending

D etermined not to miss the New Year as well as Christmas with his family after spending almost all of 1891 in the field, Hatcher hightailed it home to Long Pine on the thirty-first, finding Mrs. H. and the young bone hunter both well. He'd shipped twenty-nine crates (100–129) of both fossils and "mammal sand," some to New Haven and the rest to Long Pine, before leaving A. L. Sullins in charge at Lusk to work until January 17, sifting more sand and sending it to New Haven. As Hatcher left, Utterback was heading north, apparently to collect for "curio dealers in Hot Springs, S. Dakota." Burwell was to let Hatcher know if Utterback brought in any fossils to Lusk before February 1; Hatcher intended to confiscate them, since Marsh had paid Utterback through that date. But Hatcher suspected Utterback was trading in buffalo horns instead of fossils. Skull 29 had turned out well. The squamosals were more slender than in No. 3 but not as slender as in the *Torosaurus* specimens 19 and 19A, and the nasal horn seemed different. There was an opening on the upper side at the base of the frill about three inches long and two inches wide, and several unusual bones under the left squamosal that, during life, appeared to have been covered with a horny substance. In all, Hatcher felt well satisfied with the crew's showing and hoped Marsh would, too, since he had "pushed the work ahead with all the little energy I have hoping to demonstrate . . . that I'm still as loyal to you & have as much interest in the work as ever." He then offered several suggestions for better tools and closed by informing Marsh that he'd paid out $109.60 more than received, overdrawing his bank account considerably. He requested Marsh send $100 immediately, then he'd deduct it from next month's vouchers, which would save him from paying 18 percent interest on it, which the bank would charge.[1]

The New Year got off to a slow start, with Hatcher writing Marsh on January 3 that he'd received a letter from Peterson saying he and Wortman would work in Mexico the coming season, but Hatcher didn't believe it. Then Hatcher got very sick around the tenth and, as a result, had put in only one day picking through the quarry sand for mammals by the thirteenth. Yet he had found one nice jaw with two perfect teeth and several isolated teeth. Adding to his headache, though, was a letter he'd received from Osborn dated January 7, which Hatcher felt required a polite but firm response dated January 12:

Dear Mr. Hatcher:

Professor Marsh showed me the other day, a paper of your agreeing to stay with him until July 1st, 1891 (termination of 5 years agreement). You wrote me that your agreement with him terminated in the autumn of 1890, and I have had this understanding and acted upon it, until quite recently, when as I say, Prof. Marsh informed that your agreement had not expired by six months.

The matter can probably be explained. Will you kindly do so? I am

Yours truly,
(signed) Henry F. Osborn

Answer:

> *Prof. H. F. Osborn.*
>
> *My dear Sir:*
>
> *Yours of Jan. 7th received. I think you are mistaken in saying that I wrote you that my agreement with Prof. Marsh terminated in the Autumn of 1890. If I wrote you this it should appear in your copy of our correspondence. I have looked through carefully and find no such statement. In my first letter I state "I am ready to send in my resignation to Marsh at any time." In my letters to you this is the only reference I find to anything relating to the subject. Your so-called correspondence between us; copies of which you caused to be made and circulated last spring I think are unfair to me, for several reasons, particularly the following: you are dishonest in your quotations. I believe you quote me correctly and entirely everything I wrote, but your own letters you have so changed that in some of them the originals would not be recognized from a reading of your copies and moreover you have left out entirely one very important letter of yours. I refer to the one in which you write me asking me to meet you in New York or Princeton Showing [sic] that you were not absolutely sure of having a position for me. Why did you omit this letter if you meant to be honest with me?*
>
> Yours very truly,
(signed) J. B. Hatcher[2]

Regarding his former crew members, Hatcher related to Marsh on the eighteenth that Peterson indicated he'd be coming through on February 1 on his way to Mexico, but Hatcher thought this "only a blind." He also suspected the AMNH had engaged Utterback, despite Utterback's denials. Hatcher then submitted vouchers for January totaling $360 and informed Marsh he'd like to pay $50 on one loan and deduct the $100 already sent. Sullins had finished on the fifteenth, and Hatcher paid him through the rest of the month, because ". . . he has been at work faithfully since April 1st & never lost a day, not even Sundays." Despite being ill and the outside temperature reaching fifty-six below, Hatcher had gleaned "quite a number of mammals" from the quarry sand and would send that first batch shortly. On the twenty-second, Hatcher proudly proclaimed to Marsh, "I write to tell you that we have another young bonehunter at our house. It came along the 20th. Mother and boy doing well." The Hatchers named their new son Harold. In other business, mammals were coming more slowly, and Hatcher feared Marsh would think he wasn't working enough. On the twenty-ninth, Hatcher offered another reason for the slow pace, reporting that Anna and his older son got very sick on the twenty-fourth and had lapsed into a "dangerous condition" until they improved on the twenty-ninth. "I have not been in bed for five days & nights & I feel the effects of it too. Have spent all the time . . . waiting on the sick & going for doctor & medicine and looking for mammals." At this point, he had only found about twenty-five mammal teeth and did not specify which genera. He'd also collected "quite a number of other things" without identifying them.[3]

By February 1, Hatcher was getting fidgety and informed Marsh he'd like to start the 1892 season on March 1: "I like being at home well enough. But [Anna and the boy] are all getting along well now & I believe the field is the place for me. The time passes quicker there than anywhere else in the world." As he continued to pick through the quarry sand, he also reported he'd bought a stallion and would have sixteen mares for breeding in the spring, so his monthly payments to Marsh for his loan would need to be reduced. In all, he now had twenty-four head of horses, colts, and right mares that would have colts in spring, along with the sixteen mares to breed. Regarding the previous season's collection, he inquired about how the *Triceratops* Skulls 26 and 29 were coming along, and rather defensively declared, "You say . . . you find Had. Skel. 1 that Sullins found better than I represented; I certainly meant to say everything in praise of the specimen. I only said the front feet were gone . . . & a portion of the skull. I took greatest of pains taking it up."[4]

The market for mammals had picked up once again by the twelfth, when Hatcher had almost finished another box of sand that had produced many good teeth and several pieces of jaw, but only one jaw fragment with teeth, along with some good foot bones. In other news, he knew that

Peterson had gone west to New Mexico, instead of Mexico, and advised Marsh that there was no use worrying about interference the AMNH might instigate in the Laramie:

> *The Laramie is . . . very extensive . . . & almost all is fossiliferous. Of course, it is not pleasant to have other party . . . work in same locality in which we work & if they only knew it, it is not in their interest to work there. For as we have been working there the past three seasons with splendid results the chances of getting new things . . . are now small & I think they could do much better elsewhere. In fact I . . . recommend that we spend portion of coming season . . . in another locality farther north where I feel sure we would get much more new material. . . .*

Hatcher especially wanted to know when Marsh wanted them to start the season, since he'd need to alert Sullins and Louis Cook, who were home in Montana and Iowa, respectively. He also wanted Osborn's letters returned and asked Marsh if Baur had started at Worcester yet, because he wanted him to repay an old loan or Hatcher would send a lawyer to collect it. Always acquisitive when it came to his property, Hatcher then revealed to Marsh, in the excitable, almost breathless tone of a son asking his father to buy him a toy, the reason for needing Baur to pay up—a 160-acre parcel of land with a house and good fencing adjacent to his own spread. If Marsh would purchase it for $800, Hatcher would pay him $900 over the next year.[5]

Marsh apparently didn't respond immediately to that request but did direct Hatcher to start the season March 1, so on the seventeenth, Hatcher obediently indicated he'd write his crew to be at Long Pine then to begin work. Meanwhile, he continued to pick through sand for mammals, despite another bout with "rheumatism," but fossils were few, except for a "nice little jaw with two posterior molars" from Beecher's Quarry. Yet he was glad to hear that work on the skulls from the '91 season was going well. In closing he parried an apparent poke from Marsh about not communicating often enough: "From the tone of your message today you seem . . . somewhat put out with me. You must remember that I am seven miles from the post office & telegraph & to go there every day would mean I could do little else."[6]

The matrix from Beecher's Quarry was not particularly productive, and Hatcher told Marsh on the twenty-sixth that he had gotten almost nothing further out of it except a dozen isolated teeth, half a femur, and "a very peculiar thing, which is either a dental plate of a fish or a portion of dermal armor from a small reptile. I have never seen anything like it before." He planned to leave for Lusk the twenty-ninth; unless directed otherwise, he would first finish securing all the sand at the Peterson Quarry, then move farther north. But his "rheumatism" once again floored him, so on March 2 he remained in Long Pine while his crew, consisting of A. L. Sullins, A. E. Burrell, and Louis Cook, set out for Lusk. But Hatcher had had to scramble to staff the crew, since Anna's youngest brother, who was expected to go, quit at the last minute:

> *He agreed faithfully last fall to stay right along. I guess he thought he had me in a pinch & I would give him more wages. But I didn't & he is out of a job. I am glad he is gone & this ends all my relations with my relatives. I have never asked any favors of them & I shall never favor them again.*[7]

The season had started in earnest by March 5, but Hatcher was still harrumphing about Utterback, who had already started collecting for the AMNH and expected the rest of their crew to join him soon. Utterback promised Hatcher that he'd not come within twenty-five miles of where Hatcher was working. On the home front, Marsh had apparently declined to loan Hatcher the money for the acreage adjacent to his farm, and it had sold for more than Hatcher could afford—$840, which Hatcher would have had to borrow at 18 percent interest. Nonetheless, he still had his eye on another adjoining property. He ran into Utterback in Lusk on the eighth and was no doubt happy to hear that he'd found nothing. During their chat, Hatcher told Utterback where he intended to work and emphatically warned, Utterback that ". . . if he or any party intruded [Hatcher] should not recognize their finds." Hatcher was working for the government on government lands, and he didn't want "to have the efficiency of [his] work impaired by the interference of other parties." Utterback agreed not to work on Hatcher's territory, although Hatcher warily told Marsh, "This remains to be seen." Although formal permits are now required to collect on land owned by the US government, such was not the case in Hatcher's day. Rules regarding who could collect where were more nebulous, and as we've seen with Marsh and Cope, disputes between competing crews from different institutions collecting in the same area commonly arose. After requesting a tent and a quart of Le Page's liquid glue, Hatcher informed Marsh that Wortman and Peterson were collecting at Farmington, New Mexico. Finally on the fourteenth, Hatcher sent Marsh the first fruits of their season's efforts—the results of their search for mammals, including two humeri, one ulna, and several jaws without teeth. He somewhat defensively claimed the cache to be "of more real value than any one lot yet sent." Marsh was preparing another paper on the mammals that included over two hundred illustrations, but Hatcher couldn't tell him at the moment which localities all the teeth had come from. Nonetheless, he expressed satisfaction that Hadrosaur Skeleton No. 1 (USNM 2414), in which all the ossified tendons in the tail were preserved, was preparing out nicely, as was Skull 29. Ossified tendons, which serve to stiffen the tail so it can be used as a more effective counterbalance to the torso as the duckbill moves, are occasionally preserved, since they are hardened by calcification in contrast to regular tendons.[8]

Hatcher announced the first sensational news of the season on April 1—his discovery of another hadrosaur skeleton, which he thought would fill in the missing parts of Skeleton 1.

> ... *the tail and back portion ... stuck out & the front runs* [into] *the bank. Most of bones are in position. We have both hind feet & one front foot uncovered & portion of other front leg in sight. The front foot we have uncovered has not the phalanges in position, but the metacarpals are. They are shaped as I shall try to illustrate* [illustration included in letter] ... *there are four toes ... the two outside ones being much shorter. The one slightly out of place may possibly not be a metacarpal but I think it is. It is slightly shorter than the other short one & appears stouter.*

They hadn't gotten to the skull yet, but there was no reason to think it was not there and in excellent condition, as were all the bones except those that had been exposed. This specimen is now mounted in the Great Hall at the Peabody Museum (YPM VP 2182) and is especially noteworthy for being not only the first relatively complete dinosaur to be mounted in an American museum but also the first dinosaur to be mounted in what is now considered to be the proper bipedal posture with the head and backbone held horizontally so that the tail is raised up and not dragging along the ground. In essence, this posture for the mount, which was constructed by Beecher and Hugh Gibb in 1901, basically records the position of the bones as they were found in the ground, a fact that Beecher was able to observe, since he was part of Hatcher's crew when he collected it. The crew also brought in four more boxes and was doing very well despite enduring the most severe blizzard of the season. Since the storm would prevent work for several days, Hatcher shifted his plans and went home that night, expecting to be gone until the tenth. He supposed Wortman and Peterson would be there soon and wanted to be around when they arrived.[9]

But Hatcher was still waylaid in Long Pine on the fourteenth by a blizzard he'd "never seen the like of." It had taken him four days to get home, where he'd been cooped up inside ever since in fear of exacerbating his "rheumatism." He promised to send the hadrosaur forefoot and skull, if it was preserved, as soon as he returned, which he hoped would be on the nineteenth. Back in Lusk on the twenty-third, Hatcher was still waiting for his team and crew to come in, so he couldn't submit the monthly vouchers in time to pay them on May 1. As an aside, he informed Marsh, "The excitement over the war is dying down a little," apparently referring to the Johnson County War in northern Wyoming between powerful cattle barons, whose herds numbered in the thousands, and small operators running just enough cattle to support their families. About thirty barons and another twenty hired gunmen rode out of Casper intending to hang or gun down about seventy of the small operators. Only one small operator was murdered by the barons and their gang before several hundred Johnson County locals surrounded the "invaders" at a nearby ranch to take revenge. But before they could, Governor Amos

Barber, an ally of the barons, alerted President Benjamin Harrison about the impending bloodshed, and the government sent troops from Fort McKinney to restore order.[10]

By early May, Wyoming had turned into a mass of muck as the result of the melting snow, and although Hatcher made it in to Lusk on the ninth, he had to leave the all-important hadrosaur skull (YPM VP 2184) on the road in his wagon, which was stuck in the mud, a circumstance that must have alarmed Marsh. Hatcher had been on the road for four days facing down one snowstorm after another. Nonetheless, he was shipping crates 1–8 for the season, which, according to his list, contained mammal sand from various quarries, a turtle, and a lower jaw of a hadrosaur. He'd express the hadrosaur foreleg, then ship the rest of the skeleton soon as private freight. The skull and lower jaws were still in two large blocks and not exposed enough to assess for sure how good they were, although he had high hopes and would encase them in hard jackets for protection before digging them out, carefully packing them and shipping them to the Peabody, where they could be prepared and evaluated more fully. He made it back to camp the next day and hoped to send Sullins and Burwell in with Hadrosaur Skeleton No. 2 on the eleventh, along with the vouchers for May and a request to credit him $50 on his loan.[11]

Hatcher supposed Marsh had received the forefoot of the hadrosaur when he wrote on the twenty-first, saying he was sorry that some of the finger bones were gone, which he suspected was due to these lighter bones being transported downstream by currents in the ancient stream before the rest of the skeleton was buried by sediment and later fossilized. As is widely recognized today but not back then, he seemed surprised that the hind limbs were so much longer than the forelimbs. The crew was planning to ship nine more crates on the twenty-second and move camp about fifteen miles southwest on Doegie Creek. They had now gathered another three hundred mammal teeth, which Hatcher hoped would reveal some new forms. Wortman and Peterson were using Douglas, Wyoming, as a base, but Hatcher had no idea if they were having any luck. He'd received two or three letters from Osborn, who had hired another of Hatcher's brothers-in-law, but he didn't think they intended to work near Lusk. In addition, the still-open wounds between Hatcher and Osborn over the aborted hiring of Hatcher at the AMNH continued to fester. In a March 14 response to a letter Osborn had written Hatcher on January 18, Hatcher replied that he would be glad to "withdraw any statements in the least discourteous" to Osborn as soon as Osborn could satisfy Hatcher that he was not trying to harm him by what Hatcher alleged was Osborn's alteration of their earlier corresponence regarding the position. Hatcher also maintained that he was not "bound" to Marsh at the time negotiations for the position began because Marsh "was free to discharge me at any time." On April 25, Hatcher again wrote Osborn to rehash essentially the same argument and offer, "Whenever it appears to me that you meant me no injustice I shall be glad to withdraw any discourteous statements." Osborn fired the last salvo in this skirmish of their ongoing feud on April 29, asserting that he'd given Hatcher "a fair opportunity" to recant his repulsive language and, since Hatcher failed to do so, Hatcher had, in Osborn's eyes, "removed all the respect I had entertained for you." Apparently unphased, Hatcher focused on his fieldwork. Feeling that their present field area had been picked pretty clean, Hatcher reiterated his desire to Marsh to strike out in search of new badlands to prospect. He thought it best to reconnoiter the region to the west of where they'd been working. But he nonetheless suggested leaving Sullins and another man behind to look for something new for a few months. Only if they found a locality far to the north did Hatcher suspect that they would find numerous new forms. Using that opportunity as bait, Hatcher tried to entice Marsh to grab Charles Beecher and come out prospecting with him. But Marsh would not be manipulated and telegraphed on the thirty-first that Hatcher should proceed "with present work" and keep expenses as low as possible, preferring to delay a decision about searching for a new locality until later.[12]

Keeping his eyes peeled for interlopers, Hatcher noted that Wortman and Peterson returned to Lusk with only a few mammal teeth and planned to strike out for Miocene exposures, presumably in Nebraska or South Dakota. They also revealed that Utterback was no longer employed by the AMNH. For his part, Hatcher shipped fifteen crates weighing 5,500 pounds on June 1, including Skull 30 and two turtles—one that was extremely large and the other with a complete foot. Apparently in response to a query from Marsh, he went on to describe in detail the positioning of the bones in the hadrosaur forefoot as it had been preserved in the ground. Then he once again passionately prodded Marsh about prospecting for a new locality, grumbling, "It is a great waste of time and money to remain here longer. We are repeating same mistake we made in Kansas and Dakota. This locality is worn threadbare & we are only duplicating material." On a more personal note, he told Marsh he had a chance to trade his place in Nebraska for a new house in New Haven with fourteen rooms, bathroom, pantry and "all modern conveniences . . . stocked with choice shrubbery & fruits." Then he played his hand:

> *Now what do you think? Is there a chance for me in New Haven? If you dont* [sic] *want me there say so frankly & I will work my time out, out here & keep my property here. If you think I can do good work there & would like me there I would like to go there & will do my best to work for our mutual interests & the interests of all concerned; I wish you'd write me frankly just what you think.*
>
> *Are you willing I should work up the Laramie turtles with a view to describing them?*

Marsh must have responded as soon as he received Hatcher's proposal, writing on June 6:

> *In regard to the more important matters you mention, I will think them over and write you later when I hear definitely from Washington. You know very well that I should be glad to have you here in New Haven if you can be contented here, and in that case I should be delighted to have you take hold of the turtles and work them up. Until the uncertainty in Congress is entirely removed, I should think it would not be wise to exchange your present home for anything here, although I often feel myself that I should like to swap my ranch here for one in the West, where taxes and street committees are less oppressive.*[13]

Marsh's allusion to his problems in Washington revolved around the long-festering political disputes between Congress and the USGS, led by its director John Wesley Powell, who had appointed Marsh as the Survey's vertebrate paleontologist in 1892, much to the chagrin of Cope, who lost all his leverage for government funding to support fieldwork and publications as a result. Although both Powell and Marsh had survived Cope's attempted coup, hatched through his broadside and played out on the pages of the *New York Herald* in 1890, the Survey's difficulties did not disappear. Although Powell retained the support of Iowa senator William B. Allison, who headed up the Senate's Appropriation Committee, the annual appropriation for the Survey had long been under skeptical scrutiny by other members of Congress, especially Alabama congressman Hilary A. Herbert. Essentially, the government had for years rubber-stamped Powell's blanket request for funding without any itemization required to indicate exactly how the funds were to be spent. Basically, Powell had argued that the funds would be expended to conduct a careful study in which all of the nation would be geologically mapped in order to identify tracts of arid lands, especially in the West, that could be reclaimed by irrigation through strategically located dams and their resulting reservoirs. In 1885–86, Powell claimed to a congressional committee investigating the Survey that the mapping project would take twenty years and cost $18 million, but critics responded that at the rate the project was proceeding, it could take a century and cost $100 million. A drought in 1890 exacerbated Congress's zeal for immediate action to generate irrigation, and by 1892, the country was entering an economic downturn, which generated increased pressure on Congress to cut costs. The USGS became a prime target for cuts, and rather anecdotally, Marsh's monograph on toothed birds became a rallying cry for those cuts, especially since Harvard's influential zoologist Alexander Agassiz argued that such monographs could be published much cheaper through the private sector than through the government. Although Marsh had used his own personal money to fund the work on the lavish illustrations, Congressman Herbert dismissively held up a copy of the "sumptuous volume with morocco binding, gilt edges, wide margins [and] specially tinted paper" during one debate and proclaimed it "an excellent example of the way in which large amounts of government money were being wasted on the description of such worthless objects as 'birds with teeth.'"

Herbert's amendment requiring the cessation of all paleontological work by the Survey by July 1, 1892, was passed by a vote in the House of ninety to sixty. In the Senate, Herbert's amendment was scrapped, and salaries for paleontologists were reinserted in the Appropriations Committee's Sundry Civil Bill. But further votes followed, and in mid-July, the Senate approved an amendment slashing the annual Survey appropriation to $335,000, including salaries for four geologists and two paleontologists. Powell, in assessing the carnage caused by his defeat, sent Marsh a telegram on July 20, in which he stated, "Appropriation cut off. Please send your resignation at once." Although further attempts would be made to soften the blow to Marsh, at least to the extent of trying to help Marsh get his research projects published, the reality was that he no longer would wield power as the federal government's chief vertebrate paleontologist or benefit from the $4,000 it had provided to his annual income. Beyond that, the effects of Marsh's downfall would have enormous consequences for Hatcher, both as the rest of the 1892 field season played out and beyond.[14]

Upon receiving Marsh's June 6 response on the seventeenth, Hatcher was "somewhat disappointed by its contents." Adding to his frustration was the fact that "The 'Great American Desert' is a veritable quagmire," due to torrential rain. He could not haul crates on the muddy roads, and even if he could, the railroad had been washed out. Regardless, he had nine crates (32–40) ready to ship, including Skull 31, which was small but with nearly complete horncores and a frill that reminded him of Skulls 19 and 19A belonging to *Torosaurus*. Apparently Wortman had seen it, and Hatcher wrote, "not wishing me any bad luck he wished they had found it instead of me." Wortman and Peterson then left for regions to the north, having not succeeded in discovering any large skulls or skeletons, although they had found some mammal teeth. Hatcher still guessed they would head for Miocene exposures east of the Black Hills. Then Hatcher informed Marsh that he was making good progress on the stratigraphy of the region:

> *I've been making some observations, measurements & sketches of the Laramie. I find that the beds are not so discontinuous as I had*

supposed [and] *have been able to make out several different hori-*
zons & on the whole I think I'll be able to write a fairly creditable
paper on the geology of this region.

Hatcher eventually penned that paper in 1893. Some financial details
followed, including his request to be allowed to skip a couple of monthly
payments on his loan, since his final mortgage installment was due on
August 1.[15]

With that, Hatcher apparently fled the field temporarily to attend a
geological conference in Chicago. He continued on to New Haven in an
attempt to see Marsh, but upon his arrival, Marsh was in Washington,
dealing with the brewing political storm over USGS funding. However,
Marsh's sister, Mary, entertained Hatcher with "a dish of strawberries
and jersey cream. Quite a delicacy for an everyday 'bonehunter.'" [16]

Hatcher wended his way back to Lusk by July 8, but unfortunately,
the crew had found nothing fantastic during his absence. With Marsh
under financial pressure at the Survey, Marsh apparently presed Hatcher,
when they eventually met in New Haven, to jettison one of the crew,
but Hatcher responded, "Burrell would like very much to continue work
& it seems too bad to let him go." On the fifteenth, from the Peabody,
Marsh made his political and financial predicament clearer to Hatcher:

Dear Mr. Hatcher. –

Yours of July 8th duly received. Glad you found good weather
there, even if men found little during your absence. I think you
must be right that region is about exhausted, at least for big things.
I still have great faith in "Quarry No. 1," however, and I wish I
had a dozen boxes of sand from it, if as good as what we are now
working here. Tell Burrell that I may be able to give him some work
later, but, as we agreed when you were here, we must stop work
at the end of this month.

I do not like the look of things in Washington. The Senate appro-
priation committee, under Mr. Allison, put paleontology back, and
this passed the committee of the whole. Just before the bill passed the
Senate, a raid was made on the Geological Survey, and the whole

appropriation for it was cut down about forty percent. This may be put back in the House, or in the conference and I am inclined to think it will be, but the result no man can tell until the bill is finally passed. I will telegraph you as soon as I have any definite information. Meanwhile, let me know just where a message will reach you if you get out of reach of Lusk to go home or elsewhere.

The weather has been terribly hot since you left, and I am about worn out with trouble, anxiety, and the heat.

Hermann has been cutting down the block containing the skull of Had. No. 2. We find the head was swung around to the left side and lies on the ribs, which are in place, at least the twelve posterior ones.

Yours truly,

(signed) *O. C. Marsh*[17]

Hatcher mailed the vouchers for July on the eighteenth in preparation for wrapping up business and closing down the field operation at the end of the month: $250 for himself, $60 for Sullins, $55 for Cook, and $55 for Burrell. After receiving a telegram from Marsh on the twentieth, Hatcher indicated he'd been watching the papers in regard to the Civil Services Bill in the *Congressional Record* and was very sorry to hear of the misfortune, expressing his willingness and readiness to come to New Haven or go north into Montana at any time. He'd also rented his farm in anticipation of having to work in portions of the country from which he could not easily get home. He planned to take his family to New Haven. Still concerned about losing all of his crew, he asked if Marsh could keep Sullins on the payroll out west, then bring him east for the winter. Hatcher recommended him very highly and intimated that Sulllins would only need $50 per month and would pay his own travel expenses. With the Cross article in his hands, Hatcher had carefully surveyed the sections showing the *Triceratops* beds and those underlying and overlying them. Regardless of the stratigraphic relationships around Denver, he reported:

I nowhere find such a section as he describes there in our region. Our Triceratops beds in Converse Co. Wyoming come entirely within the

Laramie as described by King & Hayden. There is in no instance observed the slightest unconformity between the Triceratops beds & the underlying beds right down through to the Jura which is well represented in one locality to the southeast.[18]

Marsh wrote again on July 25 with more depressing news, but he also pledged to personally cover the expenses of a final prospecting trip north for the season and laid out his priorities for it:

I . . . answered your telegram of the 22d from Long Pine about work after August 1; namely, that you better go north, and I would write you more fully to Lusk.

I returned here Saturday, 23d, pretty well used up with heat and worry. I found the small can of mammal teeth, some of which were very good, and among them what I now take to be a bone of a pterodactyle sufficiently preserved to be described, although much smaller than I expected. Now we have one bone, I presume we will begin to find others, for that is the way luck usually runs.

The news from Washington is very discouraging. Two men that ought to have been friendly to the Survey, Wolcott of Colorado, and Carey of Wyoming, proved to be especially hostile, and are mainly responsible for the damage done, notwithstanding all I have done to make known the paleontology of their respective states. I have found out what the matter is with [Senator E. O.] Wolcott who is friendly to me, but cannot understand why [Senator J. M.] Carey should not be. I hope I have no enemies in Wyoming.

The probabilities now are that I shall not have a single dollar from the Survey after August 1st, during the present fiscal year. The new appropriation will be passed before March 4, but will not be available before July 1st, 1893. There is barely a possibility that the present Congress may do something better before adjournment, which will probably be the last of this week, but possibly not. There is a strong reaction in Washington in favor of the Survey, but it may be too late to help us this year, but at all events, I think we will be all right for next year.

As I shall have to pay for your northern trip myself, I wish you would keep expenses as low as possible. The three things I need most, and hope you will get on the trip, are –

> *(1) The skull of Ceratops, and other remains of the small horned Dinosaurs, the smaller the better.*
> *(2) The skull of carnivorous Laramie Dinosaur, with of course any other smaller remains.*
> *(3) Mammals and other small things from the northern horizons.*

Please send by registered mail the small things, as promptly as you can conveniently, and I enclose a lot more franks for that purpose.

Please also before you start send me your post office and telegraph address along the route, so that I can communicate with you promptly, if necessary.

I may possibly write you again before you start.

Yours very truly,[19]

Then on the twenty-eighth, Marsh wrote again from New Haven after receiving Hatcher's letter of the twenty-second from Long Pine:

I wrote you yesterday a long letter, and received today your letter of the 22d inst. from Long Pine. I am much interested in what you say about the Ceratops beds in Converse county [sic], and those above and below, and I wish we had time and money to follow the question up. I urged Powell before I left Washington to let me do this, but he said he could not promise a dollar unless Congress relented and gave him more than now promised. If that comes, you still have a good chance, but the fossils I wrote you about yesterday are more important to me if I have to pay for everything after August 1, and this may possibly be the last chance at the Laramie.

In closing work at Lusk, you may send all the fossils collected during the month of August as Government freight, but after that date, as I wrote you, either by direct freight, express, or registered mail. If you have a chance to sell at fair prices any of the things you intended to store at Lusk you may do so. I mean the buckboard and similar large things, which you spoke of.

I am sorry that I cannot now promise to give Sullins work here this winter, as the prospects look very bleak at present. As [Adam] Hermann and Thomas [Bostwick] are both cut off, I cannot take anyone else until the Survey is willing to pay for the work, much as I would otherwise like to do so, especially to oblige you and Sullins whom you speak so well of.

I send by this mail copies of my last article, which I am sure will interest you. The Hadrosaurus restoration is nearly finished, and promises to be fine.

Yours very truly, [20]

In addition to the loss of income from his position at the USGS, Marsh now faced a fragile state in his other personal finances. For decades, most of his annual income had come from two funds that had been established for his family by Marsh's uncle, George Peabody. At their zenith in the 1870s, these trusts had provided Marsh with as much as $50,000 per year; however, one trust had basically been liquidated in 1888, after Marsh received a settlement of $37,598, and the other smaller trust could only provide him with an income of about $3,000 per year. Although these amounts were extremely large in relation to the assets of most men, including Hatcher, they put a severe crimp in Marsh's lifestyle. He was eventually forced to mortgage his house to Yale for $30,000 and, for the first time, be placed on the university's payroll.[21]

From Long Pine on the twenty-eighth, Hatcher confirmed that he'd shipped seven crates of mammal-bearing sand when he left Lusk, and indicated that Wortman had written to say they'd been having very poor success. Hatcher closed with a postscript indicating he'd start north August 1 and do his best to make the trip a success. He was in Lusk on the third to meet Sullins and start north.[22]

From Lusk on the fifth, the pair headed west to Douglas, Wyoming, with Hatcher noticing on the way that the "Triceratops beds underlie the coal bearing Laramie of the Shawnee mining district." By the tenth, they had reached Buffalo, Wyoming, and despite the desiccating heat that topped out at 104, the horses were bearing up well. But to date, they had found no fossils. They reached Junction City, Montana, on the fifteenth, where Hatcher learned from Marsh that Congress had failed to appropriate any funding for paleontology. Concerned, Hatcher wondered when Marsh wanted to close the operation, as well as whether he thought they'd be able to work next season if they found a good fossil locality, since he'd need to decide what to do with the horses. He estimated expenses for August would total about $275 including travel, and requested Marsh credit him with $50 on his loans and send the rest to Junction City.[23]

Near Willow Creek, Montana, Hatcher informed Marsh on the twenty-second that they'd found numerous hadrosaur bones, but because those weren't one of Marsh's priorities, he was moving on to Cow Island in the Judith River region. Upon receiving two of Marsh's missives on the twenty-sixth, an annoyed Hatcher arched his back, retorting:

I cannot agree with you that we had "Such poor success at our old localities this season." I am well pleased with my work done there. I shipped you over 15,000 pounds of good bones from there besides many hundred mammal teeth & other small things. A better collection of Mammal teeth than the Am. Museum party got. I consider Had. Skel. 2 & Skull 31 both good finds & we got many other good things besides. Ten years ago you would have considered our success phenomenal. I shall certainly do my best for the rest of the season elsewhere & hope to send you many good things yet this fall. I work early & late, Sunday & Monday & now that I have only one man who has to stay & watch camp I have it all to do myself which does not discourage me in the least. A collector in this country has some hardship to bear, but neither bad water, hot weather, cold, chilly rains or anything else affects me as it does to find that my efforts have not been appreciated by you. It was certainly a misfortune that the box containing Skull 31 came in broken up. But this I consider no fault of mine but of the R.R. employees, for it could have only

been broken by being dumped off a platform or out of a car & I
labeled it this side up. With care, etc.

Accentuating his stress, Hatcher had received a letter from Anna saying
their oldest boy, Earl, fell and hurt his hip so he was unable to move
his leg. The doctor came twice but was unable to locate the injury or do
anything to relieve his severe and perpetual pain. Also, Hatcher was still
unable to find anything other than hadrosaur bones, of which he'd packed
a couple of crates. He informed Marsh that Burrell had undertaken collecting in the Miocene and wondered if Marsh wanted to purchase the
collection. Hatcher also seemed pleased with the man to whom he'd
rented his farm. He had a wife but no children, so he didn't think they'd
"tear up things and mar the house." Anna was boarding with them until
Hatcher returned to take her east. All in all, Hatcher seemed soured on
fieldwork, confessing,

> *I do not know that I care whether I ever work in the field again*
> *after this year. Of course I want to do whatever suits you best . . .*
> *but if . . . you do not know as you will ever do any more field work*
> *after this year, it will work no misfortune to me. . . . For I had*
> *quite as soon be in New Haven with my family.*[24]

Although rain held up Hatcher's parade through the Judith region around
the twenty-seventh, at least he received clarifying news from Anna
regarding their eldest son's injury. The doctor had finally diagnosed the
problem; his leg was broken just above the knee and had finally been
set. Unfortunately, he had had to suffer through four days and nights of
excruciating pain before the doctor used chloroform to put him under
and perform the procedure. Hatcher was also saddened to hear on the
tenth that all paleontological work had halted at the Peabody, except
for one preparator, Hugh Gibb, who was apparently on the university
payroll rather than the USGS funds. Nonetheless, Hatcher got a chuckle
out of Marsh's news that Osborn had handed over his mammals to
Cope, derisively declaring, "I presume he has learned ere this the difference between Stagodon [a small Cretaceous mammal] & Squalodon [a

Cenozoic shark-toothed whale]." Hatcher and Sullins reached Judith by September 10, but they found "nothing of importance." As with his earlier excursion to the region, he planned to work his way down the other side of the Missouri over the next two weeks. To conclude, Hatcher asked Marsh if he still wanted to sell or rent a small house he owned in New Haven, and if so, might he be willing to sell it to Hatcher, who offered to pay $500 down and the rest over the next two years. His source of funds would be the sale of his horses, which had brought in $780.[25]

Hatcher mailed a tin box containing the tooth of a large carnivorous dinosaur on the eighteenth, saying that the tooth came from freshwater beds overlying the marine beds. The only large carnivorous dinosaur tooth collected by Hatcher in 1892 is now housed at the Peabody Museum, where it is catalogued as belonging to *Tyrannosaurus* and listed as coming from the Hell Creek Formation in Montana (YPM VP 8228). He'd also found what he thought to be a hadrosaur sacrum (YPM VP 3224) with seven vertebrae attached, but bones were frustratingly sparse. Beyond that, Hatcher lamented that his once burgeoning band of bone hunters had depressingly disappeared:

> *Well I'm alone now and this is a pretty desolate country to be alone in too. Sullins left me day before yesterday. He let on to get mad because I worked so late & did not get in in time for my meals. But I think he quit to take an all winter's job here at Judith. He told me that if he could find work up in this country he would like to stay here this winter. So the time I went to Judith I spoke to Mr. Norris the man who lives there & told him what a good man Sullins was & that I would be glad if he could give him work when I got through with him. He said he needed just such a man then & would like to have him any time & that he would keep a place for him. The day he quit me he had been to Judith for the mail & I suppose had a talk with the clerk there as Norris himself was gone. So that night when I came in he had supper ready & as I went to sit down to eat he spoke for the first time & said that if I could not come in before dark for my meals I could get another cook – he'd be d—d if he'd cook for me. He'd get me my breakfast in the morning*

& that would be the last d—d meal he'd get. I just told him that there were no strings on him & he need not stay to get breakfast for me but to "pull his freight" at once as I did not want a man who could not be civil. It was only seven o'clock then & not yet dark for I took out my watch to see the time of day & could see without a light. I do not know what to do exactly. There are no men here & I do not know where I could get a man. I will work alone until the first of Oct. or longer if you think best & especially if I can find anything. But it is rather up-hill business alone. I wish you would telegraph me when you receive this letter just what you wish me to do.

On the twenty-seventh, Marsh telegraphed and tersely told Hatcher to use his best judgment about continuing work. In short, it seems that Hatcher surrendered and simply headed home. In retrospect, that seems an unbelievably unceremonious way to end a nine-year-long odyssey of fossil collecting that would go down in paleontological history and lore as among the most successful ever.[26]

Continuing his string of successful seasons in the 68- to 66-million-year-old sediments of Wyoming's Lance Creek badlands, Hatcher amassed another impressive suite of multituberculates (*Allacodon, Cimolodon, Cimolomys, Meniscoessus, Mesodma,* and "Oracodon," which is now called *Meniscoessus*); marsupials (*Alphadon, Didelphodon, Didelphops,* and *Pediomys*); and placentals (*Cimolestes* and *Gypsonictops*). The collection also contained the sturgeon *Acipenser.* Among amphibians are found the salamanders *Habrosaurus, Opisthotriton, Prodesmodon,* and *Scapherpeton.* Among the reptiles, he also tallied turtles (*Aspideretes, Axestemys,* and *Baena*); lizards (*Chamops, Contogenys, Odaxosaurus, Parasaniwa, Pelto-saurus, Leptochamops, Meniscognathus,* and "Prionosaurus," which is now called *Exostinus,* as well as "Lanceosaurus," which is now called *Chamops*); a snake (*Coniophis*); a crocodile (*Brachychampsa*); and dinosaurs (*Edmonto-saurus, Paronychodon, Aublysodon, Tyrannosaurus, Triceratops,* and *Troodon*), as well as birds such as a loon (*Gavia*).

No further documents cover correspondence that ensued during the months of October, November, or nearly all of December. Yet it's clear that the cogs of bureaucracy were churning. A draft document dated

December 31, 1892, appears in the record that states Hatcher would release Marsh from their contract one year from that date if Marsh provided Hatcher with a satisfactory recommendation and allowed Hatcher to use that recommendation to help secure another position. If Hatcher secured a position before the end of 1892, then Hatcher would release Marsh from their contract at that time. The nature of the position that Hatcher sought was initially described as an assistant geologist or paleontologist on staff of a museum in charge of field or museum work and with the liberty to publish research. The salary sought was $1,500 per college year, and Hatcher agreed to teach if required.[27]

Marsh, no doubt with Hatcher's input, then drafted by hand the required letter of recommendation on Yale University Museum letterhead, which was signed off as being satisfactory by Hatcher:

Jan 10th 1893

Mr. J. B. Hatcher, a graduate of the Sheffield Scientific School, Yale University has for nearly nine years been in my employ as assistant in Paleontology engaged in collecting vertebrate fossils and in Museum work. During all this time, he has shown great ability and industry, and has given entire satisfaction. The discoveries he has made are known to all paleontologists.

I regret that for financial reasons, I cannot retain his services, and heartily recommend him to any institution needing such an assistant.

(signed) *O. C. Marsh*[28]

Next, Hatcher hand-drafted an advertisement for the job he wanted that would be placed in Yale's *American Journal of Science* and other similar publications:

Wanted – By a graduate of the S. S. S. of Yale Univ. A position as assistant on geology and/or paleontology, especially vertebrate paleontology in any institution having a department of vertebrate paleontology or wishing to establish such. Has had nine years experience as assistant to Prof. O. C. Marsh. Will divide time between instruction, museum & field work if desired. Can furnish excellent references.

J. B. Hatcher
Yale Museum
New Haven, Ct.

Note at bottom of page:
   Hatcher started collecting for Marsh June 25, 1884 and since Hatcher "had nine years experience as assistant to Prof. O. C. Marsh" the date of the note must be 1893. I know that Hatcher quarreled much with Marsh during that year. C. Schuchert.[29]

Participation by lawyers for Yale and perhaps a lawyer for Hatcher resulted in the final memorandum of agreement, which detailed the elements required for the eventual dissolution of the contract between Marsh and Hatcher. Signed and dated on January 10, 1893, it stipulated that Hatcher would remain in Marsh's employ under the existing contractual conditions until he found a position that satisfied his stated requirements at another institution.[30] (See appendix 1)

According to Daniel L. Brinkman, current museum assistant II at Yale's Peabody Museum, there is reason to believe that Marsh did, indeed, continue to pay Hatcher for the two or so months that he spent at the Peabody Museum in late 1892 and early 1893, while writing his first two scientific publications (Hatcher 1893 a, b). In Hatcher's 1891 contract with Marsh, the two agreed that Hatcher could publish on the geology of the Ceratops and Titanotherium beds under his own name (appendix 1). Hatcher returned to the Peabody by at least Dececember 5, 1892, when he submitted his Ceratops beds paper for publication, and it appears that he was there until at least January 16, 1893, the date on which he submitted his Titanotherium beds paper. Beyond that, the terms of his revised contract with Marsh dated January 10, 1893 stated that Marsh had to keep Hatcher employed until Hatcher got a decent job offer from somewhere else. These facts shed a somewhat different light on Marsh not only as an employer but a gentleman. By (1) covering the costs of Hatcher's last few months of fieldwork out of his own pocket; (2) sticking to the terms of their 1891 and revised 1893 contracts by continuing to pay Hatcher until he found a new position while allowing him to publish on the geology of the Ceratops and Titanotherium beds; and (3) writing a supportive letter of recommendation that helped Hatcher get a new job at Princeton, Marsh appears to have been a much more loyal and supportive employer than usually portrayed. Perhaps Marsh actually took a few of his former assistants' personal jabs that appeared in the *New York Herald* articles to heart, thereby transforming him into a better employer and a better man, at least as far as his working relationship with Hatcher was concerned. The appreciation that Hatcher felt toward Marsh's treatment of him during these difficult days may also be latently reflected in a statement Hatcher made to his colleague, Charles Schuchert, who asked Hatcher, long after Hatcher had left Yale, which of the paleontologists for whom he had worked Hatcher preferred the most. "Hatcher replied, with feeling, 'Marsh was the best of them all!'" And Hatcher would amplify that sentiment more formally in print on the first page of his *Diplodocus* monograph in 1901:

> *Where a generation ago the extinct vertebrate life of America was but poorly represented in our museums by imperfect series of teeth and isolated bones, we are now able to study many of these extinct animals from more or less complete skeletons. For these improved conditions we are mainly indebted to the late Professor Marsh, either directly by reason of the vast collections acquired by him, or indirectly through the improved laboratory and field methods developed by him and his assistants.*[31]

In any event, the oft-tempestuous tandem of Hatcher and Marsh left an indelible mark that still mesmerizes paleontologists and the public. Few among us have never heard of their dinosaurian superstar, *Triceratops*, and *Torosaurus* is still the topic of impassioned scientific debate. The minuscule mammals that Hatcher discovered and Marsh described not only opened a new, 66-million-year-old window on the origins of our evolutionary cousins, with which we still share the earth; they also continue to underpin research regarding how mass extinction events, such as the one at the end of the Cretaceous, might affect our own future. These discoveries, paired with Hatcher's acute geologic insights and innovative collecting techniques, such as the gridded quarry map for the Long Island rhino site, still reverberate across many aspects of modern paleontological research.

SECTION III
1893–1900

10

From Princeton to the Plains with an Eye on Patagonia

Hatcher's quest for a new position focused on being hired permanently at a more formal, curatorial level, with privileges to publish his own research. His hunt came to a head in February 1893, with two institutions vying for his services—Princeton and the Philadelphia Academy of Sciences. On February 4, Hatcher wrote William Berryman Scott, the head of vertebrate paleontology at Princeton, with whom he'd been in negotiations, to inform him:

> *There is a very fair chance for me at Philadelphia so far as salary is concerned, but that is not the most important point for me now. From my conversation with Prof. Cope and Pres. Wistar I think I should not be justified in looking for a position there as*

permanent. . . . I think there is little doubt, but that I shall accept
your offer. Shall give you a definite reply next week.

It's interesting to note that whether Hatcher joined Cope in Philadelphia
or Cope's disciple Scott at Princeton, he would essentially be switching
sides and deserting Marsh. Furthermore, as Paul Brinkman points out,
Osborn, despite being unable to snag Hatcher's services for the AMNH,
was satisfied with having Hatcher under his friend Scott's supervision.
That would allow Osborn to obtain duplicates of specimens that Hatcher
collected, along with the locality data regarding where they were collected. Additionally, having Hatcher at Scott's poorly funded department at Princeton was much better than Hatcher working for Osborn's
wealthier rivals in Chicago or Pittsburgh.[1]

In fact, as the negotiations with Scott were proceeding, Hatcher had
made a heartfelt attempt to bury the hatchet with Osborn by penning a
three-page epistle to him on January 11. During a visit to the AMNH,
Hatcher learned "that representations were made to you . . . that in the
unfortunate affair between us some two years ago Prof. Marsh had to
raise my salary in order to retain me. In other words that he bought
me off." Hatcher pleaded for an opportunity to refute this account.
Osborn had met Hatcher in New Haven on January 7, 1891 and had
seen Hatcher's December 22, 1890 contract with Marsh in which his
salary was $1,800 per year. Apparently, during their meeting, Osborn
had given Hatcher a check to repay his loan from Marsh. Hatcher, with
Peterson in tow, immediately had taken Osborn's check to Marsh, who
refused to accept it, and apparently in an emotional attempt to retain
Hatcher's services, had "appealed to my loyalty to Yale, his own age
etc." Hatcher maintained that nothing had been said about any salary
increase and maintained that Peterson, who now worked for Osborn at
the AMNH, could testify to that fact. Hatcher had returned Osborn's
check by express the next day, and only later that afternoon had Marsh
approached Hatcher with the amendments to the December 22 contract,
which included the salary raise to $2,000 per year and other inducements.
Hatcher implored Osborn to confirm this account of events with Peterson
and Wortman, who was also familiar with the situation and then worked

for Osborn. In closing, Hatcher came clean by showing his hand in this long-running game of professional poker:

> *I wish to say that there never was one minute of the time that I did not want to go with you. In remaining with Marsh I consulted neither my own interest nor desires. I stayed with him against my own judgement & out of pure sympathy with him. I am fully convinced of how ill deserving he was of that sympathy. I am not asking or seeking sympathy from you or any other man in this matter; what I did that was wrong I am willing to bear the blame for. I should like an opportunity to explain my position.*

But Osborn, clearly feeling he held a hand to trump Hatcher's, was not ready to reconcile. He responded to Hatcher on the twentieth that the only "personal differences" between him and Hatcher remained "the offensive language in two letters, which I have already asked you to retract. I trust you will now think it best to do so . . . and I expect a very full retraction from you, before I will consent to renew our acquaintance." However, Osborn's rejection of Hatcher's peaceful entreaty prompted the pugnacious paleontologist to respond in a challenging parry:

> *I will say that if you will state that the errors and omissions in your copy of our correspondence were of a typographical nature only and not intentional on your part, I will gladly withdraw any and all accusations of dishonesty I have made against you. This I consider the fair and proper thing between us.*[2]

By February 23, the agreement between Hatcher and Scott had been finalized. Scott later wrote, "Several of my generous friends contributed to paying Hatcher's salary" before Princeton took over, and one of those "friends" was none other than the wily Osborn. Essentially, Hatcher would lead the ongoing Princeton Scientific Expeditions during the spring and summer months, during which he would instruct students in geology, paleontology, and field techniques, in addition to serving as the curator of vertebrate paleontology in the Elizabeth Marsh Museum of Geology and Archaeology at Princeton, where he would oversee the curation and preparation of the fossils, as well as conduct some research. In fact, as Scott states, the students were essential to these enterprises, for "the young men generally made their contributions large enough to finance Hatcher and enable him to begin work as soon as the weather permitted" in the field. This system led to advantages and liabilities. By all accounts, Hatcher was attentive and helpful as an instructor, and he made sure to mix business with pleasure by leading his fledglings on scenic side trips through the West; however, when the students were in the field, "there was no pretense of doing any work," at least not as much as Hatcher would have liked. In preparing for the 1893 expedition, Hatcher submitted a budget for the list of field gear that would be required to carry out his imminent collecting initiative to the White River deposits in Nebraska and South Dakota, as well as a brief foray to the Laramie in Wyoming. The list included the usual items, such as horses, harness, saddle, bridle, tarp, stove, cooking equipment, tools, packing materials, provisions and rail tickets, all totaling $314. But Hatcher requested a couple of other essential items, such as having specialized Marsh picks made at Yale, with which he'd become accustomed, along with one other addition to his outfit, inspired by Scott: "If you can get me a mattress like the one you had with you in '90, I shall be very glad of it." He also suggested acquiring another item for the Princeton lab that he'd seen at Yale—a "revolving stool on which large specimens can be placed . . . & easily turned in any position." In a keeping-up-with-the-Joneses tone, Hatcher mentioned that the AMNH had also adopted this handy apparatus. In terms of scheduling, Hatcher agreed with Marsh that he would quit at Yale on April 1, but with accrued vacation time, Hatcher would be ready to leave New York by train for the field on March 28, with some time set aside to visit his folks in Iowa, as well as Anna and the children in Long Pine.[3]

May 3 found Hatcher well ensconced in the field near Hay Springs, Nebraska, where his crew included twelve well-heeled students from Princeton—three seniors and nine juniors, as well as Scott and his colleague, William A. Libbey III, Princeton's professor of geography and the son of Elizabeth Marsh, for whom the museum at Princeton was named. Scott was dazzled with Hatcher's acumen:

Monday, Hatcher and I spent up on the buttes, getting up some fine things he lately found and in the more difficult task of getting the heavy bundles down the fearfully steep hill. It would make your hair stand on end, to see the terrible places where Hatcher would take a heavily loaded horse; places where you would not imagine it possible for a horse to go at all.

Spring snows hampered their early season collecting, but Hatcher reported they were beginning to have "better success." They had not been alone in the area, although AMNH's collector, Jacob Wortman, had just broken camp to head off to the Eocene deposits of the Bridger Basin in Wyoming. By August 15, the crew had completed work in the Big Badlands of South Dakota after packing four crates of bones. Money was short, so several students apparently decided to head home. However, before leaving, they kicked in funds to support Hatcher's thrust into Wyoming at the end of the season with the five remaining students. Until then, Hatcher and his diminished entourage broke camp and headed to Chadron, Nebraska, to continue collecting in the White River deposits.[4]

In his synopsis of the 1893 Princeton Scientific Expedition published in the *Princeton College Bulletin*, Scott seemed especially pleased with the results, proclaiming that it was conducted "very much more successfully, than any of the preceding ones—a result which is altogether due to the energy, experience and skill of Mr. Hatcher." During the first phase in April and May, which emphasized collecting in the "Loup Fork and Equus beds of northern Nebraska," Hatcher had documented an unconformity, or gap in the record of geologic time, between these two rock units that helped explain the difference in their fossilized faunas.[5]

The Equus beds, with their two species of the modern horse genus *Equus*, along with the dog genus *Canis*, the sloth *Mylodon*, and what Scott identified as *Elephas, Eschatius, Holomeniscus*, and a small deer and antelope, seemed to be Pleistocene in Scott's view, in agreement with an earlier assessment by renowned geologist Grove K. Gilbert. The crew's work in the Loup Fork beds produced the early cat named *Pseudaelurus*, along with two undetermined genera of carnivores, the rhino *Aphelops*, the horse *Protohippus*, the camels *Procamelus* and *Pliauchenia*, as well as the elephantine *Mastodon*. Scott judged these to represent a Miocene-aged fauna. Scott also argued that three distinct biostratigraphic levels could be found within the Loup Fork beds, with the middle one, which he termed Loup Fork proper, being exposed widely from Nebraska to Texas and defined by the presence of the antelope-like *Cosoryx* and the horse, *Protohippus*. The "principal part" of the expedition focused on the White River beds near the Big Badlands in South Dakota about thirty miles east of Hermosa. Collections were made from all three subdivisions of the Oligocene White River beds present in the region: the uppermost "Protoceras beds" first recognized by Wortman, the "Oreodon beds" in the middle, and the "Titanotherium beds" at the base of the sequence.[6]

However, the most unusual find of this bountiful expedition was the discovery of "two remarkably perfect skulls" of legless amphisbaenoid lizards, the first fossil specimens of this interesting limbless group ever found, which were given over to Marsh's former assistant, Georg Baur, to study in Chicago. In addition, a previously unknown dwarf species of crocodile was discovered in the "Titanotherium beds." Additional genera in the expedition's haul from the White River beds included four species of rodents, one rabbit, four carnivorans, two carnivorous creodonts, one brontothere, three rhinos, one horse, one tapir, two antelope-like ungulates, three oreodonts, a giant pig-like entelodont, a hippo-like anthracothere, and a peccary. Hatcher's late season sojourn to the Laramie in Wyoming produced "a considerable number of the extremely interesting and valuable" Cretaceous mammals.[7]

Today, all of the 257 specimens from the 1893 Princeton Scientific Expedition are housed in Yale's Peabody Museum of Natural History, following the announcement in 1985 that all of Princeton's vertebrate fossil collection would be transferred to Yale. The Peabody's specimen catalogue reveals that they are now identified as follows: Hatcher's foray to the 68-to 66-million-year-old beds of the Lance Formation yielded the bowfin fish (*Amia*), as well as the gar (*Lepisosteus*) and the mackerel shark *Myledaphus*. Salamanders are represented by *Habrosaurus*, *Scapherpeton*, and *Cuttysarkus*, which some now call *Prodesmodon*. The lizards included *Palaeosaniwa* and *Peltosaurus*, while snakes are represented by *Coniophis*.

Two crocodiles (*Brachychampsa* and *Leidyosuchus*) were found, along with the crocodile-like *Champsosaurus*. The only nonavian dinosaur collected was a specimen of the distant relative of plant-eating duckbills, *Thescelosaurus*. Birds include the shorebird, *Cimolopteryx*, and the mammals are represented by the multituberculate *Meniscoessus*.

The seemingly scant sample from the 37- to 34-million-year-old beds of the Chadron Formation contained a spectacular *Alligator* skeleton, along with a rabbit (*Palaeolagus*), a primitive camel (*Poebrotherium*), a peccary (*Perchoerus*), two rhinos (*Hyracodon* and *Subhyracodon*), and the brontotheres "Titanotherium" and "Brontotherium," which are now called *Megacerops*.

In contrast, Hatcher's payoff from prospecting in the 34- to 30-million-year-old beds of the Brule Formation produced several genera of oreodonts *Eporeodon, Merycoidodon, Leptauchenia,* and "Hadroleptauchenia," which is now called *Leptauchenia*; another ungulate (*Agriochoerus*); the anthracotheres (*Bothriodon, Heptacodon,* and *Elomeryx*); some rhinos (*Hyracodon, Subhyracodon, Metamynodon, Amphicaeonpus,* and "Caenopus," which is now called *Subhyracodon*); a tapir (*Colodon*); the carnivorous creodont *Hyaenodon*; an amphicyonid "bear dog" (*Cynodictis*); the saber-toothed carnivorans *Dinictis* and *Hoplophoneus*; the "terror pigs" *Elotherium, Scaptohyus,* and *Entelodon*; several rodents (*Eumys,* "Scottimus," and *Ischyromys*); the small deer-like *Leptomeryx* and *Protoceras*; the horses *Mesohippus* and *Miohippus*; the rabbit *Palaeolagus*; the peccary *Perchoerus*; the turtle *Stylemys*; along with the lizards *Rhineura, Hyporhineura,* and *Peltosaurus,* as well as a snake in the boa family called *Calamagrus*.

Only a single specimen of the hippo-like anthracothere *Elomeryx* was collected from the 32- to 30-million-year-old beds of the upper part of the Brule Formation called the Poleslide Member.

At other Miocene sites in Nebraska, Hatcher and his crew collected specimens of the amphicyonid "bear dog" *Aelurodon*; the oreodont *Merychyus*; the rhino *Teleoceras*; two horse genera (*Neohipparion* and *Protohippus*); the camel *Procamelus*; and the fox *Vulpes*. Some Pleistocene localities in Nebraska produced specimens of the dog *Canis*; the horse *Equus*; the small deer-like *Hayoceras*; the mastodon *Mammuthus*; the ground sloth *Mylodon*; and the turtle *Chrysemys*.

In addition to the collections, Hatcher's bibliography reveals that in accordance with his agreement with Marsh, he published scientific papers, which were submitted while he was still at Yale, on the "Ceratops" beds and the "Titanotherium" beds. (See Hatcher bibliography)

As the calendar rolled over to 1894, Hatcher and Scott put plans together for the 11th Princeton Scientific Expedition, on which one senior and nine juniors would participate beginning in mid-June. But by February 27, Hatcher was already out at the Pine Ridge Indian Agency in South Dakota, arranging for the permit to collect on Agency land, which constituted the Oglala Lakota Native American reservation. However, his title and role at Princeton were also on his mind, and he sought to clarify his position with Scott involving some potential personnel changes in the department in the wake of one staff member's departure, which had been left unresolved before he left for the field: "I should prefer to remain . . . with you in the vertebrates & be absolutely free from the other departments of the museum . . . [but] instead of being classed as "Other Officers of the University" I want to be placed with the instructors as "Assistant in Geology & Curator of Vertebrate Paleontology." Basically, another colleague in invertebrate paleontology was presently listed as "Curator of the E. M. Museum," and Hatcher chaffed that ". . . it appears as though I were under him directly." Hatcher went on to say that some of Scott's remarks made a few days before Hatcher left for the field in regard to staffing issues "created a feeling in my mind that perhaps either yourself or Prof. [William] Libbey was somewhat disappointed in me. Now if such be the case just tell me where the difficulty is & I will try to remedy it & in the event I am unable to do so will step out and let others have a chance."[8]

Aided by excellent weather, Hatcher wrote on March 9 from his camp in Big Badlands that he'd found good "Oreodon" and *Leptauchenia* skeletons, *Aceratherium* skulls and jaws, an *Elotherium*, two "Hyopotamus" skeletons, and most unusually, a partial peccary skeleton and lower jaws that someone had previously found and "knocked the stuffing out of." In all, there was already enough to fill "a good-sized box." Nearby, James W. Gidley of the AMNH was also having good success, but the "representative of the great O. C." had not shown up yet. In fact, harkening back to his days with Marsh, Hatcher was angling with Scott to hire Burwell to collect for a month in April for $25. In terms of comforts in camp, Hatcher profusely expressed his thanks to Scott: "I tell you I have a glorious bed with that mattress & the 8 blankets. It is sure fit for a queen to say nothing of a bug hunter." But those thanks were prelude to an ambitious request that followed:

> *How about that South American trip. What can be done about it! I should like immensely to go & I think it can be done with $1000, or $1500. . . . I will give $50 per month toward it from the time I start until I return with the understanding that I be remunerated for it within 5 years. By doing this I believe that if I leave Princeton with say $700 it will be sufficient. . . . The plan at present is to sail from New York about Aug. 15th. . . . I am willing to go for 9 months or one or two years. I think it a great chance & will do my best, if it can be carried out.*[9]

Three days later, despite a little snow, Hatcher recounted a maddening moment that occurred while he was collecting what he thought was an *Aceratherium* skull from an overhanging ledge of sandstone. After furiously picking and prying, "I . . . finally got the thing loose as nice as a tin whistle, but it was too much for me . . . & had to let it go over the ledge about 40 feet. I stayed with it as long as I could & then let go to save myself only to see it break in three or four pieces. Well of course I made the air about me blue for a few minutes." Disgusted, he tempestuously started off in another direction to prospect but soon thought better of it and descended to assess the damage. While trimming the block down, "a fortunate stroke of the pick brought off a slab of rock exposing the entire crest on top of the skull . . . and showed the thing to be not Aceratherium but Diceratherium or a closely allied form, at any rate it is certainly the ancestor of the John Day Diceratherium." Jolted from agony into ecstasy, Hatcher sought Scott's permission to publish on the new rhino. Nonetheless, Hatcher was concerned with his personal financial state: "My expenses last winter in Princeton were $265 more than my salary," which led him to entertain the prospect of collecting for Cope during his vacation time after the expedition was completed. But that didn't stop Hatcher from making a pitch for the Patagonian project in the same paragraph, in which he again offered to "give $50 per month and possibly more to be reimbursed in five years" after the expedition was completed. He closed by expressing sorrow if anything he'd said about the staffing issues in his February 27 letter had hurt Scott's feelings because he had not meant to. "I hope you will always feel free to discuss anything in regard to the work with me for I am sure my whole interest is in it."[10]

Hatcher's next report on the sixteenth revealed that he'd found another specimen that seemed insignificant at first glance but upon more careful examination a couple of days later "proved to be a splendid skull of Hyaenodon horridus" complete with the lower jaws and a front limb. That, in addition to an *Aceratherium* skull and lower jaws, a *Hyracodon* skull and jaws, and a peccary skull with a lower jaw, made a haul of three hefty crates. Regarding competing parties in the area, Hatcher sarcastically spewed, "Well the Great Stillwell-Marsh combination pulled in this afternoon, so there will be plenty of competition in the big camps . . . [but] bones in the sandstones that are worth taking & have not an American Museum or Princeton label on them are very scarce." By the twenty-fourth, as a blizzard hit, Hatcher's brother-in-law Peterson had arrived to bolster the AMNH crew, leading Hatcher to reassure Scott, "It will now be two to one but then we will get there." Hatcher was thrilled that Scott was pleased with the peccary fossils, for he had found more, although male *Protoceras* material was proving to be elusive in the extreme. Once again, Hatcher badgered Scott about the Patagonian expedition and implored Scott to accept his commitment of $50 per month in the calculations for the project's budget. Although the blizzard created drifts up to ten feet deep in the draws, Hatcher managed to excavate a "Hyopotamus" with a skull, lower jaws, and front limb. He'd also found another peccary skull, along with a carnivore skull and skeleton that seemed too large to belong to the saber-toothed carnivores *Hoplophoneus* or *Dinictis*, which both puzzled and intrigued him. Although Gidley had found another *Protoceras* skull, Hatcher lamented, "I seem to be out of luck on Protoceras this year." Nonetheless, he had four crates full and numerous other specimens in sight, while Marsh's crew remained shut out by the blizzard.[11]

After receiving a letter from Scott on March 25, Hatcher penned a passionate response on April 2, expressing his surprise that Scott had raised an objection to Hatcher publishing a paper on the "Diceratherium" specimen he'd found, especially after he'd prepared it for study during the blizzard. It turns out that Scott and his imperious, former Princeton classmate Osborn had arranged for Hatcher to share a camp and equipment with Gidley and Peterson from the AMNH, with each crew collecting independently for their respective institutions. Perhaps Hatcher—who was still miffed at Osborn for the conflict they'd had when Osborn tried to hire him away from Marsh and then besmirched his reputation—bristled that Scott might bow to Osborn's wish that Osborn should publish first on the "Diceratherium" material. Neither Hatcher nor the AMNH crew had known that Osborn had any *Diceratherium* specimens. Beyond that, Gidley and Peterson assured Hatcher that AMNH had "nothing like the skull I have." Hatcher chafed, "I do not see why I should take second place to [AMNH] even if they have found out since Gidley wrote them of my find that they have something which may be like it." Hatcher couldn't comprehend why Scott thought Princeton owed the AMNH anything "for the assistance they are giving us," since Hatcher felt "they are giving us nothing." He reminded Scott that the institutions were dividing the expenses of the expedition equally and the AMNH crew was using Hatcher's tent as well as the picks he'd provided. So, "I can not concede . . . that I am indebted to them . . . & do not like to be considered a parasite," which he knew neither of his field colleagues considered him to be. Since Hatcher was competing two against one, why should he and Scott make such an unjust concession? Despite this manpower disadvantage, Hatcher relished the challenge, proclaiming, "My idea is Princeton first, last, & always." That's why he wanted to describe "Diceratherium." But if Scott disagreed, he would not "do anything that might be . . . considered a breach" of Scott's authority. But Hatcher continued in the same vein regarding Patagonia:

I hope our Patagonia trip will materialize no matter what the Am. Museum people do. I had rather undertake it alone . . . & I can do it quite as cheaply alone. Let's go ahead and do it. . . . The next 10 years is our best for collecting. So why not make the best of it. By working hard we are sure to make the expeditions popular and successful which will be sure to interest some men of means. . . . So let's sail in and accomplish it regardless of the Am. Mus. $1500 will be a great plenty I am sure & it will be all the better if we do it alone.[12]

A few days later, Hatcher was surprised by Scott's generosity in sending him a new pair of boots, after asking his boss earlier if he had an old pair he could spare, since the pair he'd brought out had worn through. Hatcher then somewhat anxiously mentioned he'd bought two specimens of the intimidating carnivore *Hyaenodon horridus* from another collector, H. F. Wells. They were contained in one block, and one had a perfect skull, whereas the other had a less complete skull but most of the skeleton, although Hatcher seemed confident he could recover more of the other skeleton. In addition, he'd bought a perfect skull of *Hoplophoneus*, a skull of the carnivore "Hyaenodon cruciens," and a skull of the antilope-like *Protoceras* from near the base of the "Oreodon beds." Also included was abundant material of the rhino, *Metamynodon*, a skull, and some juvenile dentitions of the pig-like *Elotherium*, a splendid skull of "Titanotherium," and two partial horse skeletons with complete legs and feet, all from the "Metamynodon beds."[13]

Hatcher warily concluded his account of his purchase by saying, "I gave $215 for it all. I hope you will not get scared at this. It is certainly very cheap." He asked Scott to temporarily use the funds he had for purchasing fossils in order to cover the check Hatcher had written Wells. Then Hatcher laid out a plan to make reductions in the expedition's budget by providing horses of his own and not hiring laborers to care for them in order to reimburse Scott's fund for purchasing specimens. Hatcher didn't want Scott to use the funds for purchasing specimens because he wanted to save them for helping pay for the Patagonian expedition. He then hastened to emphasize that he had found an impressive set of specimens on his own, including four *Metamynodon* skulls and skeletal material, which he knew was a high priority on Scott's wish list, although he was somewhat embarrassed to admit that he'd discovered them the day after he'd purchased the collection from Wells with several *Metamynodon* specimens. He'd also found four specimens of the oreodont relative, *Agriochoerus*—all with good teeth and three with partial skeletons including the hind feet—that convinced Hatcher that *Agriochoerus* and "Artionyx" were actually the same genus. Hatcher would send these key elements, which he'd found just above the "Metamynodon beds," to Scott immediately so he could make the necessary comparisons for himself. He'd also found a nearly complete skeleton of "Hyaenodon cruciens" and three nice horse feet in the "Oredon beds."[14]

By the twenty-fourth, Hatcher had received a letter from the students who would join the expedition saying that they wanted to meet him at Chadron then visit the Pine Ridge Reservation and Agency, the Big Badlands, the Black Hills, and Yellowstone Park. Hatcher noted that this itinerary would require an overland round trip of 1,200 miles, leaving little time for prospecting and collecting. Personally, Hatcher would rather spend his time collecting, "for I want to make our collection, what it should be, the most complete and representative collection in the country." Although he'd love to see Yellowstone since he had yet to do so, he sought Scott's advice and vowed to abide by his guidance: "I will go with them to Alaska if they want to go & you think best & come back by way of Florida or the Isthmus." But he needed Scott's decision immediately so he could arrange for horses and other necessities. In Hatcher's next report, he'd discovered that one of the *Elotherium* skeletons he'd acquired in his big purchase came in a block that actually contained another skeleton of this animal.[15]

The best was "a daisy" and had a well-preserved skull and lower jaws along with the skeleton, in which "I do not think there is a bone missing." Hatcher mused, "He was a queer fellow with such a clumsy head & such slender & graceful limbs & feet. He was very tall for his length." Still trying to justify his purchase, Hatcher exclaimed, "I would not take $1000 for that skeleton alone." Besides, he was now angling to make another purchase that included specimens of a smaller *Elotherium* skull, an "A No. 1" skull and lower jaws of "Aceratherium occidentale," a *Dinictis* skull, a skull and partial skeleton of the primitive camel *Poebrotherium*, a lower jaw of "Titanotherium," and a considerable portion of a *Hyaenodon horridus* skeleton. Hatcher excitedly added, "$100 takes the whole layout," before conceding that he realized they'd already spent $300 on purchasing specimens. Hatcher had also gone across the White River to reconnoiter a nearby region and found it to be promising country for his elusive quarry, *Protoceras*. Scott had apparently decided he'd take the students to Yellowstone, which wasn't surprising, since the students' families provided funding for these expeditions, and Hatcher rationalized that since they were going that direction, he "could make a strike at the Wasatch," meaning the early Eocene deposits in the Wasatch Basin.[16]

By the twentieth, Wortman from the AMNH had joined the camp, and Hatcher had hatched a logistical plan for the Yellowstone junket; a week before they embarked from the Black Hills, he'd send the team and saddle horses to Sheridan, Wyoming. Then a few days afterward, they'd take the railroad to Sheridan, meet the horses, and drive to the park. Hatcher made all those arrangements by May 30 and set about arranging to purchase the $100 collection previously mentioned after Scott's apparent approval. He also brought up from Long Pine "as good a four horse team as ever came into this part of the country." In other business, Wortman identified one of the small *Hyaenodon* specimens Hatcher had acquired as his new species, *H. pancidens*, and Hatcher's description of the *Diceratherium* skull he found came out in the May issue of *Geologist*, thus documenting that Scott had given him approval to write and publish it.[17]

The contingent of Princeton students arrived by June 22, and everyone was doing well despite an encounter with a tornado in Chadron that destroyed several buildings and killed one of the townspeople. Upon leaving Chadron they drove to Pine Ridge, South Dakota, then set out for Wounded Knee Creek outside of Phinney. Hatcher's next report on July 5 revealed they'd collected and packed three more crates of fossils in the Badlands, making a total of thirty-two boxes weighing 9,015 pounds for the season, which would cost about $180 to ship. Hatcher had taken the students to see a "beef issue, Omaha dance & Shinny game by the Indians," and although he would have liked to collect longer, the students were "anxious to get on to the Park." So they would leave for Piedmont, Deadwood, and Lead with its Homesteak Mine and Mills, after spending only two weeks collecting in the Big Badlands region. But Hatcher was disturbed by something Wortman had said when he visited their camp, specifically that Scott had made arrangements with Osborn to send some of the fossils Princeton had purchased during the season to the AMNH. Hatcher, frankly, could not believe it, adding,

> *Now I am quite willing where we have duplicates to exchange to help them out in any way possible. But of the material I have purchased there are scarcely any duplicates. I have worked very hard & early & late this season to round out & complete our collection of White River fossils & I am sure it is now the most representative collection of the fauna of those beds in the world. In order to make it such we have both of us already made some personal sacrifices & especially yourself. As for the money I have paid out myself I had much rather stand it than to let one single specimen of which we have not better material pass out of our hands.*

With that, Hatcher tried to convince Scott to come out and take the students through Yellowstone so Hatcher could collect in the Wasatch, rather than having to serve as their tour guide himself.[18]

With the students having decided to ride across Wyoming rather than take the train, the crew found itself camped on the Powder River by July 14. "They have had splendid antelope shooting the past two days & most of them have succeeded in killing at least one. From there, they planned to invade the Big Horn Mountains for a few more days of hunting and fishing, before proceeding to the Park. Everyone was enjoying the trip immensely, although Hatcher gently groused, "I fear we will get very few more fossils, though I intend to make an attempt at the Wasatch yet." They'd arranged to ship all the crates from Hermosa at $1.57 per hundred pounds at a total cost of $141.75, or about $3,800 in modern currency, but Hatcher feared a strike by the rail workers might delay the shipment, so he requested the crates be held "until there was no danger of delay since we did not care to have them burned up." All in all, Hatcher admitted to being anxious to return to Princeton, and by August 5, after leading the students through the Shoshone Mountains to Yellowstone and providing directions to the students on how to return to Chadron, Hatcher returned to the Badlands region where he had promised to meet Baur for a month to collect. Although he regretted not being able to see the Park, he was sanguine about the decision, confiding, "I am so glad to get to doing something that will count once more." Besides, "To say that I shall be happy when I am through with the month with Baur & back at Princeton at work on our (truly wonderful) collection of this season, where I can see my family, does not express it at all. . . ." But having to wait for Baur ten days after Hatcher asked Baur to meet him in Hermosa soon ignited Hatcher's wrath, "I am not only disgusted but nearly crazy." Hatcher then boiled like a mudpot:

> *Just two months ago tomorrow we left Chadron* [for Yellowstone] *& in all that time we have packed only three boxes of fossils* [despite having] *14 in the party. It is certainly a burning shame to waste so much time & money & yet* [the party] *travels as a 'Scientific Expedition'! But nevertheless the Expedition as a whole has been wonderfully successful, but in the future I shall ask to be excused from these tail end pleasure trips, they are a great bore.*[19]

From his camp with Baur in the Big Badlands, a despondent Hatcher wrote on September 14:

> *I have been sick for the past ten days with acute diorrhoea* [sic], *fever & other complaints. Ten or a dozen doses of Squib mixture had no effect. . . . I am very weak & have no energy left. I think I shall improve right along now & be alright when I get back. Oh, I am so sick of this I wish I had never promised to stay this month. After this year I shall never attempt to collect for anyone but ourselves. . . . I have undertaken a little too much & I feel it.*

Four days later, Hatcher had perked up a bit, telling Scott that he was having reasonably good success at collecting, although he'd not found anything "startling." All in all, he related, "I am feeling first rate again & hope to be in Princeton within the next three weeks ready for a good winter's work." By the twenty-seventh, Hatcher reached Long Pine to wrap up some business regarding his property there before returning to Princeton. But in a cryptic postscript in his last letter from the field, he made reference to his old boss: "I hear that O. C. M. is on the 'prod.' I shall fix him." It's unclear what Marsh was up to, but as ever, Hatcher seemed more than willing to take him on.[20]

In any event, Hatcher assumed the role of summing up the expedition's accomplishments in the November 1894 issue of the *Princeton College Bulletin*, in which he noted that the target area had been the early Miocene White River beds just east of the Black Hills along the Cheyenne and White Rivers, where these beds crop out more extensively than anywhere else. In seeking to augment collections obtained there by earlier Princeton expeditions, "the expedition was exceptionally fortunate and successful. Several quite complete skeletons of animals as yet only known from isolated teeth and jaws were secured, as well as some forms which are doubtless new." More specifically, his listing included:

> *A complete skeleton of Elotherium; skeletons of Titanotherium, Leptomeryx and Poebrotherium; several skulls and portions of skeletons of Hyaenodon, a number of cat skeletons, good skulls and portions of the skeleton of Metamynodon, Protapirus, Perchoerus, Aceratherium, etc. A nearly complete fish skeleton was secured, the only one thus far from the White River beds. In all thirty-two boxes of good material, weighing more than 9,000 lbs., were packed and shipped to Princeton. Taken together with the collections of previous Expeditions into these beds our collection of White River fossils may now be considered as a fairly representative one of the White River fauna and second to no other in the country.*

He went on to mention that the *Agriochoerus* material collected had, indeed, allowed Scott to clarify that *Agriochoerus* and "Artionyx" were the same animal, as well as his discovery of the first specimen of the rhino *Diceratherium* from the White River beds, an animal previously known only from the John Day Formation in Oregon. He also emphasized that meticulous stratigraphic data had been kept as to where each specimen had been collected in the sequence of rock units and that two geologic units had been recognized in the region that had not been reported previously: "The Equus beds on the south slope of the divide between the White and Cheyenne rivers about six miles east of the south end of Sheep mountain; and the Cretaceous chalks . . . about three miles southeast of Hermosa, S. Dakota." But Hatcher and his crew had also kept their eyes focused on the modern flora and collected numerous specimens from the Big Horn Mountains, which were donated to the Princeton Herbarium, along with Hatcher's personal collection of 1,400 sheets of plants, representing common species from Connecticut, Nebraska, and South Dakota. In addition to Yellowstone, the crew had visited the Custer battlefield along the Little Big Horn River in Montana, and in the end, Hatcher complimented the students' efforts: "The author's best thanks . . . are due the various members of the Expedition for their generosity, which alone made it possible, and for the zealous manner with which they entered into the work."[21]

Including the purchased fossils, the Yale Peabody Museum records 311 total specimens that were collected on the 1894 Princeton Scientific Expedition. Although many of the genera had been previously collected by Marsh's field crews, these specimens helped lay the foundation for research in vertebrate paleontology at Princeton throughout most of the 1900s, and they are still referenced in research papers today. Hatcher's haul included the ten genera found in the 37- to 34-million-year-old Chadron Formation: the turtle *Trionyx*, the carnivorous creodont *Hyaenodon*, the saber-toothed carnivore *Dinictis*, and the brontothere "Titanotherium," now called *Megacerops*, the horse *Archaeotherium*, the rhinos (*Menodus* and "Caenopus," now called *Subhyracodon*), the large even-toed herbivore *Heptacodon*, and the small deer-like *Leptomeryx*.

The substantially larger suite from the 34- to 32-million-year-old lower portion of the Brule Formation consits of oreodonts and their relatives (*Agriochoerus, Eporeodon*, "Oreodon," now called *Merycoidodon*, and "Hadroleptauchenia," now called *Leptauchenia*); the anthracotheres ("Hyopotamus," now called *Bothriodon, Heptacodon*, and *Elomeryx*);

some rhinos (*Aceratherium, Diceratherium, Hyracodon,* "Menodus," *Subhyracodon,* and "Caenopus," which is now called *Subhyracodon*); along with rhino-like *Metamynodon,* the horses *Archaeotherium, Mesohippus,* and *Miohippus*; the tapirs *Colodon* and its relative *Homogalax*; the saber-toothed carnivores *Dinictis* and *Hoplophoneus*; the dog *Hesperocyon*; the "bear dog" *Daphoenus* and the creodont *Hyaenodon*; the terror pig *Entelodon*; the insectivorous *Leptictis*; several rodents (*Eumys,* "Scottimus," and *Ischyromys*); the small deer-like *Leptomeryx* and *Protoceras*; the rabbit *Palaeolagus*; the peccary *Perchoerus*; the camel *Poebrotherium*; the turtle *Stylemys,* along with the lizard *Peltosaurus.*

The younger Poleslide Member of the Brule Formation produced the horses *Mesohippus* and *Miohippus*; the rhino *Subhyracodon*; the "terror pig" *Entelodon*; the deer-like *Protoceras*; and the saber-toothed carnivore *Eusmilus.*

In addition to his fieldwork, Hatcher penned four scientific papers published in 1894 that foreshadowed the flowering of his distinguished career in paleontologic and geologic research to come. They detailed discoveries of rhinos and other vertebrates from the "Loup Fork" strata of Nebraska and the White River beds in South Dakota. (See Hatcher bibliography)

An even dozen students, including two previous graduates, four seniors, and six juniors, comprised the 12th Princeton Scientific Expedition, which Hatcher headed up in 1895. The primary goal was to collect scarce mammal fossils from the Eocene deposits of the Unita Basin in eastern Utah between 46 and 40.5 million years old. By March 22, Hatcher wrote Scott from the Ouray Agency, the administrative center for the Uncompahgre Ute reservation, to say that he had been having "fair success. That is fair success for the Unita." He anticipated acquiring a reasonably complete collection of this poorly known fauna and had already obtained specimens of "Diplacodon, Unitatherium, Paleosyops, Telmatotherium, Epihippus, Triplopus, Leptotragulus, Plesiarctomys," adding that the three partial skeletons of the latter would "give many of the skeletal features of the fellow." Although he had yet to find any skulls, he painstakingly cached any specimen with diagnostic features, given all the unknowns surrounding the fauna, and hoped his success would improve after the snow fully melted to reveal more exposures. He ended with some curatorial directives, suggesting that James Gidley, who had apparently left the AMNH to join the Princeton staff, prepare more material of the oreodont, *Leptauchenia*, and imploring that "when Mr. Adams [presumably another employee or student] puts his cat material away he would put it back in the same tray it came out of." By mid-April, results remained fair, "but the bones do not pile up very fast, owing partly to their small size & partly to their scarcity." Nonetheless, he'd just found "a very fair skull of a very peculiar Paleosyops" that had no teeth but "dandy" bone structure, and he'd found another partial skull with the dentition. He apparently again shared a camp with an AMNH crew consisting of his brother-in-law Peterson and Walter Granger, who had found a larger specimen of the same animal. In addition, Hatcher had gleaned from the ground a lower jaw of a "large Elotherium-like animal" and provided Scott with a detailed description of its morphology. Other finds included material of "Triplopus" and "Isectolophus." Somewhat frustrated with the sparse finds, Hatcher admitted, "This is not the most satisfactory collecting ground I have ever worked in . . . I hope you will be pleased with what we do get, but you must not expect too much, for as compared with last year's collection the number of boxes this year will be insignificant."[22]

A week later, Hatcher's festival of finding fossil fragments continued, although he had found "two good Telmatotherium skulls, a fairly complete but crushed skull of Mesonyx . . . a fragmentary skull of Achaenodon?, fore & hind limbs of Epihippus & an enormously big dentition of Amynodon. . ." Yet, Hatcher expressed distress with an agreement Scott had made with Osborn about guidelines for publishing on the season's finds:

> *They are a great surprise to me, and a disappointment as well. Rules 2 & 3 appear to me alright. But rule 1 if adopted last year would have prevented you from doing anything on our White River collection until, the lord knows when, for they had not their collection unpacked yet when I was in New York & probably have not yet. . . . Another thing, their party I understand is soon to be*

augmented by three more men & they contemplate staying here all summer. Now I shall have to leave here about June 1st & by the conditions of these rules it might not be impossible for them before the season closed to secure better material of everything I shall have secured in the short time at my disposal. I should like to ask if in that event you think my efforts here would be duly rewarded. I cannot understand why there should be such radical changes in these rules from those talked of when I left Princeton. To be perfectly frank I did not like the patronizing air of Prof. Osborn's letter to you in regard to this matter. There seems to be a second edition of the U. S. G. S. Palmistry springing up in New York.

Hatcher went on to say he didn't anticipate wanting to publish on any of the fossils he collected unless he found a skull or forelimb of the bronto-there *Diplacodon* and Scott passed on the opportunity. If that occurred, Hatcher would be "quite as unwilling to have anyone dictate . . . when I should describe it as I would be unwilling to set a time for them." Hatcher reminded Scott that they "had a definite understanding on this point in Jersey City before I came to Princeton & I feel sure that neither of us will violate that. . . ." Hatcher again pledged to always consult Scott before he published anything, but if he and Scott found significant new material, Hatcher was: ". . . not willing to wait to see if they [AMNH] can not find it; also, I can not conceive that anything is of more importance in science than the publishing of facts just so soon as they are known. . . ." Scott's insistence on this approach was key to Hatcher joining Princeton: "I saw that you were not only anxious to get material but equally anxious to work on it . . . & it has been with a deep sense of pleasure that I have worked, as best I could, in the field to get the material & in the museum to prepare it for study." Although Hatcher didn't see the potential for this season's work to produce much material for exhibition, he nonetheless saw great potential for signifi-cant new scientific insights, so he advanced three propositions: First, Scott should accept Osborn's suggestion that they coauthor a paper summarizing the season's results based on the best material that both crews collect; second, if that couldn't be done, let each institution use their own material to describe their specimens as best as possible, as had been done the previous two seasons; and third, if neither of his first two proposals could be achieved, Hatcher preferred "to be relieved" rather than be "controlled by outside parties." He assured Scott that he was not dissatisfied with him or Princeton, and he very much wanted to stay at Princeton "if the work can go on as it has . . . the past two years." Hatcher hoped Scott would not deem Hatcher's desires unduly "selfish" or greedy but rather in the best interests of Princeton and the people who had funded the expeditions. Regarding the collaboration with the AMNH, Hatcher lamented, "I wish we had never gone in together."[23]

Scott wrote on the fifteenth to express his delight at the rodent jaws that Hatcher had sent earlier in the month, with Hatcher rather pointedly replying on the twenty-ninth that he hoped Scott would be able to describe the specimens in print. Hatcher reassured Scott that if he could remain with Princeton "without being interfered with by others, who have no interest in me except to injure me I shall never consider any proposition even if I can increase my salary by several hundred per year." Hatcher was pleased to hear that Scott's papers on *Hyaenodon* and "Ancodus" had come out, although he'd heard nothing from Baur, presumably about the amphisbaenoid lizards. On the plus side, Hatcher had found a skull and lower jaw of his much-desired *Diplacodon*, noting that in competition with the AMNH crew, "the race for this beast has been the hottest I ever took part in, but Princeton has won by several lengths." Hatcher reiterated that he'd like to describe it if Scott didn't, since "we have fairly won the right" to do so against great odds. It had "good, large, well developed horns about 3 inches long with a fore & aft diameter of about 2½ inches and a transverse one of about 1½ inches." Overall, the skull was much more like "Titanotherium" than *Paleosyops*. Although the back of the skull was weathered and broken, Hatcher had found most of the fragments and pieced them back together. One side of the dentition was complete, so Hatcher was confident he would write a "most creditable paper on this beast" if Scott permitted. He reasoned that if Osborn was correct in calling the larger *Paleosyops*-like form from this region *Telmatotherium*, then "the latter can not be the ancestor of Diplacodon since both are found in the same horizon" or geologic level in the sequence of rock layers. Beyond that, with *Diplacodon* in hand, Hatcher felt Princeton now had a "pretty fair representation of the Unita fauna." However, he'd had bad luck with a partial *Epihippus* skeleton that he'd spent a whole day meticulously exposing and soaking with glue to keep it together, only to have "a coyote or some other beast" come and tear the skeleton all to pieces that night. In early May, Hatcher reported that things were still moving along, but slowly, since he'd been afflicted with his chronic "rheumatism" for the last month and was now "very stiff and sore."[24]

Scott's next letter near the start of May brought the sad news of the death of one of Hatcher's most respected Yale mentors, James Dwight Dana, to which Hatcher responded on May 9, "Few men can look back on a more finished life than his." Hatcher took that news and wove it into a sermon on publishing by recalling, "I worked faithfully for nine years at New Haven & it was very hard to leave there. I now feel the same attachment to Princeton (do not interpret me as meaning by New Haven O. C.). . . ." He again emphasized he did not want to leave Scott's employ and was glad to hear Scott intended to describe the Uinta rodent immediately, while once again adding that he thought the best solution to the AMNH problem would be for Scott and Osborn to publish a joint study on the Uinta collection. Although Scott had apparently offered Hatcher coauthorship on that work, Hatcher declined, stating, "I respect your ability as a vertebrate paleontologist too highly to wish to see your name coupled with mine, though I should have everything to gain by it." All Hatcher wanted was to publish on *Diplacodon*, while hastening to add, "But if this is impracticable I will willingly forego it," as long as the season's work on the Expedition wouldn't suffer from "rigid enforcement of rules which seem to me very unjust."[25]

Hatcher did not intend to be "harsh" with Scott when he expressed his criticism of the rules for publication that Scott and Osborn had modified; instead, he simply wanted "to see this work pushed for the utmost there is in it & I shall never consent to be hampered by any outside parties." In short, he didn't want Scott and Princeton "handicapped" by any rules for publishing that would diminish the credit that was due from their own efforts, and Hatcher didn't agree with the AMNH's claim that it had contributed more to their joint endeavors than Princeton had. Thus, Hatcher recommended that their institutions collect separately in the future, for Hatcher viewed several habitual expenditures of the AMNH crew in the field as "quite extravagant" and felt he could obtain equal success at a much cheaper cost. In other business, he hoped to be able to work during the coming winter not only on curating the collection but also on putting some of the material collected on the recent Expeditions on exhibition in the museum, for he felt that aspect of his responsibilities had not yet been adequately satisfied. After touching on a few other departmental matters, as he wrote amidst a "veritable sandstorm," he somewhat sheepishly stated, "Well, I suspect I have already tried your patience so will close."[26]

Having moved camp to just across the Green River from the Ouray Agency on May 15, Hatcher reported "very good" success: a nice skull and lower jaws of the primitive horse *Epihippus*, a substantial portion of the skeleton of *Triplopus*, along with a partial vertebral series and perhaps more of an animal similar to "Eplotragulus." But his "rheumatism" was still ravaging his body, making the work "very disagreeable," and with the time available before the students showed up rapidly waning, he felt forced to make "a special effort" to gather all the specimens he could. Hatcher complained about all the coordination required in collaborating with the AMNH crew; but in his estimation, they had all done well, and Princeton "has her share." He was sure he'd collected samples of all the known fossil animals from the Uinta, along with a few new forms, but he longed for two or three weeks of work on his own when he could prospect wherever he wanted without interfering ideas from others. He planned to leave for Casper in two weeks and ship his fossils from Rawlins to save money. He requested that Scott arrange for commissary and quartermaster privileges at Fort Washakie to supply the students for their Expedition. A couple days later, Hatcher received a letter from Scott saying Cope was irritated with Hatcher, but Hatcher thought Scott had misunderstood Cope because their relations had always been friendly. On another front, Hatcher was ecstatic that Scott gave him the go-ahead to describe *Diplacodon* and pledged to do it as soon as he got back and properly prepared the specimen. Hatcher had also found a skeleton of what he took to be *Triplopus*. A week later, Hatcher confirmed that he had a fairly complete skeleton of an animal, possibly "Leptotragulus," along with three feet of *Protoreodon*. He marveled at the abundance of bones and their high degree of articulation at this site near the Agency. Although the weather was dismal with rain and hail, through which he often suffered without shelter, his "rheumatism" was improving. He understood that Osborn had published a discussion of the geology of the Uinta beds, which along with Osborn and Scott's earlier publication should suffice for the subject. What Hatcher needed most was to know when the students would arrive in Casper.[27]

On June 5, Hatcher wrote from Rawlins after a rough, wet ride through rain and snow with his cache of five crates of fossils, which weighed 1,650 pounds. It cost $37.45, or about $1,000 in today's currency, to ship the season's plunder to Princeton. Hatcher hoped Scott would be pleased with the results, even though the AMNH had six crates when he left. Hatcher assured his superior that he had plenty of funds left from the students' donations to get to Casper. He hoped the students would let him use the remainder to work in the Laramie after the end of their Expedition. He'd purchased five saddle horses for the students and needed more, but those five and the team for the wagon was about all Hatcher could comfortably manage by himself. On a personal note, Hatcher told Scott that Anna had constantly been writing that their baby was in poor health, and Hatcher asked Scott to please have a Dr. Wykoff examine him thoroughly and send Hatcher his diagnosis. Apparently, Anna preferred another doctor, but Hatcher wanted a second opinion. Even though Hatcher didn't think anything was seriously wrong, he wanted "everything done for him that can be done in reason" and asked Scott to send him the bill. With that, after having been neither warm nor dry for ten days, Hatcher admitted, "I am going to treat myself to a bed at the hotel tonight." By June 12, Hatcher informed Scott that although he still had $25 of the $200 the students had given him before he left for the field, he had no personal funds and owed Scott $30 for personal incidentals purchased during the trip, which he intended to pay by July 1. But his personal finances were, seemingly as always, problematic: "If I can pull through for one more year I will be all right, but sometimes I can not see just how I am going to be able to make ends meet." Nonetheless, Hatcher said Scott wouldn't need to try and raise more funds for this season because all the field expenses to date were paid, and although he would need money to collect in the Laramie with Baur in August and ship whatever fossils he found, he would "try very hard to get it out of the Expedition" through the students. Hatcher doubted he'd make it to the White River this season, "as Mrs. Hatcher writes me that I must come home in September." Scott had summoned Wykoff to examine the Hatchers' baby by June 20 and apparently made some recommendations regarding the infant's diet. Hatcher expressed his sincere gratitude to Scott for taking the trouble to help out. The students on the Expedition arrived that day and were ready to start the next morning for Fort Washakie. Hatcher had heard from Gidley that one of the donors who had been providing $500 per year for the department at Princeton, including some for Hatcher's salary, had "dropped out," and Hatcher forthrightly inquired, "Is this going to make me a burden for you?"[28]

While on his trip with the students, Hatcher wrote from their camp along a branch of the Wind River outside Lander, Wyoming, on July 2 to suggest that if Scott wanted to collect in Utah or eastern Wyoming during the 1896 season, they should probably buy the team, wagon, harness, thirteen saddle horses, tent, and camping equipment that the students were using during the current Expedition. He'd spoken with the students, who offered to sell the outfit for $150, if Scott could find the money. With their spirits high, "All are well and enjoying themselves immensely. The ladies of Lander have tendered them a tea & hop tomorrow night. They have captured the town." Indeed, a newspaper clipping from the *Fremont Clipper* fairly reveled in their virtues: "It is needless to say that the party is composed of gentlemen of superior intelligence and that we honor ourselves when we extend to them whatever courtesies that lie in our power." The festivities also included a "hotly contested" baseball game that, although tied in the seventh inning, ended up with Lander the victor at 11–7, while "Prof. Hatcher of the Princetons gave excellent satisfaction as umpire." About five weeks later, the crew had visited Yellowstone and was returning in groups to Lander. Hatcher extolled the beauty of the whole region, calling the trip "much the finest I have ever taken," while adding that the route to the Park was even more beautiful than any sites in it:

We went by an entirely new route, following up De Noir Creek a tributary of Wind River to its head & thence upon to the continental divide which here is very high 1000 to 2000 ft. above timber line. We followed along the divide for over four days passing through Two Ocean Pass & then down onto the upper Yellowstone & down this stream to the lake & around the west shore. . . . Were in the Park three days before seeing a single person but our own party saw one band of fully 100 elk besides deer, Mtn. Sheep, antelope, bear etc.

While they were away, a spasm of violence erupted between the settlers in Wyoming and a group of Bannock warriors, and rumors spread that the Princeton crew had been captured by the Native Americans. However, the rumors were completely false, and as Hatcher wrote Scott, "It was an unfortunate affair . . . the report of our capture by Indians." From Lander, Hatcher would head to Lusk to meet Baur and collect in the Laramie, although no correspondence of this foray seems to have survived.[29]

Hatcher's summary in the *Princeton College Bulletin*, published in November 1895, listed numerous specimens "among the more interesting finds": carnivorous forms included two nearly complete skulls of the *Mesonyx*, two partial skulls possibly belonging to *Didymictis*, some material of *Miacis* and possibly *Hyaenodon*, as well as an upper dentition of the earliest known true carnivoran yet to be named. Rodents included abundant specimens of *Paramys* and the skull that Scott described of the new small form related to jumping mice, *Protoptychus*. Odd-toed ungulates, or perissodactyls related to modern horses, rhinos and tapirs, included *Telmatotherium, Amynodon, Trilopus, Isectolophus, Epihippus,* and Hatcher's favorite, *Diplacodon*, which represented the only skull of this genus then known. Hatcher also mentioned several jaws of a "small lemur," as well as some specimens of Insectivora. Even-toed ungulates, or artiodactyls related to modern pigs, hippos, camels, deer, and cattle, included a skull and lower jaws of *Achaenodon*, several skulls of the early oreodont *Protoreodon*, a skull and limbs of *Leptotragulus*, as well as skeletons of "Hyomeryx" and *Oromeryx*. In addition, *Uintatherium* represented the group of large herbivorous mammals called Dinocerata, with elaborately knobbed skulls armed with long upper canine teeth. Hatcher also elaborated extensively on the route that the students of the Expedition took to Yellowstone along the Continental Divide through the Wind River Range, which, he argued, "should be known as the 'Princeton Trail.'" That route was specifically followed, "owing to rumored Indian troubles in Jackson's Hole," leading Hatcher to choose "a route some 75 miles to the eastward, in order to avoid any possibility of trouble with the Indians, and so as to give no cause for anxiety to friends in the East." In summary, Hatcher idyllically intoned:

> *Of all the routes to the Park the 'Princeton Trail' is without rival as regards venturesome mountain climbing and picturesque scenery. The very roughness of the route precludes the possibility of its ever being much frequented; but for a party of young men, such as ours, seeking something out of the regular line and not minding "roughing it a bit," it is strongly to be recommended, and once taken will be long remembered.*[30]

Despite Hatcher's complaints, he amassed an impressive array of mammalian genera from the 46- to 40.5-million-year-old beds of the Uinta Formation. In all, the database of the Yale Peabody Museum records two hundred specimens from Hatcher's 1895 Princeton Scientific Expedition to the Uinta Basin and another thirteen specimens from Hatcher's foray into the Laramie Beds, now called the Lance Formation. The mammal specimens from the late Eocene Uinta Formation include three of the curious pig-like artiodactyl *Achaenodon*; twenty-three of the rhino-like *Amynodon*; two of the brontothere *Protitanotherium*; one of the deer-like *Camelomeryx*; three of the camel-like *Protylopus*; eleven of the rhino-like *Triplopus*; two of the carnivorous mesonychian *Mesonyx*; fourteen of the early brontothere *Diplacodon*; one of the entelodont *Elotherium* (now a subgenus of *Ammodon*); one of the early chalicothere *Eomoropus*; seven of the horse *Epihippus*; one of the omnivorous condylarth *Hyopsodus*; two of the rodent "Ischyrotomus" (now *Pseudotomus*); two of the tapir-like *Isectolophus*; two of the sheep-like oreodont *Leptoreodon*; six of the rodent *Leptotomus*; two of the antelope-like *Leptotragulus*; one of the oreodont

"Merycodesmus" (now *Leptoreodon*); two of the early brontothere *Mesati-rhinus*; one of the rodent *Mytonomys*; three of our own primate relative *Ourayia*; five of the brontothere *Palaeosyops*; one each of the rodents *Paramys* and *Plesiarctomys*; one of the enigmatic early carnivoran relative "Prodaphaenus" (now sometimes called *Miacis*); two of the rodent *Prot-optychus*; fifteen of the sheep-like oreodont *Protoreodon*; one each of the rodents *Pseudotomus* and *Reithroparamys*; three of the mesonychian mammal *Simidectes*; twenty-three of the early brontothere *Telmatherium*; six of the bizarre beast *Uintatherium*; and one of the brontothere *Meta-rhinus*. Among reptiles, he secured one specimen each of the turtles *Echmatemys* and *Baena*, two of the crocodile *Crocodylus*, and one each of the lizard *Glyptosaurus* and the monitor lizard *Saniwa*.

The late Cretaceous Laramie specimens include one of the bowfin fish *Amia*, one of crocodile-like *Champsosaurus*, one each of the early placental mammals *Cimolestes* and *Delphodon*, one of the gar *Lepisosteus*, one of the lizard *Leptochamops*, one of the mackrel shark *Myledaphus*, two of the marsupial mammal *Pediomys* and one of the three-horned dinosaur *Triceratops*. Finally, he found one specimen of the rhino *Subhyracodon* from the White River Group in South Dakota.

As evidenced in the accounts above, in the wake of his rupture with Marsh, Hatcher still held a considerable grudge. In 1896, Hatcher published a paper that contained a very direct dismissal of Marsh's diligence in establishing the regional geologic relationships between the 66-million-year-old rock layers that had produced the horned dinosaur fossils in Colorado, Wyoming, and Montana. In 1889, Marsh had claimed that these "Ceratops" beds extended in a continuous band of outcrops from near Denver, Colorado, to the confluence of the Judith and Missouri Rivers in Montana, leading Hatcher to spew sarcastically:

> *These are very widely separated localities, and no attempt has ever been made to trace the continuity of the* [rock layers] *from . . . one* [region] *to the other, nor is it at all probable that such an attempt would meet with success. . . . In a total of three and one-half days field work he seems to have found sufficient time to "carefully explore" the geological deposits of the Ceratops beds and to trace them "for eight*

hundred miles along the eastern flank of the Rocky Mountains,"
besides making numerous other observations of scientific interest.[31]

The license that Hatcher felt in leveling such a serious critique against his still prestigious former supervisor no doubt flowed from his new position at Princeton under Scott. Unlike Marsh, Scott, as noted above, placed few restrictions on what Hatcher could publish. Consequently, as noted previously, a torrent of eleven publications began to flow from Hatcher's pen between 1893 and 1896. In addition to the paper on the "Ceratops" beds, Hatcher wrote up studies on the "Titanotherium" Beds, the rhino, "Diceratherium," from the Loup Fork Beds, other vertebrates from the Loup Fork Beds of Nebraska, his treasured specimens of *Diceratherium* and *Diplacodon*, as well as his discovery of the new saber-toothed cat *Eusmilus*, not to mention the summaries of the 1894 and 1895 Expeditions, as well as a review of recent and fossil tapirs. But despite all these academic accomplishments, none of these pursuits could compete with his driving desire to explore Patagonia. (See Hatcher bibliography)

11

A Tango with the Tides among Patagonian Panoramas

atcher's feverish frenzy for collecting in Patagonia represented much more than a simple case of wanderlust. Significant scientific issues related to the ancient faunas of South America had begun to arise over collections and publications made by a pioneering pair of Argentine brothers—Florentino and Carlos Ameghino. Carlos traversed the harsh Patagonian terrain from its coastline along the Atlantic to the foothills flanking the Andes, discovering two regions of fossil-bearing rock layers. In early 1887, the white rock layers forming the shear cliffs of Barrancas Blancas near the mouth of the Río Santa Cruz yielded skeletons, appropriately called the Santacrucian fauna, characterized by unusual marsupials. In 1894, in small exposures of sedimentary rocks that filled depressions in the underlying igneous bedrock near the Río Deseado, Carlos discovered a few fragmentary fossils from the stratigraphically lower, and therefore older, *Pyrotherium* fauna. Only later, in late 1898 and 1899, did Carlos discover rock layers further inland at the Great Barranca near Lake Colhue-Huapi that contained, among other fossil mammals, abundant specimens of a hefty, somewhat rhino- or elephant-like mammal named *Pyrotherium*, a South American placental ungulate not closely related to either rhinos or elephants. After considerable research, Florentino declared the Santacrucian fauna to be of Eocene age, or about 40 million years old. He also concluded that the fauna from the *Pyrotherium* beds was Cretaceous, at least 66 million years old. At the beginning, he simply wanted them to be that old in order to support his ideas that many groups of modern mammals evolved in Argentina before they later appeared in the fossil records of Europe and North America. Later, Florentino thought Carlos found fragments of dinosaur bone in beds stratigraphically close to the *Pyrotherium* beds.[1]

These conclusions confounded North American and European paleontologists; based on their collecting, large mammals like *Pyrotherium* did not originate until long after nonavian dinosaurs went extinct at the end of the Cretaceous. Nonetheless, Florentino argued that since large mammals coexisted with nonavian dinosaurs in South America, they must have originated there long before they appeared in North America or Europe. Furthermore, Florentino concluded that because large mammals originated in South America, all mammals, including humans, must have arisen from these early, large South American mammals. These seemingly discordant declarations catalyzed Hatcher's determination to probe the outcrops of Patagonia himself. Rarely one to shy away from a dispute, Hatcher skeptically wrote:

> *The discoveries announced by the Ameghinos were of such an interesting nature, and many of the conclusions drawn were so extraordinary and so frequently opposed to conclusions believed to be well established by observed fact in the Northern Hemisphere, that paleontologists everywhere agreed as to the desirability of bringing together a representative collection of fossil vertebrates*

*and invertebrates from that region for study and comparison with
collections from North America and Europe. . . .*[2]

Hatcher emphasized that a detailed examination of the regional geology
was required to confirm the correct sequence of the fossil-bearing rock
layers in order to establish which was lower in the sequence and, therefore,
older, and which was higher in the sequence and younger. The primary
problem was that Florentino had not published detailed geographic
information describing where the collections of either the Santacrucian
or *Pyrotherium* fossils had been collected. Nonetheless, being an excellent field geologist as well as a paleontologist, Hatcher could envision no
better person for that job than himself.[3]

But, as we've seen, Hatcher had to cool his heels while Scott raised
the required funds from several "friends and alumni" of Princeton. In the
interim, Hatcher successfully poached his brother-in-law, O. A. Peterson,
who was then working at the AMNH, from the clutches of his antagonist,
Henry Fairfield Osborn, "for next to nothing" in salary to join him on the
expedition. Although Osborn and Hatcher exchanged a pair of cordial letters in the first months of 1896 regarding specimens for research, in which
Hatcher mentioned that Peterson would be joining him in Patagonia, relations between the two remained strained. In a letter to his friend Scott,
Osborn bristled about his sense that Hatcher had conducted this raid as a
hostile reaction in response to the bad blood that had flowed when Osborn
unsuccessfully attempted to hire Hatcher away from Marsh five years earlier. Scott later wrote in his autobiography that Osborn deplored Hatcher's
"absence of a clear feeling of right or wrong" in this matter.[4]

An additional complication for Scott involved the fact that Osborn, in
confidence, had told Scott several months before Hatcher sailed for South
America that Osborn wanted the AMNH to mount an expedition to
Patagonia and was demonstrably dismayed when he learned of Hatcher's
plan. Scott later wrote that this incident "came near to bringing about
the only misunderstanding that ever arose" between the two friends and
former classmates. Scott assured Osborn that at the time Osborn had told
Scott of his plans for Patagonia, "I knew nothing of [Hatcher's] scheme,
as Hatcher knew nothing of Osborn's plan."[5]

As Simpson points out, Scott's explanation seems suspect in view of Hatcher's earlier campaign of correspondence to Scott advocating that he and Scott should mount a Patagonian expedition, but perhaps Scott meant that he was unaware that Hatcher had sought funding for the enterprise from Princeton students during the 1895 Scientific Expedition, especially from the brothers John and Robert Garrett. In any event, Scott was eventually able to regain Osborn's support for Princeton's Patagonian project. In his editorial preface for Hatcher's narrative of the expedition, Scott acknowledges financial contributions from thirty-four graduates and friends of the university, including such notables as Cleveland H. Dodge, Morris K. Jessup, Henry Fairfield Osborn, and Charles Scribner, not to mention Hatcher himself. As it turned out, there would be three expeditions, and in his own introduction to his narrative, Hatcher clarified that the "chief contributors" to the first two expeditions were John W. Garrett, H. W. Garrett, M. Taylor Pyne, C. H. Dodge, F. Speir, C. C. Cuyler, Morris K. Jessup, and P. A. Rollins. Hatcher went on to note that for the most part, he supplied the funds for the third expedition. Special gratitude was offered for the generous financial support provided by Osborn's uncle and famous financier, J. Pierpont Morgan, whose "liberality alone has put it in our power to bring together in one uniform series [of publications] all the great and varied results of Mr. Hatcher's labors in South America." Echoing earlier statements, Scott summarized the goal:

> . . . the chief object of the expeditions was to make collections of the vertebrate and invertebrate fossils of Patagonia, in which the discoveries of the brothers Ameghino had so strongly aroused the interests of the scientific world. Some of the most important and far-reaching of geological and biological problems had been raised by the writings of Dr. Florentino Ameghino and it seemed most desirable to have a thoroughly representative series of the Patagonian fossils in some museum where they might be minutely studied in connection with the fossils of the northern hemisphere.[6]

In undertaking the expeditions, Hatcher clearly saw himself as following in the footsteps of one of his idols, the "master mind" Charles Darwin, who, as Hatcher noted in his introduction, visited Patagonia between 1833 and 1836 while serving as the naturalist during the voyage of the *Beagle*—an experience that eventually led to Darwin's revolutionary theory of evolution through natural selection. Hatcher lauded the broad scope of Darwin's observations in Patagonia and elsewhere, which ranged from the area's geology to its biology and included Darwin's discovery of "extinct fossil vertebrates . . . imbedded in the rocks of the sea cliffs . . . at Bahia Blanca, San Julian, and the port of Gallegos." Regarding the latter site, Darwin did not collect at Gallegos. Bartholomew J. Sulivan, who served as a lieutenant on the *Beagle* with Darwin, first discovered and collected fossils near Gallegos in 1845, while commanding a survey of the Falkland Islands for the Royal Navy. Darwin turned his specimens over to Richard Owen, the world's foremost comparative anatomist at the time, who identified them as "the first intimation of [an] entirely new world" of extinct animal life. But Hatcher was mystified that further extensive scientific exploration of the region floundered for fifty years until the "startling" discoveries and theories of the Ameghinos once again aroused the world's interest in the geologic and evolutionary history of the region. Thus, Hatcher's stated intent was to "make a thorough study of the Tertiary and Cretaceous deposits of Patagonia together with their contained fossils, in accordance with the more careful and painstaking methods which have been developed in the northern hemisphere during half a century by a great number of trained and skilled observers. . . ."[7]

With all the pieces finally in place, Hatcher and his ace assistant Peterson boarded the SS *Gallileo* at Martin's pier in Brooklyn on February 29, 1896, and after an overnight delay in New York Harbor due to fog, steamed past Sandy Hook into the tempestuous Gulf Stream, which buffeted the boat throughout the first two weeks at sea. Feigning a brave face, Hatcher, who had never before either been to sea or out of the country, later recalled, "On the second morning I enjoyed the distinction of being the only passenger at the breakfast table, and the captain paid me the doubtful complement of being a good sailor, remarking that I need never fear seasickness. He little knew how earnestly I was at that very moment striving against that very ailment."[8]

Their route would see the woozy wanderers sail south along the edge of the Sargasso Sea, with its greenish waters laced with strands of *Sargassum* seaweed, which fascinated Hatcher. Other intriguing novelties that Hatcher encountered included "Portuguese Man of War" jellyfish, "gliding upon the surface of the water like a miniature ship with most beautifully colored sails." He was transfixed by the entrancing phosphorescent light show produced by bioluminescent plankton, which provided a much-appreciated distraction from "the otherwise tedious hours" of the night. Finally, on March 25, they steamed up the Río de la Plata to Montevideo, the capital of Uruguay, where they docked to unload cargo, allowing Hatcher to explore the intriguing architecture embodied in "those low buildings constructed of solid masonry, with their tiled roofs and broad and close patios fitted with substantial if not always comfortable seats and decorated with a variety of tropical plants in fruit and flower."[9]

An overnight ride up the Plata landed Hatcher and Peterson in Buenos Aires, the Argentine capital, where they first encountered the government's "dilatory methods" as they waited several hours for the health officers to arrive. Beyond that, the crew had forgotten to retrieve the ship's health certificate from the agents in Montevideo, and only quick thinking by a medical student who suggested that another be forged allowed them to pass inspection and go through customs, where their credentials permitted a more expeditious and duty-free entry of all their firearms, ammunition, and collecting gear into the country. Having settled into their "meager" yet high-priced hotel, they made contact with the American "minister" and his consul, from whom they ascertained that the first Argentine ship to sail south along the coast to their field area around Gallegos, about thirty miles north of the entrance to the Straits of Magellan, would not leave Buenos Aires until April 16. With the ambassador's help, they secured permits for free transportation on any government steamers, although many officials recommended that they wait until after the Southern Hemisphere's winter months before commencing their work. But Hatcher would not be hindered, declaring, "We had tented it for many years on the wind-swept plains of Wyoming, Montana, and the Dakotas, often with the thermometer far below zero, and had no uneasiness as to our ability to survive successfully. . . ." To gainfully pass their time until departure, they visited the "splendid" museum in La Plata and "got a glimpse of that extinct mammalian fauna, in the remains of which we were soon to find the rocks of Patagonia so marvelously rich." [10]

On the appointed morning, Hatcher and Peterson boarded the *Villarino* and set sail for the southern coast, where on the eighteenth they awoke as they approached the port of Bahia Blanca, surrounded by "great salt marshes covered by a luxuriant growth of grass that stretched away for miles." As the ship unloaded a company of soldiers, Hatcher gazed at the flat landscape, which seemed "but recently to have been recovered from the sea" and lamented that there wouldn't be time to visit nearby Punta Alta, "where Darwin had . . . discovered the remains of Megatherium, Megalonyx, Scelidotherium, Mylodon, Toxodon, and a host of other equally interesting and long since extinct animals." Their next stop at San Blas provided Hatcher with "our first view of that great shingle formation which is everywhere found covering the Patagonian plains to a depth of from a few to more than one hundred feet," which Hatcher quickly interpreted as representing "remnants of old beaches thrown up and left by the sea during the slow process of elevation by which the land has been brought above sea level." When the prodigious thirty-foot-high tide arrived that evening, they were on their way to Port Madryn in New Bay, where they were greeted by "a line of high cliffs [that] rose sheer from the water to a height of perhaps 200 feet . . . This was our first view of that great sea wall that extends almost uninterruptedly all along the eastern coast of Patagonia . . . and with which we were shortly to become so familiar . . . as a collecting ground for both vertebrate and invertebrate fossils. . . ." A shore leave at Port Madryn afforded Hatcher and Peterson the chance to collect an array of local inhabitants from the bay, including clams, snails, sponges, and bryozoans, as well as numerous specimens of foot-long fossil oysters and other invertebrates from a blue sandstone on the beach and the face of the sea cliffs.[11]

Another three days of sailing brought the contingent to Port Desire, where Hatcher and Peterson anticipated "the splendid opportunity we should have for witnessing the wonderful dexterity of the Argentine gaucho" as the ship's supply of meat was replenished. Unfortunately, these gauchos were not up to snuff; Hatcher grimaced as two cattle were selected and one was eventually caught after "many vain attempts," then brutally immobilized by having its hamstrings cut while the gauchos struggled to catch the other. Anxious to move on, the *Villarino* arrived in Santa Cruz the next day and eventually anchored abreast a 350-foot-tall cliff at Direction Hill, "the identical cliff mentioned by Darwin and from which he made his section of the Patagonian beds published in his 'Geology of South America.'" Hatcher compared Darwin's diagram with the cliff, writing, "I was struck with the remarkable lucidity and accuracy of that great mind, and wondered whether it would be possible for me to add anything of importance to the observations made and material collected by him." [12]

Upon reaching the cliff, Hatcher indeed "found the different strata to contain the same fossils mentioned by Darwin." After four days spent by the crew erecting a signal tower, they proceeded in the company of a pod of southern right whales to Gallegos, where, as they approached Cape Fairweather, the northern shore was dominated by "a rugged line of per-pendicular cliffs, four to five hundred feet in height," with "a flat level plain above [that] terminates abruptly in the escarpment forming this sea wall." They arrived at Gallegos, the governmental center of the Territory of Santa Cruz, on April 30, as a sleety mist fell and a vigorous tidal bore rampaged past the sides of their vessel "like that of a mill race, with a velocity of six to seven miles per hour." Along with the ship's captain, Hatcher and Peterson immediately proceeded to pay their respects to the territory's genial governor, General Edlemiro Mayer, who offered to host his guests as they gathered the horses, gear, and supplies required for their foray. [13]

With winter on the horizon, the walk through mud to the governor's quarters was quite chilling, and although his library was stocked with six thousand volumes in numerous languages, Hatcher was puzzled as to why all the rooms were "cold as a barn" and lacked facilities like fireplaces to moderate the frigid temperatures. Despite a delightful dinner, Hatcher recorded that when he and Peterson retired for the night, "We knew that when once we were ready to start . . . we could, with our equipment and experience in camp life, make ourselves far more comfortable in our tent. . . ." Next morning, they perused the adjacent Río Gallegos and found that "instead of the broad sheet of water stretching uninterrupted for three miles, . . . there was now only a narrow channel.'. . . This was my first practical illustration of the enormous tides in this river, which are only exceeded by those of the Bay of Fundy and are given by some authorities as attaining a maximum of fifty-two feet."[14]

Although their gear proved to be in good shape, they needed to procure horses and a cart to carry it, which they had been told in the United States would be an easy task. But they were disappointed to discover "that the only vehicles to be had were cumbersome two-wheeled bullock carts, heavier by half than any load which they might be trusted to carry." Weighing in at about 3,500 pounds, these carts required four or six bullocks to haul a load of wool totaling 2,800 pounds. Hatcher groused, "It is difficult to understand why in a country like Patagonia, naturally so well adapted for overland travel, the inhabitants . . . are so backward in introducing more improved methods for the transportation of their wool and necessary ranch supplies to and from the different ports along the coast." Beyond that, the governor and his colleagues assured Hatcher that good horses could be easily had, but in town, Hatcher and Peterson were "besieged with parties offering [us] all sorts of nondescript horses at ridiculously high prices."[15]

Thus, the intrepid collectors eagerly accepted the governor's invitation to visit his estancia, or ranch, sixty miles to the northwest on the Río Coy. The trip, which saw Hatcher and Peterson ride on horseback rather than joining the governor in his cart, was most noteworthy for Hatcher having to help pull the governor's cart into the first waypoint at Guer Aike—much to the embarrassment of the cart's owner—where alcohol-laced jockeys staged horse races for local bettors and the traveling caravan. Quickly tiring of these spirited, yet chaotic, social festivities, Hatcher turned his attention to the surrounding landscape, where, after a short walk, he recognized that he was standing on the lower of two terraces, with the higher terrace forming an escarpment about two miles distant.[16]

From this, Hatcher deduced that several stages of recent uplift were represented: the present seafloor and mudflats on the riverbeds; the shingle deposits at the base of the sea cliffs that represented earlier beach deposits; and the two successively higher terraces representing earlier river valleys subjected to subsequent episodes of uplift. The terraces were covered with the same shingle deposits, establishing that the uplifts had occurred subsequent to the shingle being deposited on the ancient beaches. The present rivers, powered by gravity, were cutting back down through the terraces and shingle deposits to reach the sea. Far to the south, extinct volcanic craters still visible in the distance had produced black lava flows that had spread across the plain forming the upper terrace. With the sea cliffs looming to the north, Hatcher lapsed into envisioning the ancient environment, which, unlike the present, semi-arid landscape, had basked under a more moderate climate that supported a more luxuriant flora and fauna, including ungulates, sloths, armadillos, and giant, flightless birds. As he often had before, Hatcher then reflected, in what was clearly a thinly veiled and vengeful critique of both Marsh and Osborn, about the importance of making geologic and paleontologic observations in the field:

The study of nature is always instructive . . . if the student be a real lover of nature seeking for truth at first hand and for truth's sake, and not merely a fireside naturalist, who seldom goes beyond his private study . . . and either contents himself, like other parasites, with what is brought to him, or like a bird of prey forcibly seizes upon the choicest morsels of his confreres, with little or no consideration for the rights or wishes of those who have brought together the material at so great an expense of time and labor.[17]

By the time Hatcher returned to the small settlement, the partyers were still going strong amidst occasional drunken quarrels, and only toward morning did the din die down as the participants passed out. The next day saw Hatcher again rescuing the governor's cart when it and its horse got stuck in the middle while crossing the Río Gallegos. Other geologic observations lightened the long ride for Hatcher before they finally reached the governor's estancia on the Río Coy on May 5, when they were shortly afforded the opportunity to visit a nearby village of Tehuelche Indians. Although the travelers were greeted at first by a horde of seemingly ferocious dogs, the tribe soon warmly welcomed them and offered them the Patagonian drink of choice, both then and now—mate. Made from the leaves and stems of the indigenous *Ilex paraguayensis*, these are "placed in a . . . small gourd . . . then just enough water is poured in to moisten the contents, when a tube . . . usually brass . . . with a perforated bulb at the lower end . . . is pushed down to the bottom. . . . Each person . . . sucks the liquid through the tube until the contents are exhausted, then returns it to the person who has volunteered to serve mate, by whom it is refilled and handed to another, and so on indefinitely . . . for several hours at a time." Hatcher deemed this custom to be hygienically "filthy . . . and therefore much to be deplored." Nonetheless, he was fascinated by the Tehuelche, their customs, and their arts, and looked forward to meeting them again and making further observations while attempting to collect samples of their cultural artifacts.[18]

Hatcher and Peterson separated from the governor's entourage for the ride back to Gallegos so Hatcher could roam undistracted to make geologic observations and the pair could continue their quest for horses. Returning to a shepherd's shanty he had noticed on the way out, Hatcher succeeded in bargaining for "a very fair saddle horse" at the cost of seven pounds. Shortly after, he encountered a Spaniard driving a troop of horses, from which he selected another for nine pounds, giving each explorer a good mount for the field. When they reached Gallegos, their main concern was finding the most suitable wagon. Despite their trepidation, the Italian owner of the general shop kindly offered to sell his somewhat lighter-weight, more agile cart that he used to haul cargo from the port at a most reasonable price. Now all that was lacking was a horse or two to pull it, but a gaucho who had intently witnessed the cart transaction quickly jumped in to pitch Hatcher on a horse he had purchased from the Tehuelche. Initially, Hatcher was unimpressed by the appearance of this "considerably undersized and rather inferior looking animal," otherwise know as El Moro, or 'the Moor.' But after the gaucho harnessed the roan to the cart and hopped in the driver's seat, he "seized the lines, and yelling and whipping incessantly circled about over the rough and uneven country lying between us and the beach at a reckless gait. . . . Out of compassion we purchased the animal, which, however deficient he might be in physical strength, was evidently quite willing." In fact, El Moro proved to be "a tractable, docile and willing" member of the crew. Following Argentine custom, Hatcher finally purchased two cinch mares, whose job it would be to each walk along one side of the wagon, attached to the cinch rope tied to that side. Thus, on May 16, "just two and one half months after our departure from New York," Hatcher and Peterson were ready to get down to business.[19]

With their tent, stove, bedding, collecting equipment, and firearms in tow, they flew the coop of Gallegos with a month's worth of provisions, hindered slightly by having to become fluent in the local language of horse commands. Camping near Guer Aike, where they hoped to again ford the Río Gallegos when it lowered, Hatcher rode out to survey some nearby cliffs, while Peterson set traps for local rodents and hunted birds to skin. Finding no fossils, Hatcher returned with a load of calafate bushes to fuel their stove and stave off a bitter southwest wind. With the river still too high for crossing with the cart, Hatcher left Peterson to his thus far successful tasks and forded the river on his horse to spend a couple of days prospecting some promising cliffs composed of sandstone and shale on the north side. Initially finding only fragments, Hatcher proceeded about twelve miles downriver to the estancia of H. S. Felton at Killik Aike. Although Felton was away, his foreman welcomed the foreigner and invited him to stay as long as he pleased, while also assuring Hatcher that fossils were plentiful a short walk away down on the beach. After gulping down a hearty lunch of meat, vegetables, and coffee,

I set out for the beach. . . . I had scarcely clambered down over the edge of the three or four yards of silt, which forms the bottom of the small tributary valley, when at my feet . . . I discovered the jaws and teeth of a small rodent Procardia elliptica. *. . . Turning to my right I proceeded to walk along the foot of the cliff, which fronts the river and increases rapidly in height . . . until, within a short distance, it rises perpendicularly to the plain above at an altitude of four hundred and fifty feet . . . my eye caught the reflection given off by the polished enamel of a tooth protruding from the surface*

[near] *the base of the cliff . . . this proved to be . . . an almost perfect skull of* Icochilus, *a small ungulate mammal . . . belonging to the* Typotheria. *. . . . The discovery of more or less complete skulls and skeletons of other animals followed in rapid succession.*

Hatcher saw others encased in great blocks of stone that had fallen from the cliff and were being eroded by the tides, including: *Nesodon*, which resembled a small rhinoceros; *Astrapotherium*, a larger and more formidable relative; *Diadiaphorus*, a smaller horse-like ungulate; and *Prothylacinus*, a large carnivorous mammal resembling the Tasmanian wolf. Stopping to reflect in rapt awe, Hatcher mused,

Truly this vast cemetery, which for untold ages had served as nature's burial ground, was now being desecrated by her own hand, with no one present to remonstrate against her wanton destruction of those remains whose very antiquity, it would seem, should have insured them against such desecration. We are wont to speak of the kindly hand of nature and attribute all our physical ailments, at least, to a disobedience of her laws. As I stood that afternoon and calmly viewed the surrounding scene, I could not help doubting the full truth of both assumptions.[20]

Hatcher marveled at the tides' erosive power as they were propelled in solid fronts "eight to ten feet in height and several hundred yards in length" toward the sea cliffs, where they rolled "great stones of from one to two hundred pounds weight up and down the beach . . . rocking others of a ton or more, back and forth . . . ," forcing Hatcher to "seek safety at successively higher elevations" as they advanced. He mused that the tides' erosion of the cliffs mirrored scientific advances "where old theories promulgated after long and patient research are for a time accepted as truth, only to be demolished later by the discovery of new facts," and he contemplated whether the extinction of the organisms entombed in the cliffs occurred due to a catastrophic environmental event or simply as a result of natural evolutionary senility. But above all, he relished in his realization that "the success of the expedition I now felt to be assured."

In celebration, he returned to the Feltons' estancia, where he and the foreman warmed themselves in front of "a cheerful fire of good English coal" while sampling from "an abundant supply of provisions and a choice selection of liquors, wines, beer, ale [and] stout."[21]

Next morning, Hatcher gathered a few of his paleontological jewels and rushed back to Guer Aike to enlist Peterson in his collecting campaign at Felton's. Naturally, Peterson's "anxiety was no less than my own to be off at once and establish a comfortable camp somewhere within easy working distance of this newly discovered El Dorado." As they hauled their gear to their new mother lode, they were captivated by carrion hawks, or caranchas, scavenging on sheep carcasses, guanacos grazing on the grassy plain, and rheas beating a hasty retreat as their outfit rumbled into view. With their spring-side camp set and a brace of calafate brush gathered to fuel the fire, the collectors embarked on their endeavor, "working early and late and seven days to the week, for nearly a month," during which they first focused on the bluffs upstream where Hatcher had made his initial discoveries, then clambered over the cliffs downstream. What emerged was an ancient fauna with which Hatcher and Peterson were entirely unfamiliar from their previous pursuits: "Not only were the genera and species distinct . . . but the families and orders were also. . . . It was like being transferred suddenly to a new world . . . with a new fauna entirely different from that of our earth." By June 19, they had collected and packed 1.5 tons of fossils, which they loaded on the British schooner *Bootle*, which had come for a load of Felton's wool. They then moved camp downstream to the estancia of William Halliday directly across from Gallegos. There, they worked the extension of the same cliff-forming deposits exposed at Felton's and procured another crate of fossils by June 26, which were again loaded on the *Bootle* when it stopped by.[22]

With their paleontological enterprise well underway, the pair moved camp to Fitzroy Springs near Cape Fairweather to refocus on collecting specimens of the modern flora and fauna. There, grasslands studded with calafate played host to guanaco, rhea, and numerous other species. Wielding his Winchester, Hatcher soon spied a band of guanaco with fur in prime condition: "Selecting a pair that appeared especially fine, I fired two shots from my 45-90, bringing both to the earth almost in their tracks," while the rest of the group "made off across the bed of shingle in their peculiar swinging gallop . . . while swaying their long willowy necks up, down and sidewise." Upon reaching his quarry, Hatcher was confronted by "their striking large and beautiful eyes" with which "they looked up, as though imploring mercy. I almost wished I had not fired the fatal shots." So moved, he determined not to "be unnecessarily cruel . . . so, reaching for my knife, I drove the glistening blade . . . quite through the spinal cord and deep into the cranial cavity of each." As the caranchas gathered, Hatcher realized he had nothing with which to make measurements on the specimens and needed to return to camp, but by the time he returned, the caranchas "had so mutilated the skins of both animals as to render them unfit for mounting purposes." In addition, they had feasted quite fastidiously by ripping out the eyes and making an incision underneath the lower jaws through which they detached the tongue. Retreating to watch the ongoing carnage unleashed by the caranchas, Hatcher soon saw a male Andean condor gracefully swoop down, supported by his nine-foot-long wingspan: "The long primaries were motionless . . . and were each so distinct that I could without difficulty have counted the series as he soared by. The pure white of his shoulders and the delicate ruff was intensified by the deep black of the back and upper body. . . ."[23]

As the caranchas chaotically fled, the condor alighted on the nearest carcass and proceeded to puncture "though the flank and into the abdominal cavity, where at each stroke of the powerful beak consider-able sections of the intestines and other organs were torn out and eagerly devoured." After noting the condor's behavior, Hatcher realized "what an excellent specimen he would make to adorn the ornithological hall . . . at Princeton." Hoisting his Winchester, Hatcher "drew a fine sight and touched the delicate trigger. . . . The great bird sprang suddenly upward with one convulsive start, then fell and lay quite dead alongside the lifeless body of the guanaco," the loss of which Hatcher had no need to lament, since Peterson had killed and skinned three others. Universities and museums still actively collect such specimens for their scientific research, but greater attention is given to the fact that many species are endangered by current environmental and climatic changes. In Hatcher's day, the idea that then extant species were facing extinction was just beginning to be understood, as evidenced by William Hornaday's campaign to conserve the few remaining bison on the Great Plains in the late 1880s and attempt to rejuvenate the species through the establishment of dedicated preserves in 1906.[24]

Later in July, with the collection of the area's mammals and birds well in hand, Hatcher turned his attention back to prospecting for fossils in the bluffs north of Cape Fairweather but with only indifferent success for the first few days. Then, he unexpectedly encountered a huge block of sandstone lying at the base of the cliffs "literally covered with the fossil shells of gastropods, brachiopods, giant oysters and other marine invertebrates"—a fact that puzzled him, since he had previously concluded that the sea wall was composed completely of terrestrial Santa Cruz sediments that contained the mammal fossils. Upon further investigation, he established that the marine sandstone had come from a gigantic piece of the cliff, about a half mile wide and two hundred yards long, that had separated from the overlying plain and slumped down toward the beach during a landslide.[25]

Climbing to the top of the bluff, he confirmed that just underneath the shingled surface of the plain lay a thirty-foot-thick sequence of marine sandstone layers, which meant that "subsequent to the time that *Nesodon* [and] *Astrapotherium* . . . lived . . . and left their bones to be buried in the mud . . . of the streams, rivers and lakes of the Santa Cruzian epoch, this entire region had been buried beneath the ocean for the time during which these marine beds were deposited." In fact, the plate tectonic forces associated with the uplift of the Andes far to the west were also responsible for uplifting these beds once again to the earth's surface, where erosion could wear them away and expose their entombed treasure of fossils. In honor of the location in which Hatcher discovered these marine sandstones, he named them the Cape Fairweather beds. From the top of the landslide, Hatcher and Peterson were able to collect not only a full suite of fossil invertebrates but also a bevy of modern birds inhabiting the calafate and mate brush, including the brown wren, red-breasted meadow lark, black-throated sparrow, and chestnut-crowned song sparrow.[26]

Rodents also abounded, which attracted the gray, fox-like *Canis azarae*. However, Hatcher's next run-in with the condors atop the slide proved surprising. As a condor perched on the side of the cliff, Hatcher confidently loaded his double-barreled shotgun with shells containing BB shot, then approached and shot just as the "noble bird" took flight, dropping him instantly on the talus at his feet. With the bird being too heavy and cumbersome for Hatcher to carry down the steep slide to the beach two hundred feet below with his fossils and other gear, he reasoned that the condor's carcass wouldn't be damaged significantly if he just threw it off the top and let it land on the sandy shingle. "What was my surprise and disappointment, however, to see the bird almost immediately after he left my hands take to flight and go soaring off as though quite unharmed . . . ?" Peterson and Hatcher remained near Cape Fairweather, seven hundred miles farther from the equator than New York, through July and into August in order to augment their collections.[27]

Nomadically moving north along the coast on September 1 to Corrikuen Aike, about twelve miles below Coy Inlet, Hatcher and Peterson serendipitously discovered a veritable bonanza of vertebrate fossils literally imbedded in the beach. There, they daily engaged in an elaborate tango with the tides that ranks among the most unusual modes of fossil collecting ever attempted. Tidal flats of dark green sandstone over a mile long and a quarter mile wide abutted against sheer cliffs along the shoreline, and at low tide, the gently eastwardly dipping sandstone was exposed for two miles out from the shore. To Hatcher's amazement, "On walking about over the surface at low tide, there could be seen the skulls and skeletons of those prehistoric beasts protruding from the rock," including a diverse suite of Santacrucian fossils:

> *At one point the skull and skeleton of* Nesodon *would appear, at another might be seen the limbs or . . . teeth of the giant* Astrapotherium . . . *while a little farther on a skull and jaws of the little* Icochilus *grinned curiously, as though delighted with the prospect of being thus awakened from its long and uneventful sleep. On one hand, the muzzle of a skull of one of the larger carnivorous marsupials looked forth, with jaws fully extended and glistening teeth, the*

characteristic snarl of the living animal still clearly indicated, while at frequent intervals the carapace of a Glyptodon *raised its highly sculpted shell, like a rounded dome set with miniature rosettes, just above the surface of the sandstone.*

Having been buried in the sand of an ancient floodplain, these remains were sculpted from the sandstone as the powerful tidal bores, exceeding forty feet on a daily cycle, eroded away the rock. The richest collecting area was about three hundred yards wide and extended out beyond the cliffs for 1.5 miles. To gather these paleontological gems from this immense expanse required well-coordinated choreography. Hatcher and Peterson followed the tide as it waned, excavating specimens as carefully yet quickly as they could before setting them aside on the flats. Then, as the tide began to flow back in, they furiously gathered those farthest from shore and stored them at the base of the cliff above the high tide line before scrambling back across the flats to secure the next sequentially threatened batch. At times, when the excavation of a specimen took longer than anticipated, "this work of transporting the fossils to shore became the work of a rescue in every sense of the term, frequently quite exciting, and [occasionally] so entirely personal to ourselves as to become exceedingly disagreeable." After one such session, Hatcher reminisced:

> *We sat on . . . the talus-covered slope at a safe distance from the waters that dashed furiously beneath . . . while over the sandstones of the beach, from which but a few hours previously we had been excavating the remains of prehistoric animals, there now rolled a sea sufficiently deep for the safe navigation of the largest transat-lantic liner. . . . Not many experiences have left themselves so indel-ibly engraved upon my mind. At this somewhat distant perspective* [while day dreaming] *I detect myself in the midst of a most vivid mental picture . . . seated . . . on some convenient ledge . . . as the crest of each great tidal wave comes rolling in across the eastern seas and breaks with thundering force upon the rocks below, once again I am . . . transported to some favorite spot and busily engaged in my*

chosen work, only to awaken almost immediately from my reverie
to a painful consciousness of the delusion. . . .

Throughout eighteen years spent almost constantly in collecting
fossil vertebrates, during which time I have visited most of the
more important localities of the western hemisphere, I have never
seen anything to approach this locality near Corriguen Aike in
the wealth of genera, species and individuals.[28]

Hatcher and Peterson worked constantly at this site throughout the foggy month of September and into October, when they often had to rely on their yells echoing off the bluff to navigate their way back to shore. When they could see more clearly, Hatcher also reveled in the avian antics of gulls and cape pigeons that remained well out at sea to avoid the surf at high tide, as opposed to the grebes, who defied smaller breakers by bobbing over their crests, and potentially disastrous, larger waves by diving under them. High tide also brought entertaining seals and porpoises near shore. On land, the ibis excelled at hindering their sleep with its "irritating squawks and screams." Indeed, "on several occasions Mr. Peterson was so exasperated that he took the shotgun and fired several volleys into them. This only had a temporary effect, however. . . ." Several species of plovers also appeared in the spring and provided a tasty addition to their diet, while ducks, geese, and flamingos plied the nearby ponds and black-throated sparrows and brown wrens abounded. Rheas were always a welcome sight, for their eggs "provided a palatable addition to our daily menu. . . . Fried, scrambled, roasted in a bed of coals or mixed with flour and made into batter and baked as cakes, they were always relished." Although no snakes were to be found, lizards of various shapes, sizes, and hues were common, as were scorpions, beetles, small butterflies, and moths. By the end of October, Hatcher and Peterson had hauled four tons of fossils off the treacherous tidal flats to Gallegos and shipped them via the small schooner *La Patria* to Punta Arenas at 15 pesos per ton.[29]

On November 2, the pair once again moved their camp north to Coy Inlet near the mouth of the Río Coy. As Peterson set to work collecting, Hatcher felt it wise to check on the shipment of fossils to make sure it reached Punta Arenas, a task that required a ride of about 225 miles southward. The first day, he reached the Feltons' and finally had the pleasure of meeting the family, who graciously provided their legendary hospitality. But they were concerned about the risks of Hatcher's trek and offered to loan him an extra horse, which he declined after explaining, "Accustomed in our own country to making trips of five hundred to a thousand miles with one horse, I felt no alarm at undertaking so insignificant a journey as this seemed. . . ." From Felton's, he headed overland to the southwest along the Río Chico and enjoyed a similarly warm welcome at the Karks' estancia near Palli Aike, even receiving a lunch prepared by the matron for the next day's journey. Under an overcast sky with "leaden clouds" and buffeted by "a savage southwesterly wind," Hatcher halted at a grass-rimmed pool to refresh his steed, tossing the reins over his horse's head. Upon returning from a short walk, Hatcher noticed the horse had one foot caught in the reins:

> *Reaching down to take it out* . . . [the horse] *became startled and jerked his head violently upward until the reins became taut, when it was thrown down again with even greater violence just at the moment when I was rising from a stooping position, . . . and in such a manner as to strike my head with the broken shank of the Logan bit with which the bridle was fitted. This was forced through and under the scalp in such a manner as to loosen the* [scalp] *over a considerable area, at the same time rupturing some of the blood vessels and causing the wound to bleed profusely. For an hour or more I tried vainly to staunch the wound by bathing it in cold water* . . . *Not being successful* . . . *I placed a handkerchief over the wound and resumed my journey.* . . .

But when the hemorrhaging oozed unabated and he began to feel faint, he stopped and applied another handerchief, drew his Stetson down firmly over his head, wrapped himself in saddle blankets, and lay down for the night. Rising weak and famished, as well as "chilled to the marrow" by the wind, he managed to reach Ooshii Aike by midmorning, where he hoped to procure something to eat and clean his wound. But the only inhabitant there, a "surly Italian" cook, denied him entry, despite Hatcher's insistent appeals:

> *I was quite willing to pay for any accommodation that he would grant me, and . . . displayed to him my ability to do so. He remained obdurate. . . . I decided that if there was anything that would minister to my immediate necessities within the house, this "dago" should not stand between me and my needs. In an instant I declared my intentions, and shoving by him, walked through the long hall to the room in the rear which I had correctly judged to be the kitchen. . . . Making myself quite at home . . . I quickly prepared a pot of coffee, meanwhile bathing my head with warm water . . . which I then cleansed and dressed as best I could. Having refreshed myself sufficiently from the supply of bread and meat . . . I resumed my journey, not neglecting, however, to leave my card with a brief note for the foreman . . . that on my return . . . I hoped not only to make his acquaintance, but such restitution as should be thought necessary.*[30]

After another day's ride and another night camping on the trail, Hatcher reached La Posada de la Reina, or Queen's Hotel, run by a compatriot from Virginia, where he convalesced for a few days to nurse his wound as well as a cold he'd contracted. With another two days of travel, Hatcher was finally able to plop down at a miserable hotel in Punta Arenas, "about noon on the tenth day of November, suffering with a very bad cold and the wound . . . much inflamed and suppurating freely." Seeking treatment from one of the town's two physicians, Hatcher was unnerved when the doctor "suggested bleeding as the initial treatment." Thus, he purchased some quinine, carbolic acid, and cotton bandages and stayed in his room until the next morning, when he checked on his crates, which he learned had been hauled to "a hulk in the harbor." Rowing out, he found his cargo "lying about quite unprotected from the almost constant rain" before he had the crew cover them with tarps. Exhausted and ill, he holed up in his room at the Cosmos Hotel for two weeks at $6 per day: "I was permitted to occupy a small room with a single chair [and] bed, and served two very indifferent meals . . . each twenty-four hours, there was no fire. . . . Upon asking if . . . I might enjoy the comforts of a fire, I was told that, if cold, I could drink whiskey. . . . I was thunderstruck to find that the charge for one whiskey and soda was eighty cents."[31]

Returning to the Halliday estancia above Gallegos, Hatcher found that Peterson had wrapped up his sojourn near the Río Coy, having tallied another ton of Santacrucian specimens. They packed these up along with the rest of their zoological and botanical collections. In total, they'd amassed another six tons of material, which they left with Halliday for shipment to Punta Arenas on the next vessel bound there. Then they departed on December 13 on another epic leg of their expedition to the interior by retracing the steps of their initial foray through Guer Aike and General Mayer's estancia, where they would visit and dine with him for the last time. From there, they struck northwest along the north fork of the Río Coy or Río Aubone. On the nineteenth, they stopped at some springs gushing from beneath the shingle below a pampa, where they did laundry and shoed the horses in preparation for an extended trek over the lava-capped plains they expected to encounter. Heading further northwest across the pampa, they were mesmerized by mirages and bands of galloping guanaco. Another couple of days' ride brought them to a scattering of small lava fields radiating out from small volcanic cones nearby.[32]

There on December 22, Hatcher fell ill, suffering with, he stated, "a high fever and my head about the old wound . . . swollen, very much inflamed and quite painful." He had no medications, except for a few phenacetin tablets, and despite Peterson's "kindly care," the swelling "spread so rapidly over my head, face and neck that on Christmas Day both my eyes were entirely closed." Hatcher hallucinated that he was on an expedition to Greenland, even though he'd never intended to travel there. Needless to say, it was "the most miserable Christmas of my life."[33]

After resting for a few days, Hatcher began "to mend." "The inflammation subsided rapidly, taking with it, however, most of my hair." Slowly recovering his strength, they resumed their ramble to the northwest and reached the bluffs of the Río Santa Cruz on January 2, where they could see Lake Argentino in the distance. Dropping into the valley to search

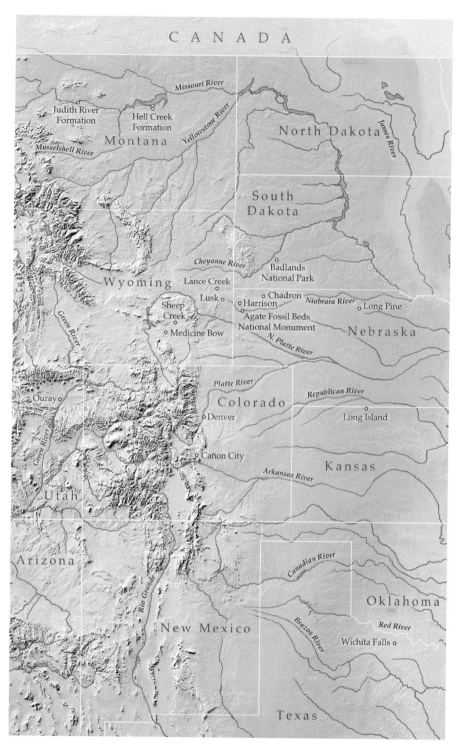

Map of primary fossil sites and localities where Hatcher and his field crews collected throughout the Rocky Mountain and Great Plains regions. *Credit: Mick Ellison.*

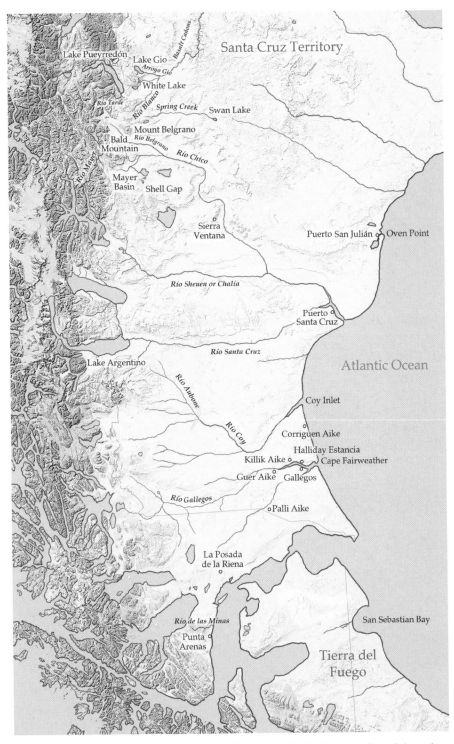

Map of primary fossil sites and localities where Hatcher and his field crews collected throughout Patagonia. *Credit: Mick Ellison.*

LEFT: John Bell Hatcher as a child, posed with chair, circa 1866. *Courtesy of John Hatcher.* BELOW: John Bell Hatcher's family circa 1890–1891: John Bell Hatcher (center back), his father John B. Hatcher and mother Margaret Columbia O'Neal (front row, second and fourth from left) along with John Bell's siblings. *Courtesy of John Hatcher.*

RIGHT: John Bell Hatcher's graduation photo. This portrait was probably taken circa 1884, when Hatcher graduated from the Sheffield Scientific School at Yale. At the bottom of the photo is printed "Pach Bros. 935 B'dway, N.Y." The Pach Brothers had a studio in New York and an outpost in New Haven that was apparently popular with Yale students and graduates. *Courtesy of John Hatcher.*

LEFT: Portrait of John Bell Hatcher taken when he was working for O. C. Marsh of Yale and the U. S. Geological Survey between 1884 and 1892. *Courtesy of the Archives; Peabody Museum of Natural History, Yale University; peabody.yale.edu.*

Specimens of *Teleoceras fossiger* comprised the great majority of fossils collected by Hatcher from Charles H. Sternberg's Rhino Quarry at Long Island, Kansas, during Hatcher's first two field seasons under the supervision of O. C. Marsh in 1894 and 1895. *Courtesy of the American Museum of Natural History Archives.*

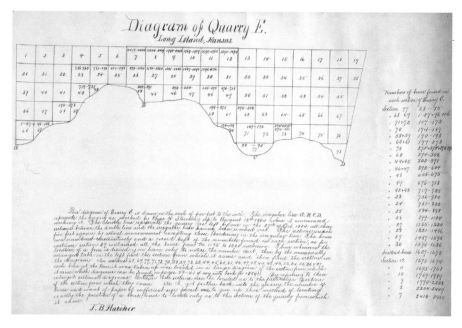

ABOVE: Hatcher's quarry map for the Long Island Rhino Quarry in Long Island, Kansas, showing the grids from which he collected and plotted individual fossils [VPAR.002371. tif]. *Courtesy of the Vertebrate Paleontology Archives; Peabody Museum of Natural History, Yale University; peabody.yale.edu.* BELOW: Hatcher's sketch of fossils found and plotted in grid Sec. 48 of his map of the Long Island Rhino Quarry in Long Island, Kansas [VPAR.000630. tif]. *Courtesy of the Vertebrate Paleontology Archives; Peabody Museum of Natural History, Yale University; peabody.yale.edu.*

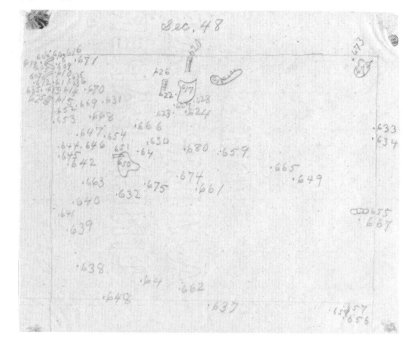

ABOVE: Eroding layers of sandstone and mudstone form a picturesque spire-pronged ridge just west of the Visitor Center in Badlands National Park, South Dakota—a region in which Hatcher and his crews collected extensively during his years with Marsh for Yale and the U. S. Geological Survey, as well as for Scott at Princeton and Holland at the Carnegie Museum. BELOW: Colorful yellow and pink exposures of the Chadron Formation underlie the more somber gray and brown layers of the Brule Formation along the eastern portion of Badlands Loop Road in Badlands National Park, South Dakota. *Both photos by Lowell Dingus.*

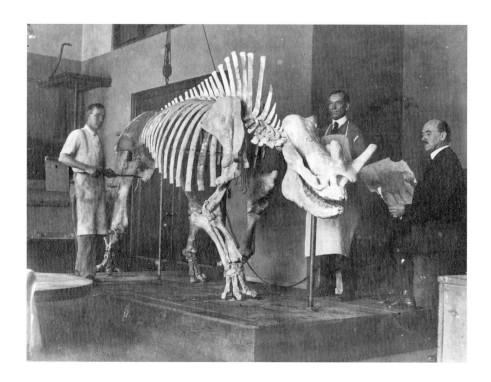

ABOVE: A 1919 photograph of the Smithsonian's National Museum of Natural History's skeletal mount of *Megacerops coloradensis* [USNM 4262], which was collected by Hatcher in 1887. *Courtesy of Smithsonian Institution Archives and Department of Paleobiology, National Museum of Natural History.* BELOW LEFT: Portrait of John Bell Hatcher and Anna Matilda Peterson Hatcher. *Courtesy of Norman Hatcher.* BELOW RIGHT: Portrait of O. A. Peterson, John Bell Hatcher's brother-in-law and Anna Matilda Peterson Hatcher's brother. *Courtesy of John Hatcher.*

ABOVE: This view of outcrops along the drainage of Lance Creek illustrates the brownish gray exposures of sandstone that represent sand bars deposited in the river channels that meandered across the ancient floodplain on which *Triceratops, Torosaurus,* and *Tyrannosaurus* lived. BELOW: Lance formation two: This view of Lance Formation outcrops near Lance Creek illustrates the light gray exposures of sandstone that represent sand bars deposited in the channels, as well as the darker gray mudstones formed when the rivers overflowed their banks. *Both photos by Lowell Dingus.*

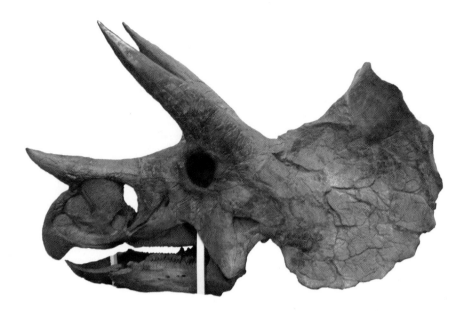

ABOVE: This side view of the imposing, horned dinosaur *Triceratops prorsus* [YPMVP.001822] clearly reveals the three horns for which this genus was named. Now on display in the Great Hall of Yale's Peabody Museum, it was discovered and collected by Hatcher in 1889, in the Lance Formation along Lance Creek in Wyoming. BELOW: Experience coming face-to-face with Hatcher's equally imposing skull of the horned dinosaur *Torosaurus latus* [YPMVP.001830], which he discovered in rock layers of the Lance Formation N of Lance Creek, Wyoming in 1891. *Both photos courtesy of the Division of Vertebrate Paleontology; Peabody Museum of Natural History, Yale University; peabody.yale.edu.*

ABOVE: This magnificent skeleton of *Edmontosaurus annectens* [YPM VPAR.000110] was collected by Hatcher in 1892 in the late Cretaceous sediments of the Lance Formation along Lance Creek north of Lusk, Wyoming. As displayed in the Great Hall of Yale's Peabody Museum, it represents the first dinosaur mount to be depicted with its backbone held more or less horizontally with the tail extended out behind off the ground. *Courtesy of the Division of Vertebrate Paleontology Archives; Peabody Museum of Natural History, Yale University; peabody. yale.edu. Scan by Alyson Heimer.* BELOW: A portion of the lower jaw of *Cimolestes incisus*, a genus of Cretaceous mammals that Hatcher discovered in the Lance Formation; this specimen was collected from the same exposures at Lance Creek, Wyoming where Hatcher and his field crews collected. [UCMP 46874 DPS 122222]; *photo by Dave Strauss, www.dscomposition.com.*

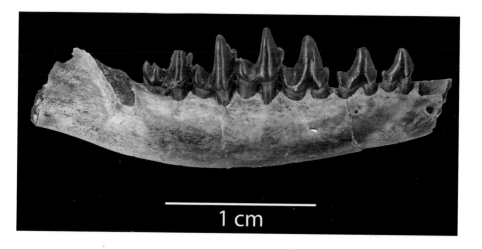

1 cm

RIGHT: Specimen of a toe bone from a horned or ceratopsian dinosaur, which Hatcher and his crews collected in 1892 at Lance Creek in Wyoming. The bone is still encased in the burlap jacket soaked in flour paste that was wrapped around the fossil bone to protect it during shipment back to Yale's Peabody Museum. [YPM VP.060174]. *Photograph by Lowell Dingus.*

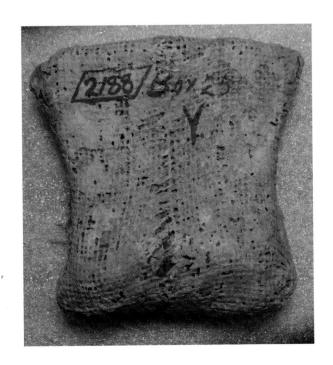

BOTTOM: John Bell Hatcher on horseback during the Princeton Scientific Expeditions between 1893 and 1895. *Courtesy of Princeton University Archives, Seeley G. Mudd Manuscript Library.*

ABOVE AND BELOW: Outcrops of the Uinta Formation along the Green River near Ouray, Utah, on the Uintah and Ouray Indian Reservation. *Photographs by Lowell Dingus.*

LEFT: John Bell Hatcher and his crew of Princeton students crating fossils during the Princeton Scientific Expeditions between 1893 and 1895. *Courtesy of Princeton University Archives, Seeley G. Mudd Manuscript Library.* BELOW: The mounted skeleton of *Diplacodon*, a relatively large Eocene mammal called a brontothere of which Hatcher found abundant fossil material in the Uinta Formation during the 1895 Princeton Scientific Expedition in Utah. *Courtesy of the Carnegie Museum of Natural History.*

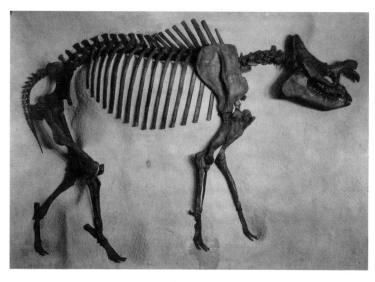

ABOVE: The exposures of the Santa Cruz Formation near Lake Pueyrredon in Patagonia as photographed by Hatcher in 1898. *Courtesy of the American Museum of Natural History Vert. Paleo. Archives; Seeley G. Mudd Manuscript Library, Princeton University Archives.* BELOW: The skull of the large herbivorous mammal named *Astrapotherium magnum* found by Hatcher near Guer Aike during his 1896–1897 Patagonian Expedition for Princeton [YPMVPPU.015332]. *Courtesy of the Division of Vertebrate Paleontology; Peabody Museum of Natural History, Yale University; peabody.yale.edu.*

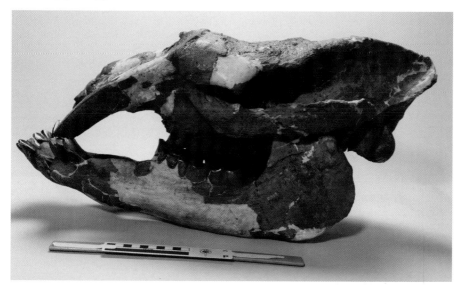

ABOVE: The skull of *Psilopterus australis*, a three-foot-tall "terror bird" that was collected by O. A. Peterson and represented one of the primary carnivores in the fauna of the Santa Cruz Formation in Patagonia between 16–18 million years ago. *Photograph by Lowell Dingus.* BELOW: Hatcher's image of his team and wagon mired in snow during the 1899 Patagonian Expedition for Princeton. *Courtesy of the American Museum of Natural History Vert. Paleo. Archives; Seeley G. Mudd Manuscript Library, Princeton University Archives.*

ABOVE LEFT: John Bell Hatcher, portrait taken during his tenure at the Carnegie Museum of Natural History from 1900-1904. *Courtesy of John Hatcher; Carnegie Museum of Natural History Archives.* ABOVE RIGHT: Portrait of Hatcher's staff in the Section of Vertebrate Paleontology at the Carnegie Museum of Natural History between 1900 and 1904: seated from left to right: Earl Douglass, Arthur S. Coggeshall, J. B. Hatcher, O. A. Peterson, and W. H. Utterback; standing from left to right: A. W. VanKirk, L. S. Coggeshall, Korman Boss, Sydney Prentice, and Charles W. Gilmore. *Courtesy of Carnegie Museum of Natural History.* BELOW: Hatcher's staff in the fossil preparation lab of the Carnegie Museum of Natural History between 1900 and 1904. *Courtesy of the Carnegie Museum of Natural History.*

ABOVE: The quarry site for the Carnegie Museum of Natural History's skeleton of *Diplodocus carnegii* in the Morrison Formation exposed along Sheep Creek north of Como Bluff and Medicine Bow, Wyoming. *Photograph by Lowell Dingus.* BELOW (BOTH IMAGES): The world-renowned skeletal mount of *Diplodocus carnegii* illustrated and reconstructed by Hatcher and his staff, as it appeared in the Carnegie Museum of Natural History when it first opened to the public in 1907, roughly three years after Hatcher's death. *Courtesy of the Carnegie Museum of Natural History.*

TOP: Mounted cast skeleton of *Diplodocus carnegii* at the Museums für Naturkunde in Berlin, Germany. *Photograph © Raimond Spekking / CC BY-SA 4.0 (http://creativecommons.org/licenses/by-sa/4.0/).* CENTER: Overview of exposures formed predominantly by the Brule and Chadron Formations taken along Badlands Loop Road in Badlands National Park, South Dakota. *Photograph by Lowell Dingus.*BOTTOM: O. A. Peterson's *Hoplophoneus primaevus* [CM 567 and 943], with its elongated, saber-shaped canine teeth, represents one of the earliest saber-toothed cats known and actually belongs to the same scientific family as living lions, cheetahs, and domestic cats—the Felidae. *Photograph by Lowell Dingus.*

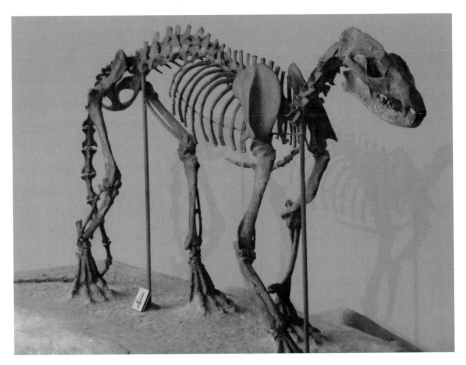

ABOVE: This skeleton of *Daphoenus felinus* [CM 492], collected by O. A. Peterson, represents a fine example of the relatively large carnivorous mammals called bear dogs, which belong to the family named Amphicyonidae. BELOW: Most of the fossils collected early on at the Agate Fossil Beds came from around the base of these two buttes—University Hill on the left, named in honor of the collecting crews from the University of Nebraska led by Erwin H. Barbour, and Carnegie Hill on the right, named in honor of O. A. Peterson and his Carnegie crew. *Both photographs by Lowell Dingus.*

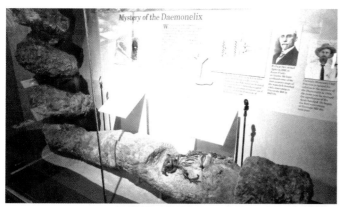

TOP: An exhibit at Agate Fossil Beds National Monument south of Harrison, Nebraska, reveals O. A. Peterson's discovery that solved the mystery of the corkscrew-shaped concretions called *Daemonelix* just before Hatcher died in 1904. Fossilized near the end of its burrow, the skeleton of an ancient beaver named *Palaeocastor* can be seen preserved in the burrow when it died. CENTER: This close up of the exhibit case demonstrates the position in which a *Palaeocastor* skeleton was found within the long, straight living chamber at the end of its corkscrew-shaped *Daemonelix* burrow. BOTTOM: Overview looking northeast at the Missouri River, with exposures of the Judith River Formation in the background, taken near where Montana State Road 236 crosses the river northwest of Winifred, Montana. *All photographs by Lowell Dingus.*

ABOVE: Steep exposures of the Judith River Formation just east of Montana State Road 236 shortly before it drops down off the bluff to cross the Missouri River northwest of Winifred, Montana. *Photograph by Lowell Dingus.* BELOW: Skull of *Deinosuchus* as reconstructed by the late Wann Langston of the University of Texas, Austin. *Courtesy of Timothy Rowe.*

ABOVE: John Bell and Anna Matilda Hatcher's house in Pittsburgh, Pennsylvania, at 3200 Elsinore Square. BELOW: John Bell Hatcher and family relaxing on porch: (Left to Right) Anna Matilda Peterson Hatcher (Wife) seated on steps, Alice Hatcher (Daughter, small girl standing on top step), Aida Peterson (standing on top step behind Anna), three unidentified women (center behind railing), Harold Hatcher (son, seated on porch railing), O. A. Peterson (Anna Matilda's brother and John Bell's brother-in-law, standing second from right), John Bell Hatcher (seated on railing). *Both images courtesy of John Hatcher.*

ABOVE: John Bell Hatcher (back) and Wife Anna Matilda (front right) pictured with their three children: Alice (held by John Bell), Earl (middle), Harold (front middle). Friends of the family, "Mrs. Ortman and child," are on the left. *Courtesy of John Hatcher.* CENTER: Portrait of Anna Matilda Peterson Hatcher. *Courtesy of Norman Hatcher.* BOTTOM: The touching headstone that marks the final resting place of John Bell Hatcher and his infant daughter Ruth is located on the grounds of the Homewood Cemetery in Pittsburgh, Pennsylvania. *Photo by Lauren Buches.*

for a place to ford, Hatcher encountered numerous terminal moraines left by the glacier that had once occupied the valley as it melted back toward the Andes. But the river was too swift and deep to cross at that point, so the duo had to descend sixty miles downstream before they found an abandoned boat. Although it was decrepit, they calked it up and left it in the water to soak and hopefully seal while they prospected in the adjacent cliffs. Finally on January 13, they disassembled and loaded the cart in the boat, drove their reluctant horses across the river by "pelting them with stones," and, with Peterson rowing while Hatcher steered, eventually navigated across the 300-yard-wide, 17-foot-deep river.[34]

After drying their gear and reassembling the cart, they managed to haul out of the valley, whose walls were formed by one enormous lava flow. They struck out to the north along the eastern edge of the river's gorge until the landscape broadened out into a high pampa, across which they could travel northwest until they reached the cliffs rising above the valley of the Río Sheuen or Río Chalia. Below, partway down to the valley, a considerable expanse of promising-looking badlands stretched before them. After a somewhat difficult descent, they set camp and hiked out to prospect: "Hardly had we reached the first exposure when I picked up a beautiful little jaw, with black, shining teeth, of *Abderites crassiramus*, a small extinct carnivorous marsupial." But despite this initial good luck, the badlands only yielded enough material to establish that they belonged to the Santa Cruz Formation. On the seventeenth, they reached the swampy valley floor, where, Hatcher writes, "throughout the night our horses and ourselves were almost literally devoured by mosquitoes," despite the fact that they wrapped themselves completely up in their tarps. Beating a hasty retreat from the bloodletting, they fled and found some intriguing invertebrate fossils on the nineteenth in exposures along the shore of a dry lake, before continuing across a pampa below cliffs of basalt teeming with bands of guanaco containing up to two hundred individuals, flocks of rhea numbering from ten to twelve, and plentiful condors perching on the adjacent bluffs of basalt. But Hatcher was most intrigued by the antics of the abundant armdillos, which, as Darwin likewise noted nearly sixty-five years earlier, proved especially tasty. By the twenty-third, after prospecting across another set of Santacrucian badlands, Hatcher and Peterson reached the Río Chico near Sierra Ventana, which represents the neck of an ancient volcano composed in part by "columns" of basalt and glassy obsidian formed as the lava cooled quickly in the crater's "throat." From the summit, Hatcher envisioned "a remote period . . . when the volcano, together with the others in the surrounding neighborhood, were in a state of violent activity and the great masses of igneous materials . . . were ejected from numerous fissures and poured out over the surface of the plain." He wondered if they had been responsible for "the extermination of that rich and varied fauna that lived and flourished . . . in Santa Cruzian times . . . but I had to confess my inability to arrive at a satisfactory answer. . . ."[35]

On the twenty-third, they began advancing up the Río Chico's valley following old Indian trails and feasting on ducks, plovers, guanaco, and rhea as they continued collecting the local fauna and flora, including flycatchers, chestnut-crowned song sparrows, Patagonian mocking birds, red-breasted meadow larks, doves, and both burrowing and short-eared owls. After several days, Hatcher clambered out of the valley to examine the "desolate . . . black, barren waste of lava" surrounding the river on all sides. Descending again to the valley, which turned west toward the Andes, they rambled over more glacial moraines that served as host for a regiment of different rodents, including a form of guinea pig, the tuco-tuco, and many others. So abundant were they that when a severe rainstorm hit the area on the first night the crew camped, so many drowned that the ground was covered in their carcasses to a depth of one inch to two feet. As Peterson tended to his traps, Hatcher climbed to the top of the ridge separating the Ríos Chico and Belgrano, where he saw a wide swath of open, well-grassed country between the lava fields to the east and the foothills of the Andes to the west, as well as an intriguing area of "bare, white bad-land hills." Following a two-day trek, the explorers passed through a narrow, stream-cut gap in a ridge of sediment formed by the Patagonian Formation that contained fossils of enormous oysters, "in which a single valve would measure a foot in length and the combined weight of . . . both upper and lower valves, could scarcely have fallen . . . short of forty pounds." In honor of these beasts, Hatcher named the passage Shell Gap, and they christened the great, beech-forested valley beyond Mayer Basin, in honor of their friend Edlemiro Mayer governor of Santa Cruz.[36]

After traipsing through a stand of "primeval Patagonian forest," attended by Chilean wrens and white-crested flycatchers, Hatcher discovered a patch of badlands composed of volcanic ash, in which the walls of one canyon "were entirely made up of the petrified trunks and branches of trees. Some of the former were several feet in diameter and many feet in length . . . interlocked with one another . . . to suggest that originally they had formed a natural dam in the current of some prehistoric stream." But he could find no vertebrate fossils in the ash and was headed back to camp when he encountered three deer, the first he had seen in Patagonia, merely twenty feet away,

> . . . *returning my expression of surprise with one of interested curiosity . . . Suddenly, remembering that we had been without fresh meat for breakfast, I deliberately, though reluctantly, drew my revolver . . . and having for a moment subdued the compassionate feeling with which I had been seized . . . dispatched one. . . . it was about as unsportsmanlike an act as could have been committed. But . . . it served the double purpose of supplying us with a supply of meat and an addition to our collection of skins. . . . The two survivors remained, unalarmed either by the report of the fatal shot, or the death struggles of their companion.*

Following a couple more days of collecting, they crossed the Continental Divide and camped below a 3,000-foot-high bluff that formed the southern border of the western half of Mayer Basin, part of which was composed of several hundred feet of variegated mudstone with occasional beds of fine sandstone. Hatcher was pleased to discover that these contained fragments of isolated dinosaur bones, and "in a pinkish colored stratum . . . I came upon the nearly complete forelimb of a large dinosaur." But since the humerus alone weighed around two hundred pounds, it would be impossible to haul it and all the other material they'd collected to the coast. Hence, he grudgingly left it in the ground in hopes of collecting it on another expedition, although it's not clear that he ever did.[37]

Hatcher and Peterson spent about ten days at this camp, with Peterson focused on collecting biological specimens near camp and Hatcher either bouncing across the bluff in a futile search for the Pyrotherium beds or hunting birds in the forest, such as the gray banded and red-headed woodpecker, brown creepers, barking birds, grebes, green parakeets, and five species of owls, as well as more deer, about which he recorded, "It was plainly evident that they were entirely unacquainted with man." Once again, they moved downstream about ten to fifteen miles to the center of Mayer Basin just south of Bald Mountain, which afforded an excellent view of the region's glaciers flowing down from the Andes. There they continued collecting zoological and botanical specimens until March 1, including night heron and a chestnut-colored goose.[38]

Stashing their wagon, Hatcher and Peterson converted their wagon team into packhorses and set off for the glaciers to the west by following and fording the braided channels of the Mayer River until they reached the terminal moraine: ". . . as we rode along the top . . . and looked upon the great white river of ice from three to five miles in width and perhaps forty in length, I thought it one of the most beautiful and impressive sites I had ever seen." Hatcher reveled in the geomorphology sculpted by the glacier, which helped him recognize some structural features he'd seen and puzzled over earlier on the trip through the interior. Entranced, the pair "built a rousing camp fire, around which we sat, until far into the night, talking alternately about our present surroundings and our experiences of the past few months, with occasional conjectures as to the health and doings of our relatives and friends at home." As they retreated downstream the next day, they collected some ammonites from an exposure of slate near the river. From there, they continued back toward their main camp in the Mayer Basin, but one of their packhorses spooked and ran off into the dense forest—an alarming event given the three hundred miles they would need to traverse back to the coast with their collections. First, Peterson set off in pursuit, while Hatcher guided the rest of the entourage. Then Hatcher, convinced that the missing horse wouldn't range far, searched near one of the camps they had used on the way out to the glacier: "As I emerged from the forest . . . I caught site of the object of my quest. Immediately the horse saw me [and] came trotting toward me with such an expression of joy depicted on his countenance as I have seldom seen in any of the dumb animals." With all accounted for, the crew reunited at their main camp in the Mayer Basin and spent a few more day collecting biological specimens among the beech forest, laced with mosses and ferns along its floor.[39]

The middle of March saw Hatcher and Peterson pack up their already heavily laden cart and head for the coast, as the first blush of the coming winter began to brush the forest leaves in shades of yellow and red and freeze the water holes at night. Scarcely a mile from the main camp, "while descending a short, steep slope, our cart turned completely upside down, breaking off both shafts close up to the body. However, we were fully prepared . . . and with axe, brace, bit [and] monkey wrench . . . in a couple of hours we had hewn and fitted a new pair of shafts . . . from the forest saplings." For the most part, they retraced their route down the Río Chico and across the divide to the Río Santa Cruz, where they sold their horses and cart and shipped their collections down to Santa Cruz in an auxiliary boat of the schooner *Cross-Owen*. Repacking their plunder for shipment to New York, they reached Gallegos in early May 1897, five months after departing for the interior. Hatcher noted, "During this time we had not only received no news of the outside world . . . but after leaving the Santa Cruz River . . . we met with no person, either Indian or white, until . . . we reached the settlements near the mouth of the Rio Chico."[40]

Tragic news awaited Hatcher and Peterson upon their arrival in Gallegos; not only had Governor Mayer unexpectedly passed but there had also been a death in their own family:

> *We received our first letters from relatives and friends at home, whom we had left fourteen months earlier. They brought news of the sad death, on the eighteenth of the preceding November, of my youngest son* [John], *a little boy just entering his fourth year, to whom both myself and his uncle, Mr. Peterson, were naturally much attached by many tender remembrances.*[41]

Upon learning that no ship heading north was soon expected, the grieving pair decided to sail around Tierra del Fuego on the *Villarino* when it arrived in two weeks. They headed for Punta Arenas on May 20, and on their voyage visited Villarino Bay, sailed through the Beagle Channel, stopped at Lapataia and Ushuaia, proceeded to Bridges Station, then on to St. John's and up the eastern coast to San Sebastian Bay. After returning to Gallegos on June 4, they loaded their remaining collections as they passed Santa Cruz and arrived at Buenos Aires on June 12. Eager to return home, the fatigued frontiersmen booked passage on the *Maskelyne* and set sail for New York on June 17, arriving a month later on July 17, 1897.[42]

After this first Patagonian foray, Hatcher published his first formal, if somewhat feeble, critique regarding the Ameghinos' contention that the Pyrotherium beds were Cretaceous:

> *I seriously question the stratigraphic position of the Pyrotherium beds as determined by the brothers Ameghino, although it may seem presumptuous on my part, since I was unable to identify the beds at all, and the explorations, travels and opportunities for observations in this region of Senor Carlos Ameghino have been far more extensive than have my own.*[43]

Clearly, more fieldwork was needed.

12

Discovery Followed by Disease and Disappointment

W hen Hatcher returned to Princeton, he was pleased with the results of his first Patagonian foray, but as he freely confided to Scott and his donors, "There remained much to be done." True to his word, Hatcher immediately began preparations for his next transcontinental trip, and by November 9, 1897, he sailed for Buenos Aires, while somewhat defensively declaring, "after a stay of nearly four months at home." Peterson preferred to stay put for a bit longer, and Hatcher was no doubt happy to have him work on preparing their most significant fossils from their first venture so they'd be ready to study and publish on when he returned. Accordingly, he turned to a taxidermist from Washington, D.C., by the name of A. E. Colburn to assist him on this odyssey. Colburn, in addition to being "a most kind and obliging young man," also brought some field experience to the enterprise, having participated on expeditions to Newfoundland and Florida. The other most noticeable change on this trip was not at all surprising, as Hatcher emphatically noted, "I took with me on the second a light two-and-three-quarter-inch mountain wagon with a good pair of double harness."[1]

Boarding the *Cacique* in New York, they sailed directly for Punta Arenas, which they reached after a voyage of thirty-two days on December 11. It took only a few days to secure the required steeds and supplies, at which point they established their first camp just north of town on the Río de las Minas. Since Hatcher hadn't collected much this far south on the first expedition, he and Colburn spent two weeks here, with Colburn hunting birds while Hatcher gathered botanical specimens and collected invertebrate fossils from the "several hundred feet of Tertiary deposits . . . exposed in the sides of this cañon." These beds were primarily of marine origin and represented several distinct horizons, but near the top a number of veins of pure lignite cropped out, suggesting a more brackish water environment.[2]

By early January 1898, the pair punched north at a leisurely pace to Gallegos, stopping to collect birds, mammals, and plants before purchasing another pair of work hoses so they could have four to pull the wagon. From there, they diverted west about seventy-five miles along the southern fork of the Río Coy to visit Indian villages, with the goal of securing "a series of photographs and procure material illustrating their arts and industries sufficient for reconstructing a family group for the United States National Museum." The first village they visited boasted a population of forty to fifty, but only about half were truly Tehulche, with the remainder either European or ethnically mixed between the two. The initial reception was rather cool, until Hatcher handed out "a judicious distribution of tobacco among the men, and raisins, sweet chocolate, ginger snaps, and other similar articles among the women and children," which notably improved the perceived estimation of the visitors and helped "establish ourselves on terms of friendly intimacy with them." Hatcher and Colburn had scant trouble acquiring common objects, such as rugs, bridles, saddles, and bolos, but "no amount of money would tempt them to part with the fur mantle, rattle, or other childish toys belonging to one of the children." Likewise, for a while, the denizens were loath to pose for photos, until Hatcher "succeeded in getting one of the young women to stand for her photograph. From this I made a few prints and gave her . . . thereafter . . . I was fairly besieged by those wanting pictures taken of themselves." But that still didn't break the barrier of obtaining childhood articles, which Hatcher desperately wanted, especially a cradle called a *tolda* for sheltering babies inside their dwelling, as well as during transport. Offers for as much as the Argentine equivalent of $75, just over $2,000 in today's currency, were roundly rejected, until,

> *fortunately, . . . on the evening previous to the day we had set for our departure the father and mother of the child to whom the cradle belonged came to us with the pleasing information that, since their child had almost outgrown the need of the cradle, and as they were, for the present at least, not expecting the arrival of another occupant, they were willing to dispose of it and for a much less sum than that which we had already offered.*

With that, the satisfied travelers consummated their deal and set off back down along the Río Coy to Gallegos, where they packed up their collections to date and left them with their friend Halliday.[3]

After a short ride up the coast to Santa Cruz, they again headed inland in search of the elusive Pyrotherium beds by way of the two-hundred-mile trek up the Río Chico that Hatcher had descended half a year earlier. A few miles below the mouth of the Río Belagrano, the wagon got stuck in the middle when they tried to ford it. "With the water running half way over the box" of the wagon, they were able to free the horses and get their supplies to shore, then eventually rescue the wagon by attaching the picket ropes to the wagon's tongue and pulling it out with the horses. However, the near disaster had cost them "most of our salt and a considerable portion of our sugar" through dissolution by the water.[4]

But their greatest concern was for their swamped matches: "Since neither of us smoked, we did not need many matches, and as we still had a few small boxes of dry ones, we decided to go on with these" and hope some of the others would work when they dried. Once underway again, they struck out northward through the valley between the basalt tableland on the west and the lava flows to the east, all the while collecting zoological and botanical specimens as condors soared overhead. A few caverns in the lava provided good collections of beetles, crickets, spiders, a centipede, and a scorpion, along with abundant black lizards on the lava itself. At the northern border of the valley extended a wide open plain, which afforded a smooth, twenty-mile pathway to the north as they passed Mount Belagrano towering to the west. Then their path was broken by the deep narrow valley of Spring Creek, into which they descended to set camp by a sparkling spring of excellent water.[5]

Again Colburn chased after birds and mammals, while Hatcher examined the geology. A significant section of rock layers composed of barren brown sandstone and dull red igneous porphyries formed the canyon walls, but no significant fossils could be found. Nonetheless, a lake at the end of Spring Creek supported gastropods, clams, ducks, plover, grebes, flamingos, and at the time of Hatcher's visit, more than a thousand swans, leading him to name the body of water Swan Lake. Proceeding to the next valley to the south, Hatcher found more exposures with a few vertebrate fossils, which, although not worthy of keeping, allowed him to identify the sediments as Santacrucian. Here, he bedded down for the night, entertained for a while by "the playful antics of a specimen of the little gray fox, *Canis azarae* . . . he ran and frisked about in a manner quite like that of a favorite domestic dog. . . . I permitted the sport to continue for several minutes, then, drawing my revolver from its scabbard, I dispatched the beautiful animal. . . ." In times past, Hatcher's campsite had also hosted native peoples, as evidenced by "numerous fragments of broken pottery, stone scrapers, drills and arrow points."[6]

After returning to check on Colburn the next morning and grabbing a fresh horse, Hatcher explored north of Spring Creek, where the plain above the valley was littered with small round hills of glacial debris. After a while, he reached a steep drop-off formed by the intimidating cliffs overlooking the broad, deep valley of the Arroyo Gio. Turning west, he traveled along the edge of these bluffs to a point where, as he later recalled,

I got my first view of the eastern extremity of Lake Pueyrredon, of which at that time I believed myself to be the discoverer, and which in a short paper I subsequently called Lake Princeton.... It had, however, been discovered during the same season, but a few months earlier, by Senor von Platen, an engineer of the Argentine Boundary Commission. Though Lake Princeton has priority of publication, I gladly relinquish it in favor of Pueyrredon, the name given by the Argentine commission after a vessel in the navy of that country. To Senor von Platen belongs the credit for the discovery of this magnificent lake, with a length of fifty miles and an average breadth of from five to ten miles.

From the bluffs of the Arroyo Gio, Hatcher spied some badlands to the northwest and descended to examine them. They turned out to be the bluffs of the Río Blanco, which were formed exclusively of glacial debris and devoid of fossils. After he climbed back out of the canyon, it was dark, and Hatcher's horse was in no condition to continue on to camp. So he bedded down under the stars by a "rousing fire" and silently reflected on his sublime surroundings, friends, family, and future plans. Settled in his own skin, he resolved, "Those who have a true love of nature must at times find this affection so strong as to drive them beyond the limits of civilization to some retreat where, unmolested, they may study her in her true form and beyond the environmental influences of man."[7]

Following Hatcher's return to camp, the crew moved their camp to the north side of the Spring Creek valley, then Hatcher set out for Lake Pueyrredon, "where from a distance I had already observed that there were considerable exposures of what appeared to be sedimentary rocks"— perhaps the mysterious Pyrotherium beds. Heading west, he reached an elevated point between Lakes White and Pueyrredon in the late afternoon. The rocks of this hogback included layers of various, brilliantly colored sandstone, including some unusual green ones that matched the "gall-green" colored pebbles described by Darwin covering the shingle in places near the coast. The surface of the hogback had been scoured by glaciers, and due to the coarse nature of the deposits, no fossils were found. The next morning, Hatcher headed on to the southwest corner of Lake Pueyrredon, where he met a crew from the Chilean Boundary Commission, with whom he briefly exchanged pleasantries. The lake occupied a deep valley less than three hundred feet above sea level, and at the southeast corner an enormous, steep bluff rose five thousand feet above the valley and was composed primarily of Cretaceous and Tertiary sediments, except for about fifty feet of basalt separating the two sedimentary units.[8]

Picketing his horse, Hatcher began an ascent armed only with his collecting tools and satchel: "The task proved a greater undertaking than I had anticipated, but . . . after several hours of hard climbing, interrupted by frequent stops to . . . collect fossils from some particularly promising exposures, I arrived at the summit." The view was supremely captivating, with the sun's rays reflecting off the mirror-like surface of the lake, and to boot, the bluff had revealed the most complete geologic section of the units present on the plains below that Hatcher had ever seen:

> *At the base were several hundred feet of Cretaceous materials . . . embracing several distinct horizons. Next followed fifty feet of basalt . . . in places . . . highly columnar. This in turn was overlaid by about one thousand feet of marine Tertiary deposits, rich in fossil remains, while above this came fifteen hundred feet of . . . the Santa Cruz formation, and at the extreme top [was] two to three hundred feet of marine beds belonging to the Cape Fairweather formation.[9]*

At first in the steeply inclined Santacrucian layers, Hatcher only found fossil forms with which he was already familiar: *Nesodon*, typotheres, armored and unarmored edentates, etc. But near the summit, he encountered a less resistant layer of mudstone that had weathered into a broad ledge, allowing him to prospect more carefully with better footing:

> *I came upon a splendid skull of Nesodon . . . Continuing a little farther, I ascended to another more extreme platform. Hardly had I reached the surface of this when I discovered an almost complete skeleton of a fossil bird about the size of the blue heron, while close at hand lay another fossilized skeleton belonging to Diadiaphorous,*

an ungulate mammal, and near at hand lay several skulls and parts
of skeletons of small carnivorous marsupials.

He excavated and packed the bird, parts of the ungulate, and a couple of the carnivorous marsupial skulls, then struggled on up to the summit, where he marveled that this block had been uplifted around five thousand feet in relatively recent geologic times as the Andes rose, before the valley below was scooped out by the similarly immense forces of ice and water. After a "thrilling descent," Hatcher tended to his horse and wrapped himself up in his saddle blanket and slicker to sleep "after one of the finest and most pleasantly and profitably spent days I experienced while in Patagonia. . . ." Although he attempted to return to his bonanza horizon the next day, a blinding, blustery snowstorm intervened halfway up his ascent, driving him back down the mountain and soaking him to his core. Although he had originally planned to be gone one day, he was again forced to camp in the freezing temperatures of the severe storm without much food. He retreated toward the main camp, about sixty-five miles distant, the next morning, and although he succeeded in shooting a deer for food, his shots were so inaccurate that he unintentionally wounded three, including a fawn; not wishing to see them suffer more, he dispatched them all. Although now supplied with venison, Hatcher struggled another couple of days through the snow. He encountered several enticing exposures that he desperately wanted to investigate. But his horse was spent, he was now almost a week late in returning to Colburn's camp, and he felt he must move on. Finally, he rode in, much to Colburn's relief.[10]

Hatcher was sorely tempted to return to the bluff by Lake Pueyrredon, but reasoning that there seemed scant chance of finding the Pyrotherium beds there, not to mention the worsening weather, he determined to push farther north. After several days of traveling through valleys by adjacent basalt bluffs, stopping to collect zoological specimens along the way, they reached the southern end of the maze of strikingly scenic, 2,000-foot-deep basalt canyons east of Lake Gio. Setting camp in a gorge drained by a clear, pristine stream stocked with fish, Colburn continued his collecting, while Hatcher searched seventy-five miles to the east and as far north as Lake Buenos Aires in vain for the Pyrotherium beds. His excursions lasted up to a week or ten days, so he stocked himself with ample supplies, including bread, rice, split peas, salt, pepper, tea, coffee, and sugar, while relying on his hunting skills for meat. In his forays among the basalt canyons to the east, he realized that they could not have been cut by the small streams now flowing through them but must have been cut by larger rivers that drained the region prior to the uplift of the Andes and the subsequent period of glaciation. The walls of these eastern canyons were formed by igneous and metamorphic rocks that had been cut into by rivers to form valleys now filled with sediments of the Patagonian and Santa Cruz Formations. These observations forced Hatcher

> to the conclusion that, during middle Tertiary times, this region existed either as a great island, or . . . a chain of islands, belonging to a former great continental land mass . . . surrounded by a shallow sea, over the bottom of which were deposited the Patagonian beds. In the later Santa Crusian epoch this region became more elevated and the island, or islands, appeared as a low mountain range above the surface of a broad level plain. It was then that the erosion began [that] produced the present deeply dissected condition of the country.[11]

Hatcher's "lonely" wanderings were accompanied by enlivening episodes of rescuing horses or ascending and descending the treacherous canyon walls that "imparted a certain spirit of adventure to the work." Especially reminiscent was one night when he was awakened by the "sudden stampeding of my horses," which he was certain had been caused by a marauding mountain lion. Alarmed by the prospect of being horseless some seventy-five miles from his base camp, which "would have proved a serious inconvenience," Hatcher grabbed his boots and scrambled off in pursuit in the pitch dark, having to rely more on hearing than eyesight; yet he knew that the canyon would confine his horses' flight. Finally, rounding a bend, he heard the sound of their hooves and approached with extreme caution so as not to spook them again. Eventually, they became aware of his presence, "after which, much to the evident delight of both the parties concerned, and which they on their part showed by a succession of friendly whinnies, I had no difficulty whatever in catching them. . . ." In addition to collecting fossils that would help determine the age of the sediments in the canyon walls, other pastimes, surrounding lunch breaks and noontime naps, included one of his most enduring fascinations—watching condors perched perilously on the jagged basaltic pinnacles or soaring effortlessly on thermals some thousands of feet above the canyon in search of carcasses to scavenge. Another denizen rarely seen on the Patagonian plains but present in these canyon lands was the Chilean deer, more typical of forested Andean habitats.[12]

To the northwest between Lakes Gio and Buenos Aires, Hatcher's work was hindered by dense smoke from forest fires set by crews of the Boundary Commissions for Argentina and Chile, making long-distance reconnaissance from high points impossible. He did return to some Santacrucian beds to the south between the base of the Andes and the interior basaltic tablelands, but snow cut that side trip short, causing him to return to camp April 29. Nonetheless, Hatcher, "since my search had been so thorough," felt reasonably sure that no Pyrotherium beds were exposed in this region—a result that he candidly characterized as making his monthlong sequence of solitary sojourns "signally unsuccessful." Throughout, he had braved the elements sleeping outside on the ground, often in damp if not soaking conditions "with inadequate equipment, considering the magnitude of the task." Given the onset of winter and the ground cover of snow starting to accumulate, it seemed pointless to persevere, so Hatcher and Colburn determined to head back to the coast, where they could more profitably pass the winter collecting fossils and waterfowl in the regions where the Santa Cruz and Patagonian beds were exposed. In all, wrote Hatcher, "Mr. Colburn had secured an excellent series of the skins and skeletons of recent birds and mammals, while I, in addition to knowledge gained in the geology and geography of the region, had made important collections of recent plants and invertebrates [as well as] vertebrate and invertebrate fossils." With their wagon fully loaded, they were ready to depart the next day.[13]

But as the day dawned, Hatcher's "left knee was considerably swollen and quite painful, while the right was somewhat affected as was also my left arm." Regardless, they set out into a "raw, cold" wind out of the southwest, since Hatcher believed these minor ailments of his chronic "rheumatism" would soon pass. By evening, they reached the valley east of Lake Gio, where Hatcher, with increasingly enflamed knees, spent a feverish night. "The following morning the pain caused by the rheumatism in my knees and elbows was so intense, that it was only with the greatest difficulty I succeeded in harnessing the horses and gaining my seat on the wagon." His pain intensified, aggravated by traversing the bumpy hillocks of glacial debris, until they arrived near Spring Creek the second evening. Persisting through the pain, Hatcher diverted toward some springs near a meadow by Swan Lake, which they reached on May 3. There, his fever was so high and his arms and legs so swollen that he couldn't continue and lay bed-ridden for six weeks as the disease spread into his feet and hands:

> I was absolutely helpless and unable to shift myself or attend to my most trivial wants. Never has an invalid received more conscientious care than did I at the hands of Mr. Colburn. His care and patience were most exemplary, although I fear they were bestowed upon a somewhat unworthy person. If at times . . . I appeared unnecessarily harsh or cross, I trust he will ascribe it to the great mental and physical pain with which I was afflicted, for looking back from this somewhat distant perspective I know and fully realize that to his tender care I am indebted for the privilege I now enjoy of making this humble, though grateful acknowledgment of his kind attention.[14]

Finally, by June 29, Hatcher could hobble along with the help of a crutch Colburn had fashioned, and they resumed their journey to Gallegos, some five hundred miles away, through the snow, shoveling it away over a patch large enough to accommodate their beds every night. They greatly feared that the Río Chico would be choked with ice when they reached it, rendering it impossible to cross, but upon their late arrival, it was frozen solid to a thickness over which they could simply drive. On July 26, the weary crew rolled into the settlements near the mouth of the Río Chico, where they first learned of the ongoing Spanish-American War. With Hatcher more or less on the mend, they pressed on, leaving their wagon and outfit there and heading for Gallegos on horseback. But upon reaching the town of Santa Cruz and learning that a steamer was due shortly, Colburn decided to take it to Punta Arenas so he could begin his voyage home, since "he had had quite enough of Patagonia."[15]

Hatcher had just set off for Gallegos alone on horseback when a ferocious rainstorm that eventually changed to snow enveloped him. Nonetheless, he persevered and reached a small estancia about thirty miles below Santa Cruz about 10:00 P.M., where he was warmly sheltered, "which, considering my benumbed and crippled condition, was indeed most welcome. . . ." By morning, the storm had morphed into a full-blown blizzard, so he couldn't press on until the next day. The icy landscape made travel treacherous: "In my crippled condition, I could walk only with the greatest difficulty, and progress on foot was not only painful but exceedingly tedious. To mount or dismount from my horse required great effort and was attended with considerable pain." His unshod horses commonly slipped and slid on the ice, and he eventually had to abandon all but one along the way. On the fifth day of his trek in late August, Hatcher stumbled into Halliday's estancia, "whose hospitality, as well as that of his wife and family, are proverbial throughout Patagonia." After recouping for several days under their care, Hatcher crossed the river to Gallegos to retrieve his mail and receive medical care. Then he holed up in Gallego's finest, yet still hellish, hotel:

> I was unable to procure what I most needed—a warm and comfortable room. Indeed, not only was there no fire anywhere . . . save the kitchen, but the building itself partook more of the nature of a dilapidated country barn than that of a habitation for human beings . . . and nothing like as comfortable as a good tent. . . . For such miserable accommodations I paid five dollars per day. . . . In order to keep myself reasonably warm, I was compelled to take to my bed throughout a greater portion of each day, arising only for my meals.

> *. . . Moreover, the additional expense incurred by my illness was*
> *rapidly depleting the at no time very plethoric funds at my disposal,*
> *so I was constantly harassed both in mind and body.*[16]

While Hatcher was thus reeling from "rheumatism," Captain Wilson, an American acquaintance who owned a small ship named *Estrella* that ferried between Gallegos and Punta Arenas, dropped by to visit. Horrified by Hatcher's condition, he implored him to join him immediately on his return south, where a steamer bound for New York was expected shortly. Hatcher reluctantly agreed, but "this decision brought me to a painful realization of the depleted state of my funds, for after paying my hotel bill and a number of other smaller accounts, I found that I only had a few dollars remaining. However, my reputation for honesty was beyond reproach, and I had no hesitancy in applying . . . for a loan of fifty dollars. . . . This request was most cheerfully complied with." Wilson shepherded Hatcher to Punta Arenas on September 21, where Hatcher requested if the agents for the Grace Line would accept a personal check on his local Princeton bank as payment for passage on the *Maori* back to New York. His request being "most assuredly" granted, a weary and physiologically wounded Hatcher departed Patagonia on the twenty-third and, "after a tedious voyage of forty-seven days," arrived in New York on November 9, 1898.[17]

Interestingly, paleontologist S. David Webb notes that Hatcher's accounts in his narrative progressively shorten during the second and third Patagonian expeditions, a trend that he attributes primarily to Hatcher's inability to find his long-sought quarry—the Pyrotherium beds. The narrative for the second expedition is but one quarter the length of that for the first, despite the fact that it was only a few months shorter, and Hatcher's description of the third expedition was merely one tenth as long as that of the first. Webb also perceives a growing sense of disorientation as Hatcher's frustration mounts in his desperate search, although Webb concedes that Hatcher's injuries and ailments, along with increasing financial strains in mounting the expeditions, could also have played roles in Hatcher's troubled state of mind.[18]

Incredibly, Hatcher truculently refused to take off more than a month at home before he once again embarked for Patagonia with Peterson in tow on December 9. Joining them on this junket was a young Barnum Brown. Henry Fairfield Osborn had arranged for Brown to collaborate and collect on behalf of the AMNH through Scott, Osborn's former classmate at Princeton. Hatcher was not at all thrilled because he had conceived of the project and did much of the work to set it up under the sponsorship of Princeton. He no doubt also still harbored ill feelings toward Osborn in the wake of their failed negotiations and their acrimonius aftermath over a possible position at the AMNH for Hatcher, as well as the complications caused by earlier collaborations with Osborn's crews during the Princeton Scientific Expeditions. Nonetheless, Hatcher eventually and grudgingly allowed Brown to participate. Osborn was especially intent upon extending the scope of the AMNH fossil mammal collections beyond the bounds of North America, and was determined that the AMNH would play a significant role in the trendy contemporary debate raised by the discoveries and research of the Ameghino brothers.[19]

Brown's participation was fortunate, at least in terms of paleontological history; he kept his own notes, which he summarized in an unpublished manuscript entitled "Patagonia: Land's End." It was written for an autobiography he never finished that provides additional insight and perspective on Hatcher and this expedition. On the morning of departure, the 25-year-old Brown awoke and trudged through a snowy New York City to his job. But unbeknownst to the newly minted paleontological assistant and fossil collector, he would not end the day in New York. As he later related:

> *I arrived at the museum at 9 o'clock as usual, but before I had taken my hat off, Professor Osborn called me into his office.*
>
> *"Brown, I want you to go to Patagonia today with the Princeton expedition. . . . The boat leaves at eleven; will you go?"*
>
> *"This is short notice, Professor Osborn, but I'll be on that boat. . . ."*

Brown, who had never been out of the country before, instantly set about gathering up his equipment with the help of members on the museum's support staff, including his "boots, saddle, bridle, winchester rifle, blankets, and heavy tarpaulin cover."[20]

The trio boarded the Grace Line freighter *Capac* for the voyage to Punta Arenas. The long cruise proved trying for Brown in more than one way; as he later admitted, he "had never been to sea before and soon was a victim of seasickness, first hoping I would die, then afraid I wouldn't. . . ." To pass the time and ease his anxiety, Brown played cards with his colleagues but was apparently unaware that Hatcher was a "master at poker." Brown describes Hatcher as "a man of average height, lean, about 35 years of age, with an uncommon knowledge of human nature." According to Brown, Hatcher's face was "inscrutable, and you never knew whether he had a bob-tail flush, or a full house." Allegedly, while participating in some poker sessions, Hatcher would lose "his entire year's salary," then vow to win it all back in the next session. Early on in the voyage, before Brown had a chance to gauge his opponent:

> *Petersen* [sic] *came up and asked if I would like to join in a poker game. Being fond of poker, I agreed but neglected to ascertain the values of the . . . chips. When this game ended . . . I was the sixteen dollar loser.* [almost $450 in modern currency]
>
> *From then on during the entire voyage we played poker night and day, everyone losing to Hatcher. "Brown," he would say, "I hate to take your money as I know your salary is only fifty dollars a month." But in the last game . . . when Petersen* [sic] *and the captain had dropped out leaving only Hatcher and myself betting, we kept raising the bets until finally Hatcher called, showing three tens to my three queens . . . I regained almost all I had lost during the voyage.*[21]

Otherwise, the monthlong voyage proved uneventful, and the crew arrived in Punta Arenas on January 10, 1899, where they immediately set about gathering their gear and supplies. Perusing the stores, the crew found them well stocked with "barrels of macaroni in all shapes . . . rice, beans; bags of sugar, coffee and Mate tea, slabs of bacon, dried smoked beef, all cuts of fresh mutton; tallow, candles; stalls of camp equipment, harnesses, bridles, leather goods; stoves, shovels, picks and crowbars; bins walled off containing whiskey . . . bottles of Italian and Spanish wines." As always, finding fit horses was challenging. In the eyes of Hatcher, as recalled by Brown, the care of some owners also lacked something to be desired: "One horse trader . . . was beating [his horse] over the head with the loaded end of his quirt [net]. 'Beat that horse once more, and you'll be a dead man,' said Hatcher, drawing his revolver; I firmly believe he would have shot the trader." [22]

While Peterson and Brown drove the cart northward to Santa Cruz via Gallegos to gather the horses Hatcher had abandoned a couple of months previously, Hatcher took a steamer to San Julian, where he made a collection of invertebrate fossils at Oven Point before joining his crew at Santa Cruz. Then, they all set out for Lake Pueyrredon, following the same trail Hatcher had traveled the previous season. Hatcher brought an extra saddle and pack animals so that while Peterson and Brown managed the wagon, he could "be spared the irksome duties of a teamster and devote my entire time as we passed along to the study of the surrounding country." Accordingly, he conducted geologic investigations into the composition of the Río Chico bluffs, the basaltic platform, and the upper boundary of the shingle. His purpose for returning to Lake Pueyrredon was to make certain he had not missed any exposures of the Pyrotherium beds, since Ameghino's publications implied they might be there. Despite spending several days on the summit of the bluff at the southeast corner of the lake being blasted by snowstorms, the crew "failed" in that "principal purpose." Nonetheless, they succeeded in securing "a considerable collection of vertebrates and invertebrates from the Santa Cruz, Cape Fairweather and Patagonian beds." Hatcher also discovered rich, new Cretaceous invertebrate localities along the Río Tarde and near Lake Blanco, which produced around thirty-six new species. [23]

In all, the crew spent two weeks near Pueyrredon before heading back to the coast, with Peterson and Brown returning by the same route and Hatcher heading south "to explore the country lying between the lake and the headwaters of the Rios Belgrano and Chico." Along the way, Hatcher encountered a mountain lion and gave chase before it disappeared into a small canyon:

> . . . I halted for a moment to reconnoiter. I knew the inability of this animal . . . to maintain any considerable speed for a long distance, and that when once beyond my sight he would seek refuge in concealment rather than flight. Over the slopes and bottom of the shallow cañon there was a considerable growth of scattered brush. By carefully scanning the ground about these I soon discovered the object of my search stretched at full length upon the ground. To dispatch him with a rifle ball was the work of but a moment and required neither skill nor courage. I preserved both skin and skeleton, and, much to my surprise, they have been considered . . . as belonging to a new subspecies.[24]

Shortly after parting ways with his other crew members, Hatcher was once again doused by rain, which created muddy flats and surging streams that forced the frontiersman to bed down unsheltered except for his slicker and tarp just southwest from the base of Mount Belagrano. Upon awaking the next morning, "the sight that greeted me was, to say the least, anything but cheerful. The storm, so far from abating, had increased in fury and presented all the aspects of a full-fledged Wyoming blizzard." As the angry winds swept down from the Andes, blowing snow obscured even the largest landmarks, creating "a most bewildering effect upon the traveler forced to continue his journey across the almost level . . . plain." Once on horseback, Hatcher hoped to reach a basaltic region to the south, where he could find a small cave in which to weather the storm.[25]

He succeeded in this quest, and the next day dawned cold but clear. So Hatcher decided to revisit the enchanting environs of Mayer Basin. There, he collected invertebrate fossils, while feasting on venison. After several days, he packed up and set off down the Río Chico for Santa Cruz, where he uneventfully arrived two weeks before his crew and spent that time "collecting invertebrate fossils from the locality in the Patagonian beds, at the mouth of the river made famous by Darwin." Much to Hatcher's delight, his efforts resulted in the discovery of "several new species."[26]

When Peterson and Brown arrived in Santa Cruz, Hatcher "turned over to the latter such of my outfit as he desired to use in continuing his work" and sent Peterson with Brown to introduce him to the exposures of the Santa Cruz Formation to the south before Peterson departed to collect elsewhere and left Brown to his work. Although paleontological lore sometimes suggests that Hatcher abandoned his young colleague in Patagonia, Brown expressed no ill feelings about being left to fend for himself in the wilds. Given Hatcher's occasionally prickly personality and Brown's predominant preference for being a loner in the field, the separation probably suited them both. But an issue was festering that would cause friction between the interests of Hatcher and Brown.[27]

On April 24, 1899, about the time that Hatcher left for home and Brown set out alone to collect along the Patagonian coast, Osborn wrote his young explorer. The letter didn't make it into Brown's hands for almost four months, and when it did, Brown was not pleased. Osborn's letter contained a revised contract regarding the terms under which Brown was participating in the expedition. In his response to Osborn, Brown stated at the outset: "Before signing this paper I wish to have a better understanding of its meaning. Also to discuss my relation to the museum." When Brown left on the expedition, Osborn and Scott had already negotiated most of the details regarding Brown's involvement in the enterprise and how the specimens that were collected would be divided. Brown, as Hatcher alluded to during the poker games, would receive a salary of at least $50 a month, a sum that equaled about $1,700 a month in today's dollars. Brown's salary would be doubled if Osborn successfully raised more funding from his friends and museum trustees. Brown also received $500 in cash for expenses, along with the understanding that another $500 could be drawn from the AMNH account during the first year as needed. Specimens collected by Hatcher and Peterson would become the property of Princeton, while those discovered by Brown would belong to the AMNH, but with a couple of provisions. As originally drafted, the agreement, according to Brown, stipulated, "material new to the Princeton Collection is to be worked up and described by myself." In other words, Brown would describe and name any new species or genera that he found. Once published, Scott and Hatcher would have the right to include that material in their own reports on the expedition.[28]

However, the revised agreement that Osborn sent in April set slightly new terms, stating that Brown could publish only new "genera of vertebrate fossils that are not contained in the Princeton collection." Brown protested directly to Osborn about that modification: "I may have any number of new species of a described genera [sic. genus] and not be able to describe them" under the revised agreement. Another change involved the publication of geologic information gleaned during the expedition. As Brown complained to Osborn in the same letter:

> *Article IV reads: "That J. B. Hatcher shall have the right to publish any observations upon the Geology of Patagonia."*
>
> *This is also vastly different from our agreement which reads "his observations" and means a great deal to me as I look over my notebook. You can readily see the position my notes are placed in at present to say nothing of future work. I want none of Mr. Hatcher's observations but I do want my own.*[29]

Brown, thoroughly isolated from discussions that involved him and apparently feeling more than a bit insecure about his prospects, decided, like the good poker player that he was, that it was time to show his hand. Thus, this instance appears to represent a seminal moment in the development of the professional relationship between Osborn and Brown. Having studied under Marsh's former assistant Williston at the University of Kansas and having just spent almost half a year traveling with Hatcher, it's difficult to imagine that Brown was unaware of the stories about how Marsh had mistreated his assistants, at least in the eyes of those assistants. Osborn, like Marsh, had conducted much of his postgraduate studies in Europe, where the major professor was master and assistants rarely participated in key decisions or publications. Although Osborn was often an "overbearing taskmaster," he was also more flexible and supportive of his assistants than Marsh, often lobbying the museum's administration for their interests and citing their accomplishments in reports on departmental activities. But somewhat like what had been said about Marsh, Osborn's name often appeared alone on papers and monographs for which his assistants had made considerable or primary contributions. Yet many of Osborn's assistants, including Brown, eventually published extensively in their own names, either with or without Osborn as a coauthor. It seems likely that all of these issues were fomenting in Brown's brain as he pondered his play in the current and potentially explosive situation. In one page, Brown diplomatically yet forcefully confronted Osborn about his performance and prospects at the AMNH. At least in some significant respects, Brown's response, including a serious confession about his recently failed academic quest for a graduate degree, set the coordinates for the rest of his career's trajectory and established a foundation of mutual trust and respect that would characterize the professional relationship, and even friendship, between Brown and Osborn for the next thirty-five years:

> *I have been with the Museum now three yeats* [sic years] *at $50 per month and assets have just about covered liabilities. Through you, I have received many kindnesses not reckoned in dollars for which I am deeply grateful. Although I failed at Columbia University (it's a bitter pill to swallow) my time there was not lost. I tried to cover too much and got swamped.*
>
> *For me to remain with the Museum I am sure I can best serve its interests in the field where physical energy and resource are most called for. After a thorough collection has been made from the different horizons in South America, . . . there is South Africa, Australia and Siberia which must eventually be represented in the American Museum. But this takes time and means, if I am the man to do the work, that I must give up other projects and interests and rely wholly on my salary from the Museum.*
>
> *I do not feel justified in doing this for less than $100 per month. I know you can get any number of men for $50. For the last two years my work has been at its best and if it is worth only $50 you will do me the greatest service yet in saying so at once. I value my time higher than that. I like the Museum, its workers and the advantages it offers a combination which I might not find elsewhere. The description of new material would count for a great deal but I have no assurance that I am even a worker in the Museum except in the field. Believe me sincerely this letter is not dictated by a spirit of greed but an awakening that I must know where I am at.*[30]

No record of Osborn's direct response has been found, but the similarities in tone and substance revealed in Brown's confrontation with Osborn, compared with Hatcher's earlier arguments with Marsh and Scott, are striking. One might even speculate that Brown had listened and learned from Hatcher discussing his own dilemmas. In any event, given that Brown continued in the service of the museum until he retired some forty years later, as well as continuing his association afterward, it's clear that a deal was reached, and Brown's bibliography does include one solely authored paper, "A new species of fossil Edentate from the Santa Cruz Formation of Patagonia."[31]

Nonetheless, the agreement regarding Brown's ability to publish on specimens he found and his own geologic observations triggered more chronically strained negotiations between Osborn and Hatcher. These ran throughout late November and December of 1899 after Hatcher returned to Princeton, leaving Brown to collect on his own. On the fourth, Osborn responded to a letter he'd received from Hatcher. Hatcher had apparently angrily protested and refused to endorse the terms Osborn and Scott had established under which the specimens Brown found would be published. Osborn wanted to meet with Hatcher in person to discuss the issues Hatcher raised, but in the meantime, he assured Hatcher, "If I have in any way been discourteous or apparently thoughtless, it has been entirely without intention," before pleading that he'd been under tremendous stress at work from juggling several demanding administrative responsibilities. Osborn went on to express his "warmest admiration for [Hatcher's] scientific achievements," and promised to try and structure the agreement for Brown "in such a manner that it will be entirely to Professor Scott and yourself. The whole arrangement with Brown in which you think I did you an injustice is capable of explanation." Osborn closed by invoking his belief that it was imperative to maintain "good will and cooperation among scientific men," which he hoped would lead to a resolution of the situation with Brown. Hatcher apparently edited the original draft of the agreement and sent it to Osborn, who again responded on December 21. Osborn suggested modifying a few clauses, but he again closed by saying he'd leave the decisions up to Hatcher and Scott. It was this modified agreement that Osborn, who'd signed it by early January

1900, sent to Brown, triggering Brown's displeasure at the changes. Brown would wander around southern Patagonia until early spring of 1900, at which point he shipped 4.5 tons of fossils back to New York for Osborn. The great majority was gleaned from the same Santacrucian beds along the coast where Hatcher and Peterson had collected.[32]

Meanwhile after leaving Brown and Peterson, Hatcher headed north to San Julian, where he spent two weeks collecting invertebrate and vertebrate fossils from the Patagonian and Cape Fairweather beds. When the steamer *Primero de Mayo* sailed past, Hatcher hopped aboard, possibly after his legendary poker game mentioned in the prologue and proceeded to Gallegos. There he made arrangements to leave Patagonia while waiting for her to circumnavigate Tierra del Fuego before he once again boarded for the trip to Buenos Aires, arriving on June 5. Peterson stayed a while longer to collect in Santa Cruz before returning by steamer to Punta Arenas and sailing for New York.[33]

However, most uncharacteristically for Hatcher, he decided he was due a proper vacation, and after returning to Buenos Aires, "started on an extended trip up the river [Río de la Plata], going as far as Asunción, the capital of Paraguay, passing and stopping at many interesting places along the way." At an old monastery in Entre Ríos, he marveled at enigmatic dinosaur bones, which Hatcher concluded had come from Triassic sediments, and chuckled to himself about the perplexed attendant, who couldn't understand why Hatcher was more interested in those bones than the more carefully curated bones representing religious relics of various saints. From Asunción, Hatcher took the "poorly-built and badly-equipped railway" into the interior, where he spent a spell in the small town of Itaguay. Unlike in Patagonia, he "obtained an excellent room and good board at five pesos, sixty-two cents a day," which led him to offer the following travel tip:

> *If any of my readers should ever feel the need of a vacation spent amid quiet but comfortable and most interesting surroundings at an exceedingly moderate expense, let me commend them to one of the country villages of Paraguay. . . . For once in my life I conquered the propensity for collecting which for years had been the one dominant and uncontrollable element within me.*[34]

After returning to Buenos Aires, Hatcher hopped a steamer and spent a few days in Rio de Janeiro before boarding the *Buffon* for New York. He arrived on August 16, 1899, about ten days before Peterson returned on September 1 with their collections. In his summary, Hatcher offered this succinct yet dichotomous declaration about the expeditions:

> *We had undergone many hardships and made considerable sacrifices in order to accomplish the work. In many respects our success had far surpassed our most sanguine expectations, while we had signally failed in one most important feature of our work, which, however, I still hope to accomplish. . . .*
>
> *Though I suffered much from the inhospitable nature of the climate of Patagonia, I am forced to confess to a certain very warm attachment to that country, and I know of no other one thing that would cause me more pain than to be forced to abandon all hope of ever visiting the region for the purpose of continuing and, if possible, completing my investigations.*[35]

The continued failure to locate the Pyrotherium beds and resolve all the related stratigraphic issues falls on the shoulders of both Florentino Ameghino and Hatcher. Florentino was unduly secretive about the location of his fossil localities. In rebuttal to Hatcher's complaint that he did not publish detailed descriptions for the locations of Carlos's fossil localities, Florentino replied, "I did not have the obligation to bring out a guide with the necessary instructions for the harvesting of fossils." But Hatcher clearly rubbed him the wrong way. Hatcher had urged Carlos to join him on a joint trip to evaluate the stratigraphy of the Pyrotherium beds when they happened to meet at Santa Cruz in 1898, and Carlos had initially agreed. However, Carlos later told Hatcher that it would be impossible for him to do so.[36]

In the wake of his three Patagonian expeditions, Hatcher published another paper, in essence refusing to recognize the Pyrotherium beds as a distinct stratigraphic unit, stating, "The Pyrotherium beds, as that term has been used by Dr. Ameghino, includes a series of deposits of varying age from Eocene to Pleistocene." In this, Hatcher proved to be incorrect.

Hatcher also bluntly stated, "There is absolutely no ground . . . that the mammalia of this region were any more advanced in early Tertiary times than were the mammals of the northern hemisphere." This is widely accepted today. Beyond that, Hatcher alleged that Carlos Ameghino had vacillated in his opinion about whether the Pyrotherium beds lay above or below the Patagonia Formation. This assertion by Hatcher was incorrect. What the Ameghinos and Hatcher referred to as the "Pyrotherium beds" are now universally recognized to be part of the Sarmiento Formation, and the Pyrotherium "fauna" is now thought to have lived during the Oligocene about 27 to 28 million years ago. Thus Hatcher was correct, and Florentino incorrect, about the age of the Pyrotherium beds being younger than Cretaceous: it was the invertebrates that Hatcher collected from the Patagonian Formation which first established that fact, when A. Ortman published on Hatcher's specimens and found them to most closely resemble invertebrate fossils that were late Oligocene or early Miocene in age. In addition, subsequent research has clearly established that the Santacrucian fauna from along the coast in Patagonia, which Florentino thought to be late Eocene in age and Hatcher thought was much younger, has now been definitively established to be early Miocene, or about 16 to 18 million years in age.[37]

In all, Hatcher's ventures produced a stunning sample comprising around sixty genera of 19- to 16-million-year-old Santacrucian mammals—the first such assemblage of ancient South American mammals ever collected for a North American museum. The collection is now housed in Yale's Peabody Museum. These remarkable animals evolved during South America's long isolation, which resulted when South America split from North America due to plate tectonic activity at least 56 million years ago, then separated from Antarctica about 34 million years ago.

By Santacrucian times, marsupials, or metatherians, included carnivorous forms from a group called Sparassodonta, such as the wolf-like *Borhyaena*, *Prothylacynus*, and *Acrocyon*, as well as the hyena-like *Sipalocyon* and *Cladosictis*. Fruit-eating forms from a group called Paucituberculata, such as *Abderites*, *Stilotherium*, *Acdestis*, and *Palaeothentes*, as well as insect-eating forms from the group called Microbiotheria, such as *Microbiotherium*, also had evolved. Placentals, or eutherians, contained a rich array of arboreal and terrestrial sloths, such as *Hapalops, Analcimorphus, Eucholoeops, Schismotherium, Planops, Nematherium, Megalonychotherium, Pelecyodon,* and *Prepotherium.*

These creatures roamed alongside tank-like, armored, entirely extinct relatives of armadillos called glyptodonts, such as *Propalaeohoplophorus, Glyptodon, Cochlops, Asterostemma, Metopotoxus,* and *Eucinepeltus.* Several types of armadillos also abounded, including *Proeutatus, Prozaedius, Peltiphilus, Stenotatus,* and *Stegotherium,* while the early anteater *Protamandua* is also recorded.

Three unique groups of herbivorous ungulates called notoungulates, litopterns, and astrapotheres, which are very distantly related to more familiar hoofed plant-eaters, such as the odd-toed, hooved horses, rhinos, and tapirs and the even-toed pigs, camels, deer, and cattle of North America also evolved. The astrapotheres included hefty herbivores, such as *Astrapotherium* and *Astrapothericulus.* Notoungulates spanned a huge range of body sizes, with some weighing in with fairly massive rhino- or hippo-like forms such as the toxodonts *Nesodon, Adinotherium,* and *Stenotephanos,* as well as the homalodothere, *Homalodotherium.* Smaller hare- or rodent-like notoungulates included the interatheres, *Interatherium,* and *Protypotherium,* and the hegetotheres *Pachyrukhos* and *Hegetotherium.* Litopterns were represented by the camel-like macrauchenid called *Theosodon* and the more horse-like proterotheriids, *Proterotherium, Thoatherium, Diadiaphorus,* and *Licaphrium.* A rich assemblage of South American rodents, called caviomorphs after the modern guinea pig, contained the genera *Neoreomys, Sciamys, Eocardia, Stichomys, Steiromys, Acaremys, Adelphomys, Schistomys,* and *Spaniomys,* while another group of rodents called eryomyids was represented by the genera *Perimys* and *Pliolagostomus.* In addition, specimens of an unusual mole-like mammal named *Necrolestes* were found. Interestingly, specimens of several genera of whales are also recorded in Hatcher and Peterson's collections from the Santa Cruz Formation, including the toothed odontocetes *Priscodelphinus, Prosqualodon,* and "Proinia," which is now called *Prosqualodon,* as well as the baleen whale *Aulocetus.*

Beyond mammals, Hatcher found fossils of frogs, including *Calytocephalella* and *Caudiverbera,* as well as "terror birds," such as *Phororhacos,*

Psilopterus, and "Pelecyornis," which some now call *Psilopterus*. These agile, avian carnivores, several feet in height, were prime predators and scavengers on the ancient Patagonian landscape. Other birds included a fossil penguin called *Palaeospheniscus* and another form called *Opisthodactylus*.

Hatcher and Scott both wanted the results published all together. As mentioned previously, they surprisingly found the financial support required from one of the world's richest men, J. Pierpont Morgan. As Scott recounted, "Hatcher made a suggestion . . . that we should attempt to raise a fund to publish the whole in a series of uniform reports, instead of scattering it through the various journals . . . of learned societies . . . Mr. Junius Morgan, then on the staff of the University Library, . . . thought that his uncle, Mr. J. Pierpont Morgan, might be so far interested in the project as to finanace it." Scott estimated it would cost $25,000. So with great trepidation, Scott, accompanied by Junius and Osborn, approached Morgan. Apparently Osborn, quite comfortable in such settings with members of New York aristocracy, including conversations with his uncle, managed to make the key argument: This was the kind of endeavor usually undertaken by governments rather than individuals, which appealed to Morgan, especially given his collection of rare manuscripts.[38]

Eventually, eight volumes, with at least twenty-six separate parts by numerous specialists, would document the research. Several decades later, Scott would reminisce, "Whenever I look at the stately row of fifteen quarto volumes, I find it a source of profound gratification . . . to bring Hatcher's greatest enterprise to so happy a conclusion." In addition to his legendary narrative of the expeditions published in 1903, Hatcher pumped out no fewer than twelve other separate scientific papers regarding the results of the Patagonian project between 1897 and 1903, ranging in topics from the fossil animals, to the regional geology and geography, and even to the tribes of indigenous peoples—not to mention another paper on the rhino *Diceratherium*.[39]

But Hatcher's feathers were still ruffled, and although the specific reasons are not documented in writing, the cause might have been related to the agreement that Scott had made with Osborn for a joint Princeton/ AMNH third Patagonian expedition against Hatcher's wishes. Tom Rea suspects that this tiff revolved around the document that gave Barnum

Brown priority to describe and publish on specimens that he found, the agreement that Osborn and Brown signed but Hatcher furiously refused to sign. In any event, as he often did, Hatcher felt underappreciated and registered his displeasure on November 17, 1899:

> . . . *in view of the fact that I am about to make application for a position elsewhere (though where I do not know) I consider it my duty to tender to you my written resignation as your assistant. . . . I confess . . . to have been partially deterred by a hope that some joint action by yourself and Prof. Osborn might be taken to explain matters and make the action unnecessary. . . . Since . . . my hopes have not been realized, there is nothing left to me except to either submit to treatment which I believe I have not merited or resign. I therefore enclose my resignation. . . .*

Although Osborn tried to alleviate Hatcher's anger by personally speaking with him face-to-face, he was unsuccessful. On January 12, 1900, Osborn reported to Scott that although Osborn had been successful in "clearing up our misunderstanding," possibly regarding the participation of Brown in the Patagonian expedition as well as the related details of who could publish on the specimens that were collected, Hatcher still had "deep feelings on the subject" and "more cause for it" than Osborn had supposed." Osborn elaborated by urging Scott as follows:

> *It is extremely important for you that Hatcher remain at Princeton, as he has done magnificent service and will continue to do so. He is just a highly sensitive organization, so I think you will have to go out of your way to express your appreciation of his work and your continued desire to give him full credit and to cooperate with him. I can explain more fully when I see you. I must say he won my sympathy by his very straightforward statements on his side of the case.*

But even though Osborn arranged for an honorary degree for Hatcher from Princeton in February 1900, for which Hatcher expressed his sincere gratitude, in the end, Osborn was helplessly left to sincerely commiserate with Scott that the departure of Hatcher constituted "a great loss to us both." Essentially, Hatcher had, once again, flown Osborn's intended coop. But Osborn's gesture to provide Hatcher with the honorary degree seems to be the act of reconciliation for which Hatcher had been waiting, and it appears to represent yet another inflection point in their sinusoidally raucous relationship. For his part, Scott was gobsmacked, later intimating that Hatcher's exodus represented "another stunning blow to me. My lack of resources had once again made itself very painfully felt." All that remained after Hatcher's latest leap was for Hatcher to locate another place to land.[40]

SECTION IV
1900–1904

13

Carnegie's Colossus

ortunately, Olaf A. Peterson, with whom Hatcher would be joined at the hip for the rest of his career, would light the way after Hatcher resigned at Princeton. At the end of 1899, Peterson himself had left Scott's employ at Princeton to join the burgeoning Department of Vertebrate Paleontology in Pittsburgh's Carnegie Museum. His decision was apparently driven by the more lucrative salary of $125 per month offered by the museum's director, William J. Holland, whom the wealthy industrialist Andrew Carnegie had hired to develop the best collection of dinosaurs and other fossil vertebrates that his money could buy. Born in Jamaica during 1848 to missionaries in the Moravian Church, Holland's childhood was spent in North Carolina before he attended Amherst College and the Princeton Theological Seminary. Upon his arrival in Pittsburgh in 1874, he assumed the duties of pastor at Bellefield Presbyterian Church, while teaching courses on ancient languages at what is now Chatham University. But his great love of butterflies led him to become one of the nation's foremost authorities on Lepidoptera, a passion he shared with the public through the publication of *The Butterfly Book* in 1898 and *The Moth Book* in 1903, which catapulted him into a position as one of the country's most prominent popularizers of science.[1]

The first suggestion of the ambitious undertaking of acquiring large dinosaur skeletons in the Carnegie's records appears in a letter from Holland to Carnegie dated November 4, 1898, in which Holland responded to a newspaper clipping that Carnegie sent him regarding a discovery of the "most colossal animal ever." The discovery had been made by William H. Reed, Marsh's former collector at Como Bluff, Wyoming, and then the assistant geologist and curator at the fledgling University of Wyoming in Laramie:

> *I noted your comments and orders on the newspaper clipping just received.*
>
> *I have telegraphed Prof. Reed asking whether a proposition to purchase would be entertained & inquiring as to condition of skeleton.*
>
> *In case he is willing to sell & the State Geological Survey of Wyoming does not object effectually to a sale shall I go to Laramie & try to make a deal? A personal inspection & a deal on the spot will beat a deal by letter in such cases every time.*
>
> *What latitude in the matter of price would you allow? Such things are scarce you know. But the greatest item of expense in the end will be for getting out the bones & setting them up.*
>
> *It is fair to remind you*
>
> *1. That if we buy this thing we may have as a term to include the employment of Reed as one of our force for a time at least. He, as the discoverer, will wish possibly to have partial supervision of the restoration.*
>
> *2. The new plans of the Museum will have to include a large hall for this display of such a monster.*
>
> *3. It will tax mechanical skill to set up such a brute in good shape & solidly, so that it will not ultimately collapse.*

40,000 lbs of stone put up on steel mountings such as are used will be the most colossal undertaking of its kind in the history of the world. I can do it, but it will cost some time, labor, & money.[2]

In a chain of correspondence through November and early December, Holland wrote Reed to inquire about purchasing the skeleton, and he offered to come out for discussions. Reed indicated that although the skeleton belonged to the University of Wyoming, they would be willing to sell it to the highest bidder. Reed claimed three other skeletons between thirty to sixty feet in length had also been discovered, all of which made him hopeful that a deal could be struck. In turn, Holland emphasized that he sought the largest skeleton ever discovered and queried Reed regarding whether any of those available were complete enough to mount without too much restoration. If so, he encouraged Reed to make a "frank" offer. Throughout, Holland consulted Carnegie and continued to counsel his patron about the inherent challenges, noting that it took Marsh's staff four years to collect and prepare his brontosaur—a reasonable amount of time given the animal's astounding size. Beyond that, the costs of mounting could "run into a good many thousands of dollars."[3]

Sensing he had Holland on the line, Reed quickly confirmed that the head of the thigh bone was 25 percent larger than any he'd previously found, but he couldn't be sure how complete the skeleton was until the spring, when he could excavate it. As Holland had suspected, the university had raised Reed's salary upon hearing of his contact with Holland and demanded that he remain on their staff. However, Reed had already been considering freelancing, because he knew the skeletons were valuable, and he encouraged Holland to come out in March to parlay over the prospects and see for himself. Holland alerted Carnegie on December 27 that he thought Reed might have a fairly complete and "magnificent" set of skeletons and sought Carnegie's approval to travel out and try to cut the best deal possible.[4]

By February 7, 1899, Holland and Carnegie were prepared to pounce, although Holland told Reed that he'd rather wait until late spring to visit in order to avoid harsh weather. In preparation, Holland needed estimates for Reed's compensation to join the staff at the museum as a collector to excavate the largest of these "Brontosaurs," the compensation for acquiring the specimen itself, and the cost of the additional hired men that would be required, preferably including some university students during the summer to reduce costs. Also, might Reed stay on the Carnegie staff to collect other specimens of the Jurassic fauna for the Carnegie and help prepare the material over the winters? Reed had agreed to become collector for the Carnegie by March 8. He was cagey about the salary required, but he did reveal that he'd need three men at $50 per month, along with a team and wagon bought at $150 to be sold at end of season for $75. Reed preferred to excavate the skeleton without compensation. Then, if it was good, he'd entertain an offer from the Carnegie. Holland suspected Reed would probably accept a salary of $1,500 to $2,000 per year, making the total cost $7,500, including other specimens that Reed would collect for a new Hall of Dinosaurs over a couple of years. Holland was feeling the heat, since the University of Wyoming had appropriated $22,000, or almost $640,000 in today's currency, for building a museum at Laramie. So Holland urged Carnegie to respond quickly.[5]

Holland wired Carnegie on March 17 that he was leaving for Wyoming. After meeting with the University of Wyoming's board of regents on the twenty-third, he sent Otto Gramm, the board president, the following written proposal:

> 1. I proposed to pay you the sum of $2000 in cash for the claim taken up & registered by Mr. W. H. Reed to the fossil remains of a certain saurian of which he has discovered the broken end of the femur.
>
> 2. I proposed to you to allow me to have the services of Mr. W. H. Reed for so long a time as might be necessary to exhume the said saurian, say six months, and agreed to pay his salary myself during that time thereby releasing your University from the necessity of paying him anything on account of salary for that time, thus saving to you the sum of $750. – his salary for 6 months.
>
> 3. I proposed in addition to pay Mr. W. H. Reed the sum of $300. for the six months in addition to his regular salary of $750.

4. I proposed to be myself at the expense of everything needed in the work of exhumation, as lumber, plaster, services of three assistants, teams, a photographic outfit, &c. &c. which I estimate will amount to the additional sum of $962.

From Holland's perspective, his offer represented a solid financial dividend to the University of Wyoming just for the privilege of digging at the claim. But the offer was not received altogether well, and Holland resented one trustee's description of the offer as "ridiculous." Holland regretted he'd need to tell Carnegie that the university had declined to consider the offer and refused to make a counteroffer, even though the Carnegie would have the first right to bid on it if the university collected the specimen and offered it for sale.[6]

After returning to Pittsburgh, Holland reported to Carnegie on the twenty-seventh that although the University of Wyoming had rejected the offer, he could "circumvent" it by securing a government patent to the land for about $3,600 that would trump the "grub stake claim" that the university had obtained. He had also reached an agreement with Reed to hire him for three years at $1,800 per annum plus collecting expenses in return for turning over his claim to the sauropod skeleton and collecting others that he'd found. But the regents of the university, convinced it was the largest skeleton in the world and worth $100,000, refused to let the specimen leave the state, since the legislature had allotted the funds to build the museum, and threatened to take the case to court. So Holland retained the best lawyer in town, former US congressman Stephen W. Downey, who dealt in land claims. Downey outlined two possible procedures—one to file a claim at the Land Office then advertise for sixty days; if no counterclaim was filed, the patent would be issued at a cost of $2.50 per acre. But the quickest way would be to purchase land scrip enough at $4.50 to $5.00 per acre, then enter scrip at the Land Office, because no advertising was needed and the transaction would be completed in a few days or weeks. Holland instructed Downey to purchase scrip at market prices and get the US surveyor to make the necessary surveys to purchase forty to eighty acres around the quarry. That total would cost $200 to $400, much less than Holland had offered the trustees. Holland's only worry was that Downey's involvement would leak out, and Downey would come under pressure from the regents and other local officials. Holland emphasized he didn't mean to be beaten and bragged to Carnegie, "He laughs best who laughs last." Although his plan would mean that the advance needed from Carnegie would increase from $7,500 to $10,000, it would be worth it to have a larger collection than either that of Osborn or Marsh. With that, Holland asked permission to proceed.[7]

The same day, Holland sent Reed his contract, which, in addition to the aforementioned salary, stipulated that Reed would receive fifteen days vacation a year and ten additional days if he worked in Pittsburgh. The Carnegie would pay railroad and hotel bills up to $50 during the first year and hire three assistants, one boy at $15 per month for two and a half months during the summer of 1899, as well as two assistants at $50 per month for as long as needed. The Carnegie would also pay for all equipment, materials, and freighting, as well as furnish a photographic outfit for photos to be taken of bones in the quarry before removal.[8]

Seemingly endless machinations ensued involving legal issues and surveying arrangements for securing the land around the sauropod quarry, as well as Reed's resignation at the University of Wyoming. But throughout, the multitasking Holland was plotting his next personnel coup. On April 1, he reported to Carnegie that he'd visited Hatcher's old competitor Jacob Wortman at the AMNH. Wortman had made arrangements with Marsh to succeed him upon Marsh's demise, but Marsh feared his death would alter the arrangement and doubted that Yale Peabody's trustees would choose Wortman as his successor. So Wortman was not satisfied with his present position. Holland thought Wortman was one of the best men in paleontology in the United States and believed he could employ both Wortman and Reed at the Carnegie. Holland had met with Carnegie's Museum Committee and suggested they set aside a sufficient amount from the general fund to hire Wortman.[9]

As Holland's courting of Wortman continued, on April 12 Holland invited Wortman to visit the Carnegie and offered to pay for the travel. Holland wrote again on the twentieth, noting Carnegie's $1,750,000 donation for the expansion of the Carnegie Institute and stating he'd decided to hire someone to take charge of work in the Department of Paleontology. Holland intimated that he intended to leave for Wyoming in a day or two to secure claims on promising property for excavating dinosaur specimens and hoped to start work with Reed in ten days or two weeks. In short, he exclaimed, "We mean business." [10]

Upon his return to Pittsburgh, Holland informed Carnegie that he and Reed had located the specimen with the US Inspector of Surveys, loaded up a wagonful of bone fragments littering the ground, and hauled them home with him. He then met with Wyoming governor DeForest Richards, Senator Francis Warren, and US district attorney Timothy Burke, who was a regent of the university, and received assurances that they would support Holland's efforts to secure the specimen for Carnegie. Since Holland offered to pay the university $2,000 for the specimen, "the Governor went so far as to speak of the action of the regents in refusing to grant what I wished in extremely uncomplimentary terms, pronouncing them in strong Western parlance d____ f____. He also said that as the appointement [sic] of these regents is with him and it will be his duty shortly to make some reappointments. . . ." They also discovered another specimen with a femur 2.5 feet long. In addition, Holland reported having hired Wortman and expressed the intent to hire another paleontologist to handle the scientific and mounting aspects of the work. [11]

Wortman wrote Holland on May 17 to suggest that he and Reed prospect separately to start the season, with Reed apparently focusing on "Happy Valley" and Wortman in the Sun Dance Hills. Wortman would send Arthur Coggeshall, an assistant he wrangled away from the AMNH, to help Reed; then, if one of the contingents failed to find good material to quarry, all three could join forces. With camera equipment purchased at a cost of $113.80, Wortman and Coggeshall were ready to set out for Wyoming as soon as Holland arranged the travel with Union Pacific. Holland responded on the twentieth that he hadn't heard from the railway agents, so Wortman and his mate should come to Pittsburgh to discuss plans. Based on the latest report he'd received from his lawyer, he was confident that the University of Wyoming would turn over to the Carnegie the specimen on the land he'd bought. In fact, a fragment of the femur had arrived at the museum. The train tickets for Wortman and

Coggeshall from Pittsburgh to Medicine Bow, Wyoming, finally arrived by the twenty-sixth.[12]

Meanwhile, Reed reported on the twenty-sixth from T. B. Ranch in Wyoming that he'd found good bones in the Sheep Creek Basin. He expressed his pleasure with Holland's hiring of Wortman and would stay at the ranch until he heard from him, but he reported that Wilbur C. Knight, apparently his replacement at the university, was collecting nearby. Wortman and Coggeshall arrived in Medicine Bow on the twenty-ninth and planned to meet Reed on the thirty-first to evaluate his prospects. Wortman had struck up a friendly relationship with the Union Pacific representatives in the area and offered to write a sketch about Wyoming and Nebraska for their advertisements, as well as participate in an excursion they were planning for paleontologists and geologists. As a result, he anticipated receiving favorable support for shipping specimens and was sure he could get Holland an invitation to come on the excursion along with several interested students.[13]

Wortman wrote Holland on June 6 that Reed's seemingly promising prospects proved disappointing, but by then they'd located six others, including one with a five-foot-long femur, tibia, fibula, ischium, two pubes, one cervical vertebra, and many ribs, which Wortman thought was probably "Morosaurus or Brontosaurus." "Morosaurus," a name Marsh coined in 1878, is now known as *Camarasaurus,* a name Cope created six months earlier in 1877. Wortman confidently identified another specimen as belonging to *Stegosaurus* and thought the chances for recovering a good part of the skeleton of this rare form were good. With other field crews soon to descend on the region, Wortman and Reed planned to travel to a locality called Troublesome about fifty miles southeast of Steamboat Springs in Colorado to prospect, although they would locate claims to hold the quarries before leaving.[14]

An article in the *Cheyenne Leader* on the eighth announced the field conference sponsored by the Union Pacific that Wortman had pledged to help advertise. Humorously billed as a "Grave Robbing Expedition," several hundred geologists, paleontologists, and students under the guidance of Wilbur C. Knight would visit Reed's skeleton of a Jurassic dinosaur 130 feet in length, 35 feet tall at the hips, 25 at the shoulder, with a skeleton weighing 40,000 pounds. Invitations were sent to 250 universities and colleges, and the Union Pacific would provide transportation to one professor and one assistant per institution, as well as reduced fares for others interested.

Wortman wrote Holland on the eighteenth that their foray to Troublesome proved unfruitful, but near the west end of the Little Medicine, they located three or four very good prospects that seemed to represent small- to medium-sized, well-preserved dinosaurs. Wortman went on to summarize the present results:

> *Quarry No. 1 (Brontosaurus) which we are now working, size of femur about 5½ feet length, Tibia-Fibula and astragalus. Pelvic bones minus Illium* [sic]. *About one dozen Ribs the largest of which is 6 feet in length. Four or five vertebrae in sight in rather poor condition. Quarry looks very favorable for many more bones of skeleton. The taking out process is slow owing to the tangled up position of bones. Quarry No. 2. (Diplodocus) Femur (5 feet) Caudal vertebra and one toe bone in sight all in good preservation. Little work done on this Quarry. Near by on same level occur many vertebrae which may belong to same individual. Chances seem favorable for something good in the way of this rare species. Quarry 3. Head of Troublesome 3 or 4 places where bones of marine Reptiles of the Ichthyosauria are exposed. This is the genus Baptanodon (Marsh) of which Yale has the only specimen. . . . Quarry 4 west end of Little Medicine anticlinal* [sic] *5 or 6 miles from Medicine Bow. Indications as above spoken of. Our Stegosaurus Quarry of which I wrote you in my last letter appears to be "n.g." although we will do a little more work there. It proved so far as at present known to only an end of a tail in very bad state of preservation.*

It should be noted that the generic name of the long-necked, quadrupedal, herbivorous sauropod *Brontosaurus* is currently in flux. Throughout most of the 1900s into the early 2000s, the name *Brontosaurus* had been declared to be scientifically invalid, since it was thought that the same animal had been first named *Apatosaurus*. But in the last few years, further scientific analysis of the animal's anatomy has led some paleon-tologists to once again argue that *Apatosaurus* and *Brontosaurus* are both valid genera, since they possess some distinct anatomical differences. *Baptanodon* is a porpoise-like ichthyosaur that lived in the Late Jurassic seas around 150 million years ago. It may or may not be a valid genus. The crew now planned to focus on excavating these prospects, which had already yielded two wagonloads of brontosaur bones and promised to produce much more soon, making what Wortman claimed would be "a fine collection and . . . a really good start in our vertebrate department." Regarding expenses, Wortman was "running as close to the wind as I can" and anticipated coming in at or under budget. He praised Reed's energy and interest. Although many field crews had already arrived, most were running short on bones. The AMNH Quarry proved disappointing, so they were prospecting for other localities.[15]

Downey informed Holland on the twenty-seventh that the University of Wyoming trustees had appointed a committee comprised of governor DeForest Richards, Gramm, and the president of the university to confer with Holland regarding his collecting proposal. They would meet before he left for the field excursion.[16]

Meanwhile, Wortman contributed some key, although disappointing, intelligence to Holland on the twenty-eighth. He and Reed had visited Reed's original sauropod quarry and found that Knight had not only removed the notice of Holland's filing for the land but had also made a 10' x 15' cut where the bones were supposed to be buried. He had collected an unknown number of bones and left a pile of bone fragments alongside the quarry. In short, Wortman concluded that if the specimen had once been good, it was no longer, especially since Knight had "gouged [them] out in the most primitive and unskillful manner." Wortman warned Holland that he "would not give 50 cents for the whole layout," adding,

When Mr. Graham [sic] *approaches you on the subject you may tell him frankly that while our collection in the subject is young and comparatively unimportant as yet but at the same time we are not exactly d—d fools on the subject of fossils. You may consider yourself exceedingly lucky that they did not accept your offer of $2000.00* *for the prospect. The whole thing has been grossly exaggerated from start to finish.*

Beyond that, all of their other prospects had failed to pan out, despite the promise they'd originally shown. Accordingly, Wortman recommended that they would check out a couple of Cretaceous dinosaur prospects that Reed had discovered a few years earlier and then move on to the Sheep Creek region. If those efforts also failed, he intended to move on to the Sun Dance Hills, where he knew of some enticing Jurassic exposures. Although he and Reed were discouraged, Wortman maintained, "It is not my intention to return in the Fall empty handed if persistent hard work will accomplish what we are after." They'd pack all the bones for shipment that they'd collected before they set out to prospect. He still felt it best for Holland to travel to Laramie for the excursion. Then the crew could have someone drive him to the camp, wherever that might be. Two days later, Wortman informed Holland that they were ready to leave for Sheep Creek, although Reed was hesitant to do so. But Wortman was convinced that the exposure where they'd been working had already been thoroughly prospected, and if they didn't succeed at Sheep Creek, they'd be near the relatively untouched Cretaceous badlands in the Sun Dance region.[17]

Not surprisingly, Holland was stunned that not only had the seemingly bountiful quarries turned out to be all but barren but Knight had also acted "in such a stupid way" at Reed's initial sauropod quarry. He wrote Wortman on July 3 that he would try to work with Downey to stop the purchase of the land and get the money spent on filing the claims refunded if possible, and he directed Wortman and Reed not to say anything to anyone there until he met with Gramm's committee. Basically, Holland wished:

> . . . *to extricate ourselves from all relations with these people at Laramie and . . . wash our hands of all connections with their enterprises. From President of University on down I have very poor opinion of whole blooming outfit; they apparently don't know how to meet manly men in a manly way, but are as full of little narrow, petty jealousies as an egg is of meat.*

He would either go to Laramie or Newcastle, Wyoming, by train, as Wortman recommended. He planned to leave on the fifteenth, but he wanted Wortman to make sure any further conveyance by horses and wagon was "first class."[18]

Holland then immediately wrote his lawyer Downey to explain the situation and have him try to abort the land purchase. He reassured Downey that he'd meet "pleasantly" with Gramm's committee but added, "Since Knight has seen fit to file a notice of claim and to destroy the specimen, he may bear whatever expense there is." Of the $350 Holland had sent Downey, Holland directed his lawyer to keep $150 for his fee and secure a refund of the rest, but to act without attracting attention. Although Holland appreciated Downey's assistance, ". . . the fates have decreed that the whole thing shall end in nothing [for] this particular specimen . . . [since it was] hewn into fragments by the hands of incompetent men, leaving nothing to science. . . ."[19]

Independence Day gave Wortman's crew something to truly celebrate, as he gleefully proclaimed to Holland from the Sheep Creek Basin about thirty miles north of Medicine Bow:

> *We have two good prospects in sight upon which we are now working. The best one is a small Brontosaur (Femur 5 ft 4 in. in length) of which femur, many vertebrae, pelvic and other limb bones are already in sight. The bones are in fine preservation and the prospect looks better every day. The second is a very large Brontosaur of which there are a large number of bones in sight with chances very favorable for many more. The difficulty with these bones however is that they are not well preserved and require the utmost care in handling. We have done more work on this one than upon the other and if we can get it to the museum in good condition it will make a superb mount. I have great hopes that we can get nearly the whole skeleton, but of course one can never tell until the last bone is out.*

A number of other prospects also appeared promising, so Wortman anticipated spending most of the season there.[20]

With Holland expected on the twenty-first, Wortman wrote on the nineteenth to confirm that a local named Fales would pick up Holland and convey him to camp. At camp, Holland would have the use of a "kind gentle saddle horse" as needed. Wortman had also ordered a first-class cornucopia of supplies to satisfy the picky proclivities of his patron: this included everything from breakfast bacon to dill pickes, plus the requisite flour, coffee, beans, and canned goods—not to mention the fresh meat the crew would supply, including sage hens and good trout. But the stars of the party would be:

> . . . *some mighty fine bones and a whole lot of them. I am almost afraid to say what I think we have but from present indications we will put in the best season I have ever had in Bone Digging business. We have "a might good stagger" at a skeleton of Diplodocus which is a "rare bird indeed" and others almost too numerous to mention.*
>
> *We have ordered lumber for a cabin and we may have it up within a few days after you get there. We will hope to see you very soon and I am certain you will have an enjoyable time in our region. I would like to go over the geology of the country with you and I know some fine sections in the Mesozoic.*[21]

A nearly monthlong lapse in correspondence ensued when Holland was in Wyoming visiting his crew and presumably participating in the paleontological excursion. But on August 15, he wrote Wortman to inform him that although he'd made it back to Pittsburgh, he was confined to his bed by an attack of appendicitis. He'd enjoyed his journey immensely, except during the trip back from camp to Medicine Bow, which was "a ride I shall never forget as long as I live. I suffered almost mortal agony on the way, and matters were not improved when, in reply to a polite request to the [driver] to push forward, I received from him a volley of oaths, he informing me that he was doing the driving and he guessed he knew how to do it better than I did." As a result of his illness, he wasn't able to attend to the business of filing claims for the land on which the fossils had been found, and he directed Wortman to stake claims under the Placer Law and Stone and Timber Laws for:

... the 20 acres in Section 11 upon which the diplodocus, stegosaur, etc. are located; the adjoining two 40 acre tracts in Section 12 are on government land, and so is the 40 acre tract in the SE corner of Section 12; the 40 acre tract in NW corner of Section 18 in [T25N R75W] *is also government land; on these four 40 acre tracts on government land, I'd file under the Stone and Timber laws, taking the land for quarrying purposes, and of course making no reference to fossils or anything of that sort; the SW 40 acre tract in Section 7,* [T25N R75W] *is railroad property and belongs to the Two-Bar Cattle outfit. I would file, as you now know the boundaries, a 20 acre Placer claim on this; can't take more than 20 acres under the Placer law; choose 20 acres that is best, and I'll leave that to your judgment; please file these claims in the Cheyenne land office. ...*

Holland remained bedridden with peritonitis on the twenty-second, relating to Wortman that his doctor quipped, "You have a first-class rattlesnake in your pocket, and my advice to you is to not disturb the animal. . . ." If his appendix ruptured, he'd have a small chance of surviving the operation. Nonetheless, he was thrilled to hear the crew had discovered the scapula and coracoid of the *Diplodocus* and advised Wortman to be sure and expand the margins of the quarry to search for the rest of the skeleton, since he deemed that currents could not have carried the missing elements far.[22]

On his end, Wortman revealed that the exposed elements of the brontosaur were about taken up and ready to ship on the twenty-ninth, and in addition to the scapula and coracoid, they'd exposed the 21st presacral. He admitted that he'd be "much disappointed" if they didn't find the rest of the skeleton and skull once they got the bone layer exposed. But hauling to Medicine Bow would cost what he felt was an "outrageous" $7.50 per ton, so he longed for the purchase of their own wagon, which would pay for itself over the course of the season, which he was confident would produce a full carload with three skeletons: *Diplodocus*, *Brontosaurus*, and *Stegosaurus*.[23]

On September 2 Holland informed Wortman that despite the great risk involved, he'd undergone an operation and was recovering fairly well, although if they had waited forty-eight hours he'd "probably be under a coffin lid." He'd need to remain in bed for two or three more weeks. Regarding the *Diplodocus*, he couldn't envision why so much of the torso was preserved yet the feet and legs were not. Thus, he remained convinced they were there somewhere and thought it well worth the time and money required to keep searching for them.[24]

With Holland sidelined, on the fourth Wortman communicated his relief to Holland's associate, C. C. Mellor, chairman of the Museum Committee of the Carnegie Institute, that Holland was recovering from "so dangerous an experience." At issue in the field was the arrangement for a boxcar with a 60,000-pound capacity in which to transport the specimens. Wortman anticipated having the carload ready by mid-September, but it would be helpful to have it on a sidetrack over ten days for loading the massive crates, some of which would weigh 3,000 pounds. Holland could inform Mellor whom to contact. Holland responded on the eleventh that he'd written the Union Pacific representative and that Wortman should contact him directly to make the arrangements, which would be free of charge.[25]

Wortman also wrote Holland on the eleventh to say he'd had the personal rail passes extended through mid-November. Although the crew had extended the quarry with a 40' x 60' cut, the sequence of vertebrae in the *Diplodocus* skeleton terminated at the 24th or 25th presacral, and the only other element found was the back of one of the lower jaws, suggesting the skull had been destroyed before it fossilized. They'd also dug fifteen feet to the south, but the rock there formed a hard, cemented mass called a concretion, so Wortman was skeptical any limb bones would be preserved there. They had taken everything they could find of that specimen as well as of the stegosaur and brontosaur. Next season they could hire a plow and scraper to further expand the quarry in search of the missing elements. For the present, he was working on the "Morosaurus" prospect, which promised well-preserved bones. Once the boxcar was loaded, he'd send the shipment along with Coggeshall to begin preparing a few bones for the upcoming Founder's Day celebration; Wortman asked for some lab space to be set aside. If the "Morosaurus" materialized, he expected to have around fifty thousand pounds of bones in all for the season, leading Wortman to proclaim, "The first paleonto-logical expedition of the Carnegie Museum will have been finished and I am not ashamed to compare results with the best of them." The crew had grown to include Reed's son, Willie, as well as a Dane named Paul Miller, who had the makings of "an extra good man with bones . . . a big strapping fellow—ingenious and a good careful worker." He was drawing $30 per month with board, and Wortman intended to hire him for $35 the following season.[26]

Holland was recovering rapidly by the nineteenth. Itching to get the specimens back to Pittsburgh, he instructed Wortman to let him know the number of the railcar as soon as he knew it so that he could communicate with the representative of the Pittsburgh, Ft. Wayne, and Chicago railroad to make sure it was sent through from Chicago. News of the Carnegie's discoveries seemed to be spreading back east, as the *New York Herald* telegraphed some associates of the museum to "get a good story on Western Fossils with pictures if possible. Want good story for Sunday to be here Friday morning."[27]

Back in Medicine Bow, Wortman wired that the car would be loaded on the twenty-seventh and asked Holland to send a check for the hauling as soon as the weight was ascertained. Wortman was leaving for the "Troublesome" region in hopes of collecting some specimens of the ichthyosaur "Baptanodon" before heading to his ranch to visit for a few days. Coggeshall had already left for Pittsburgh, and on October 10, Holland, seemingly fully recovered, instructed the chair of Carnegie's committee on buildings to make accommodations for the office Wortman would be occupying as head of the department, as well as a lab facility for preparing the fossils.[28]

With the first collecting season for the Carnegie in the books, another hiatus in correspondence ensued until January 14, 1900, when Wortman seemed to take a rather cheeky chance in writing Andrew Carnegie himself. Besides expressing his appreciation for Carnegie's broad support for the institution and science around the world, he rather obsequiously fawned over how it was useless for him to add anything regarding the importance of research as a contributor to resolving the great unsolved problems in biology, since Carnegie's associations with Marsh and acquaintance with Darwin's chief supporter, Thomas Henry Huxley, had provided Carnegie with an unusually good understanding of the whole undertaking. Wortman felt a great responsibility in his present position but refused to shrink from it, adding that it would be the great endeavor of his life to build a collection for the Carnegie equal to any in the world. To support that endeavor, he triumphantly trumpeted:

> *The acquisition of the services of Mr. O. A. Peterson recently has strengthened our department wonderfully, and we are thoroughly equipped with skillful assistants. I hope to publish in the leading scientific journal of this country the results of our discoveries from time to time in order that the world may know of . . . our work.*[29]

Although there's no concrete confirmation of the following, perhaps Wortman sensed his situation with Holland was insecure and attempted to go over Holland's head in appealing to Carnegie's sense of common purpose. But on the thirty-first, Holland, in turn, fired back over Wortman's head in a scathing letter to Mellor, who apparently wielded authority in such a dispute, to say that Wortman had been resisting Holland's "suggestions" and had "in fact, claimed for himself absolute independence from the oversight of myself as the head of the institution." Holland emphasized that he'd been patient for months and had endeavored to "show proper respect for [Wortman's] scientific attainments and to give him all the aid and encouragement which it was in my power to give him." Nonetheless, Wortman had "constantly expressed dissatisfaction" and been "extremely censorious and positively intractable." Holland reported to Mellor:

> *Matters came to a culmination yesterday when he showed me the proof of an article which he had written for the columns of* Science, *in which he made use of one or two expressions which I thought were likely to unnecessarily offend members of his own force and friends of the institution. I courteously suggested to him a modification of the paragraph in the interest of peace. He became very angry; told me to "go to hell," covered me with uncomplimentary*

epithets, and acted altogether in so ungentlemanly a manner that I felt compelled then and there to demand his resignation. He has sent it to me, and I have the honor of herewith transmitting it to the Committee that they make take whatever action in the premises seems to them to be advisable.[30]

The offending article, entitled "The New Department of Vertebrate Paleontology of the Carnegie Museum," was indeed published on February 2, 1900. In it, Wortman termed the department's establishment as an important advance in the development of the institution, as well as noting that the event was timely, given the immense paleontological potential of the exposures in the American West, which had recently shed so much new light on the evolution of Mesozoic and Tertiary vertebrate life. Given that American institutions were at the forefront of these new findings, the addition of another competitor provided the opportunity for even more significant discoveries. He noted that the staff was still small, but with Andrew Carnegie's generous support it would most probably be augmented as space for new collections became available, and those collections, which would represent the full expanse of vertebrate evolutionary history, would be assembled both by purchases and expeditions undertaken by the Carnegie staff, including himself, Reed, and Coggeshall. In fact, the expedition just completed to the Jurassic exposures in the Sheep Creek Basin:

> *. . . secured . . . the larger part of the skeleton of an herbivorous dinosaur, which was at first thought to belong to the genus Diplodocus. Of this almost the entire series of presacral vertebrae, the sacrum, and some fourteen or fifteen of the proximal caudals were secured. There are also a complete set of ribs, a scapula, coracoid, and sternum, a complete pelvic girdle lacking one ilium, and one complete femur; all in a most excellent state of preservation. The remainder of the limbs and the skull were not found, but there is much reason to believe that further excavation will bring them to light. . . .*

This material, at the present writing, is but partially worked out and prepared for study and exhibition; but from the material already prepared it would appear that the genus which it represents is most nearly allied to, if not identical with that described by Professor Marsh from the Black Hills, South Dakota, under the name of Barosaurus. If it should transpire that it belongs to Diplodocus, which is somewhat doubtful, it will prove very acceptable in that it will supply us with nearly all the missing parts of the skeleton of this interesting group of dinosaurs. Should it, on the other hand, prove to be a species of Barosaurus, it will be yet still more interesting, since the genus is known from but a few fragments of caudal vertebrae, at least so far described.

One other specimen, which is certainly that of Diplodocus, was secured, in which a few characteristic bones of the skeleton are represented. Other specimens include considerable parts of the skeleton of Brontosaurus, among which is an exceptionally perfect hind limb, most beautifully preserved. This will enable us for the first time to fix definitely the organization of the hind foot of this rather abundant group of the Sauropodous dinosaurs. . . .

Wortman went on to note that the preparation of this material, as well as the ichthyosaur specimens, was proceeding under the "skillful direction" of Coggeshall, formerly of the AMNH, and would eventually anchor the Carnegie's new paleontological hall. He also praised the hiring of Peterson, formerly of the USGS, AMNH, and Princeton, as an accomplished and experienced collector with extensive, firsthand knowledge of the fossiliferous exposures in the American West. Curiously, Wortman did not mention Reed in a similar regard, but rather launched into a tirade about whether Reed's initial specimen had been responsible for the founding of the department:

It has been stated recently in the columns of Science *that the establishment of this department in the Carnegie Museum was due to the supposed discovery of a dinosaur of extraordinary proportions in Wyoming, in 1898, by Mr. Reed. While it may be true that the newspaper accounts published at the time may have hastened action in the matter, yet I know it to be a fact that ever since the founding of the Institute, Mr. Carnegie has had it in mind to bring together a first-class collection of vertebrate fossils as a part of the Museum exhibit. . . .*

The broad basis upon which he has chosen to establish this undertaking, together with the liberal financial support which he grants to it, are sufficient evidences in themselves if no others could be had, that its inception was not due to a ridiculously exaggerated newspaper account of a bogus discovery, but to a well-conceived plan to carry into execution an important step in the growth of the Institute.

In any event, it was this verbiage that triggered Holland's wrath, as well as Andrew Carnegie's, when a summary of the skirmish appeared shortly after in a New York newspaper.[31]

On February 1, Holland, presumably backed by Mellor and his committee, informed R. B. Caldwell, who cut the salary checks for museum employees, to send Wortman's check to Holland instead of Wortman, before ominously adding "as there are some matters to be adjusted between himself and the Director of the Museum before he receives his monthly payment." Holland also sent Col. Samuel H. Church, secretary of the Trustee Committee, a written statement surrounding the recent "unfortunate situation" and informed him that Peterson, Reed, and Cogshall would all remain in their positions, with Peterson, as the most experienced, serving as lab supervisor.[32]

News of Wortman's resignation reached the popular press shortly thereafter on February 6, when a newspaper published a story with the headline DR. J. L. WORTMAN RESIGNS—DISPUTE WHETHER BONES BELONGING TO BRONTOSAURUS OR DIPSODOCUS MAGNIFICUS THE CAUSE.

Dr. J. L. Wortman has resigned the curatorship of the department of vertebrates at the Carnegie Museum and returned to his old

*place in the laboratory at Yale, owing to a disagreement with the
Rev. Dr. W. J. Holland, curator of the museum. The disagreement
arose because one of them, it is said, maintained that certain bones
dug from the fossil beds of Wyoming were those of the Brontosaurus, while the other insisted they belonged to the Dipsodocus
[sic] Magnificus.*

It may be that the correspondent meant that Wortman disputed that
Reed's *Brontosaurus* discovery, which didn't pan out, did not lead to the
inception of the Carnegie's vertebrate paleontology department and that
Wortman favored the identification of another specimen as *Barosaurus*
rather than *Diplodocus*. In any event, Wortman left for a short and equally
disappointing stay at Yale, while Holland was once again in the market
for a vertebrate paleontologist to head up his fledgling fossil consortium.[33]

14

Hatcher's Hiring and
Shenanigans at Sheep Creek

No doubt aided by Peterson's recent hiring and informed intelligence, it didn't take long for Holland to highjack his new honcho in the form of Princeton's J. B. Hatcher. On February 8, 1900, Holland wrote Mellor to inform him that, pursuant to their agreement, he had met with Hatcher and his superior, W. B. Scott, at Princeton and brought Hatcher back with him to Pittsburgh for further consultations. In the interest of due diligence, Holland meticulously listed Hatcher's references from numerous illustrious figures in American science: O. C. Marsh, who emphasized, "The discoveries he has made are known to all paleontologists"; James D. Dana, who testified "in the highest terms to Mr. Hatcher's ability" before adding that he had been "wonderfully successful"; Yale's president from 1886–1899, Rev. Timothy Dwight, who similarly praised Hatcher's ability and efficiency; as well as Hatcher's present superior, Scott:

> . . . *for the past seven years Mr. Hatcher has occupied the position of curator of vertebrate palaeontology in the Geological Museum of Princeton University and has fulfilled all its duties with the most brilliant success. He is widely known as one of the most skilful and successful collectors now living. He is an excellent and experienced field-geologist, a thoroughly trained man, fully competent to discharge the administrative duties that may devolve upon him. It is with the most unfeigned regret that I shall view his departure from Princeton.*

Consequently, Holland concluded, in praise of Hatcher and derision for Wortman:

> *I have no hesitation in view of what I have learned through the testimonials, as well as through extended conversations with Prof. Hatcher, in recommending him for the position of curator of vertebrate palaeontology recently made vacant by the resignation of Dr. J. L. Wortman. I believe him to be eminently qualified by attainments as well as experience for the duties of the position, and believe him to be a gentleman with whom pleasant relations can always be maintained, and who will not in any case transcend the limits which are imposed by considerations of official courtesy.*[1]

In the aftermath of his visit, Hatcher wrote Holland on the twelfth to confirm that he would leave Princeton on March 1 and be prepared to assume his new position on the second or third. Laudatory letters quickly followed as the news spread, including from Elmer Riggs of the Field Museum in Chicago, who congratulated Hatcher on the fifteenth but tempered his testament with his regret that, in such short order, Scott had lost the irreplaceable assistance of both Hatcher and Peterson.[2]

Through the rest of February, Peterson kept Holland abreast of Hatcher's activities as he wrapped up his responsibilities at Princeton. There would be little time for formalities in early March, as Holland intended to hold "a council of war" regarding the strategy for the upcoming collecting season as soon as Hatcher arrived, before sending Peterson and Reed to the field within a few weeks after plans had been set.[3]

With his new crew reconsolidated, Holland updated Carnegie on March 19 by crowing about how Hatcher had admirably "taken hold as successor to the 'late lamented' Wortman." The Union Pacific and Chicago Northwestern had come through with rail passes, so fossils would start flooding in as soon as weather permitted. Peterson was assigned to attack the Bridger Formation past the Red Desert in Wyoming, where neither Marsh nor Cope had ventured, while Reed and Hatcher would jam on through the Jurassic at "Camp Carnegie" in the Sheep Creek Basin. All the promising sections in the area had been purchased. Once things were rolling there, Hatcher would break off for an assault on his old haunts in the Laramie on a quest for more *Triceratops*, which Holland was especially keen to acquire, since the AMNH still didn't have any. But with the Field and the AMNH both hot after Bridger and Laramie material, Holland requested that Carnegie not say anything to his friends so his "three ablest bone sharks" in the business could search surreptitiously without their competitors following in their footsteps. Rather unrealistically, Holland worried that fossils would be hard to come by in these exposures within a decade, so his crew must work quickly. Overall, Holland was greatly pleased with the reputation his young museum had garnered, with their "work discussed in highest respect among scientific men," but that was nothing "compared to the work we hope to be able to perform."[4]

Meanwhile, congratulations for Hatcher continued to accrue. Wilbur C. Knight, apparently still miffed by his run-in the previous year with Hatcher's boss, chortled that Hatcher had landed in a "splendid place if you can handle Holland" and urged Hatcher to visit him when he came out. Beyond that, Samuel W. Williston, then dean of the University of Kansas School of Medicine and Hatcher's former field supervisor when he started for Marsh, also chimed in with kind accolades: "You have always been my ideal of a field worker in paleontology, and held up as a model to all my students and assistants. Your papers too show you to be as good in the laboratory and study as in the field, and I am glad that you have the opportunity of doing unlimited work in both directions." That last thought was clearly an inside dig at Marsh, from whom both Williston and Hatcher had broken away in order to be able to publish their own paleontological research.[5]

Hatcher spent March restoring order to the department, submitting a progress report to Holland on the thirty-first, which revealed the hiring of another lab assistant, L. S. Coggeshall, to aid his brother A. S. Coggeshall in preparing the *Diplodocus* skeleton for study and mounting. For his part, Hatcher had rearranged the lab to create more space and designed a card catalogue system, with which he had documented all the vertebrate fossils in the department. He'd also drafted a document for the railroad describing the geologic features along the Union Pacific rail line from Omaha to Ogden. The crew would deploy to their assigned areas in the field on April 3, and Hatcher, with his crew's input, prepared a detailed estimate of $2,414 for the costs of the season's fieldwork.[6]

Hatcher rendezvoused with Anna and their young "bairns" in Omaha for a visit on April 9, before heading to Laramie to meet Reed and start for Medicine Bow. Despite a blinding spring snowstorm, the crew was fanning out by the seventeenth, with Reed planning to join Peterson in the Eocene shortly to show him a cache of five skulls he'd discovered earlier. Hatcher had succeeded in purchasing two teams, wagons, and harnesses for Reed and himself at a cost of $328.15. Peterson departed from Rawlins, Wyoming, for the field on April 21, the same day Hatcher left for Sheep Creek from Medicine Bow.[7]

Finally starting work, Hatcher reported that he'd scraped an area about 100' x 30' by the twenty-eighth in order to continue searching for the missing *Diplodocus* elements belonging to the 1899 skeleton. But Hatcher's heroics transcended that task; in prospecting around the area, Hatcher discovered another partial skeleton of *Diplodocus* (CM 94), which, although slightly smaller than the one Wortman and Reed had discovered the previous season, nonetheless possessed most of the bones that were missing in the skeleton discovered in 1899. Thus, Hatcher's discovery would eventually prove equally pivotal both in Hatcher's research to scientifically describe *Diplodocus* and in the Carnegie's efforts to construct a skeletal mount of this spectacular dinosaur for exhibition. Reed had yet to return from showing Peterson where his cache of Eocene skulls was, and Hatcher wanted to spend a few days with Reed at the Sheep Creek Quarries before leaving for the Laramie near Lusk. Anna had moved on in her family visit from Omaha to Lamoni, Iowa.[8]

On May 1, Hatcher wrote what must have been a stunning letter to Holland about Hatcher's plan to join an Antarctic expedition in 1901, to continue his work in the Southern Hemisphere. He'd formulated the scheme at Princeton but had withheld discussing it with Holland until the prospects for his participation became more certain. That achieved, Hatcher forthrightly declared:

> *Now my plan is just this. During the three years & more spent in Patagonia & Tierra del Fuego I have been greatly impressed with the great thickness of the late Tertiary rocks that form the great plains of both the mainland & the Island. Moreover these rocks increase in thickness toward the S.E. in which direction they also dip. On the extreme S.E. of Tierra del Fuego they show a considerable development. As you know the question of a former land connection between S. America & the supposed Antarctic continent is a question which if definitely proven in the affirmative would go far toward the solution of many problems relating to the present and past geographical distribution of animal & vegetable life throughout the world & other biological questions as well. Considering the great thickness of these deposits & their gentle southeasterly dip I believe that they will be found on the land mass or masses that now constitute Antarctica & that they will be found in places to contain remains of that rich mammalian fauna which so abundantly characterize them in Patagonia. To find only a single one of these mammal skeletons entombed in the rocks of Antarctica would be ample proof of a former land connection which is only one of the several problems that I should propose to attack in connection with the work.*

Specifically, he intended to join the "Scottish National Antarctic Expedition" and land "S.E. of Graham land" with two assistants and devote the two summer seasons prospecting the adjacent exposures for fossils while collecting other specimens related to natural history—all for a cost not to exceed $5,000. From Hatcher's perspective, he was offering Holland a chance to fund the endeavor at some level and reap the collections obtained for the Carnegie. Hatcher hoped to leave for South America that coming autumn to complete work there before joining the Scottish expedition in the spring of 1901. He ended his pitch by demanding confidentiality from Holland and asking that he consult with Carnegie about whether the museum should sponsor him. Otherwise, he might be able to go as part of the scientific staff of the expedition, but then the Carnegie would not garner the goods collected.[9]

While waiting for Holland's response, Hatcher received a disappointing declaration from Reed at Lost Creek, Wyoming, on May 3:

> *I have nothing good to report so my letter wil be short. I made a total falure of finding the bones in the picket* [sic] *lake locality. I found the lake and the bone horison* [sic] *and we found a few bones but the two localitys* [sic] *where I saw the bones in 85 I could not find and there is so much of the bad lands in there that it would take weeks and perhaps months to find the right place so we have given it up for the present and wil* [sic] *go to the field north of the ratle snake hills* [sic] *from here.*

Adding to the dreary report, a blizzard lasting two days had buried the region, making travel impossible, so Reed couldn't return to Sheep Creek for at least a week or ten days. Peterson subsequently filed Reed's letter in the Carnegie archives in an envelope on which he wrote, "Famous letter of Reed to Hatcher excusing himself not finding the bones which he cached in 1885. He had never found them. O.A.P."[10]

Peterson provided Hatcher with his own version of events on the same day, admitting to be "much disgusted" with Reed and his antics. They'd traveled to where the cache was marked on Reed's map near the head of "Sulphur Creek" on April 25 and hunted but found nothing. Then they spent the twenty-sixth riding to Picket Lake and searched the following day for Reed's cache in a pocket near where some wild horses crossed some badlands but again found nothing significant, at which time Reed expressed doubt that he could find his "bone patch" even if they hunted for two or three weeks. The twenty-eighth and twenty-ninth were lost to a blizzard, but they continued their quest for Reed's five skulls on the thirtieth without success. Adding to Peterson's skepticism, the topography consisted of low rounded hills and long ridges without much exposure of any strata that looked fossiliferous, and since Reed "did not wish to hunt for his 'bone patch' or his cash [sic] any longer we left Picket Lake as soon as we could" in order to soldier on with the excursion to Reed's sites north of the Rattlesnake Hills. Peterson wrote Hatcher again on May 8 in extreme exasperation:

> *I have now chased aroun* [sic] *with Mr. Reed from locality to locality without he being able to show me a place of the least interest or a place with any evidence of fossils at all let alone fossils in such great abundance as he reported while in Pittsburg* [sic]. *This last locality is realy* [sic] *worst of all. We went out yesterday to the place (20 m northeast of here) where he claims he found jaws turtles and other bones anough* [sic] *to fill a barril!* [sic]
>
> *Mr. Reed and I hunted over the place till I got tired. We staied* [sic] *there close to one hour and in that time, we did not find anything but a few unimportant fragments which I have saved.*
>
> *My opinion is that the whole thing from beginning to end is a romance. But that it would be carried to such an extent is indeed surprising.*

Reed then took the stage to Rawlins to begin his journey to Sheep Creek. Peterson would write Holland the same sad story, then set off for the Henry's Fork region, where he hoped to make a representative collection from the Bridger Formation before the fall.[11]

Holland responded to Hatcher by the ninth, when Hatcher wrote back from Lusk to say he was content to let Holland and the trustees decide about the Antarctic expedition as long as they seriously considered it. In the interim, Hatcher had careened from Sheep Creek, to Cañon City to set up an operation in an old Marsh-Felch Quarry there, to Lusk. At

Sheep Creek, they'd uncovered seven new vertebrae, one humerus, and several other bones in the quarry extension, but Hatcher was skeptical that they belonged to the previous year's *Diplodocus*, because the caudals, dorsals, and cervicals were all mixed together. He chronicled the unsuccessful odyssey of Reed and Peterson before concluding:

> *I fear the entire story is fiction & that Peterson is loosing* [sic] *much valuable time. From the tone of his letter he was evidently much disgusted from being hauled about over the country for nothing. Now you know as well as I do that Mr. Reed did not tell us the truth regarding his great finds & where he said he made his cache. It never costs a man anything to tell the truth & one falsehood often costs much both in time & money. To put it frankly between you and I I am afraid Mr. Reed's veracity is not to be depended upon & for my part I do not like to be needlessly fooled or tricked by one of our own men who should have our own interest at heart. Nevertheless I am still willing to give him a fair chance as a collector, but from the nature of his work for Prof. Marsh & at the University of Wyoming I fear it is bad judgement* [sic] *to leave him in charge of so important work as that at Sheep Cr.*

Hatcher recommended using younger, yet still experienced, collectors to work with Reed, since their salaries would be cheaper. Hatcher emphasized to Holland that he wasn't prejudiced against Reed but rather lacked trust in his collecting techniques and just wanted the best specimens possible for the Carnegie.[12]

Hatcher enclosed a copy of his agreement with an M. P. Felch for working the quarry near Cañon City, where Marsh acquired some of his earliest dinosaur specimens in 1877. In fact, the Marsh-Felch Quarry is one of two in the area that represent the second earliest battlefield in the "Bone War" for dinosaurs between Marsh and Cope. The discovery of dinosaur bones near Morrison, Colorado, by Arthur Lakes shortly preceded the Cañon City discovery and initiated their acquisitive competition, and the discovery at Como Bluff in Wyoming by William Reed followed shortly after. Born in Vermont, Marshall Felch served extensively as a medic for the US Army during the Civil War before he and his wife, Amanda, married in Boston and moved to Colorado in 1866. The discovery of oil just north of Cañon City brought the couple to that area, where Marshall and his brother found a dinosaur bone in early 1877. This was shortly before O. W. Lucas and his brother, Ira, began excavating dinosaur bones for Cope from a nearby locality eventually named "Cope's Nipple." Marsh sent one of his ace field assistants, Benjamin Mudge, to investigate the area, and in August, Mudge reported that Lucas was firm in his commitment to sending Cope the bones that he'd already discovered but would consider other offers for future collecting. Mudge then began prospecting for other sites nearby.[13]

Marsh's chief field assistant, Samuel W. Williston, soon joined Mudge and worked with Felch to try and excavate a hind portion of a *Diplodocus* specimen, but the bones broke easily, making the effort and its results less than satisfactory. Soon, Marsh called off the Cañon City enterprise to focus his staff's efforts on the quarries near Morrison and then on the new discovery at Como. But Felch continued to collect at the Marsh-Felch Quarry, and in 1883, Felch and Marsh developed an agreement through which Felch collected a good deal of dinosaur material for Marsh, an operation supported by Marsh's funding from the USGS. Noteworthy specimens obtained included well-preserved skeletons of *Ceratosaurus*, *Allosaurus*, and *Stegosaurus*, which were originally shipped to Yale before being transferred to the Smithsonian after Marsh's death when his collections were divided between the two institutions. Charles Gilmore, whom Hatcher would soon hire, eventually restudied these specimens when he left the Carnegie to work at the National Museum of Natural History, and they went on display there in 1910. In addition, the quarry has yielded excellent material of *Diplodocus*, *Camarasaurus*, *Apatosaurus*, and *Haplocanthosaurus*, as well as the first specimens of mammals from the Morrison, although Quarry 9 at Como Bluff would yield a much larger and more diverse sample. When Hatcher sought to reopen the Marsh-Felch Quarry, the aging Felch was in poor physical condition, due to spinal injuries suffered at the Battle of Cedar Creek in 1864 and subsequent PTSD, as well as the death of his wife, who had been an important stabilizing factor in his life. Felch would eventually take his own life in 1902. He had shipped all his bones to Marsh just before Marsh's death, but bones were still abundant, and Hatcher felt that with some scraping, they could collect a good sample, which would only cost $25 per month for the rights to quarry.[14]

Reed reached Sheep Creek by the thirteenth. After surveying the exposed bones, he agreed they probably didn't belong to the first *Diplodocus*. Meanwhile, from Lusk, Wyoming, Hatcher attempted to reassure Holland on the eighteenth that despite the slow start, the crew understood the importance of making an excellent showing. Peterson would certainly garner a small but scientifically significant sample from the Bridger, and "AC" should be pleased with the ceratopsians Hatcher expected to excavate from the Laramie. However after reflecting on Holland's expressed concern for the season, Hatcher decided to have Peterson quit the Bridger and come to Sheep Creek to supervise that operation, even though he disliked having two experienced men making a $1,500 per year salary at the same place. Hatcher also reacted strongly to Holland's perceived implication regarding Antarctica—that Hatcher had treated the question of Antarctica lightly and had acted on impulse:

> *Let me assure you that such was not the case. It is all a plan over which I have been meditating for the past three & one half years, & that I have discussed with several of the foremost geologists & paleontologists in the country, every one of whom approved of it & recognized the logic of my reasoning. Please do not think me an adventurer in the matter as I can assure you I gave full consideration to the dangers & possibilities of the work. It was only after being fully convinced of the possibilities of making important scientific discoveries that I was willing to undergo the hardships & dangers that such an undertaking would necessarily impose.*

Hatcher also responded to Holland's draft article for *Science* regarding the number of dorsals in *Diplodocus*, saying he had no objection to Holland publishing it, provided Holland bore in mind that Hatcher had come to the Carnegie with the agreement that all vertebrate paleontology papers published would be under his charge, adding, "I shall expect to be the actual & not the nominal head of the Department, always consulting yourself as The Director in important matters, and I do not fear but that we will get along harmoniously, for there will be more than work enough for us all . . . free from petty jealousies." This shot across Holland's bow was indicative of skirmishes to come; as Paul Brinkman notes, Hatcher and Holland were not terribly "well suited for one another," given Hatcher's tempermental and straightforward nature, which would often run headlong into Holland's distaste for being challenged by subordinates. Nonetheless, Holland realized that Hatcher's extraordinary collecting skills and ability to productively manage his field crews were essential in satisfying Andrew Carnegie's high hopes for obtaining a world-class collection of dinosaurs and other fossil vertebrates. To buck Holland up a bit, Hatcher reported finding a good skull of the hog-like "terror pig" *Elotherium* with all of its teeth well preserved, which would make an excellent exhibit specimen.[15]

Hatcher also wrote Reed on the eighteenth, commencing the letter in a compassionate tone to convey his sorrow and disappointment about the Eocene effort. He might have been trying to soften the blow to come, for his next lines outlined the decision of Holland and Hatcher to abandon work in the Eocene and send Peterson to supervise Reed and the work at Sheep Creek. To save funds, one of Reed's assistants would need to be laid off—a decision Peterson would make after consulting with Reed. In closing, Hatcher suggested that working under Peterson would be of "great value" to Reed and trusted that their relations would be pleasant. Concurrently, Peterson received Hatcher's directive to head for Sheep Creek by the twenty-first. Although it would take him a couple of weeks to make the drive, he wrote Hatcher and Holland that he would start immediately, especially since he'd been having little luck in the Eocene around the Hams Fork River in southwest Wyoming near Kemmerer.[16]

About that time and still seemingly unaware of his demotion, Reed reported to Holland that before leaving for Lusk, Hatcher and crew had struck bones in the quarry extension where Reed had expected to find more of the *Diplodocus*, but he didn't think the new elements belonged to it. Nonetheless, Reed had exposed additional well-preserved but disarticulated bones: twenty-four vertebrae in all, including caudals, dorsals, and cervicals, along with some ribs, two sternal plates, and a right scapula and coracoid. He would photograph them for Holland before jacketing and crating them.[17]

Peterson reached Medicine Bow by the twenty-fifth and told Hatcher of his trepidation about supervising Reed:

> *I got here this morning and am in receipt of your registered letter with instructions. In reply I wish to again remind you of the fact that Mr. Reed expressed his unwillingness of working under my instruction shortly after Dr. Wortman's resignation. He told Dr. Holland that he would not work under my instructions in the field.*
>
> *Since my last experience with Mr. Reed in hunting for his so called cash* [sic] *of skulls, localities &c. I can not have the confidence and respect I formerly had for him and since he undoubtedly knows my feeling towards him I leave to your own judgement* [sic] *what the result may be.*[18]

Not surprisingly, Reed was indeed self-righteously incensed when Peterson gave him Hatcher's directive and immediately appealed to Holland in disbelief, starting out by saying, "You told me that you were my friend" and should come to you "if I was unjustly treated. Well now the injustice has come, and like a thunderbolt." From Reed's perspective, Hatcher's orders to turn over the specimens, equipment, and accounts to Peterson and work under Peterson's supervision directly violated the verbal agreement made between Holland, Hatcher, and himself, adding, "I cannot fully obey . . . and retain my self-respect." Reed had subordinated himself "without protest" the previous year under Wortman to learn better methods of excavating fossils and felt he was now as competent as Peterson. Beyond that, Hatcher had repeatedly promised that Reed would supervise the Sheep Creek operation; Reed had assembled his crew under that stipulation, including arranging for his son to leave the University of Wyoming to take the photos and for his wife to cook without compensation. Exasperated and resentful, he railed:

And this is my reward!

Oh, why did you ever come to Laramie? I was fairly contented there, and would give my last year's salary to be back.

Will send you a copy of the Hatcher letter, and await your decision, but one thing sure, I will never strike a pick in the ground under Mr. Peterson, - not that he is not a good man or a good collector.

Until I hear from you I will prospect around the country and try and open up some new things. But I shall not trespass on Museum grounds.

Anxiously awaiting your reply. . .[19]

Struck by the blast he had already anticipated, Peterson wrote Hatcher from Medicine Bow on the twenty-eighth to report that Reed had refused to work under him but wouldn't leave with his family until he found out what caused the coup. He warned, "You would do well to write him in full and also write to me, since relations in camp between him and I naturally have taken such turn that work can not go on smothly [sic] so long as ither [sic] one of us remain." Peterson was in town for supplies and, although "in an awkward position" that he did not appreciate, would try to continue work in the quarry until he received further word from Hatcher and Holland. Adding to Peterson's pique, Reed refused to turn over his accounts and bills. Apparently all Reed's funds on hand had been expended, so Peterson had to dip into his own salary to cover expenses. With that, Peterson also wrote Holland to relate the developments to him, adding that there were good specimens in the quarry but a thorough evaluation would require a closer survey.[20]

From his refuge in Lance Creek far removed from the carnage, Hatcher wrote Holland to submit his monthly report and reveal that although he'd found no *Triceratops* skulls yet, he had discovered duckbill material "of vastly more scientific importance" that would shed light on what dinosaur skin was like. Now identified as belonging to *Edmotosaurus annectens*, this specimen is catalogued as CM 105. He and his cook, Fales, had also collected numerous butterflies, moths, and other insects for Holland. He told Holland that he'd written Reed and Peterson to explain that they wanted Peterson to supervise the operation at Sheep Creek, but apparently Hatcher was, as yet, unaware of the implosion that had occurred there. He again argued that Reed's collecting abilities would benefit from Peterson's tutelage, and although he noted Holland's suggestion to have Peterson and Reed work in separate quarries, "I cannot approve of such a plan, as it would be equivalent to having no one directly & absolutely responsible for the work." At that point, he preferred to have Peterson solely responsible and was confident Peterson would succeed. Later, he planned to take Reed to the Cretaceous exposures at Troublesome Creek to prospect.[21]

Hatcher's monthly report for April and May detailed events already mentioned, except for the fact that he'd also collected a sample of Cretaceous mammals and a rare turtle (probably *Baena*, CM 115) from the Laramie. In addition, he revealed that the *Edmontosaurus* specimen included "most of the pelvis, sacrum & caudal vertebrae in position back to about the 25th caudal." In all, he foresaw "the greatest success" in store for the season.[22]

Apparently alerted to the situation at Sheep Creek by June 3, Hatcher, with his western empire in rather desperate disarray, telegraphed and wrote Holland from Lusk that he would leave for Medicine Bow the next day and possibly send Peterson back to the Laramie at Lance Creek. He pledged to do his utmost to forge reconciliation between Reed and Peterson; however, if Reed refused Peterson's supervision, thus resolving the issue down to one of authority, Hatcher would "insist on Mr. Reed's connection being severed with that Dept. of the Carnegie Museum of which I am the Curator." There could be no question of Hatcher's authority. Hatcher further noted he'd followed Holland's suggestion to put Peterson in charge at Sheep Creek, and Hatcher agreed that the work would proceed better under Peterson. He had closely examined Reed's work under Marsh and deemed it inferior, and Hatcher demanded better because "it simply means the destruction, rather than the preservation of rare & important material." Accordingly, Hatcher would leave behind "three prospects . . . of considerable importance" in the Laramie to return and sort things out at Sheep Creek.[23]

Acting with alacrity, Hatcher telegraphed Holland on June 6 to say that Reed had severed connections with the Carnegie on May 27 and would not resume work. Lengthy letters from Hatcher to Reed on June 6 and Hatcher to Holland on June 7 revealed how events had unfolded. Holland had sent Hatcher copies of the letters he'd received from Reed and Peterson, and Hatcher told Holland he had returned to Sheep Creek in hopes of convincing Reed to work under Peterson, but if not, Hatcher would compromise and ask Reed to work under him and send Peterson to Lusk. But since Reed had written Holland instead of Hatcher, Hatcher concluded Reed had decided to ignore him and deal with Holland directly. Hatcher indicated he'd never deny an employee under his supervision the opportunity to appeal to Holland if he felt he'd been treated unjustly, but tact, judgment, and courtesy demanded that Reed should have appealed to Hatcher first, just as Hatcher would be required to address any grievance to Holland first before appealing to the museum's trustees. Hatcher felt this breech of protocol alone would justify Reed's dismissal, but Hatcher returned to try and settle the matter directly with Reed amicably by saying he had meant no disrespect by his letter and by encouraging Reed to return to work under Peterson so he could get "full credit for the season's work." But Reed refused to acknowledge Hatcher's authority, since Reed had been hired before Hatcher. This triggered Hatcher's ire, and "I decided that to yield in the least respect to a man who professed such absurd views would only be encouraging further insubordination." So Hatcher reported to Holland that he had informed Reed "that our conference was at an end, that by his letter to you of May 27th & by his subsequent actions he had himself severed his relations with us which I believed according to his contract with you he should not have done without giving at least two months notice." Hatcher subsequently retrieved the bills in Reed's possession and paid them off. Then Reed requested a statement from Hatcher about "just how he was leaving." Hatcher drafted one in hopes of avoiding further trouble. Hatcher recounted the sequence of correspondence between Reed and Holland, including Reed's refusal, twice, to work under Peterson as Hatcher had directed. Hatcher then reasoned:

> You have by these actions set at defiance both the wishes of Director Holland as set forth in his letter to you of May 31st, 1900 & those of myself.

*I am sorry that you should have decided to abandon your work
& while I believe that according to the terms of your agreement you
should have given us at least two months notice, I shall not be rigid
on this point & will accept your withdrawal as in effect from the date
of your letter to Dr. Holland, May 27, 1900 or that being a Sunday
on the following Monday, May 28, 1900.*

Hatcher hoped Holland approved of his actions under the circumstances
and expressed his sorrow that Reed had followed the course he had, but
he didn't regret the loss to the museum, since he viewed Reed as unqualified for the work at hand. Besides, Hatcher felt they could hire three
assistants superior to Reed for the salary he commanded, and indicated
he and Holland should immediately start searching for them. With that,
Hatcher indicated that Peterson would work to expand the *Diplodocus*
Quarry, first to the east and west, where Hatcher hoped he'd find more
of that skeleton, then to the south, where he was sure they'd encounter
more bones of other skeletons. As for himself, Hatcher intended to rest
in Ogden, Utah, for a day before returning to Lusk by way of Laramie
so he could interview a prospective field assistant studying under Knight
by the name of Charles Gilmore, who would go on to become the most
accomplished vertebrate paleontologist that Hatcher would ever enlist
into his stable of trusted assistants.[24]

Holland highly approved of Hatcher's handling of matters with Reed,
and although Holland had hired Reed and kept him on under his obligations related to the contract they had signed, he was relieved to learn
Reed was no longer on staff, as he wrote on June 12:

*Reed is afflicted, as unfortunately so many partially educated
and so-called "self made" men are apt to be, with an exaggerated idea of their importance and the value of their attainments.
He is one of the long list of those who have fallen victims to
megacephalic disease.*

Holland agreed that Reed's vacated salary should be invested in new
assistants, but he urged caution when Hatcher made his selections:

I prefer the man who has had the benefit of a liberal course of training in a literary institution. Such men are far less apt to be conceited and troublesome. . . . Docility, willingness, the disposition of the soldier, who obeys orders, are needed. . . . Men who imagine that the holding of a minor position in an institution of this sort entitles them to assume the airs and to talk in the tone of men who have attained to scientific distinction and are leaders in the world of thought, are to be avoided. We have had unfortunate experiences here in the case of one or two men whom we have had with us in the past, who, having published a page or two of their exceedingly insignificant observations, have suddenly blossomed out in their own estimation as full-fledged scientists, capable of criticising [sic] the opinions of everybody from a Kelvin to a Cope. We wish no more bumptious, verdant, youths in the list of our employes [sic]. . .

Holland would counsel Coggeshall in these tenets as they looked for a lab assistant who could fit the bill at as small a salary as possible. It's interesting to compare the qualities that Hatcher sought in his field and lab assistants with those of Holland. Hatcher preferred willing, interested and modest young men, who were also agreeable. In the meantime, Holland and Hatcher needed to secure a legitimate claim on the *Diplodocus* Quarry, which Wortman had considered to be exhausted of material. Holland suspected that Reed, knowing this, might cause the Carnegie more trouble with land titles, but Holland couldn't recall the detailed location of the quarry from the claim map and sent it to Hatcher with instructions for him to put on record a claim, once they located it exactly. Holland felt that Peterson should to be able to find the corners, and with the help of the map figure out about where it was.[25]

No doubt relieved by Reed's departure, Peterson wrote Holland and Hatcher on the sixteenth that he'd opened up a 30' x 60' cut along the left side of the quarry, in which he'd discovered an additional scapula, dorsal vertebra, and pelvic bone that might belong to the original *Diplodocus*. He'd also exposed a dorsal plate and two vertebrae from the previous year's *Stegosaurus* skeleton. Local scuttlebutt suggested Reed was working on the Little Medicine River near Medicine Bow, but Peterson was unaware of any results. Walter Granger and Albert Thompson of the AMNH were due in the area shortly.[26]

Holland's map of the quarries reached Hatcher by the twenty-fifth, and Hatcher reported to Holland that he'd sent it to Peterson so he could plot the *Diplodocus* Quarry and file the required claim. Hatcher also confirmed he'd hired the aforementioned Charles Gilmore as a field assistant, who came highly recommended by way of Knight and Hatcher's old colleague Beecher, who was then at the Smithsonian's National Museum of Natural History. Hatcher described Gilmore as a "modest, capable & willing young gentleman" who had just completed his junior year in Knight's mining program, and Hatcher had been able to entice him away with a larger salary than Knight could offer—$50 per month. Unlike Reed, Gilmore had no problem working under Peterson's supervision and, as far as Hatcher could see, fit the guidelines for hires invoked by Holland quite well.[27]

With order restored to Hatcher's far-flung empire, Peterson resumed filing regular reports from Sheep Creek. On the twenty-sixth, he brought two loads of bones into Medicine Bow for shipping, after purchasing Reed's shanty at Camp Carnegie to "get rid of him." Peterson now suspected that the quarry contained a more general mix of bones and doubted that the scapula and other bones he'd mentioned actually belonged to the first *Diplodocus*. Bones of *Brontosaurus* and *Stegosaurus* were commonly mixed in with the rest. The AMNH crew was also finding stegosaur bones in their quarry. By July 2, Peterson announced the discovery of more *Diplodocus* bones, including a femur, tibia, fibula, and foot, along with another scapula and a skull base with one maxilla. So if they found a humerus, radius, ulna, and forefoot, they would be in good shape to restore a whole *Diplodocus* skeleton. He intended to prospect in the Troublesome region before returning and opening up ten to fifteen more feet of the *Diplodocus* Quarry before quitting it. Gilmore arrived on the twenty-seventh and was pleasing Peterson with his work on *Brontosaurus* bones found in the upper claims. Peterson intended to attend to all the claims, including filing one for the *Diplodocus* Quarry. Reed had a $10,000 claim near Rock Creek that Walter Granger was evaluating for Osborn, and Peter Kaisen of the AMNH indicated that Wortman also planned to work in the area that summer.[28]

On July 6, Osborn wrote Hatcher in part to alert him that Osborn had succeeded Marsh as the paleontologist for the USGS, and Osborn wanted Hatcher to take on the task of finishing Marsh's Ceratopsia monograph. Hatcher congratulated Osborn on his appointment on the twelfth and expressed interest in speaking further about the monograph in the fall, but most of Hatcher's letter sought Osborn's endorsement for the Antarctica project, which Osborn would later provide.[29]

Hatcher wrote Holland twice on the tenth, apparently in response to a newspaper article Holland had seen regarding Reed's departure. Hatcher presumed Reed had catalyzed it but reassured Holland that he need not fear a lawsuit because "he left our employ of his own accord & refused to return to work after I had urged him to do so." In addition, Reed had failed to provide two months' notice before resigning, thus violating that clause in his contract, so Hatcher was certain that Holland would be seen as the party deserving legal redress if Reed sued. In terms of collecting, three of Hatcher's prospects in the Laramie had gone bust, but he was scraping off the overburden on three more and remained hopeful of finding a *Triceratops* skull. Hatcher was content to let Holland and Coggeshall handle the hiring of a lab assistant, but he lobbied Holland to grant some vacation time to the staff, as was becoming customary: "In New York they allow three weeks & in Washington one month in each year. I hope you & the trustees will see your way clear to do as well as New York. . . ." He also issued an invitation for Holland to visit and see the operations, promising a pleasant visit. Besides, he badgered, "Lusk is only 36 hours from Pittsburg."[30]

Peterson checked in with Hatcher and Holland in mid-July to endorse Gilmore and report that they now had thirty to thirty-five vertebrae of a probable *Brontosaurus*, as well as several limb bones, including a radius and ulna together and a tibia and fibula together, along with some foot bones and many ribs. Peterson had mapped the *Diplodocus* Quarry, and excitedly exclaimed:

> *We continue to find Diplodocus bones where we left off when I first took charge of the work. As we have found so many pelvic*

bones together (two pubes, two ischii, femur and what I take to be ilium not yet uncovered) I am greatly hoping we may find the rest of the limb and foot. We have many vertebrae also in sight. I have stripped off the ground some 10 or 15 feet farther back. . . .

He had also plotted the *Diplodocus* Quarry on Holland's map and found that it was covered by the claim in Section 11 that Wortman filed the previous year.[31]

Fed up with his bad luck in the Laramie, Hatcher notified Holland that he'd temporarily fled to the *Daemonelix* beds four to five miles north of Harrison and was having "splendid success" collecting the mysterious, corkscrew-shaped, concretionary fossils for an exhibit at the Carnegie. Anna and their daughter were visiting folks in Harrison, so he'd taken the opportunity to bring his two sons out to his camp for a couple of weeks. He'd hired Utterback, his former colleague from his Marsh days, at $50 per month and resolutely recommended him for the field and lab assistant positions they were recruiting: "He is a good workman, industrious, quiet & unassuming. . . . He is a man that can be trusted anywhere, [and] he is already a good collector." Unable to suppress his curiosity any longer, Hatcher queried Holland about whether he and the trustees had made a decision about his participation in the Antarctic expedition. In his letter to Holland on August 2, Hatcher continued to pitch his initiatives to hire Utterback and create a *Daemonelix* exhibit. He envisioned reconstructing an outcrop with *Daemonelix* corkscrews sticking out of the bank, just as they did in the field. He assured Holland that he was aware of the debate between Erwin Barbour and Theodor Fuchs about the origin of *Daemonelix* and that he favored Barbour's argument for them being plant-related fossil structures. As for Utterback, Hatcher pointed out that he would be a perfect man to have working in the old Marsh-Felch Quarry in Cañon City over the winter, as Utterback was highly trained in such operations, and this would free up Peterson to help prepare material Peterson had collected back in Pittsburgh.[32]

Back at Sheep Creek, Peterson provided a revised account of material from the *Diplodocus* Quarry to Hatcher and Holland on August 2: a complete pelvic arch in position with femur, tibia, fibula, and foot, along with two sets of ischia, pubes as well as the base of a skull with a maxillary, a scapula, and fifty vertebrae, although probably not from the same individual, since a few brontosaur vertebrae were mixed in. He still hoped to discover the humerus, radius, ulna, and forefoot for the *Diplodocus* mount and would strip off another ten to fifteen feet in hopes of finding another pocket. At another outcrop across the canyon from Big Bone Quarry in the upper claims, he took out a brontosaur femur five feet six inches in length, and he had Gilmore working on four more elements. He still planned a trip to prospect in late Mesozoic exposures in the Troublesome region. A week later, on the ninth, Peterson told Hatcher the *Diplodocus* Quarry was exhausted and had been abandoned; Gilmore's site proved unfruitful as well. They were testing two more prospects, but if those didn't produce, they might have trouble finding another decent site in the area, since so many collectors had searched there. He'd seen some Jurassic exposures near Laramie Peak in 1892, but he sought Hatcher's advice about where else to prospect. He closed by wishing his sister "Mattie" and their children the best.[33]

Peterson was still pounding away at Sheep Creek in mid-August and wrote Hatcher that one of the quarries, presumably in the upper claims, was producing a number of mixed *Diplodocus* and *Brontosaurus* bones, including a scapula and a few cervicals of *Diplodocus* that he hoped might lead to the elusive front limb. To date, he thought he had a few carpals or wrist bones of *Diplodocus* but no humerus. They'd also run across a radius and ulna, but those probably belonged to *Stegosaurus*. His intent was to probe in two more prospects in the upper claims, then if nothing appeared, abandon the area. The AMNH crew had found a partial *Diplodocus* skeleton near Aurora, Wyoming, and Reed seemed to have had some success based on "the way he is blowing." Peterson was finally able to report better results on the fifteenth, having found two ischia, one pubis, the femur, tibia, two fibulae, and an astragalus of a brontosaur in the *Brontosaurus* Quarry. They hoped those would lead to a hind foot. Judging from the femur at sixty-eight inches in length, it figured to be an immense individual. Gilmore was also doing well in the other quarry, where brontosaur, *Diplodocus*, and "Morosaurus" bones were mixed together. In all, they had fifty-one boxes packed, averaging 400 pounds each. One box with *Diplodocus* ilia and sacrum weighed between 1,000 and 1,200 pounds. Reed had two quarries with some very fine things apparently, but Granger didn't purchase them for the AMNH. Instead, he had "struck it rich" near Marsh's old haunt at Como Bluff, where they had fifteen cervical and dorsal vertebrae going into a bank near the old train station at Aurora. They turned out to belong to *Diplodocus*. Peterson wondered if funds were available to buy recent skeletons, because they could get wolves, badgers, skunks, etc. from "Rattlesnake Jack." On the thirty-first, Peterson estimated that he and Gilmore would have about seventy-five crates by October 1.[34]

With Holland away in England, Hatcher cheerily checked in with Mellor on September 9 with the news that his crews had 130 crates of fossils packed, a haul that would fill two bulging boxcars. More specifically, that material would allow the construction of mounts not only for *Diplodocus* and *Brontosaurus*, but also old acquaintances from his days with Marsh, such as "Titanotherium," "Oreodon," and *Aceratherium*. Add to that the collections of modern butterflies, moths, plants, and vertebrates, and the plunder for a season that started out so scantily would end with two large chests full of treasure.[35]

Peterson updated Hatcher on the tenth with the news that they'd abandoned "Quarry E" where they'd found the brontosaur tail vertebrae and hind limb. But he was still probing the upper claims by following some stegosaur and carnivore bones into the bank. Gilmore seemed to be enjoying the best luck at "Quarry C," discovering more bones of different dinosaurs that were increasingly well preserved as he dug further into the outcrop. Again noting Granger's success at Aurora, Peterson scoffed that although Reed had some bones, he probably wouldn't get $1,000 for them because the AMNH wasn't interested.[36]

With the season winding down, Hatcher wrote Holland on the twenty-third that both crews intended to continue collecting until the weather deteriorated. He'd yet to collect a cliff with *Daemonelix* because he wasn't sure Holland approved of his plans for its exhibit, but he and Utterback were amassing an impressive array of White River mammal fossils totaling seventy-three crates that would eventually include material of *Daemonelix*, *Merycochoerus*, "Titanotherium," *Elotherium*, *Aceratherium*,

Hyaenodon, and *Hoplophoneus*. Utterback would stay until November 1 before loading the cache for shipment and heading to Cañon City to begin stripping overburden at Marsh's old Marsh-Felch Quarry. Hatcher intended to stay near Harrison until October 3, then visit Sheep Creek to assess work there and plan for the following season before arranging for the shipments with railroad officials and returning to Pittsburgh around October 10–15. Upon arrival, he'd be ready to discuss his plan to work in Patagonia and Antarctica, as well as other matters. He'd also write Earl Douglass to inquire about costs for a collection of dinosaurs that he was selling, especially the price for his best hadrosaur. Hatcher also sent his third box of butterflies to Holland, quipping that this would be the last because "the butterfly season here has closed. . . ."[37]

A letter from Peterson on the twenty-sixth informed Hatcher that the crew was still having success, so in all, the Carnegie crews might have three carloads of fossils, with two coming from Sheep Creek. Although there wasn't much more of the carnivorous dinosaur or the stegosaur, a fifth brontosaur had appeared with part of the pelvis and sacrum, along with six tail vertebrae. In all, they were now as near to having a complete *Brontosaurus* skeleton as they were to having a complete *Diplodocus*. Gilmore had excavated fourteen presacrals, many ribs, a scapula, a femur that was five feet three inches long, and thirty-eight caudals of one brontosaur from Quarry C, and they hoped to find the front limbs. Peterson had also collected more ichthyosaur bones, presumably from Troublesome, that would help finish the specimen collected the previous year.[38]

As Hatcher hit the road on October 3 for Sheep Creek, Omaha, and a visit with his brother in Iowa, Peterson and Utterback scrambled to wrap up their operations. Utterback wrote Hatcher on the tenth that "Quarry 2" had disappointed. But all the crates were now packed securely, and he'd leave between the twentieth and twenty-fifth. Peterson telegraphed Holland on the sixteenth with the number of the Union Pacific car that was nearly loaded. He recounted a harrowing incident to Hatcher on the eighteenth:

I could not get a 50 foot car and loaded the boxes in a 38 ft. They are piled up like baild [sic] *hay. The boxes being very heavy make the load top heavy a fact which I do not aprove of. The agent did not seem to think the car was overloaded which makes me somewhat more confident.*

We had an accident with the car after having it partly loaded. They set off a coal car with out a break, which bumped in to our car and broak [sic] out part of our end at top of our car. I reported to the agent who looked at the car and advised us to continue loading. He promised to have the car reported for repair at Laramie.

Peterson also confirmed he'd filed "proof of labor" statements on the claims at Sheep Creek and expected to arrive in Pittsburgh in about a week. The haul from Sheep Creek during the 1900 season was, indeed, formidable. As recorded in the Carnegie's catalogue, Peterson and Gilmore collected two specimens of *Diplodocus carnegii*, eight specimens of *Stegosaurus*, three of *Camarasaurus* (his "Morosaurus"), seven of *Brontosaurus excelsus*, along with two more probably belonging to *Brontosaurus*, and one of both *Creosaurus* and *Opthalmosaurus discus*. For his part, Utterback reported having found another "Titanotherium" skull on the twentieth, adding that he planned to "pass the rest of my sentence in the Daemonelix beds" before loading and leaving.[39]

As Holland continued to arrange free shipments with the railroads, Hatcher corresponded with M. P. Felch to set up Utterback's winter of stripping overburden and collecting at the old Marsh-Felch Quarry in Cañon City. Felch promised to show Utterback where to work to best advantage, even though the quarry's sandstone would make collecting difficult. Meanwhile, Utterback wrote Hatcher on the thirtieth to say he'd been laid up sick in Harrison for the past ten days with much of the rest of the area's population. "There has been more sickness in this vicinity the past 30 days than was ever known in the history of the country. Has been quite a number of deaths here and in Lusk since you left." Nonetheless, the camp outfit was stored, and the crates had all been loaded carefully in a cleaned-out coke car, which Utterback feared might make everything a bit dusty. He closed with a typically tongue-in-cheek quip: "Well Hatcher I hope that my work in the next month will be more satisfactory to you than this one has been to me."[40]

Hatcher also corresponded with Osborn to thank him for his endorsement of the Antarctica project and to seek more information about Osborn's plans for Hatcher to finish Marsh's Ceratopsia volume, adding, "I appreciate your kindness in even thinking of me in this connection for I had long ago reconciled myself to the idea that my nine years with Prof. Marsh were entirely lost & that the material I had collected for him was no longer accessible to me."[41]

After a quick trip to Cañon City, Utterback wrote Hatcher on November 2 to say he'd checked in at Felch's to find the old man sick and bedridden, so there was no place to board. He'd find a tent and stove to take care of himself if he could bill the Carnegie a small monthly fee. A lot of pick and shovel work on the overlying marl would be needed before he could scrape down to the bone-bearing sandstone. Then he'd need to sharpen tools, so he'd look for a portable forge. He'd spent all his spare cash on a mortgage in Harrison, so he hoped Hatcher had sent his last month's wages. With that, he noted, "There are plenty of big red apples and pretty women here [and] either takes my eye."[42]

Back in Pittsburgh, Hatcher filed his monthly report with Holland on November 8, which accounted for a total shipment of ninety-six crates from Peterson's operation at Camp Carnegie near Sheep Creek and eighty-two from Hatcher's efforts in Nebraska and central Wyoming. Since he'd returned from the West, Hatcher and his staff had helped in making preparations for the Carnegie's Founder's Day Celebration and organized the space made available for the prep lab and collection storage. The next day, Holland wrote in appreciation of Hatcher's efforts:

> . . . I desire to take this opportunity to express to you officially my entire satisfaction with the conduct of the department entrusted to your care and oversight, and especially to congratulate you upon the very successful manner in which you conducted the expedition to the Western country in quest of fossils. Not only have you entirely met our fullest expectations so far as the acquisition of valuable material for this museum is concerned, but you have verified all that we have been told in reference to yourself as a capable administrator of

affairs. Your tactful solution of several vexing and difficult matters
which came up for decision and your prudent administration of the
funds committed to your care have my highest commendation.[43]

That compliment was well deserved, as documented by the list of specimens for the 1900 season found in the catalogue for the Carnegie collections. In terms of Tertiary mammals, Hatcher collected eighteen specimens from the 37- to 34-million-year-old beds of the Chadron Formation, including the brontotheres "Brontops" and "Menodus," which are now called *Megacerops*; the rhinos *Trigonias* and "Caenopus" that is now called *Subhyracodon*; the ferocious and pig-like entelodont called *Archaeotherium*; and the small horse *Mesohippus*. Hatcher also gleaned ninety-two specimens from the 34- to 32-million-year-old beds of the Brule Formation, such as *Archaeotherium*; the chevrotain-like *Leptochoerus*; the small deer-like *Leptomeryx, Hypertragulus*, and *Hypisodus*; the large carnivorous creodont *Hyaenodon*; the pig-like oreodont *Merycoidodon*; the small early camel *Poebrotherium*; the weasel-like and possibly insectivorous *Leptictis*; the rhino *Hyracodon*; the horse *Mesohippus*; the coyote- and fox-sized dogs *Daphoenus* and *Hesperocyon*; the leopard-sized saber-tooths *Hoplophoneus* and *Dinicits*; the rodents *Ischyromys, Eumys*, and "Scottimus," which is now called *Eumys*; the rabbits *Palaeolagus* and *Megalagus*; the shrew-like *Centetodon*; the small shrew *Domnina*; the opossum-like *Peradectes*; the lizard *Peltosaurus*; and the tortoise *Stylemys*. Hatcher also collected the small, hippo-like oreodont *Promerychoerus* from the 30- to 19-million-year-old beds of the Monroe Creek Formation, as well as eleven others with incomplete field data, including *Archaeotherium*, the opossum-like *Peratherium*, and the tortoise *Testudo*. Beyond that, he lacerated the 66-million-year-old Lance Formation to retrieve fourteen specimens of dinosaurs, such as the three-horned *Triceratops*, the duckbill *Edmontosaurus*, the herbivorous *Thescelosaurus*, and everyone's favorite carnivorous villain, *Tyrannosaurus*. Among mammals, Hatcher harvested sixty-eight teeth of minute mammals, including the herbivorous multituberculates *Cimolomys, Cimolodon, Meniscoessus*, and *Mesodma*; the marsupials *Pediomys* and *Alphadon*; and the placentals *Gypsonictops* and *Cimolestes*. Finally, he gleaned seven specimens of other fish, amphibians, and reptiles, among them the bowfin fish *Amia*, the salamander *Opisthotriton*, and the lizard *Odaxosaurus*—in all, a total of 211 specimens.

Peterson pulled out a plunder of twenty mammal specimens from the Brule Formation, including the horse *Mesohippus*, the rabbit *Palaeolagus*, the relative of pocket gophers and kangaroo rats *Paradjidaumo*, the squirrel-like *Ischyromys* and the sheep-like oreodont *Merycoidodon*, as well as one specimen of the beaver *Palaeocastor* from the Miocene Harrison Formation and another specimen of the weasel-like carnivore *Miacis* from the Eocene Green River Formation. Finally, with the help of Gilmore, Peterson gleaned twenty-three specimens of dinosaurs from the 150-million-year old rock layers of the Morrison Formation, including the large, long-necked sauropod *Diplodocus* specimen that Hatcher discovered; the platy and spiked armored dinosaur *Stegosaurus*; the stocky sauropod *Camarasaurus*; the seventy-foot-long sauropod *Apatosaurus*, which is now once again called *Brontosaurus* by some paleontologists; the carnivorous "Creosaurus," which is now called *Allosaurus*; as well as a porpoise-like marnine reptile or ichthyosaur called *Opthalmosaurus* (CM 603) from the Sheep Creek region of Wyoming.

As for Utterback, he amassed thirty-one specimens: the horse *Orohippus*, the oreodont *Merycoidodon*, the rhino "Caenopus," now called *Subhyracodon*, and the brontothere "Menodus," now called *Megacerops* from the Chadron Formation; the camel *Poebrotherium*, the oreodont *Merycoidodon*, as well as the deer-like *Leptomeryx* and *Hypisodus* from the Brule Formation; the hippo-like oreodont *Promerycochoerus* from the 30- to 19-million-year-old Monroe Creek Formation; other Oligocene specimens of the brontothere "Menodus," the rhino *Aceratherium*, and the oreodont *Merycoidodon*; and a specimen of the beaver *Palaeocastor* from the early Miocene Harrison Formation.

Hatcher summarized the results of the season in an article published in *Science*, along with another paper clarifying the number of different types of neck, thoracic, sacral, and tail vertebrae in *Diplodocus*. The latter study no doubt irked Holland to some degree, since in it, Hatcher made an emphatic point of correcting several small errors that Holland had made in his *Science* paper about *Diplodocus* that had been published just six months previously. Once again, Hatcher's thrust seemed to be directed toward establishing and maintaining his dominance in terms of his authority over the scientific research in vertebrate paleontology within his department at the Carnegie.[44] (See Hatcher bibliography)

But Hatcher was already pondering yet another game of professional poker in his itinerant career, and once again, presumably unbeknownst to Holland, his prospective partner was the ever-lurking Osborn. On December 21, Hatcher wrote Osborn to say:

> *When in Washington the other day I saw Mr. Walcott & spoke to him regarding a position on the Survey, in case it were possible to revive the department of vertebrate paleontology & place it in your charge. He seemed in favor of the plan but thought it unwise to approach Congress . . . until one or two of the old proposed Marsh mongraphs were in print. He expressed . . . that in the mean time a place could be found for me in the National Museum & he volunteered to take the matter in hand for me. . . . Now it has occurred to me that you could be of great help . . . in securing a position in the National Museum & I should appreciate greatly anything you might be able to do in that respect.[45]*

15

Documenting *Diplodocus* along with a Massive Menagerie

I t would be a long, cold winter's slog for Utterback, who wrote Hatcher from Cañon City on November 12 to say he'd commenced work on the old Marsh-Felch Quarry on Felch's land. He'd need to remove overburden consisting of dirt and about fifteen feet of marl before beginning work on the fossil-bearing sandstone, so he built a fifty-foot-long trestle from the quarry to an area where he could dump the debris. It was already getting too cool to sleep in a tent, and he pressed Hatcher to approve his request for a camping outfit. That would be his biggest expense until he hired a man to help work the sandstone. By the seventeenth, Hatcher had sent $50 with a directive to strip off the entire top of the quarry to a depth of twenty-five feet, but Utterback had learned that the bone layer was confined to a strip of sandstone only thirty to forty feet wide in the quarry's center that represented the channel of an ancient stream, so cutting off the whole top would be a waste of time and money, since no bones were found at either end. He sought Hatcher's advice, adding that it would take three months to blast through the twenty-five feet of overburden above the old channel and haul it to the dump.[1]

Back in Pittsburgh, Hatcher was reviewing a set of bylaws proposed by Holland for the duties of curators and rights of the staff, as well as submitting a narrative for the historical geology of the region along the Union Pacific line out west for their promotional materials. Hatcher also submitted his monthly report to Holland on the thirtieth, which documented Utterback's work in Cañon City, acknowledged receipt of the shipments of fossils from the West, and described the preparation of mammal and dinosaur specimens in Coggeshall's lab. But most of the report represented Hatcher's response to a tempestuous tirade that Holland had apparently targeted at Hatcher regarding some unspecified difference of opinion as to the duties and rights of staff members:

I have been deeply grieved to find that my conduct of the Department placed in my charge has been so unsatisfactory as to call forth the personal abuse visited upon me, by yourself on Nov. 7th. I am also much affected by the further abuse you saw fit to administer on Nov. 28th when you called me a jack-ass & a d—d fool. Such language, it seems to me, cannot but tend to destroy that harmony, enthusiasm & interest so essential to the welfare of the institution & should therefore be discouraged. I shall earnestly strive in the future as I have in the past to so conduct myself & my department as not to merit such unqualified disapproval.

That same day, Holland requested that Hatcher speak with a reporter from Pittsburgh's *Chronicle Telegraph*, who wanted to publish information about Hatcher's department and its exploits, but Hatcher responded on December 1 that "under the existing circumstances I do not think it desirable that I should give Mr. Chilton anything for publication."[2]

Utterback checked in on December 2, having decided to fix up Felch's abode a bit so he could board there rather than buying a more expensive camp outfit. Hiring help would cost $30 to $35 per month, so Utterback suggested waiting to hire until the overburden was removed and he could more efficiently use two men to help collect in the sandstone. It was difficult labor, but Utterback was making good headway, quipping, "There is one Museum employe [sic] whose hand will not tremble when he signs for Nov wages. Even worked Thanksgiving and had bacon for dinner." [3]

By the third, the heated exchanges between Hatcher and Holland had cooled to the point where Hatcher indicated he was prepared to discuss Holland's proposed "Rules and Regulations" and hoped they could come to a mutually satisfying agreement. A week later, Hatcher was ready to begin preparing illustrations for some scientific papers about some of the specimens they had collected and asked Holland to set a limit for that budget so Hatcher could work with an illustrator. Holland even seemed to provide a small bonus for Hatcher before Christmas, writing, "Enclosed please find a trifle which will serve to put upon the table at Christmas a good, fat turkey, which you will kindly accept from me, with the best wishes of the season." [4]

As the holiday season neared in Cañon City, Utterback's work was progressing, but his correspondence to Hatcher seemed to be highjacked by the local postmaster, who Felch described as a "d—d sneak." On the seventeenth, Utterback reported that his November expenses to date totaled $78.56, but he had enough cash on hand that ". . . do not think [I] shall have to pull your leg for Jan." By the thirty-first, with the temperature plummeting to twenty-six degrees below zero, Utterback reported that he had had little time to prospect in other nearby areas. With three old bone diggers living nearby, every exposure of the bone layer had been thoroughly searched, and he felt certain that the only finds would come from sustained quarrying. To wit, Utterback's stripping would expose an area of the bone layer totaling eight hundred to one thousand square feet for collecting, and he had some photos of the quarry site taken so Hatcher could get a better sense of his quarrying strategy. [5]

Meanwhile, Osborn had put his oar in the water in an attempt to help row Hatcher out of Holland's harbor at the Carnegie by lobbying for a position in Washington, D.C., presumably at the National Museum. However, on January 11, Hatcher expressed "my thanks for your interest shown in me, although you have not met with much encouragement," leaving Hatcher momentarily resigned to another field season for Holland while he awaited "further developments." On the brighter side, Hatcher confirmed, "I should like very much to undertake the preparation of the Ceratopsia volume under you," adding that he was "greatly pleased" and thought "something is due me for the nine years I worked for Marsh." But by the fifteenth, Hatcher realized that Osborn had argued in Washington that $4,000 per year would be needed for salary and field expenses, whereas Hatcher felt only $2,750 would be required, excluding freighting costs. He concluded: "Now if there is any chance of completing arrangements on these or any other lines so that I could get away from here this coming spring I will gladly come to New York or Washington to see what can be done." Osborn apparently agreed to once again plead Hatcher's case, for which Hatcher replied on the twenty-first: "I shall anxiously await the result of your effort. . . . I think if the National Museum is at all desirous of taking up the work they will find my proposition an advantageous one." But by early February, Osborn's attempt had again come to no avail, largely for financial reasons related to congressional budgeting, leaving Hatcher to lament, "I am sorry there seems so little prospect for me." Nonetheless, Osborn conjured up a consolation prize of sorts for Hatcher in the form of hiring Hatcher to do some stratigraphic work around the Big Badlands region in South Dakota and Nebraska for Osborn's planned monograph on brontotheres, which Marsh had never finished but would still be funded and published through the USGS. Hatcher conveyed his appreciation to Osborn on February 14, soberly stating, "I am determined to hold on here [at the Carnegie] until there is an opening somewhere, though I am sorely tempted at times to throw the whole thing up."[6]

At the end of January, Utterback sent along his sympathies to Hatcher, who had been ill for a month. Although Utterback was well, he was frustrated with having to take off work to get his own supplies rather than having locals do it, because "to send in [for them] by some of these old 'Mossbacks' is agravating [sic]. Some of them would forget the rear part of their anatomy were it possible." Nonetheless, he'd completed the upper part of the stripping and was ready to start the rock work with some bones in sight. He'd need drills, a crowbar, and other supplies that would require sharpening, so he again sought a forge, which would be cheaper than sending blunt tools to town. The weather was *"mucho frio."* By February 8, he'd received $67 from Hatcher and located a forge for $22, if needed. Following Hatcher's orders, he was keeping an eye out for mammals and other bones outside the quarry, but in earlier workings he'd learned that they'd only been found in the quarry. Although Hatcher was anxious for news about the bones in sight, Utterback couldn't tell until they started quarrying, but it didn't appear that the bone layer exceeded twenty-five feet in width.[7]

Hatcher was working on a monograph about *Diplodocus* in mid-February and received a drawing from F. A. Lucas at the Smithsonian, which helped out. In return, Lucas reported that Osborn had started his monograph on brontotheres and Hatcher's field notes on Marsh's specimens had been especially helpful. The Smithsonian had acquired all the jaws for which Marsh had commissioned illustrations, along with most of the skulls, although only the Yale specimens had been engraved. The Smithsonian's *Triceratops* mount, which to this day is still nicknamed "Hatcher," was taking form from the collections Hatcher made for Marsh, and Lucas implored Hatcher to come see it.[8]

The rock in the Marsh-Felch Quarry proved even tougher than Utterback anticipated and took its toll on the tools to the point they required almost constant sharpening. Falling behind schedule, he hired an experienced quarryman on the nineteenth to work for a month at $35, but he needed more help around camp and appealed to Hatcher on the twenty-third, "How about this cooking J. B. I am getting pretty tired of it as I have had a long siege . . ." He couldn't both cook and keep pace with the quarrying. By the twenty-eighth, Utterback admitted, "This is more of an undertaking than either of us realized." But perhaps the returns would justify it, so he suggested Hatcher arrive in about three weeks.[9]

William Libbey III, Hatcher's associate in Princeton with whom he was scheming about the Antarctic expedition, wrote on March 5 that Mr. William S. Bruce, the leader of the Scottish Expedition, had accepted Hatcher as a member and wanted to know what terms Hatcher would require. Hatcher immediately attempted to enlist Osborn to provide both support and advice, especially regarding Hatcher's plans for the undertaking. Hatcher argued, "I feel sure that if I can start with the unqualified endorsement of yourself and Prof. Scott I can succeed."[10]

But back in Cañon City on the tenth, as Utterback continued to strip overburden in anticipation of Hatcher's arrival, Utterback revealed that a personal problem was pestering him. In deference, Utterback stated, "Hatcher I am aware that the average man has troubles enough of his own with-out bearing the burden of others. . ." before lamenting that he was in the throws of an acrimonious divorce. Summing up, Utterback thundered, "There is two things I will not submit to if it costs my life. She shall never have the oldest boy who refuses to live with her, neither will I pay her one red cent of my hard earned money." In order to continue working that summer, he asked Hatcher to hold his wages so his wife couldn't confiscate any of his salary; otherwise, he'd need to flee someplace where she couldn't find him. Utterback shortly received the good news that his wife couldn't collect any money from him if he stayed out of the area of jurisdiction of the court that granted the divorce, but less palatable was the fact that Hatcher wanted Utterback to continue cooking for himself to keep expenses down. On the eighteenth, Utterback wrote that the court had adjourned until next June, so no immediate action was required.[11]

Before leaving for the field, Hatcher intended to settle matters with Holland regarding the Antarctic expedition. After meeting Holland the night before, Hatcher wrote him on the twenty-first to say he would abandon the idea of participating under the Carnegie Museum's banner, since ". . . you as Director can not lend to the undertaking that hearty support which it seems to me such an undertaking should have if it is to be carried on under the auspices of this Institution." Hatcher realized the risks involved and didn't want to force the issue with the museum. Nonetheless, he believed Bruce's offer to be reasonable, and he preferred to participate in the interests of Princeton, where the endeavor was fully supported. Hatcher thanked Holland for his "conditional offer" of support but requested a leave of five days to travel to Washington to study their *Diplodocus* material and consult regarding the expedition with all expenses to be borne by Hatcher.[12]

Holland angrily responded the same day for:

> ... *arraigning me for not showing what you think to be a proper interest in your schemes for Antarctic exploration, and threatening me with withdrawal from the institution in order that you may carry out your schemes under the auspices of Princeton University. If promising to accord you* [sic. your] *leave of absence for the time that you have asked . . . one year or thereabouts on full salary, and agreeing to secure and provide the funds that are necessary for your support and for the successful prosecution of your work in connection with the expedition . . . is evincing a lack of proper interest in the same, then, I presume, I shall have to plead guilty to the charge.*

Holland felt Bruce's terms were too vague for the Carnegie to accept, and instead of having made Hatcher a firm offer, Bruce simply wanted to confirm that Princeton's William Libbey III would contribute $5,000 to the expedition if Hatcher could accompany it. Beyond that, Holland felt Bruce had all but stated that the expedition would not commence that year, since only half of the required funds had been raised. Holland implored Hatcher to write Bruce to obtain a written statement as to what Bruce was required to provide and what Hatcher would need to accomplish his objectives. Given the fund-raising still to be done, Holland doubted an immediate decision was required. Thus, after consulting with the Trustees, Holland was directed to inform Hatcher:

> *While we would be very glad to assist you and provide the money that is necessary to carry on your work successfully in connection with this Antarctic enterprise, nevertheless we do not care to be perpetually threatened by the mention of the names of other institutions, which, as you would have us infer, are waiting eagerly to take up all your suggestions while we are proving ourselves in your judgment incompetent to understand the importance of your schemes and unwilling to do what you think ought to be done.*[13]

Hatcher steadfastly responded on the twenty-third that he'd tried to see and call Holland but couldn't catch him. Nonetheless, Hatcher would leave shortly for Washington to see Lucas and examine their *Diplodocus* material before returning in a few days after also inquiring into the Antarctic expedition:

> *I hope I shall be successful for I am fully convinced of the importance of the matter. However if for financial or other reasons I am compelled to abandon it, I shall take my defeat philosophically. At any rate I wish to end one way or the other the suspense I have been in concerning this projected Antarctic trip. If I can not accomplish it now I will drop the matter for all time. One final effort though before I give it up entirely.*[14]

As March closed, Utterback informed Hatcher that he was making good progress and hoped to have a nice "layout" available for Hatcher's evaluation whenever he could get to the field. By April 6, about 1,500 square feet of the bone layer had been exposed, and there were enough well-preserved bones in sight to keep the crew busy all summer. On Hatcher's behalf, Utterback also undertook to examine some old quarries in which Cope's men had collected. However, by the twenty-third, Utterback became concerned that although he could see good bones in the Marsh-Felch Quarry, much of the ground seemed barren, but perhaps there were more buried underneath, embedded in marl.[15]

Before departing for the field, Hatcher paid a visit to Osborn at the AMNH, who had gathered all his *Diplodocus* and "Morosaurus" bones for Hatcher to study and photograph for the *Diplodocus* monograph he was preparing. Especially "remarkable" to Hatcher was the fact that Osborn had concluded that *Diplodocus* walked up on its fingers in a digitigrade mode on its front feet but more on its heels in a plantigrade mode on its hind feet. Hatcher felt deeply indebted to Osborn for sharing his insights.[16]

The field season started in earnest in early May as the Carnegie crews fanned out. Peterson arrived in Harrison, Nebraska, on the eleventh to find his outfit in good shape except for the tent. Hatcher joined Utterback in Cañon City around the same time to confirm that there were several good bones exposed in the bone layer. The area of the bone layer uncovered was equal to the size of that worked for Marsh two decades earlier, but more excavation would be required to assess whether the bones belonged to a few individuals or represented a general mix from many. Although Hatcher was hopeful, each bone would have to be partially exposed with care before being jacketed and extracted. By the thirteenth, Hatcher had started to expose an allosaur sacrum.[17]

Holland was pleased with Hatcher's initial reports when he received them on the eighteenth and in turn reported that Hatcher's *Diplodocus* memoir had been sent to the printer, with proofs expected shortly. Utterback and Hatcher had revealed the pelvis, femur, and a series of fifteen vertebrae of what looked to be a promising "Morosaurus" skeleton by the twenty-fourth, not to mention about one hundred other bones that were now in sight but as yet not fully exposed (either *Haplocanthosaurus*, CM 572 or 879). Osborn of the AMNH and Professor Eberhard Fraas of the Staatliches Museum für Naturkunde Stuttgart had visited, and Osborn had accepted some of Hatcher's conclusions regarding *Diplodocus*: Hatcher crowed, "I . . . discussed the [new] species D. carnegii & they agreed that I was perfectly justified in making the species & that my restoration was exceedingly good. You know I was myself in doubt as to the position of the feet & expected some criticism from Osborn especially, but he expressed himself as well pleased with the position I had given the feet." Hatcher envisioned *Diplodocus* as spending a good deal of its time buoyed up by the water while eating succulent vegetation in the Jurassic swamps, as did many of his contemporary colleagues, including Osborn. The Carnegie fossils now revealed that there were at least seventy vertebrae in the tail, which Hatcher and Osborn believed made it an efficient tool for swimming. The tail also, they thought, allowed the animal to rear up on its hind limbs using it as the third leg of a tripod to reach soft vegetation in the treetops. But Hatcher also believed that the elongated tail could be used like a whip to defend itself against potential predators, such as *Allosaurus*. Hatcher then joined a cushy caravan with Osborn to Green River in a railcar equipped with a "good Chef, porter & a well selected assortment of provisions, wines, cigars Etc. aboard." Intriguingly, it was along the rail route of this opulent interlude that an endlessly persistent Osborn, desperate to delegate the responsibility of arranging and overseeing his field crews, once again attempted to hire Hatcher for the AMNH as an associate curator in charge of fieldwork. This time Osborn was confident he'd succeeded, intimating to his wife, "I . . . look forward with great relief to next year when Hatcher can do the worrying and the planning . . . he is anxious to come and I think we will get on smoothly." Along the way, Hatcher noted some interesting prospects and saw a panorama of the regional geology representing the "Archean to the Laramie." In all, Hatcher was confident of success in Cañon City, Sheep Creek, and Nebraska, so he intended to prospect a bit to identify good sites for future work, including Tertiary and Cretaceous localities in Montana.[18]

Meanwhile, as Hatcher had predicted, Peterson was having success in the "oreodon beds" of Nebraska, especially concerning a dog-like skull about the size of a coyote but with a shorter face that appeared to be new (possibly *Hesperocyon*, *Temnocyon*, or the "bear dog" *Daphoenus*). Peterson hoped to find a good skull and jaws of the saber-toothed *Hoplophoneus* in order to allow them to reconstruct a skeletal mount of it, as well as possibly ones for "Oreodon," the primitive camel *Poebrotherium*, and the small, deer-like *Leptomeryx*. Peterson also planned to collect in the "lower oreodon beds" and the "Titanotherium beds."[19]

Holland sent Hatcher his proofs and seemed quite pleased that Osborn had agreed with Hatcher's reseach on *Diplodocus carnegii*, including the posture portrayed in the reconstruction of the skeleton and the fact the specimen represented a new species, adding on the twenty-ninth:

> *I am satisfied that your judgment in such matters ought to be accepted in preference to that of our esteemed friend, Professor Osborn, who, while he holds a high position and has done much good work, is nevertheless in my judgment, from what little I have observed, not as thorough a student of these matters as either yourself or Professor Scott. When it comes to a scientific proposition, you will permit me to say that I will bet on you every time as against Osborn. However, this is of course said confidentially.*

Beyond the undoubtedly pleasing praise, Paul Brinkman argues that Holland's response was seminally significant in Hatcher's decision to reject Osborn's offer of an assistant curatorship at the AMNH and stay at the Carnegie, primarily because Hatcher had gained fairly complete control of the paleontological research and fieldwork at the Carnegie, whereas if he was to work under Osborn, it would "represent a step down [in authority] to the kind of subordinate situation that he found so untolerable under Marsh at Yale."[20]

Hatcher wrote Holland on June 1 from Hot Springs, South Dakota, where he was meeting colleagues from the USGS, to confirm he'd given Peterson $200 and Utterback $300 to sustain their operations through the month, but he'd need another $500 for his own travels and to start Gilmore at Sheep Creek. Holland had dutifully deposited the funds by the fourth and would send the *Diplodocus* galley proofs to Hermosa for Hatcher to check, although he doubted there would be time to make changes. Holland had seen Lucas's *Triceratops* mount at the Pan-American Exposition in Buffalo and criticized it for being posed on the tips of its toes rather than in the more flat-footed posture that Holland and Hatcher preferred.[21]

Utterback chimed in from Cañon City on the seventh to bemoan the wet weather, which had stymied his quarrying and necessitated that he cover the "morosaur" skeleton. For his part, Peterson indicated on the twelfth that he'd gathered enough material to restore *Hoplophoneus*, "Oreodon," *Mesohippus*, and the new small dog even though the exposures near Harrison weren't nearly as rich as those in the Big Badlands. He'd also found a skull of "Titanotherium" that held the additional prospect of a whole skeleton based on the presence of five ribs, three cervicals, and a lower jaw. On a personal note, Hatcher had heard from Anna that they were all well, but she couldn't find a violin teacher for their son, Harold. Two days later, the success of Peterson and his brother continued with the discovery of a complete "Oreodon" skeleton and the skeleton of a larger dog about the size of a coyote, possibly *Hesperocyon*, *Protemnocyon*, or *Daphoenus*. Utterback then chortled that he'd managed to crate part of "skeleton A," presumably the "morosaur," by the fourteenth, including the caudals and shoulder bones, and he was now working on other bones of the skeleton.[22]

Holland proofread the galley proofs by the twenty-first and promised Hatcher to try and order a hundred extra reprints, although he feared it might be too late, since they might have gone to the printer. But he succeeded in securing the reprints by the twenty-fourth and sent the rough pulls for the plates after correcting various mistakes in the titles, along with the news that Coggeshall was progressing with a "Titanotherium" mount. This skeleton, catalogued as CM 11061 and now identified as *Brontops dispar*, is still on display in the Carnegie Museum fossil halls. By July 2, Hatcher had received the plate pulls and was ecstatic with the quality of their printing. He'd been roaming around South Dakota and collected about 1,200 pounds of specimens, including some Triassic fish and mammals from the Big Badlands. He'd also visited Lucas's locality for the type of "Stegosaurus marshii," now recognized as an armored nodosaur dinosaur called *Hoplitosaurus*, but decided it wasn't suitable for further collecting. But Hatcher's trek had taken a toll:

> *My bladder troubles me greatly. I think having to sleep in a wet bed most of the time I was with the U.S.G.S. people did me no good & then [worked] a half day in the Cheyenne river to get my outfit across. . . . Have been intending to go on to Montana . . . but if I am not better shall go to Hot Springs for a week & employ a man there to help me collect Triassic fishes. It is only a short walk from the hotel to the locality.*

Holland was concerned upon hearing of Hatcher's illness:

> *I beg you to take very good care of yourself. It is certainly hard for a man who has a tendency to internal troubles to sleep in a wet bed. . . . Do not overdo yourself. We accomplish more by persistent effort than by too strenuous exertion. An Irishman working in a railroad cut long ago taught me a useful lesson. He swung his pick slowly, but in the end, though apparently working slowly, he accomplished more than the man who rushed in and soon exhausted himself by his exertions.*

Accordingly, Hatcher holed up in Hot Springs for a few days and collected Triassic fish.[23]

Although the quarry in Cañon City continued to produce, Utterback felt on the eleventh that the results were "hardly satisfactory considering the expense." In addition to numerous isolated bones, with hard hand labor, he'd uncovered a series of twelve dorsal vertebrae and two or three plates, along with a number of other bones representing a stegosaur skeleton that continued into the bank but would require more stripping to collect. Curiously, the Carnegie catalogue does not list any specimens of *Stegosaurus* from the Marsh-Felch Quarry. He sought Hatcher's advice about whether to strip, which would require two men about a month, or just collect what was already exposed. All in all, he concluded, "With plenty of fruit forbidden and otherwise we have no occasion to kick."[24]

In Hot Springs, Hatcher forged ahead with his quest for Triassic fish, but with only modest success. His bladder was feeling better but was not completely healed, which made him wonder about the feasibility of his Antarctic excursion. He needed Holland to deposit $600, which Holland did by the thirteenth, and remained confident that this season's expenses would not exceed those of the previous one. Holland was encouraged by the reports from Cañon City and Harrison, but he'd heard nothing from Gilmore. In Pittsburgh, Coggeshall had nearly completed the "Titanotherium" mount.[25]

Hatcher pushed on to Billings to prospect near Gallatin, but the trip had aggravated his bladder problems to the point where he indicated on the seventeenth that he would head home after he finished his assessment of the area's prospects and checked in with Utterback. Holland quickly began arrangements on the twentieth for a rail pass to get Hatcher home. Utterback checked in on the twentieth as well to say his results were disappointing. Although he continued to take out good disarticulated bones, the quarry seemed to be playing out. Peterson wrote the next day to say he had found more good prospects, including a large *Merycochoerus* skeleton, but he would move to War Bonnet Creek and try to prospect in the beds at Running Water. From Gilmore's note, Peterson gathered that he was doing reasonably well at Sheep Creek, and he'd heard that the AMNH crew was gathering at Medicine Bow. Hatcher was back in Billings by the twenty-second and now intended to go directly to Harrison to meet Peterson and wait for Holland to send his rail pass. In pain, he confided to Holland, "Have seen some good localities for collecting but I am in no condition to work. I hope you will be successful in getting the pass for me from Denver to Chicago via Cañon City for I want to get home & see if I can get relief from this trouble with my bladder or whatever it is. Horseback riding aggravates it a great deal."[26]

Holland, who was not only tending remotely to an ill Hatcher but also to a very ill son at home, sent the rail pass on the twenty-fifth, along with the news that his son was improving and his fever decreased, although he was still bedridden. Hatcher empathized from Harrison on the thirtieth, sending his best wishes and noting, "The condition of our own health is always second in our own minds to that of our children." He'd been invited to guide about twenty GSA members on August 16 on a tour of the Marsh-Felch Quarry in Cañon City and the geology of the region. "I dislike to refuse but had anticipated being home by that time."[27]

By August 12, Hatcher had made it to Cañon City but found things in "a rather bad way." Felch had betrayed the Carnegie crew, and Hatcher had to "go into the real estate business here" by filing four claims under his and Holland's names to secure collecting rights by "corralling everything in sight." He intended to transfer Gilmore's assistant G. F. Axtell from Medicine Bow to work with Utterback on a 500-foot-thick sequence of freshwater Jurassic, dinosaur-bearing beds found there at many horizons. Over several years, Hatcher hoped to collect from all possible levels in the sequence, then work out the phylogeny of the different dinosaur genera through time based on where they were preserved in the sequence. "It is a great undertaking but we are in a position to do it & must not let the opportunity escape us." Hatcher formalized his feelings on this opportunity in print through his paper "The Jurassic Dinosaur Deposits Near Canyon City, Colorado" later that same year. He expected to start for Pittsburgh soon, stopping for a day or two in Iowa.[28]

On the thirteenth, Peterson reported finding a *"Procamelus"* specimen in the beds at Running Water that included the skull, lower jaws, and neck vertebrae, along with a hind limb and foot, perhaps one of the *Oxydactylus* specimens now listed in the Carnegie catalogue. Axtell reached

Cañon City to begin work with Utterback by the twenty-fourth, and by the end of August, Peterson wrote to say he was glad to know everyone was well at Hatcher's home in Pittsburgh. He'd apparently found more of the *Procamelus* skeleton, along with a small *Merycochoerus*, and he intended to prospect for a titanothere skull.[29]

Hatcher started distributing his *Diplodocus* memoir (Hatcher 1901) in early September, with Williston sending his congratulations and compliments on its beauty and excellence on the ninth from Kansas, along with news he was working on plesiosaurs. Utterback and Axtell sent their thanks on the third when they also reported finding nice specimens of a new scapula measuring five feet eight inches long, a coracoid, a radius, and a tibia from their new camp near one of Cope's old quarries. This specimen is probably of *Apatosaurus* or *Brontosaurus* (CM 2044), which is the only specimen listed from Cope's Quarry in the Carnegie catalogue. Peterson also reported more success at Running Water, including a possible cat smaller than *Hoplophoneus*, perhaps *Aleurocyon*. Horses, rhinos, large cats, and *Aleurodon* seemed rare, whereas *Procamelus* and the oreodont, *Merycochoerus*, were most abundant. He wondered if the "Loup Fork" shouldn't be subdivided into three separate units:

> *For convenience in collecting I have marked all material from Running Water locality as the upper beds. I find a distinct horizon overlaying the Cork Screw Beds in which I find all the material on Running Water. Would it not be well to divide the Loup Fork in this locality in three divisions? A lower, middle & upper. The cork screw beds seem to deserve the name of a distinct horizon and the fact that there are no cork screws in the upper beds seem also equally interesting. I am anxious to know if there is any great difference anatomically in what material we have from the lower and upper Loup Fork.*[30]

Gilmore checked in with Peterson on September 9, asking for advice regarding an offer he'd received from Elmer Riggs at the Field Museum to join them for a larger salary. He was still seeing a "good run of fortune" at Sheep Creek, including a brontosaur skeleton (CM 563) with "8 dorsals

1 cervical, 5 sacrals, 14 caudals, 1 ilium, 1 femur, 2 tibiae, few foot bones, 1 humerus, 1 radius, 13 ribs, and 5 chevrons." Axtell wrote on the thirteenth that the work in the old Cope quarries was proving unsatisfactory, with only fragments of ribs, vertebrae, a radius, and a scapula found. But Peterson announced on the fourteenth that he had fifty crates ready to ship from Harrison and would need a small boxcar. In preparation for closing the season, he'd stored his outfit in Medicine Bow. Somewhat uncomfortably, Peterson betrayed Gilmore's confidence and told Hatcher about the offer he'd received from Riggs, justifying his action by saying, "I consider it to the interest of both the institution and also to Gilmore him self [sic]. I shall tell him that I have refered [sic] the matter to you."[31]

Williston wrote on September 16 in response to Hatcher's sending a print of his *Diplodocus* restoration, which Williston wanted to frame and hang in his office. Hatcher was apparently seeking fossils from the Cretaceous chalks in Kansas, and Williston had informed a local collector that the Carnegie might be interested in purchasing some of his specimens. He bemoaned his plight at KU: "I have become very much discouraged about our own collections. I have very little means, less time, and not many facilities. We go into a new Museum soon it is true, but Paleontology is relegated to the attic to make place for spectacular displays of American mammals!"[32]

Hatcher's monthly report for September noted the operations in the Jurassic near Cañon City and Sheep Creek, as well as the Tertiary of Nebraska. Also, Coggeshall's lab at the Carnegie had prepared numerous specimens for exhibition, including a limb and foot of *Diplodocus*, a "Titanotherium" skeleton, and a *Daemonelix* corkscrew. For his part, Hatcher was busily cataloguing specimens as they were unpacked and preparing two short papers for publication. Osborn also seemed pleased with Hatcher's *Diplodocus* publication, although Hatcher pleaded with Osborn to "deal generously" with him in his review of the mongraph for *Science*, since there were several typos that Hatcher had been unable to correct because he could not proof the paper when he was in the field. Much to Hatcher's relief, Osborn penned a "complimentary notice," in which he states, "Mr. Hatcher gives . . . by far the most perfect restoration of a Sauropod which has yet been published." Osborn also wrote some notes on the Carnegie crew's field season in *Science* in September, in which he noted the collection "of some very complete horse skeletons, but these prove to belong to *Merycochoerus*, and oreodont." This proved "quite startling" to Hatcher, who had published his own account of the season's results without mentioning such details, since he had not seen the specimens. Hatcher demanded to know how Osborn had obtained this information and protested, "The only inference that can be drawn from [Osborn's report] is that I am unable to distinguish between remains of horses and oreodonts." Consequently, Hatcher requested that Osborn publish a correction to clarify the situation. Nonetheless, Hatcher also felt free to inquire, "whether or not you still wish me to become one of your staff at the American Museum & whether it has been definitely decided that I shall . . . write the Monograph on the Ceratopsidae." Osborn did not respond to Hatcher's inquiry regarding a position at the AMNH, and by the end of the year, Hatcher wrote Osborn to say that "things were going on very pleasantly" at the Carnegie, so he intended to stay there.[33]

Back in Cañon City, Axtell celebrated a "major strike" on September 20, consisting of a cervical vertebra and rib that he hoped would lead to more of a skeleton after more stripping in the quarry. But that activity would require hiring a horse team, so it wasn't until October 12 that Axtell reported that he was ready to start removing marl to expand the quarry. Utterback indicated on the fifteenth that stripping was proceeding despite an inexperienced team that disliked the collar attached to the stripper. He'd started a cut twenty feet wide by one hundred feet long on the south side of the "Nipple" where the bones were exposed. Utterback was frustrated with Axtell's lack of initiative, feeling that the stripping should have been started earlier, but Utterback submitted to working with Axtell unless Hatcher decided to replace Utterback, at which point he'd simply find other work. An oil derrick was going up nearby, so Utterback quipped, "Your forty is liable to be valuable in the near future."[34]

By the twenty-fourth, the crew had made good progress on the cut and anticipated having a large area of the bone layer to work if there were any bones there. But Utterback was still frustrated with Axtell, telling Hatcher, ". . . when I am not with him he does absolutely nothing. Now from what experience I have had unless a man takes sufficient interest in his work to keep from being driven to it he is worthless . . . you would not tolerate him one single day." But Utterback was loath to discharge Axtell, since Hatcher hired him, and even though Utterback described him as "a good natural young fellow," Utterback saw him as a "dead proposition to the Museum" unless he changed his style of work. Utterback went on to allude to more personal matters: "Allow me to congratulate you on the arrival of another daughter [Ruth]. My wife was granted divorce the 10th of Sept with possession of our youngest boy until further orders from the Court. I retain the oldest boy and pay no alimony." Axtell wrote Hatcher on the twenty-fifth to say he accepted Hatcher's arrangement for work, with Utterback in complete charge.[35]

By the end of October, Utterback had tracked down some men who had worked for Cope in his quarries, who said they'd only found a few vertebrae west of the "Ant hill" and the best part of their collection had come from sandstone two miles northwest. But Utterback intended to make another cut in the quarry where they were presently working if they found no bones in their present cut. He also planned to evaluate some prospects he'd run across southwest of Cottage Rock that were lower in the section than the Marsh-Felch Quarry and just twenty feet above the red rocks of the Triassic: "There are a large number of nice looking bones exposed in the ledge for a distance of perhaps 100 ft. The rock will be very hard to work, however hard rock assures good bones. . ." But Utterback warned, "There is one thing Mr Hatcher if you decide for me to open up this place I want permission to employ some young man that is not afraid of hard work."[36]

The monthly report for October confirmed Peterson's plunder, comprising fifty-two crates from Sioux County, Nebraska: "There is in this collection, it is believed, material sufficient for mounting skeletons of *Hoplophoneus, Daphaenus* [sic], *Mesohippus, Oreodon, Merycochoerus, & Procamelus.*" Also included were neontological materials and mineral specimens of barite, calcite, and others from the Big Badlands region. Gilmore's haul from Sheep Creek was riding the rails to Pittsburgh and expected in a few days. Utterback had closed operations in the Marsh-Felch Quarry and initiated operations at an adjacent locality familiarly known as "Cope's Nipple" that had originally been excavated for Cope—work that would continue through the winter. Coggeshall's work mentioned previously had now been put on exhibition, including a "series of skulls belonging chiefly to Oligocene & Miocene [Mammalia]." Hatcher continued to catalogue incoming material, as well as write labels for exhibition specimens.[37]

In early November, Utterback felt they would finish stripping the north side of the "Nipple" in a few days, but no bones were in sight yet. He'd concluded Axtell should be discharged, claiming he wouldn't work. On off days when Utterback released the crew to prospect, Axtell would return by 9:00 A.M., so Utterback wanted to fire him as soon as Hatcher gave the word. Axtell wrote Hatcher on the seventh, lamenting that Utterback told him he'd close operations soon and had no further use for him. That conflicted with what Hatcher had said about him having steady employment either in the field or at the museum, so he sought clarification. The next day, Utterback fired Axtell, who took it "good naturedly," but the assistant wouldn't leave until he'd heard back from Hatcher. There were still no good bones from the "Nipple." Finally, on the twenty-fifth, Utterback replaced Axtell and reported finding three vertebrae in place about thirty feet above the Triassic boundary just west of camp. The pocket contained many small bones, but no mammal teeth so far. Work at Cope's Nipple had proved a bust, but Utterback had just collected a nice, slender, three-foot-long femur from a sandstone outcrop two miles west of camp that he thought might represent *Stegosaurus*, although no such *Stegosaurus* specimens collected by Utterback are listed in the Carnegie Musuem's database. Nonetheless, Utterback was frustrated with the amount of money and time spent obtaining such scanty results:

> *There is one thing certain—no man ever worked harder than I have the past year to make this thing a success . . . parted with quite a few hard earned dollars never charged up. The sum and substance of the entire business is this, the small amount of Jurassic exposure in this locality has been prospected to a finish. The Lucas Bros worked here 5 years to say nothing of others.*

But he vowed to continue prospecting until Hatcher sent other directions.[38]

Hatcher duly recorded the events and disappointing results from Cañon City in his report for November. On the positive side, the specimens of Oligocene dogs that Peterson had discovered had been prepared and were being illustrated for a memoir before being mounted by A. S. Coggeshall and placed on exhibition. Beyond that, Peterson and Louis Coggeshall had prepared a good deal of the camel skeleton Peterson had found, and it was identified as belonging to *Protolabis*. Coggeshall and Gilmore were preparing a forelimb and front foot of the brontosaur found at Sheep Creek, and it was revealing significant new scientific information that would soon be published. A. W. VanKirk was completing the preparation of a 35-million-year-old rhino named *Trigonias osborni* that had been collected during the 1900 season, which would be mounted in the coming year for exhibition. Hatcher was writing a scientific paper based on the mounted skeleton of "Titanotherium," as well as curating the fossil plants and invertebrates until specialists were hired to curate them.[39]

The small series of vertebrae Utterback found in the lower reaches of the Jurassic now also had a sacrum attached to it, so he proposed to ship it to Hatcher by express on December 1. It's unclear if this specimen was collected, since there is apparently no listing for it in the Carnegie catalogue. Other than that, he'd not found much of importance and was concerned Hatcher might balk at the grocery bill. "You may think the grub bill pretty steep but I have had four pretty good appetites to look after and where everything is to buy $8.00 per stomache [sic] does not go very far." His luck hadn't improved by the seventh, leading Utterback to lament, "Since I wrote you last have prospected early and late far and near with no success whatever. Wherever there are any indications someone has been there before me . . . if necessary to lay me off until spring do so. If you wish me to continue in this business a few months at the Museum would be well spent." Then he sought advice about whether to sell or store the horses and outfit as the first storm of the season hit camp. Hatcher decided to provide his beleaguered bone hunter, who had been working for a year straight through, shelter in Pittsburgh over the winter, so Utterback loaded a boxcar with his meager menagerie and headed east around Christmas.[40]

The day after Christmas, Gilmore filed a field report for his season at Sheep Creek, which elaborated on earlier accounts:

> "... *we procured a large amount of miscellaneous material representing Morosaur, Brontosaur and Diplodocus* [including] *limb bones and a large number of cervical and dorsal vertebrae.* ... *The prize of the season's collection was* ... *a large isolated Brontosaur skeleton* [representing the] *greater portion of this large reptile.* ... *one of the front limbs* [was] *nearly in position* [and] *will* ... *clear up the* ... *arrangement of the bones in the fore feet of the Sauropoda. There are but two bones of the other limbs missing. The sacrum* [is] *in a fairly good state of preservation.* ... *The vertebral column is represented by seventeen pre-sacrals and eighteen caudals.*
>
> *From an upper horizon* ... *we obtained* ... *A portion of the skeleton of one of the smaller Dinosaurs* [that] *may prove a unique addition.*

It's unclear what the "smaller" dinosaur was based on the specimens recorded in the Carnegie collection.[41]

Hatcher's report for December confirmed that he'd shut down the Cañon City operation due to "unsatisfactory" results and requested that Utterback come work in the Carnegie lab. The collection, totaling 16,000 pounds of bones, was expected shortly.[42]

Although Hatcher's total reflects his increasing emphasis in time devoted to his administrative duties in the museum, he nonetheless chipped in with eight specimens of 34- to 32-million-year-old mammals from the Brule Formation, including material of the small deer-like *Leptomeryx*, the chevrontain-like *Hypertaragulus* and *Hypisodus*, the small camel *Oxydactylus*, the rhino *Trigonias*, and the carnivorous lizard *Exostinus*. Less well-documented specimens came from the pig- or hippo-like oreodont *Promerycochoerus* and the camel *Stenomylus*.

Peterson dominated the season's proceedings by procuring three specimens of the primitive camel *Poebrotherium* and the brontothere

"Menodus," now called *Megacerops*, from the 37- to 34-million-year old Chadron Formation, as well as an eye-popping 475 from the 34- to 32-million-year-old Brule Formation, such as the opossum-like marsupial *Peratherium*; the weasel-like insectivorous *Leptictis*; the shrew-like *Centetodon*; the elephant shrew *Ankylodon*; the mouse-like *Eumys*; the pocket gopher-like *Adjidaumo* and *Paradjidaumo*; the squirrel-like rodents *Oligospermophilus* and *Ischyromys*; the mountain beavers *Campestrallomys* and *Prosciurus*; the rabbits *Desmatolagus*, *Megalagus*, and *Palaeolagus*; the "terror pig" entelodont *Archaeotherium*; the hippo-like anthracothere *Bothriodon*; the herbivorous oreodonts *Limentes*, *Merycoidodon*, and *Merychyus*; the camel *Poebrotherium*; the deer-like *Leptomeryx*; the chevrotain-like *Hypertragulus* and *Hypisodus*; the browsing horse *Mesohippus*; the rhino "Caeonpus," now called *Subhyracodon*; the saber-toothed carnivores *Dinicits* and *Hoplophoneus*; the carnivorous creodont *Hyaenodon*; the "bear dogs" *Daphoenus* and "Proamphicyon," now called *Daphoenus*; the fox-like dogs *Hesperocyon* and *Protemnocyon*; the legless worm lizard *Rhineura* and the carnivorous lizards *Peltosaurus* and *Exostinus*; the boa snake *Calamagras*; and the tortoise *Stylemys*. Peterson also collected 13 specimens from the 30- to 19-million-year-old beds of the Upper Monroe Creek and Harrison Formations, including the weasel-like *Aleruocyon*; the early grazing horse *Parahippus*; the sheep-like ruminating oreodonts *Phenacocoelus*, *Mesoreodon*, and *Promerycochoerus*, as well as the beaver *Palaeocastor*. He contributed 72 from the 19- to 16-million-year-old Upper Loup Fork Beds, including the camels *Tanymykter*, *Oxydactylus*, and *Stenomylus*; the oreodonts *Cyclopedius*, *Merychyus*, *Merycochoerus*, and *Ticholeptus*; the peccary *Thinohyus*; the musk deer *Blastomeryx*; and the burrowing herbivorous tortoise *Gopherus*. Peterson also added 61 other specimens with incomplete field data, such as the coyote-sized dog *Cynodesmus*; the bone-crushing, hyaena-like dog *Aelurodon*; the rhino *Diceratherium*; the enormous herbivorous calicothere *Moropus*; and the oreodonts *Merychyus* and *Merycochoerus*.

Gilmore gleaned eight dinosaurs and one fish from the 150-million-year-old sand, silt, and mud of the Morrison Formation, such as the huge herbivorous sauropods *Apatosaurus* and "Elosaurus," now once again called *Brontosaurus* by some paleontologists, as well as *Camarasaurus*; the plated armored *Stegosaurus*; and the lungfish *Ceratodus*.

And the long-suffering Utterback cleaved ten dinosaurs and one turtle from the Morrison, including the sauropods *Haplocanthosaurus*, *Diplodocus*, and *Apatosaurus*; the imposing bipedal carnivores *Ceratosaurus* and *Allosaurus*; and the tortoise *Probaena*. Utterback also contributed four Tertiary mammals from the 37-to 35-million-year-old Chadron Formation, the 30- to 19-million-year-old Harrison Formation, and other geologic; units, including the enormous herbivorous "Brontotherium," now called *Megacerops*; the camels *Oxydactylus* and *Stenomylus*; and the oreodont *Promerycochoerus*. Thus, the eight tons of bones collected by Hatcher and his crew during the 1901 season represents an immense total of 802 specimens in the Carnegie's collection database.

In news from the prep lab, work on mounting the rhino and camel continued, while Gilmore and VanKirk began preparing the brontosaur skeleton. Hatcher had finished his two short papers, probably the ones by Hatcher on a new palm from the Laramie and the Jurassic deposits near Cañon City (Hatcher 1901a, b), and a quick note on the structure of the brontosaur front foot had already appeared in *Science* (Hatcher 1901c). In retrospect of the year's achievements, Hatcher noted the "especial value" of several quite complete skeletons of Tertiary mammals: "Cyclopidius, Oreodon, Merycochoerus, Mesohippus, Leptauchenia, Protolabis, Hyracodon, Hoplophoneus, Daphaenus, Cynodictis," as well as Gilmore's brontosaur and Utterback's "exceptionally good material pertaining to Morosaurus & Stegosaurus."[43]

The Carnegie's collection had also been enhanced by some two hundred species through specimen exchanges with the Smithsonian's National Museum of Natural History, the museums of Yale and Princeton Universities, and the Konighchen Cabinet of Stuttgart, Germany. Hatcher listed eight publications authored by members of the department (see Hatcher bibliography for 1901). Hatcher also undertook the revision of the chapter on "The Dinosauria" in the English edition of von Zittel's *Handbook of Paleontology*, and he made "considerable progress" on his assigned manuscripts for the Patagonian expeditions.[44]

Three other manuscripts were ready for publication: "*Claosaurus* & Its Synonyms"; "A Mounted Skeleton of *Titanotherium validurn Marsh*"; and "Structure of the Forelimb & Manus of *Brontosaurus*." Considerable progress had also been made in the preparation of a memoir on the Oligocene Canidae based on Peterson's specimens and on a paper for the *Annals* entitled "The Complete Osteology of *Trigonias Osborni*" based on material collected during the season of 1900 (see Hatcher bibliography for 1901 and 1902). Hatcher concluded his annual summary:

> *Taken as a whole the year 1901 may be considered as having been quite successful & as an auspicious opening of the new century. Personally I can not conceal a sense of pride & gratification in the success attained, which has been in no small measure due to the hearty support given to myself & the department as a whole by you as Director of this Museum.*[45]

Over the winter, plans were still taking shape for Hatcher to assume another taxing role in paleontology, but he relished the challenge. On January 29, Osborn wrote to say he would discuss the matter of a monograph on the horned dinosaurs with Charles D. Walcott, director of the United States Geological Survey. Since Osborn had succeeded Marsh as the USGS vertebrate paleontologist he had been given the job of assigning authors to finish many of Marsh's unfinished monographs. He chose Hatcher to complete Marsh's study of the Ceratopsia because of his seminal role in discovering and collecting Marsh's specimens. Osborn was picking up where Marsh left off on the brontotheres and visited the Carnegie to consult with Hatcher to get his insight regarding the specimens there as well as at Yale and the National Museum. As mentioned previously in relation to preliminary correspondence regarding this project, Hatcher was keen to write it, and he now felt he could do it for $3,500, including hiring a preparator to clean up the *Triceratops* material at Yale. Beyond that, he confided, "I should utilize the opportunity for paying a tribute to [the late Prof. Marsh]. I would like in some way to be permanently connected with some of the material I collected while with Marsh."[46]

Within the Carnegie, Hatcher reported that Coggeshall was still working on the rhino mount, which had been delayed by the lack of a proper base. Hatcher harangued Holland in his monthly report for

January, "Such delays would be avoided if you could find it possible to impose sufficient confidence in me as curator . . . to entrust me with the providing of these bases as needed, giving me an order on the museum carpenter authorizing him to do the necessary work which would not require at most more than a few hours of his time." Peterson was preparing to construct a mount of *Hoplophoneus*, and Gilmore was still preparing his brontosaur and "morosaur" material. Illustrations for the memoir on Oligocene canids were on the go, and casts of the brontosaur feet had been made for Beecher at Yale. To try and address the offer from Riggs, Hatcher had secured a raise for Gilmore from $60 to $65 per month, and the same increase was given to A. S. Coggeshall.[47]

Accolades continued to accumulate for Hatcher's publications in early February, with Knight of Wyoming sending thanks for the *Diplodocus* memoir and complimenting, "It is an admirable publication and allow me to congratulate on the excellency of your work." Knight was also pleased that his protégé Gilmore was working out so well and praised Hatcher for the numerous ways in which he was pushing the science of paleontology along. "You have surpassed all records of Paleontology works in the U.S. for getting material from the field into press. I hope that this good work will continue for we need a great deal of this literature at the present time." Hatcher's colleague Schuchert at Yale expressed similar sentiments. "I was much interested in that fine skull of Titanotherium, and it goes to show what can be done with fossils. Often they are as good as the skeleton of recent remains . . . I congratulate you on the splendid appearance of [the Patagonian] work . . . the results of your Patagonian explorations will be a monument to you."[48]

Despite their earlier disputes, Osborn and Hatcher had become prodigious pen pals. Osborn wrote Hatcher on February 13 to say Scott agreed that all the material Barnum Brown had collected in Patagonia should be made available to Hatcher and others for their research, and he had assigned preparators to make the specimens ready. Osborn and Scott thought Brown should be allowed to publish preliminary descriptions of material that Scott would then study in detail. Osborn sought Hatcher's approval, which Hatcher willingly granted, when he also informed Osborn that Holland had approved the hiring of an illustrator for the department. Hatcher also expressed shock at hearing that Marshall Felch had committed suicide. A month later, Osborn requested a conversation with Hatcher regarding the stratigraphy related to the brontothere specimens for his monograph. He'd also met with Walcott regarding the Ceratopsia memoir and indicated Hatcher could start in July 1902, a proposal to which Hatcher heartily agreed. Osborn hoped he could meet with Hatcher in Washington soon to discuss details. On March 20, Osborn wrote in hopes that Hatcher would be willing to fill in Utterback's discoveries on a map of the old Marsh-Felch Quarry that he had hoped to receive from Felch, adding that it would be a great help for Osborn's monograph on the Sauropoda that would complete Marsh's aborted effort and deal with his material.[49]

March had also witnessed the completion of the mount of the rhino *Trigonias* by Coggeshall, according to Hatcher's monthly chronicle, along with the preparation of the presacral vertebrae of Gilmore's brontosaur. Utterback toiled on the pelvis, scapula, and caudals of his "morosaur." For his part, Hatcher was preparing a manuscript entitled "Origin of the Oligocene & Miocene Deposits of the Great Plains," and he proudly proclaimed that his now legendary manuscript for the *Narrative & Geography of Patagonia* had gone to his editor for publication.[50]

Since Hatcher had returned from the field, the cogs at Carnegie had been churning over what role the museum might play in the Scottish Antarctic Expedition. The culmination became clear in an April 21 letter from Mellor, Holland, and Hatcher to the Executive Committee of the Carnegie Institution responding to the institution's inquiry about "any special line of scientific research" that might be advantageously supported by a donation. Hatcher and his colleagues listed three "chief purposes" in their reply:

First: To study the geology, paleontology, and biology of the lands and waters of this region, with special reference to their bearing upon the supposed former land-connection between South America and Antarctica, and to discover if possible the nature, duration, and time of such connection. Second: To make as complete collections as possible of the marine and terrestrial vertebrate and invertebrate faunas and of the floras of this region. Third: To conduct two lines of soundings, one from Cape Horn to Graham Land by way of the Dirk Gerritz Archipelago, and a second from South Georgia by way of the South Orkneys. It is proposed also to devote considerable attention to the geology and biology of the South Orkneys, South Georgia, and the Fuegian Archipelago and their waters.

Hatcher would lead this part of the effort and conduct some of the most comprehensive geologic and paleontologic research yet attempted around Antarctica, while supervising the work of invertebrate and vertebrate zoologists, with their salaries paid for by the museum. A steam whaler or other vessel with suitable sounding, dredging, and lab capabilities would be purchased or chartered for two years beginning in August 1904 to convey and support this scientific team. The requested donation to fund the purchase or engagement of the vessel was $10,000, which would be due on August 1, 1904. On the same day in 1905, two further donations of $25,000 each would be "set aside for the expenses of the expedition so far as they may be included in chartering, purchasing, equipping, and maintaining the vessel, paying the crew, and in general conducting the expedition."[51]

At the same time, Osborn was working to "get the Ceratopsia matter in shape" with Walcott at the National Museum and Beecher at Yale, part of which included a meeting with Hatcher in Washington on April 15. Osborn sent appreciation on the twenty-third for Hatcher's taking photos of two titanotheres for Osborn's illustrator, Erwin S. Christman, to draw. Osborn also expressed his support for Hatcher "pushing on with your Antarctic plans"; in relation to his role as an advisor to the Carnegie Institution, he confided, "I think our committee will be likely to recommend Carnegie Institution support." As a result of those plans, Hatcher pledged to finish the Ceratopsia monograph by July 1, 1904, just before he planned to depart. By the twenty-ninth, Christman had apparently visited the Carnegie to illustrate the titanotheres under Hatcher's supervision, for which Osborn was again most appreciative. Osborn informed Hatcher that he'd studied the ceratopsians that Lambe had collected in

Canada, and they planned to jointly publish a description of several "very interesting" forms that summer.[52]

In the prep lab, work focused on preparing the pelves of *Diplodocus*, *Brontosaurus*, and "Morosaurus," which were soon to be placed on exhibition according to Hatcher's report for April. Utterback also had the first nineteen tail vertebrae of his "morosaur" prepared, while Gilmore, L. Coggeshall, and VanKirk continued preparation of the brontosaur skeleton. Sydney Prentice had been engaged in illustrating dinosaur material for publication, and Hatcher continued to prepare his paper about Oligocene canids for publication. Hatcher also noted, "It is a source of no little pride to myself as Curator . . . that . . . the leading institutions of the country are compelled to come to us to study several of the most important groups of fossil vertebrates. Since the commencement of the year we have rendered assistance in this way to the Yale Museum, The Am. Mus. of Nat. Hist. & the U.S. Nat'l Mus."

In addition to composing the letter seeking funding for the Antarctic expedition, Hatcher revealed:

> *In the early part of the month I attended the meeting of the Am. Phil. Society in Phila., later visiting Princeton, New York & New Haven. In the middle of the month I visited Washington during the meeting of the National Academy of Science. On both these trips I was strongly urged to carry out if possible my plans for an Antarctic Expedition & was promised the support of several influential men in case I did so, who would aid in securing a grant from the Carnegie Institution Fund.*[53]

Plans for the coming field season were rapidly coming together.

16

An Eruption of Research and Astonishing Acquisitions

B y May 9, Peterson had set his camp near Adelia, close to where he intended to set up a homestead. Nearby, Wortman had bought the drugstore in Long Pine and would head out to the field once he had that enterprise running smoothly. Hatcher was apparently actively recruiting Peterson to participate on the Antarctic expedition, but Peterson was skeptical, much preferring to work on land than on the ocean. He also doubted he'd get a chance to publish his own research, since Hatcher would have several lieutenants working under him. However, he might well be interested in participating in the voyage if he got a chance to visit India. Hatcher was also recruiting B. A. Bensley, who had just completed a memoir on marsupial evolution and relished the chance to collect marsupial embryos in South America to extend his studies on the origin of the group. Meanwhile, Utterback was struggling to get to Medicine Bow, Wyoming, from Casper through deep snow and mud, plaintively mumbling, "If there was any bottom, I failed to find it."[1]

Back in Pittsburgh, Hatcher reported to Holland on the thirty-first that the Coggeshall brothers were busily preparing the sauropod pelves for exhibition, as well as a "splendid" series of dorsal vertebrae from the Cañon City "morosaur" skeleton. VanKirk had joined Peterson in Nebraska, and they had already packed eight crates of fossils, including five brontothere skulls, apparently all *Megacerops,* based on the Carnegie catalogue. Gilmore was having a slow start at Sheep Creek, and Utterback was still struggling to get to the Laramie exposures. Douglass was just leaving for southwestern Montana to collect Tertiary mammals, and Hatcher was still laboring on his memoir about Oligocene dogs.[2]

In the first half of June, Utterback reported finding two promising prospects in Jurassic exposures south of Buffalo, Wyoming. He wrote to see if Hatcher wanted him to work on them or confine himself to Laramie outcrops. A week later, on the twelfth, Utterback wrote to express sympathy and concern for an unspecified illness in Hatcher's family. He'd decided the Jurassic prospects were too labor-intensive to undertake at that point, so he was focused on prospecting Laramie beds east and north of Trabing near Buffalo, Wyoming. He'd yet to hit any promising prospects, though, and wondered how long he could keep his enthusiasm up, recalling, "Am often reminded of your remarks in regard to the Cañon City quarry, that it is better to work where we know they are than to chase all over the country after them. . . . Shall keep expenses down to the very lowest notch possible and any time you say quit alfalfa is ready to cut."[3]

Peterson stayed in touch with Hatcher throughout the latter half of June, in part because he needed Anna to send him his citizenship papers so he could complete the proof on his homestead but also because he was concerned that the Hatchers' daughter, Alice, was doing "so poorly" and hoped she'd recover soon. Despite his own case of tonsillitis and grippe, he'd discovered an *Elotherium* skeleton with good limbs and feet, along with about fifteen vertebrae and several ribs. By the twenty-second, he and VanKirk already had eighteen crates packed, even though VanKirk had been bitten by a rattler that he'd tried to catch but was evidently "not any the worse for it and is at work evry [sic] day." They planned to wrap up their work in the "lower beds" soon, unless they found another locality, and spend the rest of the summer in the "upper beds." Five days later, Peterson reported they'd found small mammals in the "Titanotherium beds," including two *Hoplophoneus* skeletons and a "hippo" skeleton, probably of the hippo-like anthracothere called *Bothriodon*, based on the entry in the Carnegie catalogue.[4]

Utterback sent his condolences and best wishes for Alice's recovery on the twenty-eighth before leveling, "Mr. Hatcher after 25 days constant rideing [sic] and prospecting in the Laramie I quit it. When a man realizes that the best part of his season is going and has accomplished nothing he is liable to become desperate." But he was now upbeat regarding his luck near Kaycee, Wyoming:

> *On the 25th made quite a find in the Jurassic and moved camp and made preparations for a summers work in this locality. After gathering up a few fragments the rain commenced to pour and at present writing is still at it. If I am not mistaken I have a good thing. Have a large number of caudal vert in position in sight and several limb bones. The bones are in fine condition and in marl and can be worked almost free from matrix. Another skeleton has gone to pieces about 300 ft from the one I shall work upon. While a good portion of that has been washed away I think we will get many good limb bones from that also.*

This specimen apparently belonged to *Diplodocus* (CM 662), as recorded in the Carnegie catalogue. Although he was struggling to find good men to hire for help, he had found a good place to board for $20 per month and vowed to work the prospects until Hatcher arrived or sent other directives. Finally, he suggested that Hatcher send Gilmore, if he wasn't having success at Sheep Creek, so he could supervise and see the geology at the site. Overall, he proclaimed, "Fine water, plenty of trout and am eating the best of venison three times per day. Bear killed two fine milk cows night before last for a ranchman near here." A week later, he had sixteen caudals ready to crate and expressed confidence that most of the skeleton was there, since the sacrum, many limb bones, as well as other vertebrae, were in sight. But no locals could be hired at any price, because they were getting $40 to $50 per month for herding sheep. So if Gilmore couldn't come and Hatcher couldn't send an assistant, he'd have to cover up the exposed bones, because he couldn't collect them by himself.[5]

Hatcher was in Hot Springs, South Dakota, by August 13, where Holland wrote him with delight at the various crews' success in the field. The illustrator Sydney Prentice had come down with a case of "walking typhoid" in Pittsburgh, and Holland was concerned at his insistence to keep working, explaining to Hatcher, "Typhoid is too treacherous a disease to permit anyone to trifle with it." In early July, Charles R. Eastman of Harvard had been commissioned to purchase as much as $500 worth of fossils for the Carnegie during a trip he was taking to Europe, especially if he could acquire a "study series" from Devonian beds in Scotland or specimens of ichthyosaurs, plesiosaurs, or pterosaurs from Germany's Solnhofen Limestone. Also, Osborn wrote gleefully with congratulations, while quoting from a USGS agreement: "You are authorized to engage . . . J. B. Hatcher for a monograph on Ceratopsia, and an allotment of $2,100 is made . . . for this purpose. It is understood that Mr. Hatcher agrees to deliver this manuscript and drawings . . . complete within two years, for the sum of $4,200 [including] all traveling and other expenses. . . ."[6]

With Utterback diverted to the Jurassic Morrison Formation, Peterson wrote on the thirtieth to say he'd taken up the quest in the Cretaceous Laramie after VanKirk had gotten into a row with the cook and returned to Pittsburgh in disgrace, leaving a frustrated Peterson without a field assistant. Nonetheless, Peterson had found two prospects near Snyder, Wyoming, one of which he was sure was *Triceratops*, and he was especially intent on finding a skull of that dinosaur in the Laramie sandstone if time permitted.[7]

Back in the Jurassic, Utterback was wrestling with a large stripping job. Although he could easily blast through the top ten feet of overburden, the last three feet had to be chopped out block by block with a hammer and chisel. On September 20, he thought he'd be done with that in five or six more days, since he'd hired a man to help, but he didn't think he'd be able to work past October 15, because the ground was already freezing at night. He now had the sacrum with both ischia, another fibula, an astragalus, and a great many vertebrae of all kinds. Both scapulae were ready to box, and he hoped to garner the greater portion of the skeleton if expense wasn't too great, about which he warned Hatcher, "Have let you down light for the past month but have your smelling salts convenient when next comes in." By October 1, both his hired men had quit to cut timber, but he'd managed to collect two cervicals, one caudal, and one dorsal, with a very fine femur and a humerus underway, along with several other bones in sight. He'd need to close camp soon and wanted Hatcher's advice as to whether he should store the outfit there for working the site next season or bring the equipment with him.[8]

Hatcher received a rare note from Andrew Carnegie, who wrote from Skibo Castle in Scotland on October 2. Hatcher had sent Carnegie a copy of his *Diplodocus* memoir with the illustrated restoration. Carnegie excitedly informed him, "The King was attracted to the Diplodocus when here. He wants one for British Museum badly." Carnegie indicated the king was "on your track now for duplicates," so perhaps Hatcher could call upon him if Hatcher came for a visit. Hatcher, having returned to Pittsburgh by mid-September, wrote Osborn to exult in Utterback's discovery of what he hoped would be "a complete skeleton of one of the Sauropoda," which turned out to be a *Diplodocus* (CM 662). He had never seen "such fine bones well preserved & not at all crushed." Hatcher also proclaimed he was ready to begin on the Ceratopsia monograph, putting in six hours a day, for 210 days per year, at $10 per day from then on. By October 1, although "making substantial progress," Hatcher realized the monograph would "develop into a considerable undertaking, perhaps more than I had anticipated," but he pledged to give it his best effort and complete it within the allotted time. Osborn expressed his pleasure with the plan and progress on October 7. By mid-October, Hatcher realized that standardizing the planned monographs for the Ceratopsia, Sauropoda, and Stegosauria that he, Osborn, and Lucas were writing would require a coordinated classification system for the Dinosauria, which Hatcher didn't feel "competent" to provide. Osborn agreed and volunteered to draft up a classification scheme revised from Marsh's earlier one, which Hatcher and Lucas could critique. Hatcher continued to update Osborn on his progress throughout the rest of the year. But not surprisingly given their former fracases, when Osborn published a note in *Science* entitled "New Vertebrates of the Mid-Cretaceous," Hatcher took exception to Osborn's statement that "the true Judith River beds certainly overlie the Ft. Pierre [beds]." Hatcher's geologic observations in the region made him uncertain of the true stratigraphic relationships, and he told Osborn he would rebut Osborn's claim in *Science*. Accurately resolving the issue would require further geologic reconnaissance, which would eventually be done with Osborn's support in conjunction with the USGS geologist T. W. Stanton during 1903.[9]

By October 7, Utterback had worked most bones out of the rock, including two cervicals and numerous foot bones. He had another radius and ulna ready to extract, but he would have to leave more vertebrae in the ground. He could haul the crates to Buffalo, Wyoming, from which he'd need to pay $20 per ton to have them hauled to the railroad at Clearmont, because parts of the road were too steep for his single team to handle. He'd assist in loading the crates to ensure their safety. A couple of days later, he expected to have the crates at Clearmont on the twenty-third and estimated that it would take two men six weeks or two months to collect the rest of the skeleton the following season. In mid-October, both Peterson and Utterback were wrestling their treasures onto the rails, but Utterback's boxcar was delayed, "owing to great rush of stock of all kinds to eastern markets the B and M are having more than they can handle. There [are] 2,000 cars of dead freight between Edgemont and Billings." He'd been trying to locate the car with his crates for three days since he arrived in Adelia from Clearmont, leading him to sarcastically state, "As Adelia is a very pleasant place especially on windy days you can easily imagine the good time am having."[10]

For all intents and purposes, Hatcher spent relatively scant time in the field during 1902, a supposition that is seemingly confirmed by the fact that the Carnegie specimen catalogue lists no fossils collected by him that year. But his crew certainly came through. Peterson recorded one specimen of the sauropod dinosaur *Camarasaurus* from the 150-million-year-old beds of the Morrison Formation, and seven mammals from the

37- to 34-million-year-old strata of the Chadron Formation, including the small "bear dog" *Brachyrhyncocyon*; brontothere beheamoths "Brontops" and "Menodus," both now called *Megacerops*; the hippo-like anthracothere *Bothriodon*; and the rhino *Trigonias*. Peterson also contributed one egg and 117 mammal fossils from the 34- to 32-million-year-old rock layers of the Brule Formation, including the opossum-like *Peratherium*; the weasel-like insectivorous *Letptictis*; the rodents *Paradjidaumo* and *Eumys*; the dogs *Protemnocyon* and *Hesperocyon*; the "bear dog" *Daphoenus*; the saber-toothed carnivores *Hoplophoneus* and *Dinictis*; the horse *Mesohippus*; the rhinos "Caeonpus," now called *Subhyracodon*, and *Hyracodon*; the "terror pig" *Archaeotherium*; the camel *Poebrotherium*; the oreodont *Merycoidodon*; the deer- and chevrotain-like *Leptomeryx*, *Hypertargulus*, and *Hypisodus*. Peterson collected six oreodont specimens of *Phenacocoelus*, *Mesoreodon*, and *Promerycochoerus* from the 30- to 19-million-year-old beds of Upper Monroe Creek Formation, as well as two other mammal fossils of the mountain beaver *Allops* and the oreodont *Merychyus* with incomplete field data.

Gilmore gathered up an impressive forty-six dinosaur specimens of the sauropods *Camarasaurus*, *Apatosaurus*, and *Diplodocus*, the armored *Stegosaurus* and the carnivorous *Allosaurus*, as well as a specimen of the porpoise-like ichthyosaur *Opthalmosaurus* from the Morrison Formation, while Utterback is credited with one ichthyosaur specimen of *Opthalmosaurus* and one specimen of the sauropod *Diplodocus*.

Douglass's collection dominated the season's tally, with one specimen of the ostrich-like dinosaur *Ornithomimus* and one specimen of the soft-shelled turtle *Trionyx* from the 84- to 72-million-year-old "Belly River" Formation. Douglass also gleaned 22 mammal specimens of the rodents *Ischyromys* and *Cylindrodon*, the rabbit *Palaeolagus*, the brontothere "Menodus," now called *Megacerops*; the horse *Mesohippus*; the tapir *Colodon*; the oreodont *Bathygenys*; and the deer-like *Leptomeryx* from the 37- to 34-million-year-old Chadron, Totson, and Renova Formations; four specimen of *Palaeolagus*, *Mesohippus*, and the oreodont *Leptauchenia* from the Brule Formation; one fossil of the dog *Mesocyon* from the 30- to 19-million-year-old beds of the John Day Formation; and one fossil of the horse *Merychippus* from an unnamed 19- to

16-million-year-old formation. But Douglass dug out an impressive 90 mammals and two tortoises from the 16- to 12.5-million-year-old strata of the Madison Valley, Deep River, and Sixmile Formations, such as the opossum-like marsupial *Peratherium*; the rabbits *Palaeolagus* and *Alphalagus*; the six-inch-long, mouse-like rodent *Eumys*; the squirrel *Palaearctomys*; the beaver *Palaeocastor*, the horned, beaver-like rodent *Mylagaulus*; the elephant-like mastodon *Mammut*, the fox-sized dog *Hesperocyon*; the "bear dog" *Daphoenus*; the three-tonned rhino *Aphelops*; the grazing horses *Merychippus* and *Protohippus*; the oreodonts *Promerycochoerus*, *Eporeodon*, *Mesoreodon*, *Cyclopedius*, and *Merycoides*; the deer-like *Leptomeryx*; the camel *Procamelus*; the antelope-like *Merycodus*; and the tortoises *Testudo* and *Stylemys*. Finally, Douglass collected five more mammal specimens of the mastodon *Mammut*, the rodent *Paradjidaumo*, the horse *Protohippus*, and the oreodont *Eporeodon* with incomplete field data. In sum, Hatcher's crew contributed 408 new specimens to the Carnegie collection.

In part, Hatcher had kept busy by canvassing fossil dealers and publishers in Europe for potential specimens and back-issue publications to purchase for the Carnegie's collection and library. In addition, his narrative of the Patagonian expeditions and study of Oligocene "canids" had come out, in which he assigned two of Peterson's specimens (CM 492 & 553) to *Daphoenus felinus*, and another to "Daphoenus dodgei" (CM 573), which is now interpreted to be a species of *Brachyrhynchocyon*. Hatcher also created new genera and species for two others—"Proamphicyon nebrascensis" (CM 491), which is now assigned to *Daphoenus vetus* (Hunt 2004), and "Protemnocyon inflatus" (CM 552), which is now known as *Daphoenus hartshornianus* (Hunt 1996). Today, these animals are not classified with true canids but rather to another group of carnivorans informally called "bear dogs," which are viewed as evolutionary relatives of true dogs. Whereas "bear dogs" walked flat-footed, or in a platigrade manner, with all the bones of their feet touching the ground, true dogs walk up on their fingers and toes in a digitigrade mode. In all, the eight papers published in 1902 varied in subject mater from the mount of "Titanotherium" to the structure of the hand in *Brontosaurus* to duckbills and the musk ox.[11]

Through November and December, Hatcher was also in touch with Charles Beecher at Yale, since he'd sent VanKirk there apparently to prepare a *Triceratops* skull for his monograph. Beecher reported that although VanKirk worked diligently, Hatcher probably wouldn't be satisfied, since the assistant wasn't very experienced in *Triceratops* preparation. Beecher, meanwhile, had pushed an initiative through the Peabody's trustees that Hatcher had proposed—to hire another man to work on preparing ceratopsian skeletons, with the costs being split evenly between the Peabody and the Carnegie.[12]

No doubt pining for a period in the field, on February 11, Hatcher was plotting with his old acquaintance, T. W. Stanton of the USGS, to travel to the Judith region for a couple of months in the summer of 1903. That same month, he was also receiving accolades for his recent publications, including ones from Lucas from the Smithsonian Institution and especially John C. Merriam from the University of California at Berkeley:

> *Your letter and the paper on the Oligocene Canidae . . . is a fine piece of work. It is much larger and more elaborate than I supposed when we were talking over the specimens. . . . I am looking forward to having a good time with your Patagonian Narrative and Geography which I know will furnish me with very good reading for some time.*[13]

A long letter from Williston arrived in Hatcher's box on the twenty-fifth, in which Williston tried to soothe Hatcher's feelings about Riggs, who had apparently tried to pilfer Hatcher's illustrator, Sydney Prentice. No doubt still seething about Riggs's attempt to hire away Gilmore the previous year, Hatcher was not amused. Williston, who had been Riggs's professor at Kansas, was now in Chicago, where Riggs was also based. Williston reassured Hatcher that Riggs surely could not have "intended anything unfriendly" and probably wrote at the suggestion of the Field's director, who was a personal friend of Prentice's. Williston reminded Hatcher that competent illustrators were in short supply, and Williston had just had to reject some work done by a local artist there. In any event, Williston wrote, "I assure you that if ever I should have a proposition to make to one of your assistants that you will hear of it first, and I am sure that you will do the same." Still unsatisfied with his own position, Williston, a gifted fellow refugee from Marsh and an academic itinerant like Hatcher, confided:

> *I may say (privately) that I suppose my relations with the museum will terminate soon. It was hoped that some effective combination could be made between the Museum and University for mutual advantage, but I have no expectation that anything will result in the immediate future. I expect to begin collecting in the Cretaceous for the University the coming summer.*
>
> *And, I am rather glad of it. Until vertebrate paleontology is put on an independent footing in the museum it will be vain to expect much advancement. . . .*
>
> *The fields that I wish particularly to work in are the Permian and the Marine Cretaceous. Of course I must get more or less Tertiary material for instruction purposes, but the strength of my department I intend to put in on the early reptiles and amphibians.*[14]

Beecher indicated on March 4 that another preparator had failed to meet standards for working on the *Triceratops* skull that Hatcher needed cleaned at Yale. Like good illustrators, competent preparators were apparently also few and far between at the time, and Beecher suggested that perhaps Marsh's old technician Hugh Gibb would be able to lend a hand by July. But Beecher presented a scheme on the seventeenth by which Gibb and another staff preparator at Yale could use their time off to work on ceratopsians, if Hatcher had funding to foot the bill at 50 cents per hour, with Yale putting in a similar amount.[15]

Better news came from Stanton on the fifth in that their planned trip to the Judith region would be part of the budget submission for the USGS, and Osborn had agreed to support it. By the sixteenth, Stanton wrote to say he was confident that the request would be approved for two months in the field beginning June 1. One imperative was to purchase the tickets soon so that the charges would go against the current budget. Given Hatcher's experience in outfitting expeditions in the region,

Stanton preferred to have Hatcher make the arrangements with someone in Havre, Montana. They hoped to visit Lambe's ceratopsian localities in Alberta. Stanton wondered if they'd have trouble crossing the border and hoped Lambe would help out to avoid the extra cost of duties.[16]

Word was getting out about the Carnegie's intent to provide the British Museum with a mounted cast of their *Diplodocus*. On the twenty-seventh, Holland received a request from the *Tribune* to provide information and imagery that they could use for a piece in their illustrated supplement, with costs to be covered by the paper.[17]

Hatcher and Stanton continued to tussle with the finances and budgetary procedures for their Judith trip throughout April and early May. Once they saw the pertinent stratigraphy and fossil sites in Montana and Alberta, they planned to split up, with Stanton going on to examine invertebrate fossil sites in Idaho and Utah. By May 3, Hatcher had struck a deal for the field outfit with a supplier in Havre for $300. Hatcher also contacted Lambe, who, on May 14, thanked Hatcher for the copy of his "splendid" memoir on Oligocene dogs and informed him that he'd try to join them for a while on the Canadian leg of their trip, in addition to providing from his papers whatever figures and illustrations he could for Hatcher's monograph on the Ceratopsia. Meanwhile, Stanton had made notes from pertinent Canadian Survey reports and planned to take copies of the associated maps.[18]

At the same time, Holland was helping to arrange transportation for Douglass back to Montana for his field season. Peterson remained in Pittsburgh during the 1903 field season, since there was a burgeoning backlog of specimens to prepare and field funds were scarce. Utterback wrote Hatcher from Mayoworth, Wyoming, on May 19 that he'd begun stripping overburden on the quarry he'd discovered the previous year. But he was a bit concerned that Riggs was conducting surveillance to figure out the exact location of Utterback's quarry by writing a friend of his in Buffalo, Wyoming. Utterback didn't object to having other crews nearby, but there were exposures just south of his quarry that he wanted to prospect because he was aware of many finds made there. He asked Hatcher to conduct some counterintelligence when he passed through Chicago. On the twenty-sixth, Hatcher confirmed he'd check in at the

Field Museum in Chicago to find out what Riggs was up to and advised Utterback to visit the exposures south of the quarry as soon as possible, then mark any significant finds with posters claiming them for Utterback and the Carnegie.[19]

Stanton and Hatcher set up an agreement on May 23 regarding the distribution of fossils they would find that stipulated that the first set of fossils, including any types for new species, would belong to the USGS, since it was the primary funder. However, Hatcher and Stanton would choose a set of duplicates for the Carnegie's collection. Before departing, Hatcher directed Peterson to continue working on the camel mount of *Oxydactylus* so it would be ready for Founder's Day, while VanKirk would continue preparation of the saber-tooths, *Hoplophoneus* and *Dinictis*, as well as the horse, *Mesohippus*, until adequate material was developed for mounting a skeleton of each. Then Hatcher wrote a memo to Holland to confirm that he'd be gone with Stanton for the months of June and July to collect and conduct geologic reconnaissance in Montana and Alberta, with the collections split as previously described. Then he'd join Utterback's operation, prospect in the Laramie near Lusk, and evaluate a brontothere prospect found two years earlier east of the Black Hills in South Dakota before returning by September 1.[20]

Utterback reported fair returns on June 1, but Quarry A was about worked out after producing six dorsals, ten caudals, both sternal bones, along with numerous foot bones, spines, and chevrons. He anticipated that Quarry B would also produce some very fine bones, and several were in sight. By the fourth, Utterback had many unspecified bones out of B with more in sight, all in all including three ischia, two pubes, about fifteen vertebrae of different kinds, as well as ribs.[21]

About a week after Hatcher hit the road, Holland wrote to say he intended to purchase the Bayet collection through C. R. Eastman of Harvard for 100,000 francs. He informed Hatcher that to keep Eastman in "good spirits" during the negotiations to come, he hoped Hatcher would be accommodating by letting Eastman, who was an ichthyologist and paleontologist, study the fish in the collection. By the tenth, Holland heard that Baron de Bayet had accepted his offer, as long as the Belgian mollusks and plants were excluded from the purchase, along with the cases that currently housed the collection. The Carnegie would be responsible for packing and shipping the collection, including the costs. Holland was desirous of acquiring the whole collection and was prepared to offer another $500, equaling 2,500 francs, to get it, but the baron was insisting that it would need to be packed and shipped in short order because he was paying rent on the house in which it was stored. Apparently, Eastman had told Holland that Hatcher had said it would be fine for him to pack up and study the collection for a year while he was in Europe; Eastman had offered to take a leave from Harvard and temporarily join the Carnegie staff to carry out the work. But Holland was skeptical that Hatcher had made such an agreement, since, during their last conversation before he left, Hatcher had expressed his disapproval for such an arrangement.[22]

In any event, Holland didn't wish to pay Eastman for a year given all the other expenses involved. On the twelfth, Holland telegraphed Hatcher to ask if he approved of Eastman studying and packing up the collection in Europe. Four days later, Eastman telegraphed Hatcher to say that Holland approved of his sailing for Brussels as soon as Hatcher approved.[23]

Hatcher finally returned to Havre from the Canadian leg of his excursion with Stanton by the twenty-second. He responded to Holland that he was greatly pleased that Mr. Carnegie had provided the funding to purchase the Bayet collection. He added:

> *I do not care how we get it just so we do get it. If you are convinced that Dr. Eastman will look out for our interests in this matter to the best possible advantage, I am quite satisfied. . . . Eastman . . . is not a close personal acquaintance of mine. I should feel much better if you or I could go over and make an invoice of the material with Eastman, who is a good paleontologist . . . but has had almost no experience in the collecting and handling of material.*
>
> *The only promise I made him was . . . he should have the privilege of working up the fishes, but without any salary in case he did so, the results to be published in the publications of our Museum. I made no promise that . . . he should be sent to Brussels. . . . He*

*told me that he was returning to Europe . . . and . . . he would be
glad to give any assistance possible in expediting matters and in
identifying material.*

Hatcher reiterated his demand that a thorough list of all the specimens
be made and suggested Holland pay rent for the place where it was stored
in order to provide the time to do so. As the curator responsible, Hatcher
offered to leave immediately to go over and handle the matter himself if
Holland wanted. But Holland decided to sail for Europe on July 8 and take
Eastman with him in order to make the inventory, verify the field collection data to the degree possible, and pack the material. This would allow
Holland to wrap up business with the baron for about two weeks before
the baron left the city. He indicated that Hatcher might need to come over
later. It seems Holland was especially keen that Hatcher get to the Judith
region so he could collect moths and butterflies, for, "from the standpoint
of the lepidopterist [the Judith was] almost a terra incognita." [24]

At the end of June, Utterback was still uncovering numerous good
bones in Quarry B and thought he had two good skeletons. Although
he couldn't identify them with certainty, he indicated one resembled
Marsh's description of *Stegosaurus*. To help Hatcher visualize his progress, he provided a sketch of his quarries, which revealed where he'd
taken out over one hundred bones from just ten square feet, making "the
bones show up so thick as to be almost impossible to work." According
to listings in the Carnegie catalogue, Utterback's haul from Quarry B
included specimens of *Diplodocus*, *Camrasaurus*, *Apatosaurus*, *Allosaurus*,
and possibly *Haplocanthosaurus*. Finding competent help still stymied
him. "Have a good man with team or pick and shovel however cares no
more for bones than a hog does for an acorn with a hole in it." Thus, he
still hadn't prospected the exposures to the south. [25]

When Hatcher wrote on July 11, he seemed pleased that Holland
was going to Brussels and requested that Holland make sure Eastman
provided labels for all the presently unlabeled specimens and packed
them securely. He was also pleased that his Judith trip had confirmed his
hypothesis about where the Judith beds fit in the stratigraphic sequence,
as opposed to the ideas held by Osborn, Williston, and Stanton. The key

question involved whether the beds of the Judith River Formation lay lower in the stratigraphic sequence of rock layers (and were, therefore, older) than the rock layers of the Laramie or Lance and Hell Creek Formations, or whether the reverse was true. Osborn, Williston, and Stanton believed the Judith beds were younger than those of the Lance and Hell Creek, but Hatcher suspected the opposite. By the end of their expedition to Montana and Alberta, Stanton had conceded the point to Hatcher and coauthored a paper to *Science* with Hatcher saying so, leading Hatcher to crow: "If some of our closet geologists would spend nineteen years almost constantly in the field, as I did, they would not presume to speak with such absolute authority on subjects of which they know nothing." [26]

By the end of July, Holland and Eastman had started slowly packing the Bayet collection, which filled eight to ten rooms and included numerous invertebrates, especially ammonites, thirteen to fourteen Solnhofen pterosaurs, an Eocene falcon, Solnhofen insects and crustaceans, mosasaurs, and several new fish. It would take two hundred crates to ship it all.[27]

Utterback reported that he'd packed twenty-two crates of bones by July 28. Barnum Brown of the AMNH had visited and spent a day prospecting before leaving for the Hell Creek region of Montana. Gilmore had written to say he'd discovered nothing significant. A few days later, Utterback had decided to close his quarry by August 10 and prospect the exposures to the south unless Hatcher had other ideas.[28]

Carnegie chimed in to Holland on August 4, proclaiming that as a result of their successes, Holland and Hatcher must be "special pets of Providence," although he couldn't understand exactly why. He was pleased that work on the duplicate of *Diplodocus* was initiated, because "I wish this for his Majesty—I do hope that Skull is coming out perfect." He marveled at what famous men Holland and Hatcher were becoming. For his part, Carnegie was considering forging a cottage industry for *Diplodocus* casts: "I think better make more than one cast of Diplodocus—If I visit all the Crowned Heads could send one to each of their National Museums," including the king of Belgium, the emperor of Germany, Russia, and Queen Wilhelmina, all of whom had sent messages inviting him to visit.[29]

Utterback was still pounding away in Quarry B on the sixth and getting more bones of the supposed stegosaur, of which he thought he'd recover a "good part." But by the tenth, he'd closed the quarry and headed for the Musselshell region of Montana as Hatcher had directed.[30]

Hatcher, having read Holland's accounts of his opulent encounters with European royalty, wrote on August 13:

> . . . *you have certainly been leading a very strenuous life of late. Lionized by the king of the Belgians & wined & dined by Barons & Baronesses is certainly too much for a retired minister, & such a "notorious" king as Leopold too. Really my dear Dr. Holland I have fears that you will return to us in a battered condition. . . . Can you not send me a case of some of that wine you have been drinking to replace some of this vile alkali water I am living on. Perhaps if you could I would get over this case of "back-door-trots" I have had the past week.*

He was delighted to hear about the "gems" in the Bayet collection, which would vault the Carnegie to the top of American museums in terms of collections of European vertebrates. But Hatcher wanted more and implored Holland to also solicit Carnegie to purchase the Filhol collection in Paris, which contained many type specimens and would be of great value in correlating American and European rock units, a problem that had "as yet never been properly attempted." Besides, it would only cost $2,000 or about $55,000 today. Hatcher was at Musselshell, Montana, where he'd found bones while traveling with Stanton, and now had several crates packed. He reported that all the crews were having good success, and he planned to return to Pittsburgh around the twentieth.[31]

When Hatcher showed up at the museum, he was no longer pleased with Holland, who had let Eastman take the falcon fossil to England with him to study and describe. Holland hurriedly informed Eastman on the thirty-first not to describe or name it, even though Eastman had pledged to name it after Holland. Holland elaborated, Hatcher "says that for me to have allowed you to take the bird, without consulting him, was to trench upon his 'sovereign rights' as Curator of Paleontology. . . . The man is very jealous of his prerogatives & of his supposed dignities." Meanwhile Eastman wrote to say he'd studied Agassiz's fossil fish types, and those in the Bayet collection were much better. He'd also found three Oligocene bird fossils from Armissan near Narbonne, but only one genus named "Taoperdix" had been described from there. One Bayet specimen, which was remarkably complete except for part of the skull, seemed to be different. Regarding the Filhol collection, the French wanted it but couldn't afford it, while the British had offered 37,500 francs and were begging the Americans not to compete.[32]

In early September, Utterback finished collecting the duckbill bones Hatcher had found near Willow Creek, Montana, and discovered a tibia, a small humerus, three metatarsals, one metacarpal, two caudals, two ribs, and some chevrons. The man hired to haul the crates "went on a high old lonesome in Billings and just returned."[33]

Hatcher had other international business to catch up on. He negotiated an exchange with F. Baron Nopcsa and Viktor Uhlig of Vienna in early September, through which Hatcher would send a pelvis and femur of an ornithopod dinosaur, while Vienna would make casts of some bones of "Struthiosaurus." Hatcher had also received a letter from his old nemesis Florentino Ameghino, to which he responded on September 3:

> *Throughout the entire discussion you have entirely misinterpreted what I have said concerning the Pyrotherium beds. If you will take the trouble to look at my paper you will see that I place the Pyrotherium beds in the Cretaceous, and that I did so on your authority, I did not then nor do I now believe that the beds from which your brother Charles collected the mammalian fauna referred to, the Pyrotherium beds are Cretaceous, and I suggested that some of them might be more recent than the Santa Cruzian. I did not then nor never have placed the Pyrotherium beds above the Santa Cruzian, I did believe and still believe that certain of the fossils described as from the Pyrotherium beds might be more recent than Santa Cruzian.*

Hatcher also disputed Ameghino's interpretation of the "Patagonian" Formation as representing a distinct horizon and Ameghino's accusation that Hatcher had mixed up the fossils he collected there. He countered,

> *Do you think that it is possible for me to have intruded the fossils into a large block of matrix which I shipped home from the mouth of the Santa Cruz River in so skillful a manner that this fraud would not have been detected by Dr. Ortmann, Professor Pillsbury, Professor Scott, Professor Osborn, Dr. Dall, or any one of the many other paleontologists who have had access to this material? Yet in each of these blocks of matrix in every instance they were finding mingled together fossils which according to you were characteristic of all three of the horizons which you claim to be able to distinguish.*

Hatcher went on to defend the care he took to collect and curate the specimens he'd collected, and pledged to publish a fuller account in papers to come. He urged that they both provide detailed descriptions, photos, and geologic sections of the localities where they collected so anyone interested could visit them and see the relationships for themselves. He felt no one had expressed more admiration for Ameghino's work than he had, and "to differ in our views and to publish those differences should never be regarded as an unfriendly act, and all criticisms and replies should, I think, be couched in friendly words."[34]

On the fourth, Hatcher wrote Osborn that he and Prentice would soon visit New Haven and New York to describe and illustrate specimens for the Ceratopsia volume. He also wrote Lambe to express his regret that he couldn't join Stanton and himself in their examination of the stratigraphy of the Belly River and Judith River beds. But Hatcher would be pleased to receive the marked-up copy of Lambe's memoir on horned dinosaurs from Canada, which would help Hatcher insert the catalogue numbers of the specimens in his Ceratopsia volume. Hatcher also expressed appreciation for Lambe's offer to loan him the original zinc blocks and ink drawings for Lambe's figures and plates. Then Hatcher asked to borrow the type of the bony-helmeted pachycephalosaur called

Stegoceras validus, because he wanted to compare it with some fossils he'd collected earlier in the summer.[35]

Closer to home, Hatcher tried to check in with Gilmore, Utterback, and Douglass on the fourth. He had not heard from Gilmore in a month and was curious about his success. He also inquired about what Gilmore would need in terms of railway passes to Pittsburgh. He directed Utterback to revisit the site where they'd collected parts of "the curious armored dinosaurs"; shovel all the loose dirt down to bedrock to see if a skeleton lay buried underneath; and pick through the debris for fragments. He added, "This is an extremely interesting and important discovery and do not be afraid of spending too much time in working over the locality. A fragment or two of the skull might be of more value than the entire cost of a month's work." As identified in the Carnegie catalogue, this specimen did not turn out to be a dinosaur but rather an enormous, thirty-foot-long alligator named *Deinosuchus* (CM 963).[36]

Once finished, Utterback was to prospect the badlands about three miles to the west, then move on to prospect at Ragged Rocks about eight to ten miles east, and finally examine the exposures about ten miles north of his camp. Everything from these localities would be new to the Carnegie collections, and the fauna was poorly known in general. At the end of the season, Utterback was to haul all the crates from Hatcher's earlier collections, as well as Utterback's own, to Billings, where they'd be combined with Douglass's crates of Tertiary fossils for shipment back to Pittsburgh. Hatcher directed Douglass to work until October 1, when the available field funds would be expended, and return to Pittsburgh, where plenty of work awaited.[37]

In other business in early September, Hatcher inquired if E. H. Sellards might be interested in joining the Carnegie staff at least for the summer as a collection manager for the invertebrate fossils, and Sellards responded on the thirteenth that he'd accept any terms Hatcher was able to arrange. However, Holland denied the request. Hatcher also told G. P. Merrill of the Smithsonian's National Museum of Natural History that it might be possible for Gilmore to visit in order to prepare their *Torosaurus* skull if Merrill could contribute $50 per month toward Gilmore's salary. He also wrote M. S. Farr at Princeton to say he'd love to receive a set of the Patagonian reports published to that point, but Farr should check with Scott first, because "from the manner in which Professor Scott has acted toward me in these and all other matters I am not sure that he would sanction your sending me a set of the reports." In fact, Scott was next on Hatcher's correspondence list, with Hatcher writing to inquire whether Scott ever intended to repay him the $75 Hatcher had paid Peterson for work at Princeton after his return from Patagonia in 1899. Hatcher ended rather sarcastically with, "I thank you very kindly for Part 1, of your Report on the Mammalia of the Santa Cruz beds. Save for my own report this is the first of any of the reports of these expeditions that I have had the pleasure of receiving." Scott responded on the ninth that he'd send at least half of the payment due in short order and expressed surprise that Hatcher hadn't received copies of the reports that had been published, since he had directed his staff to send them, before promising to "attend to the matter." Mollified, Hatcher accepted Scott's assurances.[38]

Then it was time to badger Eastman a bit by insisting that he send whatever specimens he had in Paris to the Carnegie so they could be catalogued before Eastman published on them. Hatcher also requested a complete list of the specimens Eastman had retained with an explanation of his progress in studying them. Finally, Hatcher inquired about what had become of the $100 Hatcher had given him to purchase small fossil collections in Europe, since ". . . having never received any of these small and interesting collections nor any report from you as to what you had done with them . . . I should like you to furnish me with a list of these collections and their contents and . . . a statement as to what you have done with the money entrusted to you."[39]

Hatcher finally heard from Gilmore by the seventh and seemed pleased with his "continued success" as well as the news that his new daughter was healthy. The same was true for Utterback's report of success on the ninth. Douglass checked in on the twelfth to respond that he'd try to quit on October 1, but he might not be finished collecting everything he'd located. He'd had good success, and there were good prospects for more in the future. Hatcher wrote again on the eighteenth to insist Douglass close operations by October 1. Gilmore was on his way back and provided an account of his discoveries near Winona, Kansas, on the 13th: "Last week I found a few fragments of a Plesiosaur, evidently a large one. The end of one limb bone which I take to be the humerus, measures 10 in. across the distal end. Though we searched diligently nothing more could be found. Another disarticulated skull of Clidastes with some scattering vertebrae was the most important mosasaur find." Their conversation continued on the eighteenth, with Hatcher trying to determine the rail passes that would be needed for Gilmore's trip to Pittsburgh.[40]

Beginning on the seventh, Hatcher initiated a debate with O. P. Hay of the AMNH, hectoring him for publishing his thoughts "On Some Recent Literature Bearing on the Laramie Formation" before learning of the results of Hatcher's trip with Stanton, since Hay and Hatcher had corresponded about the issue before the trip:

> Since Dr. Stanton, my at one time strongest opponent on this question now thoroughly agrees with me as you will see by a recent note in "Science," that the Judith River beds are not Laramie and do not overlie the Pierre, you will perhaps be glad to withdraw the statement made on page 116, "that Hatcher's statement avails nothing against the positive observations of many other geologists."
>
> Please accept my sincere sympathy for you in your present predicament, until such time as I may personally see you in New York, when we will lunch together and be mutually reconciled.

But Hay gamely replied on the ninth, "I am in receipt of your nervy letter of the 7th. Before replying allow me to ask a question. Do you intend to discuss my paper in any publication or are we to settle our differences privately? . . . Don't imagine that I am kicking myself. 'There are other hearts that may ache.'" Hatcher quickly followed up on the eleventh, saying he hoped Hay hadn't taken his jibes too seriously, because they were "not written in a spirit of bravado, but rather of playfulness." Then Hatcher proceeded to invite Hay to lunch as soon as Hatcher made it to New York. Ending the counterpunching, Hay wrote to say he feared Hatcher had taken his notes too seriously as well, quipping, "Don't think anyone came out of that scrimmage without some disfiguration." More to the point, he asked Hatcher what differences distinguished the Laramie and Judith River faunas.[41]

Next, Hatcher wrote Lucas of the Smithsonian on the ninth to inquire about what they paid Peter Giordani for sculpting their model of *Stegosaurus*, because Hatcher wanted him to model some missing bones of the Carnegie's *Diplodocus*. Lucas informed him that Giordani made $3.50 per day and, although not the best modeler, was very pleasant and reliable.[42]

Then on the eleventh, Hatcher sought to settle matters with Eastman, expressing delight regarding the quality of the Solnhofen and Monte Bolca fishes, as well as with Eastman's progress on studying them. He was surprised to hear of the bird fossils but dutifully promised to have the fifty crates of Bayet material, including the ones Eastman had wanted to study, brought promptly to the museum for cataloguing. He hoped to see Eastman soon in order to "arrive at some definite understanding concerning some questions about which there would seem to be some difference of opinion."[43]

Indeed, Eastman wrote the same day to register his "regret that any misapprehension should have arisen on account of my having taken with me a fossil fowl to Paris in addition to a select lot of fishes." He explained that no one, including the baron, had been aware of the bird fossils, so he'd taken the supposed falcon to Paris to compare it with other known avian fossils. But he had no intention of publishing on it because he understood from both Holland and Hatcher that a volume on the collection would be published and he didn't want to upstage what would be a most noteworthy work. In all, he acknowledged his profound appreciation for the opportunity to study the collection's fish, which would afford the scientific community with "much new information."[44]

In what must have been a blow to Hatcher, Hatcher notified W. J. McGee of the International Geological Congress on September 14 about "the results of the consultation last week with Dr. Holland and myself relating to the expedition to Patagonia. At a meeting of the Board of the Museum Committee and of the Board of Trustees, . . . it seemed to be the sense of the opinion of the trustees that they would rather not engage in this undertaking." Hatcher's bad day continued as documented in a letter to Lambe: "The types . . . of your Stegoceras validus . . . have been received, and I have to acknowledge in this connection a serious blunder on my part. What I had in mind in writing you was not Stego-ceras validus at all, but Stereocephalus tutus. I was writing entirely from memory and had, for the time being, confused these two genera. . . ." *Stegoceras* is a small, dome-headed or bony-helmeted pachycephalosaur, whereas Lambe indicated that the fossils of the armored ankylosaur, then called "Stereocephalus," were too large to send. But Hatcher could see them when he came up.[45]

On the fifteenth, Utterback and his assistant Albert C. Silberling reported having four crates of very good bones from the spring Hatcher had directed he prospect, making almost 4,000 pounds between Hatcher's and his own haul around Musselshell. But the freighter, known well for his dishonesty, wanted to bill Utterback for 5,700 pounds. To resolve the issue, Utterback got the freighting company to agree not to settle the bill until the true weight was determined when the crates were loaded on the railcar. By the twentieth, Utterback had found three more plates and several other fragments at the site of Hatcher's supposed armored dinosaur, along with parts of the jaw or skull showing the roots of some teeth. That triggered opening a quarry twenty feet long and ten feet wide, from which they extracted:

> . . . *16 more complete plates 2 dorsal vert, 1 complete rib and parts of others. Also another bone that has put both Mr S. and myself as well as O.C. Marsh's Dinosaurs of America up a stump. . . . Of the 19 plates running in size from a twenty five cent piece up there is no two the same. If anything the dorsal vert are more of a puzzle than the plates as they are so entirely different from anything I ever saw. . . .* [He wished he could identify the beast, but] *"As our pleasures in this world are largely built upon hopes and expectations you will have to await the coming of the bones themselves.*[46]

Back east, a perplexing problem arose with Osborn, who wrote on the fifteenth to say he was looking forward to Hatcher and Prentice visiting so they could discuss the Judith and Laramie work. He would also graciously make space for Prentice to draw the ceratopsians Hatcher needed and offer his advice when Hatcher wasn't there. But on the sixteenth, Beecher of Yale wrote to say Osborn's student Richard S. Lull had shown up at the Peabody "requesting the privilege of 'examining' your Triceratops skulls in connection 'with a description of our skulls.' I told him that we were under contract with you on the Triceratops material and that I could not allow him to see any of the material you had in hand." In lieu, Beecher directed him to the exhibits, where a skull of "T. prosus" was on view, but Lull left in disappointment after about fifteen minutes. Beecher sought Hatcher's advice, especially since Osborn was clearly "Vertebrate Paleontologist of the U.S.G.S. and therefore in a way in charge of all the vertebrate work, but this request to-day did not seem to me to be quite right and I therefore declined to grant it." Hatcher responded on the eighteenth with surprise that Osborn would have Lull working on ceratopsians when he'd asked Hatcher to write the official monograph and was gobsmacked that Osborn hadn't at least let him know of Lull's intentions. Hatcher would come to New Haven shortly and discuss it all but agreed with Beecher's decision, explaining:

> *As you know, I have already expended something over $500 in the payment of salaries of preparators to work on the skulls at New Haven. It does not appear to me that it would be right, in view of this fact and of the additional fact that I have already been engaged for more than a year in work upon this group, to allow others to have access to the material at New Haven for purposes of study and description. You can readily see that by such a course the results of my work during the past year and more, might very easily be anticipated by Professor Lull, and that observations made independently by me at considerable expense and trouble would be likely to be gained by him.*

But Osborn attempted to butt in again later in September, when Beecher received another request for Osborn's preparator Adam Hermann to visit Yale and make casts of ceratopsian horncores. Beecher wrote on the twenty-fourth to alert Hatcher and once again denied Osborn's request based on the "contract" Yale had with Hatcher, which reserved their ceratopsian material for Hatcher's USGS monograph. By late September, Osborn wrote Hatcher to clarify that he had only wanted the casts for a mount to be put on exhibition, and Hatcher wrote Osborn and Beecher saying he had granted the request and alerted both that he and Prentice would concentrate on studying and illustrating the Yale specimens first so that the preparation of specimens there could proceed more quickly.[47]

Eastman responded to Hatcher's directives and queries on the eighteenth from Paris, explaining that no detailed agreement existed between him and Holland regarding what groups he could study in the Bayet collection. He hoped to study the fossil fish from Monte Bolca, because Arthur Smith Woodward of the British Museum had simply listed many forms as not represented, imperfectly known, or not adequately described. Thus, since paleontology's knowledge of Eocene fish was based largely on that sample, it was imperative that a more comprehensive study of that fauna be conducted and detailed comparisons made between the fossil forms and their close living relatives. Especially concerning were some of Agassiz's previously published type specimens, in which the bones of the skull were not precisely illustrated and some parts of the anatomy had been described based on artificial restoration of those elements. Eastman followed up a week later to tell Hatcher that the three new genera and fifteen new species he'd come across in the Paris collection had generated great interest, and the director of the museum wanted Eastman to publish a study of them in France, independent of the Bayet publication being planned. But the director didn't have funding for it, and Eastman wondered if the Carnegie could help. Many of the new species were eels, and Eastman recalled having seen a number of nice eel fossils in the Bayet, which he requested Hatcher set aside as he came across them in his cataloguing. Eastman also indicated the Paris director had heard of plans for the British museum *Diplodocus* mount and wondered if Paris might acquire a mounted cast also, even giving Eastman a photo of the exhibition hall in Paris where it could be placed.[48]

Series of correspondence continued between Hatcher and several colleagues throughout the second half of September, with McGee writing to say he was disappointed with the Carnegie trustees and implored Holland to let Hatcher serve as an agent for further work in Patagonia, for which Hatcher was appreciative. Scott came through with a partial payment of his long-standing debt, much to the delight of Hatcher. He also wrote Hay to confirm that significant differences existed between the Judith and Laramie faunas, which he would detail in an upcoming paper, and confirmed with Lambe that he would visit Ottawa during the fall or winter to study Lambe's ceratopsians and the armored dinosaur "Stereocephalus," now known as *Euoplocephalus*. Finally, Hatcher notified Osborn that Prentice would arrive in New York on October 1 to begin illustrating the ceratopsian specimens he intended to include in his monograph and thanked Osborn for offering to provide Prentice with aid and advice until Hatcher arrived soon thereafter.[49]

Hatcher then turned to his field crews, coordinating with Gilmore on shipping his collection and arranging for rail passes, adding that "Mistress Hatcher will expect you and your wife and baby to make our house your home until such time as you are comfortably located." He also complimented Utterback for playing hardball with the dishonest freight hauler and endorsing his desire to have the hauling fee based on the accurate weight to be determined when the crates were loaded on the rail car. He alerted Utterback that Douglass would be shipping his crates to Billings so Utterback could combine them with the crates from the Musselshell region in the shipment. Hatcher also indicated he'd try to arrange for Utterback's trip to Pittsburgh so that Utterback could visit his family in Indianapolis, and he informed Utterback that he intended to have Silberling collect near his home near Big Timber before returning to Pittsburgh.[50]

The goal was to collect a dinosaur specimen Silberling had found in the Cretaceous Pierre Shale, along with other vertebrates he might find, then make collections from the "Red beds" and the Judith River beds. But most importantly, Silberling should "collect as complete a series as possible of mammalia from the Laramie and Ft. Union or Torrejon beds." Hatcher declared his great delight on the twenty-eighth with Utterback and Silberling's new finds of the "armored dinosaur," directing them to pack those bones in a light strong box and express them to him when they reached Billings. Silberling also stated he planned to spend three weeks in the Tertiary beds near his home and another two weeks in the Pierre, if his dinosaur prospect produced. Otherwise, he'd expand his search to other localities in the Pierre, and Hatcher agreed with his strategy. Utterback continued his tussle with the freighter, who mistakenly delivered some of the USGS crates to the passenger depot in Billings rather than the cargo depot, resulting in their loss until the freighter's employer tracked them down. Douglass shipped his crates to Billings without paying or providing their weight, so Utterback couldn't estimate how much it would cost to pay that fee and the overall freight fee to Pittsburgh. Around Musselshell, he and Silberling had collected fourteen crates in September, and there were plenty of prospects for next season. Their haul included a sacrum incorporating eight vertebrae and another vertebral series with about thirty caudals and a pubis, of which Silberling had managed to jacket eleven. They covered the rest in the quarry for the following season. Utterback had also found what he thought was a nearly complete but disarticulated skull of a duckbill dinosaur.[51]

Given the potential for continued collecting the following season, Utterback sought Hatcher's advice about storing the camp outfit near Musselshell over the winter. Hatcher agreed and congratulated Utterback on his "splendid successes," then wrote Douglass to inform Utterback about the weight of his crates. Hatcher left it to Holland to arrange the complex choreography of the rail shipments, including reserving a car at Billings for Hatcher's and Utterback's Judith, Musselshell, and Mayoworth, Wyoming, collections, as well as Douglass's Bannack, Montana, collection, then arrange for another car at Winona, Kansas, to convey Gilmore's collection. On the eighth, Hatcher asked Utterback to telegraph the number of the boxcar containing his fossils. He also wrote Gilmore to congratulate him on his discovery of a mosasaur skeleton and to provide the number for his boxcar.[52]

As Prentice finally began his illustrations of ceratopsian specimens at New Haven in early October, Hatcher confirmed he should make the drawings at half natural size. On the sixth, Prentice completed a palatal view of one specimen, but would be held up for a day because Osborn and Hermann were due to measure brontosaur specimens and make casts of *Triceratops* horns, so Beecher had covered the other ceratopsian specimens. Nonetheless, Prentice could finish the skull drawing in two more days and commence on drawings of vertebrae or go to the AMNH and begin there. On the eighth, Hatcher asked Prentice to start on Yale's ceratopsian vertebrae at one-quarter natural size after finishing the skull drawings, then do the drawings of Skull No. 2 (YPM VP 1821) and illustrations of the juvenile ceratopsian specimen. He also recommended, "Do not hesitate to take a half day off when you like either to witness some of the foot-ball games or to enjoy the magnificent scenery with which New Haven is surrounded. To my mind it is the most beautiful city in our country." Hatcher also wrote Beecher to inform him of Prentice's schedule and request that Beecher help supervise the work, for which Hatcher would be most appreciative and provide an acknowledgment in his monograph. Beecher's covering of specimens prompted Osborn to request that Hatcher provide measurements of skull specimens so the exhibition work could be completed, and he assured Hatcher that he'd get credit for directing that part of the restoration.[53]

Following Eastman's suggestion, Hatcher moved quickly to open negotiations with Marcellin Boule, the director of the Musée d'Histoire Naturelle in Paris regarding an exchange of fossils from his museum for a cast of the Carnegie's *Diplodocus*:

> *I am especially desirous of securing a representative set of the Tertiary mammals of Europe, not so much for purposes of exhibition as for purposes of study and comparison with forms from the American Tertiaries. In your immense collections. . . . you doubtless have many duplicates which you could dispose of without in any way injuring your collections. I should also, if possible, like to secure a . . . series of such dinosaurian and other reptilian remains from European horizons.*[54]

Williston wrote Hatcher on the ninth to reassure him that he wasn't offended that Hatcher had contradicted his earlier notions of the stratigraphic and faunal relationships between the Judith and the Laramie, quipping, "I have known you too long and too well to be lightly offended at criticism. I long ago made a rule, not to reply to criticism, until the subject under discussion came about in the natural course of my work, and then I usually forgot about it!" He was sure Hatcher was correct but implored him to discuss the details of the Laramie stratigraphy, not just the paleontology. He also informed Hatcher that, as foreseen, he was no longer connected with the Field Museum, bemoaning that vertebrate paleontology would not prosper there "so long as the department is subordinated to geology and in charge of one who knows no more of the subject than he does of the biology of the moon." Hatcher commiserated with his mentor's plight at the Field on the fourteenth and penned an extensive proclamation regarding the regional stratigraphy in Montana, Wyoming, and Alberta. He felt certain, based on his observations, that the Laramie occupied a position below the Tertiary Fort Union Formation and above the Cretaceous, Fox Hills Formation. There was a forty-foot-thick interval of sandstone at the base of the Laramie that was barren in vertebrate fossils but contained what Stanton thought was a brackish water invertebrate fauna typical of the Laramie. Underlying the Fox Hills was the dark gray shale of the Cretaceous marine Bearpaw Shale, which Hatcher felt was a stratigraphic equivalent of the Pierre Shale. The Judith River beds lay below the Bearpaw/Pierre Shale. Buttressing his conclusion was the following observation:

> . . . in central Montana it is possible to pass within a few miles and in a region quite undisturbed by inconformities or faults from the Judith River beds up through the overlying Pierre or Bearpaw shales through the Fox Hill sandstones and into the Laramie beds very similar both lithologically and faunally to the Congress County beds.

That is still the sequence of rock units that geologists and paleontologists recognize to be correct today, and Hatcher elaborated on his thoughts regarding these and other related stratigraphic problems in a paper he published in the *American Geologist* in 1903. More specifically in terms of geologic time, the Judith River Formation of Montana is now recognized to range in age from about 78 to 75 million years ago. In Alberta, the stratigraphically equivalent geologic unit is called the Belly River Group, which has been split into three formations: the Foremost at the base, the Oldman in the middle, and the Dinosaur Park at the top. Collectively, these three formations also range in age from about 79 to 74 million years ago. Above the Judith River Formation in Montana and the Belly River Group in Alberta lies the Bearpaw Formation, beds of dark gray marine shale that range in age from about 74 to 69 million years ago and represent a time during which the seaway that cut through the middle of North America expanded to cover the terrestrial floodplain sediments represented by the Judith River Formation and the Belly River group. But about 69 million years ago that seaway began to recede, as evidenced by the sandy beach bars represented by the Fox Hills Formation. Then by about 67 or 68 million years ago, the terrestrial floodplain sediments of the Hell Creek and Lance Formations, which Hatcher referred to as the "Laramie" Formation, were deposited in Montana and Wyoming until around 66 million years ago.[55]

Utterback regretfully closed out his season by October 13, knowing there was much more just waiting to be gleaned from the ground. He'd taken out a tibia and five femora, two of which were both four feet three inches long with "one being heavy and massive and the other quite the contrary." The tibia was associated with several other bones running into the bank, and another spot sported a sacrum with twenty other vertebrae extending into sandstone. In all, they'd tallied sixteen crates weighing 3,500 pounds around Musselshell. His crates in Clearmont weighed 8,865 pounds. With Douglass's collection, there were eighty-two crates weighing 20,445 pounds: thirty-two boxes of Judith River, twenty-one of Douglass's Tertiary fossils, and twenty-nine of Utterback's Jurassic plunder. With that, Utterback sent the load on its way on the twenty-first and headed off to visit his ill father before returning to Pittsburgh. Hatcher was greatly pleased.[56]

Correspondence between Hatcher and George P. Merrill, head curator of geology at the Smithsonian's NMNH in Washington, D.C., establishes that an agreement was struck for Charles Gilmore to work at the NMNH to prepare fossil material housed there for Hatcher's horned dinosaur monograph. The USNM would contribute $60 per month, while the Carnegie would pitch in $30. Hatcher also consoled his young field hand A. C. Silberling, upon learning from him that the dinosaur prospect that Silberling thought would be valuable turned out to be a bust. Hatcher wrote, "This is one of the everyday occurrences we have to contend with." Hatcher further corresponded with Beecher at Yale to pass along directions for his illustrator Prentice and inform Beecher that he'd spend most of November at Yale, during which he hoped Beecher could "secure for me a ticket to the Yale-Princeton football game."[57]

Also seeking to enhance the Carnegie's collection was none other than his first field crew leader, Charles H. Sternberg, who wrote Hatcher beginning early November to alert him that he would be happy to send Hatcher a list of the specimens he currently had for sale, especially fossils from the Cretaceous Niobrara Formation in Kansas. However, Hatcher gently rebuffed Sternberg's approach by clearly stating that although he'd be glad to receive a copy of Sternberg's catalogue, the high cost of his specimens would fund a field party's work "for from four to five months, in which time we usually secure one or more skeletons sufficiently complete for mounting, besides much more good material." Their correspondence would continue throughout December, with Hatcher expressing interest in purchasing a specimen of the titanic marine turtle called *Protostega* if funds allowed, but he still felt Sternberg's price was too high.[58]

Today, the catalogue for the Carnegie collections records 256 specimens attributed to Hatcher and his crew for the 1903 season. Hatcher chipped in one dinosaur specimen from the king of all predators, *Tyrannosaurus*, one specimen of the soft-shelled turtle *Trionyx*, and, with help from Utterback, the enormous alligator *Deinosuchus* from the 78- to 75-million-year-old strata of the Judith River Formation, while Peterson stayed to work in the lab.

Utterback's own odyssey unearthed thirty-seven dinosaur fossils from the 150-million-year-old rock layers of the Morrison Formation, including specimens of the long-necked, herbivorous sauropods *Diplodocus, Camarasaurus, Haplocanthosaurus,* and *Apatosaurus,* now called *Brotosaurus* by some paleontologists, as well as the astounding carnivore *Allosaurus*. Utterback also tallied a specimen of the titanic tortoise *Basilemys* from the 78- to 75-million-year-old Judith River Formation, and a duckbill dinosaur called *Edmontosaurus* from the 66-million-year-old outcrops of the Hell Creek Formation.

Gilmore not only garnered two dinosaur specimens of the sauropod *Apatosaurus* and the plated *Stegosaurus* from the Morrison Formation but also a nifty set of six giant marine monitor lizards called mosasaurs, such as *Mosasaurus, Platycarpus, Clidastes,* and *Tylosaurus,* as well as nineteen specimens of the flying pterosaur *Pteranodon* from the 87- to 82-million-year-old chalk beds of the Niobrara Formation, along with a specimen of the enormous carnivorous fish *Xiphactinus* and a specimen of the mullet fish *Syllaemus.*

Douglass dug out one shell of *Basilemys* from the Judith River Formation, as well as seventy-nine mammals, two tortoises, and a lizard from the 37- to 34-million-year-old beds of the Renova Formation, representing the opossum-like marsupial *Peratherium;* the "scaly anteater" *Epoicotherium;* the small insectivorous placental *Ictops;* the shrew-like *Micropternodus;* the rodents *Paradjidaumo, Cylindrodon, Pseudocylindrodon, Ardynomys,* and *Ischyromys;* the rabbit *Palaeolagus;* the small primitive bear *Parictis;* the carnivorous creodont *Hyaenodon;* the tapir *Colodon;* the rhinos *Trigonias* and *Hyracodon;* the brontotheres *Megacerops* and "*Menodus,*" now called *Megacerops;* the horse *Mesohippus;* the clawed herbivorous ungulate *Agriochoerus;* the oreodonts *Bathygenys, Limentes,* and *Oreonetes;* the deer-like *Hendryomeryx;* the tortoise *Testudo;* and the lizard *Glyptosaurus.* Douglass also collected four mammal specimens from the 30- to 19-million-year-old Cabbage Patch Formation, consisting of the pocket gopher *Gregorymys;* the oreodonts *Ticholeptus* and *Merychyus;* and the small "bear dog" *Temnocyon,* as well as two fossils of the oreodont *Promerycochoerus* from the 16- to 12.5-million-year-old sediments of the Deep River Formation and six specimens of *Promerycochoerus, Ticholeptus,* the antelope-like *Merycodus,* and one bird track with incomplete field data. Thus, despite limited help in the field from Hatcher, his crew chipped in with a superlative set of fossils that greatly enhanced the Carnegie collection.

Hatcher's research contined to burgeon as eleven more articles were printed and bound during 1903. Topics ranged from the discoveries about dinosaurs, including "Astrodon," *Haplocanthosaurus,* and *Diplodocus,* to the age and geologic position of the "Belly River beds" as well as the Judith River and Lance Formations. (See Hatcher bibliography)

17

The Curtain Closes

atcher continued his research on ceratopsians at Yale through November 1903. It's clear that he planned to stay into December to finish his work there, but that did not play out as planned. On December 3, Hatcher intimated to Charles Beecher, "On my arrival home . . . I found that our youngest girl was down with scarlet fever, the oldest has since been taken [sick] with the same disease." It's tragically certain that the holiday season was not a happy one; the family records document that John Bell and Anna's second daughter, Ruth, who was born in the Pittsburgh area two years earlier, tragically passed away on December 14. She was the third of the Hatcher's seven children to perish before reaching the age of four. A letter of condolence came from F. von Iterson of Princeton, who, in addition to noting that Scott intended to study the Patagonian rodents as soon as he finished his work shortly on the sloths, also commiserated, "I regret very much the misfortune that has befallen you but such is life. The Lord has given and the Lord has taken as the scripture has it. I hope you and Mrs. Hatcher and your other children are well and may you be spared for many many a year from further loss." Henry Fairfield Osborn also sent condolences, writing, "I regret to learn . . . of the sad loss which has befallen you in the death of your youngest daughter. I sympathize with you warmly."[1]

By early December, Eastman had returned from Europe and wrote Hatcher regarding other specimens that he'd purchased from an Italian collection and shipped to the Carnegie, which the Carnegie might or might not purchase. Hatcher responded that since it wasn't clear who would eventually purchase these specimens, it would have been better to ship them to Eastman's museum at Harvard so that Harvard could have paid the shipping costs. This tiff continued throughout December until New Year's Day, 1904, when Hatcher berated Holland for his alleged lack of discretion in recent conversations with Eastman:"During my conversation with Dr. Eastman yesterday afternoon he informed me that you told him yesterday that I was afraid you would discharge me to make room for him & you have on two occasions implied as much during your conversations with me." Hatcher felt wronged and feared Eastman would spread that information. Hatcher also claimed he had no such fears and had always "honestly endeavored to advance in every way possible the best interests of that department over which I was placed in charge," citing the growth of the staff and collections, as well as work on the exhibitions and research—all aspects of his tenure for which he harbored *"a certain feeling of pride."* Finally, he lectured Holland about keeping such matters within the "family" and requested that Holland withdraw his statement.[2]

In a follow-up on the eighth, Eastman informed Hatcher that he was pleased with the arrangements the two had worked out for working on the Bayet collection, and he trusted all the acrimony had been put behind them. Eastman also indicated that there was no chance he would give up his position at Harvard to replace Hatcher, and he didn't think Holland would ever seriously consider such an action. Exchanges of correspondence between Hatcher and Eastman continued throughout January, with Hatcher going so far as to "decline to continue any further intercourse" with Eastman.[3]

Hatcher was, for the most part, more magnanimous with his staff in recommending that Holland raise the monthly salaries of Sydney Prentice, Earl Douglass, and Charles Gilmore to $75; Louis Coggeshall to $65; and A. S. Coggeshall to a whopping $110. In order to maintain the same level of staff funding needed during 1903, Hatcher recommended that another employee, Norman Boss, be encouraged to seek employment elsewhere.[4]

Hatcher also wrote Sternberg on January 5 to thank his colleague, with whom he'd begun work "nearly twenty years ago," for the photos of the specimens Sternberg sent. However, Hatcher indicated that the Carnegie would be unable to purchase any of Sternberg's "very desirable" fossils, in large part because Hatcher already had "over 700 boxes of unpacked material now in storage, and with our present space for exhibitions crowded to the utmost it does not seem advisable to purchase anything further until such time as our new building is more nearly completed. . . ." Nonetheless, Hatcher and Holland eventually agreed that they should pusue the possibility of purchasing Sternberg's specimens of the gigantic fish "Portheus," now called *Xiphactinus*, as well as the leviathan, leatherback, marine turtle called *Protostega*. Accordingly, Hatcher set out for Kansas to see what he might be able to acquire for a sum of $1,000. He was successful in obtaining both, although Sternberg lamented that he had to bear the cost of crating the specimens for shipment. All in all, Sternberg stated, "I wish to congratulate you on securing from me more in actual value than any other museum in America."[5]

Also, Hatcher rang in the New Year with a complaint to Osborn that Osborn had offended both him and his coauthor on the paper regarding the Judith River beds:

> *I feel that you have been unjust to both Dr. Stanton & myself & I know that others think so. One correspondent has characterized your recent note in 'Science' as a "deliberate attempt to belittle my work on the Judith River beds & to entirely ignore that of Dr. Stanton." While I am unwilling to believe that you deliberately intended to deprive either of us of the just credit for our work, yet I think you have nonetheless done us both a decided injustice, in*

*taking for yourself the lion's share of the credit . . . in connection
with it. I hope this was quite unintentional on your part & I shall
be pleased to receive an assurance from you that you are willing to
so amend your note in 'Science' as to accord to us full recognition
for the results of our investigations. . . .*

Osborn responded by stating "regret" that Hatcher felt Osborn did him
"injustice" in a note Osborn had published in *Science* regarding the fieldwork Hatcher had done with Stanton. Osborn defended himself on the
eleventh, maintaining that what he wrote was in no way meant to either
minimize the work of Hatcher and Stanton or overstate the contribution
that Osborn had made to that research topic. He concluded:

*Throughout the report . . . I make more reference to you than to any
other paleontologist or geologist. In public and in private . . . I have
always given you the warmest possible backing. I have repeatedly
urged Yale University to give you a degree; in fact, I have always
backed you up to the utmost of my ability, and always intend to
do so. . . .*

But Hatcher refused to accept Osborn's claim that he had written the
notice in *Science* based "verbatim" on an earlier version of the report that
Hatcher had already approved. Hatcher also maintained that he would have
conducted the fieldwork regarding the stratigraphic position of the Judith
River beds whether or not Osborn had proposed coordinating that work
with the USGS. Hatcher also reported that three prominent geologists
had characterized Osborn's note as "extremely egoistic" and "a shameful
injustice," as well as an attempt to belittle Hatcher's work. Consequently,
Hatcher informed Osborn that he intended to clarify in detail and in print
who was responsible for contributing to the solution of the Judith River
problem and "I may just as well say now that I do not think that [one of]
those persons was [you] as the reader of your report in Science would certainly be led to believe." Hatcher then summed up: "I . . . will henceforth
look upon it as a simple difference of opinion between two parties perfectly
friendly to one another." For his part, Osborn, who still felt that the harsh

statements of his "geological friends" were "utterly without foundation," nonetheless promised to send Hatcher drafts of Osborn's comments on Hatcher's work before they were published to avoid similar problems in the future.[6]

Seemingly to balance the scales in this brouhaha, Osborn wrote on the eighteenth to protest that Hatcher had claimed in one of his memoirs on sauropods that Osborn thought sauropods were "aquatic reptiles." Osborn elaborated, "The fact that an animal spends part of the time in the water does not make it aquatic. Both in my description of Diplodocus and in the restoration of Brontosaurus I have represented them as land animals which made occasional incursions into the water." In response, after quoting the passage on page 213 of Osborn's memoir on *Diplodocus* that led to the offending statement, Hatcher assured Osborn that he would amend his statement in print as soon as possible, which, rather pointedly, was what he had hoped Osborn would do regarding the Judith River research. In addition, Osborn was having parts of the *Diplodocus* tail called chevrons molded so that the Carnegie could use them in constructing their skeletal mount of the animal, as well as one of the front feet so that the Carnegie could replicate it.[7]

In other business, Viktor Uhlig of Vienna wrote to thank Hatcher for the cast of the *Diplodocus* limb, which he admitted was extremely precious and more valuable than anything he'd sent in exchange—a fact he insisted he'd rectify in the future. Also, Holland wrote to R. A. Franks, a Carnegie associate in the Home Trust Company, thanking him for the notice that Carnegie had instructed him to renew his appropriation for the museum's paleontological work during 1904. With only $400 left in the fund, Holland requested that a check be sent as soon as possible to cover the $10,000 donation so he could pay the upcoming salaries due the staff. In addition, Holland requested another check of $2,000 to continue work on the *Diplodocus* mount, which Carnegie had pledged to support separately from the monies required for paleontological research. Currently, the fund for the *Diplodocus* mount stood at $240, because Holland had used $1,500 of it to purchase the Bayet collection, and Holland needed the additional $2,000 to pay the salaries for the five staff members expediting work on the mount. Intent on defending his frugality, Holland added,

I hope to accomplish this task for less than I suggested to Mr. Carnegie that it would cost. He authorized me to expend as much money as might be necessary, and our original estimate led me to suppose that it would cost anywhere from $7,500. to $10,000. to do the work. I hope to accomplish the work for a smaller figure and make not merely one, but five replicas of the original, as Mr. Carnegie suggested.

But he quickly cautioned Franks to keep those plans for more replicas a secret because Carnegie didn't want anyone to know of them. They would be produced on the sly, so "Mr. Carnegie may be in a position to honor some other institution besides the British Museum, at a later date, with the gift. . . ."[8]

Consequently, quite a kerfuffle ensued in mid-January, when Holland received a letter from Carnegie documenting that Director Boule of the Paris museum had written Carnegie requesting a *Diplodocus* mount in exchange for other material, as Hatcher had proposed. Incensed, Holland insisted he had "enjoined absolute silence" regarding the possible production of more than one replica, except for the paleontological staff that was making them. Holland informed Carnegie:

It turns out now upon investigation that two of my subordinates . . . have been corresponding with M. Boule, forgetting my injunction . . . and that [replicas] are held here subject to your order and disposition and not . . . to be used in exchange. I have admonished the offenders . . . and have informed them that acting under my prerogative as Director of the Museum I shall require them hereafter to submit to me for perusal and advice all correspondence that relates to this property, which is yours. I regret very much that in spite of my oft repeated and express injunction to maintain strict secrecy there should have been an indiscreet communication to others of the possibility of our duplicating the specimens. . . .[9]

Holland then wrote Boule to explain that those corresponding with him did not have the authority to write him and say "that a duplicate cast of

Diplodocus Carnegie [sic] is being prepared besides that destined as a gift to the British Museum." For, at that time, no such decision had been made. Yet, Holland emphasized,

> *The reproduction which is being made is being prepared in response to the suggestion of King Edward VII of England, and is intended by Mr. Carnegie to be his personal gift to the British Museum. Of course it may be that at some time . . . in the future Mr. Carnegie might instruct me to make another reproduction. . . . The matter is wholly in Mr. Carnegie's hands. I shall, however, respecting Mr. Carnegie's wish . . . place your communication in my file, and should our kind patron . . . see fit to order another replica made for the Museum in Paris, I shall be only too happy to comply. . . . and would deem this Museum honored by being permitted to place one of these wonderful reproductions under the roof of the magnificent Museum which you represent. . . .*[10]

Holland wrote Carnegie again in early March to say he and the staff were starting to look forward to having a new, larger building, for which construction was beginning. Hatcher hoped to complete the *Diplodocus* mount in August if Holland could find a large enough facility in which to assemble it. Holland hoped to secure an adequate space through Pittsburgh's Exposition Society so that the mount could be completed and set up in England sometime in September. Although the size of individuals and different species vary, the skeleton reveals that *D. carnegii* was about ninety feet long and stood about fifteen feet high at the hips. Thus, Holland cautioned, "I may not succeed in this, but we are working to this end and are getting along as rapidly as could be expected. One half at least of the work is done, and I think the most difficult half. But it is very tedious."[11]

Toward the end of February, Hatcher forthrightly wrote Florentino Ameghino to emphasize that in his geologic paper regarding the Pyrotherium beds, Hatcher had followed Ameghino in placing those beds in the Cretaceous, although "at the same time expressing a doubt as to their being of Cretaceous age." Hatcher went on to admit that he had been mistaken on another point:

Since the publication of my first paper it has been clearly shown that for the most part, at least the Pyrotherium beds and the fauna which you at first described as characterizing it, undoubtedly underlies the Patagonian formation, and there is no doubt but that I erred in considering some of the forms described by you as from the Pyrotherium beds as being the descendants or related forms in the Santa Cruzian formation. From what I can learn of the invertebrate fauna of the Pyrotherium beds, proper, and of the stratigraphic position of these beds it appears to me that there can be no reasonable doubt as to their Eocene age.

Hatcher once again implored Florentino and his brother Carlos to join him on a field trip during which they could see the key sites together in order to "come to a perfect understanding of the more important questions now in dispute between us." Hatcher hoped to conduct that expedition in the fall of 1904.[12]

Gilmore, who was working in a jointly funded position at the Smithsonian, apparently wrote Hatcher to intimate that the Smithsonian might hire him full-time, to which Hatcher responded that although he would "hate extremely" to lose Gilmore, Hatcher "could not for a moment think of standing in the way of you or any other of the men in my department, if they had an opportunity of bettering their position." Gilmore returned similar compliments on March 24, expressing his appreciation for the interest Hatcher had always shown him and adding that he'd told his mother, "If Mr. Hatcher was my father I could not ask him to do more for me than he has done since I have been connected with [his] department." In addition, Gilmore's preparation of the *Triceratops* skulls Hatcher needed for his monograph was proceeding in good order. By the twenty-sixth, Hatcher had heard from Merrill that the NMNH wanted to hire Gilmore full-time until July 1. Hatcher told Gilmore that was probably being done to alleviate the need for Gilmore to take a Civil Service examination before they hired him permanently.[13]

Hatcher's habit of paying promptly for the artwork in his publications paid off with another of his illustrators, R. Weber, who wrote on January 13 that he'd finished his drawings early because he'd set aside his work for the AMNH, since they hadn't paid yet, and taken up Hatcher's work. Beyond that, he gave Hatcher a discount for his financial punctuality. Hatcher also engaged the legendary paleontological artist Charles R. Knight to do a painting showing *Triceratops*, "Hadrosaurus," and *Dryptosaurus* both to hang in the exhibition hall and support Hatcher's pertinent publications, including the Ceratopsia monograph. Knight wrote initially on March 29 to accept the commission, provided Hatcher supplied the necessary help and data required. He suggested that he'd make a colored sketch to start, then after any issues regarding the animals and composition were worked out, he'd produce the final painting. If major changes were requested to the original, he'd charge for the time needed to make them, but minor changes would be done for no extra cost. He was familiar with *Triceratops* and "Hadrosarus," but he would need a good deal of advice and data for *Dryptosaurus*, and he asked Hatcher up front if he had preferences regarding the color of the animals. Hatcher responded that he hoped the painting could be completed by June 15 and directed Knight to have the *Dryptosaurus* partially concealed by Laramie plants, such as palmettos, "since our ignorance regarding structure is dense." By the end of April, Knight was ready to proceed and suggested making several sketches with varied compositions from which Hatcher could choose. He requested more data and rough sketches showing the proportions of *Triceratops* and *Dryptosaurus*, as well as more information on the flora, and he advised Hatcher that the image would be much more effective if it was in color. By early May, Hatcher had decided to ditch *Dryptosaurus* and substitute another *Triceratops*, which Knight felt made a better picture. The canvas was forty inches by twenty inches, making, in Knight's view, "a very long picture, but you of course have reasons for doing it."[14]

On March 22, Yale's fossil turtle specialist, George Wieland, wrote Hatcher that he'd heard from Sternberg that the Carnegie had purchased his specimen of the giant Cretaceous marine turtle *Protostega*. Wieland strongly endorsed that transaction and informed Hatcher on the sly that Hay had been pursuing a chance to publish on Yale's fossil turtles. To turn the tables on Hay, Wieland requested the opportunity to study Hatcher's newly acquired *Protostega* because, as Wieland confided, "I feel like paying him in his own coin if I get a chance."[15]

The 1904 field season started at the end of April, with Utterback checking in from near Warren, Wyoming, while he was "gathering up some of the odds and ends discovered the past season." He planned to open up some quarries as soon as the weather warmed. Apparently amused by a story in the *Pittsburgh Chronicle-Telegraph* about the Carnegie Library staff objecting to the eyesore created by the construction of the museum's new building, he advised Holland, "Ask them to vacate building entirely, and we'll build up a museum to the Queen's taste." Meanwhile, subsequent to their meeting in New York, Hatcher was recruiting Theodore Olcott to join Peterson's party in northwest Nebraska and southwest South Dakota from about May 15 to October 15 for $40 per month. Hatcher suggested Olcott come to Pittsburgh for a few days beforehand so he could meet Peterson, under whose supervision he'd serve, and accompany him to the field.[16]

In early May, Arthur Smith Woodward of the British Museum wrote Hatcher in agreement that the head and neck of the *Diplodocus* mount should be raised a little. He also approved of the forelimb posture as shown in Hatcher's published restoration.[17]

Utterback had moved on to Musselshell, Montana, by May 24, when he reported he'd been all over to the north and northeast for sixty miles without finding more Judith River beds other than those on Willow Creek and those they'd worked the previous year. He would camp fifteen miles east of Musselshell, but he noted that he'd found Laramie beds near Junction that had yielded a large portion of two ceratopsian skulls. He expected Silberling shortly and hired another local to help. Hatcher was delighted with the news of possible ceratopsians and directed Utterback to return there to prospect if the Judith exposures proved unproductive. The *Diplodocus* mount for the British Museum was taking shape at the Exposition building, and Hatcher expected it to be completed by the first of July. In early June, Utterback had managed to take out a sacrum with the ischium and ilium of the same skeleton, along with sixteen dorsal vertebrae and six associated ribs. Silberling also excavated the rest of the caudal vertebrae for specimen CM 2394, about twenty in all. These were presumably duckbills or hadrosaurs, of which Utterback is credited in the Carnegie catalogue with collecting more than a dozen from 1903 to

1904. But their prospecting had turned up nothing more, and Utterback planned to head for the Laramie to find the coveted *Triceratops* skull, "and failing shall quit the bone business forever."[18]

At the end of May, Peterson secured horses in Harrison, Nebraska, and prospected in the Gering Formation, finding only a "rotten" turtle. He didn't expect much success in the "lower beds" but had met with better success in the upper Monroe Creek beds, collecting three oreodont skulls along with partial skeletons for two of them. He'd also tallied two lower jaws of a small dog, two jaw fragments of a larger dog, and jaw fragments of a camel, possibly of the "bear dogs" *Delotrochanter, Daphenodon,* or *Ysengrinia,* and the camel, *Stenomylus* or *Oxydactylus.* A week later, he returned to where he'd found his *Promerycochoerus* oreodonts and found another just five to eight feet away. He requested a sketch or photo of his specimens at Pittsburgh so he could orient the new one in position relative to the earlier ones he'd found. Hatcher sent the drawing and was pleased with Peterson's news. Although he hoped for better luck in the Gering, Hatcher directed Peterson to focus on the underlying and overlying strata after prospecting the Gering for a week.[19]

Holland penned a letter to Carnegie on June 10, in which, after a paragraph of unaldulterated, obsequious drivel, he informed his patron that he'd notified the British Museum that the *Diplodocus* mount would be completed by July 15, so they needed to make arrangements for shipping it to London, where it would be assembled free of cost. The staff was now assembling the armature for the mount in the main building of the Western Pennsylvania Exposition Society, which had provided the space for free, and Holland was enraptured with it, especially since he was convinced it was better than the mount Osborn was erecting at the AMNH:

> *This framework I wish to say is in my judgment a very great advance upon anything of the kind that has heretofore been made. Very little iron-work will be visible, and we will avoid the unsightly and cumbrous mass of scaffolding which appears in the restoration of some of these skeletons. The beast turns out to be between 84 and 85 feet long from the tip of the nose to the tip of the tail, when the vertebral column is laid down horizontally. When*

mounted, of course, with the necessary graceful curvature which belongs to the mounted skeleton, the length is diminished, so that it covers on the floor a length of only about 78 or 80 feet. The whipcord tail adds considerably to the length, but Hatcher swears that as three tails have now been found with the bones in position and all tapering out as is the case here, that we are quite right in putting on this long tail. . . . My friend Osborn is mounting an object in plaster of Paris at the American Museum of Natural History which he calls the restoration of the skeleton of Brontosaurus. We have enough material to set up a skeleton of Brontosaurus also. When we get our Brontosaurus up it will be a very different looking thing from the caricature which one of these days you may see mounted at the American Museum. Brontosaurus was a heavier beast that [sic] Diplodocus, but it was not nearly so long. It was clumsier in shape. The trouble with Osborn is that he does not possess enough in certain portions of the frame to allow him to put the thing up as it ought to be, and he is going upon his imagination—a very dangerous thing to do in science.[20]

Knight had finished the *Triceratops* painting by the thirteenth and sent Hatcher the bill. Hatcher was curious about what Knight had done with it, but he suspected Knight had dropped it off at the Smithsonian for photographing. He promised to mail Knight's check in a few days.[21]

Despite travels to Washington, Hatcher remained in close touch with his crews through the rest of June, expressing delight with Utterback's success on the fourteenth and again endorsing his notion for striking out for the Laramie if prospects in the Judith dried up. Utterback had done just that by the twenty-sixth, informing Hatcher from Miles City that he'd left the Judith crates at Custer Station between Billings and Miles City and had been combing exposures between the Missouri and Yellowstone Rivers for two weeks without any significant success. Persistence failed to pay off, as Utterback lamented on July 1:

Never have I seen better fields for fossils or met with more encouragement than we have since starting in the Laramie. We can find everything from large skulls to the smallest of bones yet can find nothing worth saving. You must not think we are going over the ground hastily or leaving anything of value. We work each stream systematically and thoroughly satisfy ourselves before leaving a locality. . . .

We are at present prospecting down Powder river toward Terry. About 50 miles down the river from here a party found some very fine bones and brought them to Miles City where I saw them.

Unless he is like all Montanians [sic], *good liars, bones must be plentiful in that locality. If we find nothing in this section of the country am ready to vote Montana on the bum in the fossil line.*

He sought Hatcher's advice regarding his next move, cautioning that if he headed back toward Musselshell, he'd be retracing over ground recently covered by both Carnegie and AMNH crews, while if he headed for Wyoming, he'd be moving away from the rail line on which he was to return.[22]

Peterson reported continued success in the Lower Loup Fork beds around Harrison on the thirtieth and planned to move on toward Vantassle and the Reservation. He was apparently suffering from an intestinal ailment that required him to eat oatmeal and syrup rather than greasy camp cooking.[23]

But Hatcher was in no position to immediately respond to these reports, for as Holland wrote Peterson on July 1:

I dare say that you have been advised ere this of the fact that Mr. Hatcher is ill with typhoid fever. He was taken to the hospital a few days ago, and, I understand, is very sick, though not according to accounts in iminent [sic] *danger. Of course the crisis of the disease has not yet been reached, and it is impossible at this time to make any prognosis as to the results of his case, as I am informed by the authorities of the hospital. He was somewhat run down before he was taken sick, having been exerting himself very strenuously, and this is of course to a certain extent against him. However, he naturally has, as you know, a constitution which seems, in spite of the*

hardships to which he has exposed himself, to be able to resist, and
I trust that he may make a full and speedy recovery. Meanwhile,
while he is ill and unable to attend to his work, you had better com-
municate with me directly in reference to any matters that require
attention here at this end of the line.[24]

When Hatcher had first felt ill, Holland had ordered him to go home
and rest, but Hatcher had refused. There had been too much work to
do. He'd still been suffering a few days later, and Holland had again
insisted that Hatcher return home to bed. Feigning acceptance, Hatcher
had complied, but despite his 102 degree fever, he'd snuck back into the
museum that evening and locked himself in his office to keep working.
On into July, Hatcher had persisted with his work, while joking about
his sickness and willfully ignoring his doctor's directives. Finally, with
Hatcher's strength nearly spent, his doctor had ordered him loaded into
an ambulance and sent to the hospital. Holland visited him on Friday,
July 2, and checked on his condition, which the doctor determined to be
serious but not critical. Then Holland left on a long-scheduled trip to St.
Louis. Upon his return on Wednesday, July 6, he learned that Hatcher
had passed the previous Sunday night, July 3. Holland had just missed
the funeral and burial on Wednesday afternoon.[25]

18

Woe and Wrangling
in the Wake

As Hatcher lay terminally ill on July 1, Osborn and W. D. Matthew completed and shipped the first cast from their *Diplodocus* skull to Holland for the Carnegie mount, which had required a good deal of meticulous preparation in order to combine the fragments into one, light piece. Matthew sent his best wishes to Hatcher for a quick recovery, assuming the ailment resulted from "his old enemy, rheumatism."[1]

On July 4 Peterson received a telegram from Anna regarding Hatcher's death. He immediately wrote Holland the next day:

> *Last night late a telegram was brought out to my camp with the very sad news that Mr. Hatcher is dead. I just got in. Have wired Mrs. Hatcher and take this oportunity [sic] to reply on your favor*

of July 1st which I just got on to days [sic] *mail. I am extremely sorry to learn that Hatcher should depart, not only from his poor wife and children, but from what we might say a started career on a most nobel* [sic] *work, and that, at the prime of his life.*

It will now [necessitate] *be changes which will effect evry* [sic] *one conserned* [sic] *in the department. I have accordingly desided* [sic] *to close up my work here as soon as I can and come back to Pittsburgh. I wish to be there, if for nothing else to try to console and help Mrs. Hatcher as much as I can. Should it become advisable I could come out later in the season, or, the work could be resumed again next spring.*

Peterson went on to note that he had just made "some very important discoveries" and had been about to write his brother-in-law about them.[2]

Having received Peterson's letter by the eighth, Holland responded with what must have seemed to Peterson to be, at least from a modern managerial and personnel perspective, a rather heartless epistle lacking in empathy, even though it appears to have been endorsed by Peterson's sister, Anna:

I received your letter this morning in which you stated that you had decided to cease work and come home in order to at least comfort your good sister, Mrs. Hatcher. Mr. Mellor and I were at Mr. Hatcher's residence this morning, at Mrs. Hatcher's request, and we talked over the matter carefully, and it seemed to us that in view of all the circumstances it was scarcely wise for you to stop work where you are, especially in view of the fact that you tell us you have made important discoveries, and come back here. In the first place while it is no doubt true that it would be a great comfort to your sister to have you with her, nevertheless there is very little that we can see that you could just at the present time do to assist, and Mr. Mellor and I, as well as your sister, think the best thing you can do under the circumstances is to remain where you are and carry on the work that you are doing with energy. Those of us who are here will do all in our power to straighten up Mr. Hatcher's affairs in such a way that the best results possible may be secured for his good wife and family, and steps will be taken as soon as possible to collect what is due him and to adjust his affairs in such a way that Mrs. Hatcher will know what there is for her and for her children in his estate. . . . In case at a later date it should be judged necessary that you should return we can arrange for it, but I doubt very much whether it would be wise for you to pull up stakes and come back now. That would sacrifice the good results which in your letter you say you are just on the eve of achieving. Utterback reports that thus far he has accomplished nothing throughout the season, and I should regret very much to have to report to Mr. Carnegie that neither party had succeeded in accomplishing anything this summer, which would certainly be the case if you were to come back here. I promise you that everything that can possibly be done to assist Mrs. Hatcher and her family will be done by ourselves, and we will leave no stone unturned to make the best out of the small estate which he has left, and the authorities of the Museum may be relied upon to act generously under the circumstances.

Until a successor to Prof. Hatcher is secured I shall act as the head of the Section of Paleontology in the Museum, and shall expect you to report to me everything just as you were in the habit of doing to Mr. Hatcher, and to keep me fully advised of all your movements and of your necessities. Mr. Hatcher sent you $200. not long ago, and I infer that you are not in immediate need of any money.

With very kind regards, and expressing full sympathy in view of all the circumstances . . .[3]

By July 6, news of Hatcher's death had begun to ricochet around within the paleontological community to the point where it reached Knight, who expressed shock at his "sudden and untimely death." Knight sought Holland's advice about what to do regarding the painting, which Hatcher had commissioned for his Ceratopsia volume at a cost of $200.[4]

Ironically, on July 8, Osborn composed a much more compassionate note to Peterson than Holland had:

I hasten to write you of my deep sorrow and sympathy in learning of the death of Hatcher. Just by chance I saw a notice of it in the Paris Herald *yesterday and was greatly shocked, for when I last saw him he was looking very well and was full of bright plans for the future.*

This is a great personal loss for I greatly admired Hatcher's scientific ability and enthusiasm, and always felt a fresh inspiration from talking to him.

It is a hard blow to American paleontology, to which Mr. Hatcher was making such splendid contributions following his many years of magnificent work in the field—he was certainly our greatest collector. It is especially sad to think of his dying in the beginning of what promised to be the brightest and most satisfactory period of his life—when people could see his work and recognize his ability.

I hope you will express to his poor wife and children my very heartfelt sympathy.

I return early in September to take up my work, and I shall always miss Hatcher.

Believe me, always,[5]

For Osborn to proclaim Hatcher to be paleontology's greatest collector is inherently intriguing; Osborn had an ace of his own in Barnum Brown, who had just discovered the first relatively complete remains of the most famous dinosaur in the world, *Tyrannosaur rex.* But at that point, Brown had barely begun his career, which would continue for more than another half century.

Like others, Utterback was blindsided by Hatcher's death when he learned of it on the eleventh. He immediately wrote Holland:

Your message received yesterday informing me of the death of Mr. Hatcher was a sad blow indeed. Having been the warmest of friends for many years and associated with him in this work under the most trying of circumstances I feel his loss more than words can express.

I had received no word from you of his illness therefore was unprepared for such painful news.

The loss to science and to our institution will never be fully realized until an attempt is made to replace the position he so ably filled.

Unfortunately, Utterback still had no prospecting success to report but remained hopeful.[6]

Following up with Holland, Peterson wrote again on the eleventh to relate that his discovery involved the "true nature" of *Daemonelix*, the corkscrews that had so long bedeviled paleontologists, because he had found the skeleton of an ancient beaver called *Palaeocastor* inside a *Daemonelix*. He urged Holland to have Douglass round up all the related literature and send it to him so that he could write a preliminary note to *Science* before any other parties could beat him to the punch and steal the glory from the Carnegie.[7]

But behind Holland's back, Peterson was also planning for a possible escape from the Carnegie's clutches, writing Charles Schuchert and G. P. Merrill, who now both worked at the Smithsonian, about the salary and qualifications for a position that was open there. He asked Schuchert to contact Osborn or Scott, not Holland, if references were needed; as he intimated to Schuchert, he knew "nothing as yet of what changes may take place in Pittsburgh since Hatcher's death and naturally [was] on the alert should things turn uncongenially there to necessitate making a change." Schuchert responded that since Hatcher's "lamented death," he had seen Hermann at the AMNH and told him the Smithsonian had had hopes of wooing Hatcher away from the Carnegie.[8]

Hermann told Schuchert that given the circumstances, it was imperative that the Smithsonian instead hire Peterson. Schuchert had already told that to Merrill, who, Schuchert knew, would welcome Peterson's application. The position was not yet for a curator but for a chief preparator to look after specimens both on exhibition and in the collections, including mounting, assisted by Gilmore, who had left the Carnegie for the Smithsonian. Later, some fieldwork would be involved. Research time would be limited, and the salary would be $1,500 per year with a month of vacation. Applicants would need to take the Civil Service exam, consisting of "Letter writing 5%, Practical questions 45%, Experience 25%, Samples of work 25%." Schuchert ended by asking if Peterson knew if anyone was writing an obituary for Hatcher because, if not, he would undertake to do so.[9]

Peterson next wrote Osborn to thank him for his letter of condolence, agreeing that it was a pity that Hatcher passed just as he began to "reap some genuine satisfaction and pleasure" from his many years of toiling in the field. Peterson bewailed the great loss to Anna and their children as well as to science, adding, "With considerable pleasure and satisfaction not to say [pride] I watched his steady onward march to distinction, well knowing that he now occupied a place where he could with undividing energy devote his whole ambition to his most cherished work. . . ." He related how learning of Hatcher's death by reading Anna's telegram on the night of the fourth had made him "dizzy," and he had wanted to return to Pittsburgh immediately. But Holland insisted he stay in the field and report to him, all of which made him confide to Osborn,

I have no heart to do work as I did formerly. Dr. Holland is no doubt favorably disposed toward me but I know that he is not capable of the sympathy a field man crave[s] in connection with palaeontology. Not knowing what is going on or what changes are taking place in the museum I am naturally on the alert for an other place as I may on my return find that a change will be necessary.[10]

Through the rest of July, Holland continued to receive condolences from friends, such as S. Harbert Hamilton of the New Jersey Geological Survey, who grieved both over the loss of Hatcher and the great burden his passing would place on Holland's "all ready crowded and fully occupied time." More importantly, a truly heartfelt testament arrived from Andrew Carnegie on the twenty-fifth from Skibo Castle in Scotland. Regarding the passing of Hatcher, Carnegie confided, "Hatchers death haunts me. We must see to his wife & children."[11]

Based on documents and correspondence still preserved in the Carnegie Museum's archives, it's clear that several steps were taken to assist Anna and the Hatcher children following John Bell's death. Holland's assistant, Douglas Stewart, assumed the role of administrator for Hatcher's estate on July sixteenth and apparently advanced some funds to Anna in order to carry the family through in the immediate aftermath of Hatcher's death. She responded, "It was certainly very kind of you to advance money for use, and I certainly feel very grateful to you. I am sorry I am putting you to so much trouble." Stewart kept a record of the credits and expenses that accrued after the death. In short, interest payments for the $3,500 mortgage on Hatcher's house, doctor and hospital bills, funeral expenses, attorney fees, and other charges from October 1904 through April 1905 totaled about $1,181, or about $32,200 in today's currency. In terms of assets, Hatcher had about $718 in his bank account when he died, and a $3,000 life insurance policy was redeemed on October 27. In addition, the museum, through a letter from Holland to Stewart, offered to purchase Hatcher's library of scientific books and articles for $1,000—a transaction that was completed in December. Along with other deposits recorded by Stewart, the estate's assets as of the end of 1904 totaled about $4,800 or around $127,000 in current dollars. It's not clear how the mortgage was paid off, but mention is made in correspondence of selling the house with Stewart's help. In any event, it is clear that Anna and the children—Earl, Harold, Alice, and John W.—moved from Pittsburgh to Lamont, Iowa, nearby Hatcher's parents. In an undated letter to Stewart, Anna optimistically reported, "Have rented a better place now and will move next week. It is only across the street and it has a barn and more ground so the boys will have some work to do in making a garden and raising chickens. We are all well and hope this may find you enjoying life."[12]

Meanwhile, Utterback had scurried back to the Musselshell region to try and salvage the season, but by July 24 had found nothing significant. They were now concentrating on the rugged drainages that emptied into the Missouri below the mouth of the Musselshell River, where there were abundant exposures of "Laramie," now called the Hell Creek Formation. He hoped to have better news soon. By entering the realm of Hell Creek, Utterback was following in the footsteps of Barnum Brown from the AMNH, who had pioneered paleontological collecting in the region two years before. His efforts had been spurred by the serendipitous discovery of a *Triceratops* horn garnered by a settler in the region, who was encountered by William T. Hornaday. Hornaday was the former chief taxidermist at the Smithsonian, who had assumed the role of director of the New York Zoological Park, now known as the Bronx Zoo, under the sponsorship of the AMNH's Henry Fairfield Osborn. In the spring of 1902, Hornaday ventured into the depths of the Hell Creek badlands with famed western photographer Laton A. Huffman to hunt and document the lifestyle of the blacktail deer; that's when Hornaday ran into the settler who had found the horncore. When Hornaday returned to New York, he showed the fossils to Osborn and Brown, which triggered a trip by Brown to the Missouri Breaks near Hell Creek just a few months later. It was during this expedition that Brown found the first scientifically described remains of *Tyrannosaurus rex* just a few miles from where the settler and Hornaday had collected the *Triceratops* horn. So Utterback had good reason to foresee success.[13]

Silberling would finish the season but not return to the Carnegie, since he had been offered the chance to assume supervision over his mother's ranch. Utterback intimated that Hatcher hadn't been terribly pleased with Silberling's prep work in the Carnegie lab and had given Utterback license to lay him off if his fieldwork didn't improve, which it hadn't. Unless Utterback could find something significant, he confided to Holland from Jordan, Montana, "I should like very much to bring this expedition to a close sending in my resignation at the same time. I have worked early and late hard and faithful the past two months however fate is against me."[14]

Peterson continued his summer of discontent by assuring Holland on the twenty-eighth that he was having "good success" and intended to leave for a new locality the next day. He expected to have almost two tons of fossils by the end of the season, but a whole boxcar wouldn't be required. On the same day, Merrill wrote to encourage Peterson to take the exam for the Smithsonian position in the fall, although he hoped paleontological efforts at the Carnegie would continue in the wake of Hatcher's passing. On the twenty-ninth, Schuchert wrote to let Peterson know that he'd welcome him in New Haven, where he was succeeding Hatcher's friend from Yale—the late Prof. Beecher, who had passed away in February. Schuchert and Peterson would talk in more detail about the position at the Smithsonian. Schuchert again expressed his desire to write a fitting obituary for Hatcher in Peterson's name, if Peterson and Anna would help by providing information about Hatcher's life and a bibliography of Hatcher's publications. That obituary was eventually published during 1905 under Schuchert's name in the journal *American Geologist*.[15]

At the start of August, Holland wrote a long letter to Peterson, which started by trying to clarify issues regarding whether Hatcher had sent Peterson's salary to him, since the details of the transactions had become confused with Hatcher's death. Holland next sought to clear up what exactly Peterson meant in terms of the actions he wanted Holland to take in reserving space in a railcar for the collection Peterson would ship. Then there was the issue of what to do with the camp outfit. Holland requested that Peterson provide him with a detailed description of the state of the horses and other equipment, adding in no uncertain terms:

You must not imagine because Mr. Hatcher is dead that the work of the Department of Paleontology at this Museum is going to end or that we shall not have need of your services and of the services of the entire staff. While we deplore Mr. Hatcher's death most deeply, you must understand that the work of this Museum goes on forever. I wish you to stay in the field and gather all the good material that you possibly can. I know you to be an eminently successful collector, and I do not think that an early return on account of Mr. Hatcher's death will mend matters at all. The more you collect this summer the better it will be both for the institution and for your own reputation. If you have good prospects and there is material that can be acquired that is needed in the Museum, get it. I prefer to have you stay in the field as long as there is any chance to do good work. I know that Professor Hatcher's death has necessarily to some extent unsettled your mind, but you need have no discouragement on that score. As long as I am satisfied with you and well pleased it makes no difference who is Professor Hatcher's successor. You are sure of your position. I am, as you are aware, the man who is to be satisfied.

As for Peterson's discoveries regarding *Daemonelix*, Holland indicated that he'd be happy to help Peterson prepare a manuscript in Peterson's name for submission to *Science*, since all such manuscripts had to be submitted to him as the museum's director before being sent to the editor of the journal. With that, Holland reiterated that he wished Peterson to remain in the field until the late summer or fall, as long as Peterson felt it was possible to acquire good material for their collections.[16]

Emerging from his collecting slump in early August, Utterback was most pleased to report to Holland, "During the past ten days have taken out an almost complete Ceratops skull as well as some good Claosaurus material." The eight-foot-long skull was slightly crushed, but the bone was solid and would make a good exhibition specimen. The missing portions could easily be filled in with parts of other skulls they'd collected. The snout was perfect, as were the dentitions in the upper jaws and one lower jaw. Beyond that, two local brothers named Sensiba had discovered a hadrosaur skeleton the previous year that included twenty-six feet of the backbone and might well yield a complete skeleton. They'd tried to sell it to many museums, including the AMNH, who had offered them $100 based on what was showing and $300 if the skull was found with it. Utterback hadn't had time to examine it himself, but members of other crews had and vouched for its legitimacy. Utterback thought that if Holland wanted to outbid the AMNH a bit, he could secure it for the Carnegie; he sought Holland's advice.[17]

On August 10, Peterson again tried to clarify for Holland his financial transactions with Hatcher shortly before Hatcher died. Peterson also confirmed that the letter Holland proposed to send the railway depot agent should be sufficient to secure part of a car for the fossils Peterson had collected. Regarding the disposition of the horses and camp outfit, Peterson seemed confused, if not miffed, as to Holland's wishes:

> *Your letter is in part pusseling* [sic] *to me and I hardly know whether to take it seriously or as a joke. I told you—without getting a reply—in an early letter or shortly after Mr. Hatchers death, that it was the understanding I had from him (Hatcher) to despose* [sic] *of the outfit when I got through with them this season as it*

was geting [sic] *rather old and worn out. By frankly telling you Mr. Hatchers* [sic] *and my own opinion in this case I hardly expected that my meaning should be misconstrued to the extent wich* [sic] *you seem to have taken it.*

Peterson lamented that his collection for the season was not as good as he had hoped it would be. The whole season had been "a trial," not only because of Hatcher's death but also because of the "dyspepsia" he'd been suffering, which had forced him to spend time in the hospital in Fort Robinson. As a result, he'd about decided to quit collecting for a while "and have taken steps accordingly," perhaps an oblique reference to his plan to apply for the Smithsonian position. Given the hardships he'd faced, he was resolute in defending his results:

So far as our institution, The Carnegie Museum is conserned [sic] *I can say that we have a magnificent collection from this locality which when worked up should be a pride to the Museum as well as to the collectors and preparators. I am glad to say that so far as I have been able to continue this summer, we have met with good success in fact I have done some of my best work this season notwithstanding my condition.*

With that, he thanked Holland for the support he had offered to help pull the *Daemonelix* manuscript together and informed his supervisor that he planned to close out the season shortly because of his ailment.[18]

Holland wrote back in an equally antagonistic tone on the thirteenth, having now gotten a grip on the financial situation, yet still prickly with Peterson regarding the condition of the camp outfit. Noting Peterson's previous presumption that Holland sounded like he wanted to keep the horses and equipment, Holland harangued:

Please do not "imagine" things, but comply with my requests. I asked you to give me a list of what we have & to tell me whether the horses &c. are too old to keep. . . . I am not "joking" but wish a plain business-like statement, so that I can decide what to do. . . .

*I do not "misconstrue" your meaning, & do not understand what
you mean in saying so. I asked you for information which I do not
possess & you will greatly oblige me by giving me the information
I ask for, to wit: a list of things in our outfit, with a report upon
their condition, & a statement as to whether they should be in your
judgment kept or sold.*

To soften his testy soliloquy a bit, he then expressed his sorrow that
Peterson wasn't well and advised him to take care, adding, "If you find
it impossible to go on with your work, why then of course you should
return."[19]

In rather stark contrast, Utterback was merrily upbeat in his update
to Holland on the tenth, having discovered another ceratopsian skull
"far superior to No. 1." It was "perfect in every respect" except for the
lack of lower jaws. At 6.5 feet in length and perfectly symmetrical,
it would make a superb specimen for exhibition, and Utterback was
taking every precaution in crating it by doing all the work himself. At
long last, he could celebrate, for "if I have accomplished nothing more
this season have found Laramie fields that we can draw upon another
season." Although Utterback claimed to have collected two skulls, only
one—CM 1221—currently exists in the Carnegie collection database.
As Utterback had hoped, it indeed made a fine exhibition specimen and
is still on display in the renovated fossil halls at the Carnegie. The fate
of Utterback's other skull is unclear. In other news, the skull for the
Sensibas' hadrosaur had been found at the end of the entire vertebral
column, but Barnum Brown was now on the scene and had offered the
brothers $300 for the specimen. Utterback was also disappointed that
Silberling was now demanding $50 per month in salary and fifteen days'
vacation. Utterback confided that he'd had other assistants who did better
work for $40 per month, but he'd leave the decision of whether to meet
Silberling's demands up to Holland. The weather was harsh and dry,
causing problems for the crew by forcing them to travel long distances
for water to sustain themselves and the horses.[20]

Peterson had left the field for New York by the eighteenth, apparently
wishing to recover there and gather more intelligence regarding the

Smithsonian job, although he hadn't been to the AMNH yet. It also gave him a chance to write the *Daemonelix* paper, if not avoid Holland's wrath a bit longer. He sent the manuscript, entitled "Facts and Discoveries of Daemonlix [sic]," to Holland with a request that he review it, and assured Holland that the loading process for the fossils had gone fine and he'd stored the camp outfit with a reliable local in Nebraska. By the twentieth, Holland had reviewed Peterson's paper, given it a "slightly better literary form," and sent it on to *Science*. Yet Holland was not yet ready to let the issue of the outfit go, again complaining,

> *You failed to realize, as is evident from your former letter, that I was in ignorance as to the condition of the horses and outfit, all matters in relation to these things having been left entirely to Mr. Hatcher. . . . If as you state in your letter the horses are too old we had better perhaps make arrangements even yet to sell them, but I will confer with you about these things when you get back to Pittsburgh.*

He hoped Peterson would recover soon and return in good health, where work awaited him. Peterson finally filed his report on the condition of the outfit on the twenty-first, after apologizing for the delay and stating that he preferred to have "no further controversy" about it, which seems to have put the matter to rest.[21]

As the drama between Holland and Peterson played out, Utterback's crew baked amidst the rugged ridges and ravines of Hell Creek, a tributary of the Missouri thirty-five miles north of Jordan, Montana, which was one hundred miles north of the rail line at Miles City. As Utterback told Holland,

> *I question very much if you would have enjoyed camp life with us the past month. Have been camped on Hell Creek and found it every-thing its name implies . . . bad water and other disagreeable features. This is one of the roughest parts of Mont and is an ideal fossil country providing there was water. . . . Many places we cannot prospect for want of it.*

The uncomfortable conditions were due in large part to the fact that it hadn't rained since early June. Nonetheless, they'd managed to collect the skull and transport it to Jordan, although they'd had to engage in extensive "road-building" to manage it. But Utterback deemed it a fine specimen, and he believed that a pair of lower jaws he had prepared over the winter would serve well in replacing the missing parts of this new skull. Although they had seen fifty skulls that had become exposed and badly eroded, he was puzzled about why no other bones of the skeletons seemed to be preserved. Regarding the Sensibas' duckbill skeleton, the asking price had apparently escalated to $1,500, and from what Utterback had heard, the brothers had broken it badly by trying to expose it, making the whole proposition a "pig in a poke." This specimen, sometimes euphemistically referred to as "Sensiba's mule," was eventually acquired by AMNH in 1905 after a long sequence of negotiations by Barnum Brown for the much more reasonable price of $200.[22]

Throughout late August, Peterson and Holland continued to fine-tune the *Daemonelix* manuscript while they waited for the proofs. Holland also implored Peterson to rest up so he could work energetically during the fall and winter, explaining that it was "important and pressing," since they might need a new display for the new building, the foundations of which were now nearly complete. Holland was also searching for Hatcher's replacement and brought Williston in to see if he might be interested. But the salary was too small to tempt him. Williston wrote Peterson to provide him with this and other intelligence he'd gathered:

> *He discussed all possible candidates with me—Wieland, Mathews, Riggs, Case, Hay and others. He seems most disposed toward Mathews. It is not his intention to settle the matter at once, and I suspect that the condition will remain unsettled for some months. He, meanwhile, looking after the department himself. I think, however, that this is a mistake. From all that I can hear, I suspect there will be greater changes before long in the museum—perhaps for the better.*

Peterson also received a letter from Merrill at the Smithsonian on the twenty-seventh, saying the appointment for the position was now in the hands of the Civil Service Commission, and it would probably be possible for Peterson to take the exam in Pittsburgh, where Peterson planned to return in early September.[23]

Utterback had been forced to use a freighting service to transport his massive ceratopsian skulls from Jordan to Miles City, since they were heavier than his team could handle, but by September 1 the Laramie and Judith fossils had been consolidated in Miles City. The expense was great, but as Utterback noted to Holland, "The time has come when good things are not to be found within a stones throw of the rail-road." He'd amassed around three tons of fossils, but he bemoaned the fact that he hadn't discovered the Hell Creek exposures earlier because he could have had a carload of fine fossils. Regardless, the skulls were well worth the cost in his estimation, and he submitted his $18.80 bill for supplies, including oats, flour, bacon, coffee, sugar, rice, peaches, apricots, corn, tomatoes, beans, sweet potatoes, cream, syrup, soap, hominy, and onions.[24]

Over the next week, he traversed about 175 miles through the Powder River region, locating several promising prospects, including exposures of the Laramie near the head of the east fork of the Little Powder River. But, once again, a freighting firm would be required to get large fossils out to Belle Fourch on the rail line. Through the rest of the month, Utterback continued his search and made preparations to load his cache on a railcar at Miles City. On the twenty-second, he summed up his season for Holland:

> While my work for the season has not given the results as I had anticipated I believe everything considered the final outcome of the expedition will well repay us. There is no question but what I have located two very rich Laramie fields, and under ordinary circumstances should have had a much larger collection to send in. As I have written you in previous letters the drouth has been the worst known to the oldest settlers. Perhaps another season the problem of water will not [need to be contended] with.

Utterback's season closed after he sent the shipment, and on the way to Pittsburgh, he visited his aging father in Franklin, Indiana.[25]

The disturbing and depressing loss of Hatcher's guidance and direction seems clearly manifest in his crew's collection for the season, which totaled only 117 specimens. That was less than half of their next-lowest total at the Carnegie, in 1903, and only about 15 percent of their total during Hatcher's most productive season at the Carnegie in 1901. Clearly, Hatcher possessed an essentially irreplaceable knack not only for finding fossils but also inspiring his crews to perform at the highest levels of their own abilities.

Peterson soldiered on, procuring one specimen of the beaver *Palaeocastor* from the 37- to 34-million-year-old beds of the Gering Formation; seven specimens of the horse *Mesohippus*, the camel *Poebrotherium*, the oreodont *Merycoidodon*, the deer-like *Leptomeryx*, and the lizard *Peltosaurus* from the 34- to 32-million-year-old strata of the Brule Formation. But Peterson pulled an impressive eighty-two mammal fossils from the 30- to 19-million-year-old outcrops of the Harrison and Monroe Creek Formations, including the relative of bears called *Nothocyon*; the hyaena-like, bone-crushing dog *Sunkahetanka*; the "bear dogs" *Delotrochanter*, *Ysengrinia*, and *Daphenodon*; the beaver *Palaeocastor* and its corkscrew burrow *Daemonelix*; the beaver *Euhapsis*; the rhinos *Diceratherium* and *Menoceras*; the horse *Parahippus*; the large, clawed, herbivorous chalicothere *Moropus*; the terrifying "terror pig," or entelodont *Dinohyus*; the small camels *Stenomylus* and *Oxydactylus*; the oreodonts *Promerycochoerus*, *Merychyus*, *Mesoreodon*, *Sespia*, *Phenacocoelus*, *Ticholeptus*, and "Cyclopidius," now called *Leptauchenia*. Peterson also added one camel called *Stenomylus* from the 19- to 16-million-year-old sediments of the Upper Loup Fork Beds, as well as another specimen of *Stenomylus* and an oreodont called *Merycochoerus* with incomplete field data.

Douglass is credited with one rhino called *Aphelops* from the 16- to 12.5- million-year-old rock layers of the Madison Valley Formation, and as mentioned, Utterback finally found the Carnegie two *Triceratops* specimens from the 66-million-year-old outcrops of the Hell Creek Formation.

Peterson learned that he passed the Civil Service exam with an exemplary score of 91.70 during the latter half of October, but he was worried. He wrote Merrill in distress on the nineteenth. "I learn that Mr. Gidley in the Am. Muse. Nat. History N.Y. and myself passed the examination, and that you likely may call on Gidley for the place. I hardly believe this until I hear from you directly." Pressing his case, Peterson told Merrill that he'd heard Gidley didn't really want the position and might decline it even if Osborn wanted him to take it. Merrill responded on the twenty-second that he didn't know how Peterson had gotten his information because the Civil Service hadn't even sent him the exam results yet, but he expected to hear in a few days and thanked Peterson for the intelligence. Finally, S. P. Langley, secretary of the U. S. National Museum, wrote Peterson on November 21 that he had been "probationally appointed" to the position at the salary of $1,500 per year and should report on December 15 for his assignment under the head curator in the Department of Geology. But Merrill granted an extension of Peterson's start date to January 3, 1905. Accordingly, Peterson sent Holland a brief formal letter explaining his actions and decisions:

> *I hereby respectfully resign my position as field collector and assistant in the museum, to take effect on Jan. 1st, 1905.*
>
> *The reason for my action is, as you are aware, my last summers illness while in the field, and fearing the recurance* [sic] *if again similarly exposed, I had long thought of changing my field work for steady laboratory occupation, for a while, although the former is perhaps more pleasant to me.*

In the Carnegie catalogue, Peterson's last record of specimens collected is 1904. However, based on the Carnegie's staffing records, he appears to have remained at the Carnegie until 1933, ending his career as a curator of vertebrate paleontology when he passed away that same year. One might reasonably suspect that Holland simply made a better salary offer than the Smithsonian, but that inference, at this point, must remain speculative, since there is no evidence of such an offer or raise.[26]

Utterback's last record of specimens collected in the Carnegie catalogue is 1907. On April 17, 1908, Utterback wrote Douglas Stewart, who appears to have been the assistant director of the Carnegie at that time, to state, "I have decided to give up the fossil business for all time, and shall send receipts and account of all expenses to-date, in a few days."

However, the Carnegie's staffing records show that Utterback remained as a field collector and assistant preparator until 1910.[27]

Gilmore's last record of specimens collected in the Carnegie catalogue is 1903, the same year that he was hired as a vertebrate paleontologist at the Smithsonian's National Museum of Natural History. At the Smithsonian, he became one of the world's premier experts on fossil reptiles, including dinosaurs. He retired from that institution in 1945, shortly before he passed away that September.

Douglass's last record of specimens collected in the Carnegie catalogue is 1923. However, the staffing records of the Carnegie reveal that he remained at the museum as a field collector until he resigned in 1924. He discovered the famous Carnegie Quarry in the hills bordering the Green River outside of Vernal, Utah, in 1909, which led to the establishment of Dinosaur National Monument around that site in 1915. Then from 1923–1924 he worked with the USNM and the University of Utah to collect a specimen of *Barosaurus lentus* from the quarry. Then work at the quarry ended. He then joined the staff at the University of Utah, spending two years preparing specimens from the quarry for mounting, before conducting geologic work in the Unitah Basin during his final years. He passed away in 1931.[28]

Holland retired as the director of the Carnegie in 1922 and passed away in December of 1932.

One slightly silver lining surrounding the dark cloud hovering over Hatcher's death involves an effect it had on the city of Pittsburgh. The demise of such a celebrated citizen triggered by typhoid spurred the city to take new steps to clean up its water supply.

Prior to his sudden death, Hatcher left a legacy of scientific research that would be published posthumously in the ensuing years, including a detailed account of the geology and paleontology of the Judith River Formation, which was coauthored with Stanton in 1905, and a massive treatise on the horned dinosaurs—*The Ceratopsia*—which was completed by Richard Swann Lull of Yale under the direction of Henry Fairfield Osborn in 1907. Although Hatcher did not complete the scientific research and text for this latter work, he oversaw the production of a tremendous amount of the supporting illustrations, including Knight's painting of *Triceratops*; as a fitting tribute, Osborn and Lull published the monograph under the name of their fallen colleagues, John Bell Hatcher and O. C. Marsh. (See Hatcher bibliography)

Beyond that, Hatcher also left a lasting legacy for the public that, even today, still inspires visitors viewing the mounts that he and his crews discovered and constructed in museums around the world. Among them are *Diplodocus* (CM 84, 94, and 307), which represents a composite of 1899 specimens from Wortman's crew and Utterback's 1903 specimen. This first complete mount of any sauropod dinosaur, which is popularly nicknamed "Dippy," was not only finished in Pittsburgh and revealed to the public in 1907; casts of it were also shipped to museums in the United Kingdom, Germany, France, Austria, Italy, Russia, Spain, Argentina, and Mexico, thus making it one of the most viewed dinosaur skeletons in the world. In the wake of Hatcher's passing, Holland supervised these efforts, but Hatcher's chief preparator, Arthur S. Coggeshall, was the hands-on hero who helped design and construct these mounts for all to experience. Further forming the foundation of the fossil exhibitions at the Carnegie are, as identified in the exhibit, Hatcher's specimens of *Deinosuchus* (CM 963), *Opisthotriton* (CM 6468), *Meniscoessus* (CM 11623), *Teleoceras* (acquired from USNM), *Trigonias* (CM 96), *Brontops* (CM 92 and 11061), and *Merycoidodon* (CM 236); Peterson's specimens of *Tyrannosaurus* (CM 1400), *Oxydactylus, Stenomylus, Menoceras, Daphenodon, Merychyus, Trigonias, Daphoenus*, and *Hoplophoneus*; Gilmore's and Douglass's specimens of *Apatosaurus* (CM 566 and CM 3018) and Utterback's specimen of *Triceratops* (CM 1219). The Smithsonian's Natural History Museum long exhibited one of Hatcher's *Triceratops* skeletons (USNM 2580), which it affectionately nicknamed "Hatcher," as well as one of his *Edmontosaurus* specimens (USNM 2414). Further, at Yale's Peabody Museum, where Hatcher was educated and initiated his unprecedented career, the museum's Great Hall, with its magnificent mural *The Age of Reptiles* by Rudolph Zallinger, is also adorned by Hatcher's *Edmontosaurus* skeleton (YPM 2182) and no less than three of his spectacular *Triceratops* skulls (YPM 1821, 1822, and 1823), as well as one skull of the dinosaur he first truly discovered—*Torosaurus* (YPM 1830). This spectacular roster of speciemens represents a fitting and visually diverse monument to a "King of Collectors."[29]

Epilogue

At its roots, life is a gamble—a game of chance—from the genes one inherits to the experiences one encounters, whether envisioned or accidental, and it is almost exclusively so from an evolutionary perspective. Many of us reflexively retreat from these risks in an attempt to seek some protection from life's vagaries, but others enthusiastically embrace them in the pursuit of superior achievement. Hatcher embraced hazarding calculated risks. In fact, he was egregiously gonzo for such opportunities despite often holding a less than sure hand.

Fieldwork is physically demanding, and that was especially true in Hatcher's time. It involves long days of hiking across rugged terrain searching for small fossil fragments weathering out of rocky outcrops or endlessly wielding heavy picks and shovels to painstakingly extract a naturally shattered skeleton from solid rock. On top of that, these exploits are often carried out under withering weather conditions, from horrendous heat to battering hail and bone-chilling cold. This would not seem to be work well suited for a person who inherited a physiological disease that left him with weakened bones and painful joints. Nonetheless, Hatcher relished this work to the point that he could barely tolerate being home for a month or two, even if he was bedridden, before bolting back to the field. Of course, he also possessed a wealth of other strengths, even if a healthy physical constitution wasn't one of them. Yet despite his physiological frailties, he was almost demonically driven, as if from somewhere deep within he sensed that life was fleeting and he had not a moment to waste. Almost all of his peers pronounced him to be not just honest and fair-minded but also, above all, intellectually curious, analytical, intelligent, and intensely observant.

Beyond that, Hatcher's arrival among paleontologists heralded the advent of a new class of collectors and curators. Prior to Hatcher's ascent, paleontologists in Hatcher's day mostly embodied wealthy aristocrats whose natural interest and intellect led them to attain graduate degrees at prestigious universities before assuming their professional positions. They often hired relatively uneducated craftsmen, to whom they taught collecting techniques, to be their field hands. In 1990, historian Ronald Rainger relegated this dichotomous division of responsibilities within vertebrate paleontology around 1900 into a wealthier group of aristocratic "entrepreneurs" and their more menial, working-class "collectors." He took great pains to point out how collectors such as Hatcher felt increasingly frustrated at the entrepreneurs' hesitance to provide them with adequate credit for the collectors' discoveries and refusal to let them publish on their finds. Yet, despite his humble upbringing on a farm in Iowa, Hatcher himself had labored hard in nearby coal mines to set aside funds for his education at one of the most prestigious universities in the nation.

Although Marsh was his aristocratic superior and supervisor, Hatcher's true mentor appears to have been Samuel Wendell Williston, who, like Hatcher, had grown up in the Midwest near Manhattan, Kansas, in a relatively poor family that could offer him only rudimentary educational opportunities. Williston eventually wrangled these opportunities into a college degree from Kansas State Agricultural College before joining Marsh at Yale, where he became Marsh's chief field supervisor and obtained an MD and a PhD in entomology before becoming the world's foremost expert on fossil reptiles as a professor at the University of Kansas. As you'll recall, it was Williston who emancipated Hatcher from Sternberg's supervision at the Long Island Rhino Quarry, which launched the young paleontologist into his own independent collecting career. Hatcher revered Williston with deep respect from then on and continued corresponding with him throughout the rest of his life. Although Hatcher never succeeded in obtaining a formal graduate degree, he, like Williston, never abandoned his pursuit for intellectual fulfillment or search for paleontological and geological knowledge, which, as we have seen, allowed him to attain academic prominence in his chosen fields. More self-supporting, country-raised, paleontological phenoms quickly followed, such as Barnum Brown of New York's American Museum of Natural History and Elmer Riggs of Chicago's Columbian Field Museum, who were both students of Williston at the University of Kansas. Williston and his wards represented a powerful new wave of self-made paleontologists who would come to dominate the profession in the 20th century despite their modest social roots.[1]

Perhaps Hatcher's accomplishments, despite the issues of class, might not seem too surprising, given that his career involved collecting for some of the richest men and well-endowed institutions that have ever existed: O. C. Marsh of Yale and its Peabody Museum, William Berryman Scott and his supporters such as J. Pierpont Morgan at Princeton University, as well as Andrew Carnegie and his Carnegie Museum. Yet, despite working for such deeply pocketed individuals and institutions, Hatcher often found himself short of funds for his fieldwork, as seen in the anecdote involving Hatcher's proclivity for poker with which we started this story in Patagonia. In fact, this remedy for his chronic state of insufficient field funds was anything but unusual, as noted by Marsh's biographers:

> *When* [Hatcher] *rode into town for his paycheck, his idea of respite from the field was to test his skill against the best poker players that the place afforded. If a telegram arrived at the Museum, saying, "Send two hundred ammunition. Hatcher," everyone there knew what was happening; that the money was sent, regardless, is a tribute to the scrupulous honesty with which Hatcher's business was always conducted. Tales of his poker exploits reechoed from Montana to Patagonia . . .*

In any event, Hatcher always found ways to persevere and ship literally tons of valuable fossil treasures back to his employers.[2]

Having now attempted to span the impressive arc of Hatcher's short, yet eventful, career, it seems appropriate to try and assess its scientific impact. A revealing point at which to start is the sum of his paleontological pursuits. The collecting campaigns of few paleontologists have ever approached the productivity of John Bell Hatcher's. Dozens of his discoveries represented species that were new to science, and a lengthy list of others represented the first specimens of their kind ever incorporated into American collections. Below is a summary of the vertebrate paleontological specimens Hatcher and his crews collected, based on the specimen catalogue records of Yale's Peabody Museum—which now includes his Princeton collection—the Smithsonian's National Museum of Natural History, and the Carnegie Museum:

Specimen Totals Collected By J. B. Hatcher and His Crews

Year/Locality	Crates	Specimens
1884/Long Island, KS	45	708
1885/Baylor County, TX; Long Island, KS	120	1,324
1886/SD; NE; Long Island, KS; MD	114	227
1887–early 1888/SD, NE, MD, FL	78	171
1888/SD, NE, MT, WY	71	150
1889/MD, WY, SD	58	814
1890/FL, SD, WY, SC	89	403
1891/WY	141	290
1892/WY	46	391
1893/WY, SD, NE		257
1894/SD, NE?		311
1895/UT, WY		200
1896–1899/Patagonia, Argentina		1,022
1900/SD, NE, WY	178	421
1901/SD, NE, WY, CO	102+	802
1902/WY, SD, NE, CO, MT	82+	408
1903/WY, MT, KS		256
1904/SD, MT, NE		117
TOTAL		**8,272**

Although certainly impressive in and of itself, this total still seriously underestimates the quantity of material Hatcher and his crews collected for natural history institutions. From the start of his fieldwork for Marsh, his correspondence makes note of the other zoological specimens of the living fauna, as well as anthropological objects from Native Americans, that he secured for his supervisor during his field seasons. That practice continued throughout his career. As evidence, one need only recall that the primary function of his assistants Peterson and Carpenter on the Patagonian expeditions was to collect specimens of the *living* flora and fauna of the region. Further, as Hatcher's own tales document, he eagerly joined in their efforts by hunting condors, guanaco, deer, puma, and other denizens of the deserts and mountains in order to acquire specimens for the Smithsonian during his Patagonian odyssey—not to mention his negotiations with the Tehuelche to garner objects reflecting their unique culture. Then, of course, Holland hounded Hatcher and Peterson to collect butterflies, moths, and other members of the Midwest's fauna to satisfy his own true scientific passions in entomology. In fact, a quick search of the Yale Peabody Museum's online collection database simply using the search term *Hatcher* reveals that in addition to the vertebrate fossils now catalogued, there are also 1,151 invertebrate fossils, 7 invertebrate zoological specimens, 6 vertebrate zoological specimens, and 1 botanical specimen still preserved in the museum more than a century after they were collected.

Over and above the sheer number of fossils Hatcher collected, he was particularly intent on participating in the research that would clarify their scientific significance. As we have seen, this pursuit often required Hatcher to directly challenge his more powerful supervisors, including the supremely arrogant and somewhat paranoid Marsh, as well as Scott, Holland, and even the master of pomposity, Henry Fairfield Osborn. But Hatcher, as usual, forthrightly confronted all of them when he disagreed with their directives or opinions, despite the potential peril such disagreements posed for his career. He railed in print regarding their propensity for languishing in their luxurious offices instead of seeking facts for themselves in the field, and he especially despised their lack of recognition for their assistants' contributions to their research. As we've seen, these shortcomings were at the root of Hatcher's criticism of Marsh and his stratigraphic conclusions regarding the "Ceratops" beds, as well as what paleontologist S. David Webb refers to as Hatcher's "famous 'parasite' passage" in his Patagonian narrative, in which Hatcher condems any paleontologist "who seldom goes beyond his private study or dooryard, and either contents himself, like other parasites, with what is brought to him . . . with little or no consideration for the rights or wishes of those who have brought together the material at so great an expense of time and labor." Rainger very reasonably interprets Hatcher's thinly veiled vitriol as retaliation for perceived slights from Osborn, Marsh, and Scott. Another example follows:

> *It seems to me that if some of the older workers in vertebrate pale-ontology would go to the trouble to go out into the field, do their own collecting, and familiarize themselves with the laboratory work, they would have a greater appreciation for the work and efforts of others.*[3]

Through this steadfast approach, he eventually managed to make lasting contributions to our knowledge of numerous ancient and extinct animals, from *Diplodocus, Brontosaurus, Triceratops*, and *Haplocanthosaurus* to tapirs, "bear dogs," and brontotheres.

Yet, as is still true today, the study of a specimen's paleontological significance is not limited to its anatomical characteristics and evolutionary relationships. A full portrait of a fossil's paleontological significance also requires an investigation into its age and the environment in which it lived, and to glean this information about an ancient organism one must study the geology of the rocks in which the fossil was entombed. In addition to being an almost incomparable collector and insightful paleobiologist, Hatcher was a superb geologist, and as we have seen in his pointed critiques of Marsh and others, he had little patience for paleontologists who failed to venture into the field in order to gain a better understanding of the geologic settings from which their fossils came.

This insistence on meticulous geologic fieldwork and research led to some of Hatcher's most significant scientific contributions that still inform our paleontological research today. For instance, one of the most intriguing arenas of modern paleontological debate involves the cause(s) for the extinction of all dinosaurs except birds at the end of the Cretaceous around 66 million years ago, along with numerous other animals and plants both on land and in the seas. In fact, it was Hatcher who most accurately clarified the sequence of rock units that serves as the most complete geologic record leading up to that momentous extinction event.

He teamed with Stanton to establish that Judith River Formation and its fossils underlie and predate the later marine incursion represented by the Bearpaw Shale. The Bearpaw Shale, in turn, preceded the shoreline sands of the Fox Hills Formation deposited as the sea retreated before the last floodplain sediments containing the ill-fated dinosaurs of the Lance and Hell Creek Formation were deposited. In recent decades, it was by studying this key sequence of rock layers that geologists and paleontologists first discovered geologic evidence in a terrestrial geologic setting of the massive impact of an extraterrestrial object at the top of the Hell Creek Formation that played a role in the extinction of large dinosaurs.

Indeed, Hatcher's correspondence with colleagues regarding his solution to this stratigraphic enigma, which disproved the previously held views of many of them—including Hay, Osborn, his mentor Williston, and even his coauthor Stanton—reveals that he celebrated this geologic victory with at least as much profound pride as any of his fossil discoveries or the research findings related to them.

In addition, Hatcher's geologic observations on the rock units in Patagonia, which led him to suspect that South America and Australia were once connected by way of Antarctica, based on the presence of marsupials in the former two continents, has also been confirmed by recent geologic studies of plate tectonics and paleontological discoveries in Antarctica itself, belatedly justifying Hatcher's precocious desire to participate in the Antarctic expeditions of his day.

So Hatcher's professional credentials are impeccable, but in more personal terms, what can be made of him as a father and family man, given his often gruff and tempestuous personality? Compared to the vast archives documenting Hatcher's career, the materials shedding light on his personal life are decidedly scant. After John Bell married Anna Matilda, his correspondence with Marsh commonly comments on how much he misses her and his children and longs for the opportunity to spend more time with them at home. Then, in the narrative of his Patagonian expeditions, he confides in print how he and Peterson lament that they have not had any word of their families for over a year. When Holland memorialized Hatcher, he told of Hatcher's first field foray for Marsh to Long Island, during which Hatcher spent two days with his parents but refused their solicitations to spend more even though he hadn't seen them for three years because Hatcher was "filled with the highest enthusiasm for the work to which he had been called. This incident . . . casts light upon his character . . . which, though full of the warmest affection for those who were bound to him by ties of blood and friendship, he never allowed . . . to stand in the way of what he conceived to be his calling." [4]

Although there does not seem to be a large cache of personal letters between John Bell and his family, a few priceless morsels have been lovingly preserved by his descendants. The first is a highly humorous note written to his daughter Alice when he had come into Havre, Montana, while he was doing fieldwork with Stanton in 1903 to clarify the geologic sequence of late Cretaceous rock units in Montana and Alberta, Canada:

Steam Heated Electric Lighted Porcelain Baths
The Hotel Havre
A New, Modern House
$2.50 Per Day

Havre, Montana,
June 22, 1903

My dear little daughter,
    Your very welcome letter of the eighth of June I have just received after a long journey up into Canada and the mountains, lakes & rivers. There is one river up here which I know would interest you & Ruth very much. It is Milk River. Would you not like to live on a river of Milk where you could just go out any day & drink all the

nice cold milk you wanted without having to pay eight cents a quart for it? Well it is not exactly a river of milk but it looks something like it as it flows along between high bluffs of white clay which color the water & makes it white but thick & muddy.

Papa has been sleeping out doors every night with nothing but the blue skies over his bed save when a rain cloud came up, which fortunately was not often. Then there are such an interesting lot of little birds up here, just millions of them. They fly about night & day & sing all the time. O! Such a song. It goes something like this bzzzz. They are awfully funny little birds, so different from canaries. They have six legs, four wings & a long slender beak & they live on blood when they can get it. They got a good deal from us & I wonder if my little daughter can tell me the name of them. In some countries they are only around in the evenings, but here they appear in millions all day long. Glad you are having such a good time with your cousins, uncles, aunts etc. etc. But you must be a good girl & mind Mamma & Grandpa & grandma & the rest.

Papa is going off into the Bear Paw mountains today for several days then on to the Missouri River where he will get his mail at Judith for a few weeks. He will expect another letter from you & one from the boys also. Mr. Thompson wrote me that you had written him or them. Remember me to Myrtle & all & be a good girl.

Your Papa,
J.B. Hatcher.
Judith,
Montana.[5]

A second letter, written in Medicine Bow, Wyoming, on April 28, 1900, addresses "My dear Wife and Children," who were apparently visiting Hatcher's parents in Lamoni, Iowa. Hatcher goes on to complain about the weather and how it "blowed and snowed" during most of his trip out to the field, before he lapses into a leisurely discussion of family news and plans. It ends, "With kind regards to Father, Mother & all &

love & kisses for yourself & the children. I am your true husband. J. B. Hatcher."[6]

Finally, a third very touching letter was written by Hatcher's daughter Alice to her mother Anna on her fiftieth birthday, which was almost twelve years after John Bell had passed.

Tuesday, May 23, 1916

My Mother,

Fifty years ago to-day, on an old Swedish Farm set in between two big lakes—and I wonder why it is that I don't know any more about it. I do know that you raised potatoes and flax and that you spun your own thread and wove your own cloth and that you kept cattle and that you had to row across the lake to church and that you had a journeyman shoe-maker but that is about all. Oh, yes, and that you used to save your pennies to buy a great big caramel—shaped like a cushion—when you went to town. But I don't know what the house and the church looked like nor what the neighbors were like nor how near they were, nor what nor how large the town was, and if the church was in the town nor if you had a ferry or a bridge to take your teams and wagons across the lake nor even what sort of teams you drove. Well, you'll have to be remembering it all again so that you can tell us when I come home in a little over three weeks.

Well, fifty years ago she was born and even if I don't know much about the little girl, they tell me that she grew up to be a beautiful woman. And I think she had a—pretty happy time then, didn't she, from what she's said? Then, just a little later, her romance began and it's always made me very happy because I think that it lasted all the way through. It seems to me that I remember a little girl, who didn't like very well to sleep all alone in a great big bed, cuddling in between her father and mother and then, when she was almost asleep, being disturbed by two people leaning over her to kiss each other good-night! And there were the evenings too, when father rocked me and sang "Old Kentucky Home" and the "poorhouse" song with a little Alice in it and when the boys washed the dishes because he wanted you with him when he came home in the evenings. And besides that, there were very impressive times when we all went up in the library and listened while your "best man in the world" and my wonderful father got ready for one of his public lectures and we were all proud of him and loved to listen, didn't we, even if some of us didn't understand it a bit?

And now I am glad to remember a very stern Father who often had to intervene because our mother was apt to be too good to us. We always wanted our mother when we were sick, but he used to make her go to bed and sleep while he watched with us and got us drinks and things. And he wouldn't let us bother our mother for pennies when he was there and ever so many things so that I think she must always have been glad when she saw him coming down the street.

I wish you'd take a sort of holiday to-day for happy memories. And pleasant anticipations!

Birthday greetings from your daughter.

It seems, by all available accounts, that John Bell dearly loved his family and was dearly loved in return. They seemed to accept his consuming need to be in the field and understood that he loved them no less for what were, no doubt, long and difficult absences.[7]

Thus, in the end, despite a formidable set of social and genetic trump cards being stacked against him, Hatcher's other indomitable personal traits sculpted a supremely successful paleontologic and geologic scientist. He was widely recognized to be the paramount fossil collector of the pioneering phase of paleontological collecting spanning the end of the 19th and beginning of the 20th centuries. For confirmation of his pre-eminence, one must look no further than the biographers of his master, Marsh. They devoted an entire chapter to Hatcher's exploits, entitled "John Bell Hatcher, King of Collectors."

Holland memorialized Hatcher in similar terms:

Mr Hatcher's position as a paleontologist was unique. He is universally admitted by those most competent to pass judgement

to have been the best and most successful paleontological collector
whom America has ever produced. In saying this it may at once be
adimitted that he was in all probability the most successful collector
in his chosen domain who has ever lived.

Holland continued by recounting, based on his own experiences, that
Hatcher:

> . . . *had great mechanical aptitudes, and succeeded, sometimes*
> *when alone, by patient effort in accomplishing apparently impos-*
> *sible tasks in the removal of huge and weighty objects* [as large
> as a ton] *from difficult positions, which would not have been*
> *undertaken by others* . . . [and] *in which he dared great physical*
> *risks and even death* . . . *far from human companionship, in*
> *extracting large masses from their original position and moving*
> *them by a skilfil* [sic] *arrangement of levers to points where they*
> *could afterwards be taken up.*

Yet despite all of Hatcher's successful exploits, Holland reminisced:

> *Perhaps the most striking characteristic of Mr. Hatcher was his*
> *extreme modesty. He was always reticent in speaking of what he*
> *had done, and shunned publicity. . . . The notoriety which is eagerly*
> *courted by some so-called scientific men* . . . *through a diligent*
> *cultivation of the columns of the daily papers, he simply loathed,*
> *and he could not be induced, even when urged to do so, to accord*
> *an interview to the ordinary representatives of the press. Social*
> *life outside of the circle of his home had little charm for him. . . .*
> *Nevertheless, he was a most charming companion* . . . *when he could*
> *be prevailed upon to unbend and relate the stories of his adventures*
> *in strange and distant places. . . .*[8]

Barnum Brown of the AMNH, who accompanied Hatcher and
Peterson on their last Patagonian expedition, had a somewhat ambivalent
answer immediately after hearing of Hatcher's death: ". . . a sad blow

indeed for he was a strong man just in the the prime of his work. I did not admire Hatcher personally but recognized his forceful character which there are few to equal." But later, while compiling notes for his aborted autobiography, Brown certainly seemed to have mellowed, for he found much in Hatcher's professional abilities to emulate, recalling that Hatcher:

> . . . was a truly remarkable man, with few vices and more virtues than are found in most men. [Honestly], he was a paradox in some respects. He probably had had a disturbed childhood, for he said he would not trust his own father unless an agreement was signed. During our association, I found him generous to a high degree, offering any part, or all of his outfit when we separated. . . . As a worker he was indefatigable. He would ride off alone in an uncharted area, with only his blankets, revolver, and a pocket full of salt, living off the game of the land as he traveled. His geological observations were, to my knowledge, accurate; and as a collector, no one ever surpassed him.[9]

Hatcher's erstwhile competitor turned compadre, Henry Fairfield Osborn, agreed in his letter to Holland, within which he reflected on Hatcher's death:

> I can hardly tell you how shocked and grieved I am. I had often thought of the probability of Hatcher's death in the field when taking great risks and entirely away from medical and surgical attendance, but of his death at home I had not thought a moment. In his intense enthusiasm for science, and the promotion of geology and paleontology, and the tremendous sacrifices he was prepared to make, and had made, he was a truly rare and noble spirit—the sort of man that is vastly appreciated in England and Germany, but I fear very little appreciated in America. His work as a collector was magnificent—probably the greatest on record.[10]

Scott, who proclaimed that Hatcher had "a veritable genius for collecting fossils," provided further, most favorable testaments:

I was much grieved by the death of J. B. Hatcher, who . . . was a unique figure in American paleontology. One of the greatest collectors, whose original and ingenious methods raised the obtaining of fossil vertebrates to a fine art, he was much more than that and was already one of the foremost of our paleontologists. He was a thoroughly educated man . . . and gifted with a remarkable English style.

Scott also reflected in more detail on Hatcher's superior collecting strengths:

[Hatcher] *may be said to have fairly revolutionized the methods of collecting vertebrate fossils, a work which before his time had been almost wholly in the hands of untrained and unskilled men, but which he converted into a fine art. The exquisitely preserved fossils in American museums . . . are, to a large extent . . . due to* [his] *energy and skill and to the large-minded help and advice as to methods and localities which were always at the service of anyone who chose to ask for them. . . . No less than three great collections . . . owe their choicest treasures* [directly] *to the skill and devotion of Hatcher.*

All in all, Scott summarized that Hatcher possessed:

Marvelous powers of vision, at once telescopic and microscopic, a dauntless energy and fertility of resource that laughed all obstacles to scorn, and an enthusiastic devotion to his work [that] *secured for him a thoroughly well-earned success and a high reputation.*[11]

Still revered, Hatcher's modern-day successors continue to proclaim him a "King of Collectors" in spite of an untimely death that cut short his incomparable career. Contemporary historian of paleontology Paul Brinkman painted a portrait of Hatcher in the following tints of traits: ". . . determined, confident, hardworking, and often very temperamental . . . the most talented and respected field paleontologist of his generation . . . his uncanny success at finding vertebrate fossils and collecting them with great care and ingenuity earned him a wide and well-deserved reputation as a model field-worker." He further characterized Hatcher as "impetuous and strong-willed."[12]

Ronald Rainger refers to Hatcher as being "unrivaled as a collector . . . [obtaining] large and unwieldy specimens in greater numbers and finer condition than almost any of his predecessors," but he saves his superlatives for Hatcher's skills as a geologist: "Hatcher's descriptions of the geology and stratigraphy of fossil vertebrate horizons surpassed the work of other contemporary American vertebrate paleontologists." Rainger goes on to cite Marsh's admonition of Whitman Cross of the USGS when Cross belittled Hatcher's abilities as a geologist: "You do him injustice in speaking of him as a collector, and not a geologist, and you will make a great mistake if you undervalue his knowledge of the Laramie, of which formation he has probably seen more than any other man." All in all, Rainger proclaimed, "Hatcher was at the forefront of early twentieth-century American vertebrate paleontology."[13]

When Url Lanham wrote his review of legendary early collectors, he modestly entitled his chapter on Hatcher "Prince of Collectors." Nonetheless he expounded, "John Bell Hatcher stands apart as a legendary hero of vertebrate paleontology . . . the most strenuous and skillful fossil hunter ever known."[14]

In his review of paleontological work in Patagonia, the eminent evolutionary paleontologist George Gaylord Simpson describes Hatcher as a "perfectionist" and "the most successful discoverer of fossil bones and the most skillful excavator of them in his time." In reflecting on Hatcher's determination to continue working after his long ailment during the second Patagonian expedition, Simpson notes, "Still Hatcher stayed on . . . with a persistence which in retrospect seems more nearly maniacal than brave."[15]

Paleontologist S. David Webb, in summarizing Hatcher's Patagonian narrative, characterized Hatcher as being occasionally cruel in his hunting habits but imbued with "indomitable determination and courage." Calling Hatcher "surely one of the most dramatic figures in American paleontology," Webb likened him to a hero in a western: ". . . the colorful paleontologist would be the bonehunter played by Clint Eastwood, the guy in the saddle who never misses a shot."[16]

Tom Rea, who chronicled Hatcher's stunning tenure at the Carnegie Museum, simply refers to Hatcher as "brilliant."[17]

In retrospect, Hatcher stands apart within the collage of great fossil collectors that arrived around the turn of the twentieth century not because of any single attribute but because of the potent amalgamation of traits embodied within him. His relish for risk drove him to unexplored locales. But it also allowed him to speak truth to power and made him almost unfailingly straightforward and incapable of disingenuous guile. Throughout his career, he consciously bore the chip on his shoulder derived from his modest social roots and refused to passively bow to the aristocratic hierarchy that controlled the paleontological profession. His eventual success in academic pursuits flowed from his towering intellectual abilities, which along with his unrivaled aptitude for observation, allowed him to grasp both geologic and paleontologic subtlties that eluded the more mundane. In this way, Hatcher transcended the aristocracy of paleontology to attain the ultimate rank among paleontological royalty as a king of collectors.

Accordingly, it's been my privilege as a paleontologist, on behalf of my paleontological colleagues, to reintroduce the public to the man who, through all his discoveries, helped trigger the modern world's fanatic fascination and cultural curiosity about dinosaurs and other extinct creatures. Toward that goal, a more than fitting reflection of Hatcher's continuing preeminence in paleontology appeared in 1995. For nine decades after Hatcher's death, his grave in Pittsburgh's Homewood Cemetery lay unmarked. But when members of the Society of Vertebrate Paleontology convened for their annual convention in that city, a group of thoughtful colleagues redressed this neglect by having a headstone hewn with both Hatcher's name and that of his daughter Ruth, who had passed shortly before him. Together, they are attended in perpetuity by an image of an astounding dinosaur Hatcher himself discovered, *Torosaurus*.

APPENDIX 1

Contracts and Agreements Between O. C. Marsh and J. B. Hatcher

Handwritten by O. C. Marsh on Yale College Museum letterhead:

June 24th 1884
I hereby agree to work for Prof. O. C. Marsh of the U. S. Gelog. Survey from July 1st 1884 to June 30th 1885, for $50. per month, this to include everything, three months of this time to be spent in New Haven.
If required, I will continue to work as above for one year more, at the same rate, but all travelling expenses to be extra.

$\qquad$ J. B. Hatcher (signed)

New Haven June 24/84
$100
Rec'd of O. C. Marsh one hundred dollars being advance May to Sept. 1st 1884
$\qquad$ J. B. Hatcher (signed)

YPM Archives: Marsh/Hatcher Correspondence, B15F0602: 001-002

Handwritten by O. C. Marsh on Yale College Museum letterhead:

March 6th 1886
I hereby agree to remain with Prof. Marsh on U. S. Geolg. Survey till July 1st 1887 or one year from expiration of present agreement for ninety dollars

(90) per month, provided the Govt. gives the same or a greater amount for paleontology than this year.

I further agree to remain four years more, or until July 1st 1891 on above conditions, for $100 per month.

J. B. Hatcher (signed)

YPM Archives: Marsh/Hatcher Correspondence, B15F0605: 001

New Haven Ct Dec. 20, 1890

I hereby agree to remain with Prof. Marsh five years from July 1st 1891 (on to July 1st 1896) on the following conditions.

(1) My salary to be $1800 per annum, and all necessary field and travelling expenses guaranteed for five years.

(2) My position to be "Assistant in Geology."

(3) My work to be not more than six months in the field, and five in the East, with one month for vacation.

(4) My work in the East to be mainly on my own collections

J. B. Hatcher (signed)

I hereby engage Mr. Hatcher for five years on the above conditions.

O. C. Marsh (signed)

YPM Archives: Marsh/Hatcher Correspondence, B15F0619: 020

New Haven, Conn., January 8, 1891

In addition to the contract made December 22, 1890, between Mr. J. B. Hatcher and Prof. O. C. Marsh, the following agreement is hereby made:-

(1) All matters relating to the employment and control of men in the West to be left to Mr. Hatcher entirely, limited only by the amount of money available in each year.

(2) The detailed geology of the Brontotherium beds and of the Ceratops beds to be worked up by Mr. Hatcher and published under his name.

(3) The preparation and arrangement of collections made by Mr. Hatcher to be under his charge.

(4) On the termination of the contract, July 1st, 1896, if it is not renewed, a special effort is to be made by Prof. Marsh to secure an equal or better position for Mr. Hatcher; and in this effort, Prof. Marsh will seek the aid of the President of Yale, Prof. Brush, and other officers of the University.

(5) The conditions of the above contract, and the present additions; shall hold from this date, but Mr. Hatcher's salary shall be $2000.00 per annum

from January 1st, 1891; of this, $1800.00 to be paid in monthly payments of $150.00 and the remaining $200.00 in quarterly payments of $50.00 each.

J. B. Hatcher (signed)

Witness:-
R. W. Westbrook (signed)

I hereby engage Mr. Hatcher as my assistant to July 1st, 1896, on the above conditions.

O. C. Marsh (signed)

Witness:-
R. W. Westbrook (signed)

YPM Archives: Marsh/Hatcher Correspondence, B16F0620: 001–003

MEMORANDUM OF AGREEMENT by and between O. C. Marsh of New Haven, Conn., Party of the First Part and John B. Hatcher of Long Pine, Neb., Party of the Second Part, witnesseth;

Whereas the Parties hereunto did enter into a contract dated at New Haven, Conn. Dec. 22d, 1890, a copy of which is hereunto annexed and Marked exhibit A., and

Whereas the Parties hereto did on Jan. 8th, 1891 enter into a supplementary argreement to said exhibit A., a copy of which agreement is hereunto annexed and marked exhibit B., and

Whereas in accordance with the terms of said agreement. The Party of the Second Part has been and now is in the employ of the Party of the First Part;

Now therefore the Parties hereunto, each in the consideration of the agreements of the other, have agreed together as follows:

1- The Party of the First Part agrees to give immediately to the Party of the Second Part a satisfactory recommendation in writing signed by said Party of the First Part and setting forth the terms of said employment and stating that the said Party of the Second Part has fulfilled in a satisfactory manner to the Party of the First Part all of his agreements and duties in said employment.

2- The Party of the First Part further agrees that he will release the Party of the Second Part from all and each of the agreements of said contracts marked exhibit A. and exhibit B. whenever the Party of the Second Part shall have obtained and shall have entered into the duties of another employment or position satisfactory to him the said Party of the Second Part.

3- *The Party of the First Part further agrees to permit and allow the said Party of the Second Part to ask for and apply by letter or otherwise for such position or employment, and such application shall not be regarded as a violation of any and all of the stipulations of these presents or of the agreements hereinbefore referred to as exhibit A. and exhibit B.*

4- *The Party of the First Part further agrees to continue the Party of the Second Part in his present employment, under the terms of these presents and the agreements hereinbefore referred to as exhibit A. and exhibit B., until such time as the Party of the Second Part shall have obtained and shall have entered into the duties of such satisfactory position or employment hereinbefore set forth.*

5- *The Party of the Second Part agrees to continue in the employment of the Party of the First Part under the agreements of these presents and of the agreements hereinbefore referred to as exhibit A. and exhibit B., until such time as he shall have obtained such satisfactory position or employment hereunbefore* [sic] *referred to.*

6- *The Party of the Second Part further agrees to release the said Party of the First Part from all liability under and from the stipulations and agreements made in the contracts hereinbefore referred to as exhibit A. and exhibit B., in the event that he, the said Party of the Second Part, shall have obtained and shall have entered into the duties of such satisfactory position or employment as hereinbefore set forth.*

7- *It is understood and agreed by the Parties hereunto that the agreements and stipulations made in the contracts hereinbefore referred to as exhibit A. and exhibit B. shall continue in full force and effect, except insofar as the said contracts are abrogated or modified by these presents.*

8- *It is understood and agreed by the Parties hereunto that in the event that the said Party of the Second Part shall be employed upon work, under or by the direction of the Party of the First Part, for which the U. S. Geological Survey of the National Museum shall have furnished the necessary funds, that then the Party of the Second Part shall sign proper vouchers for such work at the request of the Party of the First Part.*

In Witness of the Parties hereunto have this day set their hands and seals. Dated at New Haven, this 10th day of January, A. D., 1893.

O. C. Marsh (signed and followed by initials LS): *Party of the First Part*
J. B. Hatcher (signed and followed by initials LS): *Party of the Second Part*

APPENDIX 1

EXHIBIT A.

New Haven, Conn., Dec. 22d, 1890

I hereby agree to remain with Prof. Marsh five years from July 1st, 1891 (or to
July 1st, 1896), on the following conditions: -
    (1) My salary to be $1800. per annum, and all necessary field and trav-
eling expenses guaranteed for five years.
    (2) My position to be "Assistant in Geology."
    (3) My work to be not more than six months in the field, and five in the
East, with one month vacation.
    (4) My work in the East to be mainly on my own collection.
                              (signed) J. B. Hatcher

I hereby engage Mr. Hatcher for five years on the above conditions.
                              (signed) O. C. Marsh
Witness: R. W. Westbrook

EXHIBIT B.

New Haven, Conn., January 8, 1891
    In addition to the contracts made Dec 22d, 1890, between Mr. J. B. Hatcher
and Prof. O. C. Marsh, the following agreement is hereby made: -
    (1) All matters relating to the employment and control of men in the West
to be left to Mr. Hatcher entirely, limited only by the amount of money
available each year.
    (2) The detailed geology of the Brontotherium beds and of the Cera-
tops beds to be worked up by Mr. Hatcher, and published under his
name.
    (3) The preparation and arrangement of collections, made by Mr. Hatcher,
to be under his charge.
    (4) On termination of the contract, July 1st, 1896, if it is not renewed,
a special effort is to be made by Prof. Marsh to secure an equal or
better position for Mr. Hatcher, and in this effort, Prof. Marsh will
seek the aid of the President of Yale, Prof. Brush, and other officers
of the University.
    (5) The conditions of the above contract, and the present additions, shall
hold from this date, but Mr. Hatcher's salary shall be $2000 per annum

from Jan. 1, 1891; of this $1800 to be paid in monthly payments of $150, and the remaining $200 in quarterly payments of $50 each.

(signed) *J. B. Hatcher*

Witness: R. W. Westbrook

I hereby engage Mr. Hatcher as my assistant to July 1st, 1896, on the above conditions.

(signed) *O. C. Marsh*

Witness R. W. Westbrook

YPM Archives: Marsh/Hatcher Correspondence, B16F0627: 040–044

APPENDIX 2

Year-By-Year Lists of Specimens Collected by Hatcher and His Field Crews

Note: In all the yearly lists of specimens collected, only those identified to genus in the specimen catalogues of the institutions cited are listed, except for higher taxa within the Dinosauria. Thus, in almost every yearly list, there are more specimens held in the institution's collection than are listed, which is why simply adding up the specimens for the genera listed will not add up to the "specimens total" provided in the headers for these lists. Also, in the lists below, the specimens are assigned to genera as they are currently identified in the institutions' databases. For possible generic synonomies, see text and Glossary.

1884
HATCHER
708 specimens total in USNM

Cenozoic Amphibians, Reptiles, and Mammals

Hemphillian, 9–5 MA (Republican River Formation, KS)

Aceratherium	1
Aelurodon	6
Barbourofelis	1
Bufo	6
Griphippus	3
Hesperomys	1
Hipparion	3

Mastodon	1
Merychippus	1
Microtus	9
Neohipparion	5
Palaeoelaphne	1
Palaeospiza	1
Perognathus	2
Pliohippus	3
Proictinia	1
Prosthennops	1
Protohippus	6
Tayra	1
Teleoceras	638
Terrapene	1

1885
HATCHER
1,324 specimens total in USNM and YPM

Cenezoic Amphibians, Reptiles, and Mammals

Hemphillian, 9–5 MA (Republican River Formation, KS)

Aelurodon	4
Aepycamelus	1
Aphelops	11
Aramus	1
Barbourofelis	1
Bufo	1
Epigaulus	1
Geochelone	6
Gomphotherium	7
Hemiauchenia	2
Hesperomys	1
Megatylopus	3
Merycodus	4
Pliohippus	1
"*Procamelus*"	1
Teleoceras	1,163
"*Yumaceras*"	1

APPENDIX 2

Paleozoic Reptiles, Amphibians, and Early Relatives of Mammals

Permian, Leonardian 280–270 MA (Clear Fork Group, TX)

Captorhinus	1
Diadectes	1
Dimetrodon	6
Diplocaulus	3
Edaphosaurus	4
Eryops	6
Labidosaurus	3
Lysorophus	2
Orthacanthus	2
Trimerorhachis	2

Mesozoic Reptiles

Triassic, 252–202 MA

Rutiodon	2

Note: Permian and Triassic age ranges from GSA Timescale 2012; Hemphillian age range from Tedford, et al. 2004.

1886
HATCHER
227 specimens total in USNM

Cenozoic Amphibians, Reptiles, and Mammals

Paleogene, Eocene (Chadron Formation, SD)
If from the Chadron Fm., they would be Chadronian 37–34 MA.

Hyaenodon	1
Mesohippus	5
Trigonias	3

Paleogene, Oligocene (White River Group, SD and NE)
Possibly Orellan/Whitneyan, 34–30 MA (Brule Formation)

Agriochoerus	2
Allops	4
Ancodon	1
Archaeotherium	9
Brontops	14

Brontotherium	41
Caenopus	8
Cynodictis	1
Eumys	2
Hoplophoneus	1
Hyaenodon	2
Hypertragulus	2
Hypisodus	1
Hyracodon	1
Leptomeryx	1
Megacerops	5
Menodus	39
Merycoidodon	10
Miohippus	2
Palaeolagus	9
Stylemys	8
Subhyracodon	14
Titanotherium	1
Trigonias	8

Neogene, Miocene, NE

Aphelops	1
Ischyrocyon	1
Equus	2
Pliohippus	1
Procamelus	1
Pseudhipparion	1

Cenozoic, Miocene, KS

Presumably Long Island Q: Hemphillian 9–5 MA (Republican River Formation)

Barbourofelis	1
Nimravides	1

Quaternary, NE

Equus	2
Mammuthus	1

Mesozoic Dinosaurs

Cretaceous (Potomac Group, MD)

Astrodon	1

1887 TO EARLY 1888
HATCHER
171 total specimens in USNM

Cenozoic Fish, Amphibians, Reptiles, and Mammals

Paleogene, Eocene (Chadron Formation, SD)
If from the Chadron Fm., they would be Chadronian 37–34 MA.

Allops	5
Brontops	3
Brontotherium	10
Diploconus	1
Megacerops	10
Symborodon	2
Titanops	1
Titanotherium	1

Orellan/Whitneyan, 34–30 MA (Brule Formation, SD)

Archaeotherium	1
Merycoidodon	2

Hemingfordian, 18–15 MA (Calvert Formation, MD)

Aetobatis	2
Carcharhinus	3
Carcharodon	1
Galeocerdo	1
Hemipristis	2
Isurus	3
Notorynchus	1
Rhinoptera	1

Hemphillian, 9–8 MA (Alaucha Clay, FL)

Aphelops	2
Serridentinus	2

Cretaceous 145–66 MA (Patuxent Formation, MD)

Allosaurus	1
Astrodon	62
Coelurus	1
Dryptosaurus	1

Glyptops	1
Ornithomimus	10
Priconocon	1

Prothero and Emry 2004; https://en.wikipedia.org/wiki/Calvert_Cliffs _State_Park; https://www.floridamuseum.ufl.edu/florida-vertebrate-fossils/sites /mixsons-bone-bed/

1888
HATCHER
150 specimens total, mostly in USNM

Cenozoic Amphibians, Reptiles, and Mammals

Paleogene (Chadron Formation, SD)
If from the Chadron Fm., they should be Chadronian 37–34 MA.

Allops	4
Brontops	6
Brontotherium	11
Megacerops	5
Menodus	12
"Testudo"	1
Trigonias	1

Paleogene, Oligocene (White River Group, SD, NE)
Possibly Orellan/Whitneyan, 34–30 MA (Brule Formation)

Aciprion	1
Archaeotherium (YPM)	1
Helodermoides	1
Leptictis	1
Peltosaurus	2
Rhineura	1
Saniwa	1

Paleogene, Brule Formation, SD
Possibly Orellan/Whitneyan, 34–30 MA (Brule Formation)

Eumys	1
Heliscomys	1

Cretaceous Reptiles

Cretaceous, Judith River Formation, MT

If from Judith River Fm., Late Cretaceous, 78–75 MA

Aspideretes	1
Aublysodon	1
Baena	1
Ceratops	3
Champsosaurus	1
Corythosaurus	1
Edmontonia	2
Hadrosaurus	1
Ornithomimus	2
Palaeoscincus	1
Panoplosaurus	1
Synechodus	1
Troodon	1
Tyrannosauridae (*Deinodon?*)	1

Cretaceous, Lance Formation, WY

Probably Late Cretaceous, 68–66 MA (Lance Formation)

Champsosaurus	1

Cretaceous 145–66 MA (Patuxent Formation, MD)

Astrodon	41
Goniopholis	1

1889
HATCHER
814 specimens total
Smithsonian USNM: 188 specimens total

Cenozoic Amphibians, Reptiles, and Mammals

Hemingfordian, 18–15 MA (Calvert Formation, MD)

Carcharodon	1
Odontaspis	1

Mesozoic Reptiles and Mammals

Cretaceous, Lance Formation, MT

Probably Late Cretaceous, 68–66 MA (Lance Formation)

Allacodon	2
Alphadon	8
Chamops	4
Cimolestes	1
Cimolodon	16
Cimolomys	6
Didelphodon	4
Ectoconodon	1
Gypsonictops	16
Harpagosaurus	1
Iguanavus	1
Meniscoessus	8
Mesodma	14
Odaxosaurus	1
Pachycephalosaurus	1
Pediomys	21
Peltosaurus	1
Protolambda	2
Scapherpeton	1
Stagodon	3
Triceratops	5

Cretaceous, 145–66 MA (Patuxent Formation, MD)

Astrodon	6

Late Triassic, 237–201 MA, NC

Rutiodon	1

Yale Peabody Museum: 626 specimens total collected by Hatcher

Late Jurassic, 150 MA (Morrison Formation, SD)

Barosaurus	1

Late Cretaceous, 68–66 MA (Lance Formation, WY)

Albanerpeton	1

Allacodon	4
Allognathosuchus	2
Alphadon	8
Ankylosauria	1
Aublysodon	2
Baena	1
Batodon	2
Belonostomus	3
Camptomus	4
Ceratops	1
Ceratopsia	3
Chamops	8
Cimolestes	15
Cimolodon	15
Cimolomys	68
Cimolopteryx	1
Colpodontosaurus	1
Coriops	4
Didelphodon	10
Dipriodon	2
Dromaeosauridae	3
Dryolestes	1
Enantiornithes	1
Gypsonictops	9
Hadrosauridae	1
Halodon	3
Hatcheritherium	1
Hypsolophodontidae	4
Kindleia	1
Leptoceratops	1
Leptochamops	2
Lisserpeton	7
Melvius	1
Meniscoessus	46
Mesodma	11
Nanomyops	2
Nanomys	1
Nyssodon	1
Oracodon	2
Ornithischia	4

Ornithopoda	1
Paraderma	1
Paralbula	1
Paronychodon	12
Pediomys	31
Piceoerpeton	1
Platacodon	1
Selenacodon	2
Stagodon	5
Telacodon	1
Therapoda	31
Trachodon	1
Triceratops	3
Trionyx	1
Tripriodon	2
Troodon	3
Tyrannosauridae	6
Tyrannosaurus	1

Oligocene, 34–23 MA (White River Group, SD)

Testudo	1

1890
HATCHER
403 specimens total
Smithsonian USNM: 115 specimens total

Cenozoic Mammals

Hemphillian, 9–8 MA (Alaucha Clay, FL)

Aphelops	1
Procamelus	1
Serridentinus	1
Teleoceras	14

Chadronian, 37–34 MA (Chadron Formation, SD)

Megacerops	1

Mesozoic Reptiles and Mammals

Cretaceous, Lance Formation, WY
Probably Late Cretaceous, 68–66 MA (Lance Formation)

Baena	2
Basilemys	1
Didelphodon	1
Didelphops	1
Dinosauria (indeterminate)	1
Edmontosaurus	13
Ornithomimus	2
Pediomys	5
Scapherpeton	1
Stagodon	2
Thescelosaurus	1
Thescelus	1
Triceratops	30
Troodon	1
Tyrannosaurus	1

Yale Peabody Museum: 285 specimens total

Orellan/Whitneyan, 34–30 MA (Brule Formation, SD)

Hyaenodon	1

Late Cretaceous, 68–66 MA (Lance Formation, WY)

Alphadon	11
Aublysodon	1
Belonostomus	2
Cimolodon	1
Cimolomys	17
Cimolopteryx	2
Didelphodon	3
Essonodon	1
Gypsonictops	2
Habrosaurus	2
Hadrosauridae	2
Kindleia	1
Leptoceratops	1
Lisserpeton	3

Litakis	1
Meniscoessus	14
Mesodma	11
Neornithes	1
Opisthotriton	1
Paronychodon	2
Pediomys	9
Piceoerpeton	4
Procaimanoidea	2
Prodesmodon	2
Saurornithoides	1
Stagodon	1
Stygimoloch	1
Therapoda	27
Triceratops	2
Tyrannosauridae	2

1891
HATCHER

290 specimens total
Smithsonian USNM: 195 specimens total

Mesozoic Reptiles and Mammals

Cretaceous, Lance Formation, WY
Probably Late Cretaceous, 68–66 MA (Lance Formation)

Alethesaurus	1
Allacodon	6
Alphadon	16
Batodon	1
Brachychampsa	2
Chamops	3
Cimolestes	2
Cimolomys	3
Baena	2
Basilemys	1
Didelphodon	4

Didelphops	2
Ectoconodon	2
Edmontosaurus	8
Exostinus	2
Glasbius	1
Gypsonictops	15
Habrosaurus	2
Iguanavus	1
Lanceosaurus	3
Meniscoessus	5
Mesodma	1
Opisthotriton	1
Oracodon	2
Ornithomimus	1
Pediomys	18
Protolambda	1
Scapherpeton	1
Stagodon	1
Thescelosaurus	7
Triceratops	17
Tripriodon	1
Tyrannosaurus	2

Yale Peabody Museum: 95 specimens total

Late Cretaceous, 68-66 MA (Lance Formation, WY)

Alphadon	1
Aublysodon	1
Batodon	11
Belonostomus	1
Cimolomys	9
Gypsonictops	4
Lisserpeton	1
Meniscoessus	5
Pediomys	5
Therapoda	4
Torosaurus	2
Trachodon	1
Triceratops	7
Troodon	1

1892
HATCHER
391 specimens total
Smithsonian USNM: 141 specimens total

Mesozoic Reptiles and Mammals

Cretaceous, Lance Formation, WY
Probably Late Cretaceous, 68–66 MA (Lance Formation)

Allacodon	1
Alphadon	5
Brachychampsa	3
Chamops	2
Cimolodon	8
Cimolomys	11
Coniophis	1
Didelphodon	3
Didelphops	1
Gypsonictops	3
Habrosaurus	1
Lanceosaurus	1
Meniscoessus	12
Mesodma	9
Odaxosaurus	1
Oracodon	2
Parasaniwa	2
Peltosaurus	2
Prionosaurus	2
Scapherpeton	4

Yale Peabody Museum: 250 specimens total

Late Cretaceous, 68–66 MA (Lance Formation, WY)

Acipenser	2
Alphadon	3
Aspideretes	1
Aublysodon	3
Axestemys	1
Baena	3
Chamops	2

Cimolestes	2
Cimolodon	3
Cimolomys	21
Contogenys	1
Didelphodon	1
Edmontosaurus	1
Gavia	1
Habrosaurus	1
Leptochamops	1
Meniscoessus	24
Meniscognathus	4
Opisthotriton	6
Paronychodon	1
Pediomys	19
Peltosaurus	2
Prodesmodon	2
Scapherpeton	8
Triceratops	2
Troodon	4
Tyrannosaurus	2

1893
HATCHER
257 specimens total now at YPM

Mesozoic Fish, Reptiles, and Mammals

Late Cretaceous, 68–66 MA (Lance Formation, WY)

Amia	1
Brachychampsa	1
Champsosaurus	1
Cimolopteryx	1
Coniophis	1
Cuttysarkus	1
Habrosaurus	2
Leidyosuchus	1
Lepisosteus	1
Meniscoessus	1
Myledaphus	1
Palaeosaniwa	2

Peltosaurus	1
Scapherpeton	1
Thescelosaurus	1

Cenozoic Amphibians, Reptiles, and Mammals

Chadronian, 37–34 MA (Chadron Formation, SD)

Alligator	1
Brontotherium	1
Hyracodon	1
Palaeolagus	1
Perchoerus	1
Poebrotherium	1
Subhyracodon	1
Titanotherium	8

Orellan, 34–32 MA (Brule Formation, SD)

Agriochoerus	1
Amphicaenopus	1
Bothriodon	2
Caenopus	4
Calamagras	1
Colodon	1
Cynodictis	1
Dinictis	2
Elomeryx	2
Elotherium	1
Entelodon	7
Eporeodon	27
Eumys	1
Hadroleptauchenia	2
Heptacodon	1
Hoplophoneus	1
Hyaenodon	1
Hyporhineura	1
Hyracodon	12
Ischyromys	1
Leptauchenia	21
Leptomeryx	1
Merycoidodon	5
Mesohippus	9

Metamynodon	1
Miohippus	2
Palaeolagus	1
Peltosaurus	1
Perchoerus	1
Protoceras	13
Rhineura	2
Scaptohyus	1
Scottimus	4
Stylemys	1
Subhyracodon	16

Whitneyan, 32–30 MA (Brule Formation, Poleslide Member, SD)

Elomeryx	4

Miocene, NE

Aelurodon	3
Merychyus	1
Neohipparion	2
Procamelus	1
Protohippus	1
Teleoceras	3
Vulpes	1

Pleistocene, NE

Canis	1
Chrysemys	1
Equus	14
Hayoceros	1
Mammuthus	1
Mylodon	1
Procamelus	2

1894
HATCHER
311 specimens total now at YPM

Cenozoic Reptiles and Mammals

Chadronian, 37–34 MA (Chadron Formation, SD)

Archaeotherium	1

Caenopus	1
Dinictis	1
Heptacodon	1
Hyaenodon	1
Leptomeryx	1
Menodus	1
Subhyracodon	1
Titanotherium	3
Trionyx	1

Orellan, 34–32 MA (Brule Formation)

Aceratherium	5
Agriochoerus	9
Archaeotherium	4
Bothriodon	3
Caenopus	7
Colodon	4
Daphoenus	1
Diceratherium	2
Dinictis	4
Elomeryx	1
Entelodon	3
Eporeodon	11
Hadroleptauchenia	1
Heptacodon	1
Hesperocyon	2
Homogalax	1
Hoplophoneus	3
Hyaenodon	10
Hyopotamus	1
Hyracodon	11
Ischyromys	9
Leptauchenia	8
Leptictis	7
Leptomeryx	4
Merycoidodon	28
Mesohippus	12
Metamynodon	25
Miohippus	3
Oreodon	1

Palaeolagus	3
Peltosaurus	1
Perchoerus	6
Poebrotherium	5
Protoceras	6
Stylemys	3
Subhyracodon	25

Whitneyan, 32–30 MA (Brule Formation, Poleslide Member, SD)

Entelodon	1
Eusmilus	1
Mesohippus	1
Miohippus	1
Protoceras	1
Subhyracodon	1

1895
HATCHER
200 specimens total now at YPM

Mesozoic Fish, Reptiles, and Mammals

Late Cretaceous, 68–66 MA (Lance Formation, WY)

Amia	1
Champsosaurus	1
Cimolestes	1
Delphodon	1
Lepisosteus	1
Leptochamops	1
Myledaphus	1
Pediomys	2
Triceratops	1

Cenozoic Reptiles and Mammals

Uintan, 46–40.5 MA (Uinta Formation, UT)

Achaenodon	3
Amynodon	23
Baena	1

Camelomeryx	1
Crocodylus	2
Diplacodon	14
Echmatemys	1
Elotherium	1
Eomoropus	1
Epihippus	7
Glyptosaurus	1
Hyopsodus	1
Ischyrotomus	2
Isectolophus	2
Leptoreodon	2
Leptotomus	6
Leptotragulus	2
Merycodesmus	1
Mesatirhinus	2
Mesonyx	2
Metarhinus	1
Mytonomys	1
Ourayia	3
Palaeosyops	5
Paramys	1
Plesiarctomys	1
Prodaphaenus	1
Protitanotherium	2
Protoreodon	15
Prototychus	2
Protylopus	3
Pseudotomus	1
Reithroparamys	1
Saniwa	1
Simidectes	1
Telmatherium	23
Triplopus	16
Uintatherium	6

Oligocene, White River Group, SD

Subhyracodon	1

Uinta MA: http://fossilworks.org/bridge.pl?action=displayInterval&interval_no=229

1896–1899

HATCHER PETERSON
PATAGONIAN SPECIMENS
1,022 specimens total now at YPM

Santacrucian, 19–16 MA, Santa Cruz Formation, Argentina

Abderites	3
Acaremys	9
Acdestis	4
Acrocyon	1
Adelphomys	1
Adinotherium	65
Analcimorphus	4
Asterostemma	1
Astrapothericulus	3
Astrapotherium	14
Aulocetus	1
Borhyaena	3
Calyptocephalella	2
Caudiverbera	2
Cladosictis	11
Cochlops	4
Diadiaphorus	10
Eocardia	36
Eucholoeops	3
Eucinepeltus	2
Glyptodon	8
Hapalops	88
Hegetotherium	25
Homalodotherium	10
Interatherium	44
Licaphrium	2
Megalonychotherium	1
Metopotoxus	1
Microbiotherium	2
Necrolestes	4
Nematherium	7
Neoreomys	59

Nesodon	93
Opisthodactylus	1
Pachyrukhos	24
Palaeospheniscus	1
Palaeothentes	5
Pelecyodon	2
Pelecyornis	2
Peltephilus	3
Perimys	35
Phororhacos	9
Planops	1
Pliolagostomus	8
Prepotherium	7
Priscodelphinus	1
Proeutatus	22
Proinia	2
Propalaeohoplophorus	8
Prosqualodon	1
Protamandua	1
Proterotherium	32
Prothylacynus	1
Protypotherium	80
Prozaedius	5
Psilopterus	9
Schismotherium	9
Schistomys	9
Sciamys	22
Sipalocyon	5
Spaniomys	6
Stegotherium	3
Steiromys	10
Stenotatus	4
Stenotephanos	2
Stichomys	11
Stilotherium	1
Theosodon	38
Thoatherium	21

Age: Vizcaíno. S., et al. 2012; Flynn et al. 2012

1900
421 specimens total at Carnegie Museum

HATCHER
344 specimens total

Tertiary Mammals (some with Utterback)
and Reptiles

Chadronian, 37–34 MA (Chadron Formation, SD)

Archaeotherium	1
Brontops	3
Caenopus	1
Menodus	8
Mesohippus	1
Trigonias	4

Orellan 34–32 MA (Brule Formation, SD)

Archaeotherium	2
Calamagras	1
Centetodon	1
Daphoenus	1
Dinictis	1
Domnina	1
Eumys	15
Hesperocyon	2
Hoplophoneus	3
Hyaenodon	3
Hypertragulus	3
Hypisodus	2
Hyracodon	7
Ischyromys	2
Leptictis	1
Leptochoerus	4
Leptomeryx	15
Megalagus	1
Merycoidodon	4
Mesohippus	4
Palaeolagus	2
Peltosaurus	1

Peradectes	1
Poebrotherium	12
Scottimus	2
Stylemys	1

Arikareean, 30–19 MA (Monroe Creek Formation, NE)

Promeycochoerus	1

Others

Archaeotherium	2 (No data, Oligocene)
Peratherium	1 (No data, Oligocene)
Testudo (probably)	7 (No data, Oligocene)

Late Cretaceous, 68–66 MA (Lance Formation, WY)

Dinosaurs

Edmontosaurus	5
Thescelosaurus	1
Triceratops	8
Tyrannosaurus	1

Mammals

Alphadon	1
Cimolestes	1
Cimolodon	14
Cimolomys	10
Didelphodon	3
Euangelistes	1
Gypsonictops	3
Meniscoessus	10
Mesodma	5
Pediomys	20

Other Fish, Amphibians, and Reptiles

Amia	1
Odaxosaurus	3
Opisthotriton	3

PETERSON
45 specimens total

Dinosaurs and Other Reptiles

Late Jurassic, 150 MA (Morrison Formation, WY) with Gilmore

Apatosaurus	9
Camarasaurus	3
Creosaurus	1
Diplodocus	2
Opthalmosaurus	1
Stegosaurus	8

Tertiary Mammals

Orellan, 34–32 MA (Brule Formation, SD)

Ischyromys	13
Merycoidodon	1
Mesohippus	2
Palaeolagus	3
Paradjidaumo	1

Others

Miacis	1 (Green River Formation, Eocene)
Palaeocastor	1 (Harrison Formation, Miocene)

UTTERBACK
31 specimens total

Tertiary Mammals

Chadronian, 37–34 MA (Chadron Formation, SD)

Caenopus	1
Menodus	1
Merycoidodon	1
Orohippus	1

Orellan, 34–32 MA (Brule Formation, SD)

Hypisodus	1
Leptomeryx	1
Merycoidodon	13
Poebrotherium	2

Arikareean, 30–19 MA (Monroe Creek Formation, NE)

Promerycochoerus	1

Oligocene (no field data)

Aceratherium	1
Menodus	1
Merycoidodon	2

Early Miocene (Harrison Formation, NE)

Palaeocastor	1

1901
802 specimens total at Carnegie Museum

HATCHER
12 specimens total

Tertiary Mammals and Reptiles

Orellan, 34–32 MA (Brule Formation, SD)

Exostinus	1
Hypertragulus	3
Hypisodus	1
Leptomeryx	1
Oxydactylus	1
Trigonias	1

Others

Promerycochoerus	1 (No data, Miocene)
Stenomylus	1 (No data, Miocene)

PETERSON
758 specimens total

Tertiary Mammals and Reptiles

Chadronian, 37–34 MA (Chadron Formation, SD)

Menodus	2
Poebrotherium	1

Orellan, 34–32 MA (Brule Formation, SD)

Adjidaumo	2
Ankylodon	1
Archaeotherium	3
Bothriodon	1
Caenopus	8
Calamagras	1
Campestrallomys	1
Centetodon	1
Daphoenus	7
Desmatolagus	1
Dinictis	6
Eumys	36
Exostinus	1
Hesperocyon	17
Hoplophoneus	12
Hyaenondon	15
Hypertragulus	3
Hypisodus	15
Ischyromys	66
Leptictis	11
Leptochoerus	2
Leptomeryx	41
Limenetes	1
Megalagus	1
Merychyus	1
Merycoidodon	55
Mesohippus	34
Oligospermophilus	1
Palaeolagus	62
Paradjidaumo	3

Peltosaurus	2
Peratherium	2
Poebrotherium	49
Proamphicyon	1
Prosciurus	4
Protemnocyon	1
Rhineura	5
Stylemys	3

Arikareean, 30–19 MA (Upper Monroe Creek, Harrison Formation, NE)

Mesoreodon	1
Palaeocastor	1
Phenacocoelus	3
Promerycochoerus	8

Hemingfordian, 19–16 MA (Upper Loup Fork, NE)

Aleurocyon	1
Blastomeryx	1
Cyclopedius	1
Gopherus	1
Merychyus	39
Merycochoerus	7
Oxydactylus	10
Parahippus	4
Stenomylus	5
Tanymykter	1
Thinohyus	2
Ticholeptus	1

Others

Aelurodon	1 (Upper Harrison, Middle Miocene)
Cynodesmus	1 (Loup Fork, Miocene)
Diceratherium	1 (Lower Harrison, Early Miocene)
Merychyus	43 (Upper Harrison, Middle Miocene)
Merychyus	5 (Loup Fork, Miocene)
Merycochoerus	2 (Loup Fork, Miocene)
Merycochoerus	2 (Upper Harrison, Middle Miocene)
Merycodus	1 (Upper Harrison, Middle Miocene)
Moropus	3 (Loup Fork, Upper Loup Fork, Miocene)
Teleoceras	1 (Upper Harrison, Middle Miocene)

GILMORE
21 specimens total

Dinosaurs and Fish

Late Jurassic, 150 MA (Morrison Formation, WY)

Apatosaurus	2
Camarasaurus?	2
Ceratodus	1
Elosaurus	1
Stegosaurus	3

UTTERBACK
16 specimens total

Dinosaurs and Other Reptiles

Late Jurassic, 150 MA (Morrison Formation, CO)

Allosaurus	1
Apatosaurus	2
Ceratosaurus	1
Diplodocus	1
Haplocanthosaurus	5
Probaena	1

Mammals

Chadronian, 37–34 MA (Chadron Formation, SD)

Brontotherium	1

Arikareean, 30–19 MA (Harrison Formation, NE)

Oxydactylus	1

Others

Promerycochoerus	1 (No data, Miocene)
Stenomylus	1 (No data, Miocene)

1902
408 specimens total at Carnegie Museum

HATCHER
Nothing

PETERSON
173 specimens total

Dinosaurs

Late Jurassic, 150 MA (Morrison Formation, CO)

Camarasaurus	1

Tertiary Mammals and Egg

Chadronian, 37–34 MA (Chadron Formation, SD)

Bothriodon	1
Brachyrhyncocyon	1
Brontops	3
Menodus	1
Trigonias	1

Orellan, 34–32 MA (Brule Formation, SD)

Archaeotherium	14
Caenopus	6
Daphoenus	1
Dinictis	5
Eumys	20
Hesperocyon	3
Hoplophoneus	3
Hypertragulus	2
Hypisodus	1
Hyracodon	24
Leptictis	2
Leptomeryx	1

Merycoidodon	7
Mesohippus	21
Paradjidaumo	2
Peratherium	1
Poebrotherium	3
Protemnocyon	1

Arikareean 30–19 MA (Upper Monroe Creek Formation, NE)

Mesoreodon	1
Phenacocoelus	2
Promerycochoerus	3

Others

Allops	1 (Oligocene)
Merychyus	1 (Loup Fork, Miocene)

GILMORE
48 specimens total

Dinosaurs

Late Jurassic, 150 MA (Morrison Formation, WY)

Allosaurus	1
Apatosaurus	12
Camarasaurus	27
Diplodocus	1
Opthalmosaurus	1
Stegosaurus	4

UTTERBACK
3 specimens total

Dinosaurs

Late Jurassic, 150 MA (Morrison Formation, WY)

Diplodocus	1
Opthalmosaurus	1

DOUGLASS
184 specimens total

Dinosaurs and Other Reptiles

Late Cretaceous, 84–72 MA ("Belly River" Formation, MT)

Ornithomimus	1
Trionyx	1

Tertiary Mammals and Reptiles

Chadronian, 37–34 MA (Chadron, Totson, Renova Formations, MT)

Bathygenys	2
Colodon	2
Cylindrodon	1
Ischyromys	5
Leptomeryx	7
Menodus	2
Mesohippus	2
Palaeolagus	1

Orellan, 34–32 MA (Brule Formation, MT)

Leptauchenia	1
Mesohippus	1
Palaeolagus	2

Arikareean, 30–19 MA (John Day Formation, MT)

Mesocyon	1

Hemingfordian, 19–16 MA (No formation listed)

Merychippus	1

Barstovian, 16–12.5 MA (Lower Madison Valley, Madison Valley, Deep River, Sixmile Creek Formations, MT)

Alphalagus	1
Aphelops	1
Cyclopedius	9
Daphoenus	1
Eporeodon	2

Eumys	30
Hesperocyon	1
Leptomeryx	1
Mammut	1
Merychippus	1
Merycodus	1
Merycoides	2
Mesoreodon	8
Mylagaulus	1
Palaearctomys	1
Palaeocastor	1
Palaeolagus	2
Peratherium	1
Procamelus	3
Promerycochoerus	21
Protohippus	1
Stylemys	1
Testudo	2

Others

Eporeodon	1 (White River, Oligocene)
Mammut	2 (Loup Fork, Miocene)
Paradjidaumo	1 (Early Oligocene)
Protohippus	1 (Loup Fork, Miocene)

1903
256 specimens total at Carnegie Museum

HATCHER
4 specimens total

Dinosaurs and Other Reptiles

Late Cretaceous, 78–75 MA (Judith River Formation, MT)

Deinosuchus	1 (with Utterback)
Trionyx	1
Tyrannosaurus	1

PETERSON
Nothing

UTTERBACK
55 specimens total

Dinosaurs and Other Reptiles

Late Jurassic, 150 MA (Morrison Formation, WY)

Allosaurus	1
Apatosaurus	7
Camarasaurus	24
Diplodocus	3
Haplocanthosaurus	2

Late Cretaceous, 78–75 MA (Judith River Formation, MT)

Basilemys	1

Late Cretaceous, 68–66 MA (Hell Creek Formation, MT)

Edmontosaurus	1

GILMORE
33 specimens total

Dinosaurs, Other Reptiles, and Fish

Late Jurassic, 150 MA (Morrison Formation, WY)

Apatosaurus	1
Stegosaurus	1

Late Cretaceous, 87–82 MA (Niobrara Formation, KS)

Clidastes	3
Mosasaurus	1
Platycarpus	1
Pteranodon	19
Syllaemus	1
Tylosaurus	1
Xiphactinus	1

DOUGLASS
164 specimens total

Mammals and Reptiles

Late Cretaceous, 78–75 MA (Judith River Formation, MT)

Basilemys	1

Chadronian, 37–34 MA (Renova Formation, MT)

Agriochoerus	1
Ardynomys	3
Bathygenys	1
Colodon	10
Cylindrodon	2
Epoicotherium	1
Glyptosaurus	1
Hendryomeryx	1
Hyaenodon	1
Hyracodon	4
Ictops	4
Ischyromys	1
Limenetes	13
Megacerops	1
Menodus	1
Mesohippus	5
Micropternodus	1
Oreonetes	14
Palaeolagus	4
Paradjidaumo	3
Parictis	1
Peratherium	1
Pseudocylindrodon	5
Testudo	2
Trigonias	1

Arikareean, 30–19 MA (Cabbage Patch Beds, No Data)

Gregorymys	1
Merychyus	1
Temnocyon	1
Ticholeptus	1

Barstovian, 16–12.5 MA (Deep River Formation, MT)

Promerycochoerus   2

Others

Bird tracks	2 (? White River, Madison Valley, ? Oligocene)
Merycodus	1 (Sixmile Creek Formation, Miocene)
Promerycochoerus	3 (No data, Chadronian; Unnamed, Miocene)
Ticholeptus	2 (Unnamed, Miocene)

1904
117 specimens total at Carnegie Museum

Hatcher
Nothing

Peterson
110 specimens total

Tertiary Mammals and Reptiles

Chadronian, 37–34 MA (Gering Formation, NE)

Palaeocastor   1

Orellan, 34–32 MA (Brule Formation, SD)

Leptomeryx	1
Merycoidodon	1
Mesohippus	1
Peltosaurus	1
Poebrotherium	3

Arikareean, 30–19 MA (Harrison, Monroe Creek Formations, NE)

Cyclopidius	1
Daemonelix	1
Daphenodon	1
Delotrochanter	1
Diceratherium	8
Dinohyus	1
Euhapsis	1
Menoceras	7

Merychyus	6
Mesoreodon	8
Moropus	4
Nothocyon	2
Oxydactylus	1
Palaeocastor	14
Parahippus	2
Phenacocoelus	8
Promerycochoerus	10
Protomeryx	1
Sespia	1
Stenomylus	1
Sunkahetanka	1
Ticholeptus	1
Ysengrinia	1

Hemingfordian, 19–16 MA (Upper Loup Fork, NE)

Stenomylus	1

Others

Merycochoerus	1 (Loup Fork, Miocene)
Oxydactylus	1 (Harrison, Early Miocene)

DOUGLASS
4 specimens total

Tertiary Mammals

Barstovian, 16–12.5 MA (Madison Valley Formation, MT)

Aphelops	1

UTTERBACK
3 specimens total

Dinosaurs

Late Cretaceous, 68–66 MA (Hell Creek Formation, MT)

Triceratops	2

Bibliography
for John Bell Hatcher

Hatcher, J. B. "The Ceratops Beds of Converse County, Wyoming." *Amer. Jour. Sci.*, 3rd ser., no. 45 (1893a): 135–144.

Hatcher, J. B. "The Titanotherium Beds." *Amer. Naturalist* 27 (1893b): 204–221.

Hatcher, J. B. "A Median Horned Rhinoceros from the Loup Fork Beds of Nebraska." *Amer. Geologist* 13 (1894a): 149–150.

Hatcher, J. B. "On a Small Collection of Vertebrate Fossils from the Loup Fork Beds of Northwestern Nebraska, with Note on the Geology of the Region." *Amer. Naturalist* 27 (1894b): 236–248.

Hatcher, J. B. "Discovery of *Diceratherium*, the Two-Horned Rhinoceros, in the White River Beds of South Dakota." *Amer. Geologist* 13 (1894c): 360–361.

Hatcher, J. B. "The Princeton Scientific Expedition of 1894." *The Princeton College Bulletin* 6, no. 4 (1894d): 91–92.

Hatcher, J. B. "On a New Species of *Diplacodon*, with a Discussion of the Relations of That Genus to *Telmatotherium*." *Amer. Naturalist* 29 (1895a): 1084–1090.

Hatcher, J. B. "Discovery, in the Oligocene of South Dakota, of *Eusmilus*, a Genus of Sabre-Toothed Cats New to North America." *Amer. Naturalist* 29 (1895b): 1091–1093.

Hatcher, J. B. "The Princeton Scientific Expedition of 1895." *The Princeton College Bulletin* 7, no. 4 (1895c): 95–98.

Hatcher, J. B. "Some Localities for Laramie Mammals and Horned Dinosaurs." *Amer. Naturalist* 30 (1896a): 112–120.

Hatcher, J. B. "Recent and Fossil Tapirs." *Amer. Jour. Sci* .,4th ser., v. 1 (1896b): 161–180.

Hatcher, J. B. "The Cape Fairweather Beds, a New Marine Tertiary Horizon in Southern Patagonia." *Amer. Jour. Sci.*, 4th ser., vol. 4 (1897a): 246–248.

Hatcher, J. B. "On the Geology of Southern Patagonia." *Amer. Jour. Sci.*, 4th ser., vol. 4 (1897b): 327–354.

Hatcher, J. B. "*Diceratherium proavitum.*" *Amer. Geologist* 20 (1897c): 313–316.

Hatcher, J. B. "Patagonia." *Nat. Geo.* 8 (1897d): 305–319.

Hatcher, J. B. "The Third Princeton Expedition to Patagonia." *Science* 10 (1899a): 580–581.

Hatcher, J. B. "Explorations in Patagonia." *Sci. Amer.* 81, no. 21 (1899b): 328–329.

Hatcher, J. B. "Review: The Mysterious Mammal of Patagonia, *Grypotherium domesticum.*" *Science* 10 (1899c): 814–815.

Hatcher, J. B. "The Sedimentary Rocks of Southern Patagonia." *Amer. Jour. Sci.*, 4th ser., vol. 9 (1900a): 85–108.

Hatcher. J. B. "Some Geographic Features of Southern Patagonia, with a Discussion of Their Origin." *Nat. Geo* 11 (1900b): 41–45.

Hatcher J. B. "The Carnegie Museum Paleontological Expeditions of 1900." *Science* 12 (1900c): 718–720.

Hatcher, J. B. "Vertebral Formula of *Diplodocus* (Marsh)." *Science* 12 (1900d): 828–830.

Hatcher, J. B. "The Indian Tribes of Southern Patagonia, Tierra del Fuego, and Adjoining Islands." *Nat. Geo.* 12 (1901a): 12–22.

Hatcher, J. B. "The Lake Systems of Southern Patagonia." *Bull. Geog. Soc. Philadelphia* 2 (1901b): 139–145.

Hatcher, J. B. "The Lake Systems of Southern Patagonia." *Amer. Geologist* 27 (1901c): 167–173.

Hatcher, J. B. "Some New and Little Known Fossil Vertebrates." *Ann. Carnegie Mus.* 1: (1901d): 128–144.

Hatcher, J. B. "On the Cranial Elements and the Deciduous and Permanent Dentitions of *Titanotherium.*" *Ann. Carnegie Mus.* 1 (1901e): 256–262.

Hatcher, J. B. "*Sabal rigida*, a New Species of Palm from the Laramie." *Ann. Carnegie Mus.* 1 (1901f): 263–264.

Hatcher, J. B. "The Jurassic Dinosaur Deposits Near Canyon City, Colorado." *Ann. Carnegie Mus.* 1 (1901g): 327–341.

Hatcher, J. B. "*Diplodocus* (Marsh): Its Osteology, Taxonomy, and Probable Habits, with a Restoration of the Skeleton." *Mem. Carnegie Mus.* 1 (1901h): 1–63.

Hatcher, J. B. "On the Structure of the Manus in *Brontosaurus.*" *Science* 14 (1901i): 1015–1017.

Hatcher, J. B. "A Mounted Skeleton of *Titanotherium dispar* Marsh." *Ann. Carnegie Mus.* 1 (1902a): 347–355.

Hatcher, J. B. "Structure of the Fore Limb and Manus in *Brontosaurus.*" *Ann. Carnegie Mus.* 1 (1902b): 356–376.

Hatcher, J. B. "The Genera and Species of the Trachodontidae (Hadrosauridae, Claosauridae) Marsh." *Ann. Carnegie Mus.* 1 (1902c): 377–386.

Hatcher, J. B. "Origin of the Oligocene and Miocene Deposits of the Great Plains." *Proc. Amer. Philo. Soc.* 41 (1902d): 113–131.

Hatcher, J. B. "Oligocene Canidae." *Mem. Carnegie Mus.* 1 (1902e): 65–108.

Hatcher, J. B. "Discovery of a Musk Ox Skull (*Ovis cavifrons* Leidy), in West Virginia, Near Steubenville, Ohio." *Science* 16 (1902f): 707–709.

Hatcher, J. B. "Field Work in Vertebrate Paleontology at the Carnegie Museum for 1902." *Science* 16 (1902g): 752.

Hatcher, J. B. "A Correction of Prof. Osborn's Note Entitled 'New Vertebrates of the mid-Cretaceous.'" *Science* 16 (1902h): 831–832.

Hatcher, J. B. "A New Sauropod Dinosaur from the Jurassic of Colorado." *Proc. Biol. Soc. Washington* 16 (1903a): 1–2.

Hatcher, J. B. "The Judith River Beds." *Science* 17 (1903b): 471–472.

Hatcher, J. B. "Criticism: *L'Age des formations sedimentaires de Patagonie*, by Florentino Ameghino." *Amer. Jour Sci.*, 4th ser., v. 15 (1903c): 483–486.

Hatcher, J. B. "A New Name for the Dinosaur *Haplocanthus* Hatcher." *Proc. Biol. Soc. Washington* 16 (1903d): 100.

Hatcher, J. B. "Discovery of Remains of *Astrodon* (*Pleurocoelus*) in the *Atlantosaurus* Beds of Wyoming." *Ann. Carnegie Mus.* 2 (1903e): 9–14.

Hatcher, J. B. "Relative Age of the Lance Creek (Ceratops) Beds of Converse County, Wyoming, the Judith River Beds of Montana and the Belly River Beds of Canada." *Amer. Geologist* 31 (1903f): 369–375.

Hatcher, J. B., and T. W. Stanton. "The Stratigraphic Position of the Judith River Beds and Their Correlation with the Belly River Beds." *Science* 18 (1903g): 211–212.

Hatcher, J. B. "Vertebrate Paleontology at the Carnegie Museum." *Science* 18 (1903h): 569–570.

Hatcher, J. B. "Osteology of *Haplocanthosaurus*, with a Description of a New Species, and Remarks on the Probable Habits of the Sauropoda and the Age and Origin of the Atlantosaurus Beds." *Mem. Carnegie Mus.* 2 (1903i): 1–72.

Hatcher, J. B. "Additional Remarks on *Diplodocus*." *Mem. Carnegie Mus.* 2 (1903j): 72–75.

Hatcher, J. B. "Narrative and Geography." *Reports of the Princeton University Expeditions to Patagonia, 1896–1899* 1 (1903k): 1–314.

Hatcher, J. B, and T. W. Stanton. "An Attempt to Correlate the Marine with the Non-marine Formations of the Middle West." *Proc. Amer. Philo. Soc.* 43, no. 178 (1904): 341–365.

Stanton, T. W, and J. B. Hatcher. "Geology and Paleontology of the Judith River Beds." *U.S. Geol. Soc. Bull.* 257 (1905a): 9–119.

Hatcher, J. B. "Two New Species of Ceratopsia from the Laramie of Converse County, Wyoming." Edited by R. S. Lull. *Amer. Jour. Sci.*, 4th ser., vol. 20 (1905b): 413–419.

Hatcher, J. B., O. C. Marsh, and R. S. Lull. "The Ceratopsia." *U. S. Geol. Survey Monograph* 49 (1907): 1–300.

Hatcher, J. B. *Bone Hunters in Patagonia*. Woodbridge, CT: Ox Bow Press, 1985.

References Other Than Hatcher's Publications

Baur, G. "A Review of the Charges Against the Paleontological Department of the U. S. Geological Survey, and of the Defence Made by Prof. O. C. Marsh." *Amer. Naturalist* 24, no. 279 (1890): 298–304.

Benton, R. C., et al. *The White River Badlands: Geology and Paleontology.* Bloomington, IN: Indiana Univ. Press, 2015.

Bilbey, S. A., and J. E. Hall. "Marsh and 'Megalosaurus'—Utah's First Theropod Dinosaur." In *Vertebrate Paleontology in Utah*, edited by D. D Gillette. Utah Geol. Surv, misc. pub. 99–1, (1999): 67–69.

Breithaupt, B. H. "Biography of William Harlow Reed: The Story of a Frontier Fossil Collector." *Earth Sciences History* 9, no. 1 (1990): 6–13.

Brezinski, D. K., and A. D. Kollar. "Geology of the Carnegie Museum Dinosaur Quarry Site of *Diplodocus carnegii*, Sheep Creek, Wyoming." *Ann. Carnegie Mus.* 77, no. 2 (2008): 243–252.

Brinkman, P. "Bartholomew James Sulivan's Discovery of Fossil Vertebrates in the Tertiary Beds of Patagonia." *Archives Natural History* 30, no. 1 (2003): 56–74.

Brinkman, P. D. "Charles Darwins *Beagle* voyage, fossil vertebrate succession, and 'The Gradual Birth & Death of Species,'" *Jour. History Biology*, DOI 10.1007/s10739-009-9189-9 (2009).

Brinkman, P. D. *The Second Jurassic Dinosaur Rush.* Chicago, IL: Univ. Chicago Press, 2010.

Brown, B. "A New Species of Fossil Edentate from the Santa Cruz Formation of Patagonia." *Bull. Amer. Mus. Nat. Hist.* 19 (1903): 453–457.

Brown, F. *Let's Call Him Barnum*. New York: Vantage Press, 1987.

Conniff, R. "How Science Came to Yale." *Yale Alumni Mag* 78, no. 4 (2015): https:// yalealumnimagazine.com/articles/4066-how-science-came-to-yale.

Cope, E. D. "Third Notice of Extinct Vertebrata from the Tertiary of the Plains." *Paleon. Bull* 15 (1873): 1–16.

Cope, E. D. "On Some Extinct Reptiles and Batrachia from the Judith River and Fox Hills Beds of Montana." *Proc. Philadelphia Acad. Nat. Sci.* 28 (1876): 340–359.

Cope, E. D. "On a Gigantic Saurian from the Dakota Epoch of Colorado." *Palaeontological Bulletin* 25 (1877): 5–10.

Cope, E. D. "Descriptions of Extinct Batrachia and Reptilia from the Permian Formation of Texas." *Proc. Amer. Phil. Soc.* (1878): 505–530.

Cope, E. D. "The Perissodactyla (concluded)." *Amer. Nat.* 21 (1887): 1060–1076.

Cross, C. W. "The Denver Tertiary Formation." *Colo. Sci. Soc. Pr.* 2 (1889a.): 119–33.

Cross, C. W. "The Denver Tertiary Formation." *Amer. Jour. Sc.* ser. 3, no. 37 (1889b): 261–282.

Cummins, E. D. "The Localities and Horizons of Permian Vertebrate Fossils in Texas." *Jour. Geol.* 16 (1908): 737–745.

Dana, J. D. *A System of Mineralogy*. New Haven, CT: Durrie, Peck, Herrick, Noyes, 1837.

Dana, J. D. *Manual of Mineralogy*. New Haven, CT: 1848.

Dingus, L., and M. A. Norell. *Barnum Brown: The Man Who Discovered* Tyrannosaurus rex. Berkeley, CA: Univ. California Press, 2010.

Douglass, G. E. *Speak to the Earth and It Will Teach You: The Life and Times of Earl Douglass, 1862–1931*. Charleston, SC: Booksurge LLC, 2009.

Duce, J. T. 1937. "Patter-gonia." *Atlantic Monthly*, September, v. 160: 367–373

Eberth, D. A. "Edmonton Group." In *Encyclopedia of Dinosaurs*, edited by P. J. Currie and K. Padian. San Diego, CA: Academic Press, 1997a, 199–204.

Eberth, D. A. "Judith River Wedge." In *Encyclopedia of Dinosaurs*, edited by P. J. Currie and K. Padian. San Diego, CA: Academic Press, 1997b, 379–385.

Eberth, D. A. "The Geology." In *Dinosaur Provincial Park: A Spectacular Ancient Ecosystem Revealed*, edited by P. J. Currie and E. B. Koppelhus. Bloomington, IN: Indiana Univ. Press, 2005, 54–82.

Fischer, V., et al. "New Ophthalmosaurid Ichthyosaurs from the European Lower Cretaceous Demonstrate Extensive Ichthyosaur Survival Across the Jurassic-Cretaceous Boundary." *PLoS ONE* 7, no. 1(2012): e29234.

Flower, W. H. *Introduction to the Osteology of the Mammalia*. London: MacMillan and Co., 1870.

Flynn, J. J., et al. Cenozoic Andean Faunas: Shedding New Light on South American Mammal Evolution, Biogeography, Environments, and Tectonics. 10.7208/chicago /9780226649214.003.0004, 2012. 51–75.

Gilmore, C. W. "Osteology of the Carnivorous Dinosauria in the United States National Museum, with Special Reference to the Genera *Antrodemus (Allosaurus)* and *Ceratosaurus*." *Bull. U. S. Nat. Mus.* 110 (1920): 1–154.

Grenard, D. "Marsh Felch Dinosaur Quarry Trail." http://www.gardenparkdinos.com/marsh-felch-dinosaur-quarry-trail/ (2013).

Hay, O. P. "George Baur." *Science* 8, no. 185 (1898): 68–71.

Holland, W. J. "John Bell Hatcher." *Ann. Carnegie Mus.* 2 (1904): 597–604.

Hunt, R. M. "Amphicyonidae." In *The Terrestrial Eocene-Oligocene Transition in North America*, edited by D. R. Prothero and R. J. Emry. New York: Cambridge Univ. Press, 1996, 476–485.

Hunt, R. M. "Global Climate and the Evolution of Large Mammalian Carnivores During the Later Cenozoic in North America." *Bull. Amer. Muse. Nat. Hist.* 285 (2004): 139–156.

Jacobs, L. L., et al. "Jacob Boll, Robert T. Hill and the Early History of Vertebrate Paleontology in Texas." *Historical Biology* 24, no. 4 (2012): 341–348.

Jaffe, M. *The Gilded Dinosaur.* New York: Crown Publishers, 2000.

Kelley, B. M. *Yale: A History.* New Haven, CT: Yale University Press, 1974.

Lanham, U. *The Bone Hunters.* New York: Columbia University Press, 1973.

Leidy, J. "Description of *Megacerops coloradensis.*" *Proc. Acad. Sci. Philadelphia* 22 (1870): 1–2.

Lepley, J. G., and S. Lepley. *The Vanishing West: Hornaday's Last Buffalo, the Last of the Wild Herds.* Fort Benton, MT: River and Plains Soc., 1992, 1–109.

Longrich, N. R., and D. J. Field, "*Torosaurus* Is Not *Triceratops*: Ontogeny in Chasmosaurine Ceratopsids as a Case Study in Dinosaur Taxonomy." *PLoS ONE* 7, no. 2 (2012): e32623.

Lull, R. S. "The Sauropod Dinosaur *Barosaurus* Marsh." *Mem. Connecticut Acad. Arts Sci.* 6, (1919): 1–42.

Marsh, O. C. "Notice of New Tertiary Mammals." *Amer. Jour. Sci. and Arts* 5 (1873): 1–9.

Marsh, O. C. "Notice of New Dinosaurian Reptiles." *Amer. Jour. Sci.* 15 (1878): 241–244.

Marsh, O. C. "Dinocerata: A Monograph of an Extinct Order of Gigantic Mammals." *US Geol. Sur. Monographs* 10 (1886): 1–243.

Marsh, O. C. "Notice of a New Genus of Sauropoda and Other New Dinosaurs from the Potomac Formation." *Amer. Jour. Sci.* 35 (1888): 89–94.

Marsh, O. C. "Discovery of Cretaceous Mammals." *Amer. Jour. Sci.* 38 (1889a): 81–92.

Marsh, O. C. "Notice of Gigantic Horned Dinosauria from the Cretaceous." *Amer Jour. Sci.* 38 (1889b): 173–176.

Marsh, O. C. "Discovery of Cretaceous Mammalia; Part II." *Amer. Jour. Sci.* 38 (1889c): 177–180.

Marsh, O. C. "Notice of Some Extinct Testudinata." *Amer. Jour. Sci.*, 3rd ser., no. 40 (1890): 177–179.

Marsh, O. C. "Notice of New Vertebrate Fossils." *Amer. Jour. Sci.*, 3rd ser., no. 42 (1891): 265–269.

Marsh, O. C. "Discovery of Cretaceous Mammals, Part 3." *Am. Jour. Sci.* 43 (1892): 249–262.

Mihlbachler, M. C. "Species Taxonomy, Phylogeny, and Biogeography of the Brontotheriidae (Mammalia: Perissodactyla)." *Bull. Amer. Mus. Nat. Hist.* 311 (2008): 1–475.

Osborn, H.F. "A Skeleton of *Diplodocus.*" *Memoirs of the American Museum of Natural History,* v. 1 no. 5 (1899): 191–214.

Osborn, H. F. "Recent Zoo-paleontology." *Science* 14, no. 352 (1901a): 498–499.

Osborn, H. F. "*Diplodocus* Marsh." *Science* 14, no. 353 (1901b): 531–532.

Osborn, H. F. "Recent Zoopaleontology: New Vertebrates of the Mid-Cretaceous." *Science* 16, no. 408 (1902): 673–676.

Ostrom, J. H., and J. S. McIntosh. *Marsh's Dinosaurs: The Collections from Como Bluff.* New Haven, CT: Yale University Press, 1966.

Ostrom, J. H., and P. Wellnhofer. "The Munich Specimen of *Triceratops* with a Revision of the Genus." *Zitteliana* 14 (1986): 111–158.

Otero, A., and Z. Gasperini. "The History of the Cast Skeleton of *Diplodocus carnegii* Hatcher, 1901, at the Museui De La Plata, Argentina." *Ann. Carnegie Museum* 82 (2014): 291–304.

Peterson, O. A. "Recent Observations upon *Daemonelix.*" *Science* 20 (1904): 344–345.

Peterson, O. A. "Description of New Rodents and Discussion of the Origin of *Daemonelix*." *Mem. Carnegie Mus.* 2 (1905): 139–202.

Prothero, D. R. *The Evolution of North American Rhinoceroses.* New York: Cambridge Univ. Press, 2005.

Prothero, D. R., and R. J. Emry, "The Chadronian, Orellan, and Whiteyan North American Land Mammal Ages." In *Late Cretaceous and Cenozoic Mammals of North America: Biostratigraphy and Geochronology,* edited by M. O. Woodburne. New York: Columbia Univ. Press, 2004, 156–168.

Rainger, R. "Collectors and Entrepreneurs: Hatcher, Wortman, and the Structure of American Vertebrate Paleontology circa 1900." *Earth Sci. Hist.* 9, no. 1 (1990): 14–21.

Rainger, R. *An Agenda for Antiquity: Henry Fairfield Osborn and Vertebrate Paleontology at the American Museum of Natural History, 1890–1935.* Tuscaloosa, AL: Univ. Alabama Press, 1991.

Rankin, W. M. "Recent Additions to the Herbarium." *Princeton College Bull.* 7, no. 2 (1895): 55.

Rea, T. *Bone Wars: The Excavation and Celebrity of Andrew Carnegie's Dinosaur.* Pittsburgh, PA: 2001.

Riggs, E. S. "*Brachiosaurus altithorax,* the Largest Known Dinosaur." *Amer. Jour. Sci.* v. 15 (1903): 299-306.

Rogers, R. R., et al. "Age, Correlation, and Lithostratigraphic Revision of the Upper Cretaceous (Campanian) Judith River Formation in Its Type Area (North Central Montana), with a Comparison of Low- and High-Accommodation Alluvial Records." *Jour. Geology* 124 (2016): 99–135.

Romer, A. S. "Cope versus Marsh." *Syst. Zool.* 13, no. 4 (1964): 201–207.

Ruppel, S. C., and R. R. Harrington. "Facies and Sequence Stratigraphy: Critical Tools for Reservoir Framework Definition, Fullerton Clear Fork Reservoir, Texas." *Anatomy of a giant carbonate reservoir: Fullerton Clear Fork (Lower Permian) field, Permian Basin, Texas,* edited by S. C. Ruppel. Studies in Geology 63 (2012): 5–48.

Scannella, J. B., and J. R. Horner. "*Torosaurus* Marsh, 1891 is *Triceratops* Marsh, 1889 (Ceratopsidae: Chasmosaurinae): Synonymy Through Ontogeny." *Jour. Vert. Paleont.* 30 (2010): 1157–1168.

Scannella, J. B., and J. R. Horner. "'Nedoceratops': An Example of Transitional Morphology." *PLos ONE* 6 (2011): e28705.

Schuchert, C. "John Bell Hatcher." *Amer. Geologist* 35 (1905): 131–141.

Schuchert, C. "Biographical Memoir of Othniel Charles Marsh 1831–1899." *Nat. Acad. Sci. Biograph. Mem.* 20, no. 1 (1938): 1–80.

Schuchert, C., and C. M. LeVene. *O. C. Marsh: Pioneer in Paleontology.* New Haven, CT: Yale University Press, 1940.

Scott, W. B. "The Princeton Scientific Expedition of 1893." *Princeton College Bull.* 5, no. 4 (1893): 80–84.

Scott, W. B. "John Bell Hatcher." *Science* 19 (1904 a): 139–142.

Scott, W. B. "Memoir of John Bell Hatcher." *Geol. Soc. Amer. Bull.* 16 (1904 b): 548–555.

Scott, W. B. *Some Memories of a Paleontologist.* Princeton, NJ: Princeton University Press, 1939.

Shor, E. N. *Fossils and Flies: The Life of a Compleat Scientist, Samuel Wendell Williston.* Norman, OK: Univ. of Oklahoma Press, 1971.

Shor, E. N. *The Fossil Feud.* Hicksville, NY: Exposition Press, 1974.

Simpson, G. G. *Discoverers of the Lost World.* New Haven, CT: Yale Univ. Press, 1984.

Sprain, C. J., et al. "High-Resolution Chronostratigraphy of the Terrestrial Cretaceous-Paleogene Transition and Recovery Interval in the Hell Creek Region, Montana." *Geol. Soc. Amer. Bull.* 127, no. 3–4 (2015): 393–409.

Sternberg, C. H. *The Life of a Fossil Hunter.* New York: Henry Holt and Co., 1909.

Tedford, R. H., et al. "Mammalian Biochronology of the Arikareean through Hemphillian Interval (Late Oligocene through Early Pliocene Epochs)." In *Late Cretaceous and Cenozoic Mammals of North America: Biostratigraphy and Geochronology,* edited by M. O. Woodburne. New York: Columbia Univ. Press, 2004, 169–231.

Tschopp, E., O. Mateus, and R. B. J. Benson, "A Specimen-Level Phylogenetic Analysis and Taxonomic Revision of Diplodocidae (Dinosauria, Sauropoda)." PeerJ 3 (2015): e857, DOI: 10.7717/peerj.857.

Vizcaíno. S., et al. "Background for a Paleoecological Study of the Santa Cruz Formation (late Early Miocene) on the Atlantic Coast of Patagonia." In *Early Miocene Paleobiology in Patagonia,* edited by Vizcaíno, et al. Cambridge University Press, 2012, 1–22.

Vlachos, E. "A review of the fossil record of North American turtles of the clade *Pan-Testudinoidea.*" *Bull. Peabody Mus. Nat. Hist,* v. 59, no. 1 (2018): 3–94.

Webb, S. D. "Hatcher in Patagonia." *Discovery* 19, no. 1 (1986): 20–25.

Weishampel, D. B., et al., eds. *The Dinosauria.* Berkeley, CA: Univ. California Press, 1990.

Woodburne, M. O., et al. "Paleogene Land Mammal Faunas of South America; a Response to Global Climatic Changes and Indigenous Floral Diversity." *Jour. Mamm. Evol.* 21 (2014): 1–73.

Wortman, J. "The New Department of Vertebrate Paleontology of the Carnegie Museum." *Science* 11, no. 266 (1900): 163–166.

Yale College. *17th Annual Report of the Sheffield Scientific School of Yale College.* New Haven, CT: Tuttle, Morehouse and Taylor Printers, 1883.

Yale College. *19th Annual Report of the Sheffield Scientific School of Yale College.* New Haven, CT: Tuttle, Morehouse and Taylor Printers, 1885.

Endnotes

PROLOGUE

1. Webb 1986: 21; Duce 1937: 372. James Terry Duce (1893–1965) was, like Hatcher, an American geologist who worked extensively in South America. In the oil industry, he was a vice president of Texaco and the Columbian Oil Company before going on to serve as vice president of the Arabian American Oil Company. He also served on several influential foreign policy boards and committees. https://timesmachine.nytimes.com/timesmachine/1965/08/17/96714077.html?action=click&contentCollection=Archives&module=ArticleEndCTA&region=ArchiveBody&pgtype=article&pageNumber=33.

1: BECOMING MARSH'S MINION

1. http://hatcherfamilyassn.com/getperson.php?personID=I1660&tree=QHatcher; Schuchert 1905; Holland 1904.
2. S. Powsner, pers. comm.with author, July 11, 2017; Osteogenesis Imperfecta Foundation, http://www.oif.org/site/PageServer?pagename=AOI_Facts, for information cited about the disease.
3. Scott 1904 a, b; https://www.grinnell.edu/news/historic-figu1996, res., for information cited about the Grinnell tornado.
4. Scott 1904 b.

5. Kelley 1974: 41–80.

6. Kelley 1974: 129–137; Conniff 2015.

7. Kelley 1974: 182.

8. Kelley 1974: 182–186.

9. Schuchert and LeVene 1940: 74.

10. Kelley 1974: 185; *17th Annual Report of the Sheffield Scientific School of Yale College*, 1883; http://www.in2013dollars.com/1860-dollars-in-2016?amount=100000. All conversions from past dollars to 2016 dollars will be based on this reference.

11. *17th Annual Report of the Sheffield Scientific School*, 1883: 3.

12. *17th Annual Report of the Sheffield Scientific School*, 1883: 38–39.

13. *17th Annual Report of the Sheffield Scientific School*, 1883: 41.

14. *17th Annual Report of the Sheffield Scientific School*, 1883: 41–43; *19th Annual Report of the Sheffield Scientific School* 1885: 16.

15. Schuchert and LeVene 1940: 45, 207.

2: MARSH: THE MASTER

1. Schuchert and LeVene 1940: 13–20.

2. http://peabody.yale.edu/collections/archives/biography/george-peabody.

3. http://peabody.yale.edu/collections/archives/biography/george-peabody; Schuchert and LeVene 1940: 75–82; Schuchert 1938.

4. http://peabody.yale.edu/collections/archives/biography/othniel-charles-marsh; Schuchert and LeVene 1940: 92.

5. Jaffe 2000; Shor 1974.

6. Jaffe 2000: 44–47; Shor 1974: 31.

7. Shor 1974: 30–31; Jaffe 2000: 51.

8. Jaffe 2000: 25–107; http://peabody.yale.edu/collections/archives/yale-college-scientific-expedition-1870.

9. Schuchert and LeVene 1940: 102–120; Bilbey and Hall 1999.

10. Jaffe 2000: 53, 68; Schuchert and LeVene 1940: 121–125; http://peabody.yale.edu/collections/archives/yale-college-scientific-expedition-1871.

11. Jaffe 2000: 59–62, 70.

12. Jaffe 2000: 71–76; Schuchert and LeVene 1940: 176.

13. Jaffe 2000: 76–90; Marsh 1886.

14. Jaffe 2000: 77, 91.

15. Jaffe 2000: 92.

16. Jaffe 2000: 96.

17. Jaffe 2000: 112–126.

18. Jaffe 2000: 151–153.

19. Jaffe 2000: 156–157.

20. Schuchert and LeVene 1940: 188–192.

21. Schuchert and LeVene 1940: 192–193.

22. Schuchert and LeVene 1940: 192–194.

23. Schuchert and LeVene 1940: 195–197; Ostrom and McIntosh 1966.

24. Schuchert and LeVene 1940: 201; Ostrom and McIntosh 1966: 51–59.
25. Schuchert and LeVene 1940: 248, 255.
26. Schuchert and LeVene 1940: 249–255.
27. Schuchert and LeVene 1940: 256, 261, 269.
28. Schuchert and LeVene 1940: 207.
29. YPM Archives: Marsh/Hatcher Correspondence, B15F0602: 001–002.

3: WRESTLING WITH RHINOS, AS WELL AS AUTHORITY

1. Lanham 1973: 73–78; 156–165.
2. Lanham 1973: 198–199.
3. YPM Archives: Marsh/Hatcher Correspondence, B15F0602: 004–005.
4. YPM Archives: Marsh/Hatcher Correspondence, B15F0602: 006–007.
5. YPM Archives: Marsh/Hatcher Correspondence, B15F0602: 008–009.
6. YPM Archives: Marsh/Hatcher Correspondence, B15F0602: 010.
7. YPM Archives: Marsh/Hatcher Correspondence, B15F0602: 11–14.
8. Schuchert and LeVene 1940: 172–175, 208; YPM Archives: Marsh/Hatcher Correspondence, B15F0602: 016–017, 20–21; Lanham 1973: 205.
9. YPM Archives: Marsh/Hatcher Correspondence, B15F0602: 22–28.
10. YPM Archives: Marsh/Hatcher Correspondence, B15F0602: 29–31, 36–37.
11. YPM Archives: Marsh/Hatcher Correspondence, B15F0602: 38–42.
12. YPM Archives: Marsh/Hatcher Correspondence, B15F0602: 44–50.
13. YPM Archives: Marsh/Hatcher Correspondence, B15F0602: 54–57; Schuchert and LeVene 1940: 209.
14. Lanham 1973: 199; Sternberg 1909: 132–133.
15. Prothero 2005: 113, 116; Tedford et al. 2004.

4: MESSIN' WITH TEXAS AND RETURNING FOR RHINOS

1. YPM Archives: Marsh/Hatcher Correspondence, B15F0602: 058–059; B150603: 003.
2. https://tshaonline.org/handbook/online/articles/fco65, for information cited about Cope's early collecting in Permian of Texas; Jacobs et al, 2012; Cope 1878; Cummins 1908.
3. Romer 1964.
4. YPM Archives: Marsh/Hatcher Correspondence, B15F0602: 058–059; B15F0603: 004.
5. YPM Archives: Marsh/Hatcher Correspondence, B15F0603: 001–002.
6. YPM Archives: Marsh/Hatcher Correspondence, B15F0603: 006.
7. YPM Archives: Marsh/Hatcher Correspondence, B15F0603: 008–009.
8. YPM Archives: Marsh/Hatcher Correspondence, B15F0603: 010–011.
9. YPM Archives: Marsh/Hatcher Correspondence, B15F0603: 012–013.
10. YPM Archives: Marsh/Hatcher Correspondence, B15F0603: 014–016.
11. YPM Archives: Marsh/Hatcher Correspondence, B15F0603: 020–021.
12. YPM Archives: Marsh/Hatcher Correspondence, B15F0603: 026–028.
13. YPM Archives: Marsh/Hatcher Correspondence, B15F0603: 027–028.
14. YPM Archives: Marsh/Hatcher Correspondence, B15F0603: 033.

15. http://www.stratigraphy.org/bak/geowhen/stages/Leonardian.html, for cited geologic age; Ruppel and Harrington 2012.
16. YPM Archives: Marsh/Hatcher Correspondence, B150603: 30–32, 36.
17. YPM Archives: Marsh/Hatcher Correspondence, B15F0603: 40–41; B15F0604: 001–005.
18. YPM Archives: Marsh/Hatcher Correspondence, B15F0604: 007–011.
19. YPM Archives: Marsh/Hatcher Correspondence, B15F0604: 013–014.
20. YPM Archives: Marsh/Hatcher Correspondence, B15F0604: 013–014.
21. YPM Archives: Marsh/Hatcher Correspondence, B15F0604: 013–014.
22. YPM Archives: Marsh/Hatcher Correspondence, B15F0604: 018–021.
23. YPM Archives: Marsh/Hatcher Correspondence, B15F0604: 024–025.
24. YPM Archives: Marsh/Hatcher Correspondence, B15F0604: 029–033.
25. YPM Archives: Marsh/Hatcher Correspondence, B15F0604: 035–038.
26. YPM Archives: Marsh/Hatcher Correspondence, B15F0604: 043–045.
27. YPM Archives: Marsh/Hatcher Correspondence, B15F0605: 001.

5: THUNDER BEASTS

1. Leidy 1870: 1–2; Schuchert and LeVene 1940: 107, 139–168; Cope 1873: 1–16; Mihlbachler 2008: 391; Marsh 1873: 1–9; Cope 1887: 1060–1976.
2. YPM Archives: Marsh/Hatcher Correspondence, B15F0605: 002, 005, 008.
3. YPM Archives: Marsh/Hatcher Correspondence, B15F0605: 009–010, 013; Schuchert and LeVene 1940: 134,140, 176, 211.
4. Ages in millions of years ago [MA] based on Prothero and Emry 2004: 159, fig. 5.2; Tedford et al. 2004: 180, fig. 6.2.
5. YPM Archives: Marsh/Hatcher Correspondence, B15F0605: 014–017.
6. YPM Archives: Marsh/Hatcher Correspondence, B15F0605: 023–025, 27.
7. YPM Archives: Marsh/Hatcher Correspondence, B15F0606: 001–004.
8. YPM Archives: Marsh/Hatcher Correspondence, B15F0606: 006–017.
9. YPM Archives: Marsh/Hatcher Correspondence, B15F0606: 018–023.
10. YPM Archives: Marsh/Hatcher Correspondence, B15F0606: 025–026.
11. YPM Archives: Marsh/Hatcher Correspondence, B15F0606: 028–029.
12. YPM Archives: Marsh/Hatcher Correspondence, B15F0606: 031–033.
13. YPM Archives: Marsh/Hatcher Correspondence, B15F0606: 036.
14. D. L. Brinkman, pers. comm. with author; February 2, 2018.
15. YPM Archives: Marsh/Hatcher Correspondence, B15F0606: 038; Schuchert and LeVene 1940: 211–213.
16. YPM Archives: Marsh/Hatcher Correspondence, B15F0607: 001–004; J. B. Hatcher, "Exploration of Dakota Badlands: Daily Report from Mar. 9–Aug. 31, 1887," Yale Peabody Museum, V.P. AR 000462.
17. YPM Archives: Marsh/Hatcher Correspondence, B15F0607: 006–007, 009.
18. YPM Archives: Marsh/Hatcher Correspondence, B15F0607: 010–013.
19. YPM Archives: Marsh/Hatcher Correspondence, B15F0607: 015, 016, 018–019, 023.
20. YPM Archives: Marsh/Hatcher Correspondence, B15F0607: 024–027.

21. YPM Archives: Marsh/Hatcher Correspondence, B15F0608: 001, 004.

22. YPM Archives: Marsh/Hatcher Correspondence, B15F0608: 005–006, 010.

23. YPM Archives: Marsh/Hatcher Correspondence, B15F0608: 009–014.

24. YPM Archives: Marsh/Hatcher Correspondence, B15F0608: 016–019.

25. YPM Archives: Marsh/Hatcher Correspondence, B15F0608: 020–023.

26. YPM Archives: Marsh/Hatcher Correspondence, B15F0608: 025–033; B15F0609: 003–004.

27. YPM Archives: Marsh/Hatcher Correspondence, B15F0609: 001–002.

28. YPM Archives: Marsh/Hatcher Correspondence, B15F0609: 005.

29. YPM Archives: Marsh/Hatcher Correspondence, B15F0609: 006–009.

30. YPM Archives: Marsh/Hatcher Correspondence, B15F0609: 010–015.

31. YPM Archives: Marsh/Hatcher Correspondence, B15F0609: 016–020.

32. YPM Archives: Marsh/Hatcher Correspondence, B15F0609: 022–032.

33. YPM Archives: Marsh/Hatcher Correspondence, B15F0609: 033–034; B15F0610: 001–006.

34. YPM Archives: Marsh/Hatcher Correspondence, B15F0610: 007–012.

35. YPM Archives: Marsh/Hatcher Correspondence, B15F0610: 013–018.

36. Marsh 1888, Gilmore 1920; Weishampel et al. 1990.

37. YPM Archives: Marsh/Hatcher Correspondence, B15F0610: 019–026.

38. YPM Archives: Marsh/Hatcher Correspondence, B15F0610: 027–028.

39. YPM Archives: Marsh/Hatcher Correspondence, B15F0610: 035–036; Schuchert 1905: 138.

40. YPM Archives: Marsh/Hatcher Correspondence, B15F0610: 037–039; B15F0611: 002.

41. YPM Archives: Marsh/Hatcher Correspondence, B15F0611: 001–016.

42. YPM Archives: Marsh/Hatcher Correspondence, B15F0611: 017–018.

43. YPM Archives: Marsh/Hatcher Correspondence, B15F0611: 019–027.

44. YPM Archives: Marsh/Hatcher Correspondence, B15F0611: 026.

45. YPM Archives: Marsh/Hatcher Correspondence, B15F0611: 026–031.

46. YPM Archives: Marsh/Hatcher Correspondence, B15F0611: 032–034.

47. YPM Archives: Marsh/Hatcher Correspondence, B15F0611: 036–038.

48. YPM Archives: Marsh/Hatcher Correspondence, B15F0611: 043–048.

49. Vlachos 2018: 45–46; Benton et al, 2015; Marsh 1890; D. L. Brinkman, pers. comm. with author, February 28, 2018.

50. YPM Archives: Marsh/Hatcher Correspondence, B15F0611: 50–55.

6: TRACKING *TRICERATOPS* AND MINING MINI-MAMMALS

1. YPM Archives: Marsh/Hatcher Correspondence, B15F0612: 001–006.

2. YPM Archives: Marsh/Hatcher Correspondence, B15F0612: 008–010; Lanham 1973: 204.

3. YPM Archives: Marsh/Hatcher Correspondence, B15F0612: 011–012.

4. Schuchert and LeVene 1940: 213–214.

5. YPM Archives: Marsh/Hatcher Correspondence, B15F0612: 013–014.

6.   YPM Archives: Marsh/Hatcher Correspondence, B15F0612: 015–016.
7.   YPM Archives: Marsh/Hatcher Correspondence, B15F0612: 018–019.
8.   YPM Archives: Marsh/Hatcher Correspondence, B15F0612: 021–023.
9.   YPM Archives: Marsh/Hatcher Correspondence, B15F0612: 024–025; Cross 1889a, b.
10. YPM Archives: Marsh/Hatcher Correspondence, B15F0612: 026–028.
11. YPM Archives: Marsh/Hatcher Correspondence, B15F0612: 029–034.
12. YPM Archives: Marsh/Hatcher Correspondence, B15F0612: 035–037; http://
     hatcherfamilyassn.com/getperson.php?personID=I1660&tree=QHatcher, for information
     about Hatcher's children.
13. YPM Archives: Marsh/Hatcher Correspondence, B15F0612: 038–042.
14. YPM Archives: Marsh/Hatcher Correspondence, B15F0612: 043–044; B15F0613: 001.
15. YPM Archives: Marsh/Hatcher Correspondence, B15F0613: 002–004.
16. YPM Archives: Marsh/Hatcher Correspondence, B15F0613: 005–008.
17. YPM Archives: Marsh/Hatcher Correspondence, B15F0613: 011–014.
18. YPM Archives: Marsh/Hatcher Correspondence, B15F0613: 016–020; Cope 1876.
19. YPM Archives: Marsh/Hatcher Correspondence, B15F0613: 022–027.
20. Hatcher 1896a: 119.
21. YPM Archives: Marsh/Hatcher Correspondence, B15F0613: 029–033; Ostrom and
     Wellnhofer 1986: Table 1.
22. YPM Archives: Marsh/Hatcher Correspondence, B15F0613: 035–044.
23. YPM Archives: Marsh/Hatcher Correspondence, B15F0614: 001–005.
24. YPM Archives: Marsh/Hatcher Correspondence, B15F0614: 006–013; Ostrom and
     Wellnhofer 1986: Table 1.
25. YPM Archives: Marsh/Hatcher Correspondence, B15F0614: 014–020; Marsh 1889b:
     173–176; Marsh 1889c: 177–180.
26. YPM Archives: Marsh/Hatcher Correspondence, B15F0614: 029–030.
27. YPM Archives: Marsh/Hatcher Correspondence, B15F0614: 032–035.
28. YPM Archives: Marsh/Hatcher Correspondence, B15F0614: 036–039.
29. Lull 1919.

7: PONDERING OTHER OPTIONS

1.   YPM Archives: Marsh/Hatcher Correspondence, B15F0615: 001–004; Hay 1898: 68–71.
2.   Shor 1974: 65–220; Baur 1890: 299–302.
3.   YPM Archives: Marsh/Hatcher Correspondence, B15F0615: 008–014; http://collections.
     nmnh.si.edu/search/paleo/; https://www.floridamuseum.ufl.edu/florida-vertebrate-fossils/
     sites/mixsons-bone-bed/.
4.   YPM Archives: Marsh/Hatcher Correspondence, B15F0615: 015–016.
5.   YPM Archives: Marsh/Hatcher Correspondence, B15F0615: 017–022.
6.   YPM Archives: Marsh/Hatcher Correspondence, B15F0615: 023–027.
7.   YPM Archives: Marsh/Hatcher Correspondence, B15F0615: 028–033.
8.   YPM Archives: Marsh/Hatcher Correspondence, B15F0615: 035–036.
9.   YPM Archives: Marsh/Hatcher Correspondence, B15F0615: 037–044.
10. YPM Archives: Marsh/Hatcher Correspondence, B15F0615: 045–046.

11. YPM Archives: Marsh/Hatcher Correspondence, B15F0616: 001–006.
12. YPM Archives: Marsh/Hatcher Correspondence, B15F0616: 010–012.
13. YPM Archives: Marsh/Hatcher Correspondence, B15F0616: 013–014.
14. YPM Archives: Marsh/Hatcher Correspondence, B15F0616: 016–017.
15. YPM Archives: Marsh/Hatcher Correspondence, B15F0615: 018–024.
16. YPM Archives: Marsh/Hatcher Correspondence, B15F0616: 025–032.
17. YPM Archives: Marsh/Hatcher Correspondence, B15F0617: 001–018.
18. YPM Archives: Marsh/Hatcher Correspondence, B15F0617: 019–025.
19. YPM Archives: Marsh/Hatcher Correspondence, B15F0617: 026–028.
20. YPM Archives: Marsh/Hatcher Correspondence, B15F0618: 003–013.
21. YPM Archives: Marsh/Hatcher Correspondence, B15F0618: 014–017.
22. YPM Archives: Marsh/Hatcher Correspondence, B15F0618: 019–022.
23. YPM Archives: Marsh/Hatcher Correspondence, B15F0618: 023–033; http:// hatcherfamilyassn.com/getperson.php?personID=I1660&tree=QHatcher, for information about Hatcher's children.
24. YPM Archives: Marsh/Hatcher Correspondence, B15F0619: 001–009.
25. YPM Archives: Marsh/Hatcher Correspondence, B15F0619: 010–011.
26. YPM Archives: Marsh/Hatcher Correspondence, B15F0619: 010–018.
27. YPM Archives: Marsh/Hatcher Correspondence, B15F0619: 020.
28. AMNH VP Archives, Osborn Papers, Hatcher Correspondence, VPA 1 F 46, Folder 1: Hatcher to Osborn 8/7/90, 8/19/90, 8/8/90, 9/8/90, 9/25/90, 10/28/90; Osborn to Hatcher 8/15/90, 8/28–9/1/90, 9/20/90, 9/30/90, 10/17/90; Rainger 1990: 16.
29. AMNH VP Archives, Osborn Papers, Hatcher Correspondence, VPA 1 F 46, Folder 1: Hatcher to Osborn, 12/22/90; Osborn to Hatcher, 12/24/90.

8: HAIL THE HADROSAURS AND TRUMPET *TOROSAURUS*

1. YPM Archives: Marsh/Hatcher Correspondence, B16F0620: 001–003.
2. YPM Archives: Marsh/Hatcher Correspondence, B16F0620: 004–011.
3. YPM Archives: Marsh/Hatcher Correspondence, B16F0620: 011–013.
4. YPM Archives: Marsh/Hatcher Correspondence, B16F0620: 016–043.
5. YPM Archives: Marsh/Hatcher Correspondence, B16F0620: 043–059.
6. YPM Archives: Marsh/Hatcher Correspondence, B16F0621: 001–007.
7. YPM Archives: Marsh/Hatcher Correspondence, B16F0621: 008–027.
8. AMNH VP Archives, Osborn Papers, Hatcher Correspondence, VPA 1 F 46, Folder 1: Hatcher to Osborn, 5/13/1891; YPM Archives: Marsh/Hatcher Correspondence, B16F0621: 028–034, including:

    E. M. MUSEUM OF GEOLOGY AND ARCHAEOLOGY
    PRINCETON, N. J. April 27th, 1891.
    Dear Mr. Hatcher, -

    Before this reaches you, you will have received a telegram from me announcing your appointment as Assistant in Paleontology in the American Museum of Natural History. I have experienced some difficulty to carry this through, partly because representations as to your character as well as to the consequences to the Museum, which would follow your appointment, were made to Mr. Jesup [sic] *such as caused him to hesitate to engage you.*

Some time ago I sent you a complete copy of our correspondence, in which you sought this position and accepted it upon your own terms. Now that everything that I agreed to do has been carried out, I look to you as [an] *honorable man to keep your agreement. This is a turning point in your life; if you keep your word, you will have before you a clear conscience and a bright future career. I would like to have you begin work for the Museum on May 1st in the Laramie beds. I expect to come out to see you in June or, if not then, in August.*

I am Very truly yours,

(Signed) *Henry F. Osborn*

9. Osborn Family Papers, New York Historical Society Archive, MS 474, Series II, Henry Fairfield Osborn Papers, Series II.1, H. F. Osborn to W. B. Scott: 7/24/1890, 8/14/1890, 9/2/1890; Rainger 1991: 61, 79; Rainger 1990: 17; B16F0621: 037–039, including:

New Haven, Conn., May 18, 1891.

Dear Mr. Hatcher, –

Your letter of the 13th inst. came duly, and I was very glad to learn the work was going on so successfully.

The letter you enclosed from Prof. Osborn surprised me very much, as you gave him your final answer last January. I feared he intended to make more trouble when he wrote to you for copies of his letters, and also tried to engage Utterback, but I did not think he would try to influence you again by such statements. Let me say first of all, that the statement implied in his letter that I said anything to Mr. Jesup [sic] *against your character is absolutely false, as I telegraphed you promptly on receipt of your letter. What I said to him was in your favor, if rightly understood. I met him twice accidentally and what I said was in substance the importance of your services to Yale and the Geologic Survey, and the unfairness of Osborn's attempt to make you break your written contract already signed and witnessed. When I see you, I will tell you frankly everything I said, if you wish me to do so. I return Osborn's letter, and if he attempts anything further, please let me know, at once. . . .*

With best wishes, yours truly,

10. YPM Archives: Marsh/Hatcher Correspondence, B16F0621: 040–041.
11. YPM Archives: Marsh/Hatcher Correspondence, B16F0621: 042–045; Marsh 1891: 265–269; D. L. Brinkman, pers. comm. with author, March 13, 2018.
12. YPM Archives: Marsh/Hatcher Correspondence, B16F0621: 046–047; Ostrom and Wellnhofer 1986: Table 1.
13. YPM Archives: Marsh/Hatcher Correspondence, B16F0622: 001–006.
14. YPM Archives: Marsh/Hatcher Correspondence, B16F0622: 007–009.
15. YPM Archives: Marsh/Hatcher Correspondence, B16F0622: 010–011; Schuchert and LeVene 1940: 215.
16. YPM Archives: Marsh/Hatcher Correspondence, B16F0622: 012–014.
17. YPM Archives: Marsh/Hatcher Correspondence, B16F0622: 031–034.
18. YPM Archives: Marsh/Hatcher Correspondence, B16F0622: 035–041.
19. YPM Archives: Marsh/Hatcher Correspondence, B16F0622: 042–045.
20. YPM Archives: Marsh/Hatcher Correspondence, B16F0622: 046–050.

21. YPM Archives: Marsh/Hatcher Correspondence, B16F0622: 051–054.

22. YPM Archives: Marsh/Hatcher Correspondence, B16F0623: 003–009.

23. YPM Archives: Marsh/Hatcher Correspondence, B16F0623: 010–014.

24. YPM Archives: Marsh/Hatcher Correspondence, B16F0623: 015–020.

25. YPM Archives: Marsh/Hatcher Correspondence, B16F0623: 021–029.

26. YPM Archives: Marsh/Hatcher Correspondence, B16F0624: 001–008.

27. YPM Archives: Marsh/Hatcher Correspondence, B16F0624: 012–013.

28. YPM Archives: Marsh/Hatcher Correspondence, B16F0624: 018–026.

29. YPM Archives: Marsh/Hatcher Correspondence, B16F0624: 027–034.

30. YPM Archives: Marsh/Hatcher Correspondence, B16F0624: 035–038; Ostrom and Wellnhofer 1986: Table 1.

31. YPM Archives: Marsh/Hatcher Correspondence, B16F0624: 039–040.

32. YPM Archives: Marsh/Hatcher Correspondence, B16F0624: 041–042.

33. Scannella and Horner 2010: 1157–1168; Scannella and Horner 2011: e28705; Longrich and Field 2012: e32623.

9: AN UNEXPECTED ENDING

1. YPM Archives: Marsh/Hatcher Correspondence, B16F0624: 043–051.

2. YPM Archives: Marsh/Hatcher Correspondence, B16F0625: 001–004.

3. YPM Archives: Marsh/Hatcher Correspondence, B16F0625: 006–011; http://hatcherfamilyassn.com/getperson.php?personID=I1660&tree=QHatcher, for information about Hatcher's children.

4. YPM Archives: Marsh/Hatcher Correspondence, B16F0625:012–015.

5. YPM Archives: Marsh/Hatcher Correspondence, B16F0625: 016–021.

6. YPM Archives: Marsh/Hatcher Correspondence, B16F0625: 022–025.

7. YPM Archives: Marsh/Hatcher Correspondence, B16F0625: 026–028.

8. YPM Archives: Marsh/Hatcher Correspondence, B16F0625: 030–035; Marsh 1892: 249–262.

9. YPM Archives: Marsh/Hatcher Correspondence, B16F0626: 001–006.

10. YPM Archives: Marsh/Hatcher Correspondence, B16F0626: 007–025; http://www.wyohistory.org/encyclopedia/johnson-county-war-1892-invasion-northern-wyoming.

11. YPM Archives: Marsh/Hatcher Correspondence, B16F0626: 028–034.

12. YPM Archives: Marsh/Hatcher Correspondence, B16F0626: 035–041; AMNH VP Archives, Osborn Papers, Hatcher Correspondence, VPA 1 F 46, Folder 1: Hatcher to Osborn, 3/14/92; Hatcher to Osborn, 4/25/92; Osborn to Hatcher, 4/29/92.

13. YPM Archives: Marsh/Hatcher Correspondence, B16F0626: 042–048.

14. Schuchert and LeVene 1940: 248–323.

15. YPM Archives: Marsh/Hatcher Correspondence, B16F0626: 049–050.

16. YPM Archives: Marsh/Hatcher Correspondence, B16F0626: 054–055.

17. YPM Archives: Marsh/Hatcher Correspondence, B16F0627: 001–002.

18. YPM Archives: Marsh/Hatcher Correspondence, B16F0627: 003–005; Cross 1889a: 453; Cross 1889b: 171.

19. YPM Archives: Marsh/Hatcher Correspondence, B16F0627: 006.

20. YPM Archives: Marsh/Hatcher Correspondence, B16F0627: 008.

21. Schuchert and LeVene 1940: 322–323.

22. YPM Archives: Marsh/Hatcher Correspondence, B16F0627: 009–010.

23. YPM Archives: Marsh/Hatcher Correspondence, B16F0627: 011–015.

24. YPM Archives: Marsh/Hatcher Correspondence, B16F0627: 018–021.

25. YPM Archives: Marsh/Hatcher Correspondence, B16F0627: 022–025.

26. YPM Archives: Marsh/Hatcher Correspondence, B16F0627: 026–031.

27. YPM Archives: Marsh/Hatcher Correspondence, B16F0627: 033–034.

28. YPM Archives: Marsh/Hatcher Correspondence, B16F0627: 036–038.

29. YPM Archives: Marsh/Hatcher Correspondence, B16F0627: 039.

30. YPM Archives: Marsh/Hatcher Correspondence, B16F0627: 040–044.

31. D. L. Brinkman, pers. comm. with author, March 29, 2018; Schuchert and LeVene 1940: 225; Hatcher 1901h: 1; Brinkman 2010: 231.

10: FROM PRINCETON TO THE PLAINS WITH AN EYE ON PATAGONIA

1. PU Archives: B27 F1: Hatcher to Scott, 2/4/93; Brinkman 2010: 124.

2. AMNH VP Archives, Osborn Papers, Hatcher Correspondence, VPA 1 F 46, Folder 1: Hatcher to Osborn, 1/11/93; Osborn to Hatcher, 1/20/93; Hatcher to Osborn, 1/23/93.

3. Scott 1939: 185–187; Rainger 1991: 83; PU Archives: B27 F1: Hatcher to Scott, 2/28/93.

4. PU Archives: B27 F1: Hatcher to Scott; 5/3/93, 8/15/93; Scott 1939: 186.

5. Scott 1893: 80–84.

6. Scott 1893: 80–84.

7. Scott 1893: 80–84.

8. PU Archives: B27 F1: Hatcher to Scott, 2/27/94.

9. PU Archives: B27 F1: Hatcher to Scott, 3/9/94.

10. PU Archives: B27 F1: Hatcher to Scott, 3/12/94.

11. PU Archives: B27 F1: Hatcher to Scott; 3/16/94, 3/24/94.

12. PU Archives: B27 F1: Hatcher to Scott, 4/2/94.

13. PU Archives: B27 F1: Hatcher to Scott, 4/6/94.

14. PU Archives: B27 F1: Hatcher to Scott, 4/6/94.

15. PU Archives: B27 F1: Hatcher to Scott; 5/11/94.

16. PU Archives: B27 F1: Hatcher to Scott; 5/11/94.

17. PU Archives: B27 F1: Hatcher to Scott; 5/20/94, 5/30/94.

18. PU Archives: B27 F1: Hatcher to Scott; 6/22/94, 7/5/94; "Hunting for Fossils" newspaper clipping, 7/8/94.

19. PU Archives: B27 F1: Hatcher to Scott; 7/14/94, 8/5/94, 8/19/94.

20. PU Archives: B27 F1: Hatcher to Scott; 9/14/94, 9/18/94, 9/27/94.

21. PU Archives: B27 F1: Hatcher to Scott; Hatcher 1894d: 91–92; Rankin 1895: 55.

22. PU Archives: B27 F1: Hatcher to Scott; 3/22/95, 4/14/95.

23. PU Archives: B27 F1: Hatcher to Scott; 4/22/95.

24. PU Archives: B27 F1: Hatcher to Scott; 4/29/95, 5/6/95.

25. PU Archives: B27 F1: Hatcher to Scott; 5/9/95.
26. PU Archives: B27 F1: Hatcher to Scott; 5/9/95.
27. PU Archives: B27 F1: Hatcher to Scott; 5/15/95, 5/17/95, 5/23/95.
28. PU Archives: B27 F1: Hatcher to Scott; 6/5/95, 6/12/95, 6/20/95.
29. PU Archives: B27 F1: Hatcher to Scott; 7/2/95, 8/9/95; *Freemont Clipper*, 7/5/95.
30. Hatcher 1895c: 96–98.
31. Hatcher 1896a: 115–116.

11: A TANGO WITH THE TIDES AMONG PATAGONIAN PANORAMAS

1. Simpson 1984: 62–63; 67; 70–71; 89; 90.
2. Hatcher 1985: 3.
3. Simpson 1984: 109.
4. Brinkman 2010: 27, 224–225; AMNH VP Archives, Osborn Papers, Hatcher Correspondence, VPA 1 F 46, Folder 1: Osborn to Hatcher, 1/27/96; Hatcher to Osborn, 2/12/96.
5. Scott 1939: 224–225.
6. Simpson 1984: 109; Hatcher 1985: ix–xii, 4.
7. Hatcher 1985: 1–3; Brinkman 2003: 56; Brinkman 2009.
8. Hatcher 1985: 6–7.
9. Hatcher 1985: 8–11.
10. Hatcher 1985: 12–14.
11. Hatcher 1985: 14–19.
12. Hatcher 1985: 20–24.
13. Hatcher 1985: 24–26.
14. Hatcher 1985: 27–30.
15. Hatcher 1985: 27–32.
16. Hatcher 1985: 32–36.
17. Hatcher 1985: 36–37.
18. Hatcher 1985: 39–46.
19. Hatcher 1985: 46–48.
20. Hatcher 1895: 49–53.
21. Hatcher 1985: 53–55.
22. Hatcher 1985: 56–61.
23. Hatcher 1985: 61–63.
24. Hatcher 1985: 64–65; Lepley and Lepley 1992.
25. Hatcher 1985: 66–67.
26. Hatcher 1985: 67–68.
27. Hatcher 1985: 68–71.
28. Hatcher 1985: 72–75.
29. Hatcher 1985: 75–85.
30. Hatcher 1985: 86–90.
31. Hatcher 1985: 90–94; Webb 1986: 21.
32. Hatcher 1985: 95–100.

33. Hatcher 1985: 101.
34. Hatcher 1985: 101–108.
35. Hatcher 1985: 108–119.
36. Hatcher 1985: 119–128.
37. Hatcher 1985: 128–132.
38. Hatcher 1985: 132–142.
39. Hatcher 1985: 142–145.
40. Hatcher 1985: 146–148.
41. Hatcher 1985: 149; http://hatcherfamilyassn.com/getperson.php?personID=I1660&tree =QHatcher, for information about Hatcher's children.
42. Hatcher 1985: 149–156.
43. Hatcher 1897b: 330.

12: DISCOVERY FOLLOWED BY DISEASE AND DISAPPOINTMENT

1. Hatcher 1985: 157.
2. Hatcher 1985: 157–159.
3. Hatcher 1985: 159–162.
4. Hatcher 1985: 162.
5. Hatcher 1985: 162–165.
6. Hatcher 1985: 166–168.
7. Hatcher 1985: 168–169.
8. Hatcher 1985: 170–172.
9. Hatcher 1985: 172–173.
10. Hatcher 1985: 173–178.
11. Hatcher 1985: 178–182.
12. Hatcher 1985: 182–186.
13. Hatcher 1985: 186–188.
14. Hatcher 1985: 188–189.
15. Hatcher 1985: 189–190.
16. Hatcher 1985: 190–193.
17. Hatcher 1985: 193–194.
18. Webb 1986: 22–23.
19. Hatcher 1985: 195; Rainger 1991: 92–93; Simpson 1984: 118.
20. AMNH Barnum Brown Archives 2:6 B4 F2; F. Brown 1987: 13–14; Dingus and Norell 2010: xii–xiii.
21. F. Brown 1987: 14–15; Dingus and Norell 2010: xiii.
22. Hatcher 1985: 195; AMNH Barnum Brown Archives, 2:6 B4 F2 "On the Straits of Magellan"; Dingus and Norell 2010: 65.
23. Hatcher 1985: 195–196.
24. Hatcher 1985: 196–197.
25. Hatcher 1985: 197–199.
26. Hatcher 1985: 199–201.
27. Hatcher 1985: 201.

28. AMNH Barnum Brown Archives: 2:5 B2 F3, 8/15/1899; AMNH Barnum Brown Archives: 2:5 B2 F3, Brown Patagonian Contract.

29. AMNH Barnum Brown Archives: 2:5 B2 F3, 8/15/1899.

30. Rainger 1991: 77–79; AMNH Barnum Brown Archives: 2:5 B2 F3, 8/15/1899.

31. B. Brown 1903: 453–457.

32. Simpson 1984: 121; AMNH VP Archives, Osborn Papers, Hatcher Correspondence, VPA 1 F 46, Folder 1: Osborn to Hatcher, 12/4/99; Osborn to Hatcher, 12/21/99; Osborn to Hatcher, 1/4/00; Dingus and Norell 2010: 77.

33. Hatcher 1985: 201.

34. Hatcher 1985: 201–204.

35. Hatcher 1985: 205, 209.

36. Simpson 1984: 86; Webb 1986: 25.

37. Hatcher 1897b; Hatcher 1900a: 96; Simpson 1984: 85–86; Woodburne et al. 2014: 14; Simpson 1984: 87; Vizcaíno et al. 2012: 5.

38. Scott 1939: 237–238.

39. See Hatcher bibliography; Scott 1939: 311.

40. Simpson 1984: 121–122; Brinkman 2010: 124; AMNH VPA1 (general correspondence), box 85, folder 67, W. B. Scott folder 1, Osborn to Scott, 1/12/00, 2/13/00; Scott 1939: 237; Rea 2001: 135; Rainger 1990: 17.

13: CARNEGIE'S COLOSSUS

1. Rea 2001: 43, 135; https://www.revolvy.com/main/index.php?s=William%20Jacob%20Holland&item_type=topic, for biographical information about Holland.

2. Breithaupt 1990; CM Archives: 11/4/98: Holland to Carnegie.

3. CM Archives: 11/4/98: Holland to Reed; 12/5/98: Reed to Holland; 12/10/98: Holland to Reed; 12/12/98: Holland to Carnegie.

4. CM Archives: 12/22/98: Reed to Holland; 12/27/98: Holland to Carnegie.

5. CM Archives: 2/7/99: Holland to Reed; 3/8/99: Holland to Carnegie.

6. CM Archives: 3/17/99: telegram from Holland to Carnegie; 3/23/99: Holland to Gramm.

7. CM Archives: 3/27/99: telegram from Holland to Carnegie; 3/27/99: Holland to Carnegie.

8. CM Archives: 3/27/99: Holland to Reed.

9. CM Archives: 4/1/99: Holland to Carnegie.

10. CM Archives: 4/12/99: Holland to Wortman; 4/20/99: Holland to Wortman.

11. CM Archives: 5/5/99: Holland to Carnegie,

12. CM Archives: 5/17/99: Wortman to Holland; 5/20/99: Holland to Wortman; 5/26/99: Wortman to Holland.

13. CM Archives: 5/26/99: Reed to Holland; 5/30/99: Wortman to Holland.

14. CM Archives: 6/6/99: Wortman to Holland; Cope 1877; Marsh 1878.

15. Tschopp et al. 2015; Fischer et al. 2012, see wiki *Baptamodon*; CM Archives: 6/18/99: Wortman to Holland; Riggs 1903.

16. CM Archives: 6/27/99: Downey to Holland.

17. CM Archives: 6/28/99: Wortman to Holland; 6/30/99: Wortman to Holland.

18. CM Archives: 7/3/99: Holland to Wortman.
19. CM Archives: 7/3/99: Holland to Downey.
20. CM Archives: 7/4/99: Wortman to Holland.
21. CM Archives: 7/19/99: Wortman to Holland.
22. CM Archives: 8/15/99: Holland to Wortman; 8/22/99: Holland to Wortman.
23. CM Archives: 8/29/99: Wortman to Holland.
24. CM Archives: 9/2/99: Holland to Wortman.
25. CM Archives: 9/4/99: Wortman to Mellor; 9/11/99: Holland to Wortman.
26. CM Archives: 9/11/99: Wortman to Holland.
27. CM Archives: 9/19/99: Holland to Wortman; 9/20/99: telegram from *NY Herald* to McSwigan at Carnegie Building, Pittsburgh.
28. CM Archives: 9/27/99: Wortman to Holland; 10/10/99: Holland to McClure.
29. CM Archives: 1/14/1900: Wortman to Carnegie.
30. CM Archives: 1/31/00: Holland to Mellor.
31. Wortman 1900: 163–166; Rea 2001: 121–122.
32. CM Archives: 2/1/00: Holland to R. B. Cladwell; 2/1/00: Holland to Col. Church.
33. CM Archives: 2/6/00; A. Carnegie to Holland, clipping from unidentified newspaper; Rainger 1990.

14: HATCHER'S HIRING AND SHENANIGANS AT SHEEP CREEK

1. CM Archives: 2/8/00: Holland to Mellor.
2. CM Archives: 2/12/00: Hatcher to Holland; 2/15/00: Riggs to Hatcher.
3. CM Archives: 2/24/00: Holland to Hatcher; 3/7/00: Darlow to Holland.
4. CM Archives: 3/19/00: Holland to Carnegie.
5. CM Archives: 3/19/00: Wilbur C. Knight to Hatcher; 3/27/00: S. W. Williston to Hatcher.
6. CM Archives: Note: Reed and two assistants at Sheep Creek would require $857 for six months of salaries, provisions, two tons of stucco, 3,000 feet of lumber, burlap, nails, a team and wagon along with a harness, plow, grain, shoeing, ropes and hobbles, as well as travel expenses and photo supplies. Peterson and one assistant in the Eocene of Wyoming would require $735 for a team and wagon, camp outfit, saddle horse, saddle, provisions, and travel expenses. Costs for Hatcher and his assistant in the Laramie and nearby Oligocene exposures totaled $822 for a team and wagon with harness, a saddle horse and saddle, camp outfit and supplies, travel expenses, and hauling fees for heavy skulls. Hatcher requested $650 up front, with the remaining $1,764 to be placed as a special fund in a checking account on May 1, upon which he could draw as needed. Hatcher also recommended he be given $200 for purchasing specimens from local ranchers and collectors. CM Archives: 3/31/00: Hatcher to Holland; 3/31/00: Hatcher estimate to Holland of costs for 1900 field season.
7. CM Archives: 4/9/00 and 4/17/00: Hatcher to Holland; 4/20/00: Peterson to Holland; 4/21/00: Hatcher to Holland.
8. CM Archives: 4/28/00: Hatcher to Holland; Rea 2001: 158.
9. CM Archives: 5/1/00: Hatcher to Holland.

10. CM Archives: 5/3/00: Reed to Hatcher.

11. CM Archives: 5/3/00: Peterson to Hatcher; 5/8/00: Peterson to Hatcher; 5/8/00: Peterson to Holland.

12. CM Archives: 5/9/00: Hatcher to Holland.

13. Schuchert and LeVene 1940: 188–205.

14. Schuchert and LeVene 1940: 188–205; D. Grenard, pers. comm. with author, July 13, 2017, July 24, 2017; Grenard 2013: http://www.gardenparkdinos.com/marsh-felch-dinosaur-quarry-trail/; Ostrom and McIntosh 1966.

15. CM Archives: 5/13/00: Reed to Hatcher; 5/18/00: Hatcher to Holland; Brinkman 2010: 141.

16. CM Archives: 5/18/00: Hatcher to Reed; 5/21/00: Peterson to Hatcher; 5/24/00: Peterson to Holland.

17. CM Archives: 1900 before 5/27 (undated): Reed to Holland.

18. CM Archives: 5/25/00: Peterson to Hatcher.

19. CM Archives: 5/27/00: Reed to Holland.

20. CM Archives: 5/28/00: Peterson to Hatcher; 5/28/00: Peterson to Holland.

21. CM Archives: 5/31/00: Hatcher to Holland.

22. CM Archives: 5/31/00: April and May report of Hatcher to Holland.

23. CM Archives: 6/3/00: telegram from Hatcher to Holland; 6/4/00: Hatcher to Holland.

24. CM Archives: 6/7/00: Hatcher to Holland including letter from Hatcher to Reed.

25. CM Archives: 6/12/00: Holland to Hatcher; Brinkman 2010: 226.

26. CM Archives: 6/16/00: Peterson to Holland; 6/16/00: Peterson to Hatcher.

27. CM Archives: 6/25/00: Hatcher to Holland.

28. CM Archives: 6/26/00: Peterson to Hatcher; 7/2/00: Peterson to Hatcher; 7/4/00: Peterson to Hatcher.

29. AMNH VP Archives, Osborn Papers, Hatcher Correspondence, VPA 1 F 46, Folder 1: Osborn to Hatcher 7/6/1900; Hatcher to Osborn, 7/12/00.

30. CM Archives: 7/10/00: Hatcher to Holland; 7/10/00: Hatcher to Holland.

31. CM Archives: 7/15/00: Peterson to Holland; 7/15/00: Peterson to Hatcher.

32. CM Archives: 7/25/00: Hatcher to Holland; 8/2/00: Hatcher to Holland.

33. CM Archives: 8/2/00: Peterson to Holland; 8/2/00: Peterson to Hatcher; 8/9/00: Peterson to Hatcher.

34. CM Archives: 8/15/00: Peterson to Hatcher; 8/23/00: Peterson to Hatcher; 8/31/00: Peterson to Hatcher; http://research.amnh.org/paleontology/photographs/1900-wyoming-jurassic/, for information about 1900 AMNH expedition to Wyoming.

35. CM Archives: 9/9/00: Hatcher to Mellor.

36. CM Archives: 9/10/00: Peterson to Hatcher; see Brezinski and Kollar 2008, fig. 1B for plots of Sheep Creek Quarries B, D and E.

37. CM Archives: 9/23/00: Hatcher to Holland; 9/24/00: Hatcher to Holland.

38. CM Archives: 9/26/00: Peterson to Hatcher; 9/26/00: Peterson to Holland.

39. CM Archives: 10/3/00: Hatcher to Holland; 10/10/00: Utterback to Hatcher; 10/16/00: telegram from Peterson to Holland; 10/18/00: Peterson to Hatcher; 10/20/00: Utterback to Hatcher.

40. CM Archives: 10/26/00: Burt to Holland; 10/28/00: M. P. Felch to Hatcher; 10/30/00: Utterback to Hatcher.

41. AMNH VP Archives, Osborn Papers, Hatcher Correspondence, VPA 1 F 46, Folder 1: Hatcher to Osborn, 10/28/00.
42. CM Archives: 11/2/00: Utterback to Hatcher.
43. CM Archives: 11/8/90: Hatcher to Holland; 11/9/00: Holland to Hatcher.
44. Brinkman 2010: 141–142.
45. AMNH VP Archives, Osborn Papers, Hatcher Correspondence, VPA 1 F 46, Folder 1: Hatcher to Osborn, 12/21/00.

15: DOCUMENTING *DIPLODOCUS* ALONG WITH A MASSIVE MENAGERIE

1. CM Archives: 11/12/00: Utterback to Hatcher; 11/17/00: Utterback to Hatcher.
2. CM Archives: 11/28/00: Hatcher to Holland; 11/30/00: Darlow to Hatcher; 11/30/00: Hatcher to Holland; 11/30/00: Holland to Hatcher; 12/1/00: Hatcher to Holland.
3. CM Archives: 12/2/00: Utterback to Hatcher.
4. CM Archives: 12/3/00: Hatcher to Holland; 12/10/00: Hatcher to Holland; 12/20/00: Holland to Hatcher.
5. CM Archives: 12/17/00: Utterback to Hatcher; 12/31/00: Utterback to Hatcher; 1/9/01: Utterback to Hatcher.
6. AMNH VP Archives, Osborn Papers, Hatcher Correspondence, VPA 1 F 46, Folder 1: Hatcher to Osborn, 1/11/01, 1/15/01, 1/21/01, 2/4/01, 2/14/01; Osborn to Hatcher, 2/11/01.
7. CM Archives: 1/31/01: Utterback to Hatcher; 2/8/01: Utterback to Hatcher.
8. CM Archives: 2/17/01: F. A. Lucas to Hatcher.
9. CM Archives: 2/23/01: Utterback to Hatcher; 2/28/01: Utterback to Hatcher.
10. AMNH VP Archives, Osborn Papers, Hatcher Correspondence, VPA 1 F 46, Folder 2: 3/5/01: William Libbey III to Hatcher; 3/8/01: Hatcher to Osborn.
11. CM Archives: 3/10/01: Utterback to Hatcher; 3/11/01: Utterback to Hatcher; 3/16/01: Utterback to Hatcher; 3/18/01: Utterback to Hatcher.
12. CM Archives: 3/21/01: Hatcher to Holland.
13. CM Archives: 3/21/01: Holland to Hatcher.
14. CM Archives: 3/23/01: Hatcher to Holland.
15. CM Archives: 3/30/01: Utterback to Hatcher; 4/6/01: Utterback to Hatcher; 4/23/01: Utterback to Hatcher.
16. CM Archives: 4/8/01: Osborn to Hatcher; AMNH VPA Osborn Papers; Hatcher Correspondence: 4/29/01: Hatcher to Osborn; 5/2/01: Hatcher to Osborn.
17. CM Archives: 5/11/01: Peterson to Hatcher; 5/12/01: Hatcher to Holland; 5/13/01: Hatcher to Holland.
18. CM Archives: 5/18/01: Holland to Hatcher; 5/24/01: Hatcher to Holland; Brinkman 2010: 159, 183–185; Rea 2001: 182–183.
19. CM Archives: 5/28/01: Peterson in Harrison, NE to Hatcher.
20. CM Archives: 5/29/01: Holland to Hatcher; 6/1/01: Holland to Hatcher; Brinkman 2010: 184–185.
21. CM Archives: 6/1/01: Hatcher to Holland; 6/4/01: Holland to Hatcher.
22. CM Archives: 6/7/01: Utterback to Hatcher; 6/10/01: Peterson to Hatcher; 6/12/01: Peterson to Hatcher; 6/14/01: Utterback to Hatcher.

23. CM Archives: 6/21/01; Holland to Hatcher; 6/27/01: Holland to Hatcher; 7/2/01: Hatcher to Holland; 7/5/01: Holland to Hatcher; 7/8/01: Hatcher to Holland.

24. CM Archives: 7/11/01: Utterback to Hatcher.

25. CM Archives: 7/13/01: Hatcher to Holland; 7/13/01: Holland to Hatcher.

26. CM Archives: 7/17/01: Hatcher to Holland; 7/20/01: Holland to Hatchers; 7/20/01: Utterback to Hatcher; 7/21/01: Peterson to Hatcher; 7/22/01: Hatcher to Holland.

27. CM Archives: 7/25/01: Holland to Hatcher; 7/26/01: Holland to Hatcher; 7/30/01: Hatcher to Holland.

28. CM Archives: 8/12/01: Hatcher to Holland; Hatcher 1901g.

29. CM Archives: 8/13/01: Peterson to Hatcher; 8/24/01: G. F. Axtell to Hatcher; 8/29/01: Axtell to Hatcher; 8/31/01: Peterson to Hatcher.

30. CM Archives: 9/3/01: Utterback to Hatcher; 9/3/01: Axtell to Hatcher; 9/7/01: Peterson to Hatcher; 9/7/01: Williston to Hatcher.

31. CM Archives: 9/9/01: Gilmore to Peterson; 9/13/01: Axtell to Hatcher; 9/14/01: Peterson to Hatcher.

32. CM Archives: 9/16/01: Williston to Hatcher.

33. CM Archives: 9/30/01: Hatcher to Holland; AMNH VP Archives, Osborn Papers, Hatcher Correspondence, VPA 1 F 46, Folder 2: Hatcher to Osborn, 9/18/01; Hatcher to Osborn, 9/25/01; Hatcher to Osborn, 9/28/01; Hatcher to Osborn, 10/8/01; Hatcher to Osborn, 12/9/01; Osborn 1901: 531, Osborn 1901a: 499.

34. CM Archives: 9/20/01: Axtell to Hatcher; 10/4/01: Axtell to Hatcher; 10/12/01: Axtell to Hatcher; 10/15/01: Utterback to Hatcher.

35. CM Archives: 10/24/01: Utterback to Hatcher; 10/25/01: Axtell to Hatcher.

36. CM Archives: 10/31/01: Utterback to Hatcher.

37. CM Archives: 10/31/01: Hatcher to Holland.

38. CM Archives: 11/3/01: Utterback to Hatcher; 11/7/01: Axtell to Hatcher; 11/8/01: Utterback to Hatcher; 11/25/01: Utterback to Hatcher.

39. CM Archives: 11/30/01: Hatcher to Holland; Hatcher 1902c [for Canidae]; Hatcher 1902a [for "Titanotherium"]; Hatcher 1902b [for *Brontosaurus*].

40. CM Archives: 12/1/01: Utterback to Hatcher; 12/7/01: Utterback to Hatcher; 12/23/01: Utterback to Hatcher.

41. CM Archives: 12/26/01: Gilmore to Hatcher.

42. CM Archives: 12/31/01: Hatcher to Holland.

43. CM Archives: 12/31/01: Hatcher to Holland.

44. CM Archives: 12/31/01: Hatcher to Holland.

45. CM Archives: 12/31/01: Hatcher to Holland.

46. CM Archives: 1/29/02: Osborn to Hatcher; AMNH VP Archives, Osborn Papers, Hatcher Correspondence, VPA 1 F 46, Folder 2: Hatcher to Osborn, 1/27/02.

47. CM Archives: 1/31/02: Hatcher to Holland.

48. CM Archives: 2/3/02: Wilbur C. Knight to Hatcher; 2/4/02: Charles Schuchert to Hatcher.

49. CM Archives: 2/13/02: Osborn to Hatcher; 3/13/02: Osborn to Hatcher; 3/20/02: Osborn to Hatcher; AMNH VP Archives, Osborn Papers, Hatcher Correspondence, VPA 1 F 46, Folder 2: Hatcher to Osborn, 2/15/02; Hatcher to Osborn, 3/18/02.

50. CM Archives: 3/31/02: Hatcher to Holland; Hatcher 1903k: 1–314.

51. CM Archives: 4/21/02: Mellor, Holland, Hatcher to Executive Committee of Carnegie Institution.

52. CM Archives: 4/2/02: Osborn to Hatcher; 4/23/02: Osborn to Hatcher; 4/29/02: Osborn to Hatcher; AMNH VP Archives, Osborn Papers, Hatcher Correspondence, VPA 1 F 46, Folder 2: Hatcher to Osborn, 4/21/02.

53. CM Archives: 4/30/02: Hatcher to Holland.

16: AN ERUPTION OF RESEARCH AND ASTONISHING ACQUISITIONS

1. CM Archives: 5/9/02: Peterson to Hatcher; 5/5/02: B. A. Bensley to Hatcher; 5/9/02: Bensley to Hatcher; 5/24/02: Utterback in Douglas, WY to Hatcher.

2. CM Archives: 5/31/02: Hatcher to Holland.

3. CM Archives: 6/5/02: Utterback to Hatcher; 6/12/02: Utterback to Hatcher.

4. CM Archives: 6/13/02: Peterson to Hatcher; 6/22/02: Peterson to Hatcher; 6/27/02: Peterson to Hatcher.

5. CM Archives: 6/28/02: Utterback to Hatcher; 7/3/02: Utterback to Hatcher.

6. CM Archives: 8/13/02: Holland to Hatcher; 7/7/02: agreement for Eastman to purchase fossils in Europe for Carnegie; AMNH VP Archives, Osborn Papers, Hatcher Correspondence, VPA 1 F 46, Folder 2: Osborn to Hatcher, 7/8/02.

7. CM Archives: 8/30/02: Peterson to Hatcher.

8. CM Archives: 9/20/02: Utterback to Hatcher; 10/1/02: Utterback to Hatcher.

9. CM Archives: 10/2/02: A. Carnegie to "Curator" (presumably Hatcher); AMNH VP Archives, Osborn Papers, Hatcher Correspondence, VPA 1 F 46, Folder 2: Hatcher to Osborn, 9/15/02, 9/18/02, 10/1/02, 10/16/02, 10/27/02, 12/8/02, 12/26/02; Osborn to Hatcher, 10/7/02, 10/22/02; undated but presumably latest Dec. 1902; Osborn 1902.

10. CM Archives: 10/7/02: Utterback to Hatcher; 10/9/02: Utterback to Hatcher; 10/14/02: Peterson to Hatcher; 10/27/02: Utterbac to Hatcher.

11. Hatcher 1902e: 65–108; Hunt 2004: 139–156; Hunt 1996: 476–485.

12. CM Archives: 11/15/02: Beecher to Hatcher; 11/25/02: Beecher to Hatcher; 12/8/02: Beecher to Hatcher; 12/02–2/03: several letters to Hatcher from various European fossil and mineral dealers, as well as journal publishers; 12/23/02: Beecher to Hatcher; 2/9/03: W. M. Davis to Hatcher.

13. CM Archives: 2/11/03: T. W. Stanton of USGS to Hatcher; 2/13/03: F. A. Lucas to Hatcher; 2/19/03: Merriam to Hatcher.

14. CM Archives: 2/25/03: Williston to Hatcher.

15. CM Archives: 3/4/03: Beecher to Hatcher; 3/17/03: Beecher to Hatcher.

16. CM Archives: 3/5/03: Stanton to Hatcher; 3/16/03: Stanton to Hatcher; 3/19/03: Stanton to Hatcher; 3/27/03: Stanton to Hatcher.

17. CM Archives: 3/27/03: James F. Dorrance to Holland.

18. CM Archives: 4/4/03: Stanton to Hatcher; 4/8/03: Stanton to Hatcher; 4/13/03: Stanton to Hatcher; 4/23/03: Stanton to Hatcher; 5/5/03: Stanton to Hatcher; 5/8/03: Stanton to Hatcher; 5/14/03: Laurence Lambe to Hatcher.

19. CM Archives: 5/8/03: L. Clio to Holland; 5/19/03: Utterback to Hatcher; 5/26/03: Hatcher to Utterback; Brinkman 2010: 227.

20. CM Archives: 5/23/03: Stanton to Hatcher; 5/23/03: Stanton to Hatcher; 5/26/03: Hatcher to Peterson; 5/27/03: Hatcher to Holland.

21. CM Archives: 6/1/03: Utterback to Hatcher; 6/4/03: Utterback to Hatcher.

22. CM Archives: 6/6/03: Holland to Hatcher; 6/7/03: Holland to Hatcher; 6/10/03: Holland to Hatcher.

23. CM Archives: 6/10/03: Holland to Hatcher; 6/12/03: telegram from Holland to Hatcher; 6/16/03: telegram from Eastman to Hatcher.

24. CM Archives: 6/22/03: Hatcher to Holland; 6/27/03: Holland to Hatcher.

25. CM Archives: 6/30/03: Utterback to Hatcher.

26. CM Archives: Hatcher and Stanton 1903: 211–212; 7/11/03: Hatcher to Holland.

27. CM Archives: 7/27/03: Holland to Hatcher.

28. CM Archives: 7/28/03: Utterback to Hatcher; 7/31/03: Utterback to Hatcher.

29. CM Archives: 8/4/03: A. Carnegie to Holland.

30. CM Archives: 8/6/03: Utterback to Hatcher; 8/12/03: Utterback to Hatcher.

31. CM Archives: 8/13/03: Hatcher to Holland.

32. CM Archives: 8/31/03: Holland to Eastman; 9/1/03: Eastman to Hatcher.

33. CM Archives: 9/1/03: Utterback to Hatcher.

34. CM Archives: 9/3/03: Hatcher to Nopcsa; 9/3/03: Hatcher to F. Ameghino.

35. CM Archives: 9/4/03: Hatcher to Osborn; 9/4/03: Hatcher to Lambe.

36. CM Archives: 9/4/03: Hatcher to Gilmore; 9/4/03: Hatcher to Utterback.

37. CM Archives: 9/4/03: Hatcher to Utterback; 9/4/03: Hatcher to Earl Douglass; Brinkman 2010: 227.

38. CM Archives: 9/4/03: Hatcher to E. H. Sellards; 9/13/03: E. H. Sellards to Hatcher; 10/2/03: Hatcher to Sellards; 9/5/03: Hatcher to G. P. Merrill; 9/5/03: Hatcher to M. S. Farr; 9/5/03: Hatcher to Scott; 9/9/03: Scott to Hatcher; 9/11/03: Hatcher to Scott.

39. CM Archives: 9/5/03: Hatcher to C. R. Eastman.

40. CM Archives: 9/7/03: Hatcher to Gilmore; 9/9/03: Hatcher to Utterback; 9/12/03: Douglass to Hatcher; 9/18/03: Hatcher to Douglass; 9/13/03: Gilmore to Hatcher; 9/18/03: Hatcher to Gilmore.

41. CM Archives: 9/7/03: Hatcher to O. P. Hay; 9/9/03: Hay to Hatcher; 9/11/03: Hatcher to Hay; 9/15/03: Hay to Hatcher.

42. CM Archives: 9/9/03: Hatcher to F. A. Lucas; 9/13/03: Lucas to Hatcher.

43. CM Archives: 9/11/03: Hatcher to Eastman.

44. CM Archives: 9/11/03: Eastman to Hatcher.

45. CM Archives: 9/14/03: Hatcher to W. J. McGee; 9/14/03: Hatcher to Lambe; 9/17/03: Lambe to Hatcher.

46. CM Archives: 9/14/03: Utterback to Hatcher; 9/20/03: Utterback to Hatcher.

47. CM Archives: 9/15/03: Osborn to Hatcher; 9/16/03: Beecher to Hatcher; 9/18/03: Hatcher to Beecher; 9/24/03: Beecher to Hatcher; 10/2/03: Hatcher to Beecher; 10/3/03: Hatcher to Osborn; 9/30/03: Hatcher to Beecher; 9/30/03: Hatcher to Osborn; AMNH VP Archives, Osborn Papers, Hatcher Correspondence, VPA 1 F 46, Folder 2: Osborn to Hatcher, 9/29/03, 10/8/03; Hatcher to Osborn, 10/14/03.

48. CM Archives: 9/18/03: Eastman to Hatcher; 9/25/03: Eastman to Hatcher.

49. CM Archives: 9/18/03: W. J. McGee to Hatcher; 9/21/03: Hatcher to McGee; 9/19/03: Scott to Hatcher; 9/21/03: Hatcher to Scott; 9/21/03: Hatcher to Hay; 9/21/03: Hatcher to Lambe; 9/21/03: Hatcher to Osborn.

50. CM Archives: 9/24/03: Hatcher to Gilmore; 9/30/03: Hatcher to Gilmore; 9/21/03: Hatcher to Utterback.

51. CM Archives: 9/21/03: Hatcher to Silberling; 9/28/03: Hatcher to Utterback; 10/1/03: Albert C. Silberling to Hatcher; 10/5/03: Hatcher to Silbering.

52. CM Archives: 10/1/03: Utterback to Hatcher; 10/2/03: Hatcher to Holland; 10/5/03: Hatcher to Utterback; 10/5/03: Hatcher to Douglass; 10/8/03: Hatcher to Utterback; 10/8/03: Hatcher to Gilmore.

53. CM Archives: 10/5/03: Hatcher to Prentice; 10/6/03: Prentice to Hatcher; 10/8/03: Hatcher to Prentice; 10/8/03: Hatcher to Beecher; 10/8/03: Osborn to Hatcher.

54. CM Archives: 10/8/03: Hatcher to Marcellin Boule.

55. CM Archives: 10/9/03: Williston to Hatcher; Hatcher 1903f: 369–373; Eberth 1997 a, b and 2005; Sprain et al. 2015: 393–409; Rogers et al. 2016.

56. CM Archives: 10/13/03: Utterback to Hatcher; 10/19/03: Utterback to Hatcher; 10/19/03: Hatcher to Utterback; 10/21/03: Utterback to Hatcher.

57. CM Archives: 10/19/03: Hatcher to Merrill; 10/27/03: Hatcher to Silberling.

58. CM Archives, Sternberg to Hatcher 11/2/03; Hatcher to Sternberg 12/4/03; Sternber to Hatcher 12/8/03; Hatcher to Sternberg 12/23/03.

17: THE CURTAIN CLOSES

1. CM Archives: 11/20/03: Hatcher to Holland; http://hatcherfamilyassn.com/getperson. php?personID=I1660&tree=QHatcher, for information about Hatcher's children; CM Archives: 1/12/04: F. von Iterson to Hatcher; Hatcher to Beecher 12/3/03; Osborn to Hatcher 12/28/03.

2. CM Archives: 12/5/03: Eastman to Hatcher; 12/8/03: Hatcher to Eastman; 12/10/03: Eastman to Hatcher; 12/17/03: Hatcher to Eastman; 1/1/04: Hatcher to Holland.

3. CM Archives: 1/8/04 Eastman to Hatcher; 1/8/04: Hatcher to Eastman; 1/11/04: Eastman to Hatcher; 1/14/04: Hatcher to Eastman.

4. CM Archives: 1/16/04: Hatcher to Holland.

5. CM Archives: 1/5/04: Hatcher to Sternberg; 3/11/04: Hatcher to Holland; 3/21/04, 3/21/04: Sternberg to Hatcher.

6. CM Archives: 1/5/04: Osborn to Hatcher; 1/11/04: Osborn to Hatcher; 1/26/04: Hatcher to Osborn; AMNH VP Archives, Osborn Papers, Hatcher Correspondence, VPA 1 F 46, Folder 2: Hatcher to Osborn, 1/1/04, 1/15/04; Osborn to Hatcher, 1/18/04.

7. AMNH VP Archives, Osborn Papers, Hatcher Correspondence, VPA 1 F 46, Folder 2: Osborn to Hatcher, 1/15/04, 2/25/04, 5/9/04; Hatcher to Osborn, 1/18/04, 2/23/04, 4/23/04.

8. CM Archives: 1/2/04: V. Uhlig to [presumably Hatcher]; 1/6/04: Holland to R. A. Franks.

9. CM Archives: 1/13/04: Holland to A. Carnegie.

10. CM Archives: 1/13/04: Holland to M. Boule.

11. CM Archives: 3/4/04: Holland to A. Carnegie.

12. CM Archives: 2/23/04: Hatcher to F. Ameghino.
13. CM Archives: 3/11/04: Hatcher to Gilmore; 3/24/04: Gilmore to Hatcher; 3/26/04: Hatcher to Gilmore.
14. CM Archives: 1/13/04: R. Weber to Hatcher; 3/24/04: Hatcher to Knight; 3/29/03: Knight to Hatcher; 4/2/04: Hatcher to Knight; 4/28/04: Knight to Hatcher; 5/8/04: Knight to Hatcher.
15. CM Archives: 3/22/04: Wieland to Hatcher.
16. CM Archives: 4/30/04: Utterback to Holland; 5/2/04: Hatcher to Theodore Olcott.
17. CM Archives: 5/10/04: A. Smith Woodward to Hatcher.
18. CM Archives: 5/24/04: Utterback to Hatcher; 6/4/04: Hatcher to Utterback; 6/6/04 probably: Utterback to Hatcher.
19. CM Archives: 5/30/04: Peterson to Hatcher; 5/31/04: Peterson to Hatcher; 6/6/04: Hatcher to Peterson; 6/8/04: Hatcher to Peterson.
20. CM Archives: 6/10/04: Holland to Lord Rector (A. Carnegie presumably).
21. CM Archives: 6/13/04: C. Knight to Hatcher; 6/14/04: Hatcher to Knight.
22. CM Archives: 6/14/04: Hatcher to Utterback; 6/26/04: Utterback to Hatcher; 7/1/04: Utterback to Hatcher.
23. CM Archives: 6/30/04: Peterson to Hatcher.
24. CM Archives: 7/1/04: Holland to Peterson.
25. Rea 2001: 175.

18: WOE AND WRANGLING IN THE WAKE

1. CM Archives: 7/1/04: W. D. Matthew to Holland.
2. CM Archives: 7/5/04: Peterson to Holland.
3. CM Archives: 7/8/04: Holland to Peterson.
4. CM Archives: 7/6/04: C. Knight to Holland.
5. CM Archives: 7/8/04: Osborn to Peterson.
6. CM Archives: 7/12/04: Utterback to Holland.
7. CM Archives: 7/11/04: Peterson to Holland.
8. CM Archives: 7/18/04: Peterson to Schuchert; 7/18/04: Peterson to G. P. Merrill; 7/22/04: Schuchert to Peterson.
9. CM Archives: 7/22/04: Schuchert to Peterson.
10. CM Archives: 7/25/04: Peterson to Osborn.
11. CM Archives: 7/23/04: S. Harbert Hamilton to Holland; 7/25/04: A. Carnegie to Holland.
12. CM Archives: 7/16/04: Allegheny Co., PA probate document signed by Geo. H. Stengel, register; estate of J. B. Hatcher ledger, Douglas Stewart, administrator; 11/7/04: Holland to Stewart; Rea 2001: 178; undated: Anna M. Hatcher to D. Stewart.
13. CM Archives: 7/24/04: Utterback to Holland; Dingus and Norell 2010: 84–96.
14. CM Archives: 7/24/04: Utterback to Holland.
15. 7/28/04: Peterson to Holland; 7/28/04: G. P. Merrill to Peterson (presumably); Schuchert 1905; 7/29/04: Schuchert to Peterson.
16. CM Archives: 8/1/04: Holland to Peterson.
17. CM Archives: 8/4/04: Utterback to Holland.

18. CM Archives: 8/10/04: Peterson to Holland.

19. CM Archives: 8/13/04: Holland to Peterson.

20. CM Archives: 8/10/04: Utterback to Holland; A. Henrici, pers. comm. with author, April 18, 2018.

21. CM Archives: 8/18/04: Peterson to Holland; Peterson 1904: 344–345; Peterson 1905: 139–202; 8/20/04: Holland to Peterson; 8/21/04: Peterson to Holland.

22. CM Archives: 8/22/04: Utterback to Holland; 8/25/04: Utterback to Holland; Dingus and Norell 2010: 106–110.

23. CM Archives: 8/23/04: Holland to Peterson; 8/24/04: Peterson to Holland; 8/27/04: Williston to Peterson; 8/27/04: Merrill to Peterson; 8/28/04: Peterson to Holland.

24. CM Archives: 9/1/04: Utterback to Holland; 9/1/04: Utterback's bill from Miles City dry goods and groceries store.

25. CM Archives: 9/8/04: Utterback to Holland; 9/21/04: telegram from Utterback to Holland; 9/22/04: Utterback to Holland.

26. CM Archives: 10/19/04: Peterson (presumably) to Merrill; 10/22/04: Merrill to Peterson; 11/1/04: copy of ratings report for preparatory exam, Vert. Paleo, Nat. Museum by Civil Service Commission; 11/21/04: S. P. Langley to Peterson; 11/23/04: Merrill to Peterson; 11/23/04: R. Rathburn to Peterson; 12/2/04: Peterson to Holland; Brinkman 2010: 259; Webb 1986: 22; A. Henrici, pers. comm. with author, April 18, 2018.

27. CM Archives: 4/17/08: Utterback to Stewart; A. Henrici, pers. comm. with author, April 18, 2018.

28. A. Henrici, pers. comm. with author, April 18, 2018; Douglass 2009.

29. Brinkman 2010:240–241; Rainger 1991: 162; Otero and Gasperini 2014; Rea 2004.

EPILOGUE

1. Rainger 1990; Shor 1971: 6–24.

2. Schuchert and LeVene 1940: 224.

3. Hatcher 1985: 37; Webb 1986; Rainger 1990: 18; Brinkman 2010: 227.

4. Holland 1904: 597.

5. Reprinted courtesy of John Hatcher.

6. John Hatcher, pers. comm. with author, December 2017.

7. Reprinted courtesy of John Hatcher.

8. Schuchert and LeVene 1940: 207–225; Holland 1904.

9. AMNH VPA, Barnum Brown Papers, Personal Correspondence 1896–1932, 2:5, B2, F3: 7/16/1904; AMNH VPA, Barnum Brown Papers 2:6 B4 F2: "Patagonia: Land's End": 2–3.

10. Scott 1904b: 550.

11. Scott 1939: 185, 261; Scott 1904a: 139, 141; Brinkman 2010: 199–200.

12. Brinkman 2010: 123, 141.

13. Rainger 1990: 14, 15 and 1991: 81, 185.

14. Lanham 1973: 198.

15. Simpson 1984: 118.

16. Webb 1986: 21, 23.

17. Rea 2001: 4.

Acknowledgments

A lthough the thoughts expressed within are entirely the responsibility of the author, a plethora of people provided their time, knowledge and support in this effort to bring John Bell Hatcher's tale back to life, and I am profoundly grateful for their patience and persistence.

From the start, constant support has been on offer from my steadfast literary representative Sam Fleishman of Literary Artists Representatives and my ever-encouraging editor Jessica Case at Pegasus Books. In addition, crucial aid was contributed by my relentless research assistant Ariel Revan.

In truth, there are several paleontological colleagues who know more about the animals and events inherent in Hatcher's exploits than I. But fortunately, they most willingly lent their expertise to this endeavor.

Several colleagues at Yale's Peabody Museum of Natural History passionately encouraged the undertaking of this project, including Timothy White and my esteemed classmate, Jacques Gauthier, both of whom endorsed my having access to the extensive resources related to Hatcher and Marsh in the Museum's collections and archives. Barbara Narendra supplied expert guidance to the correspondence and other related documents, and Nathan Utrup kindly scanned Hatcher's map of the Long Island Rhino Quarry. But beyond that, I owe a supreme debt of gratitude to Daniel Brinkman, who not only offered constant encouragement but also, in his review, a long series of selfless scientific and historical insights regarding both Hatcher, Marsh and their contemporaries, as well as the animals that they collected and researched. Erin Gredell also kindly gathered key images.

Matthew Lamana at the Carnegie Museum of Natural History graciously and enthusiastically granted permission to access the institution's extensive paleontological archives, and Amy Henrici provided essential guidance to the materials therein, as well as a meticulous review of that portion of the manuscript dealing with Hatcher's tenure at the Carnegie. They also provided invaluable assistance in gathering images, along with Kathleen Bodenlos, Kate Sallada, and Lauren Buches.

The numerous insightful comments and suggestions of Paul Brinkman at North Carolina State University greatly enhanced the credibility of the manuscript with a more comprehensive historical perspective regarding the paleontological personalities and perspectives of Hatcher's time.

Colleagues at the American Museum of Natural History also played essential roles in the development of the project. Mick Ellison created the marvelous maps marking the dozens of localities where Hatcher and his crews collected in the American West and Patagonia. Mark Norell and Ruth O'Leary kindly extended permission to access the archival materials in the Division of Paleontology, and Susan Bell most patiently offered hours of guidance while I explored and documented essential correspondence. The characterizations of the mammals in the yearly faunal lists collected by Hatcher and his field crews benefited greatly from a thorough review by John Flynn. Gregory Raml and Kendra Meyer ably facilitated access to imagery in the Museum's photographic archives.

Thomas Jorstad of the Smithsonian's National Museum of Natural History kindly provided information about several key specimens collected by Hatcher, as well as supplying historical imagery of their material.

Another gorgeous image of one of the Cretaceous mammals that Hatcher discovered was graciously provided by my former mentor William Clemens and his photographer, David Strauss, of the University of California Museum of Paleontology at Berkeley.

Timothy Rowe of the University of Texas at Austin considerately photographed the late Wann Langston's spectacularly reconstructed skull of *Deinosuchus*.

The staff at Princeton's Seeley G. Mudd Manuscript Library and the New-York Historical Society most politely granted permission to research pertinent correspondence and utilize archival imagery.

Likewise, Raimond Speeking graciously permitted the use of his photograph of the *Diplodocus* mount in the Museums für Naturkunde in Berlin.

Daniel Grenard thoughtfully shared his extensive knowledge regarding the development of the Marsh/Felch Quarry north of Cañon City, Colorado, and along with his associate Andrew Smith guided me on a most memorable tour of the seminal fossil sites in that area.

In addition, endless gratitude is due to Elizabeth Chapman, who most tolerantly abided the constant intrusions of Hatcher's immortal influence as I struggled to comprehend the complexities of his legendary exploits and perplexing personality.

Finally, the most unexpected, yet exhilarating, aspect of this project was the opportunity to meet and correspond with some of John Bell Hatcher's descendants, including Shelley Powsner and her family, as well as Norman and John Hatcher. All were spiritedly supportive of this endeavor and generously contributed priceless family insights, information and copies of their heirlooms. Thus, in the end, it seems most fitting to dedicate this study both to them and the other descendants of Anna Matilda and John Bell.

Index